W9-AUA-084

EXAM✓CRAM

CompTIA®
Security+
SY0-501

Fifth Edition

Diane Barrett
Marty M. Weiss

PEARSON IT
CERTIFICATION

800 East 96th Street
Indianapolis, Indiana 46240 USA

CompTIA® Security+ SY0-501 Exam Cram, Fifth Edition

Copyright © 2018 by Pearson Education, Inc.

All rights reserved. No part of this book shall be reproduced, stored in a retrieval system, or transmitted by any means, electronic, mechanical, photocopying, recording, or otherwise, without written permission from the publisher. No patent liability is assumed with respect to the use of the information contained herein. Although every precaution has been taken in the preparation of this book, the publisher and author assume no responsibility for errors or omissions. Nor is any liability assumed for damages resulting from the use of the information contained herein.

ISBN-13: 978-0-7897-5900-9
ISBN-10: 0-7897-5900-4

Library of Congress Control Number: 2017957913

Printed in the United States of America

Trademarks

All terms mentioned in this book that are known to be trademarks or service marks have been appropriately capitalized. Pearson IT Certification cannot attest to the accuracy of this information. Use of a term in this book should not be regarded as affecting the validity of any trademark or service mark.

Warning and Disclaimer

Every effort has been made to make this book as complete and as accurate as possible, but no warranty or fitness is implied. The information provided is on an "as is" basis. The authors and the publisher shall have neither liability nor responsibility to any person or entity with respect to any loss or damages arising from the information contained in this book.

Special Sales

For information about buying this title in bulk quantities, or for special sales opportunities (which may include electronic versions; custom cover designs; and content particular to your business, training goals, marketing focus, or branding interests), please contact our corporate sales department at corpsales@pearsoned.com or (800) 382-3419.

For government sales inquiries, please contact governmentsales@pearsoned.com.

For questions about sales outside the U.S., please contact intlcs@pearson.com.

Editor-in-Chief
Mark Taub

Acquisitions Editor
Michelle Newcomb

Development Editor
Christopher A. Cleveland

Managing Editor
Sandra Schroeder

Senior Project Editor
Tonya Simpson

Copy Editor
Krista Hansing Editorial Services, Inc.

Indexer
Ken Johnson

Proofreader
Larry Sulky

Technical Editor
Chris Crayton

Publishing Coordinator
Vanessa Evans

Cover Designer
Chuti Prasertsith

Compositor
codeMantra

Contents at a Glance

Elements Available Online

Glossary of Essential Terms and Components

Cram Quizzes

Note: See the "Companion Website" section in the Introduction for instructions on how to access the online elements.

Table of Contents

Elements Available Online

Glossary of Essential Terms and Components
Cram Quizzes

Note: See the "Companion Website" section in the Introduction for instructions on how to access the online elements.

About the Authors

Diane Barrett is the president of NextGard Technology and an associate professor at Bloomsburg University. She has done contract forensic and security assessment work for several years and has authored several other security and forensic books. She is a program director for ADFSL's Conference on Digital Forensics, Security, and Law; the president of the Digital Forensic Certification Board; and a volunteer on the National CyberWatch Center's Curriculum Standards Panel for Information Security Fundamentals. She holds many industry certifications, including CISSP, ISSMP, DFCP, and PCME, and also has several from CompTIA, including Security+. Diane's education includes a Ph.D. in business administration with a specialization in information security, and a master of science degree in information technology, with a specialization in information security.

Marty M. Weiss has spent most of his career in information security, risk management, and compliance, helping large organizations. Marty holds a bachelor of science degree in computer studies from the University of Maryland University College and an MBA from the Isenberg School of Management at the University of Massachusetts Amherst. He holds several certifications, including CISSP, CISA, and Security+. Marty has authored and coauthored more than a half-dozen books on information technology, many that have been described as riveting and Dostoevsky-esque in reviews by his mother. In the little free time he has left, Marty occasionally molds minds as an adjunct professor with the University of Maryland University College. A Florida native, he now lives in New England somewhere between Boston and New York City.

Dedication

To my husband, Bill, for his patience and understanding.
—Diane Barrett

To my dad. A wonderful man, and the person who first
introduced me to the security field.
—Marty M. Weiss

Acknowledgments

Publishing a book takes the collaboration and teamwork of many individuals.

Thanks to everyone involved in this process from both Waterside Productions and Pearson Education (and thanks to those who purchase this book in their quest for certification). To our editorial team and technical reviewer, thanks for making sure that our work was sound and on target. Special thanks to my coauthor, Marty, for all his hard work and dedication in making this project a success.

—Diane Barrett

Thank you—the reader of this book. It is an honor and pleasure to help others achieve a goal, and I'm thankful for that opportunity. A huge thanks to Diane. It's hard to believe we've been working together on this book for 15 years. Thank you to the entire team that helped bring this book together, from the team at Waterside Productions to everyone at Pearson. A special shout-out to Carole Jelen, Michelle Newcomb, Chris Cleveland, Chris Crayton, Vanessa Evans, and Tonya Simpson. Thank you to my wife and family that afforded me the late nights and weekends. Finally, thank you to the team at my neighborhood Dunkin' Donuts, especially Jenna and Mackenzie, for keeping me fueled on fresh dark roast while working on this book.

—Marty M. Weiss

About the Technical Reviewer

Chris Crayton (MCSE) is an author, technical consultant, and trainer. Formerly, he worked as a computer technology and networking instructor, information security director, network administrator, network engineer, and PC specialist. Chris has authored several print and online books on PC repair, CompTIA A+, CompTIA Security+, and Microsoft Windows. He has also served as the technical editor and content contributor on numerous technical titles for several leading publishing companies. Chris holds numerous industry certifications, has been recognized with many professional teaching awards, and has served as a state-level SkillsUSA competition judge.

We Want to Hear from You!

As the reader of this book, *you* are our most important critic and commentator. We value your opinion and want to know what we're doing right, what we could do better, what areas you'd like to see us publish in, and any other words of wisdom you're willing to pass our way.

We welcome your comments. You can email or write to let us know what you did or didn't like about this book—as well as what we can do to make our books better.

Please note that we cannot help you with technical problems related to the topic of this book.

When you write, please be sure to include this book's title and author as well as your name and email address. We will carefully review your comments and share them with the author and editors who worked on the book.

Email: feedback@pearsonitcertification.com

Mail: Pearson IT Certification
ATTN: Reader Feedback
          800 East 96th Street
          Indianapolis, IN 46240 USA

Reader Services

Register your copy of *CompTIA Security+ SY0-501 Exam Cram* at www.pearsonitcertification.com for convenient access to downloads, updates, and corrections as they become available. To start the registration process, go to www.pearsonitcertification.com/register and log in or create an account*. Enter the product ISBN 9780789759009 and click Submit. When the process is complete, you will find any available bonus content under Registered Products.

*Be sure to check the box that you would like to hear from us to receive exclusive discounts on future editions of this product.

Introduction

Welcome to *CompTIA Security+ SY0-501 Exam Cram*, Fifth Edition. This book helps you get ready to take and pass the CompTIA Security+ exam SY0-501.

Chapters 1–37 are designed to remind you of everything you need to know to pass the SY0-501 certification exam. The two practice exams that come with this book should give you a reasonably accurate assessment of your knowledge, and, yes, we've provided the answers and their explanations for these practice exams. Read this book, understand the material, and you'll stand a very good chance of passing the real test.

Exam Cram books help you understand and appreciate the subjects and materials you need to know to pass CompTIA certification exams. Exam Cram books are aimed strictly at test preparation and review. They do not teach you everything you need to know about a subject. Instead, the authors streamline and highlight the pertinent information by presenting and dissecting the questions and problems they've discovered that you're likely to encounter on a CompTIA test.

We strongly recommend that you spend some time installing, configuring, and working with the latest operating systems to patch and maintain them for the best and most current security possible because the Security+ exam focuses on such activities and the knowledge and skills they can provide you. Nothing beats hands-on experience and familiarity when it comes to understanding the questions you're likely to encounter on a certification test. Book learning is essential, but without a doubt, hands-on experience is the best teacher of all!

Taking a Certification Exam

After you prepare for your exam, you need to register with a testing center. At the time of this writing, the cost to take the Security+ exam is $320 USD for individuals. CompTIA corporate members receive discounts on nonmember pricing. For more information about these discounts, you can contact a local CompTIA sales representative, who can answer any questions you might have. If you don't pass, you can take the exam again for the same cost as the first attempt until you pass. In the United States and Canada, tests are administered by Prometric or VUE.

After you sign up for a test, you are told when and where the test is scheduled. You should arrive at least 15 minutes early. To be admitted into the testing room, you must supply two forms of identification, one of which must be a photo ID.

About This Book

We've structured the topics in this book to build on one another. Therefore, some topics in later chapters make the most sense after you've read earlier chapters. That's why we recommend that you read this book from front to back for your initial test preparation. If you need to brush up on a topic or if you have to bone up for a second try, you can use the index, table of contents, or Table I.1 to go straight to the topics and questions that you need to study. Beyond helping you prepare for the test, we think you'll find this book useful as a tightly focused reference on some of the most important aspects of the Security+ certification.

Chapter Format and Conventions

Every Exam Cram chapter follows a standard structure and contains graphical clues about important information. The structure of each chapter includes the following:

▶ **Opening objectives list:** This opener defines the official CompTIA Security+ exam objectives covered in the chapter.

▶ **Cram Saver questions:** Each major section begins with a Cram Saver to help you determine your current level of knowledge of the topics in that section.

▶ **Topical coverage:** The heart of the chapter explains the topics from a hands-on and a theory-based standpoint. The discussion includes in-depth descriptions geared to build your knowledge so that you can pass the exam.

▶ **Exam Alerts:** These are interspersed throughout the book and include important information on test topics. Watch out for them!

> **ExamAlert**
>
> This is what an Exam Alert looks like. Normally, an alert stresses concepts, terms, hardware, software, or activities that are likely to relate to one or more certification test questions.

▶ **Cram Quiz questions:** At the end of each part is a quiz. The quizzes and their explanations are meant to gauge your knowledge of the subjects. If you can't readily answer the questions, consider reviewing the associated chapters.

Additional Elements

Beyond the chapters are a few more elements:

▶ **Practice exams:** Two practice exams are available in the Pearson Test Prep practice test software. See the companion website instructions for how to access the Pearson Test Prep practice test software.

▶ **Cram Sheet:** The tear-out Cram Sheet is located in the beginning of the book. This is designed to jam some of the most important facts you need to know for the exam into one small sheet, allowing for easy memorization.

▶ **Glossary:** Here you find definitions of key CompTIA Security+ exam terms.

Exam Objectives

Table I.1 lists the skills the SY0-501 exam measures and the chapter in which the objective is discussed. Some objectives are covered in other chapters, too.

TABLE I.1 **CompTIA SY0-501 Exam Objectives**

Exam Objective	Chapter
Domain 1: Threats, Attacks and Vulnerabilities	
Given a scenario, analyze indicators of compromise and determine the type of malware.	1
Compare and contrast types of attacks.	2
Explain threat actor types and attributes.	3
Explain penetration testing concepts.	4
Explain vulnerability scanning concepts.	5
Explain the impact associated with types of vulnerabilities.	6
Domain 2: Technologies and Tools	
Install and configure network components, both hardware- and software-based, to support organizational security.	7

Exam Objective	Chapter
Compare and contrast various types of controls.	32
Given a scenario, carry out data security and privacy practices.	33
Domain 6: Cryptography and PKI	
Compare and contrast basic concepts of cryptography.	34
Explain cryptography algorithms and their basic characteristics.	35
Given a scenario, install and configure wireless security settings.	36
Given a scenario, implement public key infrastructure.	37

Companion Website

Register this book to get access to the Pearson Test Prep practice test software and other study materials plus additional bonus content. Check this site regularly for new and updated postings written by the author that provide further insight into the more troublesome topics on the exams. Be sure to check the box that you would like to hear from us to receive updates and exclusive discounts on future editions of this product or related products.

To access this companion website, follow these steps:

1. Go to www.pearsonITcertification.com/register and log in or create a new account.

2. Enter the ISBN 9780789759009.

3. Answer the challenge question as proof of purchase.

4. Click the **Access Bonus Content** link in the Registered Products section of your account page to go to the page where your downloadable content is available.

Note that many of our companion content files can be very large, especially image and video files.

If you are unable to locate the files for this title by following these steps, visit www.pearsonITcertification.com/contact and select the Site Problems/ Comments option. Our customer service representatives will assist you.

Pearson Test Prep Practice Test Software

As noted previously, this book comes complete with the Pearson Test Prep practice test software, including two full exams. These practice tests are available to you either online or as an offline Windows application. To access the practice exams that were developed with this book, see the instructions in the card inserted in the sleeve in the back of the book. This card includes a unique access code that enables you to activate your exams in the Pearson Test Prep practice test software.

> **Note**
>
> The cardboard sleeve in the back of this book includes a piece of paper. The paper lists the activation code for the practice exams associated with this book. Do not lose the activation code. On the opposite side of the paper from the activation code is a unique, one-time-use coupon code for the purchase of the Premium Edition eBook and Practice Test.

Accessing the Pearson Test Prep Software Online

The online version of this software can be used on any device with a browser and connectivity to the Internet, including desktop machines, tablets, and smartphones. To start using your practice exams online, simply follow these steps:

1. Go to www.PearsonTestPrep.com.

2. Select **Pearson IT Certification** as your product group.

3. Enter your email/password for your account. If you don't have an account on PearsonITCertification.com, you need to establish one by going to PearsonITCertification.com/join.

4. In the My Products tab, click the **Activate New Product** button.

5. Enter the access code printed on the insert card in the back of your book to activate your product.

6. The product will now be listed in your My Products page. Click the **Exams** button to launch the exam settings screen and start your exam.

Accessing the Pearson Test Prep Software Offline

If you want to study offline, you can download and install the Windows version of the Pearson Test Prep software. The book's companion website has a download link for this software, or you can just enter this link in your browser:

www.pearsonitcertification.com/content/downloads/pcpt/engine.zip

To access the book's companion website and the software, simply follow these steps:

1. Register your book by going to PearsonITCertification.com/register and entering the ISBN: 9780789759009.

2. Respond to the challenge questions.

3. Go to your account page and select the **Registered Products** tab.

4. Click the **Access Bonus Content** link under the product listing.

5. Click the **Install Pearson Test Prep Desktop Version** link under the Practice Exams section of the page to download the software.

6. When the software finishes downloading, unzip all the files on your computer.

7. Double-click the application file to start the installation, and follow the onscreen instructions to complete the registration.

8. When the installation is complete, launch the application and click the **Activate Exam** button on the My Products tab.

9. Click the **Activate a Product** button in the Activate Product Wizard.

10. Enter the unique access code found on the card in the sleeve in the back of your book and click the **Activate** button.

11. Click **Next**, and then click the **Finish** button to download the exam data to your application.

12. You can now start using the practice exams by selecting the product and clicking the **Open Exam** button to open the exam settings screen.

Note that the offline and online versions synch together, so saved exams and grade results recorded on one version will be available to you on the other as well.

Customizing Your Exams

When you are at the exam settings screen, you can choose to take exams in one of three modes:

▶ Study Mode

▶ Practice Exam Mode

▶ Flash Card Mode

Study Mode allows you to fully customize your exams and review answers as you are taking the exam. This is typically the mode you use first to assess your knowledge and identify information gaps. Practice Exam Mode locks certain customization options because it presents a realistic exam experience. Use this mode when you are preparing to test your exam readiness. Flash Card Mode strips out the answers and presents you with only the question stem. This mode is great for late-stage preparation when you really want to challenge yourself to provide answers without the benefit of seeing multiple-choice options. This mode does not provide the detailed score reports that the other two modes do, so do not use it if you are trying to identify knowledge gaps.

In addition to these three modes, you can select the source of your questions. You can choose to take exams that cover all the chapters, or you can narrow your selection to just a single chapter or the chapters that make up specific parts in the book. All chapters are selected by default. If you want to narrow your focus to individual chapters, simply deselect all the chapters and then select only the ones you want to focus on in the Objectives area.

You can also select the exam banks you want to focus on. Each exam bank comes complete with a full exam of questions that cover topics in every chapter. You can have the test engine serve up exams from both test banks or just from one individual bank by selecting the desired banks in the exam bank area.

You can make several other customizations to your exam from the exam settings screen, such as the time of the exam, the number of questions served up, whether to randomize questions and answers, whether to show the number of correct answers for multiple-answer questions, or whether to serve up only specific types of questions. You can also create custom test banks by selecting only questions that you have marked or questions to which you have added notes.

Updating Your Exams

If you are using the online version of the Pearson Test Prep software, you should always have access to the latest version of both the software and the exam data. If you are using the Windows desktop version, every time you launch the software, it checks to see if there are any updates to your exam data and automatically downloads any changes that were made since the last time you used the software. You must be connected to the Internet at the time you launch the software.

Sometimes the exam data does not fully download when you activate your exam. If you find that figures or exhibits are missing, you might need to manually update your exams.

To update a particular exam you have already activated and downloaded, simply select the **Tools** tab and select the **Update Products** button. Again, this is an issue only with the desktop Windows application.

If you want to check for updates to the Pearson Test Prep exam engine software, Windows desktop version, simply select the **Tools** tab and click the **Update Application** button. This will ensure that you are running the latest version of the software engine.

Assessing Exam Readiness

Exam candidates never really know whether they are adequately prepared for the exam until they have completed about 30 percent of the questions. At that point, if you are not prepared, it is too late. The best way to determine your readiness is to confidently answer (correctly) the Cram Saver quizzes at the beginning of each chapter and take the Cram Quiz at the end of each part of the book, which maps to the Security+ domains. It is best to work your way through the entire book unless you can complete each subject without having to do any research or look up any answers.

Premium Edition eBook and Practice Tests

This book also includes an exclusive offer for 70 percent off the Premium Edition eBook and Practice Tests edition of this title. See the coupon code included with the cardboard sleeve for information on how to purchase the Premium Edition.

CompTIA.

Becoming a CompTIA Certified IT Professional is Easy

It's also the best way to reach greater professional opportunities and rewards.

Why Get CompTIA Certified?

Growing Demand

Labor estimates predict some technology fields will experience growth of over 20% by the year 2020.* CompTIA certification qualifies the skills required to join this workforce.

Higher Salaries

IT professionals with certifications on their resume command better jobs, earn higher salaries and have more doors open to new multi-industry opportunities.

Verified Strengths

91% of hiring managers indicate CompTIA certifications are valuable in validating IT expertise, making certification the best way to demonstrate your competency and knowledge to employers.**

Universal Skills

CompTIA certifications are vendor neutral—which means that certified professionals can proficiently work with an extensive variety of hardware and software found in most organizations.

 **Learn**   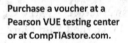 **Certify**   **Work**

Learn more about what the exam covers by reviewing the following:

- Exam objectives for key study points.
- Sample questions for a general overview of what to expect on the exam and examples of question format.
- Visit online forums, like LinkedIn, to see what other IT professionals say about CompTIA exams.

Purchase a voucher at a Pearson VUE testing center or at CompTIAstore.com.

- Register for your exam at a Pearson VUE testing center:
- Visit pearsonvue.com/CompTIA to find the closest testing center to you.
- Schedule the exam online. You will be required to enter your voucher number or provide payment information at registration.
- Take your certification exam.

Congratulations on your CompTIA certification!

- Make sure to add your certification to your resume.
- Check out the CompTIA Certification Roadmap to plan your next career move.

Learn more: Certification.CompTIA.org/securityplus

* Source: CompTIA 9th Annual Information Security Trends study: 500 U.S. IT and Business Executives Responsible for Security
** Source: CompTIA Employer Perceptions of IT Training and Certification

© 2015 CompTIA Properties, LLC, used under license by CompTIA Certifications, LLC. All rights reserved. All certification programs and education related to such programs are operated exclusively by CompTIA Certifications, LLC. CompTIA is a registered trademark of CompTIA Properties, LLC in the U.S. and internationally. Other brands and company names mentioned herein may be trademarks or service marks of CompTIA Properties, LLC or of their respective owners. Reproduction or dissemination prohibited without written consent of CompTIA Properties, LLC. Printed in the U.S. 02190-Nov2015

PART I

Threats, Attacks, and Vulnerabilities

> **This part covers the following official CompTIA Security+, SY0-501 exam objectives for Domain 1, "Threats, Attacks and Vulnerabilities":**
>
> ▶ 1.1 Given a scenario, analyze indicators of compromise and determine the type of malware.
>
> ▶ 1.2 Compare and contrast types of attacks.
>
> ▶ 1.3 Explain threat actor types and attributes.
>
> ▶ 1.4 Explain penetration testing concepts.
>
> ▶ 1.5 Explain vulnerability scanning concepts.
>
> ▶ 1.6 Explain the impact associated with types of vulnerabilities.

For more information on the official CompTIA Security+, SY0-501 exam topics, see the "About the CompTIA Security+, SY0-501 Exam" section in the Introduction.

Because networks today have become so complex and mobile, they have many points of entry. These various points can all be vulnerable, granting an intruder many points of access. With so many ways of getting into the network, the components must be divided into separate elements so that the security process becomes easier to manage. To make the best decisions about securing an environment, you must understand the threats and risks associated with the environment. The chapters in this part of the book explore those threats, risks, and associated attacks to help you navigate everyday potential dangers.

CHAPTER 1

Indicators of Compromise and Malware Types

This chapter covers the following official Security+ exam objective:

1.1 Given a scenario, analyze indicators of compromise and determine the type of malware.

- ▶ Viruses
- ▶ Crypto-malware
- ▶ Worm
- ▶ Trojan
- ▶ Rootkit
- ▶ Keylogger

- ▶ Adware
- ▶ Spyware
- ▶ Bots
- ▶ RAT
- ▶ Logic bomb
- ▶ Backdoor

For more information on the official CompTIA Security+, SY0-501 exam topics, see the "About the CompTIA Security+, SY0-501 Exam" section in the Introduction.

Essential Terms and Components

- ▶ virus
- ▶ worm
- ▶ Trojan horse
- ▶ spyware
- ▶ rootkit
- ▶ botnet
- ▶ logic bomb
- ▶ resident virus
- ▶ nonresident virus
- ▶ boot sector virus

- ▶ macro virus
- ▶ polymorphic virus
- ▶ armored virus
- ▶ stealth virus
- ▶ multipartite virus
- ▶ ransomware
- ▶ crypto-malware
- ▶ keylogger
- ▶ remote access Trojan (RAT)
- ▶ bot

CramSaver

If you can correctly answer these questions before going through this chapter, save time by skimming the Exam Alerts in this section and then completing the Cram Quiz at the end of Part I.

1. How does a virus differ from a worm?

   _____

2. What symptoms indicate that a system contains spyware?

   _____

3. What is a botnet and how does a system become part of a botnet?

   _____

4. Phishing, spear phishing, whaling, and vishing are commonly used for what purpose, and what are the technical differences between each?

   _____

Answers

1. Although worms and viruses are similar, the biggest difference is that a worm can replicate itself without any user interaction.

2. A system infested with spyware might exhibit various symptoms, such as sluggishness, changes to the web home pages, web pages automatically added to bookmarks, and websites that launch unexpectedly.

3. A botnet consists of many compromised computers that can forward transmissions to other computers outside the network. Most computers that are part of a botnet are often compromised via malicious code executed upon the system.

4. Phishing, spear phishing, whaling, and vishing are all similar. Each is a technique commonly used as part of a social engineering ploy. Phishing is commonly done through email across a large audience, whereas spear phishing targets an individual. Whaling is spear phishing that directly focuses on a high-value target. Vishing uses voice technology such as a regular phone or VoIP.

Malicious software, or malware, has become a serious problem in today's network environment. Malware is software designed to harm a user's computer or data. The target is not only the information stored on local computers, but also other resources and computers. As a security professional, you must recognize malicious code and know how to respond appropriately. This section covers the various types of malicious code you might encounter, including viruses, worms, Trojan horses, spyware, rootkits, botnets, and logic bombs.

The most serious malware typically makes use of system vulnerabilities. This makes the malware more dangerous and enables it to spread more effectively. These threats, known as blended threats, combine the characteristics of the malware items this chapter examines.

Endpoint protection technologies defend against malware by identifying and remediating security threats. Such software often provides the first line of defense by identifying that a machine has been targeted or compromised. Other symptoms of infection include unexpected system behavior and system instability. To further determine whether a system has been infected, examine the following critical areas:

▶ **Memory:** After malware is executed, it might reside in memory. Tools such as Windows Task Manager or Activity Monitor for Macs provide insight into all running processes in memory and can help identify rogue processes.

▶ **Registries:** The Windows registry, for example, provides various system settings that malware often targets. Specifically, Windows contains various entries that enable software to automatically start upon login. Malware can take advantage of these entries to ensure that malicious executables are run each time the computer starts up.

▶ **Macros:** Office applications such as Microsoft Word provide a powerful function to automate procedures. However, these macros also give malware the opportunity to automatically generate instructions when such documents launch. Office software offers an option to generate alerts when macros are being run.

Viruses

A *virus* is a program or piece of code that runs on your computer, often without your knowledge and certainly without your consent. Viruses are designed to attach themselves to other code and replicate. A virus replicates when an infected file executes or launches. It then attaches to other files, adds its code to the application's code, and continues to spread. Even a simple virus is dangerous because it can use all available resources and bring the system to a halt. Many viruses can replicate across networks and even bypass security systems.

Viruses are malicious programs that spread copies of themselves throughout a single machine. They infect other machines only if a user on another machine accesses an infected object and launches the code.

A few significant viruses have caused widespread trouble:

▶ **Melissa:** Melissa first appeared in March 1999 as a macro virus embedded in a Microsoft Word document. The recipient receives the Word document as an attachment to an email message and opens the document. The virus then sends an email to the first 50 addresses in the victim's email address book and attaches itself to each message.

▶ **Michelangelo:** Michelangelo is a master boot record virus that is based on an older virus called Stoned. The Michelangelo virus stays dormant until March 6 (its namesake's birthday), when it erases the contents of the infected drive.

▶ **Brain:** Brain is the first known stealth virus. Anytime an infected sector is accessed, Brain redirects the access to the original disk sector, to avoid detection.

> **ExamAlert**
>
> Viruses are executed by some type of action, such as running a program.

Viruses are classified and subclassified in several ways. The following classifications are based on how a virus lives in a system.

▶ **Resident virus:** This type of virus resides in memory, which means it is loaded each time the system starts and can infect other areas based on specific actions. This method allows a virus to remain active even after any host program terminates.

▶ **Nonresident virus:** Once executed, this type of virus looks for targets locally and even across the network. The virus then infects these areas and exits. Unlike a resident virus, it does not remain active.

▶ **Boot sector virus:** This type of virus is placed into the first sector of the hard drive so that when the computer boots, the virus loads into memory. As a result, the virus loads before the operating system even starts. Boot sector viruses were much more prevalent in the era of floppy disks because inserted disks supplied the means for infection and spread the virus when the computer booted up.

▶ **Macro virus:** This type of virus is inserted into a Microsoft Office document and emailed to unsuspecting users. A macro virus uses the macro language and executes when the document opens.

Finally, viruses exhibit several potential characteristics that further define their classifications.

▶ **Program and file infecting virus:** Many common viruses, particularly early ones, are this type. The virus infects executable program files and becomes active in memory. It then seeks out other files to infect. These viruses are easily identified by their binary pattern, or signature, which works essentially like a fingerprint. Similar types of file infecting files emerged in an effort to evade this signature detection, including polymorphic, stealth, and multipartite viruses (discussed next). Fortunately, security vendors are always improving their techniques as well. The evolving technology of security and antimalware vendors can help combat such attacks.

▶ **Polymorphic virus:** A polymorphic virus can change form or signature each time it is executed, to avoid detection. The prefix *poly* means "many"; *morphic* means "shape." Thus, *polymorphic* malware is malicious code capable of changing its shape. Each time a polymorphic virus infects a new file or system, for example, it changes its code. As a result, detecting the malware becomes difficult without an identifiable pattern or signature to match. Heuristic scanning is one example. Instead of looking for a specific signature, heuristic-based scanning examines the instructions running within a program.

▶ **Armored virus:** As with a polymorphic virus, the aim of an *armored virus* is to make detection difficult. As their name suggests, armored viruses go one step further by making it difficult to analyze functions, thus creating a metaphorical layer of armor around the virus. Armored viruses use various methods of operation: Most notably, in addition to seeking to defeat heuristic countermeasures, they try to prevent disassembly and debugging. If a virus succeeds in these latter aims, security researchers have more difficulty analyzing the code and designing better countermeasures.

▶ **Stealth virus:** This memory-resident virus also uses techniques to avoid detection, such as temporarily removing itself from an infected file or masking a file's size. For example, a stealth virus removes itself from an infected file and places a copy of itself in a different location.

▶ **Multipartite virus:** A multipartite virus infects executable files and also attacks the master boot record of the system. If the boot sector is not cleaned along with the infected files, the files can easily be infected again.

> **ExamAlert**
>
> Do not confuse polymorphic and armored viruses. Both try to defeat counter-measures, but armored viruses use mechanisms to keep them from being disassembled and analyzed.

Worms

Worms are similar in function and behavior to a virus, with one exception: Worms are self-replicating and do not need a host file. A worm is built to take advantage of a security hole in an existing application or operating system, then find other systems running the same software, and then automatically replicate itself to the new host. This process repeats and needs no user intervention. When the worm is successfully running on a system, it checks for Internet connectivity. If it finds connectivity, the worm tries to replicate from one system to the next. Keep in mind that the key difference between a virus and a worm is that worms do not need to attach themselves to files and programs and are capable of reproducing on their own. Common methods of replicating include spreading through email, the network, and the Internet.

Examples of worms include the following:

▶ **Morris:** This famous worm took advantage of a sendmail vulnerability and shut down the entire Internet in 1988.

▶ **Nimda:** This worm infects through several methods, including mass mailing, network share propagation, and several Microsoft vulnerabilities. Its name is *admin* spelled backward.

▶ **Code Red:** A buffer overflow exploit spreads this worm.

▶ **Blaster:** This worm made patching infected systems difficult by restarting systems. Blaster exploits a vulnerability in the Remote Procedure Call (RPC) interface.

▶ **Mydoom:** This fast-spreading worm moved through email. Spammers used it to send unsolicited mail.

▶ **Love Bug:** This worm originated in an email titled "I love you." When the attachment was launched, copies of the same email were then sent to all contacts listed in the user's address book. The worm arrived as a Visual Basic Scripting Edition (VBScript) attachment that deleted files, including MP3s, MP2s, and JPGs. It also sent usernames and passwords to the malware's author. Love Bug infected about 15 million computers and crashed servers around the world.

▶ **Stuxnet:** This worm is considered the first true cyberweapon because it targeted industrial systems. The worm spread across the network looking for software that handled a programmable logic controller.

ExamAlert

The term *virus* is often interchanged with *worm*, particularly because blended threats combine different characteristics of the two. However, remember that worms can replicate themselves without a host file.

Ransomware

Just as it sounds, *ransomware* is a form of malware that attempts to hold a user ransom, often for monetary gain. The attacker typically has already compromised a system and demands payment to prevent negative consequences such as deleting files or taking a website offline. Ransomware is actually an evolved and more demanding form of "scareware." Such scare tactics are common with fake antivirus ads that supposedly find malware on a user's machine; making a purchase simply removes the annoying notices.

CryptoLocker is an example of ransomware that became prevalent in 2013. CryptoLocker attempts to encrypt a user's data. It generates encryption keys and stores the private key on a command-and-control server. Thereafter, the ransomware demands payment in return for allowing access to the files. If the user does not pay, the ransomware threatens to delete the private key, which is required to unencrypt the files and thus restore access. Such malware is also known as *crypto-malware* because it is specifically designed to find potentially valuable data on a system and encrypt it.

In March 2017, ransomware known as WannaCry affected hundreds of thousands of systems around the world. WannaCry specifically exploited unpatched vulnerabilities on Windows systems. It even targeted hospitals, holding data hostage and demanding that infected users pay for access to their files.

ExamAlert

Ransomware is unique, in that the attacker directly demands payment, often through cryptocurrencies. The amount requested often is relatively low, to ensure a higher likelihood of payment.

Trojan Horses

Trojan horses are programs disguised as useful applications. Trojans do not rep-licate themselves as viruses do, but they can be just as destructive. Code hidden inside the application can attack your system directly or allow the code origina-tor to compromise the system. The Trojan is typically hidden, so its capability to spread depends on the popularity of the software and a user's willingness to download and install the software. Trojans can perform actions without the user's knowledge or consent, including collecting and sending data or causing the computer to malfunction. Trojans are often classified by their payload or function. The most common include backdoor, downloader, infostealer, and keylogger Trojans. Backdoor Trojans open a less obvious entry (or backdoor) into the system, for later access.

Downloader Trojans download additional, often malicious software onto infected systems. Infostealer Trojans attempt to steal information from the infected machine. *Keylogger* Trojans monitor and send keystrokes typed from the infected machine.

Examples of Trojan horses include the following:

- ▶ **Acid Rain:** When run, this old DOS Trojan deletes system files, renames folders, and creates many empty folders.

- ▶ **Nuker:** This Trojan was designed to function as a denial-of-service (DoS) attack against a workstation connected to the Internet.

- ▶ **Mocmex:** This Trojan is found in digital photo frames and collects online game passwords.

- ▶ **Simpsons:** This self-extracting batch file attempts to delete files.

- ▶ **Vundo:** This Trojan downloads and displays fraudulent advertisements.

Trojans can download other Trojans as well; this link is part of how botnets are controlled, as you see later in this chapter in the section "Bots."

Trojans are often associated with *backdoors* created intentionally as part of the Trojan. Backdoors are not malicious on their own, however; they are simply application code functions that trusted developers create either intentionally or unintentionally. During application development, software designers often add shortcut entry points to allow rapid code evaluation and testing. If the designers do not remove them before application deployment, such entry points can allow an attacker to gain unauthorized access later. Application designers might purposefully insert other backdoors as well, which present later threats to the network if no other application designer reviews them before deployment.

A backdoor Trojan is also known as a *remote access Trojan (RAT)*. Specifically, RATs installed on a system allow a remote attacker to take control of the targeted system. This approach is similar to remote control programs that allow you to personally access your computer and control it even if you are not sitting at the keyboard. Clearly, the technology itself is not malicious; only the Trojan component is because it is installed without the victim's knowledge.

> **ExamAlert**
>
> Trojans trick users by disguising their true intent to deliver a malicious payload. When executed, a remote access Trojan provides a remotely accessible backdoor for an attacker to covertly monitor the system or easily gain entry.

Rootkits

Rootkits were first documented in the early 1990s. Today they are widely used and are increasingly difficult to detect on networks. A *rootkit* is a piece of software that can be installed and hidden on a computer mainly to compromise the system and gain escalated privileges, such as administrative rights. A rootkit is usually installed on a computer when it first obtains user-level access. The rootkit then enables the attacker to gain root or privileged access to the computer, which can compromise other machines on the network as well.

A rootkit might consist of programs that view traffic and keystrokes, alter existing files to escape detection, or create a backdoor on the system.

> **ExamAlert**
>
> Rootkits can be included as part of software packages, can be installed through an unpatched vulnerability, or can be downloaded and installed by users.

Attackers are continually creating sophisticated programs that update themselves, making them harder to detect. If a rootkit has been installed, traditional antivirus software cannot always detect it because many rootkits run in the background. You can usually spot it by looking for memory processes, monitoring outbound communications, and checking for newly installed programs.

Kernel rootkits modify the kernel component of an operating system. These newer rootkits can intercept system calls passed to the kernel and can filter out queries that the rootkit software generates. Rootkits have also been known to use encryption to protect outbound communications and piggyback on commonly used ports to communicate without interrupting other applications. These tricks invalidate the usual detection methods because they make the rootkits invisible to administrators and detection tools.

Vendors do offer applications that can detect rootkits, including RootkitRevealer. Removing rootkits can be complex, however, because you must remove both the rootkit itself and the malware that the rootkit is using. Rootkits often change the Windows operating system itself, causing the system to function improperly. When a system is infected, the only definitive way to get rid of a rootkit is to completely format the computer's hard drive and reinstall the operating system. Also keep in mind that most rootkits use global hooks for stealth activity. Using security tools that prevent programs from installing global hooks and stop process injection thus prevents rootkit functionality. In addition, rootkit functionality requires full administrator rights. Therefore, you can avoid rootkit infection by running Windows from an account with lesser privileges.

Logic Bombs

A *logic bomb* is a virus or Trojan horse designed to execute malicious actions when a certain event occurs or after a certain period of time. For a virus to be considered a logic bomb, the user of the software must be unaware of the payload. A programmer might create a logic bomb to delete all code from the server on a future date, most likely after he or she has left the company. In several recent cases, ex-employees have been prosecuted for their role in this type of destruction. One of the most high-profile cases of a modern-day logic bomb involved Roger Duronio, a disgruntled computer programmer who planted a logic bomb in about 1,000 computer systems of investment bank UBS to delete critical files and prevent backups. UBS estimated the repair costs at $3.1 million, not including downtime, lost data, or lost business. The actions of the logic bomb coincided with Duronio's stock transactions, so the company added securities and mail fraud charges to the computer crime charges. Duronio was found guilty of planting a logic bomb on the systems and of securities fraud. He was sentenced to more than 8 years in jail and fined $3.1 million.

ExamAlert

A logic bomb is also referred to as slag code. The malicious code is usually planted by a disgruntled employee.

During software development, it is a good idea to evaluate the code to keep logic bombs from being inserted. Unfortunately, code evaluation cannot keep someone from planting a logic bomb *after* programming is complete.

Bots

A *bot*, short for *robot*, is an automated computer program that needs no user interaction. Bots are systems that outside sources can control. A bot provides a spam or virus originator with the venue to propagate. Many computers compromised in this way are unprotected home computers (although many computers in the corporate world are bots as well). A *botnet* is a large number of computers that forward transmissions to other computers on the Internet. You might also hear a botnet referred to as a *zombie army*.

A system is usually compromised by a virus or other malicious code that gives the attacker access. A bot can be created through a port that has been left open or an unpatched vulnerability. A small program is left on the machine for future activation. The bot master can then unleash the effects of the army by sending a single command to all the compromised machines. A computer can be part of a botnet even though it appears to be operating normally. This is because bots are hidden and usually go undetected unless you are specifically looking for certain activity. The computers that form a botnet can be programmed to conduct a distributed denial-of-service (DDoS) attack, distribute spam, or perform other malicious acts. Chapter 2, "Attack Types," has more on DDoS and other types of attacks.

Since the mid-2000s, botnets have flooded the Internet. One example, the Storm botnet, started out as an email that began circulating on January 19, 2007. It contained a link to a news story about a deadly storm. A year later, Storm remained the largest, most active botnet on the Internet at the time. It continued to be a major source of spam even years afterward. Its immense effect has now subsided largely due to patching, but on any given day, thousands of command and control botnet servers might still have millions of active connections. Storm was the first botnet to make wide use of peer-to-peer communications. It also has a self-defense mechanism. When the botnet is probed too much, it reacts automatically and starts a DoS attack against the probing entity.

Botnets can be particularly tricky and sophisticated because they can make use of social engineering. A collection of botnets known as Zbot stole millions from banks in four nations. The scammers enticed bank customers with a ruse to click a link to download an updated digital certificate. Zbot then installed a program that allowed it to see the next time the user successfully accessed the account. While the victims did their online banking, Zbot automatically completed cash transfers to other accounts.

The main issue with botnets is that they are securely hidden. The botnet masters can perform tasks, gather information, and commit crimes while remaining undetected. Worse, attackers can increase the depth and effect of their crimes by using multiple computers because each computer in a botnet can be programmed to execute the same command.

Spyware

Undesirable code sometimes arrives with commercial software distributions. *Spyware* is associated with behaviors such as advertising, collecting personal information, and changing your computer configuration without first obtaining consent. Basically, spyware is software that communicates information from a user's system to another party without notifying the user.

Similar to a Trojan horse (described in an earlier section), spyware sends information across the Internet to some unknown entity. In this case, however, spyware monitors user activity on the system, potentially including keystrokes typed, and sends this logged information to the originator. The information, such as passwords, account numbers, and other private information, then no longer is private.

Some clues indicate that a computer might contain spyware:

▶ The system is slow, especially when browsing the Internet.

▶ The Windows desktop is slow in coming up.

▶ Clicking a link does nothing or takes you to an unexpected website.

▶ The browser home page changes, and you might not be able to reset it.

▶ Web pages are automatically added to your favorites list.

> **ExamAlert**
>
> Spyware monitors user activity on the system and can include keystrokes typed. The information is then sent to the originator of the spyware.

Advertising-supported software, or *adware*, is another form of spyware that gives advertisers an online way to make a sale. Companies offer to place banner ads in their products. In exchange for the ad, a portion of the revenue from banner sales goes to the company placing the ad. However, this novel concept presents some issues for users. These companies also install tracking software on your system that remains in contact with the company through your

Internet connection. The software reports data to the company, such as your general surfing habits and the sites you visit. The company might affirm that it will not collect identifying data from your system. However, the situation is still sensitive because software on your system is sending information about you and your surfing habits to a remote location.

U.S. federal law prohibits secretly installing software that forces consumers to receive pop-ups that disrupt their computer use. Adware is legitimate only when users are informed up front that they will receive ads. In addition, if the adware gathers information about users, it must inform them. Privacy issues arise even with legitimate adware, however. For instance, although legitimate adware discloses the nature of data collected and transmitted, users have little or no control over what data is being collected and dispersed. Remember, this technology can send more than just banner statistics.

What Next?

If you want more practice on this chapter's exam objectives before you move on, remember that you can access all the Cram Quiz questions on the Pearson Test Prep software. You can also create a custom exam by objective. Note any objective you struggle with and go to that objective material in this chapter.

CHAPTER 2

Attack Types

This chapter covers the following official Security+ exam objective:

1.2 Compare and contrast types of attacks.

▶ Social engineering
  - Phishing
  - Spear phishing
  - Whaling
  - Vishing
  - Tailgating
  - Impersonation
  - Dumpster diving
  - Shoulder surfing
  - Hoax
  - Watering hole attack
  - Principles (reasons for effectiveness)
    • Authority
    • Intimidation
    • Consensus
    • Scarcity
    • Familiarity
    • Urgency
▶ Application/service attacks
  - DoS
  - DDoS
  - Man-in-the-middle
  - Buffer overflow
  - Injection
  - Cross-site scripting
  - Cross-site request forgery
  - Privilege escalation
  - ARP poisoning
  - Domain hijacking
  - Man-in-the-browser
  - Zero day
  - Replay
  - Pass the hash

- Hijacking and related attacks
  • Clickjacking
  • Session hijacking
  • URL hijacking
- Driver manipulation
  • Shimming
  • Refactoring
- MAC spoofing
- IP spoofing
▶ Wireless attacks
  - Replay
  - IV
  - Evil twin
  - Rogue AP
  - Jamming
  - WPS
  - Bluejacking
  - Bluesnarfing
  - RFID
  - NFC
  - Disassociation
▶ Cryptographic attacks
  - Birthday
  - Known plain text/cipher text
  - Rainbow tables
  - Dictionary
  - Brute force
    • Online vs. offline
  - Collision
  - Downgrade
  - Replay
  - Weak implementations

Essential Terms and Components

- social engineering
- spear phishing
- whaling
- vishing
- tailgating
- shoulder surfing
- hoax
- watering hole attack
- denial of service (DoS)
- distributed denial of service (DDOS)
- man-in-the-middle
- buffer overflow
- cross-site scripting (XSS)
- cross-site request forgery (XSRF)
- domain hijacking
- ARP poisoning
- privilege escalation
- zero day
- pass the hash
- clickjacking

- session hijacking
- URL hijacking
- typo squatting
- shimming
- refactoring
- MAC spoofing
- IP spoofing
- evil twin
- rogue access point
- jamming attack
- Wi-Fi Protected Setup (WPS)
- bluejacking
- bluesnarfing
- Radio Frequency Identification (RFID)
- Near Field Communications (NFC)
- birthday attack
- rainbow table
- dictionary attack
- brute-force attack

CramSaver

If you can correctly answer these questions before going through this chapter, save time by skimming the Exam Alerts in this section and then completing the Cram Quiz at the end of Part I.

1. Describe several different examples of social engineering attacks.

_____

2. What is the difference between bluejacking and bluesnarfing?

_____

3. Identify and explain at least two different types of code injection techniques.

_____

4. What is a zero-day attack?

_____

5. What type of attack is performed when an attacker provides the hashed password to the authenticating system for access?

_____

Answers

1. Although there are countless answers, social engineering relies on extracting useful information by tricking the target. Examples include scenarios that involve impersonating someone else, coercing someone else into divulging sensitive information without cause for concern, or convincing someone to install a malicious program to assist you.

2. Bluejacking involves sending an unsolicited broadcast message to nearby Bluetooth-enabled devices. Bluesnarfing is more nefarious: If successful, it enables the attacker to gain unauthorized access to the device. Bluejacking is commonly used to enable bluesnarfing.

3. Common code injection techniques include XSS, SQL injection, LDAP injection, and XML injection. XSS involves including a client-side script on a website for malicious purposes to exploit a vulnerability. SQL, LDAP, and XML injection are similar, in that they piggyback malicious code through an input field in the application. SQL injection is targeted at databases, LDAP injection at directories, and XML injection at XML documents and code.

4. A zero-day attack exploits a vulnerability that is unknown to others, possibly even the software developer.

5. A pass-the-hash-attack is a type of replay attack in which the attacker provides the hashed password to an accepting authentication scheme.

Today's networks are increasingly complex and mobile. Not only are there various points of entry, but the idea of a tight perimeter has been expanding and, in many cases, doesn't exist. It's important to understand the different types of attacks. Keep in mind, however, that most attacks do not succeed with just one attack. A combination of these attacks often is required. For these reasons, the idea of defense-in-depth is critical to the security of an organization. As you learn about the individual attacks in the sections that follow, compare and contrast them. Also think about how each might be used and when a combination of such attacks would be required.

Social Engineering

Social engineering has been around as long as humans. Perhaps you recall face-to-face interactions in which one individual fishes for information in a deceptive way. Legitimate users are the area of security planning that is the most difficult to adequately secure. *Social engineering* is the process by which an attacker seeks to extract useful information from users, often by just tricking them into helping the attacker. Social engineering is extremely successful because it relies on human emotions. Common examples include the following:

▶ An attacker calls a valid user and impersonates a guest, temp agent, or new user, asking for assistance in accessing the network or requesting details on the business processes of the organization.

▶ An attacker contacts a legitimate user and poses as a technical aide attempting to update some type of information. The attacker asks for identifying user details that can then be used to gain access.

▶ An attacker poses as a network administrator, directing the legitimate user to reset the password to a specific value so that an imaginary update can be applied.

▶ An attacker provides the user with a "helpful" program or agent through email, a website, or other means of distribution. This program might require the user to enter login details or personal information useful to the attacker, or it might install other programs that compromise the system's security.

Another form of social engineering has come to be known as reverse social engineering. In this situation, an attacker provides information to the legitimate user that causes the user to believe the attacker is an authorized technical assistant. This might be accomplished by obtaining an IT support badge or logo-bearing shirt to seemingly validate the attacker's legitimacy, by inserting the attacker's contact information for technical support in a secretary's files, or by making himself known for his technical skills by helping people around the office.

Many users would rather ask assistance from a nontechnical person they know to be skilled in computer support than contact a legitimate technical staff person who is perceived to be busy with more important matters. An attacker might plan and cause a minor problem, but then easily correct this problem with the users as witnesses. This enables the attacker to gain the confidence of legitimate users and also observe operational and network configuration details and login information. The attacker might even be left alone with an authorized account logged into the network.

ExamAlert

Social engineering is a common practice attackers use and is not easily countered via technology. It is important to understand that the best defense against social engineering is ongoing user awareness and education.

Next, we discuss various attacks such as phishing, whaling, and vishing. These can also be classified as social engineering, but they rely more on technical methods to accomplish the goals. These attacks, as well as several of the methods discussed next, are attacks on humans and take advantage of human psychology. People tend to trust others. People tend to want to be helpful to others in need. Because of these tendencies, adequate and ongoing training is required to counteract potential attacks.

These techniques by themselves can lead to sensitive data loss. The information acquired might not have immediate consequences, but the cumulative effect combined with other social engineering and technical attacks could have dire consequences for either the individuals or their organization.

Phishing and Related Attacks

Increasingly, social engineering attacks are combined with electronic means. Social engineering conducted via computer systems has different names based on the target and the method. One of the more common methods of social engineering via electronic communications is phishing. *Phishing* is an attempt to acquire sensitive information by masquerading as a trustworthy entity via electronic communication, usually email. Phishing attacks rely on a mix of technical deceit and social engineering practices. In most cases, the phisher must persuade the victim to intentionally perform a series of actions that provide access to confidential information. As scam artists become more sophisticated, so do their phishing email messages. The messages often include official-looking logos from real organizations and other identifying information taken directly from legitimate websites. For best protection, you must deploy proper security technologies and techniques at the client side, the server side, and the enterprise level. Ideally, users should not be able to directly access email attachments from within the email application. However, the best defense is user education.

Related methods with slight differences include the following:

▶ **Spear phishing:** This is a targeted version of phishing. Whereas phishing often involves mass emailing, spear phishing might go after a specific individual.

▶ **Whaling:** Whaling is identical to spear phishing, except for the size of the fish. Whaling employs spear phishing tactics but goes after high-profile targets such as an executive within a company.

▶ **Vishing:** This attack is also known as voice phishing. The attacker uses fake caller ID to appear as a trusted organization and attempts to get the individual to enter account details via the phone.

▶ **Smishing:** Also known as SMS phishing, this attack uses phishing methods through text messaging.

▶ **Pharming:** This term is a combination of *farming* and *phishing*. Pharming does not require the user to be tricked into clicking a link. Instead, pharming redirects victims to a bogus website, even if the user correctly entered the intended site. To accomplish this, the attacker employs another attack, such as DNS cache poisoning.

> **ExamAlert**
>
> Phishing combines technical deceit with the elements of traditional social engineering. Be sure to know the variants of phishing attacks.

Tailgating

Tailgating is a simple yet effective form of social engineering. It involves piggybacking or following closely behind someone who has authorized physical access within an environment. Tailgating involves appearing to be part of an authorized group or capitalizing on people's desire to be polite. A common example is an attacker following an authorized person and hoping that the person holds open a secure door to grant access. Many high-security facilities employ mantraps (an airlock-like mechanism that allows only one person to pass at a time) to provide entrance control and prevent tailgating.

Impersonation

Impersonation is simply a method in which someone assumes the character or appearance of someone else. The attacker pretends to be something he or she is not. Impersonation is often used in conjunction with a pretext or invented scenario. Images of private detectives might come to mind here. In many great movies, such as *Catch Me If You Can* and *Beverly Hills Cop*, the drama or humor unfolds as a result of impersonation and pretexting.

Dumpster Diving

As humans, we naturally seek the path of least resistance. Instead of shredding documents or walking them to the recycle bin, employees often throw them into the wastebasket. Workers also might put discarded equipment into the garbage if city laws do not require special disposal. Intruders know this and scavenge for discarded equipment and documents in an act called dumpster diving. They can extract sensitive information from the garbage without ever contacting anyone in the organization.

In any organization, the potential risk of an intruder gaining access to this type of information is huge. What happens when employees leave the organization? They clean out their desks. Depending on how long the employees have been there, what ends up in the garbage can be a goldmine for an intruder.

Other potential sources of discarded information include the following:

- ▶ Old company directories
- ▶ Old QA or testing analysis
- ▶ Employee manuals
- ▶ Training manuals
- ▶ Hard drives
- ▶ Floppy disks
- ▶ Optical media
- ▶ USB flash drives
- ▶ Printed emails

Proper disposal of data and equipment should be part of the organization's security policy. Companies should have a policy in place that requires shredding of all physical documents and secure erasure of all types of storage media before they may be discarded. Secure erasure is often performed via the use of disk-wiping software, which can delete the data according to different standards.

Shoulder Surfing

Shoulder surfing literally means looking over someone's shoulder to obtain information. Common situations include entering a PIN at an automated teller machine (ATM) or typing in a password at a computer system. More broadly, however, shoulder surfing includes any method of direct observation. This could include, for example, locating a camera nearby or even using binoculars from a distance. As with many of these types of methods, user awareness and training is key to prevention. However, some tools can also assist here. Many ATMs now include mirrors for users to see who might be behind them, as well as better-designed keypads to help conceal keypad entry. Even special screen overlays are available for laptop computers to prevent someone from seeing the screen at an angle. In such situations, the consequences for the perpetrator are low. Simply peering over someone's shoulder to learn the combination is less risky than, say, actually breaking open a safe or attempting to open the safe when unauthorized. In fact, the shoulder surfer might not actually be the one to initiate a subsequent attack. Information security attacks have evolved into an ecosystem. The shoulder surfer's job might be complete here because he or she simply provides or sells this information to someone else with more nefarious goals.

Hoaxes

Hoaxes are interesting because although they present a threat, the threat does not actually exist at face value. Instead, the actions people take in response to the perceived threat create the actual threats. For example, a hoax virus email can consume resources as it is forwarded on. In fact, a widely distributed and believed hoax about a computer virus can result in consequences as significant as an actual virus. Such hoaxes, particularly as they manifest themselves in the physical world, can create unnecessary fear and irrational behaviors. Most hoaxes are passed around not just via email, but also by social networks and word of mouth. Many times, the same hoax will find ways to make the rounds again even years later, perhaps altered only slightly. Snopes.com is a well-known resource that has been around since the mid-1990s. If you are ever in doubt or need help in debunking hoaxes, make this site part of your trusted arsenal.

Watering Hole Attacks

In many ways, a watering hole attack is like spear phishing, discussed earlier. However, instead of using email, the attacker attacks a site that the target frequently visits. The goal is often to compromise the larger environment—for example, the company the target works for.

Just as the lion waits hidden near the watering hole that zebras frequent, the attacker waits at the sites you frequent. In a typical scenario, the attacker first profiles and understands the victim. This includes what websites the victim visits and what type of computer and web browser are used. Next, the attacker looks for opportunities to compromise any of these sites based on existing vulnerabilities. Understanding more about the victim (for example, type of browser used and activities) helps the attacker compromise the site with the greatest chance of then exploiting the victim. Finally, such attacks are commonly used in conjunction with a zero-day exploit. Even by being able to take advantage of a cross-site scripting vulnerability on the visited site, the attacker can ensure that the trusted site helps deliver an exploit to the victim's machine.

Principles (Reasons for Effectiveness)

Ready for a psychology cram? As stated earlier, social engineering relies much on what is known about human psychology. In particular, the social engineer is looking to influence another person to gain something, which is most often not in the target's best interest. In many cases, social engineering combines influence with manipulation. Given this, let's look at the various principles of influence. The following topics are largely based on the work of Robert Cialdini, Regents Professor Emeritus of Psychology and Marketing at Arizona State University. The key challenge for the various principles of influence is that even though people might recognize the specific principle, it is not easy to see when they themselves are being illegitimately used. The following points summarize key principles of influence and highlight why they are effective:

▶ **Authority:** Job titles, uniforms, symbols, badges, and even specific expertise all represent elements we often equate with authority. With such proclaimed and believed authority, we naturally feel an obligation to comply. This could be flashing red lights that cause you to pull over. It could be the specific expertise of the IT security administrator or chief information security officer that compels you to divulge your password so that they can troubleshoot. In addition to feeling a sense of obligation, we tend to trust authoritative symbols (many of which are easily forged).

▶ **Intimidation:** Authority plays to our sense of duty, and people with authority or power above us are in a position to abuse that power. We might feel that not complying would have a negative impact. Intimidation does not need to necessarily be so severe that one fears physical harm. A social engineer would more likely use intimidation to play upon a fear of getting in trouble or getting fired, for example.

▶ **Consensus/social proof:** Based on the idea that people tend to trust like-minded people such as friends and family, this is about doing or believing what others around us believe. Think of the cliché "safety in numbers." This is why we are more likely to put a tip in a tip jar when it is not empty, for example, or why we might hesitate to eat at a restaurant that is empty. A social engineer might mention friends and colleagues—the attacker might say that these trusted people mentioned you, or that they have already complied with whatever you are being asked for. Ambiguous requests or situations are more likely to be acted on with the belief that others are doing the same thing or bought into the same situation.

▶ **Scarcity and urgency:** Scarcity is commonly used as a marketing ploy (some more effective than others). Surely you have heard the pitch about special pricing available to only the first 50 callers. Or perhaps you have heard tales of companies unable to keep up with demand (either real or just an illusion). We tend to want or value something more if we believe it is less available. We are likely to be more impulsive if we believe something is the last one. The social engineer might use the principle of scarcity to spur someone to more quickly act on a request before giving the request more thought. Scarcity tends to work when the victim desires something and, in turn, will act with a greater sense of urgency. Likewise, the social engineer can use urgency to gain support. Perhaps dreadful consequences will occur unless action takes place immediately.

▶ **Familiarity/liking:** People tend to comply with requests from those whom they like or have common ground with. Liking often leads to trust. The social engineer might try to use humor or connect more personally through shared interests or common past events and institutions. This is effective based on our fundamental desire to establish and maintain social relationships with others. Social engineers who can get you to like them often find that you will be helpful because you, too, want to be liked.

▶ **Trust:** Trust plays a large role in the previous principles. We trust those with assigned authority. We trust those with specific expertise regarding their subject. Trust typically follows liking someone. We trust the consensus. Trust further is established and plays out in the idea of reciprocation. We are taught from an early age the golden rule: Do unto others as you would have them do unto you. As a result, a social norm is established to create equity in social situations, to return favors and not feel indebted to anyone. The reciprocation that occurs and the equity that is established helps build trust.

ExamAlert

Be sure to understand how social engineers can use the previously mentioned principles for their gain and why these strategies are effective.

Application/Service Attacks

Social engineering targets humans, and by itself it might not lead attackers to their goal. Often attackers combine social engineering attacks with subsequent application and service attacks. The simplest example is an attacker tailgating into a sensitive area to gain access to conduct further attacks.

The evolution of web- or cloud-based application resources available via the HTTP and HTTPS protocols presents an "anytime/anywhere" approach to enterprise network resource availability. As more applications are migrated into the browser, attackers have an increasingly large attack surface area for interception and interaction with user input and for directed attacks against web-based resources.

It's important to understand more generalized attacks. In many cases, these attacks are not specific to wired or wireless networks; however, with the ubiquitous rollout of wireless technology across networks and devices, we need to specifically look at challenges and attacks unique to wireless networks as well.

Spoofing

Spoofing is a method of providing false identity information to gain unauthorized access. Two common methods include the following:

▶ IP spoofing

▶ MAC spoofing

IP spoofing is accomplished by modifying the source address of traffic or the source of information. Consider, for example, the IP address assigned to a specific computer. An attacker who can forge this address is essentially trying to masquerade as that system. In another example, consider the hard-coded Media Access Control (MAC) address of a network card, which is permanently assigned. Some networks might control access via this address. An attacker able to spoof this address could then gain access. You should be familiar with two specific spoofing methods:

▶ **Blind spoofing:** The attacker sends data and only makes assumptions of responses.

▶ **Informed spoofing:** The attacker can participate in a session and can monitor the bidirectional communications.

ExamAlert

IP spoofing seeks to bypass IP address filters by setting up a connection from a client and sourcing the packets with an IP address that is allowed through the filter.

Services such as email, web, and file transfer can also be spoofed. Web spoofing happens when an attacker creates a convincing but false copy of an entire website. The false site looks just like the real one, with all the same pages and links; however, the attacker controls the false site so that all network traffic between the victim's browser and the site goes through the attacker. In email spoofing, a spammer or a computer virus can forge the email packet information in an email so that it appears the email is coming from a trusted host, from one of your friends, or even from your own email address. If you leave your email address at some Internet site or exchange email with other people, a spoofer might be able to use your email address as the sender address to send spam. File-transfer spoofing involves the FTP service. FTP data is sent in clear text. An attacker can intercept the data. The data can then be viewed and altered before sending it on to the receiver. These forms of attacks are often used to get additional information from network users to complete a more aggressive attack.

You should set up a filter that denies traffic originating from the Internet if it shows an internal network address. Using the signing capabilities of certificates on servers and clients allows web and email services to be more secure. Use of IPsec can secure transmissions between critical servers and clients, to help prevent these types of attacks from taking place.

Buffer and Integer Overflows

Buffer overflows cause disruption of service and lost data. This condition occurs when the data presented to an application or service exceeds the storage space allocation that has been reserved in memory for that application or service. Poor application design might allow the input of 100 characters into a field linked to a variable that is capable of holding only 50 characters. As a result, the application does not know how to handle the extra data and becomes unstable. The overflow portion of the input data must be discarded or somehow handled by the application; otherwise, it could create undesirable results. Because no check is in place to screen out bad requests, the extra data overwrites some portions of memory that other applications use and then causes failures and crashes. A buffer overflow can result in the following:

► Data or memory storage is overwritten.

► The attack overloaded the input buffer's capability to cope with the additional data, resulting in denial of service.

► The originator can execute arbitrary code, often at a privileged level.

An *integer overflow* is another type of overflow. It is specific to whole numbers, known as *integers*. For example, 12 is an integer, but 12.1 is not. Programs that do not carefully account for integer overflows can result in undesirable behaviors and consequences. Imagine a typical vehicle odometer. Most odometers support only six digits, which go to 999,999 miles or kilometers. Many vehicles are lucky to see 200,000 miles, so what happens if one drives 1 million miles? The odometer suffers from an integer overflow and then shows that 0 miles have been driven. Put another way, a program designed to hold an integer of 8 bits could support a number up to 255 and would look like the following in binary: 11111111. The number 256 requires an extra bit and would be 100000000. If such a program designed to support only 8 bits accepted the decimal number of 256, it could interpret 256 as 0 (accepting only the last 8 bits) or as 128 (accepting only the first 8 bits).

Overflows present an opportunity for compromise using *privilege escalation*. Services require special privileges for their operation. A programming error could allow an attacker to obtain special privileges. In this situation, two possible types of privilege escalation exist: a programming error enabling a user to gain additional privileges after successful authentication, and a user gaining privileges with no authentication.

In the case of buffer overflows, good quality assurance and secure programming practices can thwart this type of attack. Currently, the most effective way to prevent an attacker from exploiting software is to keep the manufacturer's latest patches and updates applied and to monitor the web for newly discovered vulnerabilities.

Zero-Day Attack

A zero-day (or zero hour or day zero) attack or threat is a computer threat that tries to exploit computer application vulnerabilities that are unknown to others or even the software developer. (Those weaknesses are also called zero-day vulnerabilities.) Zero-day exploits (actual software that uses a security hole to carry out an attack) are used or shared by attackers before the developer of the target software knows about the vulnerability.

A zero-day attack differs from other attacks and vulnerabilities. Most attacks on vulnerable systems involve known vulnerabilities. These include vulnerabilities that developers know about, but for which a patch has not been issued. In most cases, however, attacks target known vulnerabilities for which a fix or a control exists but has not been implemented. In the case of zero-day attacks, the software developer has not even had a chance to distribute a fix for his software.

> **ExamAlert**
>
> Remember that zero-day vulnerabilities do not have a patch yet available. Keep this in mind when evaluating techniques to protect your organization. Effective security policies, training, and mitigating controls are more effective, even compared to the most aggressive patch-management strategies, when it comes to zero-day exploits.

Code Injections

Application developers and security professionals need to be aware of the different types of threats from malicious code. Using malicious *code injection*, attackers can perform a variety of attacks on systems. Proper input validation is one primary means of preventing such attacks. These attacks can result in the modification or theft of data. Examples of common code injection techniques include the following:

▶ **Cross-site scripting (XSS):** By placing a malicious client-side script on a website, an attacker can cause an unknowing browser user to conduct unauthorized access activities, expose confidential data, and log successful attacks back to the attacker without users being aware of their participation. XSS vulnerabilities can be used to hijack the user's session or to cause the user accessing malware-tainted Site A to unknowingly attack Site B on behalf of the attacker who planted code on Site A.

▶ **Cross-site request forgery (CSRF or XSRF):** This attack causes end users to execute an unwanted action on a site they are already logged into. Imagine that you are logged into a social media site. You then browse simultaneously to another site, where the site request includes code to post a status update on your social media site. Assuming that you remained logged in and the social media site is not designed to protect against such forged requests, this is entirely possible.

▶ **SQL injection:** In this attack, malicious code is inserted into strings that are later passed to a database server. The SQL server then parses and executes this code.

These attacks take advantage of coding flaws, which are preventable. In fact, many application and web development frameworks provide built-in resources and tools to prevent such errors.

Proper input validation does not prevent a code injection technique known as *DLL injection*. DLL injection inserts malicious code into a running process. This code injection technique takes advantage of dynamic link libraries (DLLs), which are designed for the running application to load at runtime. DLL injection attacks thus result when the legitimate process hooks into the malicious DLLs and then runs them. The Windows operating system now includes a protected process system to prevent such attacks by ensuring that only trusted code gets loaded. Rootkits, covered in Chapter 1, "Indicators of Compromise and Malware Types," use DLL injection to hook themselves into the Windows operating system.

Kernel-mode device drivers, which most operating systems support, run at a much lower level, with the same privilege as the operating system. Essentially, the manipulation of device drivers has the potential to completely subvert the system, making detection difficult because the system cannot be trusted. However, this is a sophisticated hack that requires installing a *shim*, a piece of code between two components that is then capable of intercepting calls and even redirecting them elsewhere. A good practice for software developers is to identify ways to make code more efficient through better design. This process, known as *refactoring*, helps improve the manageability of the code, which also helps reduce complexity and improve code extensibility. Again, however, one of the best methods of preventing such attacks is to ensure trusted code through cryptographic techniques to verify the integrity of the code components.

Hijacking and Related Attacks

You should be familiar with the various types of hijacking attacks, including URL hijacking, domain hijacking, clickjacking, and session hijacking.

URL hijacking, also known as *typo squatting*, is a simple method used frequently for benign purposes, but it is also easily used for more malicious attacks. Typo squatting most commonly relies on typographic errors users make on the Internet. It can be as simple as accidentally typing www.gooogle.com instead of www.google.com. In this example, Google owns both domain names and redirects the mistyped domain to the correct domain. However, a misspelled URL of a travel website, for instance, might take someone to a competing website. Certainly, any domain name can be slightly misspelled, but some typos are more common. Imagine that you unknowingly and mistakenly type in the wrong URL for your bank; perhaps you just accidentally transpose a couple letters.

Instead of being presented with a generic parked domain for a domain registrar (an immediate tip-off that something is wrong), you are presented with what you know and expect to be your bank. An attacker's variations and motives can vary, but the simplest attack is to easily record your login information. Perhaps after you try to log in, you simply see a message that your bank is undergoing website maintenance and will be back up in 24 hours. Meanwhile, the attacker has access to your credentials and knows which site they can be used on.

A similar yet more direct attack involves theft of the actual domain. Known as *domain hijacking*, this occurs when a domain is taken over without the original owner's knowledge or consent. This can opportunistically occur when the domain ownership expires, but direct attacks are usually the result of security issues with the domain registrar or a direct attack via social engineering or through the administration portal of the domain owner.

In another example of a hijacking attack, an attacker can hijack clicks. This attack, known as *clickjacking*, takes advantage of browser vulnerabilities and allows the attacker to redirect clicks or even keystrokes to something the user does not expect. A common method of this attack relies upon an invisible iframe layered within a web page. Thus, users think they have clicked on the intended button or link, but they have actually selected the invisible component that the attacker intended.

Session hijacking is another common attack. Browser cookies, known as session cookies, are often used to maintain an open session for users interacting within a site. These cookies ensure authentication to the remote site and are a target of attackers. With a stolen session cookie, the attacker can gain access to that site.

Additionally, because browsers access resources on a remote server using a pre-defined port (80 for HTTP or 443 for HTTPS), attackers can easily identify browser traffic. An attacker might choose to hijack legitimate user credentials and session data for unauthorized access to secured resources. Although HTTPS traffic is encrypted between endpoints, an attacker who crafts a web proxy can allow a user to connect securely to this proxy system and then establish a secured link from the proxy to the user's intended resource. The attacker could then capture plain-text data transport on the proxy system even though the user receives all appropriate responses for a secured connection.

Man-in-the-Middle

The man-in-the-middle (MITM) attack takes place when an attacker intercepts traffic and then tricks the parties at both ends into believing that they are communicating with each other. This type of attack is possible because of the nature of the three-way TCP handshake process using SYN and ACK packets. Because TCP is a connection-oriented protocol, a three-way handshake takes place when establishing a connection and when closing a session. When establishing a session, the client sends a SYN request, the server sends an acknowledgment and synchronization (SYN-ACK) to the client, and then the client sends an ACK (also referred to as SYN-ACK-ACK), completing the connection. During this process, the attacker initiates the man-in-the-middle attack. The attacker uses a program that appears to be the server to the client, and appears to be the client to the server. The attacker can also choose to alter the data or merely eavesdrop and pass it along. This attack is common in Telnet and wireless technologies. It is also generally difficult to implement because of physical routing issues, TCP sequence numbers, and speed.

If the attack is attempted on an internal network, physical access to the network is required. Be sure that access to wiring closets and switches is restricted; if possible, the area should be locked.

After you have secured the physical environment, protect the services and resources that allow a system to be inserted into a session. DNS can be compromised and used to redirect the initial request for service, providing an opportunity to execute a man-in-the-middle attack. You should restrict DNS access to read only for everyone except the administrator. The best way to prevent these types of attacks is to use encryption, secure protocols, and methods for keeping track of the user's session or device.

> **ExamAlert**
>
> A man-in-the-middle attack takes place when a computer intercepts traffic and either eavesdrops on the traffic or alters it.

MITM attacks have declined because of the prevalence of such prevention techniques. As a result, a newer type of MITM, known as man-in-the-browser (MITB), has increased. A MITB attack is a Trojan that infects web browser components such as browser plug-ins and other browser helper objects. MITB attacks are particularly dangerous because everything occurs at the application level on the user's system. These attacks are capable of avoiding web application controls that might otherwise be alerted to a traditional MITM attack at the network layer. MITB can also go beyond mere interception, to inject web code and perform other functions to interact with the user.

Replay

In a replay attack, packets are captured by using sniffers. After the pertinent information is extracted, the packets are placed back on the network. This type of attack can be used to replay bank transactions or other similar types of data transfer, in the hopes of replicating or changing activities such as deposits or transfers. Consider, for example, a password replay attack. In such a scenario, the attacker intercepts the password. Later, the attacker sends the password to authenticate as if the attacker is the original user.

Protecting yourself against replay attacks involves some type of time stamp associated with the packets or time-valued, nonrepeating serial numbers. Secure protocols such as IPsec prevent replays of data traffic in addition to providing authentication and data encryption.

Pass the Hash

Most systems do not subsequently send passwords in clear text after the user receives them. Instead, the system creates a digital fingerprint, or cryptographic hash, of the password. Knowing a hash does not allow a system to reconstruct a password; it allows it to verify that an input maps to a particular hash value. In fact, most passwords are stored as a cryptographic hashed value.

Chapter 34, "Cryptography," explores hashes more. For now, this discussion provides an overly simplified example of hashing. Imagine that each letter of the alphabet corresponds to a number (A = 1, B = 2, C = 3, and so on). If your password is ABC, then using your hashing algorithm (that is, adding up the numbers), you arrive at a value of 6. When a password is subsequently entered, it is run through the same algorithm and then compared to the stored value. If you try to enter ABD, the resulting value of 7 will not match the value stored. Of course, actual hashing algorithms are much more complicated than this, but this should help you understand the concepts further.

In a pass-the-hash attack, the attacker does not need access to a user's password. Instead, the attacker needs only the hashed value of the password. This attack is performed against systems that accept specific implementations of authentication schemes known as LM or NTLM. In this attack, the attacker does not need the password, assuming that he or she has gained access to the cryptographic hash. The attacker then can pass this hash value to a system for authentication.

ARP Poisoning

All network cards have a unique 48-bit address that is hardcoded into the network card. For network communications to occur, this hardware address must be associated with an IP address. Address Resolution Protocol (ARP), which operates at Layer 2 (data link layer) of the OSI model, associates MAC addresses to IP addresses. ARP is a simple lower-layer protocol that consists of requests and replies without validation. However, this simplicity also leads to a lack of security.

When you use a protocol analyzer to look at traffic, you see an ARP request and an ARP reply, which are the two basic parts of ARP communication. Reverse ARP (RARP) requests and RARP replies also are used. Devices maintain an ARP table that contains a cache of the IP addresses and MAC addresses the device has already correlated. The host device searches its ARP table to see whether a MAC address corresponds to the destination host IP address. When no matching entry exists, it broadcasts an ARP request to the entire network. All systems see the broadcast, but only the device that has the corresponding information replies. However, devices can accept ARP replies before even requesting them. This type of entry is known as an unsolicited entry because the information was not explicitly requested.

> ### ExamAlert
>
> ARP does not require any type of validation. Thus, as ARP requests are sent, the requesting devices believe that the incoming ARP replies are from the correct devices. This can allow a perpetrator to trick a device into thinking any IP address is related to any MAC address.

In addition, an attacker can broadcast a fake or spoofed ARP reply to an entire network and poison all computers. This is known as ARP poisoning. Put simply, the attacker deceives a device on your network, poisoning its table associations of other devices.

ARP poisoning can lead to attacks such as DoS, man-in-the-middle attacks, and MAC flooding. DoS attacks are covered in greater detail later in this chapter. MAC flooding is an attack directed at network switches. This type of attack is successful because of the way all switches and bridges work. Only a limited amount of space is allocated to store source addresses of packets. When the table becomes full, the device can no longer learn new information and becomes flooded. As a result, the switch can be forced into a hublike state that will broadcast all network traffic to every device in the network.

A lesser vulnerability of ARP is port stealing. Port stealing is a man-in-the-middle attack that exploits the binding between the port and the MAC address. The principle behind port stealing is that an attacker sends numerous packets with the source IP address of the victim and the destination MAC address of the attacker. This attack applies to broadcast networks built from switches.

ARP poisoning is limited to attacks that are locally based, so an intruder needs either physical access to your network or control of a device on your local network. To mitigate ARP poisoning on a small network, you can use static or script-based mappings for IP addresses and ARP tables. For large networks, use equipment that offers port security. By doing so, you can permit only one MAC address for each physical port on the switch. In addition, you can deploy monitoring tools or an intrusion detection system (IDS) to alert you when suspect activity occurs.

DNS Poisoning

DNS poisoning enables a perpetrator to redirect traffic by changing the IP record for a specific domain, thus permitting attackers to send legitimate traffic anywhere they choose. This not only sends a requestor to a different website, but also caches this information for a short period, distributing the attack's effect to the server users. DNS poisoning is also referred to as DNS cache poisoning because it affects the cached information.

All Internet page requests start with a DNS query. If the IP address is not known locally, the request is sent to a DNS server. Two types of DNS servers are used: authoritative and recursive. DNS servers share information, but recursive servers maintain information in cache. This means a caching or recursive server can answer queries for resource records even if it cannot resolve the request directly. A flaw in the resolution algorithm allows the poisoning of DNS records on a server. All an attacker has to do is delegate a false name to the domain server and provide a false address for the server. For example, imagine that an attacker creates a hostname called hack.example.com. After that, the attacker queries your DNS server to resolve the host example.com. The DNS server resolves the name and stores this information in its cache. Until the zone expiration, any further requests for example.com do not result in lookups but are answered by the server from its cache. It is now possible for the attacker to set your DNS server as the authoritative server for his or her zone with the domain registrar. If the attacker conducts malicious activity, the attacker can make it appear that your DNS server is being used for these malicious activities.

DNS poisoning can result in many different implications. Domain name servers can be used for DDoS attacks. Malware can be downloaded to an unsuspecting user's computer from the rogue site, and all future requests by that computer will be redirected to the fake IP address. This could be used to build an effective botnet. This method of poisoning can also allow for code injection exploits, especially because content can be pulled from multiple websites at the same time.

To minimize the effects of DNS poisoning, check the DNS setup if you are hosting your own DNS. Be sure the DNS server is not open-recursive. An open-recursive DNS server responds to any lookup request without checking where it originates. Disable recursive access for other networks to resolve names that are not in your zone files. You can also use different servers for authoritative and recursive lookups and require that caches discard information except from the com servers and the root servers. From the user perspective, education works best. However, it is becoming more difficult to spot a problem by watching the address bar on the Internet browser. Therefore, operating system vendors are adding more protection. Microsoft Windows User Account Control (UAC) notifies the user that a program is attempting to change the system's DNS settings, thus preventing the DNS cache from being poisoned.

Denial of Service

The purpose of a denial-of-service (DoS) attack is to disrupt the resources or services that a user would expect to have access to. These types of attacks are executed by manipulating protocols and can happen without the need to be validated by the network. An attack typically involves flooding a listening port on your machine with packets. The premise is to make your system so busy processing the new connections that it cannot process legitimate service requests.

Many of the tools used to produce DoS attacks are readily available on the Internet. Administrators use them to test connectivity and troubleshoot problems on the network, whereas malicious users use them to cause connectivity issues. Consider some examples of DoS attacks:

▶ **Smurf/smurfing:** This attack is based on the Internet Control Message Protocol (ICMP) echo reply function. It is more commonly known as ping, which is the command-line tool used to invoke this function. In this attack, the attacker sends ping packets to the broadcast address of the network, replacing the original source address in the ping packets with the source address of the victim. This causes a flood of traffic to be sent to the unsuspecting network device.

▶ **Fraggle:** This attack is similar to a Smurf attack. The difference is that it uses UDP instead of ICMP. The attacker sends spoofed UDP packets to broadcast addresses, as in the Smurf attack. These UDP packets are directed to port 7 (Echo) or port 19 (Chargen). When connected to port 19, a character generator attack can be run.

▶ **Ping flood:** A ping flood attempts to block service or reduce activity on a host by sending ping requests directly to the victim. A variation of this type of attack is the ping of death, in which the packet size is too large and the system does not know how to handle the packets.

▶ **SYN flood:** This attack takes advantage of the TCP three-way handshake. The source system sends a flood of SYN requests but never sends the final ACK, thus creating half-open TCP sessions. Because the TCP stack waits before resetting the port, the attack overflows the destination computer's connection buffer, making it impossible to service connection requests from valid users.

▶ **Land:** In this attack, the attacker exploits a behavior in the operating systems of several versions of Windows, Linux, macOS, and Cisco IOS with respect to their TCP/IP stacks. The attacker spoofs a TCP/IP SYN packet to the victim system with the same source and destination IP address and the same source and destination ports. This confuses the system as it tries to respond to the packet.

▶ **Teardrop:** This form of attack targets a known behavior of UDP in the TCP/IP stack of some operating systems. The Teardrop attack sends fragmented UDP packets to the victim with odd offset values in subsequent packets. When the operating system attempts to rebuild the original packets from the fragments, the fragments overwrite each other, causing confusion. Because some operating systems cannot gracefully handle the error, the system will most likely crash or reboot.

DoS attacks come in many shapes and sizes. The first step in protecting yourself from an attack is to understand the nature of the attacks in the preceding list. Although various security solutions are designed specifically to help prevent such attacks, you might consider other measures within your organization. Fundamentally, organizations should ensure that they have well-defined processes around auditing, standard operating procedures, and documented configurations. Finally, being well versed on the nature of the different types of attacks will help you make better decisions when it comes to attack recognition and implementing controls such as packet filtering and rights management.

Distributed DoS

Another form of attack is a simple expansion of a DoS attack, referred to as a distributed DoS (DDoS) attack. Masters are computers that run the client software, and zombies run software. The attacker creates masters, which, in turn, create many zombies, or recruits. The software running on the zombies can launch multiple types of attacks, such as UDP or SYN floods on a target. Figure 2.1 shows a typical DDoS attack.

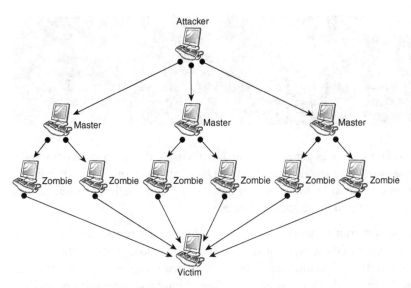

FIGURE 2.1 **A DDos Attack**

In simple terms, the attacker distributes zombie software that gives the attacker partial or full control of the infected computer system.

ExamAlert

When attackers compromise enough systems with the installed zombie software, they can initiate an attack against a victim from a wide variety of hosts. The attacks come in the form of the standard DoS attacks, but the effects are multiplied by the total number of zombie machines under the control of the attacker, resulting in a DDoS.

Often DoS and DDoS attacks take advantage of reflection—that is, the attacker takes advantage of legitimate third-party services, and the source address is spoofed to be that of the victim. As a result, any replies from the service will be directed at the victim, hiding the attacker's identity. Network time and domain name servers are common examples of third-party services used to execute such an attack. These attacks can further take advantage of amplification. As its name implies, the attack is magnified, increasing the amount of traffic sent to the victim, which is fundamental to a denial-of-service attack. Requests to an NTP time server, for example, are amplified back by a factor of more than 500 percent. Because these attacks use UDP, a connection is not required and the source is not verified.

ExamAlert

Be sure you understand how reflection and amplification factor into a DDoS attack. Consider the following analogy. Imagine that you simply ask a person for directions, but it appears as if someone else asked and that person then receives the detailed navigational response. Now imagine the computer equivalent, further compounded by a coordinated, distributed effort.

Although DDoS attacks generally come from outside the network to deny services, you must also consider the effect of DDoS attacks mounted from inside the network. Internal DDoS attacks allow disgruntled or malicious users to disrupt services without any outside influence.

To help protect your network, you can set up filters on external routers to drop packets involved in these types of attacks. You should also set up another filter that denies traffic originating from the Internet that shows an internal network address. When you do this, you incur the loss of ping and some services and utilities for testing network connectivity, but this is a small price to pay for network protection. If the operating system allows it, reduce the amount of time before the reset of an unfinished TCP connection. Doing so makes it harder to keep resources unavailable for extended periods of time.

Note

In case of a DDoS attack, your best weapon is to quickly get in touch with your upstream Internet service provider (ISP) and see whether it can divert traffic or block the traffic at a higher level.

Subscribing to security emails and checking security websites daily ensures that you keep up with the latest attacks and exploits. Applying the manufacturer's latest operating system patches or fixes can also help prevent attacks.

Cryptographic Attacks

Any resource exposed on a network can be attacked to gain unauthorized access. Cryptography plays a key role in protecting such resources. Data itself can be encrypted or access to a system can be protected by an encrypted password. Cryptographic attacks seek to break encrypted contents. The most effective attack might be breaking the cryptographic key (often a password) that unlocks everything else. However, cryptographic attacks do not necessarily need access to the unencrypted key. Although such attacks can apply in either situation, we focus the discussion here mostly on the encrypted password.

Before turning to the types of password attacks, keep in mind that passwords should not be stored in plain text, even if they can be. In fact, most passwords are stored as a cryptographic hashed value. Recall the earlier discussion about hashes regarding pass the hash.

Successful attacks on passwords often result in immediate unauthorized access to systems and potentially sensitive information. Historically, password attacks are a classic method of obtaining such access. The security of passwords largely relies upon end users. For example, an end user might opt for an easy-to-remember password instead of a complex one, despite putting organizational assets at risk. Even when technical controls are in place to ensure complex passwords, end users might simply write down their passwords for someone else to find. Because passwords provide the primary means of authentication, this is a problem. Fortunately, passwords have evolved to help thwart attacks—for example, additional controls are often used, such as examining login location or sending a secondary authentication code such as a text message to the user's phone. Of course, a tradeoff always exists between security and usability, which is why such methods are usually based on the perceived risk at that moment.

Brute Force

In some instances, passwords are written down and then retrieved, improperly shared, or easily guessed. Imagine trying every word in the dictionary to gain access to a system. This is a dictionary attack. In essence, software tools are available to automate such tasks to perform an attack on passwords. Dictionary attacks can use different and custom dictionaries. Such files can even contain lists of passwords that are not typically found within a traditional dictionary, such as 1234 and abcde. A dictionary attack is most successful on simple passwords because the attack simply tries each word within the supplied list.

The word *love*, for example, can easily be compromised through a simple dictionary attack; however, simply changing the letter *o* to a zero could counter such an attack. Brute-force attacks, however, are quite capable of defeating such passwords. Unlike a simple dictionary attack, a brute-force attack relies on cryptanalysis or algorithms capable of performing exhaustive key searches. Against short passwords, brute-force attacks are quick and can crack a password quicker than a dictionary attack. However, a brute-force attack can take a lot of time and computing power against larger, more complex passwords because it attempts to exhaust all possible combinations of letters, numbers, and symbols.

A dictionary attack might not be successful against a common word with numbers included. Yet a brute-force attack might take too long for a lengthy word with numbers included. Another attack, known as a hybrid attack, provides a compromise and is also a useful tool to help identify weak passwords and controls for audit purposes. A hybrid attack uses the dictionary attack method and then builds upon this by adding numbers to the end of the words, substituting certain letters for numbers, and capitalizing the first letter of each word.

Two well-known methods that are types of brute-force attacks are birthday attacks and the use of rainbow tables. The birthday attack is a cryptographic method against a secure hash. Keep in mind that a dictionary or brute-force attack is successful when each guess is hashed, and then the resulting hash matches a hash being cracked. A birthday attack finds collisions within hash functions, which results in a more efficient method of brute-forcing one-way hashes. So why is this called a birthday attack? It is based on what is known as the birthday paradox. Simply put, if 23 people are in a room, the probability that two of those people have the same birthday is 50 percent. Hard to believe? True. That's why it is called a paradox. Without getting into complex math, let's try to simplify the reasoning here (not easy to do!). The birthday paradox is concerned with finding any match, not necessarily a match for you. Consider that you would need 253 people in a room to have a 50 percent chance that someone else shares your birthday. Yet you need only 23 people to create 253 pairs when cross-matched with one another. That gets us to a 50 percent chance. This same theory applies to finding collisions within hash functions. Just as it would be more difficult to find someone who shares (collides with) your birthday, it is more difficult to find something that would collide with a given hash. However, just as we increase the probability of finding any two birthdays that match within the group, it is easier to find two inputs that have the same hash.

A rainbow table is another brute force method for cracking passwords that have been hashed. Rainbow tables can most easily be thought of as a very large set of precomputed hash values for every possible combination of characters. With the assumption that an attacker has enough resources to store an entire rainbow table in memory, a successful attack on passwords can occur with great efficiency. Best practices can help avoid online attacks such as locking accounts after several failed attempts, but offline attacks give the attacker the convenience of iterating through different methods and countless attempts.

Weak Implementations

The most common form of authentication and user access control is the user-name/password combination, which can be significantly weakened as a security measure if the user selects a "weak" password. Automated and social engineering assaults on passwords are easier when a password is short; lacks complexity; is derived from a common word found in the dictionary; or is derived from easily guessable personal information such as birthdays, family names, pet names, and similar details. Implementations matter.

Older and even modern poorly designed cryptographic solutions can be vulnerable to the known plain-text attack (KPA). This attack involves having a corresponding piece of both the plain text and the cipher text. The idea is that having even just a single word or phrase match can reveal further information. Consider, for example, the ease by which a single alphabetic substitution cipher is vulnerable to such an attack. For example, if *a* is substituted for *b*, and *b* for *c*, and so on, this paragraph could be analyzed by looking at the three-letter words, and basing analysis on the assumption that these words are likely to be *the*, *are*, and so forth.

This is an overly simply example, but many classic ciphers have suffered from advanced plain-text analysis. Modern ciphers such as the Advanced Encryption Standard (AES), so prominent today, are vulnerable to such an attack. This is one of the many reasons that basing ciphers and algorithms on understood and reviewed standards is important. Even the most secure cryptography solutions are weakened by poor implementations, though. Consider the following analogy of weak implementation. Suppose you buy the most secure front-door lock from the hardware store. If you leave the key under the doormat, however, the security system can easily be defeated. In another example, just because you use an alloy as strong as steel doesn't necessarily mean that a structure such as a bridge has been built to that strength.

Weak implementations manifest themselves in other ways, too. Cryptographic attacks are made simpler through downgrade attacks. The cryptographic protocols used for secure web browsing are a common example. A downgrade attack is often a result of security configurations not being updated. Often this stems from the desire to maintain backwards compatibility. When a web browser is communicating over a secure channel with a web server, the two must first agree on the version of the cryptographic protocol to use. Typically, this is Transport Layer Security (TLS) or Secure Sockets Layer (SSL). The server might require the latest and most secure version of TLS; however, if the browser does not support this method, the connection cannot happen. For this reason, security might give way to preventing operational impact. However, if the server allows negotiation to downgrade to a lesser version, the connection is susceptible to further attacks. An attacker might therefore purposely choose to use a client implementation with only less secure cryptographic versions supported.

Various countermeasures exist to help prevent and mitigate such attacks. Choosing strong cipher suites is critical. Proprietary cryptographic solutions should be avoided. Ultimately, security is a system. The cliché "You are only as strong as the weakest link" applies quite aptly to cryptography. Password security can also include such factors as multiple authentication methods—for example, combining something you know (for example, a password) with something you have (for example, a one-time-use token or code sent to a registered phone, in addition to controls already discussed, such as account lockout after three unsuccessful attempts). Finally, password hashes can use a "salt." Understand that some of the attacks mentioned here work because users who have the same password would also have the same resulting hash. This problem can be overcome by making the hashes more random. Salting adds a prefix consisting of a random string of characters to passwords before they are hashed. Such a countermeasure makes it more difficult or impractical to attack passwords unless the attacker knows the value of the salt that needs to be removed.

> ### ExamAlert
>
> Multifactor authentication mechanisms are important countermeasures to mitigate password-based attacks. These can include, for example, a token that changes every 30 seconds or a text message to a phone. Users must have something in their possession in this case, in addition to knowing the correct password or passphrase.

Wireless

Wireless networks present unique challenges to security. As with their wired counterparts, wireless networks are subject to the same types of attacks discussed (MITM, DoS, replay, crypto attacks, and so on). Such attacks have also become more prevalent because wireless networks are so common. Consider a replay attack on a wireless network. Such an attack works like the replay attack covered earlier, but the data is more readily available by using a sniffer. A wireless sniffer includes a hardware or software device capable of capturing the data or packets that traverse across the wireless channel. When traffic being sent across the network is unencrypted, packet sniffing enables the attacker to capture the data and decode it from its raw form into readable text.

Wireless networks are further susceptible to being disrupted by other radio sources. Such disruptions can merely be unintentional interference or can be a malicious attempt to jam the signal. For example, you might have personally experienced or heard stories about how the operation of microwave ovens can interfere with wireless access to the Internet. This is the result of specific wireless 802.11 devices operating at or near the same wireless band that the microwave emits. Specific attacks on wireless networks can be performed by setting up a nearby access point or even using dedicated wireless jamming devices.

> **Note**
>
> According to the Federal Communications Commission (FCC), "Federal law prohibits the operation, marketing, or sale of any type of jamming equipment, including devices that interfere with cellular and Personal Communication Services (PCS), police radar, Global Positioning Systems (GPS) and wireless networking services (Wi-Fi)."

Counteracting a jamming attack is both simple and complicated. It is simple because most jamming attacks require physical proximity. In the case of a cell phone, for example, just moving 30 feet away can make a difference. However, moving location is not always a viable option. In such cases, you must either locate the source of the jamming or boost the signal being jammed. Many enterprise-grade devices provide power levels that can be configured and have capability to identify and locate rogue devices causing the interference.

Wi-Fi

Key to Wi-Fi networks are wireless access point devices. Wireless endpoints connect to the access point. The access point typically provides the bridge to the wired network. A common attack involves the use of a rogue access point. This refers to situations in which an unauthorized wireless access point has been set up. In organizations, well-meaning insiders might use rogue access points (rogue APs) with the best of intentions. However, rogue access points can also serve as a type of man-in-the-middle attack, referred to as an evil twin. Because the client's request for connection is an omnidirectional open broadcast, it is possible for a hijacker to act as an access point to the client and to act as a client to the true network access point. This enables the hijacker to follow all data transactions and thus modify, insert, or delete packets at will. By implementing a rogue access point with stronger signal strength than more remote permanent installations, the attacker can cause a wireless client to preferentially connect to its own stronger connection nearby using the wireless device's standard roaming handoff mechanism.

> **Note**
>
> Wi-Fi is essentially synonymous with specifications defined by the IEEE 802.11 standard. Often written as *WiFi*, it is a registered trademark of the Wi-Fi Alliance.

Fortunately, detecting rogue access points is simple using software. A common method to detect rogue access points is to use wireless sniffing applications. As wireless networks have become ubiquitous and often a requirement, organizations have employed wireless site surveys. These surveys provide a well-defined process for the analysis and planning of wireless networks. Such site surveys are often associated with new deployments, but they are also conducted within existing wireless networks. During such surveys, looking for rogue access points is part of the process because these access points can negatively impact not just security, but also quality of service of the legitimate wireless network.

When rogue access points are disconnected, they receive a deauthentication frame. However, this message has been exploited in another common attack. This attack involves a denial of service between wireless users and the wireless access point. This attack is thus known as *dissociation* or *deauthentication*. Recall that a MAC address can be spoofed. By spoofing a user's MAC address, an attacker can send a deauthentication data transmission to the wireless access point.

Some Wi-Fi technologies have been shown to be easily susceptible to an IV attack. This attack uses passive statistical analysis. An IV is an input to a cryptographic algorithm, which is essentially a random number. Ideally, an IV should be unique and unpredictable. An IV attack can occur when the IV is too short, predictable, or not unique. The attack is possible when the IV is not long enough, which means it had a high probability of repeating itself after only a small number of packets. Modern wireless encryption algorithms use a longer IV, and newer protocols also use a mechanism to dynamically change keys as the system is used.

> **ExamAlert**
>
> An IV that is repeated with a given key is more subject to being attacked.

Address Resolution Protocol (ARP), covered earlier in the context of ARP poisoning, is also susceptible to replay attacks. ARP replay attacks are the foundation of many wireless attacks and provide a successful means for generating new IVs. In this attack, software listens for ARP packets to replay back to the access point. When this occurs, the access point retransmits the ARP packet along with a new IV. As this occurs repeatedly, the AP continues to retransmit the same ARP packet with a new IV. From all these new IVs, the attacker can determine the WEP key.

Wi-Fi Protected Setup (WPS), originally known as Wi-Fi Simple Config, is an extension of the wireless standards whose purpose was to make it simple for end users to establish secure wireless home networks. Originally, as Wi-Fi devices entered the mainstream, setup was complex, often resulting in users running with default configurations. Such defaults typically left these wireless networks wide open and easy to exploit. WPS provides two certified modes of operation. The first involves the use of a PIN code, which the user enters when connecting devices. The second method requires the user to simply push a button on the AP and the connecting wireless device. In 2011, however, a major security vulnerability was exposed. In fact, the vulnerability is so severe that the solution is to turn off WPS capabilities. Via brute-force attack, the PIN could be recovered in as little as 11,000 guesses or within several hours. In some cases, however, disabling WPS might not be enough to prevent such attacks, and a firmware upgrade then is required to completely disable the feature.

> **ExamAlert**
>
> Wi-Fi Protected Setup (WPS) should be disabled.

Short Range Wireless Communications

As the use of wireless networks has increased, so has the use of varying wireless technologies. Much of this growth has been spawned by computer peripherals and other smaller electronics. Consider mobile devices. Most mobile phones today provide Bluetooth and Near Field Communications (NFC) technology. If you walk into almost any store today, you can find a wide array of Bluetooth speakers music can be streamed to from any other Bluetooth-enabled device.

Bluetooth

Mobile devices equipped for Bluetooth short-range wireless connectivity, such as laptops, tablets, and cellphones, are subject to receiving text and message broadcast spam sent from a nearby Bluetooth-enabled transmitting device in an attack referred to as bluejacking. Although this act is typically benign, attackers can use this form of attack to generate messages that appear to come from the device itself. Users then follow obvious prompts and establish an open Bluetooth connection to the attacker's device. When paired with the attacker's device, the user's device makes data available for unauthorized access, modification, or deletion, which is a more aggressive attack referred to as bluesnarfing.

> **ExamAlert**
>
> Do not confuse bluejacking and bluesnarfing. Bluesnarfing is generally associated with more dangerous attacks that can expose or alter a user's information.

Near Field Communications

NFC is a set of standards for contactless communication between devices. Although NFC is considered contactless, in most practical uses, devices establish communication by being close or touching. Currently, varying use cases for NFC exist. Most individuals are familiar with NFC as a feature of their smartphone. NFC is available on most devices, such as those running the Android operating system and the Apple iPhone.

NFC chips within mobile devices generate electromagnetic fields. This allows the device to communicate with other devices, or even a tag that contains specific information that leverages the electromagnetic field as a power supply to send the information back to the device. Consider, for example, an advertisement at a bus stop embedded with a tag that is then able to communicate with a smart device.

Given NFC's limited range, the types and practicality of attacks become limited by distance. Regardless, the following list highlights potential risks of NFC:

▶ **Confidentiality:** Attacks can take advantage of the risk posed by any communications methods. This includes eavesdropping. Any sensitive data must be encrypted to mitigate such concerns.

▶ **Denial of service:** NFC could be subject to such jamming and interference disruptions causing loss of service.

▶ **Man-in-the-middle (MITM) attacks:** Theoretically, MITM attacks are possible. But again, given the limitations of proximity, such attacks present their own challenges.

▶ **Malicious code:** As with any client device, malware prevention and user awareness are key controls.

Specific concerns about NFC that have surfaced largely stem from lenient configurations. In one example, applications of NFC might provide a function to pass information such as contacts and applications, yet no confirmation is required from the receiving end. In other applications, such as device pairing, in the absence of any type of confirmation, an attacker can easily connect and run further attacks to access the device.

RFID

Radio Frequency Identification (RFID) is another wireless technology that was initially common to supply chain and inventory tracking. RFID has been around longer than NFC. In fact, NFC is based on the RFID protocols. RFID is common among various applications such as toll booths, ski resorts, passports, credit cards, key fobs, and many more. RFID chips can even be implanted into the human body for medical purposes. RFID uses electromagnetic fields and is one-way. Information is transmitted from a chip, also known as a smart tag, to an RFID reader. Two types of RFID tags include active and passive tags. Active tags can broadcast a signal over a larger distance because they contain a power source. Passive tags, on the other hand, aren't powered and are activated by a signal sent from the reader.

Cryptography is an important component for RFID security. Otherwise, RFID tags are susceptible to an attacker writing or modifying data to the tag. Arguably one of the biggest concerns surrounding RFID has been around privacy. Even when RFID tags are encrypted, an attacker can read them, for example, to track the tag's movement (or the object the tag is applied to).

> **Note**
>
> NFC is based on RFID protocols. However, NFC provides peer-to-peer communication, which sets it apart from most RFID devices. An NFC chip functions as both a reader and a tag.

What Next?

If you want more practice on this chapter's exam objectives before you move on, remember that you can access all the Cram Quiz questions on the Pearson Test Prep software. You can also create a custom exam by objective. Note any objective you struggle with and go to that objective material in this chapter.

CHAPTER 3

Threat Actor Types and Attributes

This chapter covers the following official Security+ exam objective:

1.3 Explain threat actor types and attributes.

- ▶ Types of actors
  - ■ Script kiddies
  - ■ Hacktivist
  - ■ Organized crime
  - ■ Nation states/APT
  - ■ Insiders
  - ■ Competitors

- ▶ Attributes of actors
  - ■ Internal/external
  - ■ Level of sophistication
  - ■ Resources/funding
  - ■ Intent/motivation
- ▶ Use of open-source intelligence

Essential Terms and Components

- ▶ threat actor
- ▶ script kiddie
- ▶ hacktivist

- ▶ advanced persistent threat (APT)
- ▶ open source intelligence (OSINT)

CramSaver

If you can correctly answer these questions before going through this chapter, save time by skimming the Exam Alerts in this section and then completing the Cram Quiz at the end of Part I.

1. What different types of attributes can be applied to a threat actor?

   _____

2. Name several threat actor types.

   _____

> **Answers**
>
> 1. Threat actors can be characterized by several traits, including relationship, motive, intent, and capability.
> 2. Examples of threat actors include script kiddies, insiders, hacktivists, organized crime, competitors, and nation states.

When examining threats, attacks, and vulnerabilities, understanding threat actors is important. Specifically, a threat actor is an individual, group, or entity that contributes to an incident—or, more simply, the person or entity that executes a given threat. This is not a difficult concept, but it is often overlooked, particularly when deciding how to balance security against an organization's capabilities. For example, the security mechanisms that protect your personal vehicle differ significantly from those that guard an armored truck. You might lock your doors when you leave your car, but of course, someone could still quite easily break in to it. The threat to your car likely comes from a casual passerby looking for spare change or belongings you have left behind. The armored truck, on the other hand, faces a different kind of threat actor because it transports valuables and large sums of money.

This chapter discusses the types of threat actors and their common attributes. Understanding these components enables organizations to make better decisions regarding risk and manage their vulnerabilities.

Threat Actor Attributes

When examining various threat actors, you must consider their attributes. Organizations that do so can build better threat profiles and classification systems, to deploy more relevant and proactive defenses. Common attributes include the following:

- ▶ **Relationship:** Threats can be internal or external to the organization, or might even come from a partner.

- ▶ **Motive:** Some incidents are accidental, but others are driven for specific reasons, such as financial gain or ideological differences.

- ▶ **Intent:** The threat could be malicious, with the aim to destroy data or steal information or tangible property.

- ▶ **Capability:** Several components must be considered here, including technical ability, financial means, access, political and social support, and persistence.

The relationship of a threat actor is most easily characterized as either internal or external. Script kiddies, hacktivists, organized crime, and nation state actors are all examples of external threat actors. Internal threat actors work on the inside; for example, these could be system administrators or end users.

When examining threat actor capability, you must consider the level of sophistication and both the available resources and funds. For example, some threat actors operate as businesses, with well-established roles, responsibilities, and governance. Their capabilities are often further enhanced by their technical resources and access to money for funding operations.

> **Note**
>
> When considering threat types and attributes, you might find it helpful to think about common personal situations. For example, consider your reasons for locking your personal belongings in a vehicle. What threat actors are you mitigating? What are their attributes? How does a casual passerby differ from someone with the tools and knowledge of a locksmith?

Intent is often accidental, with no motive. Other times, threat actors have a specific malicious or competitive intent. Of course, motives can vary in these cases. Consider a competitive threat. The motive could be a desire to gain a competitive advantage through espionage or even malicious destruction to the business. Financial gain is another common motive that can include directly extorting money from victims through ransomware or perhaps stealing data to sell within a criminal ecosystem for subsequent attacks. Threat actors also can be driven by ideological and political motives.

> **ExamAlert**
>
> Assessing threat actors begins with identifying their relationship to the organization—internal or external.

Threat Actor Types

Again, given a particular threat, the threat actor is the individual, group, or entity that acts to perpetrate the particular scenario. The following sections look at the most common threat actors:

▶ Script kiddies

▶ Insiders

- ▶ Hacktivists
- ▶ Organized crime
- ▶ Competitors
- ▶ Nation states

Notice that these threat actor types relate to threats from humans, not the environment. For example, the threat of a flood in a data center might stem from an impending hurricane, not a particular individual or entity.

Finally, as you review the threat actors, keep in mind that organizations need to consider how these different actors could be interrelated. For example, a terrorist group works much like hacktivists: The terrorists are driven by ideology, and hacktivists operate within the framework of organized crime. As another example, consider how organized crime might exploit script kiddies within their ecosystem to distance themselves while achieving specific goals. Similarly, some nation states might have close ties to organized crime. Finally, keep in mind that any of these threat actors can be further enabled through the compromise of an insider.

Script Kiddies

Script kiddies do not have to possess great talent. Even with few skills, they can run exploits that others have developed. Usually script kiddies cannot write sophisticated code and might not even know how to program. Still, script kiddies can undoubtedly have a huge negative impact on an organization. What makes them particularly dangerous is that they are often unaware themselves of the potential consequences of their actions. Of course, because they lack sophisticated skill, script kiddies often cannot adequately cover their tracks. Tracing their attacks is thus easier than when dealing with more sophisticated threat actors.

Script kiddies might lack sophistication and certainly financial means, but they are empowered by the number of readily available exploits and information available to them. They are often associated with website defacement attacks, but they have also been known to use DoS attacks to take down websites and even to plant Trojans and remote access tools within an organization.

Insiders

Attacks are often assumed to come from malicious outside hackers, but insider threats are a source of many breaches. In many cases, this includes employees who have the right intentions but either are unaware of an organization's security policy or simply ignore it. A common example is a well-intentioned employee who uses a personal web-based email account to send home sensitive files to work on later in the evening. These sensitive files are now in unencrypted form outside the organizational network. In another common scenario, a user brings in USB thumb drives that unknowingly have been infected with malware. Proper training and education is key to help prevent the nonmalicious insider threat.

Deliberate, malicious insider threats also can be a source of attack. These are typically motivated by financial gain, sabotage, and theft to gain a competitive advantage. Consider the case of ex-National Security Agency (NSA) contractor Edward Snowden. Formerly an insider, Snowden circulated various documents and secrets about the NSA's surveillance program. Protecting against malicious insiders is a daunting and difficult task, but organizations must have policies in place to help identify risky personnel (for example, employees who have been terminated). Perhaps most important, organizations need mechanisms for proactively monitoring network and system activities.

> **ExamAlert**
>
> Insider threat actors can be malicious, as in the case of a disgruntled employee, or simply careless.

Hacktivists

Hacktivism can have a positive or negative connotation, just as the word *hack* does, depending on how it is used. In the case of threat actors, hacktivism involves using digital tools for malicious intent based on political, social, or ideological reasoning. Hacktivists often are perceived as doing good because of their motives. For example, in early 2017, the group Anonymous took down thousands of sites related to child porn. On one hand, this can be seen as a form of vigilantism, or at least a way of targeting illegal activity. On the other hand, an animal-rights hacktivist group could also target an organization that launches a perfectly legal line of fur coats.

Organized Crime

Organized crime tends to follow the money, so it should come as no surprise that organized crime is involved in networking systems today. The United States Organized Crime Control Act from 1970 states that organized crime "is a highly sophisticated, diversified, and widespread activity that annually drains billions of dollars from America's economy by unlawful conduct and the illegal use of force, fraud, and corruption." Clearly, this threat actor is sophisticated and has adequate financial means. In fact, organized crime itself has established its own complete economy, including a system within the underworld that affects information security. The Organized Crime Control Act identifies that funding comes from such illegal activities as gambling, loan sharking, property theft, distribution of drugs, and other forms of social exploitation. Organized criminals have simply adapted to become organized cybercriminals.

The challenges of defeating organized crime are the same today as they have been for the last 45 years, particularly given the vast resources and ecosystem involved. Consider a street-level drug dealer, part of the criminal ecosystem yet with no real connection to the organized crime network. More relevant are the money mules, who are often recruited online and tasked with helping to either knowingly or unknowingly launder money.

Competitors

Competitors are generally expected to compete fairly and legally, but they do not always do so. Anticompetitive practices and industrial espionage are not new. However, the rise of the Internet and interconnected networking systems has given malicious competition a new channel of opportunity. For example, a competitor might seek to launch a DoS attack that keeps an organization from conducting business and potentially drives business to the competitor because of the downtime. Often, however, competitive threat actors are looking for information to gain an edge, or even to pilfer trade secrets and other intellectual property.

Nation States

The nation state threat actor is arguably the most sophisticated threat actor with the most resources. Nation state threat actors are government sponsored, although those ties might not always be acknowledged. This threat actor is not necessarily relevant only to government organizations: Foreign companies are often a target as well. For example, corporations might possess intellectual property that another foreign entity can use to advance its goals and objectives. This type of threat actor is also patient and targets a wide attack surface that might include partner and even customer organizations. In 2011, RSA Security, a provider of two-factor authentication tokens, was hacked. Circumstances indicated that the attack was likely targeting at least one of the company's large customers, defense contractor Lockheed Martin. Naturally, a foreign nation could gain valuable resources and intellectual property from such a contractor.

Nation state attacks have become more prevalent in recent years. Stuxnet, discovered in 2010, highlighted the sophistication and threat of nation state attacks. This costly and highly sophisticated computer worm (see Chapter 1, "Indicators of Compromise and Malware Types") is considered a cyberweapon that the United States and Israel allegedly developed to intentionally cause damage to Iran's nuclear facilities.

Advanced persistent threats (APT) are often associated with nation state threat actors. The name alone suggests sophistication. These certainly are not "smash and grab" attacks—they are generally described as "low and slow." The goal of an APT is usually to infiltrate a network and remain inside undetected. This access often provides a more strategic target or defined objective, including the capability to exfiltrate information over a long period of time.

ExamAlert

The assets or goals of an organization relate to and influence the threat actor types that present the most significant risk.

Open Source Intelligence

Open Source Intelligence (OSINT) is the term given to information available for collection from publicly available information sources. OSINT is available from varying sources and, of course, the Internet provides a treasure trove of such information. Publicly available sources can include the following:

▶ Television

▶ Newspapers and magazines

▶ Professional publications

▶ Academic publications

▶ Photos

▶ Geospatial information

In addition, certain tools and applications aggregate OSINT data or provide specific utilities for extracting it. Many resources are also readily available online. As a simple example, consider personal and professional social media web applications. An attacker can easily do reconnaissance and gather information on employees in an organization from these easily available online sites.

Despite the fact that threat actors use OSINT to discover data that helps them more easily attack a target, OSINT remains a valuable resource for organizations to defend against such attacks and also identify and prioritize potential threat actors.

Understanding threat actors' motives, capabilities, and possible actions is particularly valuable. Organizations launching a new product, sponsoring an event, or penetrating a new foreign market, for example, can use OSINT to mitigate risk by identifying potentially new threat actors and associated attributes. Without prioritizing the threats, organizations run the risk of suffering one of the main drawbacks of OSINT: information overload.

> **ExamAlert**
>
> Do not confuse open source intelligence with open source software. OSINT refers to the overt gathering of intelligence.

What Next?

If you want more practice on this chapter's exam objectives before you move on, remember that you can access all the Cram Quiz questions on the Pearson Test Prep software. You can also create a custom exam by objective. Note any objective you struggle with and go to that objective material in this chapter.

CHAPTER 4

Penetration Testing

This chapter covers the following official Security+ exam objective:

1.4 Explain penetration testing concepts.

- ▶ Active reconnaissance
- ▶ Passive reconnaissance
- ▶ Initial exploitation
- ▶ Persistence
- ▶ Escalation of privilege

- ▶ Black box
- ▶ White box
- ▶ Gray box
- ▶ Penetration testing vs. vulnerability scanning

Essential Terms and Components

- ▶ active reconnaissance
- ▶ passive reconnaissance
- ▶ initial exploitation
- ▶ persistence
- ▶ escalation of privilege

- ▶ black box
- ▶ white box
- ▶ gray box
- ▶ WHOIS

CramSaver

If you can correctly answer these questions before going through this chapter, save time by skimming the Exam Alerts in this section and then completing the Cram Quiz at the end of Part I.

1. Describe a penetration test.

   _____

2. What are the differences between a black box, a white box, and a gray box as they pertain to penetration testing?

   _____

3. Initial exploitation and escalation of privilege are the first two steps in what phase of a penetration test?

   _____

Answers

1. A penetration test, or pen test, reveals security weaknesses through real-world attacks. The results can help prioritize risk and identify areas for improvement. Penetration tests are active evaluations.

2. Each of these refers to testing performed with varying degrees of knowledge about the system or application being tested. Black box testing assumes no knowledge. White box testing provides more transparency about the inner workings. Gray box testing is a combination of both black box and white box testing.

3. Initial exploitation and escalation of privilege are the first two steps in the attack phase of a penetration test.

Penetration testing, also commonly known as pen testing, is sometimes used within an organization's information security program to better understand the systems. These tests often incorporate real-world attacks to identify methods and weaknesses within the systems, with the aim to gain deeper access or access to a specific target. Penetration test results can be valuable. For example, organizations gain further confidence in understanding how their systems tolerate real-world attacks. Identifying the required level of sophistication and the potential threats can help an organization allocate resources properly. Where required, penetration tests can also help quickly identify areas of weakness that need to be strengthened. Organizations can then quantify the adequacy of security measures in place and provide meaningful insight into specific threats against the environment. Based on the penetration test program, organizations can also measure their responses, including how quickly they can identify and mitigate attempts.

Penetration testing differs from vulnerability scanning, which the next chapter discusses. Vulnerability scanning seeks to merely programmatically identify vulnerabilities. A penetration test takes testing further by trying to exploit the vulnerabilities to gain access. As a result, penetration testing might be preceded by an attempt to assess vulnerabilities. Both vulnerability scanning and penetration testing present risk to the organization, but penetration testing is considered a much higher risk. Mimicking real-world attacks can have real-world consequences for systems, so penetration testing must follow a carefully planned program that properly understands the potential tradeoffs and risks.

Systems administrators who perform amateur or ad hoc pen tests against networks to prove a particular vulnerability or evaluate the overall security exposure of a network do so at their peril. This is a bad practice because it generates false intrusion data; can weaken the network's security level; and can even violate privacy laws, regulatory mandates, or business entity guidelines. Certainly, regularly conducted penetration tests are a good way to assess the effectiveness of an organization's controls, but these tests should always be performed within a defined program of governance that involves senior management.

Testing Methodology

Penetration testing can be conducted using various techniques classified by the following terms:

▶ Black box

▶ White box

▶ Gray box

Each category refers to varying degrees of knowledge about the systems or applications being tested. In a black box test, the assessor has no knowledge of the inner workings of the system or the source code. The assessor simply tests the application for functionality. An easy way to think about this is to imagine that you cannot see through or inside a black box. White box testing, also called *clear box* or *glass box*, provides more transparency. In white box testing, the assessor has knowledge of the inner workings of either the system or the source code. Because white box techniques are often more efficient and cost-effective, they are more common. Gray box testing combines white and black box techniques. Think of this approach as translucent: The tester has some understanding or a limited knowledge of the inner workings.

> **ExamAlert**
>
> Remember your boxes! A black box hides the contents (no knowledge). A white box is see-through (complete knowledge of inner workings). A gray box combines the two (limited knowledge).

The high-level components of a penetration test include the following:

▶ **Verify that a threat exists:** A penetration test seeks to exploit vulnerabilities. As a result, you must first understand the threat and its extent. A sheep farmer in an isolated location might be less concerned about locking his front door than about losing the sheep to wolves.

▶ **Bypass security controls:** Penetration tests should seek to bypass security controls, just as a real attacker would. Verifying that a battering ram cannot penetrate a stone wall is worthless if a back gate is left wide open. Similarly, network firewalls might be protecting the pathways into the network, but an attacker might find an easier method of entry through a rogue wireless access point or modems. Another common method of bypassing security controls is to render them ineffective. For example, a DoS attack can be mounted on security controls to overload the control, allowing for potentially easier access.

▶ **Actively test security controls:** Unlike passive techniques, active techniques include direct interaction with a specific target. Passive techniques seek to identify gaps that could lead to missing or misconfigured security controls. Active techniques, on the other hand, seek to identify whether controls are implemented properly. Consider a lock on a door. Passive reviews might uncover documentation and policies indicating that locks are installed, whereas an active test involves trying to open the door.

▶ **Exploit vulnerability:** Unlike vulnerability scanning, penetration tests do not just check for the existence of a potential vulnerability; they attempt to exploit it. A resulting exploit verifies the vulnerability and should lead to mitigation techniques and controls to deal with the security exposure. Most exploited vulnerabilities are likely the result of misconfigurations, kernel flaws, buffer overflow, input validation errors, and incorrect permissions.

Careful planning is required before conducting a penetration test, however. A penetration test involves four primary phases: planning, discovery, attack, and reporting. Figure 4.1 illustrates the flow of each stage. Also note that planning provides major input into the final reporting phase. In addition, the attack phase can lead to a loop for further discovery and subsequent attack.

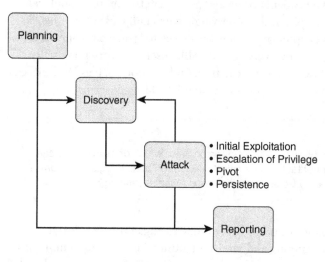

FIGURE 4.1   **Phases of a Penetration Test**

Planning

The planning phase does not involve actual tests. Its purpose is to set expectations and provide clarity regarding the plan and goals. This phase is an important part of the overall process because of the risks of penetration tests. An important output of this phase is a documented plan that includes rules and expectations.

Discovery

With planning complete, penetration testing begins with the discovery stages. Discovery consists of two fundamental areas. The first includes information gathering and scanning; the second includes vulnerability analysis.

Information gathering and scanning involves conducting reconnaissance of the target through observation and other outside discovery tools. Many techniques and tools are available for potentially gaining important information; those resources will later serve as intelligence needed for executing the attack, which is the next phase in the penetration test.

While gathering information, reconnaissance is considered either passive or active. Passive techniques are less risky because they do not require actively engaging with the targeted systems. This is similar to a burglar first staking out a neighborhood to find unoccupied homes, or even surveilling a specific home to understand when the residents come and go. A penetration test could well use similar techniques in physically observing a data center. OSINT tools, discussed in the previous chapter, are an ideal resource for passive reconnaissance. For example, an organization's website and public user directory potentially provide a great deal of pertinent information. Online tools such as WHOIS can easily gather technical contacts, host name, and IP address information.

> **Note**
>
> WHOIS is a free and publicly accessible directory from which domain names can be queried to discover contact and technical information behind registered domain names. Lookups can easily be performed at https://whois.icann.org/.

Active reconnaissance, on the other hand, requires engaging with the target. An example includes port scanning and service identification. At a minimum, port scanners identify one of two states for a port on a host system: open or closed. These scanners also identify the associated service and, potentially, the application name being run. For example, this can include the specific FTP application name running on port 21 on a specific host. Such information reveals potential targets for penetration testing.

The next step includes vulnerability identification and analysis. Databases of publicly known vulnerabilities are available. Vulnerabilities can be manually identified or automated scanners can be used. The next chapter covers vulnerability scanning using such tools.

Attack

During the attack phase, the tester tries to gain access or penetrate the system. This often is a result of exploiting an identified vulnerability during the previous phase. The idea is to at least perform an initial exploitation, even if it does not reveal the ultimate goal or data of value. During this initial exploitation, the tester commonly has only regular user access and does not have access to high-value areas. However, this initial exploit provides the opportunity for the penetration tester to escalate privileges. The tester then can gain access at a higher authorization and then conduct more advanced commands and routines. From here, the tester likely can begin to gain further access across the various systems, a process known as pivoting. Finally, the tester might try to install additional tools. Known as persistence, this enables the tester to gain additional compromising information. Achieving persistence also involves planting back doors to allow continued remote access into the systems.

ExamAlert

The following are the progressive steps during the attack phase:

1. Initial exploitation
2. Escalation of **privilege**
3. Pivoting
4. Persistence

Reporting

Reporting is an important component of the penetration test. Specifically, as activity is documented, and depending on the plan, reporting might be required within the actual discovery and attack phases. After any penetration test, a comprehensive report should be delivered that includes, at a minimum, vulnerabilities identified, actions taken and the results, mitigation techniques, and some sort of quantification of the risk.

What Next?

If you want more practice on this chapter's exam objectives before you move on, remember that you can access all the Cram Quiz questions on the Pearson Test Prep software. You can also create a custom exam by objective. Note any objective you struggle with and go to that objective material in this chapter.

CHAPTER 5
Vulnerability Scanning

This chapter covers the following official Security+ exam objective:

1.5 Explain vulnerability scanning concepts.

- ▶ Passively test security controls
- ▶ Identify vulnerability
- ▶ Identify lack of security controls
- ▶ Identify common misconfigurations

- ▶ Intrusive vs. non-intrusive
- ▶ Credentialed vs. non-credentialed
- ▶ False positives

Essential Terms and Components

- ▶ Open Vulnerability Assessment Language (OVAL)

- ▶ intrusive scan
- ▶ vulnerability scan

CramSaver

If you can correctly answer these questions before going through this chapter, save time by skimming the Exam Alerts in this section and then completing the Cram Quiz at the end of Part I.

1. A good deal of software provides automatic scanning features to help identify vulnerabilities, and the software sometimes includes built-in knowledge about the vulnerabilities. Why is it still important to properly interpret the results?

2. From the results of a vulnerability scan, what types of items are identified?

3. What type of vulnerability scan can greatly reduce false positives?

Answers

1. Vulnerabilities need to be considered within an overall structure of risk. Assets to protect vary by organization. In addition, threats and their likelihood differ according to organization. Finally, vulnerabilities must be considered within the overall goals of the organization. As a result, a vulnerability that correlates to a high risk in one area might be low in another area.

2. A vulnerability scan identifies vulnerabilities, misconfigurations, and lack of security controls.

3. A credentialed vulnerability scan helps to reduce false positives.

Identifying vulnerabilities either manually or by using vulnerability scanning tools precedes the penetration test discussed in the previous chapter. Vulnerability scanning does not involve as much risk as a comprehensive penetration test. Moreover, it is critical that organizations identify vulnerabilities across their systems, to prioritize them and to prevent real-world exploits.

Vulnerability scanning, as in port scanning, identifies hosts and open ports. However, it also looks for specific vulnerabilities and provides information and guidance. Note that although vulnerability scanners aid in interpretation, the results must be evaluated within the context of the specific business. After conducting a vulnerability assessment, the results should be organized based on the severity of the risks to the organization.

ExamAlert

The results of a vulnerability scan should be organized based on the relative security and value associated with each identified threat. An organization can then prioritize the vulnerabilities to address first.

Vulnerability assessment tools are specialized systems used to test systems for known vulnerabilities, misconfigurations, bugs, or weaknesses. The output of these tools requires careful interpretation. In many cases, several factors need to be considered. Interpretation of the results typically leads to one of three approaches:

▶ Doing nothing, either because of a false positive or because the organization faces no significant risk

▶ Fixing or eliminating the vulnerability or security gap

▶ Accepting the security gap but implementing mitigating controls

Types of Vulnerability Scans

Many network scanners are designed to be passive and non-intrusive to the target systems. Passive scanning poses minimal risk to the assessed environment because it is designed to avoid interfering with normal activity or degrade performance. However, tests against the system can still affect network and system performance. A comprehensive vulnerability scan helps organizations identify vulnerabilities, uncover common misconfigurations, and understand where further security controls are required. The following points briefly summarize these three goals:

▶ **Identify vulnerability:** This includes outdated software versions that contain flaws or even missing patches.

▶ **Identify common misconfiguration:** Vulnerability scanners can identify many common misconfigurations. Some scanners are even capable of remediation. Checking for misconfigurations is most beneficial when compared against an organization's security policies and standards.

▶ **Identify lack of security controls:** Identifying vulnerabilities provides an opportunity to remediate the weakness. In some cases, it highlights the need for further implementation of security controls to mitigate the risk.

A vulnerability scanner is a software utility that scans a range of IP addresses, testing for the presence of known vulnerabilities in software configuration and accessible services. A traditional vulnerability scanner relies on a database of known vulnerabilities. These automated tools are directed at a targeted system or systems. Unlike a system that tests for open ports, which tests only for the availability of services, vulnerability scanners can check for the version or patch level of a service to determine its level of vulnerability.

Keep in mind that a vulnerability does not necessarily indicate an issue that needs to be immediately remediated—or even remediated at all. Using an analogy, consider a home as a subject for a vulnerability assessment. A broken dead-bolt lock certainly seems like a vulnerability. Ideally, the homeowner would replace it; however, in some parts of the world, the residents do not lock their doors anyway. A smashed window is a vulnerability as well. In some cases, it might make sense to mitigate this simply by covering it with plastic to protect against the elements. Even a perfectly functioning window is a vulnerability, however. The benefit that window offers typically outweighs the other option of living without windows. Of course, this all depends on what you are trying to protect.

> **Note**
>
> Within U.S. governmental agencies, vulnerability is discussed using the Open Vulnerability Assessment Language (OVAL), sponsored by the Department of Homeland Security's National Cyber Security Division (NCSD). OVAL is intended to be an international language for representing vulnerability information. It uses an Extensible Markup Language (XML) schema for expression, allowing tools to be developed to test for identified vulnerabilities in the OVAL repository.

As you can see in the previous analogy, there isn't necessarily a quick method for determining risk based on the output of a vulnerability scanner. Relevancy to the business, tradeoffs, and identified threats and likelihoods need to be considered to accurately interpret the results.

Intrusive vs. Non-intrusive

Vulnerability tests themselves seldom disrupt systems. Instead, the initial port scans typically cause a system to fail (particularly if the implementation of a particular service does not follow proper standards). Intrusive scans combine verification of actual vulnerabilities by trying to exploit the vulnerability. Such tests can be highly intrusive, and organizations should take care before initiating such tests.

> **ExamAlert**
>
> Non-intrusive or non-invasive testing helps organizations mitigate disruptions as a result of the vulnerability assessment.

Credentialed vs. Non-credentialed

Credentials (for example, username and password) provide authorized access to the system. Scanners can be configured to run in either mode. Non-credentialed scans are less invasive and provide an outsider's point of view. With credentialed scans, however, the system can ascertain more information, which results in a more complete vulnerability status with greater certainty. Both credentialed and non-credentialed scans can mistakenly identify a vulnerability when none exists. This is known as a false positive. A large number of false positives can be time-consuming to confirm and place a burden on IT resources. Credentialed scans tend to reduce such false positives.

> **ExamAlert**
>
> Although penetration tests are always considered active, vulnerability scans can be both passive and active, to help identify weaknesses.

What Next?

If you want more practice on this chapter's exam objectives before you move on, remember that you can access all the Cram Quiz questions on the Pearson Test Prep software. You can also create a custom exam by objective. Note any objective you struggle with and go to that objective material in this chapter.

CHAPTER 6

Impacts Associated with Vulnerability Types

This chapter covers the following official Security+ exam objective:

1.6 Explain the impact associated with types of vulnerabilities.

- ▶ Race conditions
- ▶ Vulnerabilities due to:
  - ■ End-of-life systems
  - ■ Embedded systems
  - ■ Lack of vendor support
- ▶ Improper input handling
- ▶ Improper error handling
- ▶ Misconfiguration/weak configuration
- ▶ Default configuration
- ▶ Resource exhaustion
- ▶ Untrained users
- ▶ Improperly configured accounts

- ▶ Weak cipher suites and implementations
- ▶ Memory/buffer vulnerability
  - ■ Memory leak
  - ■ Integer overflow
  - ■ Buffer overflow
  - ■ Pointer dereference
  - ■ DLL injection
- ▶ System sprawl/ undocumented assets
- ▶ Architecture/design weaknesses
- ▶ New threats/zero day
- ▶ Improper certificate and key management

Essential Terms and Components

- ▶ race condition
- ▶ end-of-life (EOL)
- ▶ memory leak
- ▶ integer overflow

- ▶ buffer overflow
- ▶ pointer dereference
- ▶ DLL injection

CramSaver

If you can correctly answer these questions before going through this chapter, save time by skimming the Exam Alerts in this section and then completing the Cram Quiz at the end of Part I.

1. Describe some of the potential impacts associated with a race condition.

   _____

2. What are some of the concerns with the default configurations of systems?

   _____

3. Failing to properly handle input into an application can lead to what?

   _____

Answers

1. A race condition can result in system malfunction and unexpected results. Resulting errors can cause crashes and even allow attackers to escalate their privileges.
2. Default configurations potentially provide a larger attack surface. Default accounts and passwords also provide a simple means for an attacker to gain access to a system, resulting in several potentially negative impacts.
3. Failure to do proper input handling can lead to input that can impact data flow, allowing an attacker to gain control of a system or remotely execute commands.

Vulnerability scanners are capable of prioritizing vulnerabilities based on accepted criteria that reflect the severity of the weakness. However, each organization is unique and has varying degrees of resources to fix vulnerabilities. Keep in mind that the mere act of patching a vulnerability introduces risk because the application of the patch might negatively affect the systems. Furthermore, most organizations require resources to ensure that such fixes are properly tested.

Organizations need to consider vulnerabilities across various factors, including existing security controls, the threat likelihood, the goals of the business, and the impact on the systems and business if the vulnerability is exploited. This chapter examines the impact associated with many common vulnerability types.

Identifying vulnerabilities gives an organization the opportunity to consider the impact and criticality and to evaluate an approach to remediate the weaknesses.

However, zero-day vulnerabilities are particularly concerning because vulnerability scanners cannot initially detect them. Attackers that know about these otherwise unknown vulnerabilities can take advantage of the situation. Affected vendors then will work on a patch, and the organization might be pressured into immediately deploying a patch without adequate testing.

People and Process

Technical vulnerabilities are often the focus when assessing their impact on an organization. However, vulnerabilities related to people and process are equally important—or more so.

▶ **Business processes:** The lack of business process is a vulnerability, particularly because these processes drive policy and governance, setting the foundation for everything else covered in this chapter.

▶ **Untrained users:** Some organizations spend millions of dollars on technology, yet pay no mind to spending relatively little more to properly educate and train users. For example, an untrained user presents a grave vulnerability in attacks such as social engineering—and consequences are even worse if that user directly contributes, interacts with, configures, and maintains the technical systems.

Race Conditions

A race condition involves software, specifically the way a program executes sequences of code. A race condition typically occurs when code sequences are competing over the same resource or acting concurrently. Race conditions can result in malfunction and unexpected results. Race conditions also can cause denial of service. In fact, a race condition can cause null pointer errors in which an application dereferences a pointer that it expects to be valid but is really null, resulting in a system crash. Race conditions are also associated with allowing attackers to escalate their privileges.

ExamAlert

A race condition exploits a small window of time in which one action impacts another. These out-of-sequence actions can result in a system crash, loss of data, or unauthorized access.

Resource Exhaustion

Computing systems often have finite hardware resources available. Cloud computing systems might be more elastic in their ability to scale, but monetary costs are associated with even this scale. If software does not properly manage resources such as memory, CPU, and storage, a system might completely consume or exhaust its resources. The most obvious impact of such a situation is a denial of service. Without the required resources, users will not be able to access the system, and processing can be impacted. Resource exhaustion can also result from other unexpected events and attacks. For example, in a memory leak, discussed in the upcoming section "Leaks, Overflows, and Code Injections," all available memory is exhausted from the system, resulting in slow operations or unresponsiveness.

Architecture and Design

Improper architecture and design of systems and software can contribute to continued vulnerabilities. Most organizations follow standard good practices and use well-established frameworks, development lifecycles, and governing principles for secure design and architecture. Consider the following examples, however, which increase the likelihood of vulnerabilities:

▶ Software that allows users to perform tasks with unnecessary privileges, violating the principle of least privilege.

▶ Systems that fail open instead of failing securely. Such a system failure would allow an attacker to access resources.

▶ Security through obscurity, to prevent against only less significant threat actors.

▶ Unnecessary complexity, which makes systems management more difficult to understand and control.

The last point is particularly important as it relates to system sprawl and undocumented assets. Clear oversight for the design and architecture of systems is vital to operations and security. The design and architecture of systems can easily become poorly documented over time, often because of personnel changes, rapidly evolving needs, and disjointed operations. System sprawl and lack of clear documentation can then result in a loss of visibility and control, which can have negative impacts upon an organization. Examples include the following:

▶ Unpatched software

▶ Weak configurations

- ▶ Poor access management controls
- ▶ Lack of backups
- ▶ Downtime
- ▶ Less resiliency to change

Systems need to be managed to ensure operational efficiency and effective security practices. Organizations cannot really manage what they do not know about. This is why organizations require sound information systems governance programs and often use automated tools to constantly monitor the network to identify and ensure assets have been properly provisioned and documented.

Configuration

Configuration errors are one of the most common sources of data breaches. Configuration errors typically result from not modifying the default configurations—part of many systems—as well as generally misconfiguring systems so that they do not align with standards or best practices.

Many vendors ship their systems for ease of use and entrust the customers with applying proper configurations. A common example is the default password, a simple exploit that can have grave consequences. For example, many home routers used to ship with a default password common to all models of that particular router. Left unchanged, it provided simple access for any malicious attacker who knew the make and model of the device.

Other misconfigurations include unneeded applications and services. These services provide additional avenues for attackers, especially if default accounts are removed or changed. In addition, each additional service could carry additional flaws that might go unnoticed. Many web servers, for example, can be configured to reveal directory contents for unauthorized users to download sensitive data. These situations themselves can be harmful, but an attacker can also use them to pivot within the environment to cause even more harm.

One of the most common types of misconfigurations includes improperly configured accounts. These accounts and the associated authentication and authorization mechanisms restrict access from people who shouldn't have it. Misconfigured accounts can impact organizations in several ways, including allowing escalated privileges that then harm systems and allow attackers to exfiltrate data.

Cryptographic Management

Properly managing cryptographic keys and certificates is critical to the security of associated systems. If a digital certificate is not properly validated, for example, this can facilitate a man-in-the-middle attack. Such an attack can impact an organization's confidentiality and integrity of information. Without proper key management, data that is supposed to remain confidential is susceptible to easy decryption by an attacker.

Software and systems, especially systems that transact over the Internet, can be vulnerable to weak cipher suites and implementations. Even using standard and accepted algorithms might not be enough if the strength of the key, or key size, defaults to a client's lesser capability. In these examples, an attacker could more easily use brute force to breach confidentiality and data integrity.

> **ExamAlert**
>
> Cryptographic key size, or the number of bits an algorithm uses in a key, should be large enough to make a brute-force attack infeasible.

Embedded Systems

Embedded systems involve using specialized chips within devices that contain the operating systems themselves. Essentially, these chips are the computer. The growth of the Internet of Things (IoT) further highlights the challenges surrounding such systems. For example, consider Internet-enabled cameras. Naturally, embedded systems gain mainstream attention when a news story highlights instances of attackers taking over baby monitor cameras. Embedded systems present management challenges and can be difficult to patch. As a result, these types of systems can have a severe impact on a business if the system can be potentially completely taken over. This is especially true if such systems are also an ideal target for malware.

Lack of Vendor Support

Vulnerability scanners are quick to point out systems that the vendors no longer support or that have gone end-of-life (EOL). Unsupported software means more than just a lack of technical support or poor reliability: The vendor also is not providing patches for newly discovered vulnerabilities. For example, attackers looking for Windows XP systems might not find many, but when they do, they have an easy target. These systems potentially open the door to an attacker seeking to impact an organization in many ways, including establishing a foothold inside.

> **ExamAlert**
>
> If patches and system updates are no longer available because a system has gone end-of-life, attackers have an easy way to exploit the system.

Improper Software Handling

Software should be designed to ensure proper handling of input into the system, as well proper error handling. Both of these software errors can have an operational impact on the organization as it relates to the end user. Moreover, they can have potential security impacts:

▶ **Improper input handling:** Solutions that don't properly validate input into the system can affect data flow and expectations. An attacker might be able to gain control of a system or inject code for remote execution.

▶ **Improper error handling:** When software is not designed to properly handle errors, the result might be message and diagnostic information sensitive to the inner workings of the systems. This data can disclose details to an end user and allow an attacker to gain sufficient information to advance an attack.

> **ExamAlert**
>
> Software that is not properly designed to validate input or manage errors is vulnerable to program manipulation and could reveal information that should not be disclosed.

Leaks, Overflows, and Code Injection

At their best, memory leaks reduce the performance of a system. If left unchecked, they can cause the entire application or computer to become unresponsive, thus impacting a system's availability.

Integer overflows can facilitate malicious code or a buffer overflow. A buffer overflow can result in system crashes, impacting a system's availability. In addition, an attacker might cause a buffer overflow to execute code outside that specific application. Code injection, such as DLL injection, specifically allows an attacker to run code within the context of another process, making it more difficult for an organization to trace the attack.

This arbitrary code execution describes an attacker's ability to execute programs and commands on the attacked machine. Exploits are designed to attack bugs in software that provide the methods for running these commands. From a vulnerability standpoint, these types of bugs are significant because they allow the attacker to overtake a process. Such capability increases the likelihood that the attacker can then completely take control of the client system. A system vulnerable to such code execution is highly susceptible to malware, which does not require the owner's consent. This problem is compounded with remote code execution. Specifically, such code can run across networks and even the Internet.

Preventing these attacks begins with using secure coding practices. Unfortunately, end users are sometimes at the mercy of their software vendors. Therefore, it is important for end users to keep their systems patched and for organizations to pay attention to the types of software vulnerabilities. Arbitrary remote code execution vulnerabilities often should be prioritized in the remediation process.

What Next?

If you want more practice on this chapter's exam objectives before you move on, remember that you can access all the Cram Quiz questions on the Pearson Test Prep software. You can also create a custom exam by objective. Note any objective you struggle with and go to that objective material in this chapter.

PART I

Cram Quiz

These review questions cover material related to Chapters 1–6, which cover objectives falling under Domain 1, "Threats, Attacks and Vulnerabilities," of the Security+ exam.

1. Which of the following describes the difference between a worm and a virus?

   ○ **A.** Viruses are self-replicating.

   ○ **B.** Viruses are often malicious.

   ○ **C.** Worms are self-replicating.

   ○ **D.** Viruses are often malicious.

2. Which one of the following is not an example of a denial-of-service attack?

   ○ **A.** Fraggle

   ○ **B.** Smurf

   ○ **C.** Gargomel

   ○ **D.** Teardrop

3. Which one of the following is not a type of phishing attack?

   ○ **A.** Spear phishing

   ○ **B.** Wishing

   ○ **C.** Whaling

   ○ **D.** Smishing

4. At your place of employment, you are rushing to the door with your arms full of bags. As you approach, the woman before you scans her badge to gain entrance while holding the door for you, but not without asking to see your badge. What did she just prevent?

   ○ **A.** Phishing

   ○ **B.** Whaling

   ○ **C.** Tailgating

   ○ **D.** Door diving

5. Which of the following is an effective way to get information in crowded places such as airports, conventions, or supermarkets?

   ○ **A.** Vishing

   ○ **B.** Shoulder surfing

   ○ **C.** Reverse social engineering

   ○ **D.** Phishing

6. Which one of the following is designed to execute malicious actions when a certain event occurs or a specific time period elapses?

   ○ **A.** Logic bomb

   ○ **B.** Spyware

   ○ **C.** Botnet

   ○ **D.** DDoS

7. Which one of the following best describes a polymorphic virus?

   ○ **A.** A virus that infects EXE files

   ○ **B.** A virus that attacks the boot sector and then attacks the system files

   ○ **C.** A virus inserted into a Microsoft Office document such as Word or Excel

   ○ **D.** A virus that changes its form each time it is executed

8. You discover you are unable to access files on your computer. A message appears asking for payment to allow for the recovery of your files. Which of the following is most likely?

   ○ **A.** Your files have been deleted.

   ○ **B.** Your files have been moved to a remote server.

   ○ **C.** Your files have been encrypted.

   ○ **D.** Your files have been copied.

9. Which of the following types of attacks can result from the length of variables not being properly checked in the code of a program?

   ○ **A.** Buffer overflow

   ○ **B.** Replay

   ○ **C.** Spoofing

   ○ **D.** Denial of service

10. Which one of the following is a best practice to prevent code injection attacks?

    ○ **A.** Session cookies

    ○ **B.** Input validation

    ○ **C.** Implementing the latest security patches

    ○ **D.** Using unbound variables

11. You are the security administrator for a bank. The users are complaining about the network being slow. It is not a particularly busy time of the day, however. You capture network packets and discover that hundreds of ICMP packets have been sent to the host. What type of attack is likely being executed against your network?

    ○ **A.** Spoofing

    ○ **B.** Man-in-the-middle attack

    ○ **C.** Password attack

    ○ **D.** Denial-of-service attack

12. An initialization vector should be which of the following?

    ○ **A.** Unique and unpredictable

    ○ **B.** Unique and predictable

    ○ **C.** Repeatable and random

    ○ **D.** Repeatable and unique

13. How do relationship and capability pertain to understanding specific threat actors?

    ○ **A.** They indicate the likelihood of vulnerabilities being discovered.

    ○ **B.** They are characteristics associated with building a threat profile.

    ○ **C.** They describe attributes that apply equally to all threats.

    ○ **D.** They are the two most important attributes when analyzing threat actors.

14. With which of the following is a "low and slow" attack most associated?

    ○ **A.** APT

    ○ **B.** Ransomware

    ○ **C.** OSINT

    ○ **D.** Script kiddies

15. After conducting a vulnerability assessment, which of the following is the best action to perform?

   ○ **A.** Disable all vulnerable systems until mitigating controls can be implemented

   ○ **B.** Contact the network team to shut down all identified open ports

   ○ **C.** Immediately conduct a penetration test against identified vulnerabilities

   ○ **D.** Organize and document the results based on severity

16. You are conducting a penetration test on a software application for a client. The client provides you with details around some of the source code and development process. What type of test will you likely be conducting?

   ○ **A.** Black box

   ○ **B.** Vulnerability

   ○ **C.** White box

   ○ **D.** Answers A and C

17. Which of the following is a reason to conduct a penetration test?

   ○ **A.** To passively test security controls

   ○ **B.** To identify the vulnerabilities

   ○ **C.** To test the adequacy of security measures put in place

   ○ **D.** To steal data for malicious purposes

18. Which one of the following best describes a penetration test?

   ○ **A.** A passive evaluation and analysis of operational weaknesses using tools and techniques that a malicious source might use

   ○ **B.** An evaluation mimicking real-world attacks to identify ways to circumvent security

   ○ **C.** The monitoring of network communications and examination of header and payload data

   ○ **D.** A technique used to identify hosts and their associated vulnerabilities

19. Which one of the following best describes the four primary phases of a penetration test?

   ○ **A.** Planning, discovery, attack, reporting

   ○ **B.** Exploit, escalation, pivot, persistence

   ○ **C.** Planning, exploit, attack, persistence

   ○ **D.** Discovery, attack, pivot, reporting

20. Your team is tasked with conducting a vulnerability assessment and reports back with a high number of false positives. Which of the following might you recommend to reduce the number of false positives?

   ○ **A.** Have the team run a vulnerability scan using noncredentialed access

   ○ **B.** Have the team run a vulnerability scan using credentialed access

   ○ **C.** Have the team run a port scan across all common ports

   ○ **D.** Have the team run a port scan across all ports

21. Which of the following are potential impacts of a race condition?

   ○ **A.** System malfunction

   ○ **B.** Denial of service

   ○ **C.** Escalated privileges

   ○ **D.** All of the above

22. Which one of the following is the term given to a fraudulent wireless access point that is configured to lure connections to it?

   ○ **A.** Evil twin

   ○ **B.** ARP replay attack

   ○ **C.** Bluejacking

   ○ **D.** NFC

23. A small IT consulting firm has installed new wireless routers across all your small regional offices. Within days, you learn that you are unable to access the administrative interfaces of these routers due to an incorrect password. Which one of the following is most likely the reason?

   ○ **A.** The wireless routers were set up with the default configuration, which included a default password that was never changed.

   ○ **B.** The wireless routers are not powered on.

   ○ **C.** The wireless routers have been placed on end-of-life by the manufacturer and are no longer supported for remote login.

   ○ **D.** The wireless routers have been designed to allow improper input handling, resulting in failed password input.

24. You identify a system that becomes progressively slower over a couple days until it is unresponsive. Which of the following is most likely the reason for this behavior?

   ○ **A.** Improper error handling

   ○ **B.** Race condition

   ○ **C.** Memory leak

   ○ **D.** Untrained user

Cram Quiz Answers

1. **C.** Worms are self-replicating. Answer A is incorrect because viruses require an infected file to be executed or launched to replicate. Answers B and D are incorrect because both viruses and worms are usually malicious.

2. **C.** A Gargomel attack sounds cool, but it does not actually exist. Fraggle, Smurf, and Teardrop are names of specific denial-of-service attacks. Therefore, answers A, B, and D are incorrect.

3. **B.** Wishing is not a type of phishing attack. Answers A, C, and D are incorrect because these all do describe a type of phishing attack. Spear phishing is targeted. Whaling is spear phishing that specifically targets high-profile personnel. Smishing is SMS-based phishing.

4. **C.** Tailgating involves closely following someone with authorized physical access to gain access to the environment. Answers A and B are incorrect because these describe methods of acquiring sensitive information by masquerading as a trustworthy source. Answer D is also incorrect.

5. **B.** Shoulder surfing uses direct observation techniques. It gets its name from the tactic of looking over someone's shoulder to obtain information. Answer A is incorrect because vishing uses a phone to obtain information. Answer C is incorrect because reverse social engineering involves an attacker convincing the user that he or she is a legitimate IT authority, causing the user to solicit assistance. Answer D is incorrect because phishing is an attempt to acquire sensitive information by masquerading as a trustworthy entity via an electronic communication, usually an email.

6. **A.** Logic bombs are designed to execute after certain events, on a certain date, or after a specific time period. Answers B, C, and D are incorrect. Spyware, Botnets, and DDoS are all threats, but they do not execute malicious code after a specific event or period.

7. **D.** Polymorphic viruses can change their form each time they are run. Answers A, B, and C describe different types of viruses, such as program, multipartite, and macro, respectively, so those answers are incorrect.

8. **C.** This situation implies ransomware or crypto-malware. In this attack, files are encrypted and are essentially "held ransom" until payment is made. Answer A is incorrect because the attacker wants to ensure that you have the ability to access your files, which will further encourage others who are infected to also pay. Often, however, the attacker deletes or threatens to delete files if the ransom isn't paid after a defined period of time. Answers B and D are incorrect because the files are encrypted only on the target system.

9. **A.** Buffer overflows result from programming flaws that allow too much data to be sent. When the program does not know what to do with all this data, it crashes, leaving the machine in a state of vulnerability. Answer B is incorrect because a replay attack records and replays previously sent valid messages. Answer C is incorrect because spoofing involves modifying the source address of traffic or the source of information. Answer D is incorrect because the purpose of a DoS attack is to deny the use of resources or services to legitimate users.

10. **B.** Input validation is the one of the most important countermeasures to prevent code injection attacks. Answer A is incorrect because session cookies pertain to maintaining state within a visit to a website. Answer C is incorrect because, although ensuring that systems are patched is a good practice, it is not specifically a best practice to prevent code injection attacks. Answer D is incorrect because proper input validation to prevent code injection relies on bound variables.

11. **D.** A ping flood is a DoS attack that attempts to block service or reduce activity on a host by sending ping requests directly to the victim using ICMP. Spoofing involves modifying the source address of traffic or source of information. A man-in-the-middle attack is commonly used to gather information in transit between two hosts. A password attack attempts to gain unauthorized access by going after the authentication control for an account. Answers A, B, and C are incorrect.

12. **A.** An initialization vector (IV) should be unique and unpredictable. Answers B, C, and D do not apply to IV and are incorrect.

13. **B.** Relationship and capability are characteristics that can be attributed to threat actors. Other common attributes include motive and intent, both of which are associated with building a threat profile. Answer A is incorrect because these do not pertain to the discovery of vulnerabilities. Answer C is incorrect because each attribute varies, based on specific threat actors. Answer D is incorrect because threat actors and overall risk are unique to each organization.

14. **A.** An advanced persistent threat (APT) is a "low and slow" style of attack executed to infiltrate a network and remain inside while going undetected. Answer B is incorrect because ransomware is obvious and sends a clear message to the end user in an attempt to extort compensation from the victim. Answer C is incorrect. OSINT describes Open Source Intelligence, which is the term given to information available for collection from publicly available sources. Answer D is incorrect because script kiddies, unlike APTs, are usually not sophisticated in their methods and are usually easily detected.

15. **D.** After an assessment, the results should be organized based on the severity of risk to the organization. Answer A is incorrect because it is generally an extreme response, except in rare situations. Answer B is incorrect because many open ports are required for a network to function. Answer C is incorrect because, although a penetration test often does follow a vulnerability scan, it is not an immediate necessity and certainly is not required to be run against all identified vulnerabilities.

16. **C.** White box testing is more transparent. Because you are provided with source code, you have more knowledge about the system before you begin your penetration testing. Answer A is incorrect because black box testing assumes no prior knowledge. Answer B is incorrect because this refers to a weakness. Therefore, answer D is also incorrect.

17. **C.** A penetration test helps quantify the adequacy of security measures put in place and helps organizations understand the potential impact of threats against the environment. Answers A and B are incorrect because these describe the purpose of a vulnerability scan. Answer D is also incorrect. A penetration test is a "friendly" attack to help safeguard an organization from a real attack. A penetration test should never be used for malicious purposes, even if it succeeds in deeply penetrating an organization.

18. B. A penetration test reveals security weaknesses through real-world attacks. The results can help prioritize risk and identify areas for improvement. Penetration tests are active evaluations, so answer A is incorrect. Answer C is incorrect because it describes network sniffing. Answer D is incorrect because it describes vulnerability scanning. However, both network sniffing and vulnerability scanning can be used as part of the penetration process.

19. A. Planning, discovery, attack, and reporting are the four primary phases of a penetration attack. Answer B is incorrect because it describes the four key steps within the attack phase. Answers C and D are incorrect because they do not describe the proper four primary phases.

20. B. Noncredentialed vulnerability scans result in a greater number of false positives. This type of scan provides an outsider point-of-view, and although it might indicate what an outsider is more likely to see, it does not as effectively show the full extent of vulnerabilities. A credentialed vulnerability scan provides access into systems that might otherwise not be accessible, to further determine legitimate vulnerabilities. As a result, answer A is incorrect. Answers C and D are incorrect because vulnerability scans initially do scan specified ports as part of the process.

21. D. System malfunction, denial of service, and escalated privileges are all potential impacts because of a race condition.

22. A. An evil twin is a type of rogue access point that gets between a client and a legitimate wireless access point. The evil twin can then be used to attack the systems that connect to it. Answer B is incorrect: An ARP reply attack describes an attack against a wireless access point in an attempt to determine the key. Answer C is incorrect: Bluejacking refers to a Bluetooth wireless device sending messages to other Bluetooth-enabled devices. Answer D is incorrect because NFC refers to the communications protocol between devices within close proximity to each other.

23. A. In this scenario, the wireless routers most likely include a known default password that was never changed upon installation. This gave an outsider a simple means of access. Answer B is incorrect because, in that case, you would not be able to even attempt login. Answers C and D are also incorrect. Not being able to log in is not associated with end-of-life systems. Improper input handling refers to solutions that are not properly validating input to the system; this would more likely result in the capability to put arbitrary strings within the input fields to cause some type of undesirable behavior.

24. C. A memory leak is the most likely culprit. A memory leak occurs when an application or process continually consumes memory. Memory is usually finite; after it is consumed, the system becomes unresponsive. Answers A and B might ultimately lead to a memory leak, but these are not the best answer. Improper input handling will likely impact the data flow and expectations of the system. This can also potentially lead to a memory leak. A race condition can result in a variety of malfunctions, but this is not the best answer. Answer D is also incorrect because an untrained user is not likely the explicit reason for such a condition.

Technology and Tools

This part covers the following official CompTIA Security+ SY0-501 exam objectives for Domain 2, "Technologies and Tools":

▶ 2.1 Install and configure network components, both hardware- and software-based, to support organizational security.

▶ 2.2 Given a scenario, use appropriate software tools to assess the security posture of an organization.

▶ 2.3 Given a scenario, troubleshoot common security issues.

▶ 2.4 Given a scenario, analyze and interpret output from security technologies.

▶ 2.5 Given a scenario, deploy mobile devices securely.

▶ 2.6 Given a scenario, implement secure protocols.

(For more information on the official CompTIA Security+ SY0-501 exam topics, see the "About the CompTIA Security+ SY0-501 Exam" section in the Introduction.)

The previous part covered threats, attacks, and vulnerabilities, outlining threats, risks, and associated attacks to help you understand the potential dangers organizations face every day. This part focuses on the main principles of security technologies and tool implementation. Before you can properly secure a network, you must understand the security function, the purpose of network devices, and the technologies used to secure the network. You look at identifying the hardware- and software-based network components, selecting the appropriate software tool solution, troubleshooting security issues, interpreting security technology output, implementing secure protocols, and deploying mobile devices securely.

Knowing when and how to use security technologies and tools is necessary to protect against the threats, attacks, and vulnerabilities described in Part I, "Threats, Attacks, and Vulnerabilities." This is an important aspect of security: If you have numerous defenses in place but they are implemented incorrectly or misconfigured, the purpose of the technology or tool is defeated. To have a holistic approach to security, all working pieces should fit together and complement each other. This part explains how each type of technology and tool fits into the organization's security posture.

CHAPTER 7

Network Components

This chapter covers the following official Security+ exam objective:

2.1 Install and configure network components, both hardware- and software-based, to support organizational security.

- ▶ Firewall
  - ■ ACL
  - ■ Application-based vs. network-based
  - ■ Stateful vs. stateless
  - ■ Implicit deny
- ▶ VPN concentrator
  - ■ Remote access vs. site-to-site
  - ■ IPsec
    - • Tunnel mode
    - • Transport mode
    - • AH
    - • ESP
  - ■ Split tunnel vs. full tunnel
  - ■ TLS
  - ■ Always-on VPN
- ▶ NIPS/NIDS
  - ■ Signature-based
  - ■ Heuristic/behavioral
  - ■ Anomaly
  - ■ Inline vs. passive
  - ■ In-band vs. out-of-band
  - ■ Rules
  - ■ Analytics
    - • False positive
    - • False negative

- ▶ Router
  - ■ ACLs
  - ■ Antispoofing
- ▶ Switch
  - ■ Port security
  - ■ Layer 2 vs. Layer 3
  - ■ Loop prevention
  - ■ Flood guard
- ▶ Proxy
  - ■ Forward and reverse proxy
  - ■ Transparent
  - ■ Application/multipurpose
- ▶ Load balancer
  - ■ Scheduling
    - • Affinity
    - • Round-robin
  - ■ Active-passive
  - ■ Active-active
  - ■ Virtual IPs
- ▶ Access point
  - ■ SSID
  - ■ MAC filtering
  - ■ Signal strength
  - ■ Band selection/width
  - ■ Antenna types and placement

- Fat vs. thin
- Controller-based vs. standalone
▶ SIEM
  - Aggregation
  - Correlation
  - Automated alerting and triggers
  - Time synchronization
  - Event deduplication
  - Logs/WORM
▶ DLP
  - USB blocking
  - Cloud-based
  - Email

▶ NAC
  - Dissolvable vs. permanent
  - Host health checks
  - Agent vs. agentless
▶ Mail gateway
  - Spam filter
  - DLP
  - Encryption
▶ Bridge
▶ SSL/TLS accelerators
▶ SSL decryptors
▶ Media gateway
▶ Hardware security module

Essential Terms and Components

▶ access control list (ACL)
▶ Authentication Header (AH)
▶ behavior-based IDS
▶ behavior-based monitoring
▶ Challenge Handshake Authentication Protocol (CHAP)
▶ data-loss prevention (DLP)
▶ Encapsulating Security Payload (ESP)
▶ hardware security module (HSM)
▶ Internet Protocol Security (IPsec)

▶ intrusion detection system (IDS)
▶ network-based IDS (NIDS)
▶ network-based IPS (NIPS)
▶ router
▶ signature-based monitoring
▶ Transport Layer Security (TLS)
▶ virtual local-area network (VLAN)
▶ virtual private network (VPN)

CramSaver

If you can correctly answer these questions before going through this chapter, save time by skimming the Exam Alerts in this chapter and then completing the Cram Quiz at the end of the chapter.

1. Explain the role of SIEM in network security.

   _____

2. What is the purpose of loop protection?

   _____

3. Explain the purpose of implicit deny.

   _____

Answers

1. SIEM tools collect, correlate, and display data feeds that support response activities. SIEMs are the main element in compliance regulations such as SOX, GLBA, PCI, FISMA, and HIPAA. SIEM output is also used in a proactive manner to detect emerging threats and improve overall security by defining events of interest (EOI) and resulting actions. The purpose of SIEM is to turn a large amount of data into knowledge that can be acted upon.

2. The loop guard feature makes additional checks in Layer 2 switched networks to prevent loops. If BPDUs are not received on a nondesignated port and loop guard is enabled, that port is moved into the STP loop-inconsistent blocking state instead of the listening/learning/forwarding state. Without the loop guard feature, the port assumes the designated port role.

3. Implicit deny is an access control practice in which resource availability is restricted to only logins that are explicitly granted access; the resources remain unavailable even when logins are not explicitly denied access. This practice is used commonly in Cisco networks, where most ACLs have a default setting of implicit deny. By default, an implicit deny all clause appears at the end of every ACL. Anything that is not explicitly permitted is denied. Essentially, an implicit deny works the same as finishing the ACL with **deny ip any any**. This ensures that when access is not explicitly granted, it is automatically denied by default.

Perimeter Security

This section focuses on the network components that are used for perimeter security. Keep in mind that each organization has different needs and might use additional tools for perimeter defense. The objective of this section is to give you some idea of how the purpose of a component determines the placement of the device. Before you can properly secure a network, you must understand the security function, the purpose of network devices, and technologies used to secure the network.

Perimeter security is based on access control. Access control generally refers to the process of making resources available to accounts that should have access, while limiting that access to only what is required. Access control on perimeter devices is often done through an *access control list (ACL)*. ACLs can apply to firewalls, routers, and other devices.

Firewalls

A *firewall* is a component placed on computers and networks to help eliminate undesired access by the outside world. It can consist of hardware, software, or a combination of both. A firewall is the first line of defense for the network. The primary function of a firewall is to mitigate threats by monitoring all traffic entering or leaving a network. How firewalls are configured is important, especially for large companies. A compromised firewall might spell disaster in the form of bad publicity or a lawsuit—not only for the company, but also for the companies it does business with. For smaller companies, a firewall is an excellent investment because most small companies do not have a full-time technology staff and an intrusion could easily put them out of business. All things considered, a firewall is an important part of your defense, but you should not rely on it exclusively for network protection. Figure 7.1 shows the firewall placement in a small network.

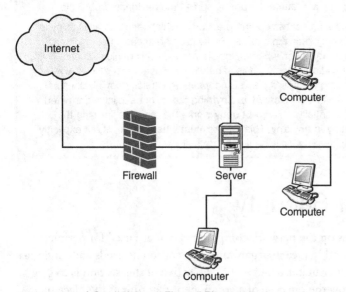

FIGURE 7.1   **A Small Network Firewall Placement**

Generally, a firewall can be described as being either stateful or stateless. Stateless firewalls tend to work as a basic access control list (ACL) filter. This type of firewall does not inspect traffic. It merely observes the traffic coming in and out of the network and then allows or denies packets based on the information in the ACL. Because this type of firewall does minimal filtering, it tends to be faster than a stateful firewall and is best for heavy traffic loads.

> **ExamAlert**
>
> Stateless firewalls tend to work as a basic ACL filter. Stateful firewalls are a deeper inspection firewall type that analyzes traffic patterns and data flows.

Stateful firewalls are a deeper inspection firewall type that analyzes traffic patterns and data flows. This allows a more dynamic access control decision because the network state is not static. Stateful firewalls are better when it comes to identifying unauthorized communication attempts because they watch the state of the connection from beginning to end, including security functions such as tunnels and encryption.

Rules can be created for either inbound traffic or outbound traffic. Inbound rules explicitly allow or explicitly block inbound network traffic that matches the criteria in the rule. Outbound rules explicitly allow or explicitly block network traffic originating from the computer that matches the criteria in the rule.

In many firewalls, the rules can be granualized and configured to specify the computers or users, program, service, or port and protocol. Rules can be configured so that they are applied when profiles are used. As soon as a network packet matches a rule, that rule is applied and processing stops. The more restrictive rules should be listed first and the least restrictive rules should follow; otherwise, if a less restrictive rule is placed before a more restrictive rule, checking stops at the first rule.

> **ExamAlert**
>
> Order of firewall rules affects application. When a less restrictive rule is placed before a more restrictive rule, checking stops at the first rule.

Implicit deny is an access control practice in which resource availability is restricted to only logins that are explicitly granted access. The resources remain unavailable even when logins are not explicitly denied access. This practice is commonly used in Cisco networks, where most ACLs have a default setting of implicit deny. By default, an implicit deny all clause appears at the end of every ACL. Anything that is not explicitly permitted is denied. Essentially, an implicit deny works the same as finishing the ACL with **deny ip any any**. This ensures that when access is not explicitly granted, it is automatically denied by default.

ExamAlert

The implicit deny is generally used by default in firewall configurations. Access lists have an implicit deny at the end of the list; unless you explicitly permit it, traffic cannot pass.

Application layer firewalls can examine application traffic and identify threats through deep packet inspection techniques. Often we do not think in terms of application-level security when discussing devices such as firewalls, IPS, IDS, and proxies. Yet most next-generation devices are capable of being application aware. To meet the changing ways organizations do business, next-generation firewalls (NGFWs) have been developed. NGFWs are considered application-aware. This means that they go beyond the traditional port and IP address examination of stateless firewalls to inspect traffic at a deeper level. Application layer firewalls integrate the functions of other network devices such as a proxy, IDS, and IPS. Many application layer firewalls use an IPS engine to provide application support. As a result, various blended techniques are used to identify applications and formulate policies based on business rules.

Application layer firewalls are preferred to network layer firewalls because they have the capability to do deep packet inspection and function at Layer 7 of the OSI model. Network layer firewalls mainly function at Layer 3 of the OSI model and, as such, are limited to basically packet forwarding.

VPN Concentrators

In the world of a mobile workforce, employers require a secure method for employees to access corporate resources while on the road or working from home. One of the most common methods implemented for this type of access is a *virtual private network (VPN)*. A *VPN concentrator* is used to allow multiple external users to access internal network resources using secure features that are built into the device. A VPN concentrator is deployed where a single device must handle a very large number of VPN tunnels. Remote-access VPN connectivity is provided using either *Internet Protocol Security (IPsec)* or Secure Sockets Layer (SSL) for the VPN. User authentication can be via RADIUS, Kerberos, Microsoft Active Directory, RSA SecurID, digital certificates, or the built-in authentication server. Chapter 22, "Identity and Access Management Concepts," covers the function and purpose of authentication services.

In a typical scenario, the VPN concentrator allows users to utilize an encrypted tunnel to securely access a corporate network or other network via the Internet. Another use is internally, to encrypt WLAN or wired traffic when the security of login and password information is paramount for high-level users and sensitive information. You can implement a VPN concentrator to prevent login and password information from being captured. A VPN concentrator also allows ACLs to be applied to remote user sessions. These scenarios use various technologies that you need to comprehend to properly implement the correct VPN solution.

VPN concentrators come in various models and allow for customized options, such as the numbers of simultaneous users, amount of throughput needed, amount of protection required, and tunnel modes. For example, Cisco VPN concentrators include components that allow for split tunneling, increased capacity, and throughput.

Internet Protocol Security

The *Internet Protocol Security* (IPsec) authentication and encapsulation standard is widely used to establish secure VPN communications. IPsec can secure transmissions between critical servers and clients. This helps prevent network-based attacks from taking place. Unlike most security systems that function within the application layer of the OSI model, IPsec functions within the network layer. IPsec provides authentication services and encapsulation of data through support of the Internet Key Exchange (IKE) protocol.

IPsec can be run in either tunnel mode or transport mode. Transport mode is used between endpoints such as a client and a server. It can also be used between a gateway and an endpoint when the gateway is being treated as an endpoint, such as in a Remote Desktop (RDP) or Telnet session.

IPsec default mode is tunnel mode. Tunnel mode is most often used between gateways such as a router and a firewall. When tunnel mode is used, the gateway acts as a proxy for the hosts. In tunnel mode, an AH or ESP header is used. The asymmetric key standard defining IPsec provides two primary security services:

▶ **Authentication Header (AH):** AH provides authentication of the data's sender, along with integrity and nonrepudiation. RFC 2402 states that AH provides authentication for as much of the IP header as possible, as well as for upper-level protocol data. However, some IP header fields might change in transit, and when the packet arrives at the receiver, the value of these fields might not be predictable by the sender. AH cannot protect the values of such fields, so the protection it provides to the IP header is somewhat piecemeal.

▶ **Encapsulating Security Payload (ESP):** ESP supports authentication of the data's sender and encryption of the data being transferred, along with confidentiality and integrity protection. ESP is used to provide confidentiality, data origin authentication, connectionless integrity, an antireplay service (a form of partial sequence integrity), and limited traffic-flow confidentiality. The set of services provided depends on options selected at the time of security association establishment and on the placement of the implementation. Confidentiality can be selected independently of all other services. However, the use of confidentiality without integrity/ authentication (either in ESP or separately in AH) might subject traffic to certain forms of active attacks that could undermine the confidentiality service.

Protocols 51 and 50 are the AH and ESP components of the IPsec protocol. IPsec inserts ESP or AH (or both) as protocol headers into an IP datagram that immediately follows an IP header.

The protocol field of the IP header is 50 for ESP or 51 for AH. If IPsec is configured to do authentication instead of encryption, you must configure an IP filter to let protocol 51 traffic pass. If IPsec uses nested AH and ESP, you can configure an IP filter to let only protocol 51 (AH) traffic pass.

IPsec supports the Internet Key Exchange (IKE) protocol, which is a key management standard used to allow separate key protocols to be specified for use during data encryption. IKE functions within the Internet Security Association and Key Management Protocol (ISAKMP), which defines the payloads used to exchange key and authentication data appended to each packet.

Part 6, "Cryptography and PKI," focuses on Domain 6 and covers the common key exchange protocols, standard encryption algorithms, and hashing algorithms used in IPsec, such as Rivest-Shamir-Adleman (RSA), International Data Encryption Algorithm (IDEA), Triple DES (3DES), and message digest 5 (MD5).

In addition to IPsec VPNs, technologies such as TLS and its predecessor, SSL, can be used to secure network communications. These VPNs use the SSL and *Transport Layer Security (TLS)* protocols to provide a secure connection between internal network resources and remote users such as bring your own device (BYOD) users, vendors, and business partners. Because TLS is a point-to-point communication encryption technology, it can be used to secure traffic in a variety of applications, including web- and email-based communications. The main advantage SSL and TLS VPNs have over IPsec VPNs is simple end-user implementation because they function via a browser and an Internet connection.

The workforce has become very mobile, allowing employees to work anytime and anywhere. This shift has caused organizations to replace traditional IPsec VPNs with SSL/TLS VPNs that include an always-on solution.

> **ExamAlert**
>
> The concept behind always-on VPNs is that the user is always on the network.

Instead of depending on the user to establish a VPN connection, the always-on VPN client immediately and automatically establishes a VPN connection when an Internet connection is made. Network authentication occurs through certificates or other enterprise solutions because the connection is transparent to the user. Examples of always-on VPN solutions include Microsoft DirectAccess and Cisco AnyConnect Secure Mobility.

So far, this chapter has mainly discussed the technologies used to secure VPN communications, but other modes and types of VPNs exist as well. When you think of VPNs, you likely relate to remote-access VPNs that connect single hosts to organizational networks.

> **ExamAlert**
>
> Besides being configured to secure traffic between the remote user and the corporate network, a VPN can be configured as a site-to-site VPN.

Site-to-site VPNs are implemented based on IPsec policies assigned to VPN topologies. These VPNs connect entire networks to each other. An example of this type of implementation might be a VPN connecting a bank branch office to the network and the main office. Individual hosts do not need VPN client software. They communicate using normal TCP/IP traffic via a VPN gateway. The VPN gateways are responsible for setting up and breaking down the encapsulation and encryption traffic.

The last item this section discusses is the mode in which the VPN operates. Two modes are available: full tunnel and split tunnel.

ExamAlert

Full tunnel works exactly as it implies: All requests are routed and encrypted through the VPN. In split tunneling, the traffic is divided. Internal traffic requests are routed over the VPN; other traffic, such as web and email traffic, directly accesses the Internet.

The traffic is split after the VPN connection is made through the client configuration settings, such as IP address range or specific protocols.

The choice to use split tunneling is mainly to reserve bandwidth while the users are on the Internet and to reduce the load on the VPN concentrator, especially when the organization has a large remote workforce. Split tunneling can also be useful when employees are treated as contractors on client sites and require access to both employer resources and client resources.

NIDS and NIPS

IDS stands for *intrusion detection system*. Intrusion detection systems are designed to analyze data, identify attacks, and respond to the intrusion by sending alerts. They differ from firewalls, which control the information that gets into and out of the network: an IDS also can identify unauthorized activity. IDSs are also designed to identify attacks in progress within the network, not just on the boundary between private and public networks. Intrusion detection is managed by two basic methods: knowledge-based and behavior-based detection.

IDSs identify attacks based on rule sets, so most IDSs have a large number of rules. Rule writing is an important and difficult part of network security monitoring. Luckily, security vendors themselves do a lot of the rule writing. For example, Proofpoint currently has more than 37,000 rules, in several popular formats, and also hosts a web page that provides a daily rule set summary. Of course, the rules still might need to be modified, to meet the needs of the organization.

The two basic types of IDSs are *network-based* and *host-based*. As the names suggest, network-based IDSs (NIDSs) look at the information exchanged between machines. Host-based IDSs (HIDSs) look at information that originates on the individual machines.

Consider some basics:

▶ NIDSs monitor the packet flow and try to locate packets that might have gotten through the firewall but are not allowed to do so. They are best at detecting DoS attacks and unauthorized user access.

▶ HIDSs monitor communications on a host-by-host basis and try to filter malicious data. These types of IDSs are good at detecting unauthorized file modifications and user activity.

ExamAlert

NIDSs try to locate packets that the firewall missed and that are not actually allowed on the network. HIDSs collect and analyze data that originates on the local machine or a computer hosting a service. NIDSs tend to be more distributed.

NIDSs and HIDSs should be used together to ensure a truly secure environment. IDSs can be located anywhere on the network. You can place them internally or between firewalls.

As with any network device, the placement of a NIDS determines the effectiveness of the technology. A NIDS can be placed outside the perimeter of the firewall as an early detection system or can be used internally as an added layer of security. Internally placed NIDSs that are near the local network switching nodes and near the access routers at the network boundary have lower false alarm rates because the NIDS doesn't have to monitor any traffic that the firewall blocks.

Intrusion detection software is reactive or passive. This means that the system detects a potential security breach, logs the information, and signals an alert after the event occurs. By the time an alert has been issued, the attack has usually occurred and has damaged the network or desktop.

This type of device is sometimes referred to as an out-of-band device.

ExamAlert

Out-of-band devices only listen passively. They do not change or affect the traffic.

Network intrusion prevention systems (NIPSs) are sometimes considered to be an extension of IDSs. NIPSs can be either hardware- or software-based, as with many other network protection devices. Intrusion prevention differs from intrusion detection because it actually prevents attacks instead of only detecting the occurrence of an attack.

ExamAlert

NIPSs are designed to sit inline with traffic flows and prevent attacks in real time. An inline NIPS sits between the systems that need to be protected and the rest of the network.

NIPSs proactively protect machines against damage from attacks that signature-based technologies cannot detect because most NIPS solutions can look at application layer protocols such HTTP, FTP, and SMTP. When implementing a NIPS, keep in mind that the sensors must be physically inline to function properly.

ExamAlert

An IDS detects and alerts. An IPS detects and prevents. Know the difference between the two concepts.

This type of device is often referred to as an in-band device. Because the device is analyzing live network traffic, an in-band device acts as the enforcement point and can prevent an attack from reaching its target. In general, in-band systems are deployed at the network perimeter, but they also can be used internally to capture traffic flows at certain network points, such as into the datacenter.

Detection Methods

Behavior-based intrusion detection methods are rooted in the premise that an intrusion can be detected by comparing the normal activity of a network to current activity. Any abnormalities from normal or expected behavior of the network are reported via an alarm. Behavior-based methods can identify attempts to exploit new or undocumented vulnerabilities, can alert to elevation or abuse of privileges, and tend to be independent of operating-system-specific processes. Behavior-based methods consider intrusive any activity that does not match a learned behavior. These methods are associated with a high false alarm rate. If a network is compromised before the learned behavior period, any malicious activity related to the compromise is not reported.

Signature-based detection methods are considered knowledge-based because the underlying mechanism is a database of known vulnerabilities. Signature-based methods monitor a network to find a pattern or signature match. When they find a match, they generate an alert. Vendors provide signature updates, similar to antivirus software updates, but generally signatures can be created anytime a particular behavior needs to be identified. Because pattern matching can be done quickly when the rule set is not extensive, the system or user notices very little intrusiveness or performance reduction.

> **ExamAlert**
>
> Signature-based methods only detect known signatures or patterns, so these events must be created for every suspicious activity. They are more reactive because an attack must be known before it can be added to the database.

Signature-based methods provide lower false alarms, compared to behavior-based methods, because all suspicious activity is in a known database. Anomaly-based detection methods are similar to behavior-based intrusion detection methods. Both are based on the concept of using a baseline for network behavior. However, a slight variation exists between the two.

In anomaly-based detection methods, after the application is trained, the established profile is used on real data to detect deviations. Training an application entails inputting and defining data criteria in a database. In a behavior-based intrusion detection method, the established profile is used as a comparison to current activity, monitoring for evidence of a compromise instead of the attack itself.

> **ExamAlert**
>
> Anomaly-based detection methods require the capability of the application engine to decode and process all monitored protocols, causing high initial overhead. After the initial protocol behavior has been defined, scalability becomes more rapid and straightforward.

The rule development process for anomaly-based methods can become complicated because of the differences in vendor protocol implementations.

Heuristic intrusion detection methods are commonly known as anomaly-based methods because heuristic algorithms are used to identify anomalies.

> **ExamAlert**
>
> Similar to anomaly-based methods, heuristic-based methods are typically rule-based and look for abnormal behavior. Heuristic rules tend to categorize activity into one of the following types: benign, suspicious, or unknown.

Similar to anomaly-based methods, heuristic-based methods are typically rule-based and look for abnormal behavior. Heuristic rules tend to categorize activity into one of the following types: benign, suspicious, or unknown. As the IDS learns network behavior, the activity category can change. This slight difference between heuristic- and anomaly-based methods is that anomaly-based methods are less specific. Anomaly-based methods target behavior that is out of the ordinary instead of classifying all behavior.

Analytics

False positives occur when a typical or expected behavior is identified as irregular or malicious. False positives generally occur when an IDS detects the presence of a newly installed application and the IDS has not yet been trained for this new behavior. Sometimes anomalous behavior in one area of an organization is acceptable; in other areas, this behavior is suspicious. False positives are one of the largest problems encountered in IDS management because they can easily prevent legitimate IDS alerts from quickly being identified. Rule sets need to be tuned to reduce the number of false positives. A single rule that generates false positives can create thousands of alerts in a short period of time. The alerts for rules that cause repeated false positives are often ignored or disabled. This increases risk to the organization because legitimate attacks might eventually be ignored, increasing the probability that the system will be compromised by the type of attack the disabled or ignored rule was actually looking for.

False negatives occur when an alert that should have been generated did not occur. In other words, an attack takes place but the IDS doesn't detect it. False negatives most often happen because the IDS is reactive and signature-based systems do not recognize new attacks. Sometimes in a signature-based system, a rule can be written to catch only a subset of an attack vector. Several risks are associated with false positives. When false positives occur, missed attacks are not mitigated, giving the organization a false sense of security. Consider one more note about false positives: In an environment that relies on anomaly detection and in a host-based intrusion detection system (HIDS) that relies on file changes, if a system was compromised at the time of IDS training, false negatives will occur for any already exploited conditions.

ExamAlert

You should be familiar with the following terms for the exam:

▶ **False positive:** A typical or expected behavior is identified as irregular or malicious.

▶ **False negative:** An alert that should have been generated did not occur.

Internal Security

After traffic has passed through the perimeter, the packets need to be properly routed. In some instances, only internal routing occurs because the traffic is strictly internal and doesn't need to leave the organization. In this case, devices are used that do not route traffic or that prevent traffic from leaving a subnet. Devices that perform this role include routers, switches, and bridges.

Routers

Routers operate at the network layer of the OSI model. They receive information from a host and forward that information to its destination on the network or the Internet. Routers maintain tables that are checked each time a packet needs to be redirected from one interface to another. The tables inside the router help speed up request resolution so that packets can reach their destination more quickly. The routes can be added manually to the routing table or can be updated automatically using the following protocols:

- ▶ Routing Information Protocol (RIP/RIPv2)
- ▶ Interior Gateway Routing Protocol (IGRP)
- ▶ Enhanced Interior Gateway Routing Protocol (EIGRP)
- ▶ Open Shortest Path First (OSPF)
- ▶ Border Gateway Protocol (BGP)
- ▶ Exterior Gateway Protocol (EGP)
- ▶ Intermediate System-to-Intermediate System (IS-IS)

Although router placement is primarily determined by the need to segment different networks or subnets, routers also have some good security features. One of the best features of a router is its capability to filter packets by source address, destination address, protocol, or port. These filters are actually access control lists (ACLs).

> **ExamAlert**
>
> In its broadest sense, an ACL is the underlying data associated with a network resource that defines the access permissions.

Part I, "Threats, Attacks, and Vulnerabilities," describes attacks such as IP spoofing and covers Domain 1 of the Security+ exam. Basic Internet routing is based on the destination IP address, so a router with a default configuration forwards packets based only on the destination IP address. In IP spoofing, an attacker gains unauthorized access to a network by making it appear (by faking the IP address) that traffic has come from a trusted source.

> **ExamAlert**
>
> Routers can also be configured to help prevent IP spoofing through antispoofing techniques. These can include creating a set of access lists that deny access to private IP addresses and local host ranges from the Internet and also using strong protocol authentication.

Because routers are the lifeblood of the network, it is important to properly secure them. The security that is configured when setting up and managing routers can make the difference between keeping data secure and providing an open invitation to hackers. The following are general recommendations for router security:

▶ Create and maintain a written router security policy. The policy should identify who is allowed to log into the router and who is allowed to configure and update it. The policy also should outline the logging and management practices.

▶ Comment and organize offline master editions of your router configuration files. Keep the offline copies of all router configurations in sync with the actual configurations running on the routers.

▶ Implement access lists that allow only the protocols, ports, and IP addresses that network users and services require. Deny everything else.

▶ Test the security of your routers regularly, especially after any major configuration changes.

Keep in mind that, no matter how secure your routing protocol is, if you never change the default password on the router, you leave yourself wide open to attacks. At the opposite end of the spectrum, a router that is too tightly locked down can turn a functional network into a completely isolated network that does not allow access to anyone.

Switches

Switches are the most common choice when it comes to connecting desktops to the wiring closet. Switches generally operate at the data link layer (Layer 2) of the OSI model. Their packet-forwarding decisions are based on Media Access Control (MAC) addresses. Switches allow LANs to be segmented, thus increasing the amount of bandwidth that goes to each device. Each segment is a separate collision domain, but all segments are in the same broadcast domain. Here are the basic functions of a switch:

▶ Filtering and forwarding frames

▶ Learning MAC addresses

▶ Preventing loops

Managed switches are configurable. You can implement sound security with your switches similarly to configuring security on a firewall or a router. Managed switches allow control over network traffic and who has access to the network. In general, you do not want to deploy managed switches using their default configuration. The default configuration often does not provide the most secure network design. In such cases, these switches require no Layer 2 functionality.

A design that properly segments the network can be accomplished using VLANs. VLANs provide a way to limit broadcast traffic in a switched network. This creates a boundary and, in essence, creates multiple, isolated LANs on one switch. VLANs are a logical separation of a physical network and often combine Layer 2 and Layer 3 switches. Layer 3 switches can best be described as routers with fast forwarding done through hardware. Layer 3 switches can perform some of the same functions as routers and offer more flexibility than Layer 2 switches.

Designing the network the proper way from the start is important to ensure that the network is stable, reliable, and scalable. Physical and virtual security controls must be in place. Locate switches in a physically secure area, if possible. Be sure that strong authentication and password policies are in place to secure access to the operating system and configuration files.

Protections

Port security is a Layer 2 traffic control feature on switches. It enables individual switch ports to be configured to allow only a specified number of source MAC addresses to come in through the port. Its primary use is to keep two or three users from sharing a single access port. You can use the port security feature to restrict input to an interface by limiting and identifying MAC addresses of the workstations that are allowed to access the port. When you assign secure MAC addresses to a secure port, the port does not forward packets with source addresses outside the group of defined addresses. If you limit the number of secure MAC addresses to one and assign a single secure MAC address, the workstation attached to that port is assured the full bandwidth of the port. By default, a port security violation forces the interface into the error-disabled state. Port security can be configured to take one of three actions upon detecting a violation. In addition to using the default shutdown mode, you can set protect mode or restrict mode. In protect mode, frames from MAC addresses other than the allowed addresses are dropped. Restrict mode is similar to protect mode, but it generates a syslog message and increases the violation counter.

> **ExamAlert**
>
> Port security is a deterrent, not a reliable security feature. MAC addresses can be spoofed, and multiple hosts can still easily be hidden behind a small router.

A flood guard is an advanced firewall guard feature used to control network activity associated with DoS attacks and distributed denial-of-service (DDoS) attacks.

> **ExamAlert**
>
> Flood guard controls how the authentication, accounting, and authorization (AAA) service handles bad login attempts that are tying up connections. It allows the firewall resources to automatically be reclaimed if the authentication subsystem runs out of resources, thereby defeating DoS and DDoS attacks.

For example, in Cisco firewalls, the **floodguard** command is enabled by default and the firewall actively reclaims TCP user resources when an inbound or outbound authorization connection is being attacked. Flood guards are available as either standalone devices or firewall components.

Bridges

Bridges are often used when two different network types need to be accessed. Bridges provide some network layer functions, such as route discovery, as well as forwarding at the data link layer. They forward packets only between networks that are destined for the other network. Several types of bridges exist:

▶ **Transparent basic bridge:** Acts similarly to a repeater. It merely stores traffic until it can move on.

▶ **Source routing bridge:** Interprets the routing information field (RIF) in the LAN frame header.

▶ **Transparent learning bridge:** Locates the routing location using the source and destination addresses in its routing table. As new destination addresses are found, they are added to the routing table.

▶ **Transparent spanning bridge:** Contains a subnet of the full topology for creating a loop-free operation.

Looping problems can occur when a site uses two or more bridges in parallel between two LANs to increase the reliability of the network. A major feature in Layer 2 devices is Spanning Tree Protocol (STP), a link-management protocol that provides path redundancy while preventing undesirable loops in the network. Multiple active paths between stations cause loops in the network. When loops occur, some devices see stations that appear on both sides of the device. This condition confuses the forwarding algorithm and allows duplicate frames to be forwarded. This situation can occur in bridges as well as Layer 2 switches.

A bridge loop occurs when data units can travel from a first LAN segment to a second LAN segment through more than one path. To eliminate bridge loops, existing bridge devices typically employ a technique referred to as the *spanning tree algorithm*. The spanning tree algorithm is implemented by bridges interchanging special messages known as bridge protocol data units (BPDUs). The STP loop guard feature provides additional protection against STP loops.

> **ExamAlert**
>
> Spanning Tree Protocol is designed to detect and prevent loops. It also helps prevent loops on managed switches.

An STP loop is created when an STP blocking port in a redundant topology erroneously transitions to the forwarding state. This usually happens because one of the ports of a physically redundant topology no longer receives STP BPDUs. In its operation, STP relies on continuous reception or transmission of BPDUs, based on the port role. The loop guard feature makes additional checks. If BPDUs are not received on a nondesignated port and loop guard is enabled, that port is moved into the STP loop-inconsistent blocking state instead of the listening/learning/forwarding state. Without the loop guard feature, the port assumes the designated port role. The port then moves to the STP forwarding state and creates a loop.

Boundary Devices

Beyond perimeter security devices and devices that provide internal security, other devices provide myriad additional services, such as acting as load balancers, proxies, and access points that improve network functionality. Many of these devices were developed for faster connectivity and to eliminate traffic bottlenecks; others were developed for convenience. As with all devices that touch the network, proper placement and security features are important considerations in their implementation.

Proxies

A *proxy server* operates on the same principle as a proxy-level firewall: It is a go-between for the network and the Internet. Proxy servers are used for security, logging, and caching. Various types of proxy servers exist, including forward, reverse, and transparent proxy servers, as well as caching, multipurpose, and application proxy servers.

In a caching proxy server, when the proxy server receives a request for an Internet service (usually on port 80 or 443), it passes through filtering requirements and checks its local cache for previously downloaded web pages. Because web pages are stored locally, response times for web pages are faster, and traffic to the Internet is substantially reduced.

The web cache can also be used to block content from websites that you do not want employees to access, such as pornography, social media, or peer-to-peer networks. You can use this type of server to rearrange web content to work for mobile devices. This strategy also provides better utilization of bandwidth because it stores all your results from requests for a period of time.

A caching server that does not require a client-side configuration is called a transparent proxy server. In this type of server, the client is unaware of a proxy server. Transparent proxies are also called inline, intercepting, or forced proxies. The proxy redirects client requests without modifying them. Transparent proxy servers are implemented primarily to reduce bandwidth usage and client configuration overhead in large networks. Transparent proxy servers are found in large enterprise organizations and ISPs. Because transparent proxies have no client overhead and can filter content, they are ideal for use in schools and libraries.

> **ExamAlert**
>
> An exposed server that provides public access to a critical service, such as a proxy, web, or email server, can be configured to isolate it from an organization's internal network and to report attack attempts to the network administrator. Such an isolated server is usually located in the DMZ and is often referred to as a *bastion host*.

Most proxy servers today are web application proxies that support protocols such as HTTP and HTTPS. When clients and the server cannot directly connect because of some type of incompatibility issue, such as security authentication, an application proxy server is used. Application proxies must support the application for which they are performing the proxy function and do not typically encrypt data. On the other hand, multipurpose proxy servers, also known as universal application level gateways, are capable of running various operating systems (such as UNIX, Windows, and Macintosh) and allowing multiple protocols to pass through (such as HTTP, FTP, NNTP, SMTP, IMAP, LDAP, and DNS). They also can convert between IPv4 and IPv6 addresses. These proxies can be used for caching, converting pass-through traffic, and handling access control. They are not restricted to a certain application or protocol.

Depending on the network size and content requirements, either a forward or reverse proxy is used. Forward and reverse proxies add a layer of security to the network by controlling traffic to and from the Internet. Both types of proxy servers are used as an intermediary for requests between source and destination hosts. A forward proxy controls traffic originating from clients on the internal network that is destined for hosts on the Internet. Because client requests are required to pass through the proxy before they are permitted to access Internet resources, forward proxy servers are primarily used to enforce security on internal client computers and are often used in conjunction with a firewall. Forward proxies can also be implemented for anonymity because they do not allow direct client access to the Internet.

Reverse proxy servers do just the opposite. A reverse proxy is a server-side concept for caching static HTTP content when the server accepts requests from external Internet clients. The primary purpose of a reverse proxy is to increase the efficiency and scalability of the web server by providing load balancing services. Full reverse proxies are capable of deep content inspection and often are implemented as a method for enforcing web application security and mitigating data leaks.

Proxy servers are used for a variety of reasons, so their placement depends on usage. You can place proxy servers between the private network and the Internet for Internet connectivity or internally for web content caching. If the organization is using the proxy server for both Internet connectivity and web content caching, you should place the proxy server between the internal network and the Internet, with access for users who are requesting the web content. In some proxy server designs, the proxy server is placed in parallel with IP routers. This design allows for network load balancing by forwarding all HTTP and FTP traffic through the proxy server and all other IP traffic through the router.

Every proxy server in your network must have at least one network interface. Proxy servers with a single network interface can provide web content caching and IP gateway services. To provide Internet connectivity, you must specify two or more network interfaces for the proxy server.

Load Balancers

Network *load balancers* are reverse proxy servers configured in a cluster to provide scalability and high availability.

Load balancing distributes IP traffic to multiple copies of a TCP/IP service, such as a web server, each running on a host within the cluster. This is used for enterprise-wide services, such as Internet sites with high traffic requirements, web, FTP, media streaming, and content delivery networks or hosted applications that use thin-client architectures, such as Windows Terminal Services or Remote Desktop Services.

ExamAlert

Network load balancing distributes the workload among multiple servers while providing a mechanism for server availability by health-checking each server. From the client's point of view, the cluster appears to be a single server.

As enterprise traffic increases, network administrators can simply plug another server into the cluster. If server or application failure occurs, a load balancer can provide automatic failover to ensure continuous availability.

Load balancing strategies work by scheduling via algorithms. Scheduling strategies are based on which tasks can be executed in parallel and where to execute these tasks. These common algorithms are used:

▶ **Round-robin:** Traffic is sent in a sequential, circular pattern to each node of a load balancer.

▶ **Random:** Traffic is sent to randomly selected nodes.

▶ **Least connections:** Traffic is sent to the node with the fewest open connections.

▶ **Weighted round-robin:** Traffic is sent in a circular pattern to each node of a load balancer, based on the assigned weight number.

▶ **Weighted least connections:** Traffic is sent to the node with the fewest open connections, based on the assigned weight number.

Each method works best in different situations. When servers that have identical equipment and capacity are used, the round-robin, random, or least connections algorithms work well. When the load balancing servers have disproportionate components such as processing power, size, or RAM, a weighted algorithm allows the servers with the maximum resources to be utilized properly.

Session affinity is a method in which all requests in a session are sent to a specific application server by overriding the load balancing algorithm. Session affinity is also called a sticky session. This ensures that all requests from the user during the session are sent to the same instance. Session affinity enhances application performance by using in-memory caching and cookies to track session information.

Some load balancers integrate IP load balancing and network intrusion prevention into one appliance. This provides failover capabilities in case of server failure, distribution of traffic across multiple servers, and integrated protection from network intrusions. Performance is also optimized for other IP services, such as Simple Mail Transfer Protocol (SMTP), Domain Name Service (DNS), Remote Authentication Dial-In User Service (RADIUS), and Trivial File Transfer Protocol (TFTP).

To mitigate risks associated with failures of the load balancers themselves, you can deploy two servers in what is called an active/passive or active/active configuration. In active/passive configuration, all traffic is sent to the active server. The passive server is promoted to active if the active server fails or is taken down for maintenance. In active/active configuration, two or more servers work together to distribute the load to network servers. Because all load balancers are active, they run almost at full capacity. If one of the load balancers fails, network traffic runs slow and user sessions time out. Virtual IPs (VIPs) are often implemented in the active/active configuration. A VIP has at least one physical server assigned but more than one virtual IP address assigned, usually through a TCP or UDP port number. Using VIPs spreads traffic among the load balancing servers. VIPs are a connection-based workload balancing solution, so if the interface cannot handle the load, traffic bottlenecks and becomes slow.

Access Points

No network is complete without wireless access points. Most businesses provide wireless access for employees and guests alike. With this expected convenience comes security implications that must be addressed to keep the network safe from the vulnerabilities and attacks described in Chapter 2, "Attack Types." This section covers basic access point types, configurations, and preventative measures an organization can implement to mitigate risk and reduce the attack surface.

Access Point Types

Wireless local-area network (WLAN) controllers are physical devices that communicate with each access point (AP) simultaneously. A centralized access controller (AC) is capable of providing management, configuration, encryption, and policy settings for WLAN access points. A controller-based WLAN design acts as a switch for wireless traffic and provides thin APs with configuration settings. Some ACs perform firewall, VPN, IDS/IPS, and monitoring functions.

The level of control and management options an AC needs to provide depends on the type of access points the organization implements. Three main types of wireless access points exist: fat, fit, and thin. Fat wireless access points are also sometimes called intelligent access points because they are all-inclusive: They contain everything needed to manage wireless clients, such as ACLs, quality of service (QoS) functions, VLAN support, and band steering. Fat APs can be used as standalone access points and do not need an AC. However, this capability makes them costly because they are built on powerful hardware and require complex software. A fit AP is a scaled-down version of a fat AP and uses an AC for control and management functions. A thin access point is nothing more than a radio and antenna controlled by a wireless switch. Thin access points are sometimes called intelligent antennas. In some instances, APs do not perform WLAN encryption; they merely transmit or receive the encrypted wireless frames. A thin AP has minimal functionality, so a controller is required. Thin APs are simple and do not require complex hardware or software.

> **ExamAlert**
>
> A fat access point is also known as an intelligent or standalone access point. A thin access point is also known as an intelligent antenna and is managed by a WLAN controller.

Antenna Types, Placement, and Power

When designing wireless networks, configure antenna types, placement, and power output for maximum coverage and minimum interference. Four basic types of antennas are commonly used in 802.11 wireless networking applications: parabolic grid, yagi, dipole, and vertical.

Wireless antenna types are either omnidirectional or directional. Omnidirectional antennas provide a 360-degree radial pattern to provide the widest possible signal coverage. An example of omnidirectional antennas is the antennas commonly found on APs. Directional antennas concentrate the wireless signal in a specific direction, limiting the coverage area. An example of a directional antenna is a yagi antenna.

The need or use determines the type of antenna required. When an organization wants to connect one building to another building, a directional antenna is used. If an organization is adding Wi-Fi internally to an office building or a warehouse, an omnidirectional antenna is used. If an organization wants to install Wi-Fi in an outdoor campus environment, a combination of both antennas is used.

APs with factory-default omni antennas cover an area that is roughly circular and is affected by RF obstacles such as walls. When using this type of antenna, common practice is to place APs in central locations or divide an office into quadrants. Many APs use multiple-input, multiple-output (MIMO) or multiuser multiple-input, multiple-output (MU-MIMO) antennas. This type of antenna takes advantage of multipath signal reflections. Ideally, locate the AP as close as possible to the antennas. The farther the signal has to travel across the cabling between the AP and the antenna, the more signal loss occurs. Loss is an important factor when deploying a wireless network, especially at higher power levels. Loss occurs as a result of the signal traveling between the wireless base unit and the antenna.

APs that require external antennas need additional consideration. You need to configure the antennas properly, consider what role the AP serves (AP or bridge), and consider where the antennas are placed. When the antenna is mounted on the outside of the building or when the interface between the wired network and the transceiver is placed in a corner, it locates the network signal in an area where it can easily be intercepted. Antenna placement should not be used as a security mechanism.

Professional site surveys for wireless network installations and proper AP placement are sometimes used to ensure coverage area and security concerns. Up-front planning takes more time and effort but can pay off in the long run, especially for large WLANs.

> **ExamAlert**
>
> Physical placement and transmit power adjustments can make it harder for intruders to stay connected to your APs—but never count on physical placement alone to stop attackers.

One of the principle requirements for wireless communication is that the transmitted wave must reach the receiver with ample power to allow the receiver to distinguish the wave from the background noise. An antenna that is too strong raises security concerns. Strong omnidirectional Wi-Fi signals are radiated to a greater distance into neighboring areas, where the signals can be readily detected and viewed. Minimizing transmission power reduces the chances your data will leak. Companies such as Cisco and Nortel have implemented dynamic power controls in their products. The system dynamically adjusts the power output of individual access points to accommodate changing network conditions, helping ensure predictable wireless performance and availability.

> **ExamAlert**
>
> Reducing the energy consumption by wireless communication devices is an important issue in WLANs. Know the mechanisms that prevent interference and increase capacity.

Transmit power control is a mechanism used to prevent too much unwanted interference between different wireless networks. Adaptive transmit power control in 802.11 WLANs on a per-link basis helps increase network capacity and improves the battery life of Wi-Fi-enabled mobile devices.

Band direction and selection are also important parts of wireless access control management. The 2.4-GHz band used for older standards such as 802.11a/b/g is crowded and subject to both interference from other wireless devices and co-channel interference from other access points because of the limited number (three) of nonoverlapping channels. Newer standards such as 802.11n and 802.11ac use the 5-GHz band, which offers 23 nonoverlapping 20-MHz channels.

Cisco wireless LAN controllers can be configured for load balancing through band direction and band selection. Band direction allows client radios capable of operating on both 2.4-GHz and 5-GHz bands to move to a 5-GHz access point for faster throughput of network transfers. In a Cisco AP, clients receive a 2.4-GHz probe response and attempt to associate with the AP before receiving a 5-GHz probe response. Band selection works by delaying client 2.4-GHz radio probe responses, causing the client to be directed toward the 5-GHz channels. 802.11n can use 2.4 GHz or 5 GHz. The main purpose of band selection is to help the 802.11n-capable dual-band clients select 5-GHz access points. Band selection can cause roaming delays and dropped calls, so it is not recommended on voice-enabled WLANs.

MAC Filter

Most wireless network routers and access points can filter devices based on their MAC address. The MAC address is a unique identifier for network adapters. *MAC filtering* is a security access control method in which the MAC address is used to determine access to the network. When MAC address filtering is used, only the devices with MAC addresses configured in the wireless router or access point are allowed to connect. MAC filtering permits and denies network access through the use of blacklists and whitelists. A *blacklist* is a list of MAC addresses that are denied access. A *whitelist* is a list of MAC addresses that are allowed access. Chapter 10, "Security Technologies," discusses blacklisting and whitelisting in further detail.

MAC addresses give a wireless network some additional protection, but they can be spoofed. An attacker can potentially capture details about a MAC address from the network and pretend to be that device to then connect. MAC filtering can be circumvented by scanning a valid MAC using a tool such as airodump-ng or Aircrack-ng Suite and then spoofing one's own MAC into a validated MAC address. When an attacker knows a MAC address that is out of the blacklist or within the whitelist, MAC filtering is almost useless.

Disable SSID Broadcast

A *service set identifier* (SSID) is used to identify WAPs on a network. The SSID is transmitted so that wireless stations searching for a network connection can find it. By default, SSID broadcast is enabled. This means that it accepts any SSID. When you disable this feature, the SSID configured in the client must match the SSID of the AP; otherwise, the client cannot connect to the AP. Having SSID broadcast enabled essentially makes your AP visible to any device searching for a wireless connection.

To improve the security of your network, change the SSIDs on your APs. Using the default SSID poses a security risk even if the AP is not broadcasting it. When changing default SSIDs, do not change the SSID to reflect your company's main names, divisions, products, or address. This just makes you an easy target for attacks such as war driving and war chalking. *War driving* is the act of a person in a moving vehicle searching for Wi-Fi wireless networks using a portable computer or other mobile device. War chalking involves drawing symbols in public places to advertise an open Wi-Fi network. Keep in mind that if an SSID name is enticing enough, it might attract hackers.

Turning off SSID broadcast does not effectively protect the network from attacks. Tools such as Kismet enable nonbroadcasting networks to be discovered almost as easily as broadcasting networks. From a security standpoint, securing a wireless network using protocols that are designed specifically to address wireless network threats is better than disabling SSID broadcast.

ExamAlert

Turning off SSID broadcast does not effectively protect the network from attacks. It is much better to secure a wireless network using protocols that are designed specifically to address wireless network threats than to disable SSID broadcast.

Enforcement Tools

Data controls include encryption, data loss prevention, and information rights management. Most enterprises implement enforcement tools to prevent sensitive information from leaving the network. These tools include security information and event management (SIEM) systems, data loss prevention (DLP) systems, network access control (NAC), gateways, and other hardware devices. This section covers these technologies and tools.

SIEM

Audit controls such as security information and event management (SIEM) systems provide the technological means to show compliance and refine security controls. SIEM tools collect, correlate, and display data feeds that support response activities. SIEMs are the main element in compliance regulations such as SOX, GLBA, PCI, FISMA, and HIPAA. SIEM output is also proactively to detect emerging threats and improve overall security by defining events of interest (EOI) and resulting actions. The purpose of SIEM is to turn a large amount of data into knowledge that can be acted upon. SIEMs are generally part of the overall security operations center (SOC) and have three basic functions:

▶ Centrally managing security events

▶ Correlating and normalizing events for context and alerting

▶ Reporting on data gathered from various applications

Just one IDS sensor or log data source can generate more than 100,000 events each day.

ExamAlert

Individual log data sources can generate more than 100,000 events each day, so answering critical questions about how much data to log from critical systems is important when deciding to use a SIEM system.

Aggregation is the process by which SIEM systems combine similar events to reduce event volume. Log management aggregates data from many network sources and consolidates the data so that crucial events are not missed. By default, events are usually aggregated based on the source IP, destination IP, and event ID. The purpose of aggregation is to reduce the event data load and improve efficiency. Conversely, if aggregation is incorrectly configured, important information could be lost. Confidence in this aggregated data is enhanced through techniques such as correlation, automated data filtering, and deduplication within the SIEM. Event aggregation alone is not enough to provide useful information in an expeditious manner. A common best practice is to use a correlation engine to automate threat detection and log analysis. The main goal of correlation is to build EOIs that can be flagged by other criteria or that allow for the creation of incident identification. To create EOIs, the correlation engine uses data that was aggregated by the following techniques:

▶ Pattern matching

▶ Anomaly detection

▶ Boolean logic

▶ A combination of Boolean logic and context-relevant data

Finding the correct balance in correlation rules is often difficult. Correlation rules that try to catch all possible attacks generate too many alerts and can produce too many false positive alerts.

The SIEM facilitates and automates alert triage to notify analysts of immediate issues. Alerts can be sent via email but are most often sent to a dashboard. SIEM systems generate a large volume of alerts and notifications, so they also provide data visualization tools. From a business perspective, reporting and alerting provide verification of continuous monitoring, auditing, and compliance. Event deduplication improves confidence in aggregated data, data throughput, and storage capacity.

Event deduplication is also important because it provides the capability to audit and collect forensic data. The centralized log management and storage of SIEM systems provide validation for regulatory compliance storage or retention requirements. Regarding forensic data and regulatory compliance, WORM (write once, read many) drives keep log data protected so that evidence cannot be altered. WORM drives permanently protect administrative data. This security measure should be implemented when an administrator with access to logs is under investigation or when an organization needs to meet for regulatory compliance (such as Payment Card Industry Data Security Standard [PCI DSS] Requirement 10).

Some SIEM systems are good at ingesting and querying flow data both in real time and retrospectively. However, with real-time analysis, significant issues are associated with time, including time synchronization, time stamping, and report time lag. For example, if the report takes 45 minutes to run, the analyst is already this far behind real time without taking into consideration the amount of time needed to read and analyze the results.

When designing a SIEM system, the volume of data generated for a single incident must be considered. SIEM systems must aggregate, correlate, and report output from devices such as firewalls, intrusion detection/prevention (IDS/IPS), access controls, and myriad network devices. Answering questions about how much data to log from critical system is important when deciding to use a SIEM system. SIEMs have a high acquisition and maintenance cost. If the daily events number in the millions per day and events are gathered from network devices, endpoints, servers, identity and access control systems, and application servers, a SIEM might be cost-effective. For smaller daily event occurrences, free or more cost-effective tools should be considered.

DLP

Data loss is a problem that all organizations face, but it can be especially challenging for global organizations that store a large volume of PII in different legal jurisdictions. Privacy issues differ by country, region, and state. Naturally, organizations implement data loss prevention tools as a way to prevent data loss. Data loss prevention (DLP) is a way of detecting and preventing confidential data from being exfiltrated physically or logically from an organization by accident or on purpose. DLP systems are basically designed to detect and prevent unauthorized use and transmission of confidential information, based on one of the three states of data: in use, in motion, or at rest. DLP systems offer a way to enforce data security policies by providing centralized management for detecting and preventing the unauthorized use and transmission of data that the organization deems confidential. A well-designed DLP strategy allows control over sensitive data, reduces the cost of data breaches, and achieves greater insight into organizational data use. International organizations should ensure that they are in compliance with local privacy regulations before implementing DLP tools and processes.

Protection of data in use is considered to be an endpoint solution. In this case, the application is run on end user workstations or servers in the organization. Endpoint systems also can monitor and control access to physical devices such as mobile devices and tablets. Protection of data in transit is considered to be a network solution, and either a hardware or software solution is installed near the network perimeter to monitor and flag policy violations. Protection of data at rest is considered to be a storage solution and is generally a software solution that monitors how confidential data is stored.

When evaluating DLP solutions, key content-filtering capabilities to look for are high performance, scalability, and the capability to accurately scan nearly anything. High performance is necessary to keep the end user from experiencing lag time and delays. The solution must readily scale as both the volume of traffic and bandwidth needs increase. The tool should also be capable of accurately scanning nearly anything.

Using an endpoint solution, here are some examples of when a user can be alerted to security policy violations, to keep sensitive information from leaving the user's desktop:

▶ Inadvertently emailing a confidential internal document to external recipients

▶ Forwarding an email with sensitive information to unauthorized recipients inside or outside the organization

▶ Sending attachments such as spreadsheets with PII to an external personal email account

▶ Accidentally selecting Reply All and emailing a sensitive document to unauthorized recipients

USB flash drives, iPods, and other portable storage devices are pervasive in the workplace and pose a real threat. They can introduce viruses or malicious code to the network and can store sensitive corporate information. Sensitive information is often stored on thumb and external hard drives, which then are lost or stolen. DLP solutions allow policies for USB blocking. This could be a policy to block the copy of any network information to removable media or a policy to block the use of unapproved USB devices.

Many organizations store sensitive data in the cloud. DLP solutions have expanded from email and local devices to include corporate data stored in the cloud. The organization must know how the cloud is being utilized before making decisions on a DLP solution:

▶ What files are being shared outside the organization

▶ What files contain sensitive data

▶ What abnormal events indicate a threat or compromise

DLP can help with the following issues in cloud implementations:

▶ Data migration control

▶ Data protection

▶ Data leakage

> **ExamAlert**
>
> In addition to DLP, organizations must address data leakage. Data leakage can occur when a data distributor gives sensitive data to a third party.

Some deployed cloud services include Office 365, Salesforce, and Box. When implementing DLP policies in the cloud, different policies apply for different cloud services. Some are merely general cloud policies. For example, a general policy centers on device access control. A specific policy for Box, for example, centers on file sharing.

DLP solutions are most successful in private or virtual private clouds. When using a public cloud, DLP solutions might not offer much value because of the lack of control; using an agent-based approach is a better solution. For example, if your DLP solution requires agents or certificates to be installed in cloud applications such as Dropbox or Google Drive, the application will interpret the agent as a man-in-the-middle attack and will not work properly. Best practices for mitigating threats related to data leakage in the cloud include active data monitoring, encryption, policy-based access controls, and centralized administration.

NAC

One the most effective ways to protect the network from malicious hosts is to use *network access control* (NAC). NAC offers a method of enforcement that helps ensure that computers are properly configured. NAC systems are available as software packages or dedicated NAC appliances, although most are dedicated appliances that include both hardware and software. Some of the main uses for NAC follow:

- ▶ Guest network services
- ▶ Endpoint baselining
- ▶ Identity-aware networking
- ▶ Monitoring and containment

The premise behind NAC is to secure the environment by examining the user's machine and then grant (or not grant) access based on the results. NAC is based on assessment and enforcement. For example, if the user's computer patches are not up to date and no desktop firewall software is installed, you can decide whether to limit access to network resources. Any host machine that does not comply with your defined policy could be relegated to a remediation server or put on a guest VLAN. The basic components of NAC products follow:

▶ **Access requestor (AR):** The AR is the device that requests access. Assessment of the device can be self-performed or delegated to another system.

▶ **Policy decision point (PDP):** The PDP is the system that assigns a policy based on the assessment. The PDP determines what access should be granted and can be the NAC's product-management system.

▶ **Policy enforcement point (PEP):** The PEP is the device that enforces the policy. This device can be a switch, firewall, or router.

NAC systems can be integrated into the network in four ways:

▶ **Inline:** Exists as an appliance in the line, usually between the access and the distribution switches

▶ **Out of band:** Intervenes and performs an assessment as hosts come online, and then grants appropriate access

▶ **Switch-based:** Works similarly to inline NAC, except that enforcement occurs on the switch itself

▶ **Host- or endpoint-based:** Relies on an installed host agent to assess and enforce access policy

NAC implementations require design considerations such as an agent or agentless integration. For example, out-of-band designs might or might not use agents, and they can use 802.1X, VLAN steering, or IP subnets. In a NAC system that uses agents, devices are enrolled in the NAC system and an agent is installed on the device. The agent reports back to a NAC policy server. Agents provide detailed information about connected devices to enforce policies. An agent might permanently reside on end devices or it might be dissolvable. If the agent is dissolvable, it provides one-time authentication and then disappears after reporting information to the NAC. Because agents can be spoofed by malware, the organization needs to be vigilant about proper malware protection or should use an agentless NAC solution.

ExamAlert

Because the user clicks on a web link to download the agent, dissolvable agents are also referred to as portal-based agents.

Agents perform more granular health checks on endpoints to ensure a greater level of compliance. When the health check is on a computer or laptop, it is often called a host health check. Health checks monitor availability and performance for proper hardware and application functionality.

Agentless solutions are mainly implemented through embedded code within an Active Directory domain controller. The NAC code verifies that the end device complies with the access policy when a user joins the domain, logs onto, or logs out of the domain. Active Directory scans cannot be scheduled, and the device is scanned only during these three actions. Another instance in which an agentless solution is deployed is through an intrusion prevention system.

Agentless solutions offer less functionality and require fewer resources. A good solution for large, diverse networks, or one in which BYOD is prevalent, is to combine both agent and agentless functionality, but use the agentless solution as a fallback. This is because agents often do not work with all devices and operating systems. An alternative might be to use a downloadable, dissolvable agent; however, some device incompatibility might still arise.

In addition to providing the capability to enforce security policy, contain noncompliant users, and mitigate threats, NAC offers business benefits. These include compliance, a better security posture, and operational cost management.

Gateways

Gateways perform many functions. At its simplest definition, a router is a gateway because it connects two different networks. Other types of gateways include mail, media, and API gateways. This section covers mail and media gateways.

Mail

Although the percentage of spam has been steadily decreasing in the past few years because of better legislative enforcement and improved products, spam is still an enormous problem for corporations. Cisco tracked spam using opt-in customer telemetry and reported that spam email accounts for 65 percent of all sent emails. Spam filters can consist of various filtering technologies, including content, header, blacklist, rule-based, permission, and challenge-response filters. Spam-filtering solutions can be deployed in a number of ways. The most common implementations use an onsite appliance such as a gateway, software installed on each individual device, and hosted or cloud-based vendor solutions.

Email security gateways prevent malicious emails from reaching their destinations. Spam-filtering products work by checking email messages when they arrive. The messages are then either directed to the user's mailbox or quarantined based on a score value. When the spam score exceeds a certain threshold, the email is sent to the junk folder. In addition to the keyword-scanning methods, which include scoring systems for emails based on multiple criteria, spam filter appliances allow for checksum technology that tracks the number of times a particular message has appeared. They also conduct message authenticity checking, which uses multiple algorithms to verify the authenticity of a message. In addition, the appliance might perform file-type attachment blocking and scanning using the built-in antivirus protection.

Besides spam filtering functions, email gateways can include additional client security controls such as email encryption, advanced content filtering, and DLP capabilities. These capabilities help protect the confidentiality and integrity of emails in transit, enforce regulatory compliance, and protect against data loss.

Media

Media gateways came about as a result of the convergence of telecommunications and data communications. Media gateways act as a bridge between different transmission technologies and add services to end-user connections. At the most basic level, a media gateway is a device that converts data from one format to another. One of the main functions of a media gateway is to convert between different transmission and coding techniques. Examples include a circuit switch, an IP gateway, and a channel bank. Media gateways work at the connectivity layer, serving as a crossing point between different networks where the desired transmission technology can be selected. For example, the media gateway might terminate channels from a circuit-switched network and stream media from a packet-switched network in an IP network. Data input such as audio and video are handled simultaneously.

In businesses, media gateways are used to convert analog communications to VoIP communications. When used in VoIP conversions, they have three main components:

▶ Media gateway

▶ Media gateway controller or softswitch

▶ Signaling gateway

One of the best examples of a media gateway in use is getting broadband cable to phones and laptops. Cable providers such as Dish, Comcast, and Cox use media gateways to distribute content to subscribers throughout their house-holds. Content distribution occurs through a gateway that converts the incoming broadband signal and delivers voice, video, and data services such as high definition and wireless codecs to consumer IP-connected devices.

Cryptographic Devices

Cryptographic hardware is used in everything from smartphones to smart TVs. Network hardware cryptographic devices include devices capable of accelerating and decrypting Secure Sockets Layer (SSL), as well as hardware devices that ensure that the information stored in the hardware is protected from external software attacks. This section discusses these technologies.

SSL/TLS Accelerators and Decryptors

SSL, the predecessor to TLS, has become the primary encryption standard for web and email transactions. SSL offloading is the process of shifting the burden of encrypting and decrypting traffic sent via SSL from the web server to another device. This process is very resource-intensive. SSL/TLS acceleration originally was done by using a separate PCI card in a computer that contained one or more application-specific integrated circuit (ASIC) coprocessors. SSL accelerators were then developed as separate network appliances. The SSL accelerator is the intermediary between a user and a server. It accepts SSL connections from the user and sends the connection to the server unencrypted.

Load balancers often handle SSL offloading. The load balancer must use CPU resources to handle SSL functions. This interferes with the other functions the load balancer is required to perform, such as distributing traffic, health checking, and content switching. To mitigate the impact of SSL processing on the load balancer, SSL acceleration/TLS acceleration is used. Load balancers are combined with SSL accelerators. This type of device is commonly referred to as an application delivery controller (ADC).

Many online banking, email, and VoIP communications are secured with SSL/TLS encryption. Even though SSL/TLS encryption helps meet data protection compliance requirements and keeps organizational data secure, encryption can be used to hide malicious activity and malware. Security and performance monitoring tools do not automatically decrypt encrypted sessions and inspect the content. SSL/TLS decryption is used for the following reasons:

▶ Monitoring of application performance

▶ Cloud services monitoring

▶ Malware detection

▶ DLP

▶ Forensic analysis

Decrypting SSL traffic is only part of the equation. After decryption, the data has to be forwarded to the appropriate device for inspection. Analysis of the decrypted content is a joint effort and includes devices such as IDS/IPS, firewalls, secure web gateways, and DLP solutions. The device the packets go to depends on the policies in place. Similar to SSL/TLS acceleration, SSL/TLS decryption can be offloaded. However, unlike SSL acceleration, decryption on a single security appliance doesn't work so well. Many other network devices might require access to the decrypted traffic. A better solution is to implement an SSL/TLS decryption method in which decrypted traffic can be forwarded to the appropriate device based on policies.

HSM

A *hardware security module (HSM)* can be described as a black-box combination of hardware and software/firmware that is attached to or contained inside a computer that is used to provide cryptographic functions for tamper protection and increased performance. HSMs support payment processing and cardholder authentication applications for PCI DSS compliance under FIPS 140-2.

ExamAlert

Basically, an HSM is a type of cryptoprocessor that manages digital keys, accelerates cryptographic processes, and provides strong access authentication for critical application encryption keys. HSMs mainly come in the form of slotted cards or external devices that can be attached directly to a network, but they can also be embedded.

The basic cryptographic operations are the same for the different types of HSMs, but the administration structure and authorization models can vary. Typically, an HSM is installed inside a server box or within an Ethernet cluster. The HSM is then wrapped by the software that provides access to the cryptographic functionality within the HSM. Traditionally, the banking sector has used HSMs to secure numerous large, bulk transactions. HSM security requirements were derived from existing ISO, ANSI, and federal standards, as well as accepted best practice recognized by the financial industry. HSMs are also found in PKI deployments to secure CA keys, handle SSL acceleration, store domain name system security extension (DNSSEC) keys, and encrypt zone records.

Two types of HSMs exist. Some are PC-based, such as PCI-e cards, and others are network-based. The main advantages of the network-attached HSM types are similar to the advantages of using a NAS. They are essentially platform-independent and can be used simultaneously from several clients. Because HSMs are often part of a mission-critical infrastructure such as a public key infrastructure or online banking application, HSMs can typically be clustered for high availability. Some HSMs feature dual power supplies. Host HSM systems are also hardware cryptographic accelerators by nature because the keys do not leave devices in an unencrypted form. The HSM must perform the common cryptographic operations so that it accelerates the intense math functions, offering better performance than a normal software-based crypto system.

HSM systems can securely back up their keys either in a wrapped form or externally. Keys protected by an HSM are only truly hardware-protected if they were generated inside the hardware itself. If a standard software-protected key is imported into an HSM, a non-hardware-protected copy of the key could still exist on old backups.

What Next?

If you want more practice on this chapter's exam objectives before you move on, remember that you can access all the Cram Quiz questions on the Pearson Test Prep software. You can also create a custom exam by objective. Note any objective you struggle with and go to that objective material in this chapter.

CHAPTER 8

Software Tools

This chapter covers the following official Security+ exam objective:

2.2 Given a scenario, use appropriate software tools to assess the security posture of an organization.

- ▶ Protocol analyzer
- ▶ Network scanners
  - ▪ Rogue system detection
  - ▪ Network mapping
- ▶ Wireless scanners/cracker
- ▶ Password cracker
- ▶ Vulnerability scanner
- ▶ Configuration compliance scanner
- ▶ Exploitation frameworks
- ▶ Data sanitization tools
- ▶ Steganography tools
- ▶ Honeypot

- ▶ Backup utilities
- ▶ Banner grabbing
- ▶ Passive vs. active
- ▶ Command line tools
  - ▪ ping
  - ▪ netstat
  - ▪ tracert
  - ▪ nslookup/dig
  - ▪ arp
  - ▪ ipconfig/ip/ifconfig
  - ▪ tcpdump
  - ▪ nmap
  - ▪ netcat

Essential Terms and Components

- ▶ Address Resolution Protocol (ARP)
- ▶ banner grabbing
- ▶ exploitation framework
- ▶ honeypot

- ▶ Internet Control Message Protocol (ICMP)
- ▶ protocol analyzer
- ▶ steganography
- ▶ vulnerability scanner

CramSaver

If you can correctly answer these questions before going through this chapter, save time by skimming the Exam Alerts in this chapter and then completing the Cram Quiz at the end of the chapter.

1. Explain how a protocol analyzer is used.

   _____

2. Explain the difference between active and passive vulnerability scanners.

   _____

3. Explain the purpose of the ARP command-line tool.

   _____

Answers

1. Protocol analyzers help you troubleshoot network issues by gathering packet-level information across the network. These applications capture packets and can conduct protocol decoding by turning the information into readable data for analysis. Protocol analyzers can do more than just look at packets. They prove useful in many other areas of network management, such as monitoring the network for unexpected, unwanted, and unnecessary traffic.

2. An active scanner sits on the network and, when scheduled, reaches out across the network to discover systems and perform a series of inquiries to identify what is running on the system. Based on that discovery, most scanners perform an iterative process of testing the system against known vulnerability signatures. However, active scanners are hampered by network and host firewalls. A passive scanner, on the other hand, doesn't actually perform scans.

3. ARP provides information from a table that contains a mapping of known Media Access Control (MAC) addresses to the associated IP addresses. ARP is necessary because the underlying hardware cannot translate IP addresses. The ARP cache maintains a table of MAC to IP addresses, so ARP is a quick way to find a machine's MAC address.

Vulnerability Assessment Tools

A variety of tools help identify vulnerabilities and together make up a complete vulnerability management program. These include protocol analyzers, vulnerability scanners, honeypots, and password crackers. This section discusses the purpose and use of these tools.

Analyzers and Scanners

To maintain a strong security posture, organizations should implement tools and processes for security monitoring. Security monitoring is not just a one-time or isolated event: It is conducted on an ongoing basis. Vulnerability assessment tools such as protocol analyzers and scanners help the organization maintain a strong security posture by finding weaknesses before attackers take advantage of them.

Protocol Analyzers

Protocol analyzers, also known as packet sniffers, help you troubleshoot network issues by gathering packet-level information across the network. This type of software utility is used on a hub, on a switch supervisory port, or in line with network connectivity to enable the analysis of network communications. Protocol analyzers can identify individual protocols, specific endpoints, and sequential access attempts. These applications capture packets and can conduct protocol decoding, turning the information into readable data for analysis. Protocol analyzers can do more than just look at packets, though. They prove useful in many other areas of network management, such as monitoring the network for unexpected, unwanted, and unnecessary traffic. For example, if the network is running slowly, a protocol analyzer can tell you whether unnecessary protocols are running on the network. You can also filter specific port numbers and types of traffic so that you can keep an eye on indicators that might cause you problems. Many protocol analyzers can be run on multiple platforms and do live traffic captures and offline analysis. Software USB protocol analyzers are also available for the development of USB devices and analysis of USB traffic.

You can place protocol analyzers in line or between the devices for which you want to capture the traffic. If you are analyzing storage-area network (SAN) traffic, you can place the analyzer outside the direct link with the use of an optical splitter. The analyzer then is placed to capture traffic between the host and the monitored device.

Some operating systems have built-in protocol analyzers. This chapter shows how you can use them to detect security-related anomalies. Windows Server operating systems come with a protocol analyzer called Microsoft Message Analyzer. In the UNIX environment, many administrators use the tools that come with the core operating system, such as ps and vmstat. Oracle Solaris has a popular utility called iostat that provides good information about I/O per-formance. You can also use other third-party programs, such as Wireshark, for network monitoring.

A sniffer and protocol analyzer are generally accepted as the same. As software packages continue to add features, the lines between the two blur. Even so, a sniffer can be considered as a tool designed to "sniff" the network and capture packets. In the simplest sense, a sniffer relies upon the user to conduct further analysis and interpretation. On the other hand, the protocol analyzer is capable of providing further details and context on the captured packets.

> **ExamAlert**
>
> A protocol analyzer is used to capture network traffic and generate statistics for creating reports. After the packets have been captured, you can view the information.

Vulnerability and Port Scanners

Port scanners are often part of a more comprehensive vulnerability assessment solution. However, port scanners also can be standalone utilities: They simply scan a range of specific ports to determine what ports are open on a system. This type of software utility scans a single machine or a range of IP addresses, checking for a response on service ports. A response on port 80, for example, might reveal the operation of an HTTP host. Port scanners are useful in creating an inventory of services hosted on networked systems. When they are applied to test ports on a single system, this is termed a port scan. A scan across multiple hosts is referred to as a port sweep. The results are valuable to system administrators and attackers alike. Port scanners typically identify one of two states for the port: open or closed. In addition, some port scanners can provide other information, such as the type of operating system running on the targeted system and services running over the ports.

Another common tool is the vulnerability scanner. Chapter 5, "Vulnerability Scanning," showed that a *vulnerability scanner* is a software utility that scans a range of IP addresses and tests for the presence of known vulnerabilities in software configuration and accessible services. A traditional vulnerability scanner relies upon a database of known vulnerabilities. These automated tools are directed at a targeted system or systems. Unlike a system that tests for open ports, which tests only for the availability of services, vulnerability scanners might check for the particular version or patch level of a service to determine its level of vulnerability. For example, Microsoft Baseline Security Analyzer (MBSA) can scan either a single system or large numbers of systems for vulnerabilities. MBSA is a software vulnerability scanner to analyze targeted Microsoft systems, to detect whether software security patches or baseline configuration settings are missing. In addition to commercial off-the-shelf vulnerability scanners, you can use some good free vulnerability scanners:

▶ **OpenVAS:** Runs only in Linux but has many good features

▶ **Nexpose Community Edition:** Can scan web applications, databases, and virtual environments, in addition to systems

▶ **Qualys FreeScan:** Checks for hidden malware and SSL issues, among other network vulnerabilities

In addition to network vulnerability scanners, some tools are built specifically for web application vulnerabilities. Web application vulnerability scanners check for vulnerabilities such as path traversal, SQL injection, and cross-site scripting. The Open Web Application Security Project (OWASP) maintains a list of the most common web application vulnerability scanners on its website.

Banner Grabbing

Banner grabbing is a technique to identify what operating system is running on a machine, as well as determine the services that are running. Active vulnerability scanning solutions use this to help identify the OS type and running services. This information helps them narrow the vulnerability signatures to scan for. An attacker can footprint an organization in much the same way. The more you understand about the specific operating systems, applications, and version information, the easier it is to identify vulnerable systems and conduct targeted attacks. Netcat is a common tool used for banner grabs. For example, from a command shell, you might type the following:

```
nc www.example.com 80
```

You simply click Enter to establish a connection, and then you just need to send a bad request. This could be as simple as typing any letter followed by pressing the Return key. Depending on the system, the results will likely provide information about the host, including the type and version of web server running and the type and version of operating systems running.

For the system administrator, this provides a handy way to identify assets. Such information also makes vulnerability management tools more intelligent. Again, it can also help an attacker know what exploit to use against the system.

Network Scanners

Network scanners identify active network hosts. One of the most common network scanning tools is a network mapper. A network mapper is a software utility used to conduct network assessments over a range of IP addresses. The network mapper compiles a listing of all systems, devices, and network hardware present within a network segment. This information can be used to identify simple points of failure, conduct a network inventory, and create graphical details suitable for reporting on network configurations. Nmap and Nessus are two of the most common network mapping software utilities used in today's networks. The upcoming section "Command-line Tools" discusses Nmap in more detail. These tools use Active Discovery to locate network hosts, open ports, and identify operating systems.

Many network scanners can do a whole lot more than just map the network. For example, they can identify rogue systems. Rogue systems present a problem for organizations because they are set up or added to the network without approval. Most rogue systems are wireless, but technically, a rogue system can be any type of unauthorized system, such as test systems, voice over IP devices, or printers. Recall from Chapter 2, "Attack Types," that rogue access refers to situations in which an unauthorized wireless access point has been set in organizations. Well-meaning insiders might use rogue access points with the best of intentions, so they are not necessarily malicious. Fortunately, detecting rogue access points is possible through the use of network scanners. Tools such as Nessus, SolarWinds, and McAfee ePolicy Orchestrator can identify rogue systems.

For example, ePolicy Orchestrator has a Rogue System Sensor as part of the Rogue System Detection architecture that identifies all network devices.

> **ExamAlert**
>
> It is important to understand that the sensor itself does not identify a system as rogue. The sensor listens passively to Layer 2 traffic and reports newly connected network device or system information to the policy server.

Configuration Compliance Scanners

Configuration compliance scanners audit network device configurations against a set policy. They are most often used in either auditing or vulnerability checking. A compliance audit and a vulnerability scan are two different concepts. Configuration compliance scanners work as an auditing tool to verify that devices meet regulatory compliance or policy requirements. Configuration compliance scanners are used in a vulnerability checking capacity to be sure that devices connected to the network are not subject to the effects of newly released vulnerabilities and that they were not missed when updates were applied, leaving the system open to known vulnerabilities.

Some of the tools mentioned in the previous section, such as Nessus and SolarWinds, have the capability to do configuration compliance checking. The extended capabilities of these tools permit the reporting of specific system information, including operating system configuration, applied hotfixes, mobile device management (MDM), and enterprise application configuration.

Knowing how a device is configured, at what level it has been patched, and what existing vulnerabilities are present helps the organization determine a course of action to mitigate risk. This is especially true at a higher level, where trends in noncompliant systems can be evaluated. Implementing a tool that has both vulnerability scanning and compliance capabilities can reduce administrative overhead and eliminate the need for two separate sets of credentials when individual tools are used.

Wireless Scanners and Crackers

The security of WLANs is important, especially in environments where wireless communication occurs with applications that host valuable data. Access points tend to be the primary rogue device on networks, so organizations should continually scan for and remove any rogue access points. Rogue access points can include points that employees put on the network for convenience or can be misconfigured company-provisioned access points. Wireless scanning hardware or software can detect rogue access points. A common method involves using wireless sniffing applications.

As stated earlier in the chapter, wireless network discovery and surveying tools are used to gather information about Wi-Fi networks, often for further reconnaissance. Some wireless tools merely monitor network activity; other tools can break WEP/WPA keys. When the latter type is used, the activity is often defined as cracking because it is similar to a direct intrusion.

Information about surrounding WAPs is obtained by passively monitoring beacon and probe response frames. Information obtained from discovered devices is usually SSID, channel, and MAC address. Some tools also report additional information, such as nonbroadcast SSIDs and location. Common wireless discovery tools include the following:

- ▶ Aerodump
- ▶ Kismet/KisMAC
- ▶ Netstumbler
- ▶ Vistumber
- ▶ inSSIDer

After discovery, Wi-Fi packet capture tools are used to capture traffic. Common packet-capture tools used in wireless networks include the following:

▶ Aircrack-ng Suite

▶ Riverbed AirPcap

▶ Airopeek

▶ Cain

▶ Wireshark

After packets are captured, wireless packet analyzers provide a way to view 802.11 WLAN traffic. During this phase, vulnerabilities such as poor configuration or weak encryption are exploited. For example, in networks whose keys are known or have already been cracked, a tool such as Commview can view captured packets by inputting the WEP/WPA key. Figure 8.1 shows the dashboard of Commview where the keys are input.

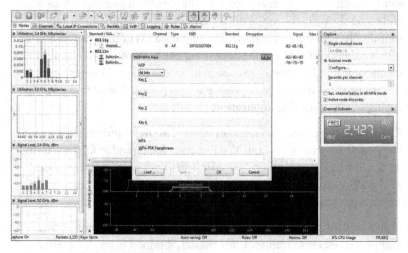

FIGURE 8.1   Commview Dashboard

Passive Versus Active Tools

One of the best ways to think about passive versus active tools is to think about the adjectives used in these terms: A passive solution only listens. On the other hand, an active solution talks. For example, consider vulnerability scanner solutions. An active scanner sits on the network and, when scheduled, reaches out across the network to discover systems and perform a series of inquiries to identify what is running on the system. Based on that discovery, most scanners perform an iterative process of testing the system against known vulnerability signatures. However, active scanners are hampered by network and host firewalls.

A passive scanner, on the other hand, doesn't actually perform scans. Instead, it sits on the wire and acts as a sniffer, collecting data from the normal flow over the network. As a result, a passive scanner can gather details between systems behind firewalls. A passive scanner might not see a system or application that isn't "talking," but it does provide greater visibility because it can see systems actively communicating that you might not have otherwise known about. Finally, even if active tools are configured to minimize any impact upon target systems, they are still invasive. Conversely, a passive scanner does nothing to interrupt the systems or the flow of information. Passive scanning tools often augment active scanning tools.

Network scanners, vulnerability scanners, and the other assessment tools mentioned in this section are used in network monitoring and protection. When these tools are used on the network, be sure that the information they gather is protected as well: That information contains valuable data for intruders.

Detection and Protection Tools

Just as tools such as protocol analyzers and scanners help the organization maintain a strong security posture, detection and protection tools can help mitigate the risk associated with a breach or damaging attack. Many organizations are breached or experience data losses because they lack proper detection and protection tools. This is especially evident in incident and data compromise reports that surface frequently.

Honeypots

Honeypots identify the level of aggressive attention directed at a network and are often used to study an attacker's common methods of attack. Honeypots are systems configured to simulate one or more services within an organization's network. They are then left exposed to network access. When an attacker accesses a honeypot system, their activities are logged and monitored by other processes so that the attacker's actions and methods can be later reviewed in detail. In the meantime, the honeypot distracts the attacker from valid network resources. Honeypots might be simple targets exposed to identify vulnerability exposure. Alternatively, they might interact with the attacker to build a better attack profile by tracking and logging the attacker's activities.

A collection of honeypots is known as a honeynet. Honeynets create functional-appearing networks that study an attacker's behavior within the network. Honeynets use specialized software agents to create seemingly normal network traffic. Honeynets and honeypots can distract attackers from valid network content and offer valuable information on an attacker's methods. They also provide an early warning of attack attempts that might later be waged against the more secure portions of the network.

> **ExamAlert**
>
> Think of honeypots and honeynets as a trap, another way to fight unauthorized system access. They distract attackers from valid network content, they enable you to study the attacker's methods, and they provide early warning of attack attempts that might later be waged against the more secure portions of the network.

Exploitation Frameworks

Exploitation frameworks are used for penetration testing and risk assessments. Each exploitation framework contains a set of exploits for known vulnerabilities that are run against a host to determine whether the host is vulnerable to the exploit. Exploitation involves the following steps:

▶ Select a target system.

▶ Select an exploit.

▶ If prior reconnaissance was conducted, determine whether the exploit might work on the target system.

▶ Select and configure the exploit payload.

▶ Select an encoding method for the payload so it can get through the IDS.

▶ Run the exploit.

Some of the most well-known exploitation frameworks are Metasploit, Canvas, and Core Impact. Exploitation frameworks exist for systems as well as specific web browsers. The Browser Exploitation Framework (BeEF) is a penetration testing tool that focuses on the exploiting vulnerabilities in web browsers by using client-side attacks.

Password Crackers

Weak passwords are easily compromised. Users must be instructed in the value of their access credentials and the potential impact of sharing their passwords and logons, using weak passwords (and identifying a strong password), and using easily guessed passwords. Even when users are educated about the dangers of using the same password for multiple accounts and when to change passwords, they often take the easy way out. As a result, it is imperative to test the passwords that employees use.

> **ExamAlert**
>
> Password crackers are software utilities that allow direct testing of user logon password strength. They conduct a brute force password test using dictionary terms, specialized lexicons, or mandatory complexity guidelines.

Chapter 2 covered the various types of password attacks. In addition to using helpful software programs, you can look for online password-cracking tools that enable you to input the hash and get the password returned in plain text. CloudCracker is an online password-cracking tool for WPA-protected Wi-Fi networks that cracks password hashes in a manner similar to other online cracking tools.

Common password cracking tools include the following:

▶ Brutus

▶ Cain and Able

▶ John the Ripper

▶ THC Hydra

When used by the organization as an assessment tool, password crackers should provide only the relative strength of a password instead of the password itself, to avoid weakening logon responsibility under evidentiary discovery actions.

Steganography

Steganography is the art or practice of concealing a message, image, or file within another message, image, or file. As with many security tools, steganography can be used for a variety of reasons. Legitimate purposes can include watermarking images for copyright protection. Digital watermarks are similar to steganography, in that they are overlaid in files that appear to be part of the original file and are thus not easily detectable. Steganography can also be used to create a substitute for a one-way hash value. Finally, steganography can help maintain the confidentiality of valuable information, to protect the data from possible sabotage, theft, or unauthorized viewing of passwords or keys.

Steganography tools use these main approaches:

► Least significant bit insertion

► Masking and filtering

► Algorithms and transformations

Common steganography tools include these:

► OpenPuff

► Camouflage

► Steghide

► rSteg

If an organization needs to detect steganography on the network, tools such as Stegdetect can help. Alternatively, manual methods such as hash or frequency distribution comparisons can be good indicators of the use of steganography.

Backup Utilities

Organization security plans and third-party contracts or agreements should address data backups. Considerations should include identifying the types of data that will be backed up, determining the backup frequency, and specifying how backups will be performed. Data backup terms should specify how to perform backups and how to link backups to contingency plan procedures. Critical data should be backed up regularly, stored in a secure off-site location to prevent loss or damage, and retained for a period that both parties approve.

Backup utilities make a copy of data and store that data elsewhere. This can be on another drive, on a NAS, or in the cloud. Backup utilities are installed on individual user machines or on servers, depending on the organizational data storage policy.

When used in an enterprise capacity, backup software utilities include deduplication, compression, and a centralized management console. Backup utilities can follow either an agent or an agentless design. Agent-based software requires an agent to be installed on each device. Agentless software runs as a service, requiring both the server and the client device to support the communication protocol the service runs on (such as SMB or SSH).

Data Sanitizing Tools

Organizations maintain data such as names, addresses, social security numbers, and possible health information. User training programs address legal or regulatory requirements for accessing, transporting, storing, and disposing of data and data storage devices. Most times the organization has a legal obligation to protect and dispose of data properly. This includes encryption systems for mobile and removable storage devices, data access logging requirements under laws such as HIPAA, and review of retention and destruction policy.

A data destruction policy spells out what happens when sensitive data contained on a device is no longer needed but the device will be repurposed. Often the device or media is sanitized.

ExamAlert

Sanitization is the process of removing the contents from the device or media as fully as possible, making it extremely difficult to restore. Sanitization can be accomplished using either a software tool or a combination of a software tool and firmware.

Sanitization falls into one of the following categories:

▶ **Clear:** Applied through standard read and write commands

▶ **Purge:** Physical or logical techniques, making recovery impossible

▶ **Destroy:** Physical or logical techniques that render the device useless

Examples of software tools are DBAN and BCWipe. Organizations that use self-encrypting drives (SEDs) also use cryptographic erase (CE). CE takes advantage of the encrypted data by sanitizing the encryption key. This is a quick and effective method that leaves only the cipher text on the media.

After sanitization, a certificate of media disposition is completed. The certificate can be either a hard copy or an ecopy stating the process and method used to sanitize the data.

NIST Special Publication 800-88: Guidelines for Media Sanitization has detailed information on how to sanitize media, based on the organization's categorization of information confidentiality.

Command-line Tools

Most organizations use monitoring and diagnostic tools to manage their networks. Diagnostic tools can be actual tools, such as cable testers and loopback connectors, or software programs and utilities. The most basic level of system monitoring tells whether something is available. The following utilities are common network command-line diagnostic tools used to assess the security posture of an organization:

▶ **IPConfig/Ifconfig/ip:** IPConfig displays the TCP/IP settings on a Windows machine. It can display the IP address, subnet mask, default gateway, Windows Internet Naming Service (WINS), DNS, and MAC information. It is useful in verifying that the Transmission Control Protocol/Internet Protocol (TCP/IP) configuration is correct if connectivity issues arise. IPConfig works on Windows-based systems; Ifconfig works on Macintosh and Linux-based systems. The newer **ip** command is used in a manner similar to IPConfig but has more functionality.

▶ **ping:** Packet Internet Groper (ping) is a utility that tests network connectivity by sending an *Internet Control Message Protocol (ICMP)* echo request to a host. It is a good troubleshooting tool to tell whether a route is available to a host.

▶ **ARP:** ARP provides information from a table that contains a mapping of known MAC addresses to the associated IP addresses. ARP is necessary because the underlying hardware cannot translate IP addresses. The ARP cache maintains a table of MAC-to-IP addresses, so ARP is a quick way to find a machine's MAC address.

▶ **tracert/traceroute:** This utility traces the route a packet takes and records the hops along the way. It is a good tool to use to find out where a packet is getting hung up. The tracert utility works on Windows-based systems; traceroute works on Macintosh and Linux-based systems.

▶ **nslookup/dig:** This command-line utility troubleshoots a Domain Name System (DNS) database. It queries the DNS server to check whether the correct information is in the zone database. nslookup is used on Windows-based systems; dig, which stands for Domain Information Groper, is used on Macintosh and Linux-based systems.

▶ **netstat/nbtstat:** The netstat utility displays all the ports on which the computer is listening. It can also display the routing table and pre-protocol statistics. Nbtstat is a diagnostic tool for NetBIOS over TCP/IP primarily designed is to help troubleshoot NetBIOS name resolution problems in Windows operating systems.

▶ **Telnet:** Telnet is a terminal emulation program used to access remote routers and UNIX systems. It is an excellent tool for determining whether the port on a host computer is working properly.

▶ **tcpdump:** The tcpdump utility is a command-line packet analyzer tool that captures TCP/IP packets sent and received on a specific interface. The tcpdump tool is used on Macintosh and Linux-based systems; Windump is used on Windows-based systems.

▶ **Nmap:** Network Mapper (Nmap) is a network scanning tool used for locating network hosts, detecting operating systems, and identifying services. Nmap is most often used in security auditing but can also be useful for routine administrative tasks such as monitoring host uptime or host inventory.

▶ **Netcat:** Netcat is a network utility for gathering information from TCP and UDP network connections. It is a versatile tool that can be used for functions such as port scanning, monitoring, and file copying. Netcat is Linux based, but versions are available for Windows machines.

ExamAlert

Know the different utilities for troubleshooting networks and what they are used for.

Many of the command-line utilities in the preceding list rely on underlying technologies. For example, ping and traceroute rely on ICMP. Internet Control Message Protocol (ICMP) is meant to be an aid for other protocols (as well as system administrators) to test connectivity and search for configuration errors in a network. Ping uses the ICMP echo function and is the lowest-level test of whether a remote host is alive. A small packet containing an ICMP echo message is sent through the network to a particular IP address. The computer that sent the packet then waits for a return packet. If the connections are good and the target computer is up, the echo message return packet will be received. Ping is one of the most useful network tools because it tests the most basic function of an IP network. It also shows the time to live (TTL) value and the amount of time it takes for a packet to make the complete trip—also known as the round-trip time (RTT)—in milliseconds (ms). Figure 8.2 shows an example of how ping is used.

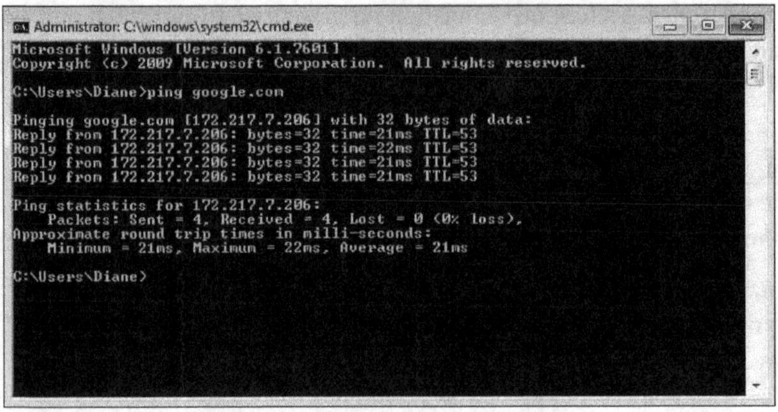

FIGURE 8.2   **Using ping**

The traceroute tool uses an ICMP echo request packet to find the path. It sends an echo reply with the TTL value set to 1. When the first router sees the packet with TTL 1, it decreases it by one, to 0, and discards the packet. As a result, it sends an ICMP time exceeded message back to the source address. The source address of the ICMP error message is the first router address. Now the source knows the address of the first router. Generally, three packets are sent at each TTL and the RTT is measured for each one. Most implementations of traceroute keep working until they have gone 30 hops, but this can be extended over up to 254 routers.

Ping relies on ARP to identify IP addresses because 48-bit MAC addresses must be mapped to an IP address for devices on different networks to communicate. Some of the Layer 3 protocols used to perform the MAC to IP mapping follow:

▶ Address Resolution Protocol (ARP)

▶ Reverse ARP (RARP)

▶ Serial Line ARP (SLARP)

▶ Inverse ARP

The output from command-line tools can be saved and imported into other tools. For example, the output from tcpdump is often saved and imported into Wireshark for easier interpretation. Command-line tools can also provide some of the same functionality as other tools, without all the overhead. For example, netcat can establish a TCP connection to a web server and then grab the banner to fingerprint the OS the server is running. Both dig and nslookup can map IP address to domain name and other related information, including mail exchanges and nameservers.

What Next?

If you want more practice on this chapter's exam objectives before you move on, remember that you can access all the Cram Quiz questions on the Pearson Test Prep software. You can also create a custom exam by objective. Note any objective you struggle with and go to that objective material in this chapter.

CHAPTER 9

Security Issues

This chapter covers the following official Security+ exam objective:

2.3 Given a scenario, troubleshoot common security issues.

- ▶ Unencrypted credentials/ clear text
- ▶ Logs and events anomalies
- ▶ Permission issues
- ▶ Access violations
- ▶ Certificate issues
- ▶ Data exfiltration
- ▶ Misconfigured devices
  - ▪ Firewall
  - ▪ Content filter
  - ▪ Access points
- ▶ Weak security configurations
- ▶ Personnel issues
  - ▪ Policy violation
  - ▪ Insider threat
  - ▪ Social engineering
  - ▪ Social media
  - ▪ Personal email
- ▶ Unauthorized software
- ▶ Baseline deviation
- ▶ License compliance violation (availability/integrity)
- ▶ Asset management
- ▶ Authentication issues

Essential Terms and Components

- ▶ application logging
- ▶ auditing
- ▶ baseline
- ▶ data exfiltration
- ▶ security baseline
- ▶ system logging

CramSaver

If you can correctly answer these questions before going through this chapter, save time by skimming the Exam Alerts in this chapter and then completing the Cram Quiz at the end of Part II.

1. Explain why auditing is used and how it is implemented.

   _____

2. Identify the most common firewall configuration errors and tell how to mitigate them.

   _____

3. What can an organization do to reduce the impact of policy violations and insider threat?

   _____

Answers

1. Auditing user permissions is one way to identify access violations and issues. Auditing user permissions is generally a two-step process that involves turning on auditing within the operating system and then specifying the resources to be audited. After you enable auditing, you also need to monitor the logs that are generated.

2. The most common firewall configuration errors include permitting traffic from any source to any destination, running unnecessary services, allowing weak authentication, and permitting log file negligence. To reduce these misconfiguration errors, organizations should allow only the minimal level of privilege that is needed for a user or service to function; harden devices; implement strong, uniform authentication mechanisms; and centralize and analyze log files.

3. Having the proper technologies in place to enforce policies and spot policy violations is paramount to keeping sensitive information from improper access. Technology can go a long way toward not only spotting policy violations, but also helping with personnel issues such as insider threats.

Authentication, Authorization, and Access

Authentication and authorization issues such as unencrypted credentials, incorrect permissions, and access violations leave the organization vulnerable. Sometimes not even organizational configurations are exposing the credentials. For example, the Starbucks iOS mobile app sent user passwords in clear text for most of a year before the app was fixed. The vulnerability happened because of the way crash information data was produced. Users often reuse passwords, so a mobile app vulnerability like this could well lead to the compromise of organizational data.

Unencrypted Credentials and Clear Text

Weak passwords often are discovered when using security tools such as those described in the previous chapter. In the previous Starbucks example, an organization can mitigate this type of exposure in several ways. Chapter 11, "Mobile Devices," covers mobile apps and security, so this section focuses on sending unencrypted and plain-text passwords in general.

Authentication alone is typically not sufficient when weak passwords are used. When an application or service stores or sends passwords in clear text, risk to the organization can be reduced by sending the credentials via an encrypted channel such as HTTPS. This prevents malicious users from capturing the clear text passwords.

Probably one of the most unintentional exposures of a password in clear text occurs when a user logs in and types the password into the username field. In a Windows environment, failed logins record the clear text password in the security log. Because most web applications log unsuccessful login attempts, the same can happen with web-based applications. Although an attacker would need additional information to obtain the associated username, it could be possible. For example, when users log in incorrectly, they usually immediately attempt to log in again. Chances are pretty good that the next successful login is the username associated with the previous failed login. This method of association has a greater success rate in a small environment. The best defense against this type of exposure is to educate users about the vulnerability this presents and have them change the password.

Permission Issues

When trying to access resources, you have likely seen the message "Access Denied" at some point. This notification is a sign that permissions are set to deny access to the requested resource. These common user activities tend to have permission issues:

- ▶ Reading, modifying, and deleting files
- ▶ Accessing shared folders on the network
- ▶ Using services such as remote access or remote desktop services
- ▶ Using devices such as printers

These activities can be restricted by design or because of misconfigured user account permissions.

ExamAlert

The biggest security issue with incorrect user account permissions is that they could grant access to information that a user should not be able to access.

For example, the user could have access to employee records or customer data that should be restricted to a small group of upper management. One of the best examples of misconfigured user access involves Bradley (Chelsea) Manning. Misconfiguration of permissions allowed Manning to exfiltrate sensitive data. Misconfigured permissions leave the network vulnerable and can violate regulatory compliance.

Auditing user permissions is one way of identifying access violations and issues. Auditing user permissions is generally a two-step process that involves turning on auditing within the operating system and then specifying the resources to be audited. After you enable auditing, you also need to monitor the logs that are generated. Auditing should include both privilege and use. Access use and rights changes should be audited to prevent unauthorized or unintentional access or an escalation of privileges that, for example, might give a guest or restricted user account access to sensitive or protected resources.

When configuring an audit policy, it is important to monitor both successful and failed access attempts. Failure events enable you to identify unauthorized access attempts. Successful events can reveal an accidental or intentional escalation of access rights.

In a Windows environment, user permissions are generally assigned via group policy. Group policies can get complex, causing permission issues. The easiest method to determine what group policies have been applied is to use GPResult, a command-line utility that determines the resultant set of policy for a given user or computer. Another helpful tool for troubleshooting permission issues for users or groups is AccessChk. It shows the permissions specific users and groups have for files, folders, registry keys, Windows services, and other objects. Using AccessChk is a quick way to determine whether the proper level of security has been applied.

Access Violations

You already know that too much access creates risk for the organization, and too little access slows productivity. Just as user access can be managed via auditing, access violations can be managed through enterprise-level software. In a

Windows environment, Microsoft Operations Manager (MOM) has an Audit Collection Services (ACS) function that collects audit events in a database that can then be queried. ACS provides two preconfigured reports:

▶ Access Violation Account Locked Report

▶ Access Violation Unsuccessful Logon Attempts Report

In addition to OS available tools, vendors provide software to manage access violations. For example, the Greenlight SAP Access Violation Management software enables organizations to automate the recognition and notification of access permission violations so that they then can calculate the financial impact of the violations.

Authentication Issues

All regular users have likely experienced authentication issues. Perhaps the most annoying problem arises when a frequently visited site makes changes and a user's password no longer works. In this instance, both the username and password are correct; other factors are causing the authentication issue. The most common authentication issues follow:

▶ Incorrect username

▶ Incorrect password

▶ Disabled or deleted account

▶ Restricted user rights

▶ Computer not in the domain

▶ Domain controller not available

To resolve the authentication issues in the preceding list, the first item to check as you begin the troubleshooting process is that the correct username and password have been entered. Then verify that the user's password has not expired or that the account has not been disabled. Finally, check to be sure no basic connectivity issues exist between the client machine and the domain controller.

Even if no local machine and network issues are present, authentication issues can occur. For example, Microsoft had authentication issues that prevented access to related applications for anyone with a cloud-based account. In this instance, only the service provider can resolve the authentication issue.

Certificate Issues

You have most likely seen the warning "There is a problem with this website's security certificate" when attempting to access a website. One of the most common causes of this error is an incorrect date and time or time zone on the machine. For example, suppose that the user set the date and time to 1/1/1970. In this instance, any website that uses certificates that the user attempts to access will show this error because the certificates rely on the correct date and time to function properly. Other suggested activities for troubleshooting certificate errors follow:

▶ Clear the browser cache.

▶ Verify the browser settings.

▶ Check the client configuration for valid server credentials.

▶ Test the credentials path.

For Windows-based machines, the computer Event Viewer logs can provide additional information that can help troubleshoot the problem.

Certificate issues affect not only external website access, but also internal users when a PKI is used. PKI certificate issues fall into these categories:

▶ Trust between the two parties

▶ Inability to verify the validity of the certificate

▶ Algorithm mismatch

▶ Intended purpose incorrect

For Windows-based servers, the Certificates Microsoft Management Console (MMC) snap-in can provide additional information to troubleshoot the problem.

When client machines cannot view an IIS web page that uses SSL, the error "This page can't be displayed" results. This is a server-side error related to the certificate. The first step in troubleshooting the error is to see if the client can connect via HTTP. If so, the most common way to troubleshoot is to use a network packet-capture tool such as Wireshark or Microsoft Message Analyzer.

Misconfigurations and Deviations

Misconfigured devices and weak security configurations are among the most common security issues an organization faces. These issues can have dire consequences. For example, in early 2017, a misconfigured firewall resulted in a ransomware attack that affected a hospital's ability to do business for four days.

Firewall

Gartner research suggests that the majority of firewall breaches are attributable to simple firewall misconfigurations. With the complexity of today's networks, it is no surprise that human error is the cause of most firewall misconfigurations.

ExamAlert

Firewall misconfigurations occur most often during the change management process when a new rule is added or an existing one is changed.

To reduce the risk of misconfiguration, organizations should follow a strong change management process. Chapter 28, "Risk Management Processes and Concepts," describes this process in more detail.

Some of the most common firewall configuration errors follow:

▶ Traffic permitted from any source to any destination

▶ Unnecessary services running

▶ Weak authentication

▶ Log file negligence

To reduce these misconfiguration errors, organizations should allow only the minimal level of privilege that is needed for a user or service to function; harden devices; implement strong, uniform authentication mechanisms; and centralize and analyze log files.

Content Filter

Content filters control Internet content that is available for use in the organizational environment. Internet content filters use a collection of terms, words, and phrases that they then compare to content from browsers and applications. This type of software can filter content from various Internet activites and applications, such as instant messaging, email, and Microsoft Office documents. Content filtering reports only on violations identified in the specified applications listed for the filtering application. In other words, if the application filters only Microsoft Office documents and a user chooses to use Office, the content is filtered. If the user chooses to use something other than Office, that content is not filtered. Internet content filtering works by analyzing data against a database contained in the software. If a match occurs, the data can be addressed in one of several ways, including filtering, capturing, or blocking the content and closing the application. Windows Parental Controls is an example of such software.

Unlike antivirus and antispyware applications, content monitoring does not require daily updates to keep the database effective and current. On the downside, content filtering needs to be "trained."

> **ExamAlert**
>
> A misconfigured web content filter can either prevent legitimate content or allow prohibited content. For example, if the IP addresses or domains of customers are accidentally blocked, customers become blacklisted.

Accidentally blacklisting customers can have a very detrimental effect on business. The issue with most content filters is that they look at only HTTP traffic and filter based on a database of words.

Content filters can be bypassed by using HTTPS, a filter evasion application such as TOR, or a web proxy service. To prevent a content filter from being bypassed, select a solution that is used inline, has the capability to decrypt HTTPS, and uses real-time analysis to detect proxy website behavior.

Access Points

Misconfigured wireless APs are most often found in smaller business environments. As with firewall misconfigurations, human error is a common reason for misconfigured APs. APs often are set up quickly and left with weak security settings. These settings include factory default username and passwords that attackers can easily obtain on the Internet. Other misconfiguration errors also can leave the organization vulnerable:

▶ Using WEP instead of WPA

▶ Allowing rogue access points to connect

▶ Allowing ad hoc connections

As a preventive security measure, organizations should conduct ongoing site surveys to monitor the wireless environment. A *site survey* is necessary to optimize network layout within each unique location. This is particularly important in distributed wireless network configurations that span multiple buildings or open natural areas, where imposing structures and tree growth might affect network access in key areas.

A site survey should review the desired physical and logical structure of the network, the selection of possible technologies, and several other factors:

▶ Federal, state, and local laws and regulations relating to the proposed network solution.

▶ Potential sources of radio frequency (RF) interference, including local broadcast systems, motors, fans, and other types of equipment that generate radio frequency interference. An analysis of potential channel overlap between wireless access point hardware is needed.

▶ Available locations for AP hardware installation and physical network integration connectivity.

▶ Any special requirements of users, applications, and network equipment that must function over the proposed wireless network solution.

▶ Information on whether a point-to-point (ad hoc or wireless bridge) or multipoint wireless solution is required. In most solutions, point-to-multipoint connectivity is required to support multiple wireless clients from each wireless access point connected to the physical network.

ExamAlert

All wireless networks share several common security vulnerabilities related to their use of radio frequency broadcasts. These can potentially be detected and compromised without the network administrator's knowledge.

Data transported over this medium is available to anyone with the proper equipment. Therefore, it must be secured through encryption and encapsulation mechanisms that are not subject to public compromise.

VPNs are commonly used to securely connect employees to corporate networks when they are not in the office by using an Internet connection. More organizations are requiring hotspot visitors to use a VPN to connect to the organizational network because they have no control over the security used in public Wi-Fi hotspots. The same principles that apply to wired VPNs can be applied to VPNs over open wireless networks. The use of a VPN over public Wi-Fi hotspots can increase privacy and provide data protection. A VPN that is used over an open wireless network is not always immune to man-in-the-middle attacks. This access method can also be susceptible to Wi-Fi-based attacks and VPN-based attacks.

Baseline Deviation

One way to reduce the chance of misconfiguration is to implement measures that provide a secure configuration. Baselines are the measure of normal activity. Organizations should have a secure baseline build for all systems and components, for use as a point of reference when something on the computer goes awry. Without a baseline, determining the problem is difficult because you do not know what is normal. Baselines should also include software applications.

Baseline deviations occur because either a real issue is occurring or the baseline has not been updated to reflect the new normal. Baselines must be updated regularly—and certainly when the computer has changed or new technology has been deployed. Baselining should be done for both host and application processes so that you can tell whether a hardware or software issue is to blame. Host software baselining can be done for a variety of reasons, including monitoring for malware and creating system images.

Detecting baseline deviation is not always easy, especially in an ever-changing network environment. For this reason dynamic baselining is more effective than static baselining. Dynamic baselining uses predictive analytics and patterns instead of static thresholds. It is ideal for analyzing the following:

▶ Varying workloads across different days

▶ Application performance based on seasonal usage

▶ Individual locations

By looking at patterns and contrasts over time, you are better equipped to identify actual anomalies. Dynamic baselining allows organizations to set deviation variables and reduce false positives.

Proper and effective reporting is critical to the overall health and security of an organization. Reporting should be subject to a policy governing the overall risk of the infrastructure and data. This helps define what types of reports are required, the frequency of the reports, and how often they are examined. Adequate reporting should also include the following mechanisms:

▶ **Alarms:** The purpose of an alarm is to report a critical event that typically requires some type of immediate response. Consider the common analogy of a bank. A report might include details on each specific time the safe is accessed, but that might not necessitate an alarm; however, a broken window after hours would trigger an alarm for immediate response.

▶ **Alerts:** An alert is similar to an alarm, but it is less critical and likely does not require an immediate response. For example, several failed logon attempts would likely generate an alert. At a minimum, an alert should generate a log file, but depending on the situation, it could merely provide some sort of notification to an administrator. Alerts can be used in conjunction with an alarm. For example, several alerts might be correlated to form a condition that deems an alarm necessary.

▶ **Trends:** Identifying and understanding trends is vital to detecting and responding to incidents. Furthermore, trends help prevent the unnecessary response to something that initially seems warranted but is actually not. Trends become more apparent when considered within a time frame. For example, in a week-long period, an abnormal activity might occur on Sunday. That might not be a worrisome situation. However, if during a month-long period it becomes evident that this activity occurs every Sunday, perhaps due to a weekly processing event, a response would be necessary.

Weak Security Configurations and Data Exfiltration

Theft of data is a major concern for organizations, not only from insiders, but also from malicious actors. Weak security configurations can easily lead to *data exfiltration*, or the unauthorized transfer of data. A more basic definition of data exfiltration is data theft. One of the most well-known cases of data exfiltration occurred in the Edward Snowden case. Snowden created and used self-signed certificates to copy data to an external file share over encrypted channels.

> **ExamAlert**
>
> Data exfiltration and data breach are two different concepts. Data exfiltration is the unauthorized transfer of data. A data breach is the release of private or confidential information.

A security posture includes an organization's overall plan for protecting itself against threats. This should also include the activities required for the ongoing monitoring and reactions required of security incidents. One of these functions involves looking for and remediating weak security configurations. Weak security configurations can result in data exfiltration from the following sources:

▶ Databases

▶ Files

▶ Email

▶ Source code

Data loss prevention (DLP) products can help prevent data exfiltration, but organizations must recognize that when data is stolen, damage has already been done. A better strategy is to use proactive measures instead of reactive ones. The risk assessment measures in Chapter 33, "Data Security and Privacy Practices," provide guidance on how to implement proactive measures to prevent data exfiltration.

An overall approach to avoiding weak security configurations must focus on setting baseline standards. To establish effective security baselines, enterprise network security management requires a measure of commonality between systems. Mandatory settings, standard application suites, and initial setup configuration details all factor into the security stance of an enterprise network.

You should be familiar with these types of security configuration settings:

▶ **Group policies:** Group policies are collections of configuration settings that are applied to a system based on computer or user group membership. They can influence the level, type, and extent of access provided.

▶ **Security templates:** These sets of configurations reflect a particular role or standard established either through industry guidelines or within an organization. They are assigned to fulfill a particular purpose. Examples include assigning a minimum-access configuration template to limited-access kiosk systems while assigning a high-security template to systems that require more stringent logon and access control mechanisms.

▶ **Configuration baselines:** Many industries must meet specific criteria that are established as a baseline measure of security. For example, the healthcare industry must comply with a lengthy set of requirements for information technology specified in the Health Insurance Portability and Accountability Act (HIPAA) security standards. Unless the mandated security baseline is met, an organization can face penalties and fines. Security baselines are often established by governmental mandate, regulatory bodies, or industry representatives. For example, businesses in the credit card industry must meet Payment Card Industry (PCI) requirements if they collect and transact using credit information.

Chapter 15, "Secure Systems Design," discusses secure configurations in greater detail.

Personnel

It has been said, "An Enterprise could be nearly perfect, except for all the users." As in a chain, a network is only as secure as its weakest link. Users have a variety of bad habits, a vast range of knowledge and skill, and varying intent in data access. Personnel issues present one of the most challenging organizational security issues because human behavior cannot be predicted.

Policy Violation

Proper user education can go a long way toward mitigating risk in the enterprise. Policy violations are one of the most common personnel issues an organization faces. Employees might violate policies based on perceived benefit, their moral beliefs, and resulting consequences.

Regulations such as HIPAA and GLBA make policy enforcement mandatory. An organization can have excellent, well-defined security policies in place, but they are useless unless employees adhere to them. To encourage employees to follow policy, organizations should educate users about why policies exist, why they must comply, and the consequences of policy violations.

Having the proper technologies in place to enforce policies and spot policy violations is paramount to keeping sensitive information from improperly being accessed. Technologies such as those discussed in the next chapter can make large gains to not only spot policy violations, but also help with issues such as insider threat.

Insider Threat

Chapter 3, "Threat Actor Types and Attributes," describes insiders and insider threat. This is one of the biggest risks to an organization. When access is not properly set, great damage can be done, as noted in this chapter's earlier section "Authentication, Authorization, and Access." Most unauthorized access involves organizational employees, usually after employment separation. Employees might try to take with them sensitive or confidential information that the employer owns when they leave the organization. Insiders also can pose a threat via social media and personal email, covered later in this section.

Social Engineering

Chapter 2, "Attack Types," describes social engineering attacks in great detail. Social engineering plays on human behavior and how we interact with one another, so it does not feel like an attack at all. As a matter of fact, we teach our employees to be customer-service-oriented, so they might think they are being helpful and simply doing the right thing instead of opening themselves to social engineering attacks. Social engineering has definitely become more advanced and harder to spot.

Unsecured equipment is also vulnerable to social engineering attacks. An attacker can much more easily walk into a reception area, say she has arrived to do some work on the server, and be given access to the server room without any questions asked, other than completing the guest sign-in and sign-out sheet.

Human behavior is difficult, if not impossible, to predict. The best defense against personnel issues such as social engineering is user education.

> **ExamAlert**
>
> Adding an integrated antiphishing tool and teaching users basic ways to spot scams (such as mouseover skills) can help reduce the success of social engineering attacks.

Social Media

Employee use of social media can be problematic for several reasons. For starters, employees can negatively impact business if they post detrimental material about their place of employment or while they are at work. In addition, social media issues can affect productivity, for instance if employees use Facebook and Twitter excessively. Furthermore, social media used at work can bypass traditional network defenses, potentially exposing the enterprise to unexpected avenues by which malware can enter or providing uncontrolled pathways by which data can be exfiltrated. Of course, social media services are increasingly used for business purposes, so separating business and personal accounts becomes critical if the organization faces a legal motion for discovery that requires access to personally controlled data resources. Social media services accessed through encrypted web access also open the organization to inadvertent disclosure of protected information. Normal content review systems such as content filtering would offer no help.

The best defense against personnel issues is policy creation and user education. Organizations can reduce potential problems with a functional social media policy:

- ▶ Encourage employees to discuss workplace grievances with the proper authority before taking to social media.

- ▶ Define confidential information.

▶ Address what is considered illegal content.

▶ Spell out employee consequences of social media use and posting.

▶ Emulate the company's security posture and culture.

Personal Email

Personal email use by employees poses several threats to an organization because this is one of the most common ways for data to leave an organization. Because personal email accounts are beyond the organization's control, issues ranging from improper backups to compliance and e-discovery problems can occur.

For example, imagine that an organization has a 90-day data retention policy on emails. After 90 days, an email is deleted from the server. An employee that doesn't like the policy and wants to save email might then forward important emails to a personal email account. Now imagine that the organization becomes involved in litigation, and this employee is discovered to have been forwarding emails to a personal account for more than 5 years. The forwarded emails suddenly become a legal issue for the organization.

As with all items in this section, setting strict policies against the use of personal email for business and educating users is the best course of action. Consider some additional suggestions to alleviate personnel issues:

▶ Formally communicate policies.

▶ Establish a security awareness program.

▶ Audit for compliance.

▶ Perform continuous monitoring.

Logs and Event Anomalies

Logging is the process of collecting data to be used for monitoring and auditing purposes. The log files themselves are documentation, but how do you properly set up a log? You should develop standards for each platform, application, and server type to make this a checklist or monitoring function. When choosing what to log, carefully consider your options. Logs take up disk space and use system resources. They also have to be read; if you log too much, the system bogs down and weeding through the log files to determine what is important takes a long time. Be sure to mandate a common storage location for all logs. Documentation also should state the proper methods for archiving and reviewing logs.

All devices, operating systems, and applications have log files. For example, application log files contain error messages, operational data, and usage information that can help manage applications and servers. Analyzing web application logs enables you to understand who visited the application, on what pages, and how often, and it also provides information on errors and performance problems of the web application. Analyzing logs from web servers such as Apache, IIS, ISA, and Tomcat is automatic and can contribute important insight into website and web application quality and availability. Web server logs are usually access logs, common error logs, custom logs, and W3C logs. W3C logs are used mainly by web servers to log web-related events, including web logs.

Unlike the security log, the application and system logs are available for all users to view. You can use the application log to tell how well an application is running. The system log shows events that occur on the individual system. You can configure settings such as the size of the file and filtering of events. Event logging is used for troubleshooting or notifying administrators of unusual circumstances. Be sure that you have the log file size set properly, that the size is monitored, and that the logs are periodically archived and cleared.

ExamAlert

Carefully consider where you store log files, to keep intruders from having access to them. By doing so, you eliminate the ability for intruders to cover their tracks.

Table 9.1 lists the fields and definitions of Windows events.

TABLE 9.1 **Windows Events**

Field Name	Field Description
Type	The type of the event, such as error, warning, or information
Time	The date and time of the local computer when the event occurred
Computer	The computer on which the event occurred
Provider Type	The type of event that generated the event, such as a Windows event log
Provider Name	The name of the event, such as Application or Security

Field Name	Field Description
Source	The application that logged the event, such as MS SQL Server
Event ID	The Windows event number
Description	The description of the event

The Event ID and Description fields are important to note. The Event ID is the easiest way to research the event in the Microsoft Knowledge Base, and the Description text usually explains what happened in simple language.

Other operating systems also have built-in and downloadable tools that enable you to view statistics about the system, such as CPU usage, memory usage, hard drive space, bandwidth usage, temperature, fan speeds, battery usage, uptime, and the top five processes. In addition, third-party programs can monitor network health. These programs can monitor the entire network and include devices such as modems, printers, routers, switches, and hubs.

To monitor the health of all systems, you install agents on the machines and then monitor those agents from a central location. For example, Simple Network Management Protocol (SNMP) is an application layer protocol whose purpose is to collect statistics from TCP/IP devices.

The nuances of system logging and monitoring are varied and detailed, but system logs are broadly classified as the following:

- ▶ **System event logs:** These logs record the events that occur across the system and, most notably, are related to the operating system. Keep in mind that these logs are specific to the system, not the user interacting with the system. Examples include hardware failures, drivers that do not load properly, and issues related to performance.

- ▶ **Audit logs:** Audit logs help ensure proper process and provide a useful record for auditors. Such logs provide relevant security information such as successful and unsuccessful login attempts, user creation and deletion, log data deletion, user privilege modification, and file access. These logs also provide accountability and, in the case of an incident, give a record of what occurred for forensics and recovery purposes.

- ▶ **Security logs:** These logs contain the events specific to systems and application security. Security solutions deployed within the network are a major source of such logs. This includes, for example, antimalware software, intrusion detection systems, remote access software, vulnerability management software, authentication servers, network quarantine systems, routers, and firewalls.

▶ **Access logs:** These logs provide information about requests and connections between systems. For example, this can include connections between an LDAP client and a directory server (which might include details such as the IP address) and records related to the binding operation. Web servers are another common source of access logs. For example, a web server will log access to each resource such as a page or image. Included in the log entry are details such as IP address, browser, operating system, referring page, and a date and time stamp.

ExamAlert

System logs vary. Be able to recognize event, audit, security, and access logs, and be sure you understand when each would be used in specific scenarios.

Systems generate large sizable logs. When dealing with such a large volume of logs and events, anomalies will occur. The problem lies in finding or recognizing the anomalies. Intrusion detection system logs tend to have better automatic processing to find anomalies in network traffic than system and event logs.

To detect log file anomalies, the data is collected, cleaned, structured, and then analyzed. Anomaly detection deduces dynamic thresholds by learning a baseline or pattern of events. Data mining techniques are often used in the analysis phase. Because systems don't always stay static, dynamic rules are combined with data mining techniques to produce valid anomalies.

The capability to correlate information across various data sources is paramount. Event correlation helps identify anomalies and behaviors that warrant additional investigation. Although anomaly-detection tools automate log anomaly detection, never underestimate that value of understanding of the system. Sometimes manual analysis is still required to detect anomalies.

Assets and Licensing

Asset tracking effectively manages assets so that the device location is known at all times. Applications that allow the use of an asset's ID or barcode provide reliable inventory control and an up-to-date status on assets. Automated asset discovery and management software can alert the organization to software license compliance violations.

Asset Management

Asset tracking and management is important to quickly identify a device when it is lost or stolen. Inventory control helps the organization keep a firm handle on how many devices are on hand and how many are issued, and to ensure that devices are returned upon employment termination. This is especially important when the organization issues items such external hard drives, USB drives, and mobile devices.

Asset management includes both hardware and software. Software asset management is similar to hardware asset management, but instead of tracking hardware, it tracks software licenses, versions, and installation location.

License Compliance Violation

When a company is unaware of the software that is installed and used in the environment, the resulting consequences can range from unauthorized software installations to large fines. Violating software licensing agreements is illegal and represents a significant business risk. For example, the city of Denver was threatened with a potential $10 million penalty for overuse of Oracle software after the city admitted it had violated its licensing agreement.

If Oracle had decided to cut off all connections that exceeded the initial agreement, the *A* in the CIA triad would have been affected and the software would not have been available to many users. Additionally, when software licensing agreements have been violated, the integrity of the software is at issue because the endpoints might not have received proper updates or patches.

Unauthorized Software

Unauthorized software increases the attack surface of the organization because, as with software installations that violate licensing agreements, the organization might not have the correct configuration, updates, and patches. A key way to prevent unauthorized software from being installed is application whitelisting. Another option is to implement strong security controls that block files with extensions of known executables.

General guidelines for proper asset management and licensing compliance include the following:

▶ Implement a policy for software acquisitions.

▶ Read all license agreements.

▶ Maintain an inventory list.

▶ Audit for compliance.

What Next?

If you want more practice on this chapter's exam objectives before you move on, remember that you can access all the Cram Quiz questions on the Pearson Test Prep software. You can also create a custom exam by objective. Note any objective you struggle with and go to that objective material in this chapter.

CHAPTER 10
Security Technologies

This chapter covers the following official Security+ exam objective:

2.4 Given a scenario, analyze and interpret output from security technologies.

- ▶ HIDS/HIPS
- ▶ Antivirus
- ▶ File integrity check
- ▶ Host-based firewall
- ▶ Application whitelisting
- ▶ Removable media control

- ▶ Advanced malware tools
- ▶ Patch management tools
- ▶ UTM
- ▶ DLP
- ▶ Data execution prevention
- ▶ Web application firewall

Essential Terms and Components

- ▶ antispam
- ▶ antivirus
- ▶ data execution prevention
- ▶ file integrity checker
- ▶ Group Policy

- ▶ host-based IDS (HIDS)
- ▶ host-based IPS (HIPS)
- ▶ pop-up blocker
- ▶ web application firewall

CramSaver

If you can correctly answer these questions before going through this chapter, save time by skimming the Exam Alerts in this chapter and then completing the Cram Quiz at the end of the chapter.

1. Explain the difference between NIDS and NIPS.

   _____

2. Explain how data execution prevention works.

   _____

3. Explain how UTM can help in enterprise risk mitigation.

   _____

Answers

1. Network intrusion detection systems (NIDS) examine data traffic to identify unauthorized access attempts and generate alerts. Network intrusion prevention systems (NIPS) solutions are intended to provide direct protection against identified attacks. A NIDS solution might be configured to automatically drop connections from a range of IP addresses during a DoS attack, for example.

2. Data Execution Prevention (DEP) is a security technology that can prevent security threats from executing code on a system. DEP works by preventing malware from executing in memory space reserved for operating system processes. DEP can be either hardware- or software-based.

3. Unified threat management (UTM) security appliances contain spam-filtering functions and can also provide antivirus protection. For example, the Barracuda Spam & Virus Firewall has antivirus protection built in. Another example is the Cisco Web Security appliance.

Security Technologies

The security hardware and assessment tools discussed in Chapters 7, "Network Components," and 8, "Software Tools," are specialized systems and tools used to protect systems from known vulnerabilities or weaknesses. The output of these tools requires careful interpretation. In many cases, you must consider several factors. The overall interpretation typically results in one of three options:

▶ Doing nothing, either because of a false positive or because the organization faces no significant risk

▶ Fixing or eliminating the vulnerability or security gap

▶ Accepting the security gap but implementing mitigating controls

This chapter discusses the process of analyzing and interpreting output from these security technologies so that you can select and act upon the proper option.

Host Technologies

Organizational attacks will likely increase in complexity, and all host devices must have some type of malware protection. Malicious code authors are using the dark parts of the Internet to create smarter, shadier, and stealthier threats. Worse, those authors can adeptly camouflage their work.

Firewalls and HIPS/HIDS

Desktops and laptops need to have layered security just like servers. However, many organizations stop this protection at antivirus software. In today's environment, that might not be enough to ward off malware, phishing, and rootkits. One of the most common ways to protect desktops and laptops is to use a host firewall. Firewalls can consist of hardware, software, or a combination of both. For the purposes of this section, the discussion focuses on software firewalls that can be implemented into the user environment.

The potential for hackers to access data through a user's machine has grown substantially because hacking tools have become more sophisticated and difficult to spot. This is especially true for telecommuters' machines. Always-connected computers, typical with cable modems, give attackers plenty of time to discover and exploit system vulnerabilities. Many software firewalls are available, and most operating systems come with them. Users can opt for the OS vendor firewall or can install a separate one.

As with most other solutions, firewalls have strengths and weaknesses. By design, firewalls close off systems to scanning and entry by blocking ports or nontrusted services and applications. However, firewalls must be properly configured. Typically, the first time a program tries to access the Internet, a software firewall asks whether it should permit the communication. Some users might find this annoying and, consequently, either disable the firewall or else allow all communications because they do not understand what the software is asking. Another caveat is that some firewalls monitor only for incoming connections, not outgoing ones. Monitoring outbound connections is important in the case of malware that "phones home." Without this type of protection, the environment is not properly protected. Remember that even a good firewall cannot protect you if users do not think before downloading and do not exercise a proper level of caution. No system is foolproof, but software firewalls installed on user systems can help make the computing environment safer.

Host-based IDS solutions involve processes running on a host monitoring event, application logs, port access, and other running processes to identify signatures or behaviors that indicate an attack or unauthorized access attempt. Some host-based IDS solutions involve deploying individual client applications on each host that relay their findings to a central IDS server, which then is responsible for compiling the data to identify distributed trends.

Table 10.1 details some strengths of host-based IDS solutions.

TABLE 10.1 **Strengths of Host-based IDS Solutions**

Strength	Description
Low number of false positives	Because host-based IDS solutions analyze logged events, both success and failure events can be monitored, with alerts generated only after passing a proper threshold.
Change monitoring auditing	Host-based IDS solutions can monitor individual processes on each host, including changes to the auditing process itself.
Non-network attack detection	Host-based IDS solutions can be used to monitor events on standalone systems, including access from the keyboard.
Encrypted communication monitoring	Some attacks make use of encrypted or encapsulated data communications, bypassing network-based IDS.
Cost savings by directed monitoring	Unlike network-based IDS systems, which must monitor all data traffic across the monitored network, host-based solutions require no additional hardware purchasing and can be deployed on systems that require only an IDS.
Single-point monitoring	Within large switched networks, network-based IDS solutions can be inadvertently or purposefully bypassed by using a secondary access route. Host-based IDS solutions are not limited to a particular communications path for detection.

Host intrusion prevention systems (HIPS) are a necessity in any enterprise environment. HIPS protects hosts against known and unknown malicious attacks from the network layer up through the application layer. HIPS technologies can be categorized by what they scan for, how they recognize an attack, and at what layer they attempt to detect the attack. HIPS systems encompass many technologies to protect servers, desktops, and laptops. They are often used as an all-in-one solution that includes everything from traditional signature-based antivirus technology to behavior analysis.

ExamAlert

The exam might use two different acronyms in intrusion detection questions: NIDS and NIPS. Network intrusion detection systems (NIDS) examine data traffic to identify unauthorized access attempts and generate alerts. Network intrusion prevention systems (NIPS) solutions are intended to provide direct protection against identified attacks. A NIDS solution might be configured to automatically drop connections from a range of IP addresses during a DoS attack, for example.

When using HIDS/HIPS, you leave the security decisions up to the user. When a program runs with elevated privileges or for the first time, it gives the user the option to either allow or block the action. The system is only as good as the user's response. Most users will choose the Allow option, inadvertently infecting the system.

In analyzing the output from HIDS and HIPS, the biggest issue is false positives. For example, HIPS monitors changes that other software programs attempt to make on the local system. Registry keys are problematic because many legitimate programs add a key upon installation, and this can be flagged as a malicious action.

Often a file integrity checker is included as part of an IDS. For example, Advanced Intrusion Detection Environment (AIDE) is a file and directory integrity checker for use on Linux-based systems.

ExamAlert

A file integrity checker tool computes a cryptographic hash such as SHA-1 or MD5 for all selected files and creates a database of the hashes. The hashes are periodically recalculated and compared to the hashes in the database, to check for modification.

The primary purpose of a file integrity checker is to detect when a file has been improperly modified. Probably the most well-known integrity checker tool is Tripwire.

As with HIDS/HIPS solutions, the biggest issue is false positives. Files often make changes when an application is updated or OS updates are applied. Keeping the hash database current is challenging, especially if it does not run in real time or is not run on a regular basis. File checkers serve a good purpose, of course, and even if the file integrity checker was run only once, the database information can still provide a baseline record to let you know whether a file was modified. This brings us to another problem with file integrity checkers: File integrity checkers should be run when the system is first installed, to create a clean database. If they are run after the system hits the Internet and a user starts downloading or installing files, the system might already be compromised. It is also a good security practice to store the hash database on a server offline so that attackers cannot alter it.

Antivirus and Other Host Protections

A necessary software program for protecting the user environment is antivirus software. *Antivirus* software scans for malicious code in email and downloaded files. Antivirus software actually works backward. Virus writers release a virus, it is reported, and then antivirus vendors reverse-engineer the code to find a solution. After the virus has been analyzed, the antivirus software can look for specific characteristics of the virus. Remember that, for a virus to be successful, it must replicate its code.

The most common method used in an antivirus program is scanning. Scanning searches files in memory, the boot sector, and the hard drive and removable media for identifiable virus code. Scanning identifies virus code based on a unique string of characters known as a signature. When the virus software detects the signature, it isolates the file. Then depending on the software settings, the antivirus software either quarantines it or permanently deletes it. Interception software detects virus-like behavior and pops up a warning to the user; however, because the software looks only at file changes, it might also detect legitimate files.

In the past, antivirus engines used a heuristic engine to detect virus structures or used integrity checking as a method of file comparison. A false positive occurs when the software classifies an action as a possible intrusion when it is actually a nonthreatening action.

ExamAlert

Heuristic scanning looks for instructions or commands that are not typically found in application programs. However, these methods are susceptible to false positives and cannot identify new viruses until the database is updated.

Antivirus software vendors update their virus signatures on a regular basis. Most antivirus software connects to the vendor website to check the software database for updates and then automatically downloads and installs them as they become available. Besides setting your antivirus software for automatic updates, you should set the machine to automatically scan at least once a week.

If a machine does become infected, the first step is to remove it from the network so that it cannot damage other machines. The best defense against virus infection is user education. Most antivirus software used today is fairly effective, but only if it is kept updated and the user practices safe computing habits, such as not opening unfamiliar documents or programs. Despite all this, antivirus software cannot protect against brand new viruses. Furthermore, users often do not take the necessary precautions and might even disable antivirus software because it interferes with programs that are currently installed on the machine. Be sure to guard against this type of incident.

Antispam software is often part of antivirus software or a host security suite. Antispam software can add another layer of defense to the infrastructure. The most common installation locations are at the email server or email client. When the software and updates are installed on a central server and pushed out to the client machines, this is a centralized solution. When the updates are left up to the individual users, you have a decentralized environment. The main component of antispam software is heuristic filtering. Recall from Chapter 7 that heuristic filtering has a predefined rule set that compares incoming email information against the rule set. The software reads the contents of each message and compares the words in that message against the words in typical spam messages. Each rule assigns a numeric score to the probability that the message is spam. This score is then used to determine whether the message meets the acceptable level set. If many of the same words from the rule set are in the message being examined, the message is marked as spam. Specific spam filtering levels can be set on the user's email account. If the setting is high, more spam will be filtered, but this can also trigger false positives and filter legitimate email as spam.

ExamAlert

Naturally, software cannot assign meaning to the words it examines. It simply tracks and compares the words used.

Additional settings can be used in the rule set. An email address that you add to the approved list is never considered spam. As mentioned previously, this is also known as a whitelist. Using whitelists gives you more flexibility in the type of email you receive. For example, adding the addresses of your relatives or friends to your whitelist allows you to receive any type of content from them. Conversely, an email address that you add to the blocked list is always considered spam. This is also known as a blacklist. Other factors might affect the ability to receive email on a whitelist. For example, if attachments are not allowed and the email has an attachment, the message might be filtered even if the address is on the approved list.

For additional host protection, many spyware eliminator programs are available. These programs scan your machine, similar to how antivirus software scans for viruses. As with antivirus software, you should keep spyware eliminator programs updated and regularly run scans. Configuration options on antispyware software allow the program to check for updates on a regularly scheduled basis. The antispyware software should be set to load upon startup and to automatically update spyware definitions.

Most online toolbars come with pop-up blockers. In addition, various downloadable pop-up blocking software programs are available; the browsers included with some operating systems, such as Windows, can block pop-ups. As with much of the other defensive software discussed so far, pop-up blockers have settings that you can adjust. Try setting the software to medium level so that it will block most automatic pop-ups but still allow functionality. Keep in mind that you can adjust the settings on pop-up blockers to meet organizational policy or to best protect the user environment.

Several caveats apply when using pop-up blockers. Remember that some pop-ups are helpful, and some web-based programmed application installers actually use pop-ups to install software.

> **ExamAlert**
>
> If all pop-ups are blocked, the user might not be able to install certain applications or programs.

You can also circumvent pop-up blockers in various ways. Most pop-up blockers block only the JavaScript; therefore, other technologies such as Flash bypass the pop-up blocker. On some Internet browsers, holding down the Ctrl key while clicking a link allows the browser to bypass the pop-up filter.

Data Execution Prevention

Data Execution Prevention (DEP) is a security technology that can prevent security threats from executing code on a system.

ExamAlert

DEP works by preventing malware from executing in memory space that is reserved for operating system processes. DEP can be either hardware- or software-based.

Hardware-based DEP prevents code from being executed by using processor hardware to set a memory attribute designating that code should not run in that memory space. Both Advanced Micro Devices (AMD) and Intel platforms have DEP hardware capabilities for Windows-based systems. Software-based DEP prevents malicious code from taking advantage of exception-handling mechanisms in Windows by throwing an exception when the injected code attempts to run. This essentially blocks the malware from running the injected code.

Software-based DEP works regardless of hardware DEP but is more limited. Its main function is to block malicious programs that use exception-handling mechanisms in Windows for execution. Figure 10.1 shows the configuration option in Windows for DEP.

FIGURE 10.1 **Windows DEP Configuration Option**

Sometimes older, non-malicious programs will trigger DEP because of faulty coding.

Enterprise Technologies

In addition to host-based technologies, enterprise technologies are used to protect the host environment. Some of the technologies that the previous section mentioned can also be used from an enterprise perspective. For example, with host-based IDS/IPS, the host applications can report back to a centralized location, making administration and control much easier.

Web Application Firewall

In response to the onslaught of web-based attacks, many organizations have implemented a web application firewall in addition to network firewalls. Put simply, a *web application firewall* is software or a hardware appliance used to protect the organization's web server from attack. A web application firewall can be an appliance, server plug-in, or filter that is used specifically for preventing execution of common web-based attacks such as Cross-Site Scripting (XSS) and SQL injection on a web server. Chapter 2, "Attack Types," covers these and other attack methods. Web application firewalls can be either signature based or anomaly based. Some look for particular attack signatures to try to identify an attack, whereas others look for abnormal behavior outside the website's normal traffic patterns. The device sits between a web client and a web server and analyzes communication at the application layer, much like a network stateful-inspection firewall. Web application firewalls are placed in front of a web server, in an effort to shield it from incoming attacks. Web application firewalls are sometimes referred to as *deep packet inspection (DPI) firewalls* because they can look at every request and response within web service layers.

UTM

Spyware, malware, worms, and viruses pose a serious threat to both system integrity and user privacy. The prevalence of such malicious programs can also threaten the stability of critical systems and networks. Vendors have responded by offering unified threat management (UTM) security appliances that contain spam-filtering functions and can also provide antivirus protection. For example, the Barracuda Spam & Virus Firewall has antivirus protection built in. Another example is the Cisco Web Security appliance. In these devices, updates are posted hourly to ensure that the latest definitions are in place. As with any appliance that provides multiple functions, UTM is a single point of failure. To maintain availability, organizations might need to have two units deployed in automatic failover mode.

A malware inspection filter is basically a web filter applied to traffic that uses HTTP. The body of all HTTP requests and responses is inspected. Malicious content is blocked, and legitimate content passes through unaltered. Passing files can be hashed and matched against the signatures stored in a malware signature database. Other approaches include caching files for running a heuristic scan later within the file cache. If the scan finds a malicious file within the file cache, the signature is inserted in the malware signature database so that it can be blocked in the future. The context for malware inspection comes from scanning downloaded content allowed by web access rules, to inspect web pages and files downloaded over HTTP from external websites.

Application Whitelisting

In application whitelisting, an organization approves software applications that are permitted to be used on assets. Only those approved applications can be run. The primary purpose of whitelisting is to protect resources from harmful applications. For example, in Microsoft environments, AppLocker can be used to whitelist applications based on the following three conditions:

▶ Publisher, for digitally signed files

▶ Path, which identifies an application by its location

▶ File hash, which uses a system-computed cryptographic hash

AppLocker rules merely allow or prevent an application from launching. They have no control over how an application behaves after it is launched.

ExamAlert

Application whitelisting is useful in preventing users and attackers from executing unauthorized applications, but it does not prevent malicious code from executing.

As with many other control technologies, false positives can result when applications are updated or new applications are installed. Whitelist information thus needs to stay updated. The administrative and maintenance overhead associated with complex solutions is therefore higher, as is the overhead when the whitelist is not automated.

Patch Management Tools

The patch management infrastructure of an organization includes all tools and technologies that are used to assess, test, deploy, and install software updates. This infrastructure is an essential tool for keeping the entire environment secure and reliable, so it must be managed and maintained properly. When it comes to managing your infrastructure, chances are good that your network includes many types of clients and thus might have different needs regarding updates and hot fixes.

> **ExamAlert**
>
> The most efficient way to update client machines is to use automated processes and products. Many vendors provide regular updates for installed products, managed through automated deployment tools or by manual update procedures that a system user carries out.

Regular maintenance is required to meet emerging security threats, whether you are applying an updated RPM (Red Hat Package Manager, a file format used to distribute Linux applications and update packages) by hand or using fully automated "call home for updates" options, such as those in many commercial operating systems and applications.

Systems Management Server (SMS) assists you in security patch management by scanning computers remotely throughout your network and reporting the results to a central repository. The results can then be assessed and compared to determine which computers need additional patches.

Microsoft maintains the Automatic Updates website, which contains all the latest security updates. Starting with Windows 10, the user configuration options have changed so that, by default, updates are automatically downloaded and installed. Unless the update setting is changed manually or through Group Policy, all client computers will receive updates as soon as they come out.

Advanced Malware Tools

Advanced malware, such as ransomware, is complex malware that includes components such as command and control, data exfiltration, and payload execution. This type of malware makes antivirus programs ineffective because the malware uses a variety of techniques to obscure and avoid detection.

> **ExamAlert**
>
> Advanced malware tools use behavior-based and context-based detection methods instead of signature-based methods.

Advanced malware tools employ various methods to detect malware, including sandboxing and indicator of compromise (IoC) capabilities. Characteristics include continuous analysis and big data analytics. The main point to remember about advanced malware tools is that they tend to be complex enterprise solutions that are built to protect organizations before, during, and after a malware attack. For example, Cisco's Advanced Malware Protection uses real-time threat intelligence and dynamic malware analytics, along with continuous analysis. This tool can be deployed on endpoints, networks, and firewalls, as well as in cloud-based environments.

DLP

DLP is necessary for organizations to meet regulatory compliance requirements, as well as to protect assets. To properly implement a DLP solution, an organization must understand what kind of sensitive data it has and then perform a risk assessment to determine what happens if data is exposed or falls into the wrong hands. The organization then can begin DLP product integration.

DLP products identify confidential or sensitive information through content analysis. Content analysis techniques include rule-based, database, exact file or data matching, partial document matching, and statistical analysis.

When a DLP solution is implemented across the whole organization in a blanket solution, a large number of false positives will result. It is important to accurately identify sensitive data, to lower false positives and fine-tune DLP policies, especially when rule-based or statistical analysis solutions are used. Implementing a DLP solution that is divided into different phases gives you a much better chance of reducing false positives.

> ### ExamAlert
>
> Although some DLP solutions provide remediation processes, an incident generally means that data has been lost. Be sure the proper protections are put into place.

Removable Media Control

As Chapter 7 discussed, most DLP solutions have the capability to control or manage removable media such as USB devices, mobile devices, email, and storage media. In many instances, banning USB and not permitting copying to devices is not an acceptable solution. For example, thumb drives were banned after malicious software infected thousands of military computers and networks. The ban was a major inconvenience for those who relied on thumb drives. Aircraft and vehicle technicians stored manuals on thumb drives. Medical records of wounded troops were sometimes stored on thumb drives and accompanied patients from field hospitals in foreign countries to their final U.S.-based hospitals. Pilots used thumb drives to transfer mission plans from operations rooms to aircraft computers.

When employees must use removable drives, finding a way to secure data that is taken outside a managed environment is part of doing business. Encryption is essential. Some disk encryption products protect only the local drive, not USB devices. Other encryption products automatically encrypt data that is copied or written to removable media. Other solutions include antivirus software that actively scans removable media and grants access to only approved devices. In a Windows environment, group policy objects (GPOs) offer another solution.

What Next?

If you want more practice on this chapter's exam objectives before you move on, remember that you can access all the Cram Quiz questions on the Pearson Test Prep software. You can also create a custom exam by objective. Note any objective you struggle with and go to that objective material in this chapter.

CHAPTER 11

Mobile Devices

This chapter covers the following official Security+ exam objective:

2.5 Given a scenario, deploy mobile devices securely.

- ▶ Connection methods
  - Cellular
  - Wi-Fi
  - SATCOM
  - Bluetooth
  - NFC
  - ANT
  - Infrared
  - USB
- ▶ Mobile device management concepts
  - Application management
  - Content management
  - Remote wipe
  - Geofencing
  - Geolocation
  - Screen locks
  - Push notification services
  - Passwords and pins
  - Biometrics
  - Context-aware authentication
  - Containerization
  - Storage segmentation
  - Full device encryption

- ▶ Enforcement and monitoring for:
  - Third-party app stores
  - Rooting/jailbreaking
  - Sideloading
  - Custom firmware
  - Carrier unlocking
  - Firmware OTA updates
  - Camera use
  - SMS/MMS
  - External media
  - USB OTG
  - Recording microphone
  - GPS tagging
  - Wi-Fi direct/ad hoc
  - Tethering
  - Payment methods
- ▶ Deployment models
  - BYOD
  - COPE
  - CYOD
  - Corporate-owned
  - VDI

Essential Terms and Components

- bring your own device (BYOD)
- choose your own device (CYOD)
- corporate owned, personally enabled (COPE)
- geofencing
- jailbreaking
- plain old telephone service (POTS)
- remote wipe
- rooting
- sideloading
- Short Message Service (SMS)
- tethering

CramSaver

If you can correctly answer these questions before going through this section, save time by skimming the Exam Alerts in this section and then completing the Cram Quiz at the end of the section.

1. Explain what measures can be taken to secure handheld mobile devices.

   _____

2. Explain what measures can be taken to secure applications on handheld mobile devices.

   _____

3. Explain what areas to consider when implementing a BYOD, CYOD, or COPE program.

   _____

Answers

1. A screen lock or passcode is used to prevent access to the device. Because passwords are one of the best methods of acquiring access, password length is an important consideration for mobile devices. As with data on hard drives, data on mobile devices can be encrypted. Remote wipe allows the handheld's data to be remotely deleted in case the device is lost or stolen. Mobile voice encryption allows executives and employees alike to discuss sensitive information without having to travel to secure company locations. If a mobile device is lost, GPS tracking can help find it.

2. Recommendations for application security include restricting which applications may be installed through whitelisting, digitally signing applications to ensure that only applications from trusted entities are installed on the device, and distributing the organization's applications from a dedicated mobile application store.

3. Formulating a BYOD, CYOD, or COPE program requires a security model that provides differentiated levels of access by device, user, application, and location. Implementing of a BYOD, CYOD, or COPE program and related policies deals with several realms, including general technical considerations, financial responsibility, technical support, and corporate liability.

Communication Methods

Just about every technology magazine and article published mentions a new mobile device, operating system release, or service provider merger. We are racing toward 5G (fifth generation of cellular wireless standards) technology that provides capabilities beyond today's 4G LTE mobile networks to accommodate real-time applications across billions of interconnected devices. Mobile devices contain a full file system, applications, and data. These devices need to be protected in a similar manner to regular computers. The composition of a mobile device is different than that of a regular computer because it is an embedded device, so security is a bit more challenging. There Mobile devices can communicate using several methods, including cellular, Bluetooth, Wi-Fi, and near field communication.

Cellular communications are the main mode that a mobile device uses to connect to the service provider network. A cellular network consists of the following components:

▶ The cellular layout (towers)

▶ The base station (connects to the tower)

▶ The mobile switching office (centerpiece of the operation)

▶ The public switched telephone network (PSTN)

Today wireless providers transmit voice calls over this traditional circuit-switched network design, and subscribers use the newer IP-based 4G LTE network to access the Internet and other data services.

ExamAlert

Two cellular voice technologies are currently used: Code Division Multiple Access (CDMA) and Global Systems Mobile (GSM). GSM is the dominant technology and is used in more than 100 countries, mostly in Asia and Europe.

GSM devices use a subscriber identity module (SIM) to communicate with the provider network. CDMA relies on a soft hand-off, allowing for fewer dropped calls and providing a more secure underlying technology. Currently, AT&T and T-Mobile run on GSM networks, while Sprint and Verizon Wireless use CDMA.

Long-Term Evolution (LTE) is used for faster data transfers and higher capacity. Different variations of LTE networks exist across carriers that use different frequencies. Sprint, T-Mobile, Verizon, and AT&T all have their own bands of LTE.

For users who lack traditional landline or cellular coverage, satellite communication (SATCOM) is an option for mobile device use. SATCOM uses an artificial satellite for telecommunication by transmitting radio signals. It can cover far more distance and wider areas than most other radio technologies. Because satellite phones do not rely on phone transmission lines or cellular towers, they function in remote locations. Most satellite phones have limited connectivity to the Internet and data rates tend to be slow, but they come with GPS capabilities to indicate your position in real time.

ExamAlert

Satellite phones generally require line-of-site with the sky to receive a signal for service. Dense structures such as buildings and mountains negatively affect the signal.

The most common satellite phones are Inmarsat, Iridium, Globalstar, and Thuraya. Satellite phones might or might not use a SIM card. For example, Globalstar does not use SIM cards, whereas Inmarsat and Iridium do.

Mobile devices also communicate via wireless signals. The most common are Wi-Fi and Bluetooth. Mobile Wi-Fi connectivity basically works just like connecting your laptop to a wireless router for Internet access. Through the device's Settings menu, you access available Wi-Fi networks. Additional capabilities of Wi-Fi are described later in this chapter.

Mobile devices are equipped for Bluetooth, which is short-range wireless connectivity. A common cellular use for Bluetooth is listening to music. Users also can pair a cellphone with a car infotainment center so they can talk on the phone "hands-free" while driving. In fact, drivers sometimes wear wireless headsets for the same purpose.

Bluetooth uses a spread spectrum, frequency hopping, full-duplex signal. An antenna-equipped chip in each device that wants to communicate sends and receives signals at a specific frequency range defined for short-range communication. For Bluetooth devices to communicate, they pair with each other to form a personal-area network (PAN) also known as a *piconet*. This process is done through discovery, with one device making itself discoverable by the other device. Bluetooth is a common mobile connectivity method because it has low power consumption requirements and a short-range signal.

> ### ExamAlert
> If Bluetooth is necessary for an organization's mobile devices, it should be set to nondiscoverable.

As defined in Chapter 2, "Attack Types," near field communication (NFC) is a set of standards for contactless communication between devices. NFC chips within mobile devices generate electromagnetic fields. This allows the device to communicate with other devices. Although NFC is considered contactless, in most practical uses, devices establish communication by being close or even touching. Contactless payment systems such as those found in coffee shops, train stations, and some supermarkets allow payment through the phone's NFC chip by simply holding the phone close to the payment terminal.

The NFC standard has three modes of operation:

▶ **Peer-to-peer mode:** Two mobile devices exchange data.

▶ **Read/write mode:** An active device receives data from a passive device.

▶ **Card emulation:** The device is used as a contactless credit card.

Most users are familiar with NFC as a feature of their smartphone. The NFC technology makes tap-and-go services such as Apple Pay and Google Wallet work. Apple will finally allow third-party application developers to access the NFC chip in the iPhone 7/Plus with the release of iOS 11 in fall 2017. To date, only Apple Pay has been allowed to use the NFC chip.

Many Android mobile devices natively support ANT+. ANT is a proprietary multicast wireless sensor technology developed by ANT Wireless.

> **ExamAlert**
>
> ANT technology enables you to view fitness and health monitoring data in real time on your mobile device. ANT is a wireless protocol for use over short distances by creating personal-area networks similar to Bluetooth.

For example, the ANT+ heart rate belt has the capability to communicate with Garmin sports watches. The main difference between ANT and Bluetooth is that ANT tends to have a lower power consumption rate and is geared toward sensor usage.

Another wireless mobile technology used for device communication over a short range is infrared (IR). IR transceivers are relatively cheap and provide short-range communication solutions. IR communication is most commonly used in mobile technology with IR cameras. IR technologies are quickly advancing, and soon smartphones might have IR cameras built in. The FLIR One is an example of an infrared camera attachment for an iPhone, Android smartphone or tablet. Recent Apple patents and design rumors indicate that future iPhones could use infrared technology to provide sophisticated cameras or embed a fingerprint scanner that uses infrared emitters and sensors. In 2015, Peel Technologies was granted a patent for IR technology that allows users to control their TV through their cellphone. Many vendors, such as Fluke, have developed IR cameras for night vision recording that can be used with a hand-held device. In addition, fire and police departments use IR for thermal sensing to find people in burning buildings and locate suspects at night or in heavily wooded areas.

The last communication method mobile devices use USB. USB communications allow a cellphone to be used as data, audio, or a mass storage device. The most popular use of USB communication is as a hotspot by connecting a laptop to the phone for Internet connectivity. Often this method is used for security reasons when Internet access is needed but only untrusted public Wi-Fi networks such as those in an airport, hotel, or coffee shop are available. USB connectivity also allows the mobile device to act as a modem, fax, or extension interface to plug into other USB devices. Additionally, the mobile USB port is used for connecting to forensic acquisition devices when information needs to be gathered for an investigation.

Mobile Device Management Concepts

The commingling of personal and organizational data on mobile devices is inevitable unless some safeguards are in place, such as keeping sensitive data only on secure servers and accessing it remotely using secure communication techniques outlined in the security policy. Another option is to separate the user and organizational data on the device. This limits business risk associated with enterprise data on mobile devices by compartmentalizing the data. It leaves employees' private information untouched and enforces policies and compliance at the application level.

Device, Application, and Content Management

Managing mobile device access and usage in an organization is a challenging endeavor. Businesses take various approaches to these handheld devices, and each business has different needs. Coupled with the fact that handheld technology moves at a much faster pace than computer technology, administrative nightmares can happen quickly. Mobile management is necessary to protect organizational assets at various levels, including the device itself, applications, and content. This section discusses these three concepts.

Mobile Device Management

Mobile device management (MDM) differs from mobile application management.

> **ExamAlert**
>
> MAM focuses on application management. MDM solutions provide a more comprehensive level of device management, managing applications and application data all the way down to device firmware and configuration settings.

MDM provides functionality and control over enterprise devices by allowing the enrollment of enterprise devices for management functions such as provisioning devices, tracking inventory, changing configurations, updating, managing applications, and enforcing policies. For example, VPN and passcode settings can be pushed out to users, saving support a lot of time and effort.

Both iOS and Android isolate applications and sensitive operating system features using a method called sandboxing. *Sandboxing* is a security method that keeps running applications separate. Although this design reduces the threat surface, malware or spyware can still potentially be installed. The mobile threat landscape increases with ambiguous applications, such as those that require excessive privileges or that access sensitive data. Too often, users click through permission requests when installing an application, giving full access to information on the device.

ExamAlert

In a corporate environment, applications can be managed by provisioning and controlling access to available mobile applications. This is called *mobile application management* (MAM).

Mobile Content Management

One of the biggest security risks involves applications that share data across environments such as Dropbox, Box, Google Drive, OneDrive, and iCloud. Organizations should carefully consider what apps to allow on their production networks.

When dealing with shared data, mobile content management (MCM) comes into play. MCM has several different definitions, but in the context of this discussion, it refers to access to content from mobile devices that are not managing content for a mobile-accessible website. An MCM system is used to control access to the file storage and sharing capabilities of services. These services can be cloud based, as with Office 365 and Box, or can function as middleware connecting the mobile device with existing data repositories. Many of these services are used for collaboration and better workflow by interfacing with other productivity applications. One such example is the capability for real-time coauthoring in Office Online through Box. As you can see, several layers of access exist, not only for the mobile user, but also for the applications and services. An MCM solution must incorporate identity management, so it offers control over what data end users are able to access. Many MCM products provide enhanced security features by using secure storage containers to secure organizational data downloaded to a mobile device.

Mobile Application Management

In addition to device security, you need to consider mobile application security. The primary attack points on mobile devices are data storage, key stores, the application file system, application databases, caches, and configuration files. Recommendations for application security include restricting which applications may be installed through whitelisting, digitally signing applications to ensure that only applications from trusted entities are installed on the device, and distributing the organization's applications from a dedicated mobile application store.

Access controls rely on credentials to validate the identities of users, applications, and devices. Credentials for applications such as usernames and passwords are stored in databases on the device, and many times the credentials are not encrypted. MDM solutions allow organizations to employ ways to manage application credentials that reduce the risk of compromised credentials, protect data more effectively, reduce operational costs, and improve efficiency.

Security best practices require strong authentication credentials so that a device can be trusted both on the enterprise's network and with access to enterprise applications. Passwords are one of the primary methods of acquiring access. For applications that require authentication, password length and complexity is an important consideration. Using strong passwords lowers the overall risk of a security breach, but strong passwords do not replace the need for other effective security controls.

> **ExamAlert**
>
> Using static passwords for authentication is a flawed security practice because passwords can be guessed, forgotten, or written down.

Mobile phones that are capable of running Java applets are common, so a mobile phone can be used as an authentication token. Many vendors offer one-time passwords (OTPs) as an authentication solution for Java-capable mobile devices. An application might require an OTP for performing highly sensitive operations such as fund transfers. OTPs can be either Short Messaging Service (SMS) generated or device generated. Device-generated OTPs are better than SMS OTPs because they eliminate the sniffing and delivery time issues associated with SMS OTP.

Managing mobile applications is a top security concern for organizations. Applications can be managed by whitelisting or blacklisting. The general concept behind application whitelisting differs from that of blacklisting. Instead of attempting to block malicious files and activity as blacklisting does, application whitelisting permits only known good apps.

ExamAlert

When security is a concern, whitelisting applications is a better option because it allows organizations to maintain strict control over the apps employees are approved to use.

Whitelisting apps can be controlled through various degrees of MDM polices. One of the most effective techniques for managing a whitelist is to automatically trust certain publishers of software. Whitelisting increases administrative overhead but offers better control. In a highly secure environment, maintaining a whitelist also entails exerting strict device control, preventing pairing over USB, deploying only in-house enterprise apps, and removing user capability to install or delete apps.

The concept of transitive trust for mobile devices is similar to identity federation but can cross boundaries of authentication domains at the application layer. Identity federation defines a set of technologies used to provide authentication (sign-in) services for applications. Transitive trusts enable decentralized authentication through trusted agents.

ExamAlert

Application transitive trusts and authentication can be used to improve the availability of service access, but they can present security issues. When applications interact with each other, restricting one application can create an environment for data to still leave the mobile device through the other application. An application with only local permissions could then send sensitive data through third-party applications to external destinations.

You might want to encrypt data from a mobile application for several reasons. Application data is encrypted to make sure that files exported to shared storage, such as the device's SD card, are not easily accessible to other applications. Some applications store sensitive data on mobile devices and require encryption. Application encryption is used to encrypt sensitive information stored by the app or to limit content accessibility to users who have the appropriate access key. Some encryption options for encrypting applications are to use MDM to allow the device itself to encrypt the data, thus enabling the application to provide its own encryption scheme, or to use an MDM application-wrapping technology that wraps system calls and automatically performs encryption and decryption on the application data.

When data is encrypted, procedures for key management and key recovery must be in place. Encryption key management systems can be console-based software or hardware appliances.

> **ExamAlert**
>
> Key management is intended to provide a single point of management for keys and to enable users to both manage the life cycle of keys and store them securely. It also makes key distribution easier.

Some mobile operating systems have built-in application key management features. In iOS, the keychain provides storage for encryption keys and certificates. After an application requests access to a keychain, it can store and retrieve sensitive data. Android has a similar keychain capability. On a mobile device, extracting a key and decrypting data is easy when the key is stored either with the encrypted data or as a file private to the application, especially if the device is rooted. This weakness could give unauthorized applications access to sensitive information. To better protect the keys, one solution is not to store keys, but to derive them from user-entered passwords.

Protections

The risk areas associated with mobile devices are physical risk (including theft or loss), unauthorized access risk, operating system or application risk, network risk, and mobile device data storage risk. To mitigate these risks, many of the same protections that apply to computers apply to mobile devices. Safeguards include screen locks, encryption, remote wipes, GPS tracking, and proper access. This section discusses these protections.

Screen Locks, Passwords, and PINs

All mobile phones have the capability to lock the phone, requiring the user to input a PIN/passcode or password to access the phone and applications. Figure 11.1 shows the passcode unlock screen of a mobile device. A screen lock prevents access to the device by requiring the user to input a PIN/passcode before granting access to the device content.

FIGURE 11.1 **Passcode Unlock Screen**

> **ExamAlert**
>
> PINs/passcodes and pattern locks are a basic form of security and a first line of defense. They should be required on all devices that access corporate resources.

This is similar to a password-protected screensaver on a computer. The lock code usually consists of a four-digit code or PIN. The pattern lock uses a pattern drawn on the screen instead of requiring a PIN/passcode. Android devices usually refer to this four-digit code as a PIN, whereas iOS devices refer to it as a passcode.

Figure 11.2 shows the pattern unlock screen of a mobile device.

FIGURE 11.2 **Pattern Unlock Screen**

Screen locks should be configured to automatically lock the device screen after a brief period of inactivity.

ExamAlert

A screen lock only locks users out of the user interface. It does not encrypt data.

A screen lock only locks users out of the user interface. It does not encrypt data. The number of times a user can attempt to input a password or code depends on the OS or corporate policy. For example, by default, the vendor might allow seven bad attempts before the device is locked. If the user fails to enter the correct passcode or password on the screen after seven attempts, the phone prompts the user to wait for 30 seconds before trying again. For a reset, the user is required to provide the original email account name and password used to set up the phone. Corporate policies might be more restrictive and tend to lean more toward five bad attempts before the phone becomes locked.

One caveat: You need your Gmail/Google account credentials to reset the security lock if you forget it, so be sure to set up a valid Gmail/Google account beforehand. Security Applications available in the Android application marketplace can add additional security measures.

Biometrics and Context-aware Authentication

Biometric authentication methods have been a part of security practices for a while. Biometric authentication is based on some type of physical characteristic that is unique to an individual. Biometric methods embedded in mobile phones include fingerprint, face, iris, voice, and signature recognition. Chapter 24, "Identity and Access Controls," discusses biometrics in greater detail, so this section does not define associated methods.

Apple leads the way with the implementation of mobile biometrics, but any Android device running since version 6.0 (Marshmallow) has support for fingerprint scanners. This is currently the most common biometric method used in mobile devices. In the future, facial and voice recognition biometrics will be more prevalent because they don't require the additional internal hardware that fingerprint biometrics do and are thus easier to implement. For example, face recognition does not require additional hardware because phones already have cameras. Similarly, voice recognition can be integrated into existing interactive voice response systems.

Biometric methods are not foolproof. Some fingerprint recognition technologies can be fooled by a copy of a person's fingerprint and facial recognition technologies can be defeated using a three-dimensional image of a user's social media photo. Still, biometric authentication is more secure than weak passwords. The best approach to mobile device security is to combine biometric authentication with a strong password or PIN.

A shift is taking place to context-aware authentication for mobile devices. The idea behind context-aware authentication is to use machine learning to determine whether a user resource request is correct or whether the account was compromised. In simplest terms, this is done by basing an access decision on what is considered learned normal behavior for the user. More technically, machine learning algorithms determine a confidence level that the access request is the real user and not a malicious actor. This is a more preferred method for authentication because environments are more fluid. Static methods do not have the capability to understand the context of a login attempt, calculate risk based on the context analysis, and change requirements appropriately.

The risks associated with cloud computing and BYOD have made context-aware security a more viable approach. Context-aware authentication more effectively protects against fraudulent and unauthorized access attempts because it assesses risk for resources that the user accesses. An extension of context-aware authentication is Google's Trust API, which uses proximity-based authentication on mobile devices. A trust score is calculated based on user-specific data points.

Remote Wiping

The data stored on a mobile device is worth a lot more than the device itself. Mobile devices carry a variety of personal and business information, so preventing them from getting into the wrong hands is critical. Many of today's smartphones support a mobile kill switch or remote wipe capability.

> ## ExamAlert
>
> *Remote wipe* allows the handheld's data to be remotely deleted if the device is lost or stolen. All the major smartphone platforms have this capability. The most common ways to remote wipe are using applications installed on the handset, working through an IT management console, and using a cloud-based service.

Several vendors offer services to Apple users that allow a remote wipe on a lost or stolen iPhone. Other options can erase all data on the iPhone after a certain number of failed passcode attempts. iPhone models using iOS 8 and above include hardware encryption, and all data is encrypted on-the-fly. This means that, for newer iOS versions, you do not need to actually wipe the phone's entire contents; remote wiping the encryption key works. Via remote administration, any BlackBerry Enterprise Server (BES) handset can be erased, reset to factory default settings, or set to retain its previous IT policy. This is done via the Erase Data and Disable Handheld command over the wireless network. By default, the device deletes all data after ten bad password attempts. Microsoft's My Phone Windows Phone service enables users to locate lost handhelds via GPS and erase their data remotely. To enable remote wipe on enterprise Android phones, the phone must have the Google Apps Device Policy app installed. This is similar in functionality to the remote control features for a

BES. Blackberry has extended its MDM capabilities to include Android and iOS within BES.

Remote wipes are not fail-safe. If someone finds the phone before the remote wipe occurs and either takes the device off the network or force-reboots and restores the device, that person can still recover sensitive data. In the case of BlackBerry devices, if the device is turned off or taken outside the coverage area, the remote wipe command is queued on the BES until the device can be contacted. If a user is removed from the BES before the command has reached the smartphone, data will not be erased from the device.

In addition to enterprise or built-in remote wiping tools, third-party products can be used to remove sensitive information. Some products are good solutions for a particular device type, whereas others cover all three major mobile device types. Most solutions can securely wipe media cards, be configured to wipe data remotely from a device that has been lost or stolen, automatically wipe the device clean when there is an attempt to insert another SIM card, or disable the phone functionality.

Geolocation, Geofencing, and Push Notifications

If a mobile device is lost, you can use geolocation to track it. Geolocation uses Global Positioning System (GPS) tracking to find the location of a device. More commonly, employers use this feature to locate employees through their devices.

ExamAlert

GPS tracking features can be used on company-issued devices as a deterrent to prevent the unauthorized, personal use of vehicles and the practice of taking unauthorized, unscheduled breaks.

In the case of serious crimes, such as the hijacking of an armored vehicle, GPS-enabled devices can help locate and recover the stolen vehicle and possibly save the lives of the guards.

The location of a mobile phone can be tracked in a few ways. Some applications use General Packet Radio Service (GPRS) and allow the GPS coordinates to be downloaded in a variety of formats. This makes it easy to import the coordinates into mapping software or create archives. Some software programs use a BES and BlackBerry's push technology to enable

IT administrators to track devices through a web-based mapping platform, accessible from any computer or cellphone with an Internet connection. Applications such as Phone Tracker and Find My Device can reveal any geographic locations visited.

Services also provide GPS tracking for devices. For example, the AccuTracking online GPS cellphone tracking service provides real-time device locations for a monthly service charge. Software is installed on the phone, a PC is used to add the device to the vendor's web interface, the phone communicates with the server, and then the device can be tracked through the vendor website.

The best example of geolocation is apps such as Foursquare that are installed on devices. These apps report device location to other app users so they can find nearby friends. Geofencing takes geolocation one step further and uses GPS coordinates or radio frequency identification (RFID) to define a geographic perimeter. When a device enters or exits the perimeter, an alert or notification is sent. The Find My Friends app through Apple allows geofence-based notifications, to inform users when someone enters or leaves a designated area. Geofencing is commonly used to alert local businesses to users' locations so they can use push advertising.

> **ExamAlert**
>
> Geofencing can be used on company-issued devices as a virtual time clock and can deter time theft.

Various geofencing applications provide automated employee time tracking. Some also integrate with third-party solutions such as QuickBooks so that employee time sheets can go directly into an accounting system for payroll.

Push technology began with BlackBerry. As soon as a device connected to the cellular network, new emails or updates were automatically pushed to the device. When a mobile app is installed, a user can opt in to receive notification whenever new content is available. A push notification is a brief message or alert that is sent through the installed application to the users who opted in for notifications. Push notification services have three main components:

▶ Operating system push notification service (OSPNS)

▶ App publisher

▶ Client app

Push notification services are often used in conjunction with geolocation and geofencing. Advertisers target users according to location by setting up geofenced messages. As soon as the device enters the geofence, an advertisement is pushed to the user's device. Most airline apps use push notifications to remind customers when to check in. Other businesses use geotargeting and assess user histories for push notifications.

Push notifications have become popular in the business environment for internal communication as a way to engage employees and to notify employees of important events or emergency situations. Push notifications can also help in HR processes such as onboarding, paperwork deadlines, recognition, training sessions, and benefit programs.

Storage Segmentation and Containerization

Malware and security risks such as data leakage have greatly increased in the past few years, putting at risk sensitive corporate information on user devices. Storage segmentation and containerization separate personal and business content on the device.

> **ExamAlert**
>
> Storage segmentation protects business content from security risks introduced by personal usage.

Security and data protection policies are applied to a segmented business container on a personal or company-owned device.

Segmentation and containerization are necessary when an organization has a BYOD environment. These approaches are used in conjunction with MAM as a way to apply policies to mobile devices. They provide an authenticated, encrypted area of the mobile device that can be used to separate sensitive corporate information from the user's personal use of the device. Additional benefits of containerization are capabilities to do the following:

- Isolate apps
- Control app functions
- Delete container information
- Remotely wipe the device

Applications such as those provided by Good Technology offer a security container that separates company and personal information. The enterprise container securely houses enterprise data and applications on the device, encrypting all data with strong Advanced Encryption Standard (AES) 192-bit encryption. This solution also encrypts any data in transit between the device and servers behind the organization's firewall.

The downside to segmentation and containerization is that they are third-party solutions and tend to be costly if an organization lacks the infrastructure required. Secure containers also can limit the apps that employees can use, for compatibility issues, and some solutions do not provide adequate protection because they rely on device-level controls. This means that if a weak passcode is used and the device is compromised, the data is also compromised.

Full Device Encryption

As with data on hard drives, data on mobile devices can be encrypted. However, this presents some challenges. For starters, entering complex passwords on small keyboards is difficult, and multifactor authentication is often unfeasible. In addition, the limited processing power of mobile devices means that the extra computation required for encryption could cause them to suffer performance issues. The always-on nature of these devices also means that encryption can easily break functionality. Another consideration is that because of the variety of devices, a company might have to implement multiple encryption methods. For example, BlackBerry Enterprise Server can be used to manage built-in data encryption, whereas Windows Android and Windows mobile devices can use a third-party encryption solution.

Mobile voice encryption can allow executives and employees alike to discuss sensitive information without having to travel to secure company locations. A number of options are available for voice encryption. Secusmart makes microSD flash cards that fit into certain mobile devices. The software is installed on the phone when the card is first inserted into a device. Another hardware option is *embedded encryption*, offered in KoolSpan's TrustChip solution. TrustChip consists of three main components:

- ▶ Embedded encryption software on the chip
- ▶ Linux-based management server
- ▶ TrustChip software development kit (SDK)

Third-party software applications can provide secure VoIP communication for iPhone, Android, and BlackBerry devices by using 256-bit AES military-grade encryption to encrypt calls between users. For added security, 1024-bit RSA encryption can be used during the symmetric key exchange. This type of application can provide VoIP connectivity for secure calls over several networks, including 3G, 4G, and Wi-Fi.

When using voice encryption software, keep in mind that it must be installed on each mobile phone to create a secure connection. You cannot create a secure encrypted connection between a device that has software installed and one that does not. The same is true for hardware solutions. For example, TrustChip encrypts voice only when the phone calls another TrustChip phone. The user sees an icon on the display informing him that the call is encrypted.

As with many other solutions, using voice encryption is not an end-all solution. Many commercially available mobile voice encryption products can be intercepted and compromised using a little ingenuity and creativity. Some applications can be compromised in as little as a few minutes.

Enterprise-level encryption solutions are also available and encompass various different devices. For example, Sophos Mobile Control provides device protection on iOS, Android, and Windows mobile devices. It can secure mobile devices by centrally configuring security settings and enabling lockdown of unwanted features; furthermore, it offers remote over-the-air locking or wiping if a device is lost or stolen, and it has a self-service portal that allows end users to register new devices and either lock or wipe lost or stolen phones.

Enforcement and Monitoring

Both enterprise administrators and users need to be aware of the growing risks associated with the convenience of having the Internet and the corporate network data in the palm of your hand. The most effective way to secure restricted data is not to store it on mobile devices. Of course, this is easier said than done.

MDM provides functionality and control over enterprise devices by allowing the organization to manage, secure, and monitor employee devices. MDM is one part of an overall enterprise mobility management (EMM) approach. EMM typically includes MDM, MAM, and identity management. This section covers these additional tools and technologies for mobile device enforcement and monitoring.

EMM allows an organization to perform advanced management of devices:

▶ Restricting changes to mobile network, Wi-Fi, or VPN access

▶ Controlling USB transfers, as well as transfers to external media

▶ Restricting users from sharing their location in an app

▶ Preventing users from resetting devices to factory reset

Jailbreaking and Rooting

Jailbreaking and rooting are similar because they alter the device capability. However, they have different functionality and apply to different mobile operating systems.

> **ExamAlert**
>
> Jailbreaking is associated with Apple devices. Rooting is associated with Android devices.

Apple controls iOS apps by using a private key for app authorization to protect the devices from risks associated with questionable apps. Users often want to run apps that they feel are safe but that Apple has not authorized. To run these apps, the device must be jailbroken. Essentially, jailbreaking removes the restriction that the device must run only Apple-authorized apps. Jailbreaking is done by installing a custom kernel that allows root access to the device through applications such as RedSn0w, which then uses a package manager such as Cydia to allow unauthorized application installation. Jailbreaking can be classified as either tethered or untethered. In tethered jailbreaking, the user must start the device from a software installation on a computer. In untethered jailbreaking, the device does not need to be connected to a computer in order to start; the device is altered so that it can start on its own.

With an Android OS, if a user wants to run apps that are not available on the Google Play Store, the choices are either rooting the device or sideloading the app. The next section discusses sideloading. Rooting allows complete access to the device. Root-level access allows a user to configure the device to run unauthorized apps and set different permissions by circumventing Android's security architecture.

Rooted or jailbroken devices pose a risk to organizational data. In a bring your own device (BYOD) environment, the organization might not know if or when users jailbreak or root devices. To mitigate this vulnerability, most EMM solutions have the capability to detect jailbroken and rooted devices. Detection is done by identifying indicators such as the existence of Cydia on iOS devices, or having an alert sent when an app invokes the superuser APK in Android systems. The device is then marked as noncompliant and can be removed from the network or denied access to enterprise apps. The associated data authorized for the device then can be prohibited.

Custom Firmware, Carrier Unlocking, and OTA Updates

Technically, there is difference between rooting and jailbreaking a device and loading custom firmware or unlocking a device. The most common scenario for installing custom firmware installation on a device is for forensic acquisition. Most forensic tools require a deep level of access to the device, so the acquisition process can sometimes involve the installation of custom firmware.

Users might want to load custom firmware on their devices so that they can use a different language, switch from the manufacturer-induced skin to a different look, or get rid of the unnecessary applications installed by default so they can free up space on the device. Installing a custom ROM requires using a custom bootloader and a custom recovery manager. Root access is not necessarily required. Alternately, the Replicant OS, a free Android distribution, can give users the flexibility they are looking for in custom firmware.

Carrier unlocking is the process by which users modify a device so that they do not have to use the original carrier or service provider. Carrier unlocking is done mainly because most service providers require two-year contracts with customers. Many consumers complained about this practice. In 2014, President Obama signed the Unlocking Consumer Choice and Wireless Competition Act, which makes it legal for consumers to unlock their phones.

> **ExamAlert**
>
> Unlocking allows users to select whatever wireless provider they choose without having to purchase a new device.

When a device is unlocked, the new service provider must have compatible technology with the device hardware. For example, an original Verizon device using CMDA technology cannot necessarily be activated on an AT&T GSM network because the device might not have the required SIM slot.

Most U.S. carriers will unlock the device upon request, as long as the contract is fully paid, so the organization might not be aware of changes, especially in a BYOD environment. EMM solutions allow the organization to look at device monitoring and usage thresholds that indicate a carrier switch. When an organization is reimbursing employees for associated costs, the organization can help the employee choose the right option when switching carrier plans, as long as it is done legally instead of through jailbreaking or rooting the device.

Mobile devices have the capability to receive and install over-the-air (OTA) systems and application updates that are pushed over Wi-Fi to the device. Device users are notified that an update is available so that they can either install or postpone the update. OTA firmware updates are done through the device's recovery partition, which has the required software to unpack the update package and run it on the system.

OTA updates can be managed through EMM. For example, with an Android OS, a device policy controller (DPC) app can be deployed to mobile devices. This gives the organization control over when the OTA updates are installed through a local OTA policy. When the OTA policy is set, the updates are installed according to the policy settings and users have no control over when the updates are installed; users also are not notified of updates.

Third-Party App Stores and Sideloading

Less invasive processes than rooting or jailbreaking a device are also available to users who want to install apps that are not authorized by their OS vendor. For example, users can download from third-party apps stores such as Amazon, Getjar, Appbrain, and Appolicious. On Android devices, users can easily install third-party apps by changing the option in the device's security settings, even though it is disabled by default. Third-party apps stores are problematic for organizations because often the apps are not properly vetted. To prevent downloaded apps from third-party app stores, EMM solutions can be configured to not allow users to modify settings or to allow only whitelisted apps to be installed on the device. Another option, albeit a more costly one, is for organizations to provide their own enterprise app store. As part of a mobile application management (MAM) strategy, an organization can provide its own app store, hosting IT-approved apps and allowing only apps from the enterprise app store to be installed on the device.

Sideloading is a process in which a user goes around the approved app marketplace and device settings to install unapproved apps. Before sideloading can be done an Android device, users must enable the installation from unknown sources in the system security settings. Sideloading on an Android device can be done one of three ways:

▶ **Manual:** Using a USB connection and a file manager application

▶ **Android debug bridge (ADB):** Using a command-line installation similar to Linux-based installs

▶ **AirDroid:** Using a drag-and-drop application installer

Sideloading on iOS devices can be done by using the Cydia Impactor tool. As with the installation of third-party app stores, sideloading an app poses a risk to the organization because those apps have not been vetted and thus could introduce malicious software and compromise sensitive corporate data. The organizational protections are the same as for third-party apps. MAM configurations prevent the installation of apps from untrusted sources. EMM implementations can further lock down the device by applying policies that are capable of deleting apps and wiping a device.

Removable Storage and USB OTG

Most mobile devices have an external media card used for storage. Most devices support USB Host Mode, also known as USB on-the-go (OTG). USB OTG is a standard that enables mobile devices to communicate with each other through a USB cable that users attach. Examples of USB and USB OTG functions include importing camera data from the device, copying files onto a USB drive, and attaching a full-size USB keyboard or mouse. To mitigate this vulnerability, most EMM solutions can prevent users from accessing unauthorized sources such as USB storage or file-sharing sites.

The data on the media card needs to be encrypted as well. Full device encryption is an added feature that enables users to secure sensitive information on a mobile device's removable flash memory storage card. The data is accessible only when the card is installed in a particular mobile device. If the card is ever lost or stolen, the information remains secure because it is encrypted.

Enforcement for Normal Device Functions

Many organizations produce and store proprietary information. Allowing employee-owned devices on the network that can instantly share location, take pictures, text, and record video and audio poses security risks. Policies should cover the use of camera, video, texting, and audio recordings as they relate to the organizational work environment.

Geotagging location services are based on GPS positions and coordinates.

> **ExamAlert**
>
> The security risks associated with geotagging are unwanted advertising, spying, stalking, and theft. Some social networking sites and services show the location of logged use.

Geotagging allows location data to be attached to images, videos, SMS messages, and website postings, providing permanent and searchable data. Geotagging can be limited by turning off features in social network accounts, disabling location services, and selectively using location features.

Texting and sending pictures via text (MMS) is a growing concern for most organizations. Excessive texting during work hours can interfere with employee productivity. Texting policies might be required in situations where personal information could be disclosed, such as health or financial services. The Final Omnibus Rule of March 2013 introduced a new HIPAA texting policy. The revisions apply not only to the healthcare providers, but also to third-party healthcare industry service providers and business associates. The HIPAA texting policy was written to address the risk associated with sending patient health information via SMS and placing patient health information on mobile devices. In environments where SMS/MMS communications contain sensitive information, encrypted messaging must be used to keep these communications secure and to comply with regulations. Employees should be made aware of policies on corporate texting and pictures sent via text (MMS).

Unused features on the mobile devices should be disabled. Depending on the organizational needs, disabling other features on the devices might be advisable as well. For example, if an employee works with highly confidential or trade secret information, the organization might require that the camera and microphone on corporate devices be disabled.

> **ExamAlert**
>
> A comprehensive mobile policy should clearly state restrictions on the use of cameras, video, audio, or location sharing and other applications and services.

Employees might be trustworthy, but if the device is lost or stolen, proprietary information can still be compromised. In high-security areas, employees might have to surrender the mobile device if it is equipped with any of these features. As with most of the features discussed in this section, the settings associated with them can be disabled or controlled through EMM implementations.

Wi-Fi Methods, Tethering, and Payments

Wi-Fi has been a mobile communication method for a while. A mobile device can use two different Wi-Fi methods to connect to another device: direct and ad hoc. Both allow two devices to directly connect without the use of a wireless access point.

The principle behind the Wi-Fi Direct standard is a quick connection with effortless setup through peer-to-peer wireless networking. When Wi-Fi Direct is used, one device acts as a wireless access point and the other devices connect to it. The device acting as the access point is called the Group Owner (GO). Other devices connect to it as clients in station mode. Devices discover each other the same way a device finds a wireless network. Connected devices are not limited to Wi-Fi Direct, so devices that are not Wi-Fi Direct enabled can connect as well. Wi-Fi Direct uses the Wi-Fi Protected Setup (WPS) protocol to exchange credentials, so users do not need to know a shared password. To connect, the user only needs to enter a PIN code or push a device button. Wi-Fi Direct can be used to perform such tasks as print to a wireless printer, transfer photos between devices, or send files to a computer. Wi-Fi Direct is made for easily connecting a small number of devices for a short period of time.

Wi-Fi Direct device connections can happen anywhere, anytime, and do not require access to a Wi-Fi network. The use of WPS is a major security concern because it has been proven insecure. The Wi-Fi Direct Alliance recommends that, when using Wi-Fi Direct, device connections be protected by WPA2 instead of WPS.

An ad hoc mobile network (MANET) is part of the IEEE 802.11 standard called Independent Basic Service Set (IBSS). No hierarchy governs IBSS devices, so all the devices are called nodes. The IBSS nodes regularly send beacons to announce the existence of the network. IBSS networks have no security requirement, so security can range from no encryption to WEP, WPA, or WPA2. The concept of MANET is simple, but because many configuration options are available, inexperienced users tend to find it hard to use.

ExamAlert

An ad hoc mobile network is more flexible than one that uses Wi-Fi Direct because it can be used with upper-level protocols to create large networks.

MANET is most often used by the military and emergency services. It can also be used by education institutions for classrooms and labs.

Depending on the manufacturer of the organization's WLAN equipment, organizational policy might control the capability to use Wi-Fi Direct. For example, Cisco Wireless LAN controllers can be used to configure the Wi-Fi Direct Client Policy to disallow this type of connection, or to allow the connection but not allow the setup of a peer-to-peer connection. In Windows networks, MANET can be controlled through group policy.

Tethering is sharing a device's Internet connection with other devices through Wi-Fi, Bluetooth, or a USB cable. This technique basically allows the device to act as a modem. Tethering is used when no other method exists for connecting to the Internet. Tethering can be especially useful when traveling, but it has some downsides: Speed can be slower, the battery of the tethering device drains more quickly, and, depending on the carrier, additional data charges might apply.

Organizational policy on tethering might differ from restrictions on mobile device use in general. Unsecured public Wi-Fi networks are not considered safe. An organization might prefer to absorb the extra cost and keep data more secure by sending it directly through an employees-tethered mobile device. When this is the case, the additional cost must be monitored, especially when employees travel overseas. EMM solutions can help keep an eye on costs associated with tethering and provide flexible tethering controls.

Users can also use mobile devices to make payments for meals and other expenses and to transfer money. Mobile payments can be made in several ways, including with mobile wallets, contactless payments, carrier billing, and card payments. Mobile payments generally fall into several categories:

▶ **Daily transactions:** Most often associated with a mobile wallet

▶ **Point-of-sale (POS) payments:** Goods and services vendors

▶ **Carrier payments:** Billed directly through your carrier, most often associated with charitable donations via text

▶ **Mobile card reader:** Often associated with small businesses that accept credit card payment via a tablet

Each type of payment has apps used for the payment processing. For example, POS systems often support Apple Pay, Samsung Pay, and Android Pay. The NFC reader in the POS terminal takes care of the payment details by merely holding the device near the POS. When organizations issue employees company credit cards and want to mitigate vulnerabilities associated with mobile payment systems, MDM or EMM systems provide the required control. This is done by disabling the services or apps associated with mobile payment systems.

Deployment Models

More employees are using personal devices for critical job functions, requiring organizations to seek better control over mobile devices and to implement solutions such as MDM and MAM. Mobile device management, secure access to data, and application control all require a holistic security approach. Human factors combined with role-based management can help protect the organization against data loss and threats, as well as ensure that the organization is meeting compliance requirements. This section discusses the current mobile deployment models and consideration factors.

BYOD, CYOD, COPE and Corporate-owned Devices

Bring your own device (BYOD) focuses on reducing corporate costs and increasing productivity by allowing employees, partners, and guests to connect to the corporate network for access to resources. BYOD gives employees freedom to choose the device, applications, and services that best meet their needs. When employees can use their own personal devices, productivity usually increases. From a management perspective, BYOD has increased administrative overhead because many different devices are in use and the organization has no control over the software or applications users have installed.

Employers sometimes offer reimbursement for business use of a personal device. In some states, the reimbursement is required by law. For example, California Labor Code Section 2802 states that employers are required to reimburse employees for necessary expenses, including all reasonable costs. This translates to reimbursement for the percentage of the cost associated with business calls.

In *choose your own device* (CYOD), the organization controls which devices an employee can choose by providing a list of approved devices. This option is more restrictive that BYOD and gives the organization greater control over which devices are allowed on the network. The flexibility in this option is that employees still have some control over the device because they are still responsible for the cost and maintenance of the device. In most implementations of CYOD, the organization purchases the device and pays the data usage costs. Device ownership thus rests with the organization, so employees must surrender their devices when they leave or are terminated. This method of managing user devices can reduce the hardware and management costs of corporate-owned devices, but it cannot completely eliminate them.

With corporate-owned devices, organizations issue the employees a device they can use. This model is sometimes called use what you are told (UWYT). In this model, the mobile devices available for use are predetermined. Users are issued a device based on corporate policy, which often depends on the role of the employee. Corporate-owned devices provide a clear separation of employees' personal and business lives. This is often inconvenient for users because they are required to carry two mobiles, one for each function.

Corporate-owned, personally enabled (COPE), or company-issued business only (COBO), is similar in principle to corporate-owned devices but allows personal use of the device. With COPE, the devices are the organization's responsibility, so monitoring policies must be in place and devices must be kept up to date. As with corporate-owned devices, this deployment model allows the organization to disconnect devices from the network in case of a compromise or malware infection. Financial institutions and healthcare providers tend to choose COPE to meet regulatory compliance requirements. Because the organization has to supply, update, and monitor the device, the cost of this implementation method is much higher than with BYOD or CYOD; it is generally not cost effective for small businesses.

VDI

Virtual desktop infrastructure (VDI) is the process by which an organization hosts virtual desktops on a centralized server. Generally, employees use a client app to securely connect to the virtual infrastructure that hosts a user's desktop. VDI allows the organization to securely publish personalized desktops for each user through a managed infrastructure. Organizations are extending their VDI to mobile devices, referred to as virtual mobile infrastructure (VMI) or mobile VDI. In this implementation model, instead of using a hosted desktop, the user receives a hosted mobile device OS. There are two different methods for setting up a client to access a mobile VDI:

▶ **Client-based mobile VDI:** A mobile VDI client must be installed on each mobile device.

▶ **Browser-based mobile VDI:** A web browser is used to access a mobile VDI client.

Mobile VDI is especially useful in BYOD environments because it gives access to both organizational and personal data without the inherent risk of commingled data. Security for EMM and BYOD is already built into mobile VDI because data and applications are stored on the organization's infrastructure, there is little to no data transfer to the mobile device, and users might have no need for client software on the mobile device. This can reduce the risk associated with lost devices and the need for remote wipes on those lost devices. However, if a mobile VDI experiences an infrastructure failure, users will not be able to access resources.

Deployment Strategies

Implementing a mobile deployment program and associated policies requires considering several realms, including general technical considerations, financial responsibility, technical support, and corporate liability. BYOD, CYOD, and COPE deployments vary among organizations.

> **ExamAlert**
>
> Formulating a BYOD, COPE, or CYOD program requires a security model that provides differentiated levels of access by device, user, application, and location.

One of the primary differences in BYOD, CYOD, and COPE deployment is the associated cost. For COPE and CYOD, all costs reside with the organization; BYOD users pay their own device costs but might receive reimbursement for associated business costs. In addition to the cost, organizations must address some overall challenges related to securing sensitive data in any deployment method, to protect organizational resources.

Architecture/Infrastructure Considerations

Implementing a BYOD, CYOD, or COPE program requires planning and understanding the access methods and device management options for the devices. In addition to looking at the 802.11 infrastructure, organizations should consider bandwidth, network saturation, and scalability. Devices might need to be manually provisioned, but the design architecture usually includes some type of MDM solution so that security, management of mobile endpoints, self-service for enterprise applications, and onboarding can more easily be managed. Most MDM solutions offer management capabilities through virtualization architecture, identity-based access and provisioning, device identification, authentication, authorization, single sign-on, and policy enforcement. When choosing a centralized MDM strategy, the organization can use a solution offered by a mobile device vendor or use a product from a third party. Both approaches are similar and use a typical client/server architecture.

Adherence to Corporate Policies and Acceptable Use

Many organizations use a self-service method through a preconfigured profile to minimize IT intervention. This offers a simplified way to identify domain user groups that are permitted to onboard their devices. When an employee is terminated, retires, or quits, segregating and retrieving organizational data and applications might be difficult. The BYOD, CYOD, or COPE policy should address how data and corporate-owned applications will be retrieved in this situation. In some instances, the organization might opt for a total device wipe.

When implementing a BYOD, CYOD, or COPE policy, employees need to be made aware of, understand, and accept the BYOD policy as it relates to an organization's policies. Many organizations stipulate that they have the right to wipe a device at any time and will not assume responsibility for any loss of data if the device is wiped. Some organizations require employees to install software that provides additional security. Corporate policies might ban rooted or jailbroken devices, as well as the use of file-sharing sites such as Dropbox, Google Drive, OneDrive, or iCloud. Users who are part of the BYOD, CYOD, or COPE program are expected to adhere to all corporate policies.

In a BYOD, CYOD, or COPE environment, an organization might choose to use a personal device use policy in addition the organizational acceptable use policy. A personal device use policy defines responsibilities, guidelines, and terms of use for employee-owned devices accessing the organizational network. Often a personal device use policy is created to address expense limitations and because access to the Internet, applications, and peer-to-peer file sharing is subject to different policies when the use is for personal purposes instead of corporate purposes.

Employee consent or user acceptance of the BYOD, CYOD, or COPE policy helps protect the organization in case security measures need to be implemented that affect the device. These measures can include seizing the device and deleting all device data.

> **ExamAlert**
>
> Employees should provide written consent to all terms and conditions of the BYOD, CYOD, or COPE policy so that the organization can easily refute any claim of policy unawareness.

The signed agreements should be kept on file in case the organization needs to take future action that pertains to the device.

Legal Concerns

Legal concerns for implementing a BYOD, CYOD, or COPE program and related policies include whether the policies will be enforceable, whether data privacy laws will restrict security controls and required user consent, whether laws and regulations could limit the ability to audit and monitor activity on personally owned devices, and consent to access the device for business purposes. Furthermore, some legal ramifications relate to determining the liability of the organization for application usage, licensing, removing sensitive data and organizational applications, and wiping data from a personal device. All legal concerns should be addressed prior to program implementation.

Privacy

Data privacy is a concern (not only for the individual, but also for the organization) when employees bring their own devices to the corporate network. This is especially true in organizations that are bound by legal requirements regarding the storage of private personal information, such as in the medical and financial industries. Privacy concerns should be addressed in BYOD, CYOD, or COPE policies. The BYOD, CYOD, or COPE policy might need to contain language prohibiting or limiting remote access for certain categories of sensitive data.

Employees should be notified of the organization's monitoring and personal data access capabilities. The BYOD, CYOD, or COPE policy should clearly disclose how the organization will access an employee's personal data. If the organization offers device data backup, the policy also should state whether personal data will be stored on backup media. In many cases, the organizational BYOD, CYOD, or COPE policy clearly indicates that the organization does not guarantee employee privacy when an employee chooses to be part of the BYOD, CYOD, or COPE workforce.

Data and Support Ownership

Data ownership on an employee-owned device used on a corporate network becomes tricky because of the combination of corporate data and personal data. Many organizations approach this issue by using either containerization or MDM solutions. When formulating a BYOD, CYOD, or COPE policy, the organization should clearly state who owns the data stored on the device, specifically addressing what data belongs to the organization. The policy should include language stipulating that the organization will remotely wipe data if the employee violates the BYOD, CYOD, or COPE policy; terminates employment; or purchases a new device. Some organizations also reiterate user responsibility for backing up any personal data stored on the device.

Many organizations save IT support costs because implementing BYOD programs entail fewer device support obligations. Support time is minimal and mostly limited to helping employees initially get the devices up and running on the network. Most BYOD policies state that employees are responsible for voice and data plan billing and for maintenance of their devices, whereas CYOD and COPE policies establish what types of devices are permitted to access the network and what support is provided.

Patch and Antivirus Management

When corporate data resides on a personal device, it faces risk from viruses, malware, and OS-related vulnerabilities.

> **ExamAlert**
>
> In a BYOD environment, the organization sets minimum security requirements or mandates security as a condition for giving personal devices access to network resources.

Policy should clearly state the requirements for installing updates, patches, and antivirus software. Policy options might include the approval of updates and patches or specific antivirus software, as well as mandatory reporting of any suspected instances of malware infection. In addition, the policy might include material on policy compliance, state that IT may push updates as required, and detail the responsibility for antivirus software costs.

Forensics

A key issue in BYOD, CYOD, and COPE is how to handle device data when an investigation is required. Any captured data will likely include an employee's personal information along with corporate data. Although tools can be used to record WLAN data from capture points for forensics, many times the device itself requires imaging. Organizations can try to limit the scope of an investigation or perform data capture when a personal device is involved. However, prevailing litigation consequences for failing to preserve data might take precedence.

> **ExamAlert**
>
> In a BYOD, CYOD, or COPE environment, legal requirements take precedence. In an investigation, the employee might be temporarily unable to use the device during the investigation period.

Organizations need to address this scenario when creating BYOD, CYOD, or COPE policies, being sure that proper BYOD, CYOD, and COPE incident response procedures are formulated and communicated to the users.

What Next?

If you want more practice on this chapter's exam objectives before you move on, remember that you can access all the Cram Quiz questions on the Pearson Test Prep software. You can also create a custom exam by objective. Note any objective you struggle with and go to that objective material in this chapter.

CHAPTER 12

Secure Protocols

This chapter covers the following official Security+ exam objective:

2.6 Given a scenario, implement secure protocols.

- ▶ Protocols
  - DNSSEC
  - SSH
  - S/MIME
  - SRTP
  - LDAPS
  - FTPS
  - SFTP
  - SNMPv3
  - SSL/TLS
  - HTTPS
  - Secure POP/IMAP

- ▶ Use cases
  - Voice and video
  - Time synchronization
  - Email and web
  - File transfer
  - Directory services
  - Remote access
  - Domain name resolution
  - Routing and switching
  - Network address allocation
  - Subscription services

Essential Terms and Components

- ▶ Domain Name Service (DNS)
- ▶ File Transfer Protocol (FTP)
- ▶ Hypertext Transfer Protocol (HTTP)
- ▶ Hypertext Transfer Protocol over Secure Sockets Layer (HTTPS)
- ▶ Lightweight Directory Access Protocol (LDAP)
- ▶ Network Time Protocol (NTP)
- ▶ Secure Hypertext Transfer Protocol (S-HTTP)
- ▶ Secure/Multipurpose Internet Mail Extensions (S/MIME)
- ▶ Secure Shell (SSH)
- ▶ Secure Sockets Layer (SSL)
- ▶ Simple Network Management Protocol (SNMP)
- ▶ voice over IP (VoIP)

CramSaver

If you can correctly answer these questions before going through this chapter, save time by skimming the Exam Alerts in this chapter and then completing the Cram Quiz at the end of the chapter.

1. Explain how HTTP can be secured.

   _____

2. Describe how voice and video communications can be secured.

   _____

3. Provide a use case for securing directory services with LDAPS.

   _____

Answers

1. Basic web connectivity using Hypertext Transfer Protocol (HTTP) occurs over TCP port 80, providing no security against interception of transacted data sent in clear text. An alternative to this involves the use of SSL transport protocols operating on port 443, which creates an encrypted pipe through which HTTP traffic can be conducted securely.

2. SRTP (Secure Real-Time Transport Protocol, or Secure RTP) is an extension to RTP that incorporates enhanced security features. As with RTP, it is intended particularly for voice over IP (VoIP) or video network communications. SRTP encrypts RTP data for unicast and multicast applications. This adds confidentiality, message authentication, and replay protection to the communication exchange.

3. Organizations generally use LDAPS to protect the authentication session when an application authenticates with Active Directory Domain Services (AD DS). A well-documented use case for using LDAPS with AD-integrated applications is Oracle PeopleSoft.

Secure Protocols

The network infrastructure is subject to myriad internal and external attacks through services, protocols, and open ports. Older protocols that are still in use might leave the network vulnerable. Protocols such as Simple Network Management Protocol (SNMP) and Domain Name Service (DNS) that were developed a long time ago and have been widely deployed can pose security risks, too. You must understand how to properly secure these protocols, especially if the network has been in existence for a while and newer or more secure versions have been developed. This section helps you understand how to use the proper network implementation of secure protocols to protect and mitigate threats against network infrastructure.

Securing Web Protocols

Basic web connectivity using Hypertext Transfer Protocol (HTTP) occurs over TCP port 80. No security is provided against the interception of transacted data sent in clear text. Web protocol security is usually implemented at two layers: the transport layer and the application layer.

ExamAlert

To secure against web communication interception, transport layer security protocols such as Secure Socket Layer (SSL) and Transport Layer Security (TLS) are used.

A more secure way to conduct web communication involves using SSL transport protocols operating on port 443, which creates an encrypted pipe through which HTTP traffic can be conducted securely. To differentiate a call to port 80 (http://servername/), HTTP over SSL calls on port 443 using HTTPS as the URL port designator (https://servername/).

HTTPS was originally created by the Netscape Corporation. It used a 40-bit RC4 stream encryption algorithm to establish a secure connection encapsulating data transferred between the client and web server. However, it can also support the use of X.509 digital certificates to allow the user to authenticate the sender. Now 256-bit encryption keys have become the accepted level of secure connectivity for online banking and electronic commerce transactions.

ExamAlert

An alternative to HTTPS is the Secure Hypertext Transfer Protocol (S-HTTP), which was developed to support connectivity for banking transactions and other secure web communications. S-HTTP supports DES, 3DES, RC2, and RSA2 encryption, along with CHAP authentication; however, the early web browser developers (for example, Netscape and Microsoft) did not adopt it, so it remains less common than the HTTPS standard.

Although HTTPS encrypts communication between the client and server, it doesn't guarantee that the merchant is trustworthy or that the merchant's server is secure. SSL/TLS is designed to positively identify the merchant's server and encrypt communication between the client and the server. When organizations use OpenSSL, version 1.0.1g or newer must be used, to avoid vulnerability to the heartbleed bug.

Secure Sockets Layer (SSL) protocol communications occur between the HTTP (application) and TCP (transport) layers of Internet communications.

Millions of websites use SSL to protect their online transactions with their customers. SSL is a public-key-based security protocol that Internet services and clients use for authentication, message integrity, and confidentiality. The SSL process uses certificates for authentication and encryption for message integrity and confidentiality. SSL establishes a *stateful connection*, in which both ends set up and maintain information about the session itself during its life. This is different from a stateless connection, in which no prior connection has been set up. The SSL stateful connection is negotiated by a handshaking procedure between client and server. During this handshake, the client and server exchange the specifications for the cipher that will be used for that session. SSL communicates using an asymmetric key with a cipher strength of 40 or 128 bits.

SSL works by establishing a secure channel using public key infrastructure (PKI). This can eliminate the vast majority of attacks, such as session hijackings and information theft. As a general rule, SSL is not as flexible as IPsec from an application perspective but is more flexible for access from any location. Organizations must determine the usage requirements for each class of user and then decide on the best approach.

Another asymmetric key encapsulation (and currently considered the successor to SSL) is the Transport Layer Security (TLS) protocol, based on Netscape's Secure Sockets Layer 3.0 (SSL3) transport protocol. TLS provides encryption using stronger encryption methods, such as DES. It can work without encryption altogether if it is desired for authentication only. SSL and TLS transport are similar but not entirely interoperable. TLS also provides confidentiality and data integrity.

TLS has two layers of operation:

▶ **TLS Record Protocol:** Allows the client and server to communicate using some form of encryption algorithm (or without encryption, if desired)

▶ **TLS Handshake Protocol:** Allows the client and server to authenticate one another and exchange encryption keys to be used during the session

The *domain name service* (DNS) was originally designed as an open protocol. (Note that CompTIA uses this terminology; ICANN and other entities use the term *domain name system*.) DNS servers are organized in a hierarchy. At the top level of the hierarchy, root servers store the complete database of Internet domain names and their corresponding IP addresses. Different types of DNS servers exist. The most common types follow:

▶ **Authoritative servers:** These servers are definitive for particular domains and provide information about only those domains. An authoritative-only name server returns answers to queries about just the domain names that have been specifically configured.

▶ **Caching or recursive servers:** These servers use recursion to resolve a given name, starting with the DNS root through to the authoritative name servers of the queried domain.

The terms *SSL* and *TLS* are often used interchangeably and are denoted as *SSL/TLS* except when there is a need to refer to one of the protocols separately.

DNS does not check for credentials before accepting an answer. Attackers exploit this basic vulnerability. An attacker can cause DNS poisoning by delegating a false name to the domain server and providing a false address for the server (see Chapter 2, "Attack Types"). To prevent this from happening, the DNS Security Extensions (DNSSEC) protocol was developed. DNSSEC protects against such attacks by providing a validation path for records.

> **ExamAlert**
>
> DNSSEC does not encrypt data; it provides a way to validate the address of a site by using a sequence of digital signatures through the DNS hierarchy. All individual domain levels are in control of their own signature-generating keys.

Validation is done through the use of a key and a signature. To properly validate the path, DNSSEC must be implemented at each domain level. The higher organization level signs the key of the lower domain level. Using the domain www.CompTIA.org as an example, the root level signs the .org key, and the .org level signs the CompTIA.org key. DNSSEC follows the chain of trust from the lowest-level domain to the top-level domain, validating the keys at each level along the way.

Securing File Transfer Protocols

FTP passes the username and password in a plain-text form. Attackers can thus use packet sniffing on the network traffic to read these values and possibly use them to gain unauthorized access to the server. FTPS, also known as FTP Secure and FTP-SSL, is an FTP extension that adds support for TLS and SSL. FTPS supports channel encryption, as defined in RFC 2228.

With FTPS, data transfers take place so that both parties can authenticate each other. It also prevents eavesdropping, tampering, and forgery on the messages exchanged. FTPS includes full support for the TLS and SSL cryptographic protocols, including the use of server-side public key authentication certificates and client-side authorization certificates. In addition, FTPS supports compatible ciphers, including AES, RC4, RC2, Triple DES, and DES. It supports the hash functions SHA1, MD5, MD4, and MD2.

Secure variations of the FTP protocol ensure that data cannot be intercepted during transfer and allow the use of more secure transfer of user access credentials during FTP logon. SFTP, or secure FTP, is a program that uses SSH to transfer files. Unlike standard FTP, it encrypts both commands and data, preventing passwords and sensitive information from being transmitted in the clear over the network. It is functionally similar to FTP, but it uses a different protocol. Therefore, a standard FTP client cannot talk to an SFTP server, nor can an FTP server connect to a client that supports only SFTP.

> **ExamAlert**
>
> A more secure version of FTP (SFTP) has been developed that includes SSL encapsulation. This version is referred to as FTP over SSH. It uses the Secure Shell (SSH) TCP port 22.

Do not confuse SFTP with FTPS (FTP over SSL). FTPS uses more than one port and can be either implicit or explicit. FTPS (Implicit) uses TCP port 990 for command and passive ports for data. FTPS (Explicit) uses TCP port 21 for command and passive ports for data. Either the SFTP or FTPS protocols can be used in an enterprise network.

Securing Email Protocols

The Multipurpose Internet Mail Extension (MIME) protocol extended the capability of the original Simple Mail Transfer Protocol (SMTP) to allow the inclusion of nontextual data within an email message. Embedding data within an email message is an easy way to send images, audio and video files, and many other types of non-ASCII text. To provide a secure method of transmission, the Secure Multipurpose Internet Mail Extension (S/MIME) protocol was developed. S/MIME is a widely accepted technology for sending digitally signed and encrypted messages that provides authentication, message integrity, and nonrepudiation. S/MIME is based on the following standards:

▶ Asymmetric Cryptography using the following algorithms: RSA, DSA, or Elliptic Curve

▶ Symmetric Cryptography using Advanced Encryption Standard (AES)

▶ Cryptographic Messaging Standard that provides the underlying key security

For more detailed information on how asymmetric and symmetric cryptography work, see Part VI, "Cryptography and PKI." When S/MIME is used to secure email, the technology behind it increases security and verifies that the message received is the exact message sent.

Other email protocols, such as Post Office Protocol version 3 (POP3) and Internet Message Access Protocol (IMAP), can also be used in a more secure way. One of the biggest security issues with POP and IMAP is that login credentials are transmitted in clear text over unencrypted connections. In secure POP3 or IMAP mail, the communication occurs over an SSL/TLS session, which mitigates this insecurity. Encrypting mail during transmission protects the communication and makes reading the email more difficult for an attacker.

> **ExamAlert**
>
> Using POP3S or IMAPS allows the data from the client to be encrypted because it is sent to the server over an SSL/TLS session.

Because a certificate is used to verify the identity of the server to the client, the connection fails if a valid certificate is not present.

The ports used by secure versions of protocols differ from the ports used by unsecured protocols. POP3 communicates over port 110 while POP3S uses port 995. IMAP communicates over port 143, while IMAPS uses port 993.

Many sites disable IMAP and POP3 completely, forcing the use of an SSL/TLS-encrypted connection.

Securing Internal Protocols

As a more secure replacement for the common command-line terminal utility Telnet, the *Secure Shell* (SSH) utility establishes a session between the client and host computers using an authenticated and encrypted connection. SSH requires encryption of all data, including the login portion. SSH uses the asymmetric (public key) RSA cryptography method to provide both connection and authentication.

Data encryption is accomplished using one of the following algorithms:

▶ **International Data Encryption Algorithm (IDEA):** The default encryption algorithm used by SSH, which uses a 128-bit symmetric key block cipher.

▶ **Blowfish:** A symmetric (private key) encryption algorithm using a variable 32- to 448-bit secret key.

▶ **Data Encryption Standard (DES):** A symmetric key encryption algorithm using a random key selected from a large number of shared keys. Most forms of this algorithm cannot be used in products meant for export from the United States.

▶ **Triple Data Encryption Standard (3DES):** A symmetric key encryption algorithm that dramatically improves upon the DES by using the DES algorithm three times with three distinct keys.

Using SSH helps guard against attacks such as eavesdropping, man-in-the-middle attacks, and spoofing. Attempts to spoof the identity of either side of a communication can be thwarted because each packet is encrypted using a key known only by the local and remote systems.

> **ExamAlert**
>
> Some versions of SSH, including the Secure Shell for Windows Server, provide a secure version of the File Transfer Protocol (SFTP) along with the other common SSH utilities.

Lightweight Directory Access Protocol (LDAP) is a directory services protocol for use on IP networks. By default, LDAP traffic is unsecured—that is, attackers can use network monitoring programs to view LDAP traffic, including Active Directory (AD)–associated services that use LDAP to authenticate. Encryption is recommended when LDAP is used over a network that is not secure.

ExamAlert

LDAP over SSL (LDAPS) is a method to secure Lightweight Directory Access Protocol (LDAP) by enabling communication over SSL/TLS.

As with web, mail, and FTP protocols, SSL/TLS establishes an encrypted tunnel to prevent traffic from being read. With LDAPS, the encrypted tunnel occurs between an LDAP client and a Windows AD domain controller. This is the process used for LDAPS communication:

▶ An LDAP session is started between a client and the LDAP server commonly referred to as Directory System Agent (DSA) on default port 636. The Global Catalog is accessed via 3269.

▶ The server sends a client operation request response. The various requests a client can make include bind, search, and entry editing.

The DSA is the database that stores information hierarchically for easy retrieval. Information is encoded pursuant to the Basic Encoding Rules (BER) used by X.500 directories and is specified in RFC 4522.

The Real-Time Transport Protocol (RTP) is used for video and audio communications on IP networks. As with many of the other protocols discussed previously, the design is inherently insecure, allowing for eavesdropping and communication interception. Support for RTP encryption in service provider gateways is lacking because of the inherent design. It is not possible to provide privacy and security for calls that go over the public switched telephone network (PSTN). The most common use for RTP is VoIP. VoIP network communications are subject to the same attacks as other Internet communication methods.

SRTP (Secure Real-Time Transport Protocol or Secure RTP) is an extension to RTP that incorporates enhanced security features. As with RTP, it is intended particularly for voice over IP (VoIP) or video network communications.

> **ExamAlert**
>
> SRTP is used to protect VoIP traffic because when it is used with header compression, IP quality of service (QoS) does not suffer. SRTP encrypts RTP data for unicast and multicast applications.

This adds confidentiality, message authentication, and replay protection to the communication exchange. UDP is still used as the RTP transport protocol, but keys are exchanged to enable encryption, similar to the HTTPS process used for secure web mail.

SNMP is an application layer protocol whose purpose is to collect statistics from TCP/IP devices. SNMP is used to monitor the health of network equipment, computer equipment and devices such as uninterruptible power supplies (UPSs).

SNMPv3 is the current standard, but some devices still use SNMPv1 or SNMPv2. The SNMP management infrastructure consists of three components:

- ▶ SNMP managed node
- ▶ SNMP agent
- ▶ SNMP network management station

The device loads the agent, which collects the information and forwards it to the management station. Network management stations collect a massive amount of critical network information and are likely targets of intruders. Using SNMP can help malicious users learn a lot about your system.

Many of the vulnerabilities associated with SNMP stem from using SNMPv1. Although these vulnerabilities were discovered 15 years ago, vulnerabilities are still being reported with current SNMP components. The only security measure SNMPv1 has in place is its community name, which is similar to a password. By default, this is *public* and often is not changed, thus leaving the information wide open to intruders.

SNMPv2 focused on performance more than security. One improvement was the implementation of Message Digest Algorithm 5 (MD5) for authentication between the server and the agent. SNMPv2 did not provide a way to authenticate the source of a management message, nor did it provide encryption. The plain-text password could still be sniffed from network traffic and was subject to replay attacks. SNMPv3 attempted to address the deficiencies in SNMPv2 by defining an overall SNMP architecture that included a set of security capabilities.

SNMPv3 changed the structure to include access control, authentication, and privacy. SNMPv3 uses the same ports as SNMPv1 and SNMPv2. UDP port 161 is required for polling, and 162 is required for notifications. SNMPv3 can also run over TCP. Figure 12.1 shows the layout of SNMPv3.

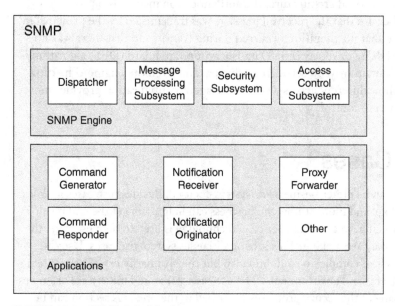

FIGURE 12.1 **SNMPv3 Architecture**

RFC 2271 defines these components of an SNMP entity (refer to Figure 12.1):

▶ **Dispatcher:** Allows for concurrent support of multiple versions of SNMP messages

▶ **SNMP message processing subsystem:** Prepares messages for sending and extracts data from received messages

▶ **SNMP security subsystem:** Provides message security services

▶ **SNMP access control subsystem:** Provides authorization services

▶ **SNMP command generator:** Initiates request PDUs and processes the response

▶ **SNMP command responder:** Receives request PDUs destined for the local system

▶ **SNMP notification originator:** Monitors a system and generates trap messages

▶ **SNMP notification receiver:** Listens for notification messages and generates response messages

▶ **SNMP proxy forwarder:** Forwards SNMP messages

With this improved architecture, the authentication mechanism provides a check to be sure that the received message was transmitted by the principal in the header, that no alteration occurred during transit, and that there was no purposeful delay or replay. The Data Encryption Standard (DES) algorithm is used to maintain privacy between a principal and a remote engine. The capability to allow different access levels in the agent configuration provides more granular access control.

Use Cases

Use cases can be either business- or system-focused. Business use cases look less at technology and more at how the business can help users get the end result they are seeking. In a system user case, technology is used to help users get the end result they are seeking. This section discusses system use cases. Use cases vary in levels of complexity and difficulty, but they primarily explain the interaction of systems and environments. The use cases presented merely are examples of how many of the secure protocols described in the previous section can be applied.

Secure Web Communication

Web communication security is paramount in any organization because so much of our daily activity is conducted via the Internet. Depending on the protocol used, web communication security can involve one or more of the following: authentication, authorization, and message protection.

Using HTTPS for Web Communication

Use cases for deploying HTTPS in web communications are numerous. Whenever a website has any kind of nonpublic information such as logins, HTTPS should be used. Some basic uses follow:

▶ **Use case #1:** A website that includes logins used only by administrators, such as an internal Wordpress website.

▶ **Use case #2:** User credentials are required in a transaction, such as on bank websites, on sites that accept credit card payments, and with medical information access. One of the most well-known examples is PayPal.

▶ **Use case #3:** Session cookies in which user credentials are stored.

▶ **Use case #4:** Cloud-based environment communications.

▶ **Use case #5:** Media streaming to protect privacy and to keep third-party analytics from collecting viewer data. Perhaps the most well-known implementation example is Netflix.

▶ **Use case #6:** A method to prevent man-in-the-middle content hijacking.

▶ **Use case #7:** A way to prohibit phishing websites and protect brand identity.

By far the most common use case for HTTPS is secure communication for sites that collect sensitive data. Generally, use of HTTPS has become the norm. According to Google's Transparency report, more than 50 percent of web pages loaded by desktop users are over HTTPS. In January 2017, Google began flagging HTTP pages that collect sensitive data as nonsecure.

Using SSL/TLS for Remote Access

Most devices inherently support SSL/TLS, so organizations do not need to install client-side software. The main purpose of SSL/TLS is to secure data in transit. SSL/TLS can be used in many different ways. The following use cases are particular to securing remote access communications:

▶ **Use case #1:** Virtual environment application access

▶ **Use case #2:** Remote administrative functions

▶ **Use case #3:** SSL VPN

▶ **Use case #4:** Connection to an internal application over HTTPS

The most common use case for using SSL/TLS for remote access is an SSL VPN. SSL VPNs, which work at Layers 5 and 6 of the OSI model, are the preferred choice for remote access. Because SSL/TLS VPN access can be initiated via a web browser, organizations can take advantage of an IT cost reduction benefit.

Using DNSSEC for Domain Name Resolution

As the previous section stated, DNS by design is inherently unsecure. The principle behind DNSSEC is that it functions as a way to provide a new PKI for authenticating Internet services. As DNSSEC becomes the foundation for secure Internet communication, use cases will continue to grow. Consider the most common DNSSEC use cases:

▶ **Use case #1:** Protection from DNS cache poisoning

▶ **Use case #2:** PKI usage within DNS

▶ **Use case #3:** DNS-Based Authentication of Named Entities (DANE), allowing the validation of X.509 certificates tied to TLS using DNSSEC lookups

▶ **Use case #4:** SSH host fingerprint posting (SSHFP) in DNS

The most common use case for DNSSEC for DNS is protection from DNS poisoning. According to the Internet Society's 2016 year-end report, 89 percent of top-level domains (TLDs) zones are signed and about 88 percent of measured zones in the .gov domain are signed.

Secure File Transfer Communication

FTP is not considered a secure protocol because it does not provide for any type of encryption during data transfer. In March 2017, the FBI issued a Private Industry Notification to healthcare providers outlining how cybercriminals are gaining access to personally identifiable information (PII) patient data via anonymous access on FTP servers.

Using FTPS and SFTP for File Transfers

SFTP and FTPS are more secure file transfer options with strong authentication capabilities. Organizations should use FTPS when they need to transfer sensitive or confidential data between a client and a server that is configured to use SSL for secure transactions.

SFTP is easier to implement in regard to firewalls because only port 22 needs to be opened. FTPS, on the other hand, uses multiple port numbers because it uses a control channel and opens new connections for the data transfer. Here are some of the most common use cases for FTPS and SFTP:

▶ **Use case #1:** Publishing files on an internal web portal

▶ **Use case #2:** Performing transparent FTP tunneling

▶ **Use case #3:** Downloading files from servers that are located on the Internet through a DMZ

▶ **Use case #4:** Reducing risks during data exchanges

▶ **Use case #5:** Compliance requirements

▶ **Use case #6:** Performing server-to-server file transfer

▶ **Use case #7:** Large or bulk file transfers

One of the most common use cases for the implementation of FTPS and SFTP is compliance. Laws such as HIPAA, PCI DSS, SOX, and GLBA require secure file transfers to protect confidential data. The ramifications for not implementing proper protections include penalties and reputation damage.

Some organizations opt for using a managed file transfer (MFT) service or application to secure FTP communications. Using this type of solution provides secure file transfers for internal, external, and ad-hoc file transfers. Some of the most prominent MFT solutions are GoAnywhere, MOVEit, and IBM Managed File Transfer. Many industries use managed file transfer solutions, including healthcare, accounting, engineering, insurance, legal, and manufacturing.

Secure Email Communication

As with file transfer protocols, email protocols were not built with security in mind. Unprotected email leaves the organization vulnerable to attacks and disclosure of confidential data. Email can be secured via S/MIME, POP3S, and IMAPS.

Using S/MIME, POP3S, and IMAPS for Email

S/MIME requires a PKI infrastructure so that clients can be issued certificates. S/MIME is used for confidentiality and integrity. POP3S and IMAPS use SSL as a method to secure emails in transit between a POP or an IMAP server and the client. Because no control governs how the message is transferred between external servers, end-to-end message protection is not guaranteed. Here are some common use cases for secured email:

▶ **Use case #1:** Protecting confidential user information such as credit card numbers

▶ **Use case #2:** Encrypting messages to prevent identity theft

▶ **Use case #3:** Securing internal client messages

▶ **Use case #4:** Protecting email passwords from easily being read by someone intercepting the traffic between a client computer and an email server

Because S/MIME is a client-based protocol, the most common use case for this protocol is securing internal client messages. The client side is responsible for protecting the message. The message is protected until the authorized recipient opens it. Organizations choose S/MIME when they want to secure messages from client to client because it is a cost-effective way to implement encryption and digital signing of email.

ExamAlert

POP3S and IMAPS are mainly used as a method to secure connections between client machines and their associated servers.

For example, Microsoft strongly recommends using TLS and SSL to secure communications between POP3 and IMAP clients and the Exchange Client Access Server. This use case is associated with use case #4, protecting email passwords from easily being read by someone intercepting the traffic between a client computer and an email server.

Mail servers can also use DNSSEC verification to ensure that the MX record is authentic and then retrieve the certificate fingerprint using DANE.

Secured Internal Communication

Internal communications need to be secured not only from external threats, but from internal threats as well. When business partners and vendors are able to access the same network and organizational users, additional measures to secure communication must be implemented. According to a recent Kaspersky report, 52 percent of businesses admit that the careless actions of employees put IT security at risk.

Using SRTP for Voice and Video

SRTP can secure voice and video. RFC 7201 lists several use cases in which SRTP can be implemented to secure voice and video:

▶ **Use case #1:** Media security for SIP-established sessions. This framework uses SIP with SDP procedures to exchange network addresses when the server endpoint has an SRTP-enabled server running.

▶ **Use case #2:** Media security for WebRTC sessions. In this implementation, JavaScript web application real-time media is transported using RTP and protected using a mandatory application of SRTP.

▶ **Use case #3:** IP Multimedia Subsystem (IMS) security. IMS media security uses end-to-access-edge security. SRTP is terminated in the first node in the core network.

▶ **Use case #4:** Real-time Streaming Protocol. Using TLS-protected signaling, the client and server agree on the secure media transport of SRTP over UDP when doing the SETUP request and response.

Perhaps the most common use case for securing voice and video with SRTP is the first use case: security for SIP-established sessions. Cisco has published an extensive white paper on securing Internet telephony media with SRTP and SDP. This is a guide for applying SRTP to voice, fax, and other IP telephony media for engineers and network administrators.

An everyday use case for SRTP is videoconferencing with Skype Connect. Skype Connect uses TLS and SRTP to encrypt SIP messages and media streams between Skype and the organization's communication platform.

Using LDAPS for Directory Services

Much of organization communication is not restricted to the internal infrastructure, so encryption is recommended when LDAP is used over an insecure network. Chapter 23, "Identity and Access Services," discusses uses for LDAPS implementation with identity and access management. LDAPS works by using TLS to authenticate the connection between the LDAP client and the LDAP server. The data exchanges are then encrypted by a TLS-supported cipher suite.

▶ **Use case #1:** Establishing an encrypted tunnel between an LDAP client and a Windows domain controller (DC)

▶ **Use case #2:** Securing LDAP subprotocols such as LDAP bind

▶ **Use case #3:** Preventing attackers from using network-monitoring software to read LDAP traffic between clients and DCs

▶ **Use case #4:** Using an application that integrates with AD and thus requires LDAP communication to be encrypted

ExamAlert

Organizations generally use LDAPS to protect the authentication session when an application authenticates with Active Directory Domain Services (AD DS).

A well-documented use case for using LDAPS with AD-integrated applications is Oracle PeopleSoft. An SSL connection is established between PeopleSoft and LDAP. For this to work correctly, SSL must be configured in both PeopleSoft and on the directory server.

Using SNMPv3 with Routing and Switching

SNMPv3 is designed to provide added security to earlier versions of the SNMP protocol. When the network is publicly accessible, it is best to use SNMPv3, which provides more secure access and encryption. Keep in mind that added security features on routers and switches result in reduced performance. Consider some use cases for SNMPv3 with routing and switching devices:

▶ **Use case #1:** Verifying that the message originated from a trusted source

▶ **Use case #2:** Validating that a packet has not been modified in transit

▶ **Use case #3:** Eliminating plain-text SNMP data on the network

▶ **Use case #4:** Securely monitoring interface counters, bandwidth usage, CPU load, and traps

▶ **Use case #5:** Securely backing up configuration files

The most common use case for SNMPv3 with routing and switching is to eliminate plain-text SNMP data on the network. SNMPv3 allows for granular control and advanced security mechanisms. It also does away with having to use the default read-write public community string that is accessible from anywhere. When SNMPv3 is used with routing and switching, common configurations include enforcing an SNMP view that restricts the download of full IP routing and ARP tables, using the maximum security level supported by SNMP managers, and using encrypted communication wherever possible.

Network Address Allocation

Approach network address allocation with security in mind. Proper planning of IP address space across all layers of the organizational network is critical to good traffic flow and adequate protection. Planning network address allocation entails dividing the network into subnets. Subnetting can be done for several reasons. If you have an IPv4 Class C address and 1,000 clients, you need to subnet the network or use a custom subnet mask to accommodate all the hosts.

Use cases for subnetting include the following:

▶ **Use case #1:** Network traffic control

▶ **Use case #2:** Improved network security

▶ **Use case #3:** Hosts arranged into the different logical groups that isolate each subnet into its own mini-network

▶ **Use case #4:** Divisions based on business goals and security policy objectives

▶ **Use case #5:** Separation of branch offices

▶ **Use case #6:** Separation of intranets and extranets

The most common use case for network subnetting is to control network traffic. Splitting one network into two or more and using routers to connect each subnet means that broadcasts can be limited to each subnet. However, often networks are subnetted to improve network security, not just performance. Subnet divisions can be based on business goals and security policy objectives. For example, perhaps you use contract workers and want to keep them separated from the organizational employees. Organizations with branches often use subnets to keep each branch separate. Other instances of subnetting include intranets and extranets (see Chapter 14, "Network Architecture").

When subnetting for IPv4 is done, an IP address usually originates from one of the IP address classes and default subnet masks listed in Table 12.1.

TABLE 12.1 **IPv4 Address Class, IP Range, and Default Subnet Mask**

Address Class	IP Address Range	Default Subnet Mask
Class A	0.0.0.0 to 126.255.255.255	255.0.0.0
Class B	128.0.0.0 to 191.255.255.255	255.255.0.0
Class C	192.0.0.0 to 223.255.255.255	255.255.255.0

Notice that the 127 network address is missing. Although the 127.0.0.0 network is technically in the Class A area, using addresses in this range causes the protocol software to return data without sending traffic across a network. For example, the address 127.0.0.1 is used for TCP/IPv4 loopback testing, and the address 127.0.0.2 is used for testing purposes.

Special ranges in each IP address class are used specifically for private addressing. These addresses are considered not routable on the Internet.

Take a look at the private address ranges:

▶ **Class A:** 10.0.0.0 network. Valid host IDs are from 10.0.0.1 to 10.255.255.254.

▶ **Class B**: 172.16.0.0 through 172.31.0.0 networks. Valid host IDs are from 172.16.0.1 through 172.31.255.254.

▶ **Class C:** 192.168.0.0 network. Valid host IDs are from 192.168.0.1 to 192.168.255.254.

To denote the network prefix for the subnet mask, the number of bits in the prefix is appended to the address with a slash (/) separator. This type of notation is called classless interdomain routing (CIDR). Consider an example: A Class C internal address of 192.168.0.0 with a subnet mask of 255.255.255.0 is written as 192.168.0.0/24.

IPv6 is designed to replace IPv4. Addresses are 128 bits instead of the 32 bits used in IPv4. IPv6 addresses are represented in hexadecimal. In IPv6, subnets use IPv6 addresses with 64 bits for the host portion. These addresses can be further subnetted, just as in IPv4. IPv6 is based on the concepts of variable-length subnet masking (VLSM) and CIDR. A VLSM allocates IP addresses to subnets based on individual need instead of a general network-wide rule. An example of CIDR notation for IPv6 is 2001:db8::/32, designating the address 2001:db8:: with a network prefix that consists of the most significant 32 bits. Just as in IPv4, blocks of addresses are set aside in IPv6 for private addresses. In IPv6, internal addresses are called unique local addresses (ULA). Addresses starting with fe80: are called link-local addresses and are routable only in the local link area.

Figure 12.2 shows an internal network with two different subnets. This is an example of use case #3. Notice the IP addresses, subnet masks, and default gateway.

ExamAlert

Watch for scenarios or examples similar to Figure 12.2, asking you to identify a correct or incorrect subnet mask, default gateway address, or router.

IP address: 192.168.1.15
Subnet mask: 255.255.255.0
Default Gateway: 192.168.1.1

IP address: 192.168.2.15
Subnet mask: 255.255.255.0
Default Gateway: 192.168.2.1

Subnet
192.168.1.0

Subnet
192.168.2.0

IP address: 192.168.1.25
Subnet mask: 255.255.255.0
Default Gateway: 192.168.1.1

IP address: 192.168.2.25
Subnet mask: 255.255.255.0
Default Gateway: 192.168.2.1

FIGURE 12.2   **A Segmented Network**

Notice in Figure 12.2 that the subnets 192.168.1.0 and 192.168.2.0 are identified next to the router. These are not valid IP addresses for a network router; they are used to identify the 192.168.1.x and 192.168.2.x networks in routing tables.

Allocating network addresses can be done as either static or dynamic. Often client addresses are assigned via Dynamic Host Configuration Protocol (DHCP). This method is much easier than manual configuration, and DHCP has the capability to push out DNS configuration changes. DHCP servers share many of the same security problems associated with other network services, such as DNS servers. Chapter 14 discusses DHCP scope configurations.

Time Synchronization

Network Time Protocol (NTP) is a UDP communication protocol used to synchronize devices with a network time server. NTP time servers are arranged in a hierarchy similar to domain name servers. Accurate time is necessary for many network operations. Here are some use cases for time synchronization:

- ▶ **Use case #1:** Time-synchronized encryption and protocols such as Kerberos
- ▶ **Use case #2:** Timestamps in logs to track security breaches
- ▶ **Use case #3:** The modification times in shared filesystems
- ▶ **Use case #4:** Billing services and applications
- ▶ **Use case #5:** Regulatory mandates that require accurate time stamping
- ▶ **Use case #6:** Channel-based audio
- ▶ **Use case #7:** Surgical operations run simultaneously
- ▶ **Use case #8:** Digital certificates

As with many older protocols, NTP contains weaknesses. Exploitation of NTP weaknesses can result in time alterations and DoS attacks that shut down the server. In 2007, the Internet Engineering Task Force (IETF) began work on Network Time Security (NTS), a mechanism for using Transport Layer Security (TLS) and Authenticated Encryption with Associated Data (AEAD) to provide cryptographic security for NTP. It is now in version 9, which was submitted in June 2017 for review.

Subscription Services

Technology is advancing at a very fast rate, and organizations often have a hard time keeping up. We now have Everything as a Service (XaaS) to help. With this business model, companies offer services that are delivered via the Internet. Subscription services are part of XaaS and are offered so that organizations avoid the expense of upgrading hardware and software. The organization pays a monthly fee for a certain number of users or devices, and the service provider takes care of the software or hardware requirements. One of the most prominent subscription services is Microsoft Office 365. Microsoft has taken its subscription services one step further in offering Microsoft 365, bundling Office 365 with Windows 10. Consider some additional use cases for subscription services:

▶ **Use case #1:** Gateway antivirus and antispyware

▶ **Use case #2:** Web and application filtering

▶ **Use case #3:** IPS/IDS

▶ **Use case #4:** Network automation and data analytics

▶ **Use case #5:** Malware detection and quarantine

▶ **Use case #6:** Desktop and server hardware

Using a subscription model for IT offers direct benefits. For example, subscription services might be good for smaller organizations that would never be able to afford the outright purchase of hardware or software. Subscription services can also benefit larger organizations, especially with hardware.

For example, take a look at the Microsoft 365 use case. If an organization has to replace thousands of PCs to meet the hardware requirements of Windows 10, it must provide the cost of the new machines and then deal with all the old hardware. Under a subscription service, Microsoft takes care of having equipment to run the OS; the user merely needs a browser.

Regarding security and subscription services, organizations choose a provider they can trust. Uptime, level of service, and security are all spelled out in a service level agreement (SLA). Chapter 26, "Policies, Plans, and Procedures Related to Organizational Security," covers this.

What Next?

If you want more practice on this chapter's exam objectives before you move on, remember that you can access all the Cram Quiz questions on the Pearson Test Prep software. You can also create a custom exam by objective. Note any objective you struggle with and go to that objective material in this chapter.

PART II
Cram Quiz

This Cram Quiz covers material related to Chapters 7–12, which cover objectives falling under Domain 2, "Technologies and Tools," of the Security+ exam.

1. Which of the following is a use for a VPN concentrator?
   - ○ **A.** Intrusion detection
   - ○ **B.** Internet connectivity
   - ○ **C.** Load balancing
   - ○ **D.** Remote access

2. If the organization requires a firewall feature that controls network activity associated with DoS attacks, which of the following safeguards should be implemented?
   - ○ **A.** Loop protection
   - ○ **B.** Flood guard
   - ○ **C.** Implicit deny
   - ○ **D.** Port security

3. Wired traffic must be encrypted because there is concern about protecting the security of login and password information for internal high-level users. Which technology should you implement?
   - ○ **A.** DMZ
   - ○ **B.** VPN
   - ○ **C.** VLAN
   - ○ **D.** NAT

4. Which of the following are uses for proxy servers? (Choose all correct answers.)
   - ○ **A.** Intrusion detection
   - ○ **B.** Internet connectivity
   - ○ **C.** Load balancing
   - ○ **D.** Web content caching

5. If the organization requires a switch feature that makes additional checks in Layer 2 networks to prevent STP issues, which of the following safeguards should be implemented?

- ○ **A.** Loop protection
- ○ **B.** Flood guard
- ○ **C.** Implicit deny
- ○ **D.** Port security

6. You are setting remote access for users and want to be sure a secure channel is used. Which technology should you implement?

- ○ **A.** DMZ
- ○ **B.** VPN
- ○ **C.** VLAN
- ○ **D.** NAT

7. Which of the following uses a secure cryptoprocessor that accelerates cryptographic processes and provides strong access authentication for critical application encryption keys?

- ○ **A.** Hardware security module
- ○ **B.** Full disk encryption
- ○ **C.** File-level encryption
- ○ **D.** Public key infrastructure

8. You have recently had problems with clients in one particular area of the network not being able to connect to a server. Which of the following tools should you use to begin troubleshooting?

- ○ **A.** Ping
- ○ **B.** Nslookup
- ○ **C.** Telnet
- ○ **D.** Netstat

9. You have been tasked with testing the strength of user passwords. Which of the following tools is the best choice to help accomplish this task?

- ○ **A.** Metasploit
- ○ **B.** Brutus
- ○ **C.** Nmap
- ○ **D.** OpenPuff

10. Which of the following is used for penetrating testing and risk assessments?

- ○ **A.** Honeypot
- ○ **B.** Configuration compliance scanner
- ○ **C.** Exploitation framework
- ○ **D.** Banner grabbing

11. Which of the following is used to help troubleshoot network issues by gathering packet-level information across the network?

- ○ **A.** Protocol analyzer
- ○ **B.** Vulnerability scanner
- ○ **C.** Port scanner
- ○ **D.** Data sanitation tools

12. You have recently had problems with clients not being able to resolve domain names correctly. Which of the following tools should you use?

- ○ **A.** Ping
- ○ **B.** Nslookup
- ○ **C.** Ifconfig
- ○ **D.** Netstat

13. It has been reported that some weak user passwords from your organization have shown up on the Internet. Which of the following tools would provide information to confirm or deny this allegation?

- ○ **A.** Tcpdump
- ○ **B.** Camouflage
- ○ **C.** SolarWinds
- ○ **D.** Cain and Abel

14. Which of the following is used to identify the level of aggressive attention directed at a network and to study and learn from an attacker's common methods of attack?

- ○ **A.** Honeypot
- ○ **B.** Configuration compliance scanner
- ○ **C.** Vulnerability scanner
- ○ **D.** Banner grabbing

15. You are required to check user permissions for the finance group that includes specific registry keys. Which of the following should you choose?

- ○ **A.** Content filter
- ○ **B.** Audit user permissions

    ◯ **C.** HTTPS

    ◯ **D.** DNS

16. Which of the following is associated with certificate issues?

    ◯ **A.** Unauthorized transfer of data

    ◯ **B.** Release of private or confidential information

    ◯ **C.** Algorithm mismatch error

    ◯ **D.** Prevention of legitimate content

17. You are required to implement a solution to identify baseline deviations for varying workloads across different days. Which of the following should you choose?

    ◯ **A.** Static baselining

    ◯ **B.** Alarms

    ◯ **C.** Alerts

    ◯ **D.** Dynamic baselining

18. Recently, some employees have fallen victim to social engineering. Which of the following is the best way to manage this personnel issue?

    ◯ **A.** Termination

    ◯ **B.** Awareness training

    ◯ **C.** Written warning

    ◯ **D.** A new policy

19. It has been reported that some clear-text passwords are being transmitted within your organization. Which of the following can mitigate this situation?

    ◯ **A.** Auditing of user permissions

    ◯ **B.** Content filtering

    ◯ **C.** HTTPS

    ◯ **D.** DNS

20. Which of the following best describes data exfiltration?

    ◯ **A.** Unauthorized transfer of data

    ◯ **B.** Release of private or confidential information

    ◯ **C.** Algorithm mismatch error

    ◯ **D.** Prevention of legitimate content

21. An organization is looking to add a layer of security by implementing a solution that protects hosts against known and unknown malicious attacks from the network layer up through the application layer. Which of the following fulfills this requirement?

○ **A.** HIPS

○ **B.** Encryption

○ **C.** DLP

○ **D.** Whitelisting

22. Which of the following types of antivirus scanning looks for instructions or commands that are not typically found in application programs?

○ **A.** Manual

○ **B.** Heuristic

○ **C.** Static

○ **D.** Pattern matching

23. Which of the following is useful in preventing users and attackers from executing unauthorized applications but does not prevent malicious code from executing?

○ **A.** DLP

○ **B.** Patch management

○ **C.** Application whitelisting

○ **D.** Malware inspection filter

24. An organization is looking to add a layer of security by maintaining strict control over the devices employees are approved to use. Which of the following fulfills this requirement?

○ **A.** HIPS

○ **B.** Encryption

○ **C.** DLP

○ **D.** Whitelisting

25. Advanced malware tools use which of the following analysis methods?

○ **A.** Static analysis

○ **B.** Context based

○ **C.** Signature analysis

○ **D.** Manual analysis

26. A Windows system is software DEP-enabled. An attacker runs an exploit that injects code into a program, and the program uses known memory space. What will the result be?

   ○ **A.** The code will run with limited functionality.

   ○ **B.** The machine will automatically blue-screen and shut down.

   ○ **C.** The malware will be blocked from running the injected code.

   ○ **D.** The malware code will run because it was injected into a known process.

27. Which of the following enables decentralized authentication through trusted agents?

   ○ **A.** Key management

   ○ **B.** Data ownership

   ○ **C.** Credential management

   ○ **D.** Transitive trusts

28. An organization wants to be sure that certain application data is protected. Which of the following fulfills this requirement?

   ○ **A.** Blacklisting

   ○ **B.** Encryption

   ○ **C.** Lockout

   ○ **D.** Whitelisting

29. An organization is looking for a mobile solution that will allow data to be deleted if a device is lost or stolen. Which of the following fulfills this requirement?

   ○ **A.** GPS tracking

   ○ **B.** Remote wipe

   ○ **C.** Voice encryption

   ○ **D.** Passcode policy

30. Which of the following are used as a most basic form of security in handheld devices? (Choose two correct answers.)

   ○ **A.** Encryption

   ○ **B.** PIN

   ○ **C.** Passcode

   ○ **D.** Fingerprint biometrics

31. Which of the following is included in a BYOD, CYOD, or COPE policy?

   ○ **A.** Key management

   ○ **B.** Data ownership

    ○ **C.** Credential management

    ○ **D.** Transitive trusts

32. An organization is looking to add a layer of security and maintain strict control over the apps employees are approved to use. Which of the following fulfills this requirement?

    ○ **A.** Blacklisting

    ○ **B.** Encryption

    ○ **C.** Lockout

    ○ **D.** Whitelisting

33. Which of the following is necessary to implement an effective BYOD, CYOD, or COPE program? (Choose two correct answers.)

    ○ **A.** Key management

    ○ **B.** Legal considerations

    ○ **C.** Infrastructure considerations

    ○ **D.** Storage limitations

34. Which standard port is used to establish an FTP connection?

    ○ **A.** 21

    ○ **B.** 80

    ○ **C.** 443

    ○ **D.** 8250

35. Which of the following is a protocol that incorporates enhanced security features for VoIP (Voice over IP) or video network communications?

    ○ **A.** LDAPS

    ○ **B.** HTTPS

    ○ **C.** NTP

    ○ **D.** SRTP

36. Which of the following should be used to establish a session between client and host computers using an authenticated and encrypted connection?

    ○ **A.** SFTP

    ○ **B.** S/MIME

    ○ **C.** SNMP

    ○ **D.** SSH

37. Which of the following is a use case for subnetting?

    ○ A. Regulatory mandates that require accurate time stamping
    ○ B. Host arrangement into the different logical groups that isolate each subnet
    ○ C. Subscription services
    ○ D. Reduced risks during data exchanges

38. Which standard port is used to establish a web connection using the 40-bit RC4 encryption protocol?

    ○ A. 21
    ○ B. 80
    ○ C. 443
    ○ D. 8250

39. Which of the following protocols is used to secure email?

    ○ A. SFTP
    ○ B. S/MIME
    ○ C. SNMP
    ○ D. SSH

40. Which of the following is a use case for subscription services?

    ○ A. Regulatory mandates that require accurate time stamping
    ○ B. Arrangement of hosts into the different logical groups that isolate each subnet
    ○ C. Network automation and data analytics
    ○ D. Reduced risks during data exchanges

Cram Quiz Answers

1. **D.** A VPN concentrator is used to allow multiple external users to access internal network resources. It uses secure features that are built into the device and are deployed where a single device must handle a very large number of VPN tunnels. Answer A is incorrect because VPN concentrators are not used for intrusion detection. Answers B and C are incorrect because they are uses for a proxy server.

2. **B.** A flood guard is a firewall feature to control network activity associated with DoS attacks. Answer A is incorrect because a loop guard feature makes additional checks in Layer 2 switched networks to prevent loops. Answer C is incorrect because implicit deny is an access control practice in which resource availability is restricted to only logons that are explicitly granted access. Answer D is

incorrect because port security is a Layer 2 traffic control feature on Cisco Catalyst switches. It enables individual switch ports to be configured to allow only a specified number of source MAC addresses to come in through the port.

3. **B.** A VPN concentrator can be used internally to encrypt WLAN or wired traffic, where there is concern about protecting the security of login and password information for high-level users and sensitive information. Answer A is incorrect because a DMZ is a small network between the internal network and the Internet that provides a layer of security and privacy. Answer C is incorrect because the purpose of a VLAN is to unite network nodes logically into the same broadcast domain, regardless of their physical attachment to the network. Answer D is incorrect because NAT acts as a liaison between an internal network and the Internet.

4. **B, C, and D.** You can place proxy servers between the private network and the Internet for Internet connectivity or internally for web content caching. If the organization is using the proxy server for both Internet connectivity and web content caching, you should place the proxy server between the internal network and the Internet, with access for users who are requesting the web content. In some proxy server designs, the proxy server is placed in parallel with IP routers. This facilitates network load balancing by forwarding all HTTP and FTP traffic through the proxy server and forwarding all other IP traffic through the router. Answer A is incorrect because proxy servers are not used for intrusion detection.

5. **A.** The loop guard feature makes additional checks in Layer 2 switched networks to prevent loops. Answer B is incorrect because a flood guard is a firewall feature to control network activity associated with DoS attacks. Answer C is incorrect because implicit deny is an access control practice in which resource availability is restricted to only logons that are explicitly granted access. Answer D is incorrect because port security is a Layer 2 traffic control feature on Cisco Catalyst switches. It enables individual switch ports to be configured to allow only a specified number of source MAC addresses to come in through the port.

6. **B.** A VPN is a network connection that grants you access via a secure tunnel created through an Internet connection. Answer A is incorrect because a DMZ is a small network between the internal network and the Internet that provides a layer of security and privacy. Answer C is incorrect because the purpose of a VLAN is to unite network nodes logically into the same broadcast domain, regardless of their physical attachment to the network. Answer D is incorrect because NAT acts as a liaison between an internal network and the Internet.

7. **A.** An HSM is a type of cryptoprocessor that manages digital keys, accelerates cryptographic processes, and provides strong access authentication for critical application encryption keys. Answer B is incorrect because full-disk encryption involves encrypting the operating system partition on a computer and then booting and running with the system drive encrypted at all times. Answer C is incorrect because in file- or folder-level encryption, individual files or directories are encrypted by the file system itself. Answer D is incorrect because PKI is a set of hardware, software, people, policies, and procedures needed to create, manage, distribute, use, store, and revoke digital certificates.

8. **A.** Packet Internet Grouper (ping) is a utility that tests network connectivity by sending an Internet Control Message Protocol (ICMP) echo request to a host. Answer B is incorrect because Nslookup is a command-line utility used to

troubleshoot a Domain Name Service (DNS) database. It queries the DNS server to check whether the correct information is in the zone database. Answer C is incorrect because Telnet is a terminal emulation program used to access remote routers and UNIX systems. Answer D is incorrect because Netstat displays all the ports on which the computer is listening. It can also be used to display the routing table and preprotocol statistics.

9. **B.** Brutus is a common password cracker. Password crackers are software utilities that allow direct testing of user logon password strength by conducting a brute force password test using dictionary terms, specialized lexicons, or mandatory complexity guidelines. Answer A is incorrect because Metasploit is an exploitation framework. Answer C is incorrect because Network Mapper (Nmap) is a network scanning tool used for locating network hosts, detecting operating systems, and identifying services. Answer D is incorrect because OpenPuff is a common steganography tool.

10. **C.** Exploitation frameworks are used for penetrating testing and risk assessments. Each exploitation framework contains a set of exploits for known vulnerabilities that are run against a host to determine whether the host is vulnerable to the exploit. Answer A is incorrect because honeypots are often used to identify the level of aggressive attention directed at a network and to study and learn from an attacker's common methods of attack. Answer B is incorrect because a configuration compliance scanner audits network device configurations against a set policy. Answer D is incorrect because banner grabbing describes a technique to identify what operating system is running on a machine, as well as the services that are running.

11. **A.** A protocol analyzer is used to capture network traffic and generate statistics for creating reports. Answer B is incorrect because a vulnerability scanner is a software utility that scans a range of IP addresses, testing for the presence of known vulnerabilities in software configuration and accessible services. Answer C is incorrect because port scanners are useful in creating an inventory of services hosted on networked systems. Answer D is incorrect because data-sanitizing tools are used for removing the contents from the device or media as fully as possible, making it extremely difficult to restore.

12. **B.** Nslookup is a command-line utility used to troubleshoot a Domain Name Server (DNS) database. It queries the DNS server to check whether the correct information is in the zone database. Answer A is incorrect because Packet Internet Grouper (ping) is a utility that tests network connectivity by sending an Internet Control Message Protocol (ICMP) echo request to a host. Answer C is incorrect because Ifconfig is used for a network interface configuration. Answer D is incorrect because Netstat displays all the ports on which the computer is listening. It can also be used to display the routing table and preprotocol statistics.

13. **D.** Cain and Abel is a password cracker. Password crackers are software utilities that allow direct testing of user logon password strength by conducting a brute force password test using dictionary terms, specialized lexicons, or mandatory complexity guidelines. Answer A is incorrect because Tcpdump is a command-line packet analyzer tool that captures TCP/IP packets sent and received on a specific interface. Answer B is incorrect because Camouflage is a common steganography tool. Answer C is incorrect because SolarWinds is a configuration compliance scanner.

14. **A.** Honeypots are often used to identify the level of aggressive attention directed at a network and to study and learn from an attacker's common methods of attack. Answer B is incorrect because configuration compliance scanners audit network device configurations against a set policy. *They are most often used in either auditing or vulnerability checking.* Answer C is incorrect because a vulnerability scanner is a software utility that scans a range of IP addresses, testing for the presence of known vulnerabilities in software configuration and accessible services. Answer D is incorrect because banner grabbing describes a technique to identify what operating system is running on a machine, as well as the services that are running.

15. **B.** Auditing user permissions identifies access violations and issues. Tools such as AccessChk show the permissions specific users and groups have for files, folders, registry keys, Windows services, and other objects. Answer A is incorrect because content filters are used to control Internet content that is available for use in the organizational environment. Answer C is incorrect because HTTPS helps prevent malicious users from capturing clear-text passwords. Answer D is incorrect because DNS is used to resolve IP addresses and domain names.

16. **C.** An algorithm mismatch is associated with certificate issues. Answer A is incorrect because data exfiltration is the unauthorized transfer of data. A more basic definition is data theft. Answer B is incorrect because a data breach is the release of private or confidential information. Answer D is incorrect because prevention of legitimate content is associated with a misconfigured web content filter.

17. **D.** Dynamic baselining is ideal for analyzing varying workloads across different days or application performance based on seasonal usage. Answer A is incorrect because static thresholds are not good for analyzing varying workloads across different days. Answer B is incorrect because the purpose of an alarm is to report a critical event that typically requires some type of immediate response. Answer C is incorrect because an alert is similar to an alarm, but it is less critical and likely does not require an immediate response.

18. **B.** The best defense against personnel issues such as social engineering is user education and awareness training. Answers A and C are incorrect because social engineering plays on human behavior and interactions; it doesn't feel like an attack, so it is difficult to spot. Answer D is incorrect because writing a new policy cannot control human behavior.

19. **C.** When an application or service stores or sends passwords in clear text, risk to the organization can be reduced by sending the credentials via an encrypted channel such as HTTPS. This helps prevent malicious users from capturing the clear-text passwords. Answer A is incorrect because auditing user permissions works for identifying access violations and issues. Answer B is incorrect because content filters are used to control Internet content that is available for use in the organizational environment. Answer D is incorrect because DNS is used to resolve IP addresses and domain names.

20. **A.** Data exfiltration is the unauthorized transfer of data. A more basic definition is data theft. Answer B is incorrect because a data breach is the release of private or confidential information. Answer C is incorrect because an algorithm mismatch is associated with certificate issues. Answer D is incorrect because prevention of legitimate content is associated with a misconfigured web content filter.

21. **A.** A HIPS protects hosts against known and unknown malicious attacks from the network layer up through the application layer. Answer B is incorrect because encrypting media devices does not provide the same functionality as controlling use of the media device. Answer C is incorrect because DLP solutions are used to prevent data loss by controlling removable media such as USB devices, mobile devices, email, and storage media. Application whitelisting is a process in which the organization approves software applications to be used on assets; only those approved applications can be run, making answer D incorrect.

22. **B.** Heuristic scanning looks for instructions or commands that are not typically found in application programs. Therefore, manual, static, and pattern matching analysis methods do not perform this function, making answers A, C, and D incorrect.

23. **C.** Application whitelisting is useful in preventing users and attackers from executing unauthorized applications, but it does not prevent malicious code from executing. Answer A is incorrect because DLP products identify confidential or sensitive information through content analysis. Answer B is incorrect because patch management is used to assess, test, deploy, and install software updates. Answer D is incorrect. A malware inspection filter is basically a web filter applied to traffic that uses HTTP.

24. **C.** Most DLP solutions have the capability to control or manage removable media such as USB devices, mobile devices, email, and storage media. Answer A is incorrect because a HIPS protects hosts against known and unknown malicious attacks from the network layer up through the application layer. Answer B is incorrect because encrypting media devices does not provide the same functionality as the capability to control use of the media device. Application whitelisting is a process in which the organization approves software applications to be used on assets; only those approved applications can be run, making answer D incorrect.

25. **B.** Advanced malware tools use behavior- and context-based detection methods instead of signature-based methods. Advanced malware tools tend to be complex enterprise solutions that are built to protect organizations before, during, and after a malware attack. Therefore, static, signature, and manual analysis methods are not effective, making answers A, C, and D incorrect.

26. **C.** Software-based DEP prevents malicious code from taking advantage of exception-handling mechanisms in Windows by throwing an exception when the injected code attempts to run. This essentially blocks the malware from running the injected code. Based on this explanation, answers A, B, and D are incorrect.

27. **D.** Transitive trusts enable decentralized authentication through trusted agents. Answer A is incorrect because key management is intended to provide a single point of management for keys and to enable users to both manage the life cycle of keys and store them securely; it also makes key distribution easier. Answer B is incorrect because ownership of data stored on the device is part of a BYOD or CYOD policy. Answer C is incorrect because credentials validate the identities of users, applications, and devices.

28. **B.** Application encryption is used to encrypt sensitive information stored by the app or to limit content accessibility to users who have the appropriate access key. Answer A is incorrect because although blacklisting is an option, it is not as

effective as whitelisting. Answer C is incorrect because lockout has to do with the number of times a user can enter a passcode. Answer D is incorrect because application whitelisting permits only known good apps to be installed.

29. **B.** A remote wipe allows mobile device data to be remotely deleted if the device is lost or stolen. Answer A is incorrect because if a mobile device is lost, GPS tracking can be used to find the location. Answer C is incorrect because mobile voice encryption can allow executives and employees alike to discuss sensitive information without having to travel to secure company locations. Answer D is incorrect because a screen lock or passcode is used to prevent access to the phone.

30. **B and C.** PINs/passcodes and pattern locks are used as a most basic form of security and a first line of defense. Answer A is incorrect because mobile device encryption is difficult to implement. Answer D is incorrect because fingerprint biometrics require additional internal hardware.

31. **B.** When formulating a BYOD, CYOD, or COPE policy, the organization should clearly state who owns the data stored on the device, specifically addressing what data belongs to the organization. Answer A is incorrect because key management is intended to provide a single point of management for keys and to enable users to both manage the life cycle of keys and store them securely; it also makes key distribution easier. Answer C is incorrect because the use of credentials is to validate the identities of users, applications, and devices. Answer D is incorrect because transitive trusts enable decentralized authentication through trusted agents.

32. **D.** Application whitelisting permits only known good apps. When security is a concern, whitelisting applications is a better option because it allows organizations to maintain strict control over the apps employees are approved to use. Answer A is incorrect because although blacklisting is an option, it is not as effective as whitelisting. Answer B is incorrect because encryption has nothing to do with restricting application usage. Answer C is incorrect because lockout has to do with the number of times a user can enter a passcode.

33. **B and C.** To establish an effective BYOD, CYOD, or COPE program, all legal concerns should be addressed before program implementation. Implementing a BYOD, CYOD, or COPE program requires planning and understanding the infrastructure considerations such as access methods and device management options for the devices. Answer A is incorrect because key management is intended to provide a single point of management for keys and to enable users to both manage the life cycle of keys and store them securely; it also makes key distribution easier. Answer D is incorrect because storage limitations are not a primary consideration in BYOD, CYOD, or COPE.

34. **A.** Port 21 is used for FTP connections. Answer B is incorrect because port 80 is used for unsecure plain-text HTTP communications. Answer C is incorrect because a connection using the HTTP protocol over SSL (HTTPS) is made using port 443. Answer D is incorrect because port 8250 is not designated to a particular TCP/IP protocol.

35. **D.** SRTP is an extension to RTP that incorporates enhanced security features. As with RTP, it is intended particularly for VoIP (voice over IP) or video network communications. Answer A is incorrect because LDAPS is used to protect the

authentication session when an application authenticates with Active Directory Domain Services (AD DS). Answer B is incorrect because HTTPS is used to establish a secured connection between a client and a web server. Answer C is incorrect because Network Time Protocol (NTP) is a UDP communication protocol used to synchronize devices with a network time server.

36. **D.** The Secure Shell (SSH) utility establishes a session between the client and host computers using an authenticated and encrypted connection. Answer A is incorrect because SFTP, or secure FTP, is a program that uses SSL to transfer files. Answer B is incorrect because S/MIME is a widely accepted technology for sending digitally signed and encrypted messages that provides authentication, message integrity, and nonrepudiation for email. Answer C is incorrect because SNMP is an application layer protocol whose purpose is to collect statistics from TCP/IP devices.

37. **B.** Splitting one network into two or more and using routers to connect each subnet together is a function of subnetting and network address allocation. Answer A is incorrect because timestamping is a time function, and this is a use case for NTP. Answer C is incorrect because subscription services are a monthly fee to a service provider for a certain number of users or devices. Answer D is incorrect because reducing risks during data exchanges is a common use case for the implementation of FTPS and SFTP.

38. **C.** A connection using the HTTP protocol over SSL (HTTPS) is made using the RC4 cipher and port 443. Answer A is incorrect because port 21 is used for FTP connections. Answer B is incorrect because port 80 is used for unsecure plaintext HTTP communications. Answer D is incorrect because port 8250 is not designated to a particular TCP/IP protocol.

39. **B.** S/MIME is a widely accepted technology for sending digitally signed and encrypted messages that provides authentication, message integrity, and nonrepudiation for email. Answer A is incorrect: SFTP, or secure FTP, is a program that uses SSH to transfer files. Answer C is incorrect because *SNMP* is an application layer protocol whose purpose is to collect statistics from TCP/IP devices. SNMP is used to monitor the health of network equipment, computer equipment, and devices such as uninterruptible power supplies (UPSs). Answer D is incorrect because the Secure Shell (SSH) utility establishes a session between the client and host computers using an authenticated and encrypted connection.

40. **C.** Network automation and data analytics subscription services are part of XaaS and are offered so that organizations do not have the expense of upgrading hardware and software. The organization pays a monthly fee for a certain number of users or devices, and the service provider takes care of the software or hardware requirements. Answer A is incorrect because timestamping is a time function, and this is a use case for NTP. Answer B is incorrect because splitting one network into two or more and using routers to connect each subnet is a function of subnetting and network address allocation. Answer D is incorrect because reducing risks during data exchanges is a common use case for the implementation of FTPS and SFTP.

PART III

Architecture and Design

For more information on the official CompTIA Security+ SY0-501 exam topics, see the "About the CompTIA Security+ SY0-501 Exam" section in the Introduction.

The previous part covered the main principles of security technologies and tool implementation so that you can become familiar with solutions organizations can use to mitigate the potential dangers they face every day. This part focuses on the main principles of secure architecture and design.

To properly secure a network, you must understand the principles of secure design. This part covers selecting the correct security framework, implementing secure network architecture and systems, and achieving secure application development and deployment, along with the security implications of embedded systems, virtualization, and cloud environments. It also addresses reducing risk through resiliency and automation.

Planning a secure architecture and design is critical to ensure that proper controls are in place to meet organizational goals and reduce risk. Secure network architecture and systems design are based on frameworks, best practices, and guides. Secure design is holistic, encompassing physical security controls, logical controls, and additional internal and external systems. This part explains how architecture and design fit into the organization's security posture.

CHAPTER 13

Use Cases, Frameworks, and Best Practices

This chapter covers the following official Security+ exam objective:

3.1 Explain use cases and purpose for frameworks, best practices and secure configuration guides.

- ▶ Industry-standard frameworks and reference architectures
  - ■ Regulatory
  - ■ Non-regulatory
  - ■ National vs. international
  - ■ Industry-specific frameworks
- ▶ Benchmarks/secure configuration guides
  - ■ Platform/vendor-specific guides
    - • Web server
    - • Operating system
  - • Application server
  - • Network infrastructure devices
  - ■ General purpose guides
- ▶ Defense-in-depth/layered security
  - ■ Vendor diversity
  - ■ Control diversity
    - • Administrative
    - • Technical
  - ■ User training

Essential Terms and Components

- ▶ defense-in-depth
- ▶ framework
- ▶ guide
- ▶ International Organization for Standardization (ISO)
- ▶ layered security
- ▶ National Institute of Standards & Technology (NIST)
- ▶ standard
- ▶ Challenge Handshake Authentication Protocol (CHAP)
- ▶ data-loss prevention (DLP)

CramSaver

If you can correctly answer these questions before going through this chapter, save time by skimming the Exam Alerts in this chapter and then completing the Cram Quiz at the end of Part 3.

1. Define non-regulatory requirements.

   _____

2. What is a framework and how is it used?

   _____

3. What is the purpose of a security benchmark?

   _____

Answers

1. Non-regulatory requirements are developed by agencies that provide technology, metrics, and standards development for the betterment of the science and technology industry.

2. Frameworks provide the foundation to strengthen an organization's security posture and guide regulation compliance. Organizations use frameworks to ensure legal compliance, demonstrate security posture, and reduce liability.

3. Benchmarks provide guidance for creating a secure configuration posture for an organization.

Industry-standard Frameworks and Reference Architectures

The security architecture of an organization is based on some type of security framework. Often the organization is bound by regulations and must base the security architecture on these regulations. When an organization is multinational or does business in another country, the organization could be subject to additional restrictions, based on regulatory compliance in that country.

When designing the organizational security architecture in addition to regulations, the components taken into consideration include standards, frameworks, and guides. *Standards* describe specific mandatory controls based on policies. *Guides*, or guidelines, provide recommendations or good practices. A *framework* generally includes more components than a guide and is used as a basis for the implementation and management of security controls.

Regulatory and Non-regulatory

Regulatory requirements are created by governmental agencies and are mandated by law. Regulation can exist on an international, national, or local level. Noncompliance with regulatory requirements can result in serious consequences for organizations, including financial implications such as fines or a negative impact on stock value and investor relations. Examples of regulatory requirements for U.S. organizations include the following:

▶ The Health Insurance Portability and Accountability Act (HIPAA) of 1996 sets national standards for protecting health information.

▶ The Gramm-Leach-Bliley Act (GLBA) establishes privacy rules for the financial industry.

▶ The Payment Card Industry Data Security Standard (PCI DSS) is designed to reduce fraud and protect customer credit card information.

▶ Sarbanes-Oxley (SOX) governs financial and accounting disclosure information.

Non-regulatory requirements are developed by agencies that provide technology, metrics, and standards development for the betterment of the science and technology industry. *The National Institute of Standards and Technology* (NIST) is an example of a U.S. non-regulatory organization. The European Union Agency for Network and Information Security (ENISA) is a similar organization that focuses on information security expertise for the E.U.

ExamAlert

Many non-regulatory bodies assist organizations by offering guidance in implementing legislation and improving the overall security of critical information infrastructure and networks.

National vs. International

The first data breach notification law in the United States was California's S.B. 1386, a bill that was enacted in August 2002 and put into effect in July 2003. Almost all U.S. states and territories now have enacted breach notification laws that require organizations to notify consumers whose personal information has been compromised. Beyond state and federal data breach notification, organizations formed in the United States are also bound by laws that cover the protection and proper disclosure of data (see the previous section).

When organizations operate at a multinational level, they generally must comply with both national and international regulations. For example, U.S. entities that have data transactions within the European Union need to meet General Data Protection Regulation (GDPR) requirements. Because some of the GDPR provisions are stricter than U.S. laws and regulations, initial organizational data protection standards might not be strong enough to comply with E.U. regulations. For example, U.S. organizations must be aware of these international privacy laws, among others:

▶ **Australia:** Privacy Act and Privacy Amendment Act

▶ **Canada:** Personal Information Protection and Electronics Document Act

▶ **UK:** Data Protection Act

▶ **EU:** Privacy Directive

▶ **Japan:** Computer Processed Personal Data Protection Act

▶ **Germany:** Federal Protection Act

Different countries have different approaches to notifying customers. This is especially important in a global economy. Notification of affected customers should be a part of an organization's incident response plan. If an organization resides in an area that is not subject to a specific notification law, it should adhere to common law liability and treat each incident on a case-by-case basis.

Additionally, state and provincial laws might require compliance.

> **ExamAlert**
>
> National laws and federal regulations supersede state and provincial laws.

Regulations can affect many aspects of security planning. For example, changes to the Federal Rules of Civil Procedure (FRCP) made requests for electronic data a standard part of the discovery process during federal lawsuits. This means that organizations need to have a record-retention policy.

It is imperative to know the legal ramifications of any incident that occurs. Be sure to check the state laws concerning privacy, liability, and spam.

Consider an example of what can happen. Imagine that your state has a strict antispam law. The company email server was misconfigured and has an open relay that allows it to be used for spamming purposes. A spammer sends email on the price of gasoline in Europe to 500,000 people. This could prove fatal to the company. First, all email would cease. Your ISP would put the company's

IP address on the spammers list. The open relay would have to be fixed and validated before you could send any email. You have would also been reported for spamming, with an associated fine of $10 per email. This could put your company out of business. The company likely would have insurance, but there's a good chance the insurance company would not cover this type of incident.

Finally, compliance with laws and regulations comes into play during complex third-party relationships. As part of a comprehensive monitoring program, the organization should periodically conduct a regular assessment of business relationships, to verify that all third parties conform to laws, regulations, and established policies and procedures.

Industry-specific Frameworks

Frameworks provide the foundation to strengthen an organization's security posture and guide regulation compliance. Organizations use frameworks to ensure legal compliance, demonstrate security posture, and reduce liability. An organization's decision to use a particular framework might depend on the industry, its location, or its size. Common security frameworks include the following:

▶ The International Organization for Standardization (ISO) and the International Electrotechnical Commission (IEC) 27002 provide best practice recommendations on information security management.

▶ The National Institute of Standards and Technology (NIST) is a U.S. government–based entity that provides a cybersecurity framework for various industries.

▶ Control Objectives for Information and Related Technology (COBIT) is a set of best practices for IT management.

▶ The Committee of Sponsoring Organizations (COSO) of the Treadway Commission is a widely accepted control framework for enterprise governance and risk management.

▶ The Health Information Trust Alliance Common Security Framework (HITRUST CSF) is a security framework developed specifically for healthcare information.

ExamAlert

Industries tend to have their own cultures and terms. Working groups and research labs often work together to provide industry-specific frameworks.

For example, the U.S. Department of Energy's Sandia National Laboratories is responsible for providing the framework for supervisory control and data acquisition (SCADA) security policy that is specific to SCADA systems. On the international front, the G7 finance ministers and central bank governors issued a set of fundamental elements of cybersecurity for the financial sector. This guidance was produced to help banks improve cybersecurity and promote the consistency of cybersecurity approaches among G7 partners.

Of course, organizations have different regulatory compliance goals, so choosing the correct framework is important to the overall security posture of the organization. Some general observations about frameworks follow:

▶ ISO/IEC 27002 can be used for any industry but tends to be used by cloud providers that want to validate an active security program.

▶ NIST is specific to U.S. government agencies but can be applied in just about any other industry.

▶ COBIT is most commonly used to attain compliance with Sarbanes-Oxley (SOX).

Myriad other frameworks work for different industries. For example, educational institutions might choose Operationally Critical Threat, Asset and Vulnerability Evaluation (OCTAVE). OCTAVE was developed by Carnegie Mellon University's computer emergency response team (CERT) and has a more strategic approach to information security.

> **ExamAlert**
>
> The choice of framework is subject to many factors. The alternative of not using any framework creates a haphazard approach to managing risk and reducing vulnerabilities.

Benchmarks and Secure Configuration Guides

Benchmarking typically determines how much of a load a system, device, or server can handle by comparing two or more systems or components of a system. The most common use of a benchmark is to measure performance. Applying that concept to security is the principle behind security benchmarks and secure configuration guides. Perhaps the most widely used resource for benchmarks is the Center of Internet Security (CIS). CIS is the main provider of more than 100 configuration guides and comprehensive checklists for various platforms that help organizations mitigate security vulnerabilities.

The benchmarks and guides prove useful because they include desirable characteristics. For example, they are based on use cases in which security is paramount and they take technology performance into consideration. CIS benchmarks and secure configuration guides are based on international best practices and are commended by industry vendors and governing bodies.

Platform and Vendor-specific Guides

CIS benchmarks provide guidance on creating a secure configuration posture for an organization. Each CIS benchmark undergoes two phases of consensus review by subject matter experts and allows for feedback from the community. Some of the benchmark categories follow:

▶ Desktops and web browsers

▶ Mobile devices

▶ Network devices

▶ Security metrics

▶ Servers

▶ Operating systems

▶ Virtualization platforms and cloud

In addition to the CIS benchmarks, many vendors provide platform- and product-specific guides that cover web and application servers, operating systems, and network infrastructure devices. For example, the Microsoft Security TechCenter provides prescriptive guidance, and Cisco provides a wide library of documents and best practices on securing Cisco devices. Additionally, NIST produces specific guides that include such documents as *Guidelines on Securing Public Web Servers*.

General Purpose Guides

General purpose security guides are available as guidance for organizations that might just want some guidance on servers that are used for general purposes. For example, NIST publishes a *Guide to General Server Security* that addresses the general security issues of typical servers. The guide addresses the underlying operating system, server software, and ways to maintain a secure configuration.

The *General Purpose Operating System Security Requirements Guide* (SRG) and the *Operating System Security Requirements Guide* are informational tools to improve the security of Department of Defense (DoD) systems. The *General-Purpose Operating System Protection Profile* (OSPP) guide also is available. This guide was created in a joint effort between the National Information Assurance Partnership (NIAP) and the British Standards Institution (BSI) to develop a Common Criteria Protection Profile that is often used in the certification process in accordance with ISO/IEC 15408 and the Common Criteria.

Defense in Depth and Layered Security

Layered security is based on the premise that implementing security at different levels or layers to form a complete security strategy provides better protection than implementing an individual security defense. A layered security approach includes using firewalls, intrusion detection systems, content filters, encryption, and auditing procedures. Each component provides a different type of security protection, so when they are implemented together, they help improve the overall security posture of the organization.

> **ExamAlert**
>
> Defense-in-depth is a comprehensive security approach for protecting the integrity of organizational information assets.

Defense-in-depth is rooted in military strategy and requires a balanced emphasis on people, technology, and operations to maintain information assurance (IA). Defense-in-depth stems from a philosophy that complete security against threats can never be achieved; the components that comprise a layered security strategy only impede threat progress until either the attacker gives up or the organization can respond to the threat.

Although they are closely related, layered security and defense-in-depth are two different concepts. Layered security can be considered a subset of defense-in-depth. Layered security focuses on protecting IT resources. Defense-in-depth

focuses on a wider, holistic approach that includes components such as disaster recovery and forensic analysis.

With layered security, the idea is to create rational security layers within the environment for improved security. Security layers can be logical, physical, or a combination of both, allowing proper alignment between resources and security requirements. For example, applications can be monitored for anomalous activity by being placed behind heuristic engines. Implementing layered security begins with understanding the organization's current risk, mapping the architecture, and then implementing security layers. Layered security can be a good alternative solution for mainframes. Enforcing security policies, using perimeter devices with access control lists, detecting malicious activity, mitigating vulnerabilities, and patching systems can all be considered layers of security.

Vendor Diversity

Vendor diversity is a business concept that requires a variety of suppliers for the purchase of goods and services for the organization. This approach keeps organizations from relying on a small number of vendors or possibly only one particular vendor for their technology needs.

> **ExamAlert**
>
> It is a common misconception that the smaller number of vendors the organization uses, the less risk the organization faces.

Dependence on a small number of vendors can create risks for the organization:

- ▶ Technological inefficiency
- ▶ High equipment and service costs
- ▶ Supply chain rigidity
- ▶ Lack of innovation
- ▶ Increased risk

Having a larger, more diversified list of vendors helps to mitigate risk, reduces single point of failure, and lessens the likelihood of unnecessary or unplanned expenditures.

Control Diversity

Organizations face growing challenges to safeguarding confidential data and proprietary information. It might seem that simply following policies and procedures can protect data, but organizations need controls in place to supplement policies and procedures. Hardening the network perimeter and implementing proper access controls mitigates threats and vulnerabilities from outside threats. With the large volumes and mobility of data made available to users, the biggest threat of data loss often comes from inside the organization. Technology and data access have become so intertwined that users unintentionally release confidential data quite easily. Technical and administrative controls need to be put in place after users have been granted permission to access information, to restrict their ability to redistribute or modify data.

Administrative and Technical Controls

Administrative controls consist of management constraints, operational procedures, and supplemental administrative controls established to provide an acceptable level of protection for resources. Administrative controls tend to be action that employees may do, or must always do, or cannot do. Preventive administrative controls are personnel-oriented techniques for controlling people's behavior to ensure the confidentiality, integrity, and availability of computing data and programs.

Technology controls consist of the type of control and the control points.

> **ExamAlert**
>
> Technical controls include encryption, data loss prevention, and information rights management.

Technical controls are sometimes referred to as logical controls. For example, encryption might be used on devices such as laptop or desktop hard drives. Access controls provide both authentication and authorization including technology such as web access management and two-factor authentication. Technical access controls can be implemented at the host level to ensure that only authorized users and machines have access to key information. Preventive technical controls keep unauthorized personnel or programs from gaining remote access to computing resources.

Control diversity is important in any environment. Consider the importance of having both administrative controls and technical controls. In a perfect world, we would need only one type of control. Unfortunately, however, not all

malicious activity can be prevented. Control diversity must be part of a layered security approach. As an example, the best protected banks in the world use both administrative and technical controls. In addition to performing employee till audits, the bank has various technical controls in place, such as two-factor authentication and access controls.

User Training

Training end users is one of the most important steps in a successful security program. Security awareness programs and policies are required for regulatory compliance with PCI DSS and HIPAA, as well as other compliance purposes. Organizations must establish clear and detailed security programs and policies that are ratified by management and brought to the attention of users.

Policies and training that users have no knowledge of are rarely effective. Similarly, policies that lack management support might be unenforceable. User training programs should be flexible enough to change as technology and organizational business goals change. Affecting the formulation of those policies and programs are current and pending legislation, frameworks, and best practice guides adopted by the organization.

What Next?

If you want more practice on this chapter's exam objectives before you move on, remember that you can access all the Cram Quiz questions on the Pearson Test Prep software. You can also create a custom exam by objective. Note any objective you struggle with and go to that objective material in this chapter.

CHAPTER 14

Network Architecture

This chapter covers the following official Security+ exam objective:

3.2 Given a scenario, implement secure network architecture concepts.

- ▶ Zones/topologies
  - ■ DMZ
  - ■ Extranet
  - ■ Intranet
  - ■ Wireless
  - ■ Guest
  - ■ Honeynets
  - ■ NAT
  - ■ Ad hoc
  - ■ Network mapping
- ▶ Segregation/segmentation/ isolation
  - ■ Physical
  - ■ Logical (VLAN)
  - ■ Virtualization
  - ■ Air gaps
- ▶ Tunneling/VPN
  - ■ Site-to-site
  - ■ Remote access

- ▶ Security device/technology placement
  - ■ Sensors
  - ■ Collectors
  - ■ Correlation engines
  - ■ Filters
  - ■ Proxies
  - ■ Firewalls
  - ■ VPN concentrators
  - ■ SSL accelerators
  - ■ Load balancers
  - ■ DDoS mitigator
  - ■ Aggregation switches
  - ■ Taps and port mirror
- ▶ SDN

Essential Terms and Components

- ▶ demilitarized zone (DMZ)
- ▶ extranet
- ▶ intranet
- ▶ sensor

- ▶ software-defined networking (SDN)
- ▶ virtual local-area network (VLAN)

CramSaver

If you can correctly answer these questions before going through this chapter, save time by skimming the Exam Alerts in this chapter and then completing the Cram Quiz at the end of Part 3.

1. You are setting up a switched network and want to group users by department. Which network design element should you implement?

   _____

2. You are setting up a web server that both internal employees and external customers need to access. What type of architecture should you implement?

   _____

3. Define software-defined networking.

   _____

Answers

1. The purpose of a VLAN is to unite network nodes logically into the same broadcast domain, regardless of their physical attachment to the network. VLANs provide a way to limit broadcast traffic in a switched network. This creates a boundary and, in essence, creates multiple, isolated LANs on one switch so that the users can be grouped by department.

2. The DMZ is an area that allows external users to access information that the organization deems necessary but will not compromise any internal organizational information. This configuration permits outside access yet prevents external users from directly accessing a server that holds internal organizational data.

3. Software-defined networking (SDN) is a method by which organizations can manage network services thorough a decoupled underlying infrastructure. It facilitates quick adjustments to changing business requirements.

Zones and Topologies

As you create a network security policy, you must define procedures to defend your network and users against harm and loss. With this objective in mind, network design and its included components play an important role in implementing the overall security of the organization. An overall security solution includes design elements such as zones and topologies that distinguish private networks, intranets, and the Internet. This section discusses these elements and helps you both tell them apart and understand their place in the security of the network.

DMZ, Intranet, and Extranet

A *demilitarized zone (DMZ)* is a small network between the internal network and the Internet that provides a layer of security and privacy. Both internal and external users might have limited access to the servers in the DMZ. Figure 14.1 depicts a DMZ.

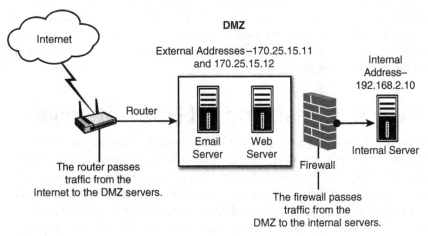

FIGURE 14.1 **A DMZ**

Web and mail servers often are placed in the DMZ. Because these devices are exposed to the Internet, it is important that they be hardened and kept current with patches. The DMZ allows external users to access information that the organization deems necessary but will not compromise any internal organizational information. This configuration permits outside access yet prevents external users from directly accessing a server that holds internal organizational data.

> **ExamAlert**
>
> An exposed server or segmented network that provides public access to a critical service, such as a web or email server, can be configured to isolate it from an organization's network while reporting attack attempts to the network administrator. Such a network is called a DMZ.

In addition to a DMZ, many organizations have intranets and extranets. An *intranet* is a subnet portion or segmented zone of the internal network that uses web-based technologies. The information is stored on web servers and accessed using browsers. The web servers don't necessarily have to be accessible to the outside world. This is possible because the IP addresses of the servers are reserved for private internal use. If the intranet can be accessed from public networks, it should be done through a virtual private network (VPN), for security reasons. VPNs and VPN concentrators are discussed later in this chapter, in the "VPN Tunneling" section.

An *extranet* is a subnet or segmented zone of the public portion of the company's IT infrastructure that grants resource access by partners and resellers that have proper authorization and authentication. This type of arrangement is commonly used in business-to-business relationships. An extranet can provide liability for a company, so care must be taken to properly configure VPNs and firewalls to strictly enforce security policies.

Wireless, Guest, and Ad Hoc Networks

All organizations have some type of wireless network. As with wired networks, wireless networks should have separate zones. Access to the internal zone can be controlled through MAC filtering. Each device on the network has a MAC address that identifies the network interface. A common control, albeit one that shouldn't be solely relied upon to prevent rogue machine access, is MAC limiting and filtering. This control provides further capability to limit what can access a network or service. Wireless access points, for example, can easily be configured to accept connections only from specific MAC addresses. The reason for additional measures is that MAC addresses can easily be spoofed. Although it is a worthy control to prevent users from bringing in their own devices, it will not likely prevent an attacker who wants to gain access.

Devices that need to connect to an internal wireless network can also be controlled via the IEEE standard, 802.1X. Do not confuse this with 802.11. 802.1X provides standards for port-based access control, whereas 802.11 is specific to wireless technology. 802.1X provides a method for authenticating a device to another system via an authentication server. The standard essentially facilitates the use of various authentication methods such as RADIUS, digital certificates, and one-time password devices.

Many places offer wireless guest access for customer convenience. A solution such as MAC filtering does not work for guest access. Guest wireless networks should have defined separation from the internal network through a wireless firewall for separate networks. A guest network user should only be able to access the Internet gateway to surf the web and check email.

To have some control over guest networks, captive portals are often used. They are widely used in businesses that offer free Wi-Fi hotspots to Internet users, such as hotels and restaurants. A captive portal web page can be used to require authentication, complete payment for usage, or display some type of policy or agreement. Chapter 36, "Wireless Security Settings," explains captive portals further.

An ad hoc wireless network (WANET) is a decentralized wireless network similar to the MANET description in Chapter 11, "Mobile Devices." Ad hoc mode offers minimal security and should not be allowed on the internal network or any area where sensitive information is stored because an attacker can easily connect to an ad hoc network. To protect organizational internal laptops and devices, ad hoc settings can be controlled via a wireless network group policy.

NAT

Network Address Translation (NAT) acts as a liaison between an internal network and the Internet. It allows multiple computers to connect to the Internet using one IP address. An important security aspect of NAT is that it hides the internal network from the outside world. In this situation, the internal network uses a private IP address.

For smaller companies, NAT can be used in the form of Windows Internet Connection Sharing (ICS), in which all machines share one Internet connection, such as a broadband modem. NAT can also be used for address translation among multiple protocols, which improves security and provides more interoperability in heterogeneous networks.

NAT is not generally used with secure protocols such as DNSSEC or IPsec because of its lack of support for TCP segment reassembly. IPsec uses cryptography to protect communications. NAT has to replace the headers of the incoming packet with its own headers before sending the packet. This might not be possible because IPsec information is encrypted.

IPv6 was developed before NAT was in general use. Because IPv6 has an almost infinite number of addresses, having to provide renumbering makes NAT unnecessary. However, Network Address Translation—Protocol Translation (NAT-PT, RFC 2766) was developed as a means for hosts that run IPv6 to communicate with hosts that run IPv4.

Honeynet

Chapter 8, "Software Tools," defined honeynets. Honeynets and honey-pots are used to distract attackers from valid network content, to study the attacker's methods, and to provide early warning of attack attempts. Honey-pots can be VMs or actual machines. Honeynets are segregated from the rest of the network. In a honeynet, a firewall is generally placed before a honey-pot. This provides access control and allows only legitimate traffic into the honeynet so that the honeypot is not overwhelmed with traffic. Configuring the firewall to prevent outgoing traffic traps the attacker in the honeynet after he or she infiltrates the internal network. The honeypots in the hon-eynet should be configured to log and gather information on any attacks if gathering information is the primary purpose. Honeynets can collect a high volume of data.

Segregation, Segmentation, and Isolation

Designing the network the proper way from the start is important to ensure that the network is stable, reliable, and scalable. Physical, logical, and virtual security controls must be in place. Controls include segregation, segmenta-tion, and isolation. The network should be segmented to separate informa-tion and infrastructure based on organizational security requirements.

Network segregation, isolation, and segmentation are some of the most effective controls an organization can implement to mitigate the effect of a network intrusion. Properly implemented, these controls are a preventative measure to protect sensitive information. In sensitive systems such as SCADA networks, applying segmentation in layers, from the data link layer through the application layer, can go a long way in protecting vital infrastructure services. Segmentation, isolation, and segregation entail more than just segmenting net-works via firewalls. They also include restricting intersystem communication to specific ports or protocols. The next chapter covers these concepts.

> ## ExamAlert
>
> Some key considerations for implementing good network segmentation, segrega-tion, and isolation are knowing how users and systems interact and communicate with each other, implementing least privilege and need-to-know principles, using whitelisting instead of blacklisting, and addressing all layers of the OSI model.

Physical

When your computers are on separate physical networks, you can divide your network into subnets that enable you to use one block of addresses on multiple physical networks. If an incident happens and you notice it quickly, you can usually contain the issue to that particular subnet.

In addition to securing internal connectivity, you should secure connections between interconnecting networks. This situation might come into play when an organization establishes network interconnections with partners as in an extranet or an actual connection between the involved organizations because of a merger, acquisition, or joint project. Business partners can include government agencies and commercial organizations. Although this type of interconnection increases functionality and reduces costs, it can result in security risks. These risks include compromise of all connected systems and any network connected to those systems, along with exposure of data the systems handle. With interconnected networks, the potential for damage greatly increases because one compromised system on one network can easily spread to other networks. Networks that partners, vendors, or departments share should have clear separation boundaries.

Air Gaps

Air gaps are physically isolated machines or networks. Chapter 21, "Physical Security Controls," explains air gaps in greater detail. Because air gaps are physically isolated, they should not have any connection to the Internet or any machine that connects to the Internet. Even when an organization implements an air gap, there are still risks to the environment. For example, files such as patches and updates must be exchanged with the outside world, employees connect personal devices to the network, and misconfigurations can cause vulnerabilities.

Related to the subject of physical isolation, make sure you do not neglect physical security. Place switches in a physically secure area, if possible. Make sure that network management stations are secure both physically and on the network. You might even consider using a separate management subnet and protecting it using a router with an access list.

Logical (VLAN)

A design that properly segments the network can be accomplished using VLANs. The purpose of a *virtual local-area network (VLAN)* is to unite network nodes logically into the same broadcast domain, regardless of their physical attachment to the network. VLANs are a logical separation of a physical network. A VLAN is basically a software solution that supports creating unique tag identifiers to be assigned to different ports on the switch.

VLANs provide a way to limit broadcast traffic in a switched network. This creates a boundary and, in essence, creates multiple, isolated LANs on one switch. When the hosts in one VLAN need to communicate with hosts in another VLAN, the traffic must be routed between them. This is called inter-VLAN routing. When a Layer 2 (data link layer) switch is used, a router is required to pass the traffic from one VLAN to another. When a Layer 3 (network layer) switch is used, inter-VLAN routing is done through Layer 3 interfaces.

> **ExamAlert**
>
> The purpose of a VLAN is to logically group network nodes, regardless of their physical location.

The most notable benefit of using a VLAN is that it can span multiple switches. Because users on the same VLAN do not have to be associated by physical location, they can be grouped logically. VLANs provide the following benefits:

▶ Users can be grouped by logical department instead of physical location.

▶ Moving and adding users is simplified. No matter where a user physically moves, changes are made to the software configuration in the switch.

▶ Because VLANs allow users to be grouped, applying security policies becomes easier.

When working with VLANs, you have various configurations and considerations. For example, when mapping VLANs onto a new hierarchical network design, check the subnetting scheme that has been applied to the network and associate a VLAN to each subnet. Allocating IP address spaces in contiguous blocks allows each switch block to be summarized into one large address block. In addition, different types of traffic might exist on the network, so organizations should consider this before they implement device placement and VLAN configuration.

Ideally, a VLAN should be limited to one access switch or switch stack. However, it might be necessary to extend a VLAN across multiple access switches within a switch block to support a capability such as wireless mobility. In this situation, if you are using multiple switches from various vendors to be connected, some switch features might be supported on only one vendor's switches (but not on other vendors' switches). You need to consider such points as

VLAN Trunking Protocol (VTP) domain management and inter-VLAN routing when you have two or more switches in the network.

Keep in mind that use of a VLAN is not an absolute safeguard against security infringements. It does not provide the same level of security as a router. A VLAN is a software solution and cannot take the place of a well-subnetted or routed network. It is possible to make frames hop from one VLAN to another. This takes skill and knowledge on the part of an attacker, but it is possible.

Virtualization

To secure a virtualized environment, machines should be segmented by the sensitivity of the information they contain. A policy should be in place specifying that hardware is not shared for test environments and sensitive data. Another way to secure a virtualized environment is to use standard locked-down images. Other areas that present issues for a virtualized environment are deploying financial applications on virtualized shared hosting and securing storage on storage-area network (SAN) technologies.

Organizations should have the same security controls in place for virtualized operating systems as they have for the same operating systems running directly on hardware. If the organization has a security policy for an application, it should apply the same policy whether the application is running on an OS within a hypervisor or on an OS running on hardware.

To protect the environment, use network security tools such as IPS/IDS to monitor access and traffic in the virtual network between the host server virtual machines and enforce policy between virtual machines and network connections. This can be accomplished by monitoring the traffic between VMs and applying the access controls needed to block unwanted protocols.

VPN Tunneling

The previous domain focused on VPN concentrators and technologies. VPN tunneling is the method VPNs use to establish and maintain a logical network connection. In tunneling, packets are assembled in a specified VPN protocol format, encapsulated with a carrier protocol, transmitted between the client and server, and then unencapsulated at the other end.

Recall from Chapter 7, "Network Components," that a VPN can be configured as a site-to-site VPN. An example of this type of implementation is connecting a bank branch office to the network and the main office. With site-to-site tunneling, individual hosts do not need VPN client software; they communicate using normal TCP/IP traffic via a VPN gateway.

Remote-access VPNs connect individual hosts to private networks. Remote Access Services (RAS) lets you connect your computer from a remote location, such as your home or any on-the-road location, to a corporate network. Many organizations maintain RAS servers to provide direct connectivity for remote users or administrators. RAS is achieved primarily through VPNs using IPsec or SSL or other Remote Access software. A remote-access VPN provides secure access to corporate resources using an encrypted tunnel over the Internet. In addition to using hardware such as VPN concentrators (discussed in Chapter 7), you can establish remote access with Routing and Remote Access (RRAS), a network service available on Microsoft Server installations that allows the deployment of VPNs and dial-up remote access services.

> **ExamAlert**
>
> Remote-access VPNs are mainly used for teleworkers or employees who travel frequently and require secure access to the organizational network. Site-to-site VPN solutions connect networks with each other and are often used in organizations with multiple locations.

The type of service you choose depends on many factors, such as cost, connect and transfer speeds, reliability, and availability.

Security Device and Technology Placement

A variety of devices and technologies work to secure a network. Placement of those devices and technologies is paramount to properly protecting the network and organizational resources. The organizational security strategy should first identify the organization's most important assets and determine the priority of protection. After the assets have been identified and prioritized, the correct network architecture can be planned, allowing the best possible protection through strategic placement of devices and technology.

Sensors, Collectors, and Correlation Engines

NIDSs are an important part of network security, and their placement is an integral part of network architecture design. As with any network device, placing a NIDS determines the effectiveness of the technology. A typical NIDS consists of sensors to monitor packet traffic, a server for management functions, and a management console.

A *sensor* collects information about your network and can really be anything from a network tap to a firewall log. Sensors are found in both NIDS and NIPS and have real-time network awareness. Generally, sensor placement depends on what the organization wants to protect, the calculated risk, and traffic flows. Sensors should be placed closest to assets identified as high priority or most important.

Other considerations for sensor placement follow:

▶ Use or purpose of the sensor

▶ Bandwidth utilization

▶ Distance from protected assets

Sensors can be placed outside the perimeter of the firewall as an early detection system or can be used internally as an added layer of security. Using sensors outside the perimeter firewall generates a lot of noise. This is not typically the ideal placement, but it can occasionally work for fine-tuning security policy. Internally placed sensors that are near the local network switching nodes and near the access routers at the network boundary have reduced false alarm rates because the sensor does not have to monitor any traffic blocked by the firewall. Sensors should be placed in the DMZ because it could lead to a compromise of the internal network in case a machine here is compromised.

Network flow collectors are used in monitoring and analyzing network traffic data. Flow collectors monitor internal switches in a single data center or in conjunction with probes when monitoring border routers of large distributed networks. Flow collectors are most often used for these purposes:

▶ Simple network performance monitoring

▶ Supplemental passive traffic monitoring

▶ Ad hoc network problem troubleshooting

Because collectors generate a large amount of data, it is important to evaluate placement relative to router location and network traffic monitoring requirements. When collectors are implemented, the network will experience an increase in packets coming from the routers and additional SNMP traffic generated when the routers are polled. Placing the collector so that it does not send the additional traffic over critical areas of the network or busy WAN links reduces overhead and helps prevent latency. The location of a collector relative to the report server should be given the same consideration. At every monitoring interval, data is sent to the report server.

SIEMs fall under correlation engines because they gather and correlate data. The main purpose of a correlation engine is to aggregate events and analyze event relationships to reduce alert noise. Each organization has unique needs, and correlation engines should be implemented based on those needs.

Because correlation is based on logs and events, log management is required before implementation. The next steps to good implementation follow:

▶ Establish goals and requirements.

▶ Require functionality and features.

▶ Define the scope of data to be collected.

▶ Establish the bounds.

▶ Design in the overall architecture.

When a correlation engine is implemented, the organization must have the capability to respond to alerts, perform ongoing periodic monitoring, and continuously tune the deployed correlation tool.

Firewalls, Proxies, and Filters

The main objective for the placement of network firewalls is to allow only traffic that the organization deems necessary and provide notification of suspicious behavior. Most organizations deploy at least two firewalls. The first firewall is placed in front of the *demilitarized zone (DMZ)* to allow requests destined for servers in the DMZ or to route requests to an authentication proxy. The second firewall is placed between the DMZ and the internal network to allow outbound requests. All initial necessary connections are located on the DMZ machines. For example, a RADIUS server might be running in the DMZ for improved performance and enhanced security, even though its database resides inside the company intranet. DMZ is covered in more detail later in this chapter, and RADIUS is covered in Chapter 23, "Identity and Access Services." Most organizations have many firewalls; the level of protection is strongest where it is closest to the outside edge of the environment. Figure 14.2 shows an example.

ExamAlert

Watch for scenarios that ask you to select the proper firewall placement based on organizational need.

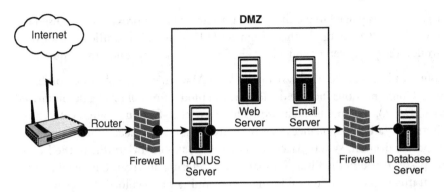

FIGURE 14.2 **A Network with Two Firewalls**

When deploying multiple firewalls, you might experience network latency. If you do, check the placement of the firewalls and possibly reconsider the topology, to be sure you get the most out of the firewalls. Another factor to think about is the use of a SAN or network-area storage (NAS) behind a firewall. Because most storage environments span multiple networks, this creates a virtual bridge that can counteract a firewall, providing a channel into the storage environment if a system is compromised in the DMZ.

For better security, segment the wireless network by placing a firewall between the WLAN and the rest of the network. Because IPsec is a solution to securely authenticate and encrypt network IP packets, you can use IPsec to provide strong security between a Remote Authentication Dial-In User Service (RADIUS) server and a domain controller, or to secure traffic to a partner organization's RADIUS servers. RADIUS provides authentication and access control within an enterprise network and is explained in greater detail in Chapter 23. Many of the VPN solutions use IPsec, which, as with a virtual private network (VPN), is an excellent solution in many circumstances. However, it should not be a direct alternative for WLAN protection implemented at the network hardware layer.

Recall from Chapter 7 that proxy servers are used for a variety of reasons. Their placement depends on their use:

▶ Placing proxy servers between the private network and the Internet for Internet connectivity

▶ Placing proxy servers internally for web content caching

The proxy server should be placed between the internal network and the Internet when the proxy server is used for both Internet connectivity and web content caching, with access for users who are requesting the web content. The proxy server is placed in parallel with IP routers when a proxy server is used for network load balancing. In this design, all HTTP and FTP traffic is forwarded through the proxy server and all other IP traffic is sent through the router.

Content filters can be hardware or software. Many network solutions combine both. Configurations include deployment behind a firewall or in a demilitarized zone (DMZ), with public addresses behind a packet-filtering router. Content filters and gateway appliances that filter are most often placed inline behind a corporate firewall. When placed directly inline, all network traffic to the Internet passes through the filter. This facilitates filtering and scanning of all Internet traffic requests, content filtering and scanning of downloads for spyware and viruses, and application filtering. Other available modes for filters follow:

▶ One network interface, with the client configured in proxy mode

▶ One network interface in routed proxy mode

▶ Two network interfaces in pass-through mode

▶ Two network interfaces, with the client configured in proxy mode

Hardware appliances are usually connected to the same network segment as the users they monitor. These appliances use access control filtering software on the dedicated filtering appliance. The device monitors every packet of traffic that passes over a network. In a multisegmented network, the filter must be installed in a location where it can both receive and manage Internet requests from the filter and communicate with installed agents.

Accelerators, Concentrators, and Balancers

VPN concentrators can be deployed in different ways, based on trusted and untrusted segmentation. The most secure option is to use a double-DMZ approach. Untrusted segments are usually deployed in a DMZ using public IP addresses and are protected by a firewall. Trusted segments should be run through a separate firewall instead of directly into the internal network. This allows decrypted traffic to be firewalled and subject to policy control. Placement of the concentrator should be close to the authentication server, to avoid communication issues.

Load balancer placement depends on the purpose of the balancer and what traffic the balancer is directing. For example, firewalls used in a load balancing capacity have different placement than load balancers for web and application traffic.

Generally, web and application load balancers are often placed parallel to firewalls. The load balancer is placed in front of web and application servers to maximize availability, security, and application acceleration. Three possible physical topologies follow:

▶ **One-armed mode:** Implemented off to the side of the data/network layer infrastructure, and receives only traffic that is specifically destined for it

▶ **Routed mode:** Acts as a Layer 3 device and routes traffic flows between clients and servers

▶ **Single VLAN one-armed mode:** Resides on the same network as the actual servers and clients

Routed mode is the most common deployment method; one-armed mode is the simplest. Because load balancers are used for high availability, usually two balancers are used, one primary and one secondary. The secondary load balancer takes over if the primary fails.

SSL accelerators are devices that accept SSL connections from users and then send the connection to the server unencrypted. They are typically positioned inline between the users and a server. Load balancers are often combined with SSL accelerators. These combined devices are commonly referred to as an application delivery controller (ADC). Some SSL decryption solutions use shared hardware resources for SSL decryption and IPS inspection. Cisco SSL architecture separates these two processes so that they run on different systems. This provides better IPS performance and scalability because the decryption and encryption function is offloaded.

An SSL accelerator can be positioned so that it is performing SSL termination, inbound SSL pass-through, or outbound SSL visibility. To protect high availability, organizations have some options for SSL failover: SSL session mirroring, SSL connection mirroring, and SSL session tickets.

DDoS mitigation appliances can be implemented through external ISP-based solutions, on-premises solutions, or third-party based solutions. In an on-premises solution, the DDoS mitigation appliance can be placed inline, out-of-band, or in the NetFlow stream.

Inline appliances are usually deployed near the network firewall. They are located in the network traffic flow and can view all inbound network traffic. When the DDoS mitigation appliance is placed out-of-band, it is usually at the Internet edge layer of the network. The appliance receives traffic information through switched port analyzer (SPAN) ports, discussed in the next section. Incoming traffic is mirrored to the detection engine of the DDoS mitigation appliance so that the appliance can be serviced without affecting the network. When used via the NetFlow protocol supported in routers and switches, the implementation is similar to the out-of-band implementation and does not interfere with normal network traffic.

Switches, Taps, and Mirroring

Combining network taps and aggregation devices in the network architecture design improves visibility and redundancy, while reducing system complexity and costs. Aggregation switches are most often found in data centers or large networks. An aggregation switch is used in a manner similar to a load balancer. Other switches are connected to the aggregation switch, which is then connected to a router or other device. Large networks contain a distribution layer, which is an additional layer of switching that aggregates the edge switches. This is done primarily to reduce cabling and network management. Essentially, aggregation takes the multitude of edge switch uplinks and aggregates them into higher-speed links.

ExamAlert

The main methods used to get network traffic to network monitoring tools are taps and SPAN, or mirror ports.

The main methods used to get network traffic to network monitoring tools are taps and SPAN ports. SPAN ports, also known as mirror ports, access traffic moving through a SPAN-supporting network switch. Configuration is done by mirroring traffic from selected ports or VLANs to the SPAN port. When configuration is complete, network monitoring tools are attached. When port mirroring is used, the switch sends a copy of the network packets from a port or VLAN to another port where the packets can then be analyzed.

SPAN ports tend to have the following issues:

▶ Tendency to drop packets

▶ Required switch configuration

▶ Security vulnerabilities

▶ Effect on performance because they are not passive

To avoid these SPAN port issues, network test access points (TAPs) are often used for access to the network traffic. A tap is designed to copy the information in a network connection, thereby eliminating it as a point of failure in the network. A tap also can provide copies to multiple tools for data analysis. By design, taps provide traffic visibility without impacting monitored traffic.

A tap is typically placed where the most critical information in the network is located. Taps are based on a latency-minimizing hardware architecture, so they can be deployed anywhere in the network. Some other common locations for taps are inside the firewall and on critical server links.

SDN

Software-defined networking (SDN) is a method by which organizations can manage network services through a decoupled underlying infrastructure, allowing quick adjustments to changing business requirements. In the SDN architecture, the control and data planes are decoupled. The system that makes decisions about where traffic is sent is the control plane, and the underlying system that forwards the traffic is the data plane. Separating control of the network from the elements involved in forwarding the packets provides a holistic view of the network.

SDN came about because mobile devices, server virtualization, and cloud services made traditional network architectures obsolete. The SDN layer sits between the applications and the infrastructure. The network appears as one logical switch to applications because all network intelligence is centralized in software-based SDN controllers. Network devices no longer need to understand a multitude of protocol standards because instructions come from the SDN controllers. The SDN layer can be configured instead of having to configure an array of devices in various locations. Figure 14.3 depicts the SDN architecture.

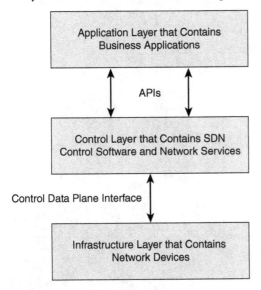

FIGURE 14.3 **SDN Architecture**

> **ExamAlert**
>
> SDN encompasses multiple types of network technologies, making it possible to build highly scalable, adaptable, and flexible networks that can easily handle changing business requirements.

SDN architecture supports APIs that allow common network services and policy management to be specifically tailored to meet the changing business objectives of the organization. An SDN approach fosters network virtualization, enabling IT staff to manage their servers, applications, storage, and networks with a common approach and tool set. Whether in a carrier environment or an enterprise data center and campus, SDN adoption can improve network manageability, scalability, and agility.

What Next?

If you want more practice on this chapter's exam objectives before you move on, remember that you can access all the Cram Quiz questions on the Pearson Test Prep software. You can also create a custom exam by objective. Note any objective you struggle with and go to that objective material in this chapter.

CHAPTER 15

Secure Systems Design

This chapter covers the following official Security+ exam objective:

3.3 Given a scenario, implement secure systems design.

- ▶ Hardware/firmware security
  - ■ FDE/SED
  - ■ TPM
  - ■ HSM
  - ■ UEFI/BIOS
  - ■ Secure boot and attestation
  - ■ Supply chain
  - ■ Hardware root of trust
  - ■ EMI/EMP
- ▶ Operating systems
  - ■ Types
    - • Network
    - • Server
    - • Workstation
    - • Appliance
    - • Kiosk
    - • Mobile OS
  - ■ Patch management

- ■ Disabling unnecessary ports and services
- ■ Least functionality
- ■ Secure configurations
- ■ Trusted operating system
- ■ Application whitelisting/ blacklisting
- ■ Disable default accounts/ passwords
- ▶ Peripherals
  - ■ Wireless keyboards
  - ■ Wireless mice
  - ■ Displays
  - ■ Wi-Fi–enabled MicroSD cards
  - ■ Printers/MFDs
  - ■ External storage devices
  - ■ Digital cameras

Essential Terms and Components

▶ electromagnetic interference (EMI)
▶ electromagnetic pulse (EMP)
▶ least functionality
▶ root of trust
▶ secure boot

▶ self-encrypting drive (SED)
▶ Trusted Platform Module (TPM)
▶ Unified Extensible Firmware Interface (UEFI)

CramSaver

If you can correctly answer these questions before going through this chapter, save time by skimming the Exam Alerts in this chapter and then completing the Cram Quiz at the end of the chapter.

1. Explain what TPM is and how it can be used to secure data.

   _____

2. Explain what is included in hardening a host operating system.

   _____

3. Explain root of trust and provide some examples of hardware roots or trust.

   _____

Answers

1. TPM refers to a secure cryptoprocessor that authenticates hardware devices such as a PC or laptop. The idea behind TPM is to allow any encryption-enabled application to take advantage of the chip. Therefore, TCM has many possible applications, including network access control (NAC), secure remote access, secure transmission of data, whole disk encryption, software license enforcement, digital rights management (DRM), and credential protection. Part of what makes TPM effective is that the TPM module is given a unique ID and master key that even the owner of the system does not control or have knowledge of.

2. Hardening of the operating system includes planning against both accidental and directed attacks, such as the use of fault-tolerant hardware and software solutions. In addition, implementing an effective system for file-level security is important. This includes encrypted file support and secure file system selection that provides the proper level of access control. For example, the Microsoft New Technology File System (NTFS) allows file-level access control and encryption, whereas older File Allocation Table (FAT)–based file systems allow only share-level access control, without encryption. Organizations also must include regular update reviews for all deployed operating systems to address newly identified exploits and apply security patches, hotfixes, and service packs.

3. Roots of trust are basically hardware or software components that are inherently trusted. Examples of hardware roots of trust include SEDs, TPMs, virtual TPMs, and HSMs.

Hardware and Firmware Security

Security begins at the hardware level. When a device is infected at the hardware or firmware level, the root cause might avoid detection for an extended period of time simply because people tend to implicitly trust hardware and firmware. In today's environment, however, hardware and firmware are no longer trustworthy and also need to be secured. With the advent of the Internet of Things (IoT), firmware- and hardware-based exploits will become more common in the very near future.

FDE and SED

Full disk encryption (FDE), also called whole disk encryption, has become popular to mitigate the risks associated with lost or stolen mobile devices and accompanying disclosure laws.

ExamAlert

FDE can be either hardware- or software-based. Unlike file- or folder-level encryption, FDE is meant to encrypt the entire contents of the drive—even temporary files and memory.

FDE involves encrypting the operating system partition on a computer and then booting and running with the system drive encrypted at all times. If the device is stolen or lost, the OS and all the data on the drive become unreadable without the decryption key.

Unlike selective file encryption, which might require the end user to take responsibility for encrypting files, encrypting the contents of the entire drive takes the onus off individual users.

An example of FDE is BitLocker. BitLocker is a full disk encryption feature included with Microsoft Windows OSs. Bitlocker is available for all Windows versions starting with Windows Vista. It is designed to protect data by providing encryption for entire volumes. By default, BitLocker uses the AES encryption algorithm.

The Encrypting File System (EFS) is a feature of Microsoft Windows OSs that provides filesystem-level encryption. EFS enables files to be transparently encrypted to protect confidential data from attackers with physical access to the computer. By default, no files are encrypted, so the encryption must be enabled. The user then encypts files on a per-file, per-directory, or per-drive basis. Some EFS settings can be implemented through Group Policy in Windows domain environments, giving the organization a bit more control.

It is not unusual for end users to sacrifice security for convenience, especially when they do not fully understand the associated risks. Nevertheless, along with the benefits of whole disk encryption come certain tradeoffs. For example, key management becomes increasingly important; loss of the decryption keys could render the data unrecoverable. In addition, although FDE might make it easier for an organization to deal with a stolen or lost device, the fact that the entire drive is encrypted could present management challenges, including not being able to effectively control who has unauthorized access to sensitive data.

> **ExamAlert**
>
> After the device is booted and running, it is just as vulnerable as a drive that has no encryption on it.

The term *self-encrypting drive* (SED) is often used when referring to FDE on hard disks. The Trusted Computing Group (TCG) security subsystem storage standard Opal provides industry-accepted standardization SEDs. SEDs automatically encrypt all data in the drive, preventing attackers from accessing the data through the operating system. SED vendors include Seagate Technology, Hitachi, Western Digital, Samsung, and Toshiba.

Firmware and hardware implement common cryptographic functions. Disk encryption that is embedded in the hard drive provides performance that is very close to that of unencrypted disk drives; the user sees no noticeable difference from using an unencrypted disk. Advantages of hardware hard drive encryption include faster setup time, enhanced scalability, improved portability, and better system performance. Disadvantages include lack of management software and weak authentication components. Coupled with the TPM's public key infrastructure (PKI) capability, an SED can achieve strong authentication. You can use hardware drive encryption to protect data at rest because all the data, even the OS, is encrypted with a secure mode of AES.

> **ExamAlert**
>
> With hardware drive encryption, authentication happens on drive power-up either through a software preboot authentication environment or with a BIOS password. Enhanced firmware and special-purpose cryptographic hardware are built into the hard drive.

To effectively use FDE products, you should also use a preboot authentication mechanism—that is, the user attempting to log on must provide authentication before the actual operating system boots. Thus, the encryption key is decrypted only after another key is input into this preboot environment. Most vendors typically offer different options, such as the following:

▶ Username and password. This is typically the least secure option.

▶ Smart card or smart card–enabled USB token along with a PIN. This option provides two-factor functionality and can often be the same token or smart card currently used for access elsewhere.

▶ A Trusted Platform Module to store the decryption key (discussed in the next section of this chapter).

Full disk encryption is most useful when you're dealing with a device that is taken on the road by people such as traveling executives, sales managers, or insurance agents. For example, on Windows based laptops, FDE implementations could include combining technologies such as a TPM and BitLocker. Because encryption adds overhead, its' less productive for a computer in a fixed location with strong physical access control, unless the data is extremely sensitive and must be protected at all costs.

TPM and HSM

Some organizations turn to hardware-based encryption devices because of factors such as the need for a highly secure environment, the unreliability of software, and an increased frequency of complex attacks. Hardware-based encryption basically allows IT administrators to move certificate authentication (CA) software components to hardware. Authentication is performed based on the user providing a credential to the hardware on the machine. This delivers a hardware-based authentication solution for wireless networks and virtual private networks (VPNs) and eliminates the possibility of users sharing keys.

The Trusted Computing Group is responsible for the *Trusted Platform Module (TPM)* specification.

ExamAlert

TPM refers to using a secure cryptoprocessor to authenticate hardware devices such as PCs, laptops, and tablets.

At the most basic level, TPM provides for the secure storage of keys, passwords, and digital certificates. It is hardware-based and is typically attached to the circuit board of the system. In addition, TPM can ensure that a system is authenticated and has not been altered or breached.

TPM consists of various components. You should be familiar with some key TPM concepts, including the following:

▶ **Endorsement key (EK):** A 2048-bit asymmetric key pair created at the time of manufacturing. It cannot be changed.

▶ **Storage root key (SRK):** A 2048-bit asymmetric key pair generated within a TPM and used to provide encrypted storage.

▶ **Sealed storage:** Protects information by binding it to the system. This means that the information can be read only by the same system in a particular described state.

▶ **Attestation:** Vouches for the accuracy of the system.

Computers that use a TPM have the capability to create and encrypt cryptographic keys through a process called *wrapping*. Each TPM has a root wrapping key, called the *storage root key (SRK)*, that is stored within the TPM itself. Additionally, TPM-enabled computers can create and tie a key to certain platform measurements. This type of key can be unwrapped only when the platform measurements have the same values that they had when the key was created. This process is called *sealing* the key to the TPM. Decrypting it is called *unsealing*. Attestation and other TPM functions do not transmit users' personal information.

The idea behind TPM is to allow any encryption-enabled application to take advantage of the chip. Therefore, TPM has many possible applications, such as network access control (NAC), secure remote access, secure transmission of data, whole disk encryption, software license enforcement, digital rights management (DRM), and credential protection. Interestingly, part of what makes TPM effective is that the TPM module is given a unique ID and master key that even the owner of the system neither controls nor has knowledge of. On the other hand, critics of TPM argue that this security architecture puts too much control into the hands of the people who design the related systems and software. Concerns thus arise about several issues, including DRM, loss of end user control, loss of anonymity, and interoperability. If standards and shared specifications do not exist, components of the trusted environment cannot interoperate and trusted computing applications cannot be implemented to work on all platforms. It is also important to understand that TPM can store pre-run-time configuration parameters but does not control the software running on a device. If something happens to the TPM or the motherboard, you need a separate recovery key to access your data simply when connecting the hard drive to another computer.

> **ExamAlert**
>
> A TPM can offer greater security protection for processes such as digital signing, mission-critical applications, and businesses that require high security. Trusted modules can also be used in mobile phones and network equipment.

The nature of hardware-based cryptography ensures that the information stored in hardware is better protected from external software attacks. Newer Windows systems incorporate a TPM Management console. This function can be used to administer the TPM security hardware through a TPM Management console and an API called TPM Base Services (TBS).

Whereas a TPM is an embedded chip, a hardware security module (HSM) is a removable or external device used in asymmetric encryption. Recall from Chapter 7, "Network Components," that an HSM can be described as a black-box combination of hardware and software and/or firmware that is attached or contained inside a computer used to provide cryptographic functions for tamper protection and increased performance. The main focus of HSMs is performance and key storage space. Hardware security modules (HSMs) can also enforce separation of duties for key management by separating database and security administration. For example, HSMs support payment processing and cardholder authentication applications for PCI DSS compliance under FIPS 140-2.

Hardware can better protect encryption keys because it stores the cryptographic keys inside a hardened, tamper-resistant device. Some additional reasons hardware is better at protecting encryption keys are that the application does not directly handle the key; the key does not leave the device; and because the host OS is not storing the key, it cannot be compromised on the host system.

BIOS and UEFI

The basic input/output system (BIOS) consists of firmware or software instructions about basic computer functions, stored on a small memory chip on the motherboard. Unified Extensible Firmware Interface (UEFI) is a newer version of BIOS. Both BIOS and UEFI are the first program that runs when a computer is turned on.

UEFI is an industry-wide standard managed by the Unified Extended Firmware Interface Forum. UEFI defines a standard interface between the OS, firmware, and external devices. Figure 15.1 shows how UEFI interacts with the OS and firmware.

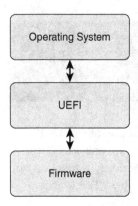

FIGURE 15.1   **UEFI OS and Firmware Interaction**

The UEFI firmware enables OS boot loaders and UEFI applications to be called from the UEFI preboot environment.

UEFI is more compatible with today's PCs, and the majority of computers use UEFI instead of BIOS. UEFI supports security features, larger-capacity hard drives, and faster boot times. UEFI-enabled OSs are preferred over BIOS-enabled OSs because they can run in 64-bit mode and provide better support for external devices and boot targets. Sophisticated attacks can occur with traditional boot processes. Combining UEFI with a TPM establishes certainty that the system is trusted when the OS loads.

Secure Boot

Boot drive encryption solutions require a secure boot or preboot authentication component. Today's PCs ship with a feature called secure boot, which UEFI supports. The premise behind secure boot is that the PC will boot using only trusted software from the PC manufacturer. Secure boot is basically an extension of UEFI. It was added to the UEFI specification in version 2.2 as an optional component.

Most PC manufacturers that install current Windows OSs are required by Microsoft to enable secure boot. Secure boot uses a series of sequential image verification steps in the boot sequence to prevent unauthorized code from running. Software images are authenticated by previously verified software before they are executed. This sequence is the beginning of what is called the chain or root of trust. It starts with the software that is executed from the read-only-memory (ROM). The ROM bootloader cryptographically verifies the signature of the next bootloader. That bootloader cryptographically verifies the signature of the next software image, and so on, until the full OS is loaded. This level of trust provides an authentication chain and validates the integrity of the rest of the system.

Attestation

The trustworthiness of a platform is based on attestation. Secure boot permits a platform to record evidence that can be presented to a remote party in a platform attestation. The purpose of attestation is to give you confidence in the identity and trustworthiness of a target device before you interact with the device. Consider some general examples of when attestation is used:

▶ A device can access a network only if it is up-to-date and contains all OS patches.

▶ A laptop is allowed to access an enterprise environment only if it is running authorized software.

▶ A gaming machine can join the gaming network only if its game client is unmodified.

Applying this concept, you can look at how TPMs are used in the attestation process. Recall from the section on TPMs that the first component of a TPM includes an endorsement key (EK). The EK is created at time of manufacture. It cannot be changed and is used for attestation. An attestation identity key (AIK) also is created. The AIK is a private key known only by the TPM. Also used in attestation is a set of-special purpose platform configuration registers (PCRs). The purpose of PCRs is to record the aggregate platform state.

To perform attestation, the attesting platform's TPM signs a new challenge and PCR values with the AIK. The challenger then verifies information before deciding whether to trust the attesting platform. Here are the actual steps in attestation:

▶ The requesting party sends a message to the attesting platform, asking for evidence of authenticity.

▶ A platform agent gathers the requested information.

▶ The platform agent returns the information and credentials to the challenger.

▶ The relying party verifies and validates the returned information, establishing identity and configuration of the platform.

▶ If the relying party trusts the information provided to vouch for the attesting platform, it compares the attested configuration to configuration information that is already deemed trustworthy.

ExamAlert

Attestation is merely a disclosure about the trustworthiness of a platform at a given point in time. It does not provide validation about the running state of a system.

Supply Chain

Original equipment manufacturers (OEMs) rely on global operations in their supply chains for manufacturing and shipping. The end product can cross several international borders and storage facilities along the way. This becomes problematic because it provides opportunities for product tampering before reaching the end user.

During manufacturing, it is critical to ensure that any root of trust device is programmed securely. To mitigate supply chain threats and risks, manufacturers often implement root of trust measures to be sure that their products boot only authenticated code. One approach is to tie secure boot to the system by loading a component with secure boot logic, making it CPU independent. Control of the system is more reliable because the approach uses existing components. The likelihood that an attacker would remove and replace components to defeat secure boot capabilities is greatly reduced. A system approach that supports key revocation with in-band or out-of-band management can be implemented as well.

Creating a key hierarchy to secure supply chains starts by building a root of trust at the very beginning level of the system and then using the secure boot process to validate the integrity of all software that executes on the platform. Secure boot has been proven to reduce the risks associated with global manufacturing operations and remote deployment. For example, Cisco developed a supply chain security process that takes a holistic approach spanning engineering, manufacturing, technical services, and suppliers. Additionally, Cisco implements secure boot across its entire product line, including switches, routers, security appliances, and collaboration platforms.

Hardware Root of Trust

So far, in this chapter we have discussed roots of trust in regard to hardware such as TPMs and software such as UEFI that supports secure boot. Roots of trust are basically hardware or software components that are inherently trusted. Secure boot is considered a root of trust. Roots of trust are inherently trusted and must be secure by design, which is why many roots of trust are implemented in hardware. This is because malware can embed itself at a level lower than the OS or can be disguised as an OS loader or third-party boot driver.

TPMs and HSMs are good examples of hardware roots of trust. TPM is now embedded in all types of devices from most major vendors. Consider two implementation examples of how organizations are using hardware roots of trust:

▶ The Google Chromebook uses TPM to find and correct corruption in firmware.

▶ Price Waterhouse Cooper uses a TPM-aware cryptographic service provider (CSP) installed under a Microsoft Cryptography API in its PCs to import identity certificates.

Examples of hardware roots of trust include SEDs, TPMs, virtual TPMs, and HSMs. Hardware roots of trust are used extensively in virtual environments. According to NIST, hardware roots of trusts are preferred because they are less susceptible to change, have smaller attack surfaces, and exhibit more reliable behavior.

EMI and EMP

One risk that is often overlooked comes from electronic interference (EMI) and electromagnetic emissions. Electrical equipment generally gives off electrical signals. Monitors, printers, fax machines, and even keyboards use electricity. These electronic signals are said to "leak" from computer and electronic equipment. Shielding seeks to reduce this output. The shielding can be local, can cover an entire room, or can cover a whole building, depending on the perceived threat.

An early specification called TEMPEST is an acronym built from the Transient Electromagnetic Pulse Emanation Standard. It describes standards used to limit or block electromagnetic emanation (radiation) from electronic equipment. TEMPEST has grown in its definition to include the study of this radiation. Individual pieces of equipment are protected through extra shielding that helps prevent electrical signals from emanating. This extra shielding is a metallic sheath that surrounds connection wires for mouse devices, keyboards, and video monitor connectors. It can also be a completely shielded case for the motherboard, CPU, hard drive, and video display system. This protection prevents the transfer of signals through the air or nearby conductors, such as copper pipes, electrical wires, and phone wires. You are most likely to find TEMPEST-certified equipment in government, military, and corporate environments that process government/military classified information. TEMPEST can be costly to implement, so protecting an area within a building makes more sense than protecting individual pieces of equipment.

An electromagnetic pulse (EMP) occurs when a source emits a short-duration pulse of energy. The energy is usually broadband. EMP events include the following:

▶ Switching action of electrical circuitry

▶ Electrostatic discharge (ESD)

▶ Lightning electromagnetic pulse (LEMP)

▶ Power line surges/pulses

At the most catastrophic end, an EMP attack could have dire effects on a nation's electronic systems and infrastructure. The EMP generated by a high-altitude nuclear explosion could instantaneously degrade or shut down all or part of the electric power grid in the geographic area of EMP exposure.

For everyday use, one protection for electronically sensitive equipment is the Faraday cage, discussed in Chapter 21, "Physical Security Controls." Another protective measure for electronic devices is to use surge protectors and lightning arrestors.

Operating Systems

Operating systems come in various shapes and forms and are the essence of the computing environment. Many exploits occur from vulnerabilities in operating system code that allow attackers to steal information and damage the system. Operating system security is of utmost importance because it involves the main platform of the computer. Additionally, several areas must be secured because the OS communicates with the hardware, performs common application required tasks, and serves as an interface with programs and applications. Some of the most common operating system spaces to be secured are listed here:

▶ **Network:** Supports local-area network (LAN) connections for workstations, personal computers, and sometimes legacy terminals

▶ **Server:** Runs on specialized machines that are operating in a client/server architecture and used specifically for responding to network client requests

▶ **Workstation:** Runs applications for a single end user on computer hardware

▶ **Appliance:** Contains software and/or an operating system to run on industry-standard hardware or in a virtual machine

▶ **Kiosk:** Consists of specialized hardware and software that provides access to information and applications in a locked-down environment to protect the kiosk

▶ **Mobile OS:** Runs applications for a single end user on a mobile device

Security planning and protection covers all devices connected to the network. Each OS is configured differently and has its own security considerations. For example, securing a web server involves different security considerations than securing an airport ticket kiosk.

Patch Management

Improperly programmed software can be exploited. Software exploitation is a method of searching for specific problems, weaknesses, or security holes in software code. It takes advantage of a program's flawed code. The most effective way to prevent an attacker from exploiting software bugs is to keep the latest manufacturer's patches and service packs applied, as well as monitor the web for new vulnerabilities.

Because of the emergence of blended-threat malware, which targets multiple vulnerabilities within a single attack, all major operating systems and application solutions must be considered in system-hardening plans. Automated reverse engineering of newly released patches has significantly reduced the time from an update's initial release until its first exploits are seen in the wild. Whereas unpatched applications previously could be targeted in a matter of months, now the threat can materialize in only hours.

You should be familiar with the following types of updates:

▶ **Hotfixes:** Small, specific-purpose updates that alter the behavior of installed applications in a limited manner. Hotfixes are the most common type of update.

▶ **Service packs:** A tested, cumulative set of all hotfixes, security updates, critical updates, and updates.

▶ **Updates:** An update that addresses a noncritical, non-security-related bug and is usually a fix for a specific problem. Although the term *updates* is used in a generic manner, this category can consist of various types of updates and address critical issues. For example, Microsoft divides its update categories into critical, definition, and security types. Security updates address a fix for a product-specific, security-related vulnerability; a critical update addresses a fix for a specific problem that is a critical, non-security-related bug.

> **ExamAlert**
>
> To make the patching process easier, Microsoft releases its security-only updates, or monthly rollup, on a regular schedule. Any system running Microsoft products in your enterprise should be evaluated for the release requirements.

Updates are now released on a schedule, which makes it easier to put a sensible plan into place. If an attacker learns of a vulnerability and releases an exploit for it before the update date, the security updates are posted ahead of schedule if the situation warrants.

Disabling Unnecessary Ports and Services

In security terms, *hardening* a system refers to reducing its security exposure and strengthening its defenses against unauthorized access attempts and other forms of malicious attention. A "soft" system is one that is installed with default configurations or unnecessary services, or one that is not maintained to include emerging security updates. No "completely safe" system exists; the process of hardening simply reflects attention to security thresholds.

Systems installed in default configurations often include many unnecessary services that are configured automatically. These provide many potential avenues for unauthorized access to a system or network. Many services have known vulnerabilities that require specific action to make them more secure or ones that could actually impair system function by causing additional processing overhead. Default configurations also allow for unauthorized access and exploitation.

> **Note**
>
> A denial-of-service (DoS) attack against an unneeded web service is one example of how a nonessential service can potentially cause problems for an otherwise functional system.

Common default configuration exploits include both services (such as anonymous-access FTP servers) and network protocols (such as the Simple Network Management Protocol [SNMP]). Others exploit vendor-supplied default logon/password combinations.

> **ExamAlert**
>
> When you are presented with a scenario on the exam, you might be tempted to keep all services enabled to cover all requirements. Be wary of this option; you might be installing unnecessary services or protocols.

A computer can communicate through 65,535 TCP and UDP ports. The port numbers are divided into three ranges:

▶ **Well-known ports:** The well-known ports are 0 through 1,023.

▶ **Registered ports:** The registered ports are from 1,024 through 49,151.

▶ **Dynamic/private ports:** The dynamic/private ports are 49,152 through 65,535.

Often these ports are not secured and, as a result, become used for exploitation. Table 15.1 lists some of the most commonly used ports and the services and protocols that use them. Many of these ports and services have vulnerabilities associated with them. You should know what common ports are used by network protocols and how to securely implement services on these ports.

ExamAlert

Know the differences in the various ports that are used for network services and protocols.

TABLE 15.1   **Commonly Used Ports**

Port	Service/Protocol
15	Netstat
20	FTP-Data transfer
21	FTP-Control (command)
22	SSH/SFTP/SCP
23	Telnet
25	SMTP
53	DNS
67, 68	DHCP
69	TFTP
80	HTTP
110	POP3
123	NTP
137, 138, 139	NetBIOS
143	IMAP
161/162	SNMP
389	LDAP
443	HTTPS
445	SMB
636	LDAPS
989/990	FTPS
1812	RADIUS
3389	RDP

Table 15.1 includes a list of protocols that might be currently in use on a network. These protocols, along with some older or antiquated protocols, could be configured open by default by the machine manufacturer or when an operating system is installed. Every operating system requires different services to operate

properly. If ports are open for manufacturer-installed tools, the manufacturer should have the services listed in the documentation. Ports for older protocols such as Chargen (port 19) and Telnet (port 23) might still be accessible. For example, Finger, which uses port 79, was widely used during the early days of the Internet, but today's sites no longer offer the service. However, you might still find some old implementations of Eudora mail that use the Finger protocol. Worse, the mail clients have long since been upgraded, but the port used 10 years ago was somehow left open. The quickest way to tell which ports are open and which services are running is to do a Netstat scan on the machine. You can also run local or online port scans.

The best way to protect the network infrastructure from attacks aimed at antiquated or unused ports and protocols is to remove any unnecessary protocols and create access control lists to allow traffic on necessary ports only. By doing so, you eliminate the possibility of exploiting unused and antiquated protocols and minimize the threat of an attack.

Least Functionality

Least functionality is based on the principle that, by default, systems provide a wide variety of functions and services, some of which are not necessary to support the essential operation of the organization. Least functionality prevents an organization from using a single system to provide multiple services and thus increase risk. Where feasible, organizations must limit component functionality to a single function per device and must disable any unnecessary protocols, ports, or services. Any functionality that does not support a business need should be removed or disabled.

The term *least functionality* comes from NIST 800-53 and is defined as configuration management 7 (CM-7), which states that an organization must configure an information system to provide only essential capabilities and specifically prohibits or restricts the use of certain ports, protocols, or services. Network scanning tools can identify prohibited functions, ports, protocols, and services. Enforcement is accomplished through IPSs, firewalls, and endpoint protections.

Secure Configurations

Secure configurations are imperative to prevent malware from infiltrating the network. Hardening an operating system is a large part of making sure that systems have secure configurations. Hardening the operating system includes planning against both accidental data deletion and directed attacks, such as the use of fault-tolerant hardware and software solutions. In addition, organizations must implement an effective system for file-level security, including encrypted file support and secured file system selection that allows the proper level of access control. For example, NTFS allows file-level access control and encryption, whereas most FAT-based file systems allow only share-level access control, without encryption.

Organizations also must include regular update reviews for all deployed operating systems, to address newly identified exploits and apply security updates, hotfixes, and service packs. Many automated attacks make use of common vulnerabilities, often ones for which patches and hotfixes are already available but not yet applied. Failure to update applications on a regular basis or perform regular auditing can result in an unsecure solution that gives an attacker access to additional resources throughout an organization's network.

IP Security (IPsec) and public key infrastructure (PKI) implementations must also be properly configured and updated to maintain key and ticket stores. Some systems can be hardened to include specific levels of access, gaining the C2 security rating that many government deployment scenarios require. The Trusted Computer System Evaluation Criteria (TCSEC) rating of C2 indicates a discretionary access control (DAC) environment with additional requirements such as individual logon accounts and access logging.

Operating system hardening includes configuring log files and auditing, changing default administrator account names and default passwords, and instituting account lockout and password policies to guarantee strong passwords that can resist brute force attacks. File-level security and access control mechanisms isolate access attempts within the operating system environment. Make sure you understand the principle of least privilege, which states that every user or service of a system should operate with only the minimal set of privileges required to fulfill their job duty or function.

Trusted Operating System

The trusted operating system concept was developed in the early 1980s and is based on technical standards of the DoD Trusted Computer System Evaluation Criteria (TCSEC). Trusted operating systems are security-enhanced operating system versions and have access segmented through compartmentalization, role, least privilege, and kernel-level enforcement. Individual components are locked down to protect memory and files, restrict object access, and enforce user authentication. Some applications cannot work on a trusted OS because of the strict security settings.

An operating system is called trusted if it meets the intended security requirements. A certain level of trust can be assigned to an operating system depending on the degree to which it meets a specific set of requirements. A trusted operating system is designed from the beginning with security in mind. Evaluating the level of trust depends on security policy enforcement and the sufficiency of the operating system's measures and mechanisms. Trusted operating system (OS) authentication is a feature that allows the existing OS authentication to log onto system architecture. The user is not prompted for a user login to connect the second architecture.

Application Whitelisting/Blacklisting

Organizations control application installations by either blacklisting or whitelisting them. Blacklisting applications is listing all applications that the organization deems undesirable or banned and then preventing those applications from being installed. The concept of blacklisting applications is similar to the way antivirus software works. Blacklisting is generally done to reduce security-related issues, but organizations also can blacklist time-wasting or bandwidth-intensive applications. File-sharing apps such as Dropbox, SugarSync, Box, Facebook, and Google Drive are the most commonly blacklisted apps in the enterprise.

> **ExamAlert**
>
> Whitelisting applications tends to make an environment more closed by allowing only approved applications to be installed.

A whitelisting approach uses a list of approved applications. If the application is not on the approved list of software, the application installation is denied or restricted. Application whitelisting is the preferred method of restricting applications because the approved apps can be allowed to run using numerous methods of trust. This decreases the risk of infection and improves system stability.

Disable Default Accounts and Passwords

Devices often are left with default passwords or default accounts that have not been disabled. Certain accounts are installed by default. Administrators should know what accounts these are so they can determine which ones are really needed and which ones can be disabled to make the system more secure. You should also know which accounts, if any, are installed with blank passwords.

The security settings in many of the newer operating systems do not allow blank passwords, but older operating systems might.

Renaming or disabling the administrator account and guest account in each domain is advisable to prevent attacks on your domains. Default credentials and unmonitored accounts such as the guest or admin accounts commonly established in older equipment and software soften security because they give attackers one component of access credentials. Attempts to compromise both the account and its associated password are more difficult.

This also applies to routers and other network devices. Equipment manufacturers typically use a simple default password on their equipment, with the expectation that the purchaser will change the password. Default login and passwords are freely available on the Internet, and leaving them in place poses a huge security risk.

Peripherals

Unsecured peripherals can also present security issues. Peripherals that have wireless connectivity present a greater risk because they are connected to your network. Attackers who can access the device can potentially gain access to your entire network.

Wireless Keyboards and Mice

Wireless keyboards connect to computers through a USB dongle and encrypt the communication to prevent attackers from sniffing the traffic in hopes of obtaining sensitive information such as passwords. Wireless keyboard manufacturers use 128-bit AES encryption to secure the communication between the keyboard and the USB dongle. Vulnerabilities of wireless keyboards and mice include an exploit called mousejacking. Mousejacking is based on flaws in a propriety protocol used in the dongle. A wireless keyboard or mouse has a unique radio frequency address. Keyboard dongles do not authenticate communicating devices and do not always require that the data be encrypted. Mouse manufacturers do not encrypt their clicks. Thus, an attacker could use an inexpensive USB dongle to sniff the data packets. After gathering the appropriate information, the attacker could transmit keystroke packets to the dongle as if he or she were the rightful user of the computer. Most product manufacturers have responded to this exploit by releasing a software update to the dongle to make it more secure.

Displays

The first level of display protection involves physically obscuring the viewing area of a monitor by using privacy screens. Vulnerabilities that can affect a system often come through the display drivers. For example, a recent CVE bulletin stated that NVIDIA Windows GPU Display Driver contains vulnerabilities that can lead to denial of service or possible escalation of privileges. The biggest security issue with display drivers is that they communicate at a lower level, giving an attacker more privileged access to the system. Graphics drivers often have direct memory access (DMA), and vulnerabilities could be used to overwrite system memory and exploit the system. The best preventative method for securing displays is to watch for vulnerabilities and keep drivers up to date.

WiFi-Enabled MicroSD Cards and Digital Cameras

A wireless SD card is just what it says it is: an SD card with built-in Wi-Fi capabilities. Mobile devices and other Wi-Fi-enabled devices can connect to the SD card through its network. The card comes with a transfer utility that can range from a simple web interface to an actual desktop application. Because the SD card itself handles the Wi-Fi capabilities, the cards are compatible with most devices and are mainly used in digital cameras.

Several security issues relate to these cards. The first is physical security. If the card is lost or stolen, information can be compromised. Another concern is the card's wireless capabilities. The SD card is basically a hotspot. Some models have two modes of connection to the card: direct share and Internet mode. With direct share, the Wi-Fi-enabled device is connected to the card. In Internet mode, the card itself is connected to a Wi-Fi device such as a hotspot or cellphone. Direct share mode provides a default SSID and password. Users typically do not change this information, so access to all files on the card can be obtained by entering the default username and password for the admin panel or by connecting and then browsing the card.

Digital cameras can pose a security risk to an organization as well. Most digital cameras have high-resolution cameras. If unauthorized pictures are taken, even from afar, there is a good chance that organizational information can be compromised. If digital cameras are allowed to connect to the network via either wireless or USB technology, sensitive information can be copied to the storage in the camera.

Protection mechanisms include changing the default access information. In an enterprise setting, group policy or MDM can prevent unauthorized devices from connecting to the wireless network or devices. When an organization uses digital cameras in their business, the security policy should address theft or loss of the device or the SD card.

Printers and MFDs

Most organizations have a multitude of printers and multifunction devices (MFDs) connected to the network. These devices are just as susceptible to attacks as the PCs and devices that send print jobs to them, but they are often overlooked when it comes to security and employee security awareness training.

The following security issues arise from use of printers and MFDs:

▶ Improper IP addressing

▶ Unsecured wireless printers

▶ Unattended sensitive information printouts

▶ Unpatched OSs

▶ Unnecessary services running

▶ Exclusion from data destruction policies

▶ Default login and passwords that have not been changed

Enterprise printers and MFDs need to be included in security policies and protected just like any other network device. Often security tools neglect to block access from a printer running old, vulnerable firmware. In addition to addressing the listed vulnerabilities, the organization should use encrypted connections for printing and accessing administrative control panels. If the budget allows, companies should replace outdated models that have known vulnerabilities with newer models that provide better security options.

External Storage Devices

The use of external storage devices can increase the risk of data loss, data exposure, and network-based attacks. The biggest risk associated with external devices is the large capacity and the amount of content that can be stored on the device. If confidential information on an external storage device is lost or illicit data is placed on the network through an external storage device, the organization is legally liable for that information. This can result in large fines or even criminal prosecution.

When an organization allows external storage devices to be used, the devices should be encrypted to protect any sensitive data, in case the devices are lost or stolen. Addressing data protection is critical so that the information is not compromised. As with most of the devices discussed in this section, in an enterprise setting, both group policy and MDM solutions can prevent unauthorized devices from connecting to the network or other devices. Some other protective measures an organization can put in place include implementing tools and processes that track the movement of data and how it is accessed, identifying the types of data that require unique protection, and specifically addressing the use of external storage devices in policies.

What Next?

If you want more practice on this chapter's exam objectives before you move on, remember that you can access all the Cram Quiz questions on the Pearson Test Prep software. You can also create a custom exam by objective. Note any objective you struggle with and go to that objective material in this chapter.

CHAPTER 16

Secure Staging Deployment

This chapter covers the following official Security+ exam objective:

3.4 Explain the importance of secure staging deployment concepts.

- ▶ Sandboxing
- ▶ Environment
  - ■ Development
  - ■ Test
- ■ Staging
- ■ Production
- ▶ Secure baseline
- ▶ Integrity measurement

Essential Terms and Components

- ▶ Core-Root-of-Trust-Measurement (CRTM)
- ▶ sandboxing
- ▶ staging environment
- ▶ integrity measure

CramSaver

If you can correctly answer these questions before going through this chapter, save time by skimming the Exam Alerts in this chapter and then completing the Cram Quiz at the end of Part 3.

1. Explain how sandboxing is used.

   _____

2. Explain what is needed to establish effective security baselines for host systems.

   _____

3. What is integrity measurement?

   _____

Answers

1. The basic idea of sandboxing is to provide a safe execution environment for untrusted programs. Running a program in a sandbox contains it so that it can be tested and reduces some security issues because it cannot harm the host.

2. To establish effective security baselines, enterprise network security management requires a measure of commonality between systems. Mandatory settings, standard application suites, and initial setup configuration details all factor into the security stance of an enterprise network.

3. Integrity measurement is a method that uses attestation challenges from computed hashes of system or application information to obtain confidence in the trustworthiness and identity of a platform or software.

Sandboxing

Although sandboxing and virtualization are commonly thought to be the same, they are two different technologies. The basic idea of *sandboxing* is to provide a safe execution environment for untrusted programs. Sandboxing allows programs and processes to be run in an isolated environment to limit access to files and the host system. Running a program or file in a sandbox contains it so that it can be tested and also reduces some security issues because the program or file cannot harm the host or make any changes to the host. In this respect, sandboxing is similar to virtualization because actions within the sandbox are contained to that environment. Generally, programs or files running inside a sandbox appear normal.

Whether or not you realize it, web pages you visit run in a sandbox. Web pages are restricted to running in a browser. In most browsers, all HTML rendering and JavaScript executions are isolated in their own class of processes. PDF files run in a sandbox, and Group Policy allows Microsoft Office 2016 to block macros using sandbox mode. When macro-blocking is enabled, it prevents users from exiting the Protected View sandbox when opening Word documents in Outlook.

ExamAlert

Web applications are launched in a sandbox, meaning that they run in their own browser windows, without the capability to read or write files from sensitive areas.

Often when an endpoint has a cloud-enhanced antivirus product installed, the antivirus product employs an Internet-connected sandbox as part of its cloud service so that suspicious programs are automatically run in a virtual environment. Both iOS and Android isolate applications and sensitive operating system features using sandboxing.

Third-party and free programs are also available to run programs sandboxed. One such popular program is Sandboxie (see Figure 16.1).

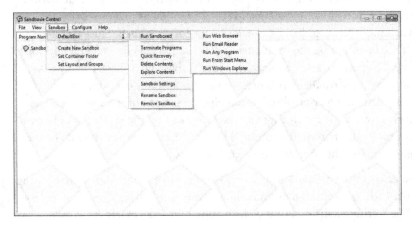

FIGURE 16.1 **Sandboxie Interface**

Sandboxing is mainly used for security, but another common use is malware analysis. For example, for individual analysis, Cuckoo Sandbox can examine a suspicious file and quickly provide detailed results of the file's actions when executed inside the isolated environment. On the enterprise level, Blue Coat Malware Analysis and sandboxing capabilities can provide an emulation sandbox for analyzing files that detect virtual environments and refuse to run, as well as a virtualization sandbox for both PC and mobile environments. Enterprise solutions often integrate with other tools to interact with malware, gather intelligence, and provide remediation.

Environment

Organizations that develop software tend to separate the process into various phases or environments. Separate environments can also be used as a way to implement software application and operating system updates, especially in the test, staging, and production phases. For example, many organizations that have an application deployment life cycle test applications before deploying them. Separate environments are required because when applications are developed in production environments, programming mistakes can disable features, cause errors, or crash the application. Smaller organizations commonly use three environments, whereas larger organizations typically use four: development, test, staging, and production.

Development and Test

Organizations generally implement physical isolation or VLAN segmentation between the different environments. In the development phase of software, the environment tends to be less restrictive for local rights because deeper levels of access might be required during development. When several developers are working on the same project, it is often advisable to have them work in a sandboxed or virtual environment so that code is not overwritten as it is developed. Versioning control software helps keep track of the software. Code gets checked out of a version control repository so that the system maintains a record of the code changes that occur. The development environment consolidates and validates the project team's work so that it can be tested.

The test environment should be isolated from development. During the testing phase, the code is tested to determine how it interacts with a normal environment. The testing environment is a clean copy of the development environment used for integration testing. The testing environment also measures the performance characteristics of the software.

In a physical isolation environment, a firewall normally separates the environments from each other and the outside world. In VLAN segmentation, VLANs are often mapped into security zones. Traffic between zones must pass through a firewall that enforces the segmentation rules between the environments.

Test and development environments often have lower security levels. Keeping them separate or isolated from the staging and production environments provides segregation and prevents untested code from accidently being deployed. Development and testing environments often are deployed using a public cloud provider, and staging and production environments are deployed within an organization's private network.

Staging and Production

A staging environment is often implemented to reduce the risk of introducing issues upon deployment in the production environment. The staging environment is primarily used to unit test the actual deployment of code. The staging environment should closely match the production environment. The staging environment can also verify that the software runs under security settings. Although the staging environment should be closely matched to the production environment, using virtual machines in the staging environment might be acceptable as long as they are not measuring performance. The staging environment can also be used as a demonstration or training environment.

The developers should be able to deploy code to the staging environment. Care must be taken to be sure that versioning control is employed and that the proper version of the software is ported over. Staging basically provides one last opportunity to find and remove flaws or features that are not intended for production.

After the code has been thoroughly tested and run through the staging environment, it can be deployed to production. The production environment is the final stage in the process and the actual "live" environment that will be running the code. The production environment should contain only applications that have already been developed, tested, and staged in the other environments. All pertinent security settings should apply, and access to the production environment should be limited to a few experienced developers.

Secure Baseline

No one-size-fits-all approach to security exists, even within a single organization across various systems. On the other hand, it is important to consider a minimum or baseline standard of security for systems, components, and applications.

Recall from Chapter 9, "Security Issues," that baselines are necessary to reduce the chances of misconfiguration. Good security practice dictates creating a secure baseline build for all systems, components, and software applications, as a point of reference. Security system baselines are often established by governmental mandate, regulatory bodies, or industry guidance. For example, NIST SP 800-70 Rev. 3 is a repository of publicly available security checklists that provide guidance on the security configuration settings of operating systems and applications.

Generally, the environment needs of an organization follow the legacy, enterprise, or high-security client levels. A legacy client has the lowest lockdown level. A good baseline is needed for these computers because of their vulnerability and lack of capability to configure tightened security settings. The enterprise client environment is designed to provide solid security for the organization and allows the use of more restrictive security templates, for added security. Using security templates also allows the organization to introduce additional roles on top of the baseline template, for easier implementation. In a high-security environment, the settings are restrictive and many applications might not function under this type of configuration. Therefore, having a baseline is important. Baselines must be updated regularly, certainly when the network has changed or new technology has been deployed.

Application baselining is similar to operating system baselining because it provides a reference point for normal and abnormal activity. Applications must also be maintained in a current state by regularly reviewing applied updates and applying those that are required for the network configuration solutions in use. An initial baseline should be done for both network and application processes so that you can tell whether you have a hardware or software issue. Sometimes applications have memory leaks or a new version causes performance issues. Access rights also should be reviewed regularly and permissions granted on a group structure similar to Active Directory.

> **ExamAlert**
>
> Baselines establish patterns of use and can identify variations that could indicate unauthorized access attempts.

Keep in mind that security monitoring should be conducted during baseline creation. An ongoing attack during the baselining process could register as the normal level of activity.

Integrity Measurement

When a program is run on a system, no indication shows how the code has affected the system on which the program is run. You do not know for sure that, after the program is run, the system is still exactly the same as it was beforehand. With malware being able to infiltrate systems at a very low level, organizations need to be able to securely identify the software running on the system.

The way in which data about a system's hardware, configuration settings, or software is collected is referred to as measurement. *Integrity measurement* uses attestation challenges from computed hashes of system or application information to obtain confidence in the trustworthiness and identity of a platform or software. Remember from Chapter 15, "Secure Systems Design," that the purpose of attestation is to obtain confidence in the trustworthiness and identity of a platform or software. Integrity measurement uses attestation challenges to query the integrity status of software.

Integrity measurement is done through the Trusted Platform Module (TPM) at load time. When an executable loads, a hash function is used to fingerprint information. This could be the executable itself, the executable along with its input data, or a sequence of related files. The hash values are then used to establish code identity to verifiers through attestation. Additionally, these hash values can be used along with a feature called sealed storage. Sealed storage uses cryptographically secure secrets so that only a specific application can open data files.

ExamAlert

The TPM collects measurements, but it does not calculate the measurement and cannot take action on them.

Linux-based systems have the capability to implement the Integrity Measurement Architecture (IMA) through a kernel module. The IMA maintains a kernel trust chain. The IMA subsystem calculates the hash of a program before loading the program and validates the hash to a predefined list. When the system has a hardware TPM, the IMA maintains both a runtime measurement list and an aggregate integrity value over the list. This helps prevent undetectable software attacks.

Integrity measurement mechanisms that have been proposed and developed include the Trusted Computing Group (TCG). As noted in Chapter 15, the TCG is responsible for publishing the transitive trust concept with hardware root-of-trust for TPM. It has also defined the Core-Root-of-Trust-Measurement (CRTM), the first action executed when booting. The CRTM measures the bootloader and sends the hash value to the TPM for storage in one of the Platform Configuration Registers (PCR) before execution. After bootloader execution and before OS execution, the OS image is measured and the value is stored in a PCR extension. This process continues for all loaded applications. When an attestation challenge occurs, the TPM signs a set of PCR values with an attestation identity key (AIK). The challenger decides on the integrity and trust status of the platform by comparing the returned result against known-good values.

ExamAlert

Trust in all subsequent measurements is based on the integrity of the CRTM. If the CRTM is compromised, no further measurements can be trusted.

What Next?

If you want more practice on this chapter's exam objectives before you move on, remember that you can access all the Cram Quiz questions on the Pearson Test Prep software. You can also create a custom exam by objective. Note any objective you struggle with and go to that objective material in this chapter.

CHAPTER 17

Embedded Systems

This chapter covers the following official Security+ exam objective:

3.5 Explain the security implications of embedded systems.

- ▶ SCADA/ICS
- ▶ Smart devices/IoT
  - ▪ Wearable technology
  - ▪ Home automation
- ▶ HVAC
- ▶ SoC
- ▶ RTOS
- ▶ Printers/MFDs
- ▶ Camera systems
- ▶ Special purpose
  - ▪ Medical devices
  - ▪ Vehicles
  - ▪ Aircraft/UAV

Essential Terms and Components

- ▶ ICS
- ▶ RTOS
- ▶ SCADA
- ▶ SoC
- ▶ UAV

CramSaver

If you can correctly answer these questions before going through this chapter, save time by skimming the Exam Alerts in this chapter and then completing the Cram Quiz at the end of Part 3.

1. Explain why a separate security group might be required with SCADA systems.

   _____

2. Explain SoC technology.

   _____

3. Explain what protections should be put in place for embedded MFD.

   _____

Answers

1. Ideally, two separate security and IT groups should manage the network infrastructure and the ICS or SCADA network. Because ICS security requirements are different, IT architects and managers who do not have experience on this type of system need to be trained specifically in ICS security and must be familiar with guidance documents.

2. System-on-a-chip (SoC) technology is found in many electronic devices. This is basically a hardware module in small form factor. SoC devices have very good processing power, and the small footprint makes them ideal for reduced power consumption, lower cost, and better performance than larger components.

3. Protections for MFDs include proper access control to the device and functions, inclusion of printers and MFDs in security planning and policies, and implementation of protections for both data in transit and data at rest.

SCADA and ICS

In some areas, an organization might be able to exert better control over the management of security risks because the environment is considered static or less fluid than a cloud or virtualized environment. Environments such as SCADA systems, some embedded systems, and mainframe sytems are considered static because the technology behind them has been around for a long time. Thanks to business needs and vendor access, many of these sytems that previously were on their own secure networks have become targets because they are connected to the Internet.

Supervisory control and data acquisition (SCADA) systems and industrial control systems (ICS) include critical infrastructure systems such as networks related to manufacturing, logistics and transportation, energy and utilities, telecommunication services, agriculture, and food production. SCADA is a subset of ICS. An ICS is managed via a SCADA system that provides a Human-Machine Interface (HMI) for operators to monitor the status of a system. Other ICS systems include industrial automation and control systems (IACS), distributed control systems (DCS), programmable logic controllers (PLCs), and remote terminal units (RTUs).

Targeted terrorist attacks against an ICS poses a threat to the infrastructure. Ideally, two separate security and IT groups should manage the network infrastructure and the ICS or SCADA network. Because ICS security requirements differ, IT architects and managers who do not have previous experience on this type of system need to be trained specifically in ICS security and must be familiar with guidance documents. Otherwise, the stronger security controls required for an ICS might be inadvertently missed, putting both the organization and the community at increased risk. In addressing SCADA security concerns, one of the first lines of defense against attacks is to implement physical segregation of internal and external networks, to reduce the attack surface by segregating the SCADA network from the corporate LAN. The SCADA LAN can be further segregated from the field device network containing the remote terminal units (RTUs) and programmable logic controllers (PLCs) by establishing an electronic security perimeter.

Guidance for proper security and established best practices for SCADA systems is found in *ISA99—Industrial Automation and Control Systems Security*, *North American Electric Reliability Corporation (NERC)—Critical Infrastructure Protection (CIP)*, and *NIST Special Publication 800-82: Guide to Industrial Control Systems (ICS) Security*.

> **ExamAlert**
>
> A key control against attacks on SCADA systems is to implement physical segregation of internal and external networks, to reduce the attack surface by segregating the SCADA network from the corporate LAN.

Smart Devices and IoT

Thanks to the Internet of Things (IoT), your smartphone can control household devices and your voice can instruct devices to find information or perform certain functions. IoT is described as enabling embedded system devices or components to interact with physical devices for the collection and exchange of data.

Gartner predicts that 8.4 billion IoT devices will be connected in 2017, increasing to 25 billion by 2020. All these devices collect or store data that must be protected.

Wearable Technology

Wearable technology has been around since the 1980s in the form of wearable heart rate monitors for athletes. The Fitbit debuted in 2011, and wearable technology came to the forefront with the release of the Apple Watch in 2015. Since then, other manufacturers have released smart watches and even wearable GPS trackers for pets. Perhaps the most recent technology of this type is wearable and body-mounted cameras that many police departments now require.

> **ExamAlert**
>
> Wearable technology was not developed to be secure and generally does not have any security protection, such as a PIN, authentication, or encryption. If the device is lost or stolen, anyone can access the data stored on the device.

Device manufacturers are being pushed to strengthen user data protection and implement security in designs, to secure wearable technology. For organizations that use wearable technology in their everyday business, many devices can be controlled through policy. For example, organizations that use wearables to capture video and audio can create an acceptable use policy outlining parameters for use. Policy enforcement controls should also be put in place. Other areas of concern include the following:

▶ Bluetooth and Wi-Fi communication between wearable devices and smartphones

▶ Sale of sensitive information tracked by wearable devices

▶ Wearable device information stored in a public cloud

Organizations can restrict wearable device capabilities by disabling certain features through MDM and restricting locations where wearable technology is allowed through geofencing.

Home Automation

Home automation devices are rapidly growing. The first widely used home automation device was the Roomba robot vacuum; it can be scheduled to automatically start whether or not the owner is near. One of the most popular home automation devices is the Amazon Echo. The Echo technically is a Bluetooth speaker, but it uses a digital assistant that can perform a variety of functions. This technology has even found its way into court cases. For example, recently Amazon handed over data from an Echo pertaining to a 2015 murder case.

Other home automation devices include smart thermostats, smart lighting, and smart locks. Interestingly, many of the home automation devices involve kitchen appliances such as refrigerators, coffee makers, garbage cans, and crock pots. Smart forks can even track what you eat. The home automation market is expected to reach $79.57 billion by 2022.

Home automation devices need to be protected. If an attacker can compromise your smart lock, house entry is possible without lock picking. Even without the inherent dangers of compromise, an unsecured device could be taken over with malware and used to participate in DDoS attacks.

ExamAlert

An easy way to tell whether any home automation devices are susceptible to public attack is to use an Internet of Things scanner.

Several IoT scanners are available. The most widely used is Shodan, which is basically a search engine that looks for publicly accessible devices.

Consider these tips for securing home automation devices:

▶ Secure the wireless network

▶ Know the devices that are communicating on the network and what they do

▶ Install security software on devices that offer that option

▶ Secure the smartphones and mobile apps that communicate with IoT devices

Technology advancements enable useful home automation capabilities, but you must be sure to secure your devices and protect your assets.

SoC and RTOS

System-on-a-chip (SoC) technology is basically a hardware module in small form factor. SoC devices have good processing power, and the small footprint makes this technology ideal for reduced power consumption, lower cost, and better performance than larger components. Some examples of developing technologies that take advantage of this are nanorobots, video devices for the visually impaired, and wireless antennas.

SoC is integration between a microcontroller, an application or microprocessor, and peripherals. The peripherals could be a GPU, a Wi-Fi module, or a coprocessor. The processor is usually powerful enough to run an OS such as Windows, Linux, Android, or Real-Time Operating System (RTOS). Intel's Curie module is about the size of a shirt button and contains all the components required to provide power for wearable devices.

SoC designs integrate intellectual property (IP) blocks, which are often acquired from untrusted third-party vendors. Although the design of SoC requires a security architecture, it relies on third-party vendors and little standardization of the security architecture in the design. An IP that contains a security vulnerability can make the entire SoC untrustworthy, and the lack of standardization allows for actions such as device jailbreaking and DRM overriding.

Suggestions for making the SoC design more secure follow:

▶ The device should be shielded from electromagnetic interference at the maximum level.

▶ Sensitive data should not be stored in the register or cache after processing.

▶ A separate security verification tool should be used to check the design.

The level of security built into SoC devices should take into consideration how easily a known vulnerability can be exploited and the amount of damage that can occur if the security of the device is compromised.

A real-time operating system (RTOS) is a small operating system used in embedded systems and IoT applications that are typically run in a SoC environment. The primary purpose of an RTOS is to allow the rapid switching of tasks, with a focus on timing instead of throughput. An RTOS allows applications to run with precise timing and high reliability. RTOS systems are used in microcontrollers and implemented in wearable and medical devices, as well as in-vehicle systems and home automation devices.

Vulnerabilities associated with RTOS include the following:

▶ Exploitation of shared memory

▶ Priority inversion

▶ Interprocess communication (IPC) attacks

▶ Code injection

▶ DoS attacks

HVAC

Heating, ventilation, and air conditioning (HVAC) devices use embedded systems to efficiently run environmental systems and reduce wasted energy. This is done by allowing them to be switched on only when necessary through the control of individual circuits. Circuits are switched off when no guests, visitors, or employees are present.

In large-scale systems, the embedded system controls work as PC-based system on a chip (SoC) boxes located near the HVAC elements they control. The boxes are usually rugged enough to function reliably in extreme-temperature locations and have extensive communication capabilities.

ExamAlert

Some HVAC monitoring software is not well updated or runs on older vulnerable versions of software. In addition, organizations often connect their HVAC equipment to the rest of their network, leaving the network vulnerable.

The Target intrusion case is a great example. The initial intrusion into Target's systems was traced back to network credentials that were stolen from a third-party vendor. Target had given the HVAC subcontractor remote access to perform energy-consumption monitoring for regulating store temperatures.

Printers, MFDs, and Camera Systems

Chapter 15, "Secure Systems Design," covered the vulnerabilities associated with printers and MFDs. Embedded applications such as Follow Me Print extend single sign-on capabilities to allow users to log into MFDs with their network password and print to virtually any printer. The embedded enabled MFD device integrates with the directory services of all major OS vendors. The embedded copier interface allows users to immediately see the cost of print jobs.

Organizations must realize that these systems are actual computers that have a hard drive, run an embedded operating system, and provide network services. They are subject to the same attacks as other network devices and embedded systems, including information leakage and buffer overflows.

Protections for these devices include the following:

▶ Proper access control to the device and functions

▶ Inclusion of printers and MFDs in security planning and policies

▶ Implementation of protections for data-in-transit and data-at-rest

The use of camera systems has grown significantly in the last few years. The current market for smart cameras and camera systems is expected to grow about 24 percent from now until 2020. These systems will be used for video surveillance, traffic monitoring, human interaction, and industrial automation.

The camera systems use smart cameras, which are basically video cameras that use an embedded system. Camera systems can contain embedded lighting, lenses, sensors, and processors.

Because these systems collect, store, and transit data, they require the same security considerations as any other device that holds sensitive data.

Noted camera system vulnerabilities include the following:

▶ Buffer overflows

▶ Disconnection of the camera from the Wi-Fi network

▶ Backdoors that allow the remote enabling of the Telnet/SSH service

Vulnerabilities can be exploited through hard-coded default credentials or default usernames and passwords that have not been changed. Additionally, the camera firmware and software should be regularly updated just as in any other networked device.

Special-Purpose Devices

The embedded systems discussed so far work in a variety of industries. Special-purpose embedded systems are devised for one industry in particular. The architecture is often based on a single-purpose processor and is designed to execute exactly one program. These special-purpose embedded devices are common in the medical, automotive, and aviation fields.

Medical Devices

Perhaps one of the fastest-growing IoT implementation industries is the healthcare sector. Medical advancements have encouraged hospitals to deploy more IoT devices. These advancements include uses such as a neural-machine interface (NMI) for artificial legs that can decode an amputee's intended movement in real time. The attacker community has also taken notice, and more incidents in recent years have taken place in the healthcare sector than in the financial sector. Medical devices have the capability for wireless connectivity, remote monitoring, and near field communication.

In 2013, concerns arose that Vice President Dick Cheney's pacemaker could be hacked, causing his death. In another instance, Johnson & Johnson publicly released a warning in 2016 to diabetic patients about an insulin pump security vulnerability. Shortly afterward, a team of researchers found several potentially fatal security flaws in various medical implants and defibrillators.

> **ExamAlert**
>
> Vulnerabilities in embedded medical devices present not only patient safety issues, but also the risk of lateral movement within the network.

If an attacker were able to exploit a vulnerability in a medical device and laterally move within the network, sensitive medical records could be at risk. According to industry professionals, U.S. hospitals currently average 10 to 15 connected devices per bed, amounting to 10 million to 15 million medical devices. A recent quick Internet search using Shodan revealed more than 36,000 publicly discoverable healthcare-related devices in the United States.

Government regulators such as the FDA have responded to recent incidents with a fact sheet on cybersecurity. They offer the following recommendations for the mitigation and management of cybersecurity threats to medical devices:

▶ Medical device manufacturers and healthcare facilities should apply appropriate device safeguards and risk mitigation.

▶ Hospitals and healthcare facilities should evaluate network security and protect their hospital systems.

As with all other embedded devices, medical devices require security and updates. Because this area relies on third-party components that could be vulnerable, robust security protections must be implemented from the start.

Vehicles

Automobile in-vehicle computing systems have been inaccessible to attackers. But the landscape is changing, thanks to the implementation of wireless networks such as Global System for Mobile communications (GSM) and Bluetooth integrated into automobiles. Current in-vehicle systems are capable of producing and storing data necessary for vehicle operation and maintenance, safety protection, and emergency contact transmission. Most in-vehicle systems have a wireless interface that connects to the Internet and have an on-board diagnostics interface for physical access. Many vehicles have data recorders inside the vehicle system that record vehicle speed, location, and braking maneuvers. Many insurance companies make use of this system to offer a discount for safe driving. A device inserted into the on-board diagnostics (OBD) port of the vehicle sends the collected data to the insurance company for analysis.

All communication between controllers is done in plain text. Because in-vehicle communications do not follow basic security practices, risks include unauthorized tracking, wireless jamming, and spoofing. A lot has been published regarding the capability to override a vehicle's Controller Area Network (CAN) bus communications. For example, researchers Charlie Miller and Chris Valasek attached themselves remotely to a Jeep Cherokee and were able to disable both the transmission and the brakes.

Risk mitigation recommendations include secure system software design practices, basic encryption, authentication of incoming data, and implementation of a firewall on the wireless gateway.

Aircraft and UAV

An aircraft has many embedded control systems, ranging from the flight control system to the galley microwave. A highly publicized article in 2016 highlighted a security researcher that used a flaw in an in-flight entertainment system to access a plane's controls. (Aviation experts asserted that this was technically impossible because the design isolates the infotainment system from the other systems performing critical functions.) Another vulnerability found in aviation control equipment is the use of hardcoded logon credentials that grant access to a plane's communications system using a single username and password. Other security issues are similar to those of medical embedded systems: use of undocumented or insecure protocols, weak credential protections, and the use of backdoors.

The technology associated with Unmanned Aerial Vehicles (UAVs), or drones, has been widely used in areas such as the military, agriculture, and cartography. Drones are most often used for aerial photography, surveillance, and surveying. They have become mainstream and now are proposed for delivery services such as Amazon. The first drone service delivery occurred in New Zealand in 2016, with a Domino's Pizza. FAA rules for drone delivery are set to be finalized in 2018, and commercial deliveries should begin in 2020.

Drones have many of the same vulnerabilities as other embedded systems and lack strong security. Drones are susceptible to hijacking, Wi-Fi attacks, GPS spoofing attacks, jamming, and deauthentication attacks. These attacks can allow an attacker to intercept or disable the drone and access its data.

Protecting Embedded Systems

Embedded systems that are used to capture, store, and access data of a sensitive nature pose some unique and interesting security challenges. Embedded systems are found in printers, smart TVs, and HVAC control systems, among other devices.

Security protocols and encryption address security considerations from a functional perspective, but most embedded systems are constrained by the environments in which they operate and the resources they use. Attacks against embedded systems rely on exploiting security vulnerabilities in the software and hardware components of the implementation and are susceptible to timing and side-channel attacks. Nonvolatile memory chips are found in many hardware devices, including TV tuners, fax machines, cameras, radios, antilock brakes, keyless entry systems, printers and copiers, modems, HVAC controls, satellite receivers, barcode readers, point-of-sale terminals, medical devices, smart cards, lock boxes, and garage door openers. The best protections for maintaining embedded device security include requiring software and hardware vendors to provide evidence that the software has no security weaknesses, perform remote attestation to verify that firmware has not been modified, and maintain secure configuration management processes when servicing field devices or updating firmware. Additionally, organizations must provide proper security oversight and monitor the contractors and vendors that perform work on installed systems.

What Next?

If you want more practice on this chapter's exam objectives before you move on, remember that you can access all the Cram Quiz questions on the Pearson Test Prep software. You can also create a custom exam by objective. Note any objective you struggle with and go to that objective material in this chapter.

CHAPTER 18

Secure Application Development and Deployment

This chapter covers the following official Security+ exam objective:

3.6 Summarize secure application development and deployment concepts.

▶ Development life-cycle models

- Waterfall vs. Agile

▶ Secure DevOps

- Security automation
- Continuous integration
- Baselining
- Immutable systems
- Infrastructure as code

▶ Version control and change management

▶ Provisioning and deprovisioning

▶ Secure coding techniques

- Proper error handling
- Proper input validation
- Normalization
- Stored procedures

- Code signing
- Encryption
- Obfuscation/camouflage
- Code reuse/dead code
- Server-side vs. client-side execution and validation
- Memory management
- Use of third-party libraries and SDKs
- Data exposure

▶ Code quality and testing

- Static code analyzers
- Dynamic analysis (e.g., fuzzing)
- Stress testing
- Sandboxing
- Model verification

▶ Compiled vs. runtime code

Essential Terms and Components

▶ Agile
▶ DevOps
▶ fuzzing
▶ infrastructure as code

▶ model verification
▶ normalization
▶ Waterfall

CramSaver

If you can correctly answer these questions before going through this chapter, save time by skimming the Exam Alerts in this chapter and then completing the Cram Quiz at the end of Part 3.

1. Explain the difference between the Waterfall and Agile methods of software development.

   _____

2. Explain the concept of continuous integration.

   _____

3. Explain how dynamic code analysis works.

   _____

Answers

1. The main differences between the Waterfall and Agile models have to do with planning and adjustments. The Waterfall SDLC model is traditional, starting with a defined set of requirements and a well-developed plan, and confining adjustments to the current development stage. The Agile SDLC model starts with less rigorous guidelines and allows for adjustments during the entire process.

2. Continuous integration (CI) is a process in which the source code updates from all developers working on the same project are continually monitored and merged from a central repository when a new commit is detected. CI avoids code merging conflicts, which occur when developers keep a working local copy of a software project for a long period of time.

3. Dynamic code analysis is based on observing how the code behaves during execution. Dynamic analysis uses a technique called fuzzing, which enables an attacker to inject random-looking data into a program to see if it can cause the program to crash.

Development Life-cycle Models

The software development life cycle (SDLC) is used in the software industry to produce high-quality software products. The SDLC framework, based on ISO/IEC 12207, defines the functions and steps necessary for the development and maintenance of software. The SDLC consists of the following six basic steps:

▶ Planning and analyzing requirements

▶ Defining and documenting requirements

▶ Designing the architecture

▶ Developing the software product

▶ Testing the software product

▶ Deploying and maintaining the software product

Multiple software development life cycle models or methodologies (SDLM) can be used during the software development process. Each model is unique and has advantages and disadvantages. These models include Waterfall, V-Shaped, Iterative, Spiral, Big Bang, and Agile.

Waterfall vs. Agile

Perhaps the oldest and most structured SDLC model is Waterfall. The Waterfall method is also referred to as a linear-sequential life cycle model. It is simple to understand and use but is slower and more rigid than some other models. Each individual phase is completed before the next phase starts because the outcome of each phase acts as the input for the next phase (hence the name Waterfall). If the first phase gets behind schedule, the entire project ends up behind. Additionally, when a phase is completed, there is no going back to make adjustments. Changes cannot be made until the software is in the maintenance phase. This model should not be chosen for long, ongoing projects or when flexibility is a primary requirement.

The Agile SDLC model breaks the development into cycles. Agile combines iterative and incremental process models, to achieve rapid delivery of a working product. This tends to be a more realistic development approach. The Agile method is well suited for applications that are updated frequently, such as with PayPal and Google apps. The Agile method provides ongoing releases, and each release contains incremental changes. Testing is conducted with each new release or iteration. Iterations generally last one to three weeks. The Agile model relies heavily on customer interaction and can easily be derailed if customer direction is not clear. The model is not suitable for products that require complex dependencies.

ExamAlert

The main differences between Waterfall and Agile have to do with planning and adjustments. The Waterfall SDLC model is traditional: It starts with a defined set of requirements and a well-developed plan, and it confines adjustments to the current development stage. The Agile SDLC model starts with less rigorous guidelines and allows for adjustments during the entire process.

Secure DevOps

Development and Operation (DevOps) originated from the recognition that organizational infrastructure should support development of the SDLC along with production capacity. Secure DevOps includes security in the SDLC, which was not always a major concern in developing software applications. When the topic was initially introduced, software developers had a negative reaction because it meant greater programming effort and delays in development and release cycles. The evolvement of secure DevOps has produced some best practices for increased security of developed applications, including the following:

▶ Address security concerns at the beginning of projects.

▶ Reduce faults by standardizing the integration cycle.

▶ Add automated security testing techniques to the SDLC.

From a secure DevOps perspective, software should be secure and resilient. Developers should be proficient with the tools and thought processes to develop software that can withstand attacks and continue to function instead of ones that only seek to prevent attacks. This offers more flexibility in mitigating attack risks. A secure SDLC requires the organization to focus on practices such as security automation, continuous integration, and infrastructure as code.

Continuous Integration and Security Automation

A main DevOps concept is continuous integration (CI), a process in which the source code updates from all developers working on the same project are continually monitored and merged from a central repository. The repository is updated when a new commit or permanent change is detected. Software builds are triggered by every commit to the repository. CI helps avoid code merging conflicts that can arise when developers keep a working local copy of a software project for a long period of time.

The CI process is automated. A centralized server continually pulls in new source code changes as they are committed by developers. It then builds the software application and runs unit test suites for the project. When a process fails, the CI server fails the build and immediately notifies the project team of the failure.

ExamAlert

CI servers are also called build servers because of their main function. A CI server compiles, builds, and tests each new version of code committed to the central repository without user interaction.

All members of the team are notified when code in the repository fails. This prevents a loss in team productivity by limiting the chance for merge issues and rework due to a broken codebase. The CI process is based on automated configuration and deployment scripts. Automated processes are critical to ensure that software operates as intended.

DevOps includes more rigor and testing so that the process itself can inherently foster a more secure environment. Automation frameworks such as Chef and Puppet are already used for IT infrastructure. Continuous delivery for secure code using security automation is similar to the automation of IT infrastructure.

Scripting and automation are a large part of DevOps, and security automation is no exception. Security testing is automated so that security concerns are designed into systems at the beginning of the process and then are continually checked as part of the software development process. The primary benefits of security automation follow:

▶ A more holistic approach to security because it is part of the build process

▶ Proactive scanning for common vulnerabilities during the entire process

▶ Available list of version control security checks with deployments

Security automation within the SDLC provides more secure, higher-quality code, at a faster rate.

Baselining

An SDLC baseline is a reference point in the process that is noted by the completion and subsequent approval of a set of predefined project requirements. The primary goal of a baseline is to prevent uncontrolled change and lessen project vulnerability. This is accomplished by implementing formal change control processes for key deliverables at critical points in the SDLC. Baselines provide the following:

▶ Measurable progress points

▶ A foundation for change control in phases that follow

▶ A sound reference point for future projects, including intermediate as well as final points

A typical project contains baselines such as functional, allocated, design, several testing points, product, and operational. They can also be used to establish the required software and hardware components necessary for a specific release. In DevOps, baselines and metrics are typically used to record and track progress.

Immutable Systems

Mutable means that after something has been created, if changes are needed, you modify the one you already put in place. This is done primarily to avoid the cost associated with creating a new one. Traditional software programs and servers function in this way. Mutability is a leading cause of software bugs and configuration errors.

Immutability means that a value, program, configuration, or server is never modified in place. If changes are needed, a new one is built or configured and the old one is removed.

> **ExamAlert**
>
> Immutability increases the reliability of system and software behavior while reducing software development and deployment time.

The concept of immutability has grown with DevOps because replacement and deployment costs have become very inexpensive. This produces more frequent, repeatable updates and more reliable services, with less downtime. An immutable server has a known, documented, repeatable configuration that is source controlled. A new development server is exactly the same as a new production server because both were created using the same deployment files. This process also makes adding servers easier when the workload increases and supports a faster recovery from disaster because the same deployment files are used in new deployments.

Infrastructure As Code

Infrastructure as code (IaC) is also known as programmable infrastructure. This means that infrastructure configuration can be incorporated into application code. IaC enables DevOps teams to test applications in production-like environments from the beginning of the development cycle. Validation and testing can then prevent common deployment issues.

The previously mentioned automation frameworks Chef and Puppet (along with other tools, such as Ansible and Docker) provide the capability to automatically configure the infrastructure layer and operating system layers through scripts or code. Developers write the infrastructure that the application code runs on into the program. Basically, all configurations are written into the script or code, eliminating the need for a full environment. IaC provides the following benefits:

- ▶ Acts as a documentation reference point for the application infrastructure

- ▶ Provides a consistent starting point for deployments

- ▶ Supports infrastructure independence

- ▶ Avoids infrastructure inconsistencies

IaC is based on using proven coding techniques that encompass infrastructure.

Change Management and Version Control

The software change management process is similar to the IT change management process. Change management processes are used to properly control and manage changes to software. The primary function of change management is managing project or product changes so they meet both the defined scope and customer expectations. The capability to manage changes is a necessary component for quality in software products.

In an Agile or DevOps environment, change management has a stronger focus on responsiveness to requests for change and swift implementation of approved change requests. This is accomplished by using advanced automation and control tools, to streamline the change and release management process. Different types of management often are consolidated into one pipeline.

Change management goes hand in hand with version control, and change management tools often are used to handle version control. Version control, or source control, is part of software configuration or change management and manages changes to collections of information. Version control tracks changes in the source code and provides software integrity during development stages of the SDLC. Strict version control prevents tampering with the source code or executables.

Version control is done though a system, software tools, or applications that track software file changes and provide a way to manage changes to source code over time. Most version control systems use some form of distributed storage. For example, one tool might use one master server, while other tools might use a network of distributed servers.

Version control benefits include the following:

▶ Historical data on changes to files

▶ Branching and merging capabilities

▶ Traceability

When used in a DevOps environment, version control is generally used as a predictor of performance because it can provide metrics for process improvement.

Provisioning and Deprovisioning

Provisioning is the creation or update of a resource. Deprovisioning is the removal of a resource. Provisioning and deprovisioning are part of organizational lifecycle management and can affect any number of assets. Software provisioning and deprovisioning are generally automated processes in which software packages are made available to computers and users through a self-service portal. Provisioning can be integrated with other technologies as well. This is especially true in cloud-based environments. For example, in one particular implementation, VMware used a private cloud based on a software-defined data center architecture to automate the provisioning process. The results included a reduction in application environment provisioning time, an increase in developer productivity, improved capacity, and significant cost savings.

Secure Coding Techniques

Attacks against software vulnerabilities are becoming more sophisticated. Many times a vendor misses a vulnerability and then, when it is discovered, does not address it for quite some time. The vendor decides how and when to patch a vulnerability. As a result, users have become increasingly concerned about the integrity, security, and reliability of commercial software. *Software assurance* describes vendor efforts to reduce vulnerabilities, improve resistance to attack, and protect the integrity of products. Software assurance is especially important in organizations where users require a high level of confidence that commercial software is as secure as possible. Secure software is achieved when it is created using best practices for secure software development.

The security of software code has come to the forefront in recent years, and coalitions have been formed to improve it. Additionally, the industry offers certifications in software security. The Software Assurance Forum for Excellence in Code (SAFECode) works to identify and promote best practices for developing and delivering more secure and reliable software, hardware, and services. It was founded by EMC, Juniper Networks, Microsoft, SAP, and Symantec. Organizations such as (ISC)² offer a certification specifically geared toward secure code design, such as the Certified Secure Software Lifecycle Professional (CSSLP). The various stages of secure software include design, coding, source code handling, and testing.

Security must be implemented from the very beginning. In the early design phase, potential threats to the application must be identified and addressed. Organizations must take into consideration ways to reduce the associated risks. These objectives can be accomplished in a variety of ways, such as threat modeling and mitigation planning, including analyzing potential vulnerabilities and attack vectors from an attacker's point of view. When the design is complete, the secure programming practices must be implemented. Secure coding skills require inspecting an application's source code to identify vulnerabilities created by coding errors.

ExamAlert

Organizations should implement secure programming practices that reduce the frequency and severity of errors. Source code review should combine manual analysis and automated analysis tools.

Using automated tools along with manual review can reduce the vulnerabilities that might be missed using only one method.

When the coding is done and has been reviewed, you must carefully handle the source code. Procedures for the secure handling of code include strict change management, tracking, and confidentiality protection of the code. To prevent malicious insiders from introducing vulnerabilities, only authorized persons should be permitted to view or modify the code. Additional consideration for the protection of code includes protecting the systems and code repositories from unauthorized access. When the development is outsourced, you should conduct internal design and code reviews to prevent malicious code from being introduced. The final step in secure code development is testing. In the testing phase, particular attention should be given to validating that the security requirements were met and the design and coding specifications were followed. Testing processes can include applying testing techniques such as fuzzing and using a variety of inputs to identify possible buffer overflows or other vulnerabilities. Some software vendors submit their products for external testing in addition to doing internal testing because an unbiased, independent test might uncover vulnerabilities that would not be detectable using internal processes. The secure code testing phase can include the important black box, white box, or gray box testing methods discussed in previous chapters.

Proper Error Handling

Many of the software exploits that have emerged in the past few years were a direct result of poor or incorrect input validation or mishandled exceptions. Common programming flaws include trusting input when designing an application and not performing proper exception checking in the code. These practices allow attacks such as buffer overflows, format string vulnerabilities, and utilization of shell escape codes. To reduce these programming flaws, organizations should review authentication, authorization, logging and auditing, code dependencies, error messages, and code comment practices.

Authentication strength is vital to the security of the application. Relinquish common practices such as hard-coding credentials into an application or storing them in clear text, in favor of encrypting authentication credentials. This is especially important for a web application that uses cookies to store session and authentication information. In web applications or multilayered systems in which the identity is often propagated to other contexts, authorization control should form a strong link to the identity through the life cycle of the authenticated session. Logging and auditing should be designed to include configurable logging and auditing capabilities. This facilitates the flexibility of collecting detailed information when necessary. Using libraries from established vendors minimizes the risk of unknown vulnerabilities, especially when using object-oriented programming that relies on the use of third-party libraries.

Take care when programming error messages. Although error messages are important to determine the problem, they should not divulge specific system or application information. Attackers usually gather information before they try to break into an application, so outputting detailed error messages can give an attacker the necessary information to escalate an attack. Information output in error messages should be on a need-to-know basis. Exception handling should log the error and provide the user with a standard message. Do not use comments in public viewable code that could reveal valuable information about the application or system, especially in web applications where the code and associated comments reside on the browser.

Proper Input Validation

Input validation tests whether an application properly handles input from a source outside the application that is destined for internal processing.

ExamAlert

The most common result of improper input validation is buffer overflow exploitation. Additional types of input validation errors result in format string and denial-of-service (DoS) exploits.

Application field input should always include a default value and character limitations to avoid these types of exploits. Although software developers can overlook input validation, testing the code by sending varying amounts of both properly and improperly formatted data into the application helps determine whether this application is potentially vulnerable to exploits. Various methods can test input validation, including automated testing, session management validation, race condition analysis, cryptographic analysis, and code coverage analysis.

An automated program can randomly perform input validation against the target, based on the program's capability to handle input without any established criteria for external interfaces of the application. This means that any component of the application can be tested with randomly generated data without a set order or reason. Testing an application for session management vulnerabilities consists of attempting to modify any session state variables to evoke undesirable results from the application. Access can be gained to other communication channels through modified variables, leading to privilege escalation, loss of data confidentiality, and unauthorized access to resources. When time elapses between a security operation and the general function it applies to, a window of opportunity is created that might allow an attacker to circumvent security measures. This is known as a race condition. Testing for race conditions attempts to access the file between the time the application creates the file and when the application actually applies the security. Sensitive data such as passwords and credit card information is frequently protected by cryptographic methods. Knowing what algorithm an application uses might exploit its weaknesses. Additionally, if strong encryption is used but the vendor implementation is incorrect, the data might not be properly protected; this could result in errors such as improper creation or storage of the cryptographic keys and key management. Code coverage analysis verifies that proper security measures are taken on all possible paths of code execution. Some paths might enable security to be bypassed, leaving the system in a vulnerable state. This type of analysis can be resource intensive and should be done in stages during application development.

Normalization

Applications often accept untrusted input strings and instead use techniques such as validation methods and input filtering. These methods are based on the strings' character data and are similar to blacklisting. Although they are not really sufficient for complete input validation and sanitization, these methods do provide some level of security. For example, an application might be programmed to forbid certain tags in input, to mitigate cross-site scripting (XSS) vulnerabilities. When an application uses this type of method, after it is accepted, the input should be normalized before it is validated. Normalization is the conversion of data to its anticipated, simplest known form. This provides assurance that all equivalent strings have a unique binary representation. This is necessary because, in Unicode, the same string can have many different representations.

If the data is accepted merely because strings can have different representations, then the application can accept malicious code. Using normalization, when the input is validated, the malicious input is correctly identified.

> **ExamAlert**
>
> Validating input before normalization allows attackers to bypass security mechanisms, resulting in the execution of malicious code.

Stored Procedures

Stored procedures are most often associated with databases and database queries. Stored procedures are combinations of precompiled SQL statements, stored in the database, that execute some task. The purpose of a stored procedure is to allow the acceptance of input parameters so that one procedure can be used by many clients using varied input data. This produces faster results and reduces network traffic.

Stored procedures can be used for security by encapsulating certain logic in server-side persistent modules. Client or user database communication is then restricted to use only server-side stored procedures. To increase security and reduce SQL injection vulnerabilities, data manipulation statements such as SELECT or DELETE have to go through the stored procedures before returning data. SQL injection vulnerabilities are reduced because stored procedures can be written so that the stored procedure has execute rights without the client or user needing to have read/write permission on the underlying tables. Using stored procedures does not necessarily eliminate SQL injections, however: When dynamic SQL is allowed to be created inside the stored procedure, SQL injection can still occur.

Code Signing

The most common example of code signing is drivers. For example, by default, Microsoft operating systems block the installation of unsigned drivers. Code signing consists of signing executables using a certificate-based digital signature. This is done to provide trustworthiness in the executable. Code signing proves the author's identity and provides reasonable assurance that the code has not been tampered with since it was signed.

The two types of code signing certificates are organizational code signing certificates, which are issued to organizations, and individual code signing certificates, which identify independent developers. The certificate is issued by a Certificate Authority (CA) that validates the legitimacy of the issuer. If a nefarious person steals a legitimate certificate, that certificate can be used to sign malware. This makes the program seem legitimate to unsuspecting users. For this reason, many cybercriminals and cybercriminal groups such as Suckfly are stealing certificates and using them in malicious attacks.

Encryption, Obfuscation, and Camouflage

Encryption tends to be a catch-all solution. When in doubt, encrypt. Encryption, obfuscation, and camouflage are used in the software development process to prevent the software from being reverse-engineered. These practices protect the trade secrets and intellectual property of organizations.

Encoding technologies have been developed that effectively hide executable program code in plain sight and do not require the code to be decrypted before it is run. This allows the software to run but not be reverse-engineered.

Obfuscation has been used for a long time in interpreted languages. This is often done by shortening function and variable names and removing whitespace. The best way to see the prevalence of this technique is to view the source code of a web home page such as Google. When used in a malicious manner, obfuscation usually goes one step further by encrypting the underlying source code, which is then decrypted on the fly when the code is run.

> **ExamAlert**
>
> Camouflage can also protect software from reverse engineering. Whereas obfuscation uses the process of hiding original data with random characters or data, camouflage replaces sensitive data with realistic fictional data.

Camouflage can protect software from reverse engineering. Fake source code is created by modifying a piece of original source code. When an attacker analyzes the program, the attacker sees the fake code, but the program executes the original when it is run.

Use of these techniques can affect the functionality of the software and programs. For example, if SQL Server objects, procedures, or functions are encrypted, the source cannot be retrieved from the SQL Server.

Code Reuse and Dead Code

Code reuse is the practice of using existing software to build new software. A great deal of the code used in software development is reused to save time and development costs. Although this is beneficial because much of the work is already done, it can introduce security flaws and vulnerabilities into the product. Developers sometimes use vulnerable or nonpatched versions of reused components even after vulnerabilities are made public and more secure versions are available. Much of this code comes from third parties, allowing an attacker to target one component vulnerability that many applications might have used.

In examples such as OpenSSL Heartbleed and GNU Bash Shellshock, libraries and frameworks that contained unpatched vulnerabilities were used in applications. Either the development team lacks due diligence in these cases or a vulnerability is discovered in code that was previously considered reliable. To mitigate the effects of introducing vulnerabilities through code reuse, organizations must exercise due diligence, keep components patched, and continually strive to find reliable sources of code when creating new products.

Dead code is code contained in a program that can be executed but no longer provides a useful resulting action. Dead code often occurs because software requirements change and developers did not take the time to clean up the old code. As a common programming practice, dead code should be deleted or removed.

The execution of dead code can exhaust resources such as computation time and memory. More troubling is that it can cost an organization millions of dollars if dead code is awakened. For example, flag reuse of a flag that hadn't been used in eight years triggered the execution of a version of the code that still had a dependency on the old flag. This misstep actually ended in bankrupting the organization.

Use of Third-Party Libraries and SDKs

As mentioned previously, much of the code used to create applications comes from third-party libraries. When using third-party libraries, the organization must exercise due diligence by keeping track of and implementing library updates and security measures. Most critical vulnerabilities in third-party libraries are disclosed as Common Vulnerabilities and Exposures (CVEs), making them quite visible for organizations to locate and track.

A software development kit (SDK) is a set of tools for creating applications using a certain software package. For example, if you are creating an Android application, you would use the Android SDK. SDKs present the same security issues as the use of third-party libraries. Known vulnerabilities in SDKs are also published via CVEs. The biggest problem with vulnerabilities in third-party libraries and SDKs is that they can potentially affect millions of applications. This is why attackers have recently shifted efforts to this area.

Server-side vs. Client-side Execution and Validation

Client-side validation occurs when the data entered into a form is validated through a web page script via the user's browser before the form is posted back to the originating server. Client-side validation is often used for convenience because it gives immediate feedback to the user if incorrect data is input. Client-side validation is an insecure form of validation in web applications because it places trust in the browser. This form of validation allows the client to execute validation and can be easily bypassed or altered; in addition, it allows the user to view the page code through built-in browser capabilities. When an application accepts input from the client, the input should be validated on the server for type, length, and range.

Server-side validation occurs on the server where the application resides. Server-side validation helps protect against malicious attempts by a user to bypass validation or submit unsafe input information to the server. Server-side checks are more difficult to bypass and are a more secure form of input validation. Several techniques on the server side can improve validation, including identifying the acceptable data input type that is being passed from the client, defining the input format and type, building a validator routine for each input type, and situating the validator routines at the trust boundary of the application. A recommended approach is to initially perform client-side validation and then, after the input form has posted to the server, perform the validation a second time using server-side validation.

Memory Management

Memory management optimizes performance by assigning blocks of memory to various processes and programs. It makes sure that sufficient memory is available for any currently running program or process. Memory management is used in all computing functions and plays an integral part in programming applications. Application memory management is based on allocation and recycling. Programs are written to request blocks of memory, and the allocator is used to assign that block to the program. When the program no longer needs the data in the assigned allocated memory blocks, the blocks can be reassigned.

Proper memory management in software development is imperative because many vulnerabilities take advantage of improper memory management techniques. For example, buffer overflow vulnerabilities are based on the capability to overflow the memory allocated for a variable. Suggestions for mitigating vulnerabilities such as buffer overflows include the following:

▶ Verify that the buffer is as large as specified.

▶ Use input and output control for data that is untrusted.

▶ Properly free allocated memory upon completion of the functions.

▶ Do not use known vulnerable functions.

Clearing sensitive information stored in memory to avoid unintentional disclosure should also be included in the memory management practices.

Data Exposure

According to best practices, sensitive data should be encrypted at all times, including while in transit and at rest. Data exposure often occurs in applications because sensitive data such as credit card numbers, personal health information, and authentication credentials are not protected during transit. Other times, sensitive application data is stored unprotected, exposing the data.

Mitigation of data exposure should be addressed using an SDLC framework along with best practices. Addressing data exposure in both the requirements and design phases permits the organization to take a holistic approach to mitigation. Security best practices dictate that the following methods be included when building applications:

▶ Data validation

▶ Authentication and authorization

▶ Encryption

In particular, organizations should address the following three areas: exposed data that might mistakenly be uploaded, weak cryptography, and browser caching controls.

Compiled vs. Runtime Code

Before the coding process is complete, developers need a method of making sure that the code will actually execute. This can happen through either a compiled or run-time environment. The environment depends on the programming language used to create the code. Some languages are considered compiled, which means that the code goes through a compiler to run. Other languages are considered interpreted, which means that the code can be run using a command as long as a program is installed on the machine that can interpret the code.

In a compiled program, certain checks are done at compile time before the program is actually run. This allows coding errors to be fixed before a fully running program is ready for use. Compiled code generally runs faster than interpreted code. In a run-time program, the program code is translated through an interpreter. Interpreted code runs more slowly than compiled code because the interpreter actively turns the code into machine-readable commands on the fly.

Interpreted languages make development easier and coding faster. Generally, interpreters are less secure than compiled programs because they need to execute arbitrary code and make untrusted writeable memory regions executable. Interpreter security can be improved through explicit support by the OS.

Code Quality and Testing

Quality assurance and testing processes directly affect code quality. The earlier defects in software are found, the easier and cheaper they are to fix. The benefits of implementing a sound QA and testing process far outweigh the associated costs. The SDLC must include quality code and testing: Reports of website vulnerabilities and data breaches are reported in the news almost daily. Providing quality software also builds a positive reputation for the organization and provides customers confidence in the products they are purchasing.

Static Code Analyzers

Static analysis is performed in a nonruntime environment. Typically, a static analysis tool inspects the code for all possible runtime behaviors and looks for problematic code such as back doors or malicious code.

> **ExamAlert**
>
> Static analysis is a white box software testing process for detecting bugs. The idea behind static analysis is to take a thorough approach to bug detection in the early stages of program development.

The same kind of compiler is used in static code analyzers that is used to compile code. Integrating a source code analyzer into a compiler makes the best use of the compiler and reduces complexity. The code analyzer can use pre-existing compiler data flow algorithms to perform analysis. The analysis is a complete program analysis that checks complex code interactions. Static code analyzers can detect a wide array of vulnerabilities, including memory leaks.

Dynamic Analysis

As noted in the previous section, static code analysis is performed without executing any code. Dynamic code analysis is based on observing how the code behaves during execution. Dynamic analysis is done while the program is in operation and monitors functional behavior and overall performance. Dynamic analysis uses a technique called *fuzzing*, which enables an attacker to inject random-looking data into a program to see if it can cause the program to crash.

ExamAlert

Fuzzing is a black-box software-testing process in which semirandom data is injected into a program or protocol stack to detect bugs. Fuzzing is based on the assumption that every program has bugs.

A systematic discovery approach should find application bugs sooner or later. The data generation part consists of generators. Generators typically use combinations of static fuzzing vectors or totally random data. The vulnerability identification relies on debugging tools. Most fuzzers are either protocol/file format dependent or data type dependent. New generation fuzzers use genetic algorithms to link injected data and observed impact. OWASP provides a fuzz vector resource section, which is a great source for fuzzing methodology and real-life fuzzing vectors examples.

Several different types of fuzzing exist:

▶ **Application fuzzing:** Attack vectors are within its I/O—for example, the user interface, the command-line options, URLs, forms, user-generated content, and RPC requests.

▶ **Protocol fuzzing:** Forged packets are sent to the tested application, which can act as a proxy and modify requests on the fly and then replay them.

▶ **File format fuzzing:** Multiple malformed samples are generated and then opened sequentially. When the program crashes, debug information is kept for further investigation.

An advantage of fuzzing is that the test design is generally very simple, without any presumptions about system behavior. This approach makes it possible to find bugs that human testing would have missed. In some closed application instances, fuzzing might be the only means of reviewing the security quality of the program. The simplicity can be a disadvantage because more advanced bugs will not be found. Additionally, if a fuzzer is very protocol aware, it will tend to miss odd errors. A random approach is still a good idea for best results. Fuzzing can add another dimension to normal software-testing techniques.

Stress Testing

Stress testing tests how much stress an application or program can withstand before it breaks. Stress testing uses methods to overload the existing resources in an attempt to break the application. The primary purpose of stress testing is to assess the behavior of the application beyond normal conditions. It serves the following purposes:

▶ Offers a method of nonfunctional testing

▶ Identifies the breaking point of the application

▶ Determines application stability

▶ Provides statistics on application availability and error handling under high usage

▶ Produces information on crash conditions under lack of resources

Stress testing provides a reference point for application robustness and stability.

Sandboxing

Recall from Chapter 16, "Secure Staging Deployment," that sandboxing allows programs and processes to be run in an isolated environment, to limit access to files and the host system. Running a program or file in a sandbox contains it so that it can be tested, and this reduces some security issues because the program or file cannot harm the host or make any changes to the host. In software development, especially when Agile methods are used, common best practice is to ensure that developers work in their own sandbox. A sandbox is basically a technical environment whose scope is well defined and respected. Sandboxing reduces the risk of programming errors adversely affecting the entire team. In software development, the following types of sandboxes can be used:

▶ Development

▶ Project integration

▶ Demo

▶ Preproduction test or QA

▶ Production

Organizations that use development sandboxes have the distinct advantage of being able to scan applications more frequently and early in the SDLC. This provides an environment that encourages development teams to be cognizant of application security, detects issues early in the process, and reduces risk to the organization.

Model Verification

Model-based development uses modeling languages to allow developers to create a model of the system. The model can then be executed, analyzed, and used to generate code and test cases.

Model checking is an algorithmic approach to the analysis of system states that automatically verifies the correctness of properties associated with finite-state systems. This concept has been ported to be applicable to the analysis of software.

Model checking for software verification is based on a constructed model of how the software should perform. Model verification is used for checking software with these characteristics:

▶ Contains complex data structures

▶ Based on an object-oriented design

▶ Uses complex coordination between software components

▶ Has synchronous or asynchronous execution

Model checking automatically and thoroughly checks whether a model meets a given specification. Model checkers improve the quality of code because they perform exhaustive testing by considering every possible combination of inputs and state.

What Next?

If you want more practice on this chapter's exam objectives before you move on, remember that you can access all the Cram Quiz questions on the Pearson Test Prep software. You can also create a custom exam by objective. Note any objective you struggle with and go to that objective material in this chapter.

CHAPTER 19

Cloud and Virtualization

This chapter covers the following official Security+ exam objective:

3.7 Summarize cloud and virtualization concepts.

- ▶ Hypervisor
  - Type I
  - Type II
  - Application cells/ containers
- ▶ VM sprawl avoidance
- ▶ VM escape protection
- ▶ Cloud storage
- ▶ Cloud deployment models
  - SaaS
  - PaaS

- IaaS
- Private
- Public
- Hybrid
- Community
- ▶ On-premise vs. hosted vs. cloud
- ▶ VDI/VDE
- ▶ Cloud access security broker
- ▶ Security as a Service

Essential Terms and Components

- ▶ cloud access security broker
- ▶ hypervisor
- ▶ Infrastructure as a Service (IaaS)
- ▶ Platform as a Service (PaaS)
- ▶ Security as a Service (SecaaS)
- ▶ Software as a Service (SaaS)

- ▶ virtual desktop environment (VDE)
- ▶ virtual desktop infrastructure (VDI)
- ▶ virtualization technology
- ▶ VM escape
- ▶ VM sprawl

CramSaver

If you can correctly answer these questions before going through this chapter, save time by skimming the Exam Alerts in this chapter and then completing the Cram Quiz at the end of Part 3.

1. Explain what a hypervisor is.

   _____

2. Describe cloud computing.

   _____

3. Define a cloud access security broker (CASB).

   _____

Answers

1. A hypervisor is a software- or hardware-layer program that permits the use of many instances of an operating system or instances of different operating systems on the same machine, independent of each other.

2. *Cloud computing* as it is used today is a general term that basically describes anything that involves delivering hosted computing services over the Internet.

3. CASB is a Gartner-created term that describes a cloud cybersecurity layer focused on visibility, compliance, data security, and threat protection.

Virtualization Concepts

With power becoming more expensive and society placing more emphasis on becoming environmentally friendly, virtualization offers attractive cost benefits by decreasing the number of physical machines required within an environment. This applies to both servers and desktops. On the client side, the capability to run multiple operating environments allows a machine to support applications and services for an operating environment other than the primary environment. Currently, many implementations of virtual environments are available to run on just about everything from servers and routers to USB thumb drives.

The security concerns of virtual environments begin on the guest operating system. If a virtual machine is compromised, an intruder can gain control of all the guest operating systems. In addition, because hardware is shared, most virtual machines run with very high privileges. This can allow an intruder who compromises a virtual machine to compromise the host machine, too. Just as with regular host-installed environments, vulnerabilities also come into play with virtualization. The section "VM Escape Protection" covers the VENOM vulnerability. Virtual machine environments need to be patched just like host environments and are susceptible to the same issues as a host operating system. You should be cognizant of sharing files among guest and host operating systems.

> **ExamAlert**
>
> If compromised, virtualized environments can provide access to not only the network, but also any virtualization infrastructure. This puts a lot of data at risk.

Hypervisors

For virtualization to work, a hypervisor is used. A *hypervisor* is a software- or hardware-layer program that permits the use of many instances of an operating system or instances of different operating systems on the same machine, independent of each other. This section discusses virtualization methods.

Type I

A Type I native hypervisor, or bare-metal hypervisor, is software that runs directly on a hardware platform. The guest operating system runs at the second level above the hardware. These hardware-bound virtual machine emulators rely on the real, underlying CPU to execute nonsensitive instructions at native speed. In hardware virtualization, a guest operating system is run under the control of a host system, where the guest has been ported to a virtual architecture that is almost like the hardware it is actually running on. The guest OS is not aware that it is being virtualized and requires no modification. The hypervisor translates all operating system instructions on the fly and caches the results for future use, while user-level instructions run unmodified at native speed.

Type II

A Type II hypervisor, or hosted hypervisor, is software that runs within an operating system environment with the guest operating system running at the third level above the hardware. The hypervisor runs as an application or shell on another operating system that is already running. Operating systems running on the hypervisor are then called guest or virtual operating systems. This type of virtual machine consists entirely of software and contains no hardware components whatsoever. Thus, the host can boot to completion and launch any number of applications as usual, with one of them being the virtual machine emulator. That emulator then sets up CPU-specific control structures and uses a CPU instruction to place the operating system into a virtualized state. A virtual machine monitor (VMM) provides a layer of software between the operating system(s) and the hardware of a machine to create the illusion of one or more virtual machines (VMs) on a single physical platform. A virtual machine entirely encapsulates the state of the guest operating system running inside it. Because virtual machines consist entirely of software and contain no hardware components, virtual machines offer distinct advantages over physical hardware.

Figure 19.1 shows the difference between a Type I and a Type II hypervisor.

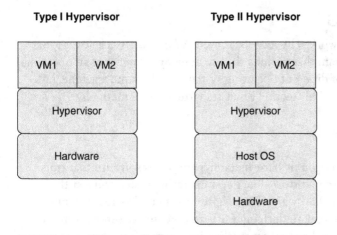

FIGURE 19.1   Difference Between a Type I and a Type II Hypervisor

The distinction between Type I and Type II hypervisors has to do with whether an underlying operating system is present:

▶ **Type I:** Runs directly on the hardware, with VM resources provided by the hypervisor. VMware ESXi and Citrix XenServer are Type 1 hypervisors.

▶ **Type II:** Runs on a host operating system to provide virtualization services. VirtualBox, VMware Server, and Microsoft Virtual PC are Type 2 hypervisors.

Hyper-V stand-alone or integrated Windows Servers are considered Type 1 hypervisors.

> **ExamAlert**
>
> Type I hypervisors offer better management tools and performance and are used in larger environments. Type II hypervisors present more security implications because of their reliance on the underlying OS.

Type II hypervisors tend to have better hardware compatibility because they use software-based virtualization.

Containers and Application Cells

Preconfigured virtual environments are preconfigured virtual appliances that are available from a variety of vendors, including VMware, Microsoft, and Parallels. Virtual appliances come ready to start up. They have a preinstalled, preconfigured OS inside a virtual machine environment. The user merely downloads the container and loads it. Virtual appliances are created using virtual appliance authoring tools and then the appliance is posted for use.

Virtual containers are spawned from virtual appliances. Virtual containers operate differently from appliances because they contain only applications and follow the minimal requirements to run the application in the container package. Containers do not require a hypervisor or separate OS instances because they share the same OS kernel as the host. This makes them more efficient and permits the host to run many containers simultaneously. Double to triple the number of applications generally can run on a single server with containers instead of full VMs.

The downside of containers is that because they use the same OS host kernel, the underlying operating system can theoretically be compromised if a user or application has elevated privileges within the container. The same quality assurance problem exists with containers as with VM marketplaces. Without properly vetting the container, the organization can open itself to malware infection.

Virtualization has found its way into handheld devices as well. Application cells are individual VM cells used to stage and run applications. This environment is most commonly found in Android mobile applications. Each application runs in its own Java virtual machine (JVM), to prevent the applications from affecting each other. The security problem with this design is that when apps are installed, they often ask for access to other apps or information. If access is granted, exfiltration of data can take place between the apps.

Taking this one step further, entire virtual smartphones and tablets can be run simultaneously on the same physical device using an open-source virtualization architecture called Cells. Another way virtualization is affecting handheld devices is through cellular technology virtualization, which is based on the Cloud/Centralized Radio Access Network (C-RAN) architecture. C-RAN centralizes the base station function for many radios into a single location. C-RAN functions similarly to network functions virtualization (NFV), providing more flexibility and efficiency.

VDE/VDI

Virtual desktop environments (VDE) are similar in form to server virtualization, but with some differences in their usage and the performance demands made on them. Desktop virtualization is often the most dynamic of all the virtualized environments because far more changes are made inside the environment both locally and over the network than with a virtualized server. With virtual desktops, user desktop environments are stored remotely on a server. This facilitates configurations that can be created, deleted, copied, archived, and downloaded over a network or can be remotely hosted very quickly.

Most VDEs include software for managing the virtual desktops. *Virtual desktop infrastructure (VDI)* is the server-based *virtualization technology* that hosts and manages the virtual desktops. Functions include creating the desktop images, managing the desktops on the servers, and providing client network access for the desktop.

Managing and deploying a VDI requires different skills than basic network management. Desktop virtualization requires high availability and storage capacity for a multitude of desktop clients and applications. If designed properly, resource utilization can be maximized while reducing management costs. Improper management can result in security risks and loss of productivity.

VM Sprawl Avoidance

One drawback associated with virtual environments is *VM sprawl*. VM sprawl is mainly associated with servers. In this situation, multiple, underutilized virtualized servers take up more space and consume more resources than is justified by their workload. VM sprawl can be confined to a single server room, but it also can spread across multiple facilities in different geographical locations, especially where one company has acquired another or where two companies have merged.

VM sprawl occurs mainly because VMs are omitted from the change/lifecycle management processes. This can be mitigated with these actions:

▶ Following the change control process

▶ Enforcing automatic deployment and configuration

▶ Decommissioning, archiving, or deleting virtual machines

▶ Using management agents

VM sprawl control is necessary to reduce hardware and licensing costs, enhance security, and conserve resource consumption. This can be accomplished by real-locating and better provisioning existing resources, along with formulating a strategy to address existing virtual machine sprawl and prevent its reoccurrence.

VM Escape Protection

The idea of VM guest escape has been discussed for many years. A VM is essentially an isolated guest operating system that runs independently on an operating system. *VM escape* happens when the virtual machine breaks out of or escapes from isolation and can interact with the host operating system. VM escape does not affect bare-metal platforms; it affects only hosted platforms. A full VM escape happened with the Virtualized Environment Neglected Operations Manipulation (VENOM) exploit, which used malformed commands sent to the virtual floppy drives in VMs to create a buffer overflow that subsequently allowed a guest to escape. The exploit demonstrated that attackers inside a guest VM can execute instructions in the memory space of the host operating system. In another instance, a virtual machine escape at the Pwn2Own hacking contest used a combination of three separate exploits.

The most obvious ways to prevent VM escape follow:

▶ Keep up to date on VM CVEs and immediately apply patches

▶ Contact cloud service providers to inquire about patching affected products

Virtual environment security is concerned with anything that directly or indi-rectly touches the hypervisor, so securing the hypervisor is critical. Organiza-tions can approach hypervisor security through either architectural options or configuration choices.

Cloud Concepts

The term *cloud computing* arose from the cloud symbol that commonly represents the Internet in network diagrams. Although cloud computing has come to the forefront over the past couple years, its concept can be traced back to mainframe computing. Multiple users were given small slices of the computer's time to run whatever program they needed at that time. Today the typical cloud computing provider delivers computing power, storage, and common applications online to users who access them from a web browser or portal. In essence, cloud computing blends virtualization, distributed computing, and prevalent high-speed bandwidth.

As it is used today, *cloud computing* is a very general term that basically describes anything that involves delivering hosted computing services over the Internet. Cloud computing and virtualization are different, although the terms are often used interchangeably. Virtualization separates physical infrastructures to create various dedicated resources. Cloud computing provides services not inherent in virtualization:

▶ Self-service capability

▶ Elasticity

▶ Automated management

▶ Scalability

▶ Pay as you go

Some clouds, such as bare-metal clouds, do not include virtualization. Cloud computing falls into a variety of categories and models, which the following sections discuss.

Cloud Storage

Cloud computing includes various flavors and uses of technology, such as Desktops as a Service and Streaming Operating Systems. These environments have huge potential for a dramatically simplified IT infrastructure with more cost-effective IT management and utilization. But along with that comes the potential for enormous data loss if the data is not properly encrypted. Having highly available cloud data is risky because multiple copies of your data can be in various locations. When you delete files, successful deletion of trace data becomes next to impossible.

Traditional encryption solutions for the purpose of data security protection cannot be adopted for the cloud as a result of this loss of control of data. Because various kinds of data are stored in the cloud and long-term continuous assurance of data security is needed, verifying the correctness of data stored in the cloud becomes even more challenging. Although encryption is far from a total solution for all cloud data security issues, when used properly and in combination with other controls, it provides effective security. In cloud implementations, encryption might help alleviate the security issues related to multitenancy, public clouds, and remote or outsourced hosting. Encrypting data stored in the cloud also helps prevent data from being modified and can reduce the risk of a compromise when cloud storage devices are sold to another user but still contain organizational information.

Cloud Deployment Models

Cloud computing includes the capabilities of almost all existing technologies. Cloud computing has a layered architecture of cloud infrastructures that uses both deployment and service models. The three cloud service models are the well-recognized models of Infrastructure as a Service (IaaS), Platform as a Service (PaaS), and Software as a Service (SaaS). The four cloud deployment models are community, hybrid, public, and private. The following section discusses these models.

IaaS

Infrastructure as a Service (IaaS) delivers the computer infrastructure in a hosted service model over the Internet. This method of cloud computing allows the client to literally outsource everything that would normally be found in a typical IT department. Data center space, servers, networking equipment, and software can all be purchased as a service. IaaS follows the same model as power and water: You're billed for how much you use. Thus, it falls under the category of utility computing. IaaS implementations typically have Internet connectivity, computer networking, servers or grid computing, and hardware virtualization.

ExamAlert

Watch for scenarios or examples asking you to identify a correct or incorrect cloud service type or service implementation choice.

PaaS

Platform as a Service (PaaS) delivers a computing platform—often an operating system with associated services—over the Internet without downloads or installation. PaaS systems often are development platforms designed to operate specifically in the cloud environment. Google Apps are examples. PaaS implementations typically have integrated development environment services, interface creation tools, and web and database integration.

SaaS

Software as a Service (SaaS) delivers a licensed application to customers over the Internet for use as a service on demand. A SaaS vendor hosts an application and allows the customer to use the application for a set period of time, after which the application becomes inactive. This model is useful to give individuals and businesses the right to access a certain application without having to purchase a full license. This on-demand licensing environment allows for all the benefits of the full application without the up-front costs and maintenance associated with traditional software purchases.

Public

A public cloud is an environment in which the services and infrastructure are hosted at a service provider's off-site facility and can be accessed over the Internet, based on a monthly or yearly usage fee. Many organizations share the main infrastructure, but each organization's data is logically separated. This is referred to as multitenancy. The advantages of using a public cloud include lower infrastructure, maintenance, and administrative costs; greater level of hardware efficiency; reduced implementation time; and availability of short-term usage. The disadvantages of a public cloud are greater vulnerable risk (because of multitenancy), diminished control of organizational data and the environment (because the environment is hosted at a service provider's facility), and reduced bandwidth (because data transfer capability is limited to that of the Internet Service Provider). A public cloud is the best choice when an organization requires scalability, wants reduced costs, lacks in-house administrative personnel, or has a high-maintenance, distributed network.

Private

A private cloud is a hosted infrastructure on a private platform. It is sometimes referred to as an internal, corporate, or enterprise cloud. Because it is hosted on a private platform, this type of cloud affords organizations more control over the infrastructure and is usually restricted to organizational employees and business partners. A private cloud offers the capability to add applications and services on demand, similar to a public cloud. The advantages of using a private cloud design include better control over organizational data, higher levels of security and customization (because of flexibility in design specifications), better performance (because the private cloud is deployed separately), and easier access to compliance data (because the information is readily available). The disadvantages of a private cloud include building capacity limitations, along with higher costs for infrastructure, maintenance, and administration. A private cloud is the best choice for an organization that needs strict control of business-critical data or highly regulated businesses such as financial institutions.

Hybrid

A hybrid cloud is a combination of public and private clouds. A private cloud ensures control of data, while other functions are hosted using a public cloud. This approach allows the organization to leverage the advantages of both environment types. A hybrid cloud environment is the best choice when an organization offers services that need to be configured for diverse vertical markets or wants to use a SaaS application but is concerned about security.

Community

Community clouds are designed to accommodate the mutual needs of a particular business community. This is generally industry specific, such as with healthcare or energy companies or in the public sector. Community clouds provide collaborative business processes in a cloud environment while maintaining a higher level of security using a hybrid cloud. A community cloud is best suited for organizations that want to increase cross-organizational or collaborative processes when in-house implementation is not possible because of conditions such as geographically distributed participants, fluctuating resource requirements, or resource limitations. An example of a community cloud is Google's implementation of Google Apps for U.S. government agencies.

ExamAlert

Watch for scenarios or examples asking you to identify the best cloud choice based on public, private, hybrid, or community features.

On-premises vs. Hosted vs. Cloud

When an organization decides on a service and deployment model, it must take certain factors into account, such as regulations, accessibility, and security. These considerations can be deciding factors in whether the organization implements a cloud environment on-premises, chooses a hosting service, or opts for a large cloud environment such as Amazon Web Services (AWS) or Rackspace.

The primary benefit of an on-premises solution is control. When an organization chooses this model, it has confidence that all critical business infrastructure is protected and that the organization does not have to depend on someone else to be sure that its data is secure and its operations are running smoothly. The organization has complete control over who accesses its data and resources.

On-premises solutions tend to be costly for hardware and software. The organization might have difficulty keeping up storage requirements, implementing new product features, or detecting insider breaches.

In a hosted environment, the organization employs the services of a data center provider. This model frees up internal resources for other uses, reduces infrastructure costs, and taps the expertise of the services provider for security, availability, and maintenance. A hosted environment offers additional benefits as well:

- ▶ Secure rack cabinets

- ▶ Higher bandwidth

- ▶ Controlled cooling

- ▶ Tight physical security

- ▶ Continual monitoring and support at all hours

- ▶ Offsite backups

- ▶ Lower latency

The disadvantages of using a hosted environment include increased reliance on the data center provider for proper security, due diligence issues that the service level agreement might not have addressed, and an inability to recover quickly in case of a natural disaster because of the size of the environment.

A cloud environment is similar to a hosted environment, with a few differences. Cloud systems tend to have fewer service disruptions. Because cloud services have different service models, service level varies. Most cloud providers offer pay-as-you-go pricing so that the organization pays only for what it uses. Business productivity is also enhanced because cloud-based applications can be accessed from a browser anywhere in the world. With cloud-based services, an environment can be spun in a short period of time, increasing speed. Environments also can be spun down as easily as spun up, so scalability increases. This is particularly conducive to organizations that experience seasonal surges in business. Cloud services also provide dashboard and reporting functions, which frees up internal manpower and enables the organization to focus more on innovating than managing resources.

One of the biggest drawbacks of using a cloud environment involves the level of trust. Trust issues are generally the most difficult for executives to overcome, especially when an organization is bound by regulatory requirements. Security can also be a legitimate concern when choosing to store data and apps in the cloud.

Cloud Access Security Broker

According to Gartner, in just a few short years, 85 percent of large enterprises will use a cloud access security broker (CASB).

> **ExamAlert**
>
> CASB is a Gartner-created term that describes a cloud cybersecurity layer that focuses on visibility, compliance, data security, and threat protection.

The four pillars of CASB are visibility, compliance, data security, and threat protection:

▶ Visibility is the capability to see risk in the environment.

▶ Compliance is the capability to meet regulatory requirements.

▶ Data security is identifying, monitoring, and securing sensitive data.

▶ Threat protection is protection against cloud-native malware and account compromise.

The primary approach to CASB is a central security application directly integrated with the cloud platform. Basically, CASB is a security policy enforcement point that inserts enterprise security policies between a cloud service consumer and a cloud service provider as cloud-based resources are accessed. This approach provides scalability with no end user impact.

CASBs can run in a corporate data center, in hybrid data center/cloud mode, or in the cloud. The three CASB deployment methods are as a reverse proxy, as a forward proxy, or in API mode. Some CASB approaches use API integration, which provides retroactive monitoring of cloud data at rest upon deployment, as well as the capability to secure applications on any service model platform (PaaS, IaaS, or SaaS). Large enterprise CASB vendors include Symantec and Cisco.

Security as a Service

Security as a Service (SecaaS) is based on other cloud services models. In SecaaS, a security service provider uses a subscription-based model to implement security for the organization. SecaaS can be delivered using any of the other cloud service models (PaaS, IaaS, or SaaS), depending on the level of protection the organization requires.

SecaaS providers offer a wide variety of security services, including but not limited to the following:

▶ Identity and access management (IAM)

▶ Email security

▶ Encryption

▶ Firewall management

▶ IDS/IPS

▶ SIEM

▶ Vulnerability and compliance assessments

▶ Website security

SecaaS does raise some ownership and compliance issues related to regulations.

ExamAlert

Using a SecaaS provider does not relieve the organization of the responsibility for information security.

The organization can outsource information security services, but the accountability for security remains with the organization. Be sure to carefully review the service level agreement (SLA). Security must be actively managed at all times, with appropriate expertise.

What Next?

If you want more practice on this chapter's exam objectives before you move on, remember that you can access all the Cram Quiz questions on the Pearson Test Prep software. You can also create a custom exam by objective. Note any objective you struggle with and go to that objective material in this chapter.

CHAPTER 20

Reducing Risk

This chapter covers the following official Security+ exam objective:

3.8 Explain how resiliency and automation strategies reduce risk.

- ▶ Automation/scripting
  - ■ Automated courses of action
  - ■ Continuous monitoring
  - ■ Configuration validation
- ▶ Templates
- ▶ Master image
- ▶ Non-persistence
  - ■ Snapshots
  - ■ Revert to known state
- ■ Rollback to known configuration
- ■ Live boot media
- ▶ Elasticity
- ▶ Scalability
- ▶ Distributive allocation
- ▶ Redundancy
- ▶ Fault tolerance
- ▶ High availability
- ▶ RAID

Essential Terms and Components

- ▶ elasticity
- ▶ RAID
- ▶ redundancy
- ▶ scalability
- ▶ snapshots

CramSaver

If you can correctly answer these questions before going through this chapter, save time by skimming the Exam Alerts in this chapter and then completing the Cram Quiz at the end of Part 3.

1. Explain the purpose of continuous monitoring.

   _____

2. Explain the difference between scalability and elasticity.

   _____

3. How can an organization compensate for the high vulnerability to disk failures in large disk arrays?

   _____

Answers

1. The purpose of continuous monitoring is to ensure that the processes are followed and enforced, to detect organizational compliance and risk. In certain instances, continuous monitoring is required. Industry regulations might require continuous monitoring.

2. The main difference between scalability and elasticity has to do with the resources. Scalability is based on the capability to handle the changing needs of a system, process, or application within the confines of the current resources. Elasticity is the capability to expand and reduce resources as needed at any given point in time.

3. Large disk arrays are highly vulnerable to disk failures. To solve this problem, an organization can use redundancy in the form of error-correcting codes to tolerate disk failures. With this method, a redundant disk array can retain data for a much longer period of time than an unprotected single disk. With multiple disks and a RAID scheme, a system can stay up and running when a disk fails and during the time both the replacement disk is being installed and data is being restored.

Automation and Scripting

Resiliency and automation strategies help mitigate organizational risk. Resilience is the organizational capacity to continue acceptable levels of service when disruption to vital processes or systems occurs. Automation can range anywhere from basic scripting to automated collective action systems. It includes functions such as courses of action, continuous monitoring, and configuration validation.

Automation greatly increases an organization's capability to detect and respond to threats. Automation systems or frameworks are used for courses of action and require the following:

▶ Characteristics of interoperability, extensibility, and industry standards based

▶ Built-in privacy protections from the ground up

▶ Based on international technical standards

▶ Capability to deal with system attack attempts

▶ Capability to effectively identify false positives

This type of system combines machine learning with automation to respond to threats and maintain critical operations. Automated collection systems are meant to be resilient and more secure because devices work together in near–real time to anticipate and prevent attacks. These systems can be considered an extension of continuous monitoring, which the next section describes.

Organizations have the option to automate individual areas as part of a holistic approach to automation. For example, an organization can automate infrastructure buildout to reduce the chance of security mistakes or can include automated security monitoring in system deployments as part of the configuration process.

ExamAlert

Automation makes managing and securing the environment easier. However, when done incorrectly, automation breaks more than it fixes.

On a smaller scale, organizations can use scripting and vendor-provided tools for automated courses of action such as security and network tasks. Automation scripts for management and provisioning are done through command-line interfaces (CLIs) and APIs. Automated configuration and provisioning capabilities are already built into devices from most major vendors. For example, Cisco IOS software provides embedded automation capabilities. Windows Power-Shell Scripting is used to automate Windows administration and security tasks.

The purpose of continuous monitoring is to ensure that the processes are followed and enforced so that they detect organizational compliance and risk. In certain instances, such as to comply with industry regulations, continuous monitoring is required. For example, PCI DSS compliance requires that an organization have well-defined processes in place to review and reassess security practices, even in highly dynamic business environments. FedRAMP, which focuses on cloud service providers (CSPs), requires that CSPs continuously monitor the cloud service offering to detect changes in the security posture of the system.

Tools often provide scripts to help with continuous monitoring. For example, Solar Winds maintains more than 100 predefined automation scripts in its script library. PowerShell can be used to implement continuous monitoring as well.

Configuration validation for organizations can be done through the Security Content Automation Protocol (SCAP), developed by NIST to enable automated vulnerability management and policy compliance. Configuration Assessment as a Service (COAS) is a method developed within the European Union for automated validation and assessment of configuration settings over distributed environments. Configuration validation scripts can be written, depending on the target, and PowerShell can be used for configuration validation as well. For Windows machines, the Security Configuration and Analysis (SCA) snap-in works to validate configurations.

Additionally, scripting languages such as Python can be used either alone or in combination with other scripts or tools. For example, Cisco DevNet has readily available scripts that leverage Cisco-provided Python libraries for device automation.

Templates and Master Images

Recall from Chapter 9, "Security Issues," that security templates are used as a basis for device configurations. Configuration settings for templates can be based on industry standards or organization parameters. Templates ensure consistency in deployments and meet requirements that reduce organizational risk. Templates can be based on the OS or security requirements. For example, limited-access kiosk systems use a template with lower security settings than a system that is used in financial transactions. The Microsoft Security Compliance Toolkit consists of configuration baselines for different releases of Windows.

Templates can also be used to define standard network designs and device implementation, ranging from wiring closets to VPN concentrators. In high-risk environments, templates can contain an entire network specification that includes topology, installation requirements, and device configurations for all cabling, hardware, and software. This type of template reduces the organizational risk level by providing some assurance that no additional risk is introduced through variations in equipment. Automation tools such as Chef or Puppet can be used to apply security configuration changes to templates and images.

A golden image or master image is a template used for hard disks, virtual machines (VMs), or servers. Master images are often used in a self-service provisioning environment. For example, when a new remote employee begins employment, the employee's laptop accesses the organizational network and the master image is downloaded to the laptop. The advantage of using a master image is that the environment is set up exactly the way it is needed and then saved. Changes are made only to the master image. This saves time and provides consistency.

A master VM is typically created as a virtual desktop template. When the master VM is created, the hardware and software parameters are specified so that all created VMs in the managed virtual desktop environment have the same settings. For example, if the master VM is assigned 8 GB of RAM, then each created VM in the managed environment will be assigned 8 GB of RAM. This makes it easy to create and manage hundreds or thousands of VMs using a single master VM as the template.

Non-persistence

A persistent system is one that is generally still removable in the event of a failure. For example, if a CPU dies, the system information and data are generally recoverable when the system is restored. In a non-persistent system, if a failure occurs, the information is lost. This is similar to what happens to memory contents when a system is shut down. Cloud environments tend to be fluid and work differently than physical desktop environments. Persistent cloud environments tend to be more difficult to support than non-persistent environments, especially with data storage or volumes. Sometimes persistence is not desired. Non-persistence is part of the concept of elasticity, which the next section discusses. Because cloud environments are so fluid, snapshots actually provide a way to capture persistence.

Snapshots

A snapshot preserves the entire state and data of the virtual machine at the time it is taken. A snapshot includes the virtual machine settings and the state of the machine's virtual drives. The contents of the virtual machine's memory can also be included in the snapshot, but it is not recommended and rarely needed.

> **ExamAlert**
>
> Snapshots can capture sensitive data that is present on the system at the time and can inadvertently put personal information at risk.

Snapshots eliminate the need to create multiple VMs if an organization repeatedly needs to return a machine to the same state. In an environment that uses VM templates, disk-based snapshots are a quick way to make a new VM from the template for provisioning.

Snapshots can also be used as a restore point when testing software or configuration changes. When you take a snapshot of a virtual machine, a new child disk is created for each attached disk. Keep in mind that, for a snapshot to work, the base disk is needed. Therefore, snapshots should not be used as a backup solution. Best practice for performance is to keep only two or three snapshots, and only for a short period of time. Inherent changes occur in the VM, and the snapshot file can grow quickly, filling up space in the datastore. Restoring a snapshot is often done using software automation.

Although VMware is the most popular product for VMs, Microsoft also offers a virtualized solution in Hyper-V. The Microsoft Hyper-V term for a snapshot is a checkpoint. Checkpoints work the same way as snapshots in VMware, with certain limitations. For example, they cannot be used in a VM designated as an Active Directory Domain Services role such as a domain controller.

Revert to Known State and Rollback to Known Configuration

The primary purpose of a snapshot is to allow the user to revert back to an earlier state if something causes the VM to not work properly. The parent snapshot of a virtual machine is the snapshot on which the current state is based. When the first snapshot is taken, that stored state becomes the parent snapshot of the VM.

When you revert to a known state in a VM, you can revert or go to an earlier snapshot. Revert is used to go to the parent snapshot of the VM. Revert immediately discards the current disk and memory states and then reverts to the disk and memory states of the parent snapshot. Some VM products have an option to use a "go to" feature that allows the user to choose any snapshot, not just the parent one. This can be used in a software development environment where several snapshots are used to test changes to a program or product. Options also can enable you to automatically revert to the parent snapshot whenever the machine is powered off.

ExamAlert

When the system reverts to an earlier snapshot, the reverted snapshot becomes the parent snapshot of the virtual machine.

In a non-persistent or cloud environment, sometimes virtual networking components change or are misconfigured. Rollback is used to prevent loss of connectivity to a host by rolling back to a previous valid or known configuration. This is similar to Windows Roll Back Driver, except that it relates to the network instead of individual machine drivers. Networking events that can cause a rollback are host networking changes and modifications to distributed switches. Invalid host networking configuration changes cause host networking rollbacks. Network change that disconnects a host, such as when updating DNS and routing settings, also triggers a rollback. Invalid updates to distributed switches can cause rollbacks to occur as well. For example, VLAN changes in a distributed port group can cause one or more hosts to be out of synchronization with the distributed switch. If the situation cannot be manually fixed, you can roll back the switch or port group to a previous configuration.

Live Boot Media

Live boot media is considered non-persistent because actions that occur between reboots do not persist. With live boot media, system RAM acts as a disk. When the media is removed and the system reboots, the RAM is cleared. Live boot media keeps the original media configuration. USB drives can be created with persistent storage through a persistent overlay file. Although there is some room for persistence, it has limitations and might not work with all OS distributions.

A saved VM such as a virtual disk can be booted using a CD or USB device, but live boot media is often used in instances when an organization needs a very secure environment in an unsecure location. For example, Bootable Media (BootMe) is a Live CD that creates a secure, non-persistent environment on a personal or public computer. BootMe provides a trusted environment for remotely accessing sensitive government services on non-government equipment.

Live boot media can reduce risk in areas that are considered high risk. Bootable media has been used to provide civilians, contractors, and military personnel secure remote access to government systems for some time. Such solutions are designed with security in mind, running from read-only media and without any persistent storage.

Scalability and Elasticity

Although they are somewhat related, scalability and elasticity are two different concepts. Scalability is the capacity to expand the amount of production from the current infrastructure without negatively impacting performance. Scalability issues can cause failures in many areas, such as systems, applications, networks, and businesses.

Scalability can refer to systems or software applications and can be vertical or horizontal. Vertical scalability refers to the capability to scale up within a system; horizontal scalability refers to scaling linearly or scaling out to multiple systems. Applications are generally built with the capability to scale either vertical or horizontal so that lack of resources does not affect performance.

> **ExamAlert**
>
> Scalability can involve the capacity to decrease as well as increase services or resources.

Elasticity is the capacity to dynamically expand or reduce infrastructure resources by autonomously adjusting to workload changes to maximize resources. NIST defines elasticity as the capability for rapid, automatic, and elastic provisioning of resources to quickly scale out, as well as the capability to be rapidly released to quickly scale in. Because elasticity is used in scale-out solutions, allowing resources to be dynamically added or removed, it results in infrastructure costs savings.

This is particularly useful when dealing with virtualized environments because host availability is a concern. With elasticity, resources can be purchased as needed based on timeframe, platform, or operating system.

> **ExamAlert**
>
> Elasticity is most often found in cloud environments, where resources can be purchased for a short period of time based on demand and then deleted when no longer needed.

Organizations that have cyclical business periods often choose this option because it saves costs and administrative overhead. Security challenges in an elastic model include enforcing proper configuration, change management, and adequate administrative separation between virtual customer environments.

The main difference between elasticity and scalability has to do with the resources. Scalability is based on the capability to handle the changing needs of a system, process, or application within the confines of the current resources. Elasticity is the capability to expand and reduce resources as needed at any given point in time.

Distributive Allocation

Various principles determine how available resources are distributed. In a cloud environment, this is even more important, especially with elasticity. The idea behind distributive allocation is to distribute the environment among different providers or components. Approaches to distributive allocation range from resource throttling to a federation of multiple clouds.

Improper resource allocation management can allow attacks such as DoS. If an organization does not have the capability to recognize when a malicious resource consumption event is taking place, legitimate users will be denied access to resources. Proper resource allocation planning is key. Proper resource allocation management will require a greater number of resources for an attacker to mount a successful attack. Distributive allocation helps ensure that resources are properly distributed to handle workloads and provide availability.

In a cloud environment, quota management mechanisms are often used to control distributed resources. These mechanisms track costs and keep budget allocations in check, while also influencing performance and availability. Distributive allocation helps handle availability and avoid over- or underprovisioning resources. When planning for distributive allocation, consider the following infrastructure items:

▶ Design goals

▶ Traffic requirements

▶ Component configurations

Cloud providers have limited resources and service many customers. On-demand environments cause usage to fluctuate, and a single cloud provider generally cannot provide unlimited services. The cloud provider's physical resources can handle only a certain level of service. Distributive allocation uses multiple cloud providers or a federation of clouds. Each cloud provider might have a different pricing model and different resource allocation strategies, so selecting the most appropriate provider for application and service hosting becomes an important part of organizational risk mitigation strategies.

Fault Tolerance and Redundancy

Equipment will fail—as one movie character has suggested, "The world is an imperfect place." When a single drive crashes, sometimes the only way to sustain operations is to have another copy of all the data. Redundancy and diversity are commonly applied principles for fault tolerance against accidental faults. Fault tolerance allows a system to continue functioning even when one of the components has failed. Common fault-tolerant solutions include RAID solutions, which maintain duplicated data across multiple disks so that the loss of one disk does not cause the loss of data. Many of these solutions can also support hot-swapping failed drives and redundant power supplies so that replacement hardware can be installed without ever taking the server offline.

Diversity refers to having multiple versions of software packages in which redundant software versions are different. Redundancy is replication of a component in identical copies to compensate for random hardware failures. Multiple versions are used to protect against software failures. Maintaining multiple diverse versions will hopefully cover any individual software faults. Redundancy and diversity should be designed into critical facilities and applications. Chapter 31, "Disaster Recovery and Continuity of Operations," discusses additional redundancy planning options, such as hot, warm, and cold sites.

In the next chapter, you see that human life is always the most important asset when planning for physical and environmental safety controls. Perhaps the next biggest asset an organization has is its data. Planning for every server setup should consider how to salvage the data in case a component fails. Deciding how to store and protect data depends on how the organization uses its data. The main goal of preventing and effectively dealing with any type of disruption is to ensure availability. This is often accomplished through redundancy. Redundancy is usually dispersed geographically, as well as through backup equipment and databases, or hot sparing of system components. Of course, you can use RAID, UPS equipment, and clustering to accomplish and ensure availability as well, but neglecting single points of failure can prove disastrous. A single point of failure is any piece of equipment that can bring down your operation if it stops working. To determine the number of single points of failure in the organization, start with a good map of everything the organization uses to operate. Pay special attention to items such as the Internet connection, routers, switches, and proprietary business equipment.

After you identify the single points of failure, perform a risk analysis. In other words, compare the consequences of the device failing to the cost of redundancy. For example, if all your business is web based, it is a good idea to have some redundancy in case the Internet connection goes down. However, if the majority of your business is telephone based, you might look for redundancy in the phone system instead of the ISP. In some cases, the ISP might supply both the Internet and the phone services. The point here is to be aware of where your organization is vulnerable and understand the risk so you can devise an appropriate backup plan.

In disaster recovery planning, you might need to consider redundant connections between branches or sites. Internally, for total redundancy, you might need two network cards in computers connected to different switches. With redundant connections, all devices are connected to each other more than once, to create fault tolerance. A single device or cable failure does not affect the performance because the devices are connected by more than one means. This setup is more expensive because it requires more hardware and cabling. This type of topology can also be found in enterprise-wide networks, with routers connected to other routers for fault tolerance.

Along with power and equipment loss, telephone and Internet communications might be out of service for a while when a disaster strikes. Organizations must consider this factor when formulating a disaster recovery plan. Relying on a single Internet connection for critical business functions could prove disastrous to your business. With a redundant ISP, a backup ISP could be standing by in case an outage at the main ISP occurs. Traffic then could be switched over to the redundant ISP, and the organization could continue to do business without any interruptions.

Although using multiple ISPs is mostly considered for disaster recovery purposes, it can also relieve network traffic congestion and provide network isolation for applications. As organizations become global, dealing with natural disasters will become more common. Solutions such as wireless ISPs used in conjunction with VoIP to quickly restore phone and data services are being looked at more closely. Organizations might look to ISP redundancy to prevent application performance failure and supplier diversity. For example, businesses that transfer large files can use multiple ISPs to segregate voice and file transfer traffic to a specific ISP. More organizations are implementing technologies such as VoIP. When planning deployment, explore using different ISPs for better network traffic performance, for disaster recovery, and to ensure a quality level of service.

For risk mitigation, some redundancy and diversity controls that can be implemented against threats are replication to different data centers, replication to different geographic areas, redundant components, replication software systems, distinct security zones, different administrative control, and different organizational control.

High Availability

One way to increase availability or provide high availability is to use server clustering. A server cluster is the combination of two or more servers so that they appear as one. Clustering increases availability by ensuring that if a server is out of commission because of failure or planned downtime, another server in the cluster takes over the workload. To provide load balancing to avoid functionality loss because of directed attacks meant to prevent valid access, continuity planning might include clustering solutions that allow multiple nodes to perform support while transparently acting as a single host to the user. High-availability clustering might also be used to ensure that automatic failover occurs in case hardware failure renders the primary node incapable of providing normal service.

Load balancing is the primary reason to implement server clustering. Load balancing provides high availability by distributing workloads across multiple computing resources. Load balancing aims to optimize the use of resources, maximize throughput, minimize response time, and avoid overload of any single resource. This proves especially useful when traffic volume is high: It prevents one server from being overloaded while another sits idle. Load balancing can be implemented with hardware, software, or a combination of both. Typically, load balancing occurs in organizations with high website traffic, as well as in cloud-based environments.

You might need to set up redundant servers so that the business can still function in case of hardware or software failure. If a single server hosts vital applications, a simple equipment failure could result in days of downtime as the problem is repaired. In addition, some manufacturers provide redundant power supplies in mission-critical servers.

To ensure high availability and reliability, server redundancy is implemented. This means multiple servers are used to perform the same task. For example, if you have a web-based business with more than one server hosting your site, when one of the servers crashes, the requests can be redirected to another server. This provides a highly available website. If you do not host your own website, confirm whether the vendor you are using provides high availability and reliability.

> **ExamAlert**
>
> In today's world, mission-critical businesses demand 100 percent uptime 24 hours a day, 7 days a week. Availability is vital, and many businesses cannot function without redundancy. Redundancy can take several forms, including automatic failover, failback, and virtualization. Perhaps the most notable advantage of server redundancy is load balancing.

Cross-site replication might be included for high-availability solutions that also require high levels of fault tolerance. In addition, individual servers can be configured to allow for the continued function of key services even in the case of hardware failure.

RAID

The most common approach to data availability and redundancy is Redundant Array of Inexpensive Disks (RAID). RAID organizes multiple disks into a large, high-performance logical disk. In other words, if you have three hard drives, you can configure them to look like one large drive. Disk arrays are created to stripe data across multiple disks and access them in parallel, which allows the following:

- ▶ Higher data transfer rates on large data accesses
- ▶ Higher I/O rates on small data accesses
- ▶ Uniform load balancing across all the disks

Large disk arrays are highly vulnerable to disk failures. To solve this problem, you can use redundancy in the form of error-correcting codes to tolerate disk failures. With this method, a redundant disk array can retain data for a much longer time than an unprotected single disk. With multiple disks and a RAID scheme, a system can stay up and running when a disk fails, as well as during the time the replacement disk is being installed and data is being restored. Figure 20.1 shows common types of RAID configurations.

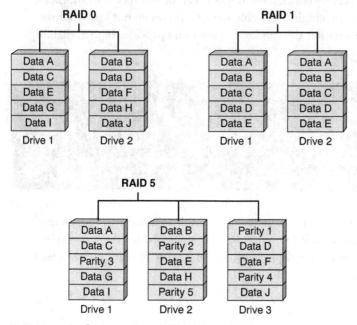

FIGURE 20.1 **Common Types of RAID Configurations**

The two major goals when implementing disk arrays are data striping for better performance and redundancy for better reliability. RAID comes in many flavors; the more common ones follow:

▶ **RAID Level 0: Striped disk array without fault tolerance:** RAID 0 implements a striped disk array. The data is broken into blocks, and each block is written to a separate disk drive. This requires a minimum of two disks to implement.

▶ **RAID Level 1: Mirroring and duplexing:** This solution, called mirroring or duplexing, requires a minimum of two disks and offers 100 percent redundancy because all data is written to both disks. The difference between mirroring and duplexing is the number of controllers. Mirroring uses one controller, whereas duplexing uses one controller for each disk. In RAID 1, disk usage is 50 percent; the other 50 percent is for redundancy.

▶ **RAID Level 2: Hamming code error correcting code (ECC):** In RAID 2, each bit of a data word is written to a disk. RAID 2 requires the use of extra disks to store an error-correcting code. A typical setup requires ten data disks and four ECC disks. All modern disk drives incorporate ECC, so this offers little additional protection. No commercial implementations exist today. The controller required is complex, specialized, and expensive, and the performance is not very good.

▶ **RAID Level 3: Parallel transfer with parity:** In RAID 3, the data block is striped and written on the data disks. This requires a minimum of three drives to implement. In a parallel transfer with parity, data is interleaved bit-wise over the data disks, and a single parity disk is added to tolerate any single disk failure.

▶ **RAID Level 4: Independent data disks with shared parity disk:** Entire blocks are written onto a data disk. RAID 4 requires a minimum of three drives to implement. RAID 4 is similar to RAID 3, except that data is interleaved across disks of arbitrary size instead of in bits.

▶ **RAID Level 5: Independent data disks with distributed parity blocks:** In RAID 5, each entire block of the data and the parity is striped. RAID 5 requires a minimum of three disks. Because it writes both the data and the parity over all the disks, it has the best small read, large write performance of any redundancy disk array.

▶ **RAID Level 6: Independent data disks with two independent parity schemes:** This extension of RAID 5 allows for additional fault tolerance by using two-dimensional parity. RAID 6 uses Reed-Solomon codes to protect against up to two disk failures using the bare minimum of two redundant disk arrays.

▶ **RAID Level 10 (also called 1+0): High reliability combined with high performance:** RAID 10 combines RAID 1 and RAID 0 and requires a minimum of four disks to implement. A variant of RAID 10 is called 0+1. This solution is a striped array that has RAID 1 arrays. Disks are mirrored in pairs for redundancy and improved performance, and then data is striped across multiple disks. Both versions provide fault tolerance and increased performance.

ExamAlert

Know the different levels of RAID and the number of disks required to implement each one. The following are the most common forms of RAID:

▶ **RAID 0:** Spanned volume, no redundancy, highest write speed, highest performance.

▶ **RAID 1:** Mirroring, 100 percent duplication of data across all drives, lowest performance.

▶ **RAID 3:** Parallel transfer with parity bit, minimum of three drives, data written to all drives simultaneously while parity is calculated and written to its own nonredundant drive.

▶ **RAID 5:** Parallel transfer with distributed parity, data written to all drives simultaneously, parity written in segments across all drives for redundancy of parity as well as data segments, highest read rates.

▶ **RAID 10:** (Also called 1+0.) Combines RAID 1 and RAID 0. A variant exists, called 0+1. Both provide fault tolerance and increased performance.

When choosing a method of redundancy, opt for a level of RAID that the operating system supports. Not all operating systems support all versions of RAID. For example, Microsoft Windows Servers support RAID levels 0, 1, and 5. In addition to hardware RAID, you can use software RAID. Software RAID is the best option when the expense of additional drives is not included in the budget or if the organization is using older servers. Software RAID can provide more flexibility, but it requires more CPU cycles and power to run. It operates on a partition-by-partition basis and tends to be slightly more complicated.

Another point to remember is that even though you set up the server for redundancy, you must still back up your data. RAID does not protect you from multiple disk failures. Regular tape backups enable you to recover from data loss that results from errors unrelated to disk failure (such as human, hardware, and software errors). Chapter 31 discusses the different types and methods of backups.

What Next?

If you want more practice on this chapter's exam objectives before you move on, remember that you can access all the Cram Quiz questions on the Pearson Test Prep software. You can also create a custom exam by objective. Note any objective you struggle with and go to that objective material in this chapter.

CHAPTER 21

Physical Security Controls

This chapter covers the following official Security+ exam objective:

3.9 Explain the importance of physical security controls.

- ▶ Lighting
- ▶ Signs
- ▶ Fencing/gate/cage
- ▶ Security guards
- ▶ Alarms
- ▶ Safe
- ▶ Secure cabinets/enclosures
- ▶ Protected distribution/ Protected cabling
- ▶ Air gap
- ▶ Mantrap
- ▶ Faraday cage
- ▶ Lock types
- ▶ Biometrics

- ▶ Barricades/bollards
- ▶ Tokens/cards
- ▶ Environmental controls
  - ▪ HVAC
  - ▪ Hot and cold aisles
  - ▪ Fire suppression
- ▶ Cable locks
- ▶ Screen filters
- ▶ Cameras
- ▶ Motion detection
- ▶ Logs
- ▶ Infrared detection
- ▶ Key management

Essential Terms and Components

- ▶ air gap
- ▶ cold site
- ▶ dry-pipe fire suppression
- ▶ heating, ventilation, and air conditioning (HVAC)

- ▶ hot site
- ▶ mantrap
- ▶ warm site
- ▶ wet-pipe fire suppression

CramSaver

If you can correctly answer these questions before going through this chapter, save time by skimming the Exam Alerts in this chapter and then completing the Cram Quiz at the end of Part 3.

1. What is the most important asset that must be protected by physical and environmental security controls?

   _____

2. What is an air gap?

   _____

3. Explain how hot and cold aisles work.

   _____

Answers

1. Human life is always the most important asset when planning for physical and environmental safety controls.

2. An air gap is a physical isolation gap between a system or network and the outside world. No system is connected to the Internet or connected to any other system that has Internet access. In a true air-gapped system, data is transferred to the system via removable media or a direct connection to another computer.

3. Data centers and server farms might make use of an alternating arrangement of server racks, with alternating rows facing opposing directions. Fan intakes draw in cool air vented to racks facing the cold aisle, and then fan output of hot air is vented to the alternating hot aisles for removal from the data center.

Perimeter Security

When planning security for network scenarios, many organizations overlook physical security. In many smaller organizations, the servers, switches, routers, and patch panels are placed as a matter of convenience because of space restrictions. This can cause security issues. Speaking from experience, this equipment ends up in the oddest places, such as in the coat closet by the receptionist's desk in the lobby, in the room with the copy machine, or in a storage room with a back-door exit that is unlocked most of the time. Securing physical access and ensuring that access requires proper authentication is necessary to avoid accidental exposure of sensitive data to attackers performing physical profiling of a target organization.

ExamAlert

Be familiar with physical security descriptions that indicate potential security flaws. Watch for descriptions that include physical details or organizational processes. Be particularly careful when questions address processes that use the same physical area for both common business traffic and data transport media, or when data resources are placed in publicly accessible areas.

Physical access to a system creates many avenues for a breach in security. Unsecured equipment is also vulnerable to social engineering attacks. It is much easier for an attacker to walk into a reception area, say he or she is there to do some work on the server, and get access to the server in an unsecured area than it is for the attacker to get into a physically secured area with a guest sign-in/sign-out sheet. In a secure design, physical security controls parallel data controls. When physical security is considered, the most obvious element to control is physical access to systems and resources. Your goal is to allow only trusted use of these resources via positive identification that the entity accessing the systems is someone or something that has permission to do so, based on the security model you have chosen. The following section briefly describes physical security components used to protect the perimeter.

Signs, Fencing, and Gates

Organizations might be bound by regulations to warn employees and visitors about workplace hazards. One of the most common ways to accomplish this is to use signs. Warning signs can be both informative and deterring. For example, if the organization deals in caustic chemicals, signs warning of the chemicals can inform visitors while also deterring intruders. Agencies such as OSHA, ANSI, and the National Electrical Manufacturers Association (NEMA) have specific established specifications for safety signs.

A common deterrent is a fence or similar device that surrounds the entire building. A fence keeps out unwanted vehicles and people. One factor to consider in fencing is the height. The higher the fence, the harder it is to get over. To deter intruders, fence height should be 6 to 7 feet. For areas that need to be more secure, or to provide protection against a determined intruder, the fence height should be 8 feet with barbed wire on top.

Another factor to consider is the material for the fence. Removing wooden slats or cutting a chain-link fence with bolt cutters is much easier than drilling through concrete or block. Keep in mind that if the fence is not maintained or the area around it is not well lit, the fence can easily be compromised.

Gates usually control access through fencing. These can be manned or unmanned. One of the main advantages of using automatic gates is the capability to use keycard readers and touchpad systems to control entry and exit. Unmanned gates allow entry only to people who have clearance to enter an area. An additional benefit of using an automatic gate with keycard readers is that the system maintains a log of all area entries and exits. Hybrid manned and automatic systems use a feature that checks entry via intercom; then the gate can be opened upon verification. This type of system is often used for visitors and outside vendors.

Another form of fencing is data center cage fencing, a secure cage that provides an additional physical security layer. See the section "Internal Security" for more on data center cages.

Lighting

From a safety perspective, too little light can provide an opportunity for a criminal, yet too much light can create glare and blind spots, resulting in potential risks. Protective lighting improves visibility for checking badges and people at entrances, inspecting vehicles, and detecting intruders both outside and inside buildings and grounds. Protective lighting should be located where it will illuminate dark areas and be directed at probable routes of intrusion.

Proper placement and positioning of fixtures can dramatically reduce glare. In areas where crime is a concern, install lamps with a higher color rendering index. If areas are brightly lit and have cameras, they are less likely to have unauthorized access attempts. A good design provides uniform lighting, minimizes glare, is compatible with CCTV, and complies with local light pollution and light trespass ordinances. Regular maintenance ensures that the safety and security of both people and property is not compromised. Twice annually, conduct an audit of all exterior lighting.

Barricades and Bollards

To enhance the security of critical or vulnerable facilities, physical access control structures or barricades can be used to protect against unauthorized people, vehicles, explosives, and other threats. Barricades provide a high level of protection and can withstand direct-impact forces. Vehicle barricades often are used in restricted areas to stop a vehicle from entering without proper authorization. A common barricade found in many environments is a *bollard*, a short post that prevents vehicles from entering an area. Crash-rated barriers and bollards provide the best security but are more costly. Examples of vehicle barricades include drop-arm gates, active bollard systems, planters, and crash barrier gates.

Cameras

Cameras and closed-circuit television (CCTV) are the most common method of perimeter surveillance. The video signal is processed and then transmitted for viewing at a central monitoring point. Traditionally, CCTV has been analog; however, recent technologies have taken advantage of the digital format, including IP video surveillance that uses TCP/IP for remote or wireless recording and monitoring. CCTV is a critical component of a comprehensive security program. It is important to appropriately plan and set clear measurable objectives for a CCTV system. Failing to do so from the outset can be costly.

Many types of CCTV systems are available. Organizations should take technical, administrative, and legal considerations (including privacy) into account before and during the implementation of a CCTV system.

Security Guards

The presence of security guards can be reassuring to employees and can discourage intruders. Security guards are often armed, so they must be trained properly. The range of duties for guards can include manning security gates, checking credentials, conducting active patrols, and monitoring CCTV feeds. Guards tend to be a greater visual deterrent than cameras alone and are often used in combination with other measures, such as deterrent signs.

ExamAlert

The exam might include questions about the various physical barrier techniques. Be sure you are familiar with the methods previously listed.

Perimeter security deterrents do not necessarily have to be designed to stop unauthorized access. As the name implies, they need to help deter the access. That is, the potential attacker might think twice about the attempt; even an attacker considers the concept of risk/reward. Common examples include a sign indicating that the property is alarmed or protected by a dog. Lighting, locks, dogs, cleared zones around the perimeter, and even life-size cut-outs of law enforcement officers can make a location appear less inviting to potential attackers.

Internal Security

Mandatory physical access controls are commonly found in government facilities and military installations, where users are closely monitored and very restricted. Because they are being monitored by security personnel and devices, users cannot modify entry methods or let others in. Discretionary physical control to a building or room is delegated to parties responsible for that building or room. In role-based access methods for physical control, groups of people who have common access needs are predetermined and access to different locations is allowed with the same key or swipe card. In this model, users generally have some security training and are often allowed to grant access to others by serving as an escort or by issuing a guest badge. The security department coordinates the secure setup of the facility and surrounding areas, identifies the groups allowed to enter various areas, and grants access based on group membership.

Internally, security guards, surveillance cameras, motion detectors, limited-access zones, token-based and biometric access requirements for restricted areas, and many other considerations could be involved in physical security planning. In addition, users must be educated about each measure taken to prevent circumvention and improve ease of normal access. The following section briefly describes physical security components used to protect the organization when a person gets past the perimeter of the property.

Alarms

Alarm systems detect intrusions and monitor or record intruders. Electronic alarm systems are designed to detect, determine, and deter criminal activity or other threatening situations. An alarm system can detect an event such as an invasion, fire, gas leak, or environmental change; determine whether the event poses a threat; and then send a notification about the event. Alarm systems can also be combined with closed-circuit television surveillance systems to automatically record the activities of intruders. Alarm systems also can interface with access control systems to electrically lock doors, for example.

Motion and Infrared Detection

The main purpose of a motion detector is to provide security against intruders by alerting security personnel to an unexpected presence or suspicious activity on the company's premises. Motion detectors contain a sensor that is integrated with other technologies to trigger an alert when a moving object is in the sensor's field of view. Motion detectors can be based on light, sound, infrared, or ultrasonic technology.

Infrared detection is based on an electrical signal that uses infrared light beams connected to a detector. It can be either active or passive. In active infrared detection, an alarm goes off when a constant light beam is interrupted. In passive infrared detection, a heat source event must trigger the alarm. Because infrared detectors pick up movement, they are useful when a high level of security must be maintained, such as in banks and restricted military facilities. These devices must be properly configured because they are extremely sensitive and can issue false alarms if they are set too stringently.

Mantraps

A mantrap is a holding area between two entry points that gives security personnel time to view a person before allowing him into the internal building. One door of a mantrap cannot be unlocked and opened until the opposite door has been closed and locked. In the most basic implementation of a mantrap, one door connects to the nonsecured area and the other door connects the portal to the secure area. Mantraps are often used to prevent tailgating and are found in areas such as data centers. Mantrap doors are operated mainly via RFID cards and can be sophisticated enough to record a person's weight coming in and out—for example, to trigger an alarm if the person might be taking equipment from the data center.

Locks and Lock Types

Locks must be easy to operate yet deter intruders. Beyond the normal key locks, several different types can be considered. A cipher lock has a punch-code entry system. A wireless lock is opened by a receiver mechanism that reads the card when it is held close to the receiver. A swipe card lock requires a card to be inserted into the lock; many hotels use these. Factors to consider are strength, material, and cost.

Access can be controlled by physically securing a system within a locked room or cabinet; attaching the system to fixed, unmovable furniture using cable locks or restraints; or locking the case itself to prevent the removal of key components. Nonstandard case screws add another layer of security for publicly accessible terminals. Other secured-area considerations include ensuring that air ducts, drop ceilings, and raised floors do not provide unauthorized avenues for physical access.

Of course, you can have the most secure lock on the door and use biometric devices for identification, but if the walls don't go up all the way and ceiling tiles can be removed to access rooms with sensitive equipment in them, someone can easily walk off with equipment and sensitive data. Be sure to consider all areas of the room.

Cards, Tokens, and Biometrics

Employees should have access to facilities based on their role or function. This includes visitor control and access control to software programs for testing and revision. Access list restrictions specifically align a person's access to information with his or her role or function in the organization. Functional or role-based access control determines which persons should have access to certain locations within the facility. Access can be granted via cards, tokens, or biometrics.

Most modern access control systems use proximity cards that enable users to gain access into restricted areas. Proximity cards store details of the holder's identity similar to how chip and PIN bank cards do. The difference is that proximity readers can read the information using radio frequency communication, making actual contact with the card unnecessary. Simply holding the card close to the reader enables its details to be read and checked quickly.

Security tokens can be used to grant access to computers and devices. A security token is a small, easy-to-carry, tamper-resistant physical object. Many times, the token is used in addition to a PIN or password so that if the token falls into the wrong hands, it is useless without the corresponding information. One of the most common physical security tokens is a key fob.

Physical security can also integrate biometric methods into a door-lock mechanism. Biometrics can use a variety of methods. See Table 24.1 in Chapter 24, "Identity and Access Controls," for a review of these technologies.

> **ExamAlert**
>
> When using biometrics, remember that each method has its own degree of error ratios. Some methods might seem invasive to the users and thus might not be accepted gracefully.

Retinal scans, for example, require that a user place an eye in contact with the imaging aperture. Some users might feel squeamish at the potential for contagious disease or be concerned with potential injury.

Key Management

Although many organizations try to avoid using physical keys, it is almost impossible not to have some keys within an organization. The keys found in organizations range from office cabinet keys to company vehicle keys. Nothing is more unsettling than to find that keys to areas that hold valuable information are missing from the key pegboard. All organizations should have some type of key management policy in place. When formulating a key management policy, items to consider include the following:

▶ Protecting master keys from leaving the site

▶ Grouping keys that are used together

▶ Determining which employees are permitted to use keys

▶ Formulating misuse and loss policies

▶ Providing a secure key location

Key-management systems are available with options such as cabinets that unlock only with correct authentication and that allow only the authorized keys to be removed. Others make use of biometric access features, automated logging, and alarming.

Logs

Locks and alarms provide a good measure of security, but in a layered security approach, logs are also used. Most organizations have a log book for visitors to sign in and out. Many times the log book is accompanied by security guards or a reception desk. Often the visitor is given a proximity access card or ID badge and must supply a valid ID, such as a driver's license that is kept until the ID badge or card is returned.

Manual sign-in and sign-out sheets tend to be resource-intensive and can be problematic if the information is not verified. Physical access logs might be required, depending on the type of business the organization conducts. For example, the Federal Financial Institutions Examination Council (FFIEC), which regulates and oversees financial institutions, requires physical security logs for visitors who enter secured areas. Companies can meet this requirement by using a badge system with a key card, but the system must be configured to maintain an access log.

Equipment Security

The next layer of physical security is the security of equipment. Physical access to a system creates avenues for a breach in security. Many tools can be used to extract password and account information that can then be used to access secured network resources. Given the capability to reboot a system and load software from a USB drive, attackers might be able to access data or implant Trojan horses and other applications intended to weaken or compromise network security.

A more serious threat is theft or loss. Laptops and handheld devices are easy targets for thieves. Theft of laptops and handheld devices in an office setting is nearly as high as theft in cars and other forms of transportation. To prevent theft or loss, you must safeguard the equipment in your organization.

Cable Locks

To protect organizational resources and minimize liability costs, each employee should take responsibility for securing office equipment. Laptops should never be left in an area where anyone can have easy access to them. Laptops, Apple iMacs, and any easily transportable office computers should be physically secured. Security cables with combination locks can provide such security and are easy to use. The cable is used to attach the computer to an immovable object. Computers have one and sometimes two security cable slots. The security cable slots allow you to attach a commercially available antitheft device to the computer. Computer locks commonly use steel cables to secure the PC to a desk; they are most commonly found in computer labs and Internet cafes. Laptop locks are meant to protect both privacy and the computer. They come in different types: cable locks, case locks, and twist locks. The most common type of antitheft devices for portable computers usually include a length of metal-stranded cable with an attached locking device and associated key. The cable is looped around an immovable object and the locking device is inserted into a security cable slot.

Antitheft devices differ in design, so be sure yours is compatible with the security cable slot on the computer. Never leave a laptop unsecured. If the area is not safe, do not leave a laptop even if it is secured by a cable-locking device. Thieves have driven off with whole ATM machines so they can find a way to bypass the lock later.

Cages and Safes

Tower-style computers can also be targets for thieves, not only because they have a higher resale value than laptops, but also because of the data they might hold. For example, financial businesses have been hit hard by theft of desktop computers because they hold a lot of personal data. Secure computer towers and server cages that bolt to the floor can improve physical security and prevent theft. In machines that are bolted to the floor, drive access can be either completely restricted or left available for ease of use. Server cages are most often found in data centers to protect server equipment and separate customer equipment. Colocation data centers can host the information of multiple customers, so typically a standard data center cage made of rigid metal is used. Cages can be modified based on customer specifications, such as stronger locks, restricted backside access, or military-grade requirements.

Some laptop safe security cases have special features to protect an organization's computers and data out in the field. For example, Flexysafe Digital makes a safe that is designed for people who take their laptop computers home from work. Also available are high-security laptop safes, which store laptops in a manner similar to bank vault storage. Individual storage accommodates laptops in locking compartments, and those compartments can then be additionally secured behind the high-security main safe door when required. The open compartment version offers open shelves (usually one laptop per shelf) for storage that can be secured by the safe's main door. Other computer safe options include types made to securely store laptops and carry cases, plus other valuable equipment in reception areas; mobile car safes made to prevent smash-and-grab attacks; and home computer safes with an electronic lock similar to the safes provided in hotel rooms.

Locking Cabinets and Enclosures

A locked cabinet or enclosure is another alternative for laptop equipment that is not used or that does not have to be physically accessed on a regular, daily basis. Vendors provide solutions such as a security cabinet locker that secures CPU towers. The housing is made of durable, heavy-duty steel for strength that lasts. The sides and door are ventilated to reduce risk of overheating. Another option is a wood laminate security computer cabinet that provides a computer workstation that can be locked away into a cabinet for space as well as security. Computer cabinets include a keyboard drawer and adjustable top shelf. A slide-out bottom shelf accommodates a CPU and printer. It has built-in cable management grommets. Depending on what needs to be secured, some computer enclosures can hold everything from LCD/LED flat screens to entire systems. This type of security is often used for training rooms, where the computers can be secured without having to remove them after each training session.

Screen Filters

A computer privacy screen filter might be a requirement, depending on the type of business the organization conducts. For example, HIPAA has stringent standards for patient privacy protection and requires medical, insurance, and other healthcare businesses and practitioners to protect the privacy and security of medical information. This includes information that is visible on computer screens. A computer screen filter limits the reading radius of the screen so that someone looking at the screen from the side cannot read what is onscreen. Many organizations require screen filters to shield important documents. Privacy screen filters are often used by employees while traveling to protect information while sitting in airports, using public transportation, or working from other public places.

Air Gap

An *air gap* is a physical isolation gap between a system or network and the outside world. No system is connected to the Internet or connected to any other system that has Internet access. In a true air-gapped system, data is transferred to the system via removable media or a direct connection to another computer. Air gaps prevent unauthorized access and keep malware away from the systems. Air gaps are often found in industrial control systems (ICS), military classified networks, and credit and debit card payment networks. Air-gapped systems can give you a false sense of security, however, because they can be compromised even though they are not connected to the Internet. Perhaps the most high-profile case involving the infection of an air-gapped system is Stuxnet.

Environmental Controls

Not all incidents arise from attacks, illegal activities, or other forms of directed threats to an enterprise. Many threats emerge from physical and environmental factors that require additional consideration in planning for security controls. The location of everything from the actual building to wireless antennas affects security. When picking a location for a building, an organization should investigate the type of neighborhood, population, crime rate, and emergency response times. This helps in planning the physical barriers needed, such as fencing, lighting, and security personnel. An organization must also analyze the potential dangers from natural disasters and plan to reduce their effect when possible.

When protecting computers, wiring closets, and other devices from physical damage from either natural or man-made disasters, you must select locations carefully. Proper placement of the equipment might cost a company a little money upfront, but it will provide significant protection from possible loss of data due to electrical damage, flooding, or fire.

Protected Cabling, Protected Distribution, and Faraday Cages

Also take shielding into consideration when choosing cable types and placement of cable. Coaxial cable was the first type of cable used in network computers. Coaxial cables are made of a thick copper core with an outer metallic shield to reduce interference. Coaxial cables have no physical transmission security and are simple to tap without being noticed or interrupting regular transmissions. The electric signal, conducted by a single core wire, can easily be tapped by piercing the sheath. An attacker then can eavesdrop on the conversations of all hosts attached to the segment because coaxial cabling implements broadband transmission technology and assumes that many hosts are connected to the same wire. Another security concern of coaxial cable is reliability. Because no focal point such as a switch or hub is involved, a single faulty cable can bring down the whole network. Missing terminators or improperly functioning transceivers can cause poor network performance and transmission errors.

Twisted-pair cable is used in most of today's network topologies. Twisted-pair cabling is either unshielded (UTP) or shielded (STP). UTP is popular because it is inexpensive and easy to install. UTP consists of eight wires twisted into four pairs. The design cancels much of the overflow and interference from one wire to the next, but UTP is subject to interference from outside electromagnetic sources and is prone to radio frequency interference (RFI) and electromagnetic interference (EMI), as well as crosstalk. Longer cable lengths transfer a more significant environmental measure of noise because wires can inadvertently act as an "antenna" for broadcast emanations.

STP is different from UTP because it has shielding surrounding the cable's wires. Some STP has shielding around the individual wires, which helps prevent crosstalk. STP is more resistant to EMI and is considered a bit more secure because the shielding makes wire-tapping more difficult.

ExamAlert

Both UTP and STP are possible to tap, although it is physically a little trickier to do so than tapping coaxial cable because of the physical structure of STP and UTP cable. With UTP and STP, a bigger danger lies in the fact that adding devices to the network via open ports is easy on unsecured hubs and switches.

These devices should be secured from unauthorized access, and cables should be clearly marked so a visual inspection can let you know whether something is awry. Software programs also can help detect unauthorized devices and the ports on which they will accept attempts at connection.

The plenum is the space between the ceiling and the floor of a building's next level. It is commonly used to run network cables. The cables must be of plenum grade, to comply with fire codes. The outer casing is more fire resistant than in regular twisted-pair cable.

Fiber optic cabling was designed for transmissions at higher speeds over longer distances, such as in underwater intercontinental telecommunications applications. Fiber uses light pulses for signal transmission, making it immune to RFI, EMI, and eavesdropping without specialized equipment capable of detecting transient optical emission at a fiber join or bend. Fiber optic wire has a plastic or glass center, surrounded by another layer of plastic or glass with a protective outer coating. On the downside, fiber is still quite expensive compared to more traditional cabling, it is more difficult to install, and fixing breaks can be time intensive and costly with hundreds or thousands of individual fibers in a single bundle. As far as security is concerned, fiber cabling eliminates the signal tapping that is possible with coaxial cabling. Tapping fiber is impossible without interrupting the service and using specially constructed equipment. This makes it more difficult for an attacker to eavesdrop or steal service.

Secure Internet Protocol Router Network (SIPRNET) and Non-Classified but Sensitive Internet Protocol Router Network (NIPRNET) are private government-run networks used for exchanging sensitive information in a secure manner. SIPRNET carries classified information up to the level of secret. These systems use a protected distribution system (PDS) of copper or optical cables that are protected from unauthorized physical or electronic access. The purpose of a PDS is to deter, detect, and make difficult physical access to the communication lines carrying national security information.

Simple distribution PDSs are afforded a reduced level of physical security protection, compared to a hardened distribution PDS. They use a simple carrier system. The following means are acceptable under CNSSI 7003:

▶ The data cables should be installed in a carrier.

▶ The carrier can be constructed of any material (wood, PVT, EMT, ferrous conduit, and so on).

▶ The joints and access points should be secured and controlled by personnel cleared to the highest level of data handled by the PDS.

▶ The carrier must be inspected in accordance with the requirements of CNSSI 7003.

A more efficient way to protect a large quantity of equipment from electronic eavesdropping is to place the equipment in a well-grounded metal box of conductive material, called a Faraday cage. Named after its inventor, Dr. Michael Faraday, this box can be small enough for a cellphone or can encompass an entire building. The idea behind it is to protect the contents from electromagnetic fields. The cage surrounds an object with interconnected and well-grounded metal, typically a copper mesh that is attached to the walls and covered with plaster or drywall. The wire mesh acts as a net for stray electric signals either inside or outside the box. New forms of wall treatment (wallpaper) can be used to embed a Faraday mesh atop existing structural materials, retrofitting older buildings with Faraday-style protections to create cellphone-free zones in restaurants and theaters.

HVAC

When doing facilities planning, you need to take into consideration the cooling requirements of computer data centers and server rooms. The amount of heat generated by some of this equipment is extreme and highly variable. Depending on the size of the space, age, and type of equipment the room contains, energy consumption typically ranges from 20 to 100 watts per square foot. Despite being smaller and more powerful, newer servers might consume even more energy. Some high-end facilities with state-of-the-art technology can require up to 400 watts per square foot. These spaces consume many times more energy than office facilities of equivalent size and must be planned for accordingly. Smaller, more powerful IT equipment is considerably hotter than older systems, making heat management a major challenge.

> **ExamAlert**
>
> When monitoring the HVAC (heating, ventilation, and air conditioning) system, keep in mind that overcooling causes condensation on equipment and too-dry environments lead to excessive static.

Monitor the area for hot spots and cold spots, where one exchange is frigid cold under a vent and still hot elsewhere. Water or drain pipes above facilities also raise a concern about upper-floor drains clogging. One solution is to use rubberized floors above the data center or server room. Above all else, timely air conditioning maintenance is required.

Fire Suppression

Fire is a danger common to all business environments and must be planned for well in advance of any possible occurrence. The first step in a fire safety program is fire prevention.

The best way to prevent fires is to train employees to recognize dangerous situations and report them immediately. Knowing where a fire extinguisher is and how to use it can stop a small fire from becoming a major catastrophe. Many of the newer motion- and ultrasonic-detection systems also include heat and smoke detection for fire prevention. These systems alert the monitoring station of smoke or a rapid increase in temperature. If a fire does break out somewhere within the facility, a proper fire-suppression system can avoid major damage. Keep in mind that laws and ordinances apply to the deployment and monitoring of a fire-suppression system. The company has the responsibility to ensure that these codes are properly met. In addition, the organization should have safe evacuation procedures and periodic fire drills to protect its most important investment: human life.

Fire requires three main components to exist: heat, oxygen, and fuel. If you eliminate any of these components, the fire goes out. A common way to fight fire is with water. Water attempts to take away oxygen and heat. A wet-pipe fire-suppression system is the one most people think of when discussing an indoor sprinkler system. The term *wet* describes the state of the pipe during normal operations. The pipe in the wet-pipe system has water under pressure in it at all times. The pipes are interconnected and have sprinkler heads attached at regularly spaced intervals. The sprinkler heads have a stopper held in place with a bonding agent designed to melt at an appropriate temperature. When the stopper melts, it opens the valve and allows water to flow from the sprinkler head to extinguish the fire. Keep in mind that electronic equipment and water don't get along well. Fires that start outside electrical areas are well served by water-based sprinkler systems, but all these systems should have both manual activation and manual shutoff capabilities. You want to be able to turn off a sprinkler system to prevent potential water damage. Most systems are designed to activate only one head at a time. This works effectively to put out fires in the early stages.

Dry-pipe systems work in exactly the same way as wet-pipe systems, except that the pipes are filled with pressurized air instead of water. The stoppers work on the same principle. When the stopper melts, the air pressure is released and a valve in the system opens. One reason for using a dry-pipe system is that, when the outside temperature drops below freezing, any water in the pipes can freeze, causing them to burst. Another reason for justifying a dry-pipe system is the delay associated between the system activation and the actual water deployment. Some laws require a sprinkler system even in areas of the building that house electrical equipment, so there should be enough of a delay for someone to manually deactivate the system before water starts to flow. In such a case, a company could deploy a dry-pipe system and a chemical system together. The delay in the dry-pipe system could be used to deploy the chemical system first and avoid serious damage to the running equipment from a water-based sprinkler system.

Fire suppression systems are rated according to class:

▶ For Class A fires (trash, wood, and paper), water decreases the fire's temperature and extinguishes its flames.

▶ For Class B fires, foam extinguishes flames fueled by flammable liquids, gases, and greases. Liquid foam mixes with air while passing through the hose and the foam.

▶ Class C fires (energized electrical equipment, electrical fires, and burning wires) are put out using extinguishers based on carbon dioxide or halon. Halon was once used as a reliable, effective, and safe fire-protection tool, but in 1987, an international agreement known as the Montreal Protocol mandated the phase-out of environmentally damaging halons in developed countries due to emissions concerns. Therefore, carbon dioxide extinguishers have replaced halon extinguishers in all but a few locations. Carbon dioxide extinguishers do not leave a harmful residue, and exposure can be tolerated for a while without extreme protective measures, making them a good choice for an electrical fire in a data center or in other electronic devices.

▶ Class D fires are fires that involve combustible metals such as magnesium, titanium, and sodium. The two types of extinguishing agents for Class D fires are sodium chloride and a copper-based dry powder.

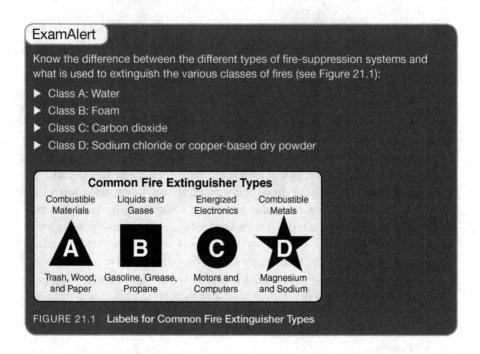

> **ExamAlert**
>
> Know the difference between the different types of fire-suppression systems and what is used to extinguish the various classes of fires (see Figure 21.1):
>
> ▶ Class A: Water
> ▶ Class B: Foam
> ▶ Class C: Carbon dioxide
> ▶ Class D: Sodium chloride or copper-based dry powder
>
> **Common Fire Extinguisher Types**
>
> | Combustible Materials | Liquids and Gases | Energized Electronics | Combustible Metals |
> |---|---|---|---|
> | **A** | **B** | **C** | **D** |
> | Trash, Wood, and Paper | Gasoline, Grease, Propane | Motors and Computers | Magnesium and Sodium |
>
> FIGURE 21.1   Labels for Common Fire Extinguisher Types

Hot and Cold Aisles

Data centers and server farms can make use of an alternating arrangement of server racks, with alternating rows facing opposing directions. Fan intakes draw in cool air vented to racks facing the cold aisle, and then fan output of hot air is vented to the alternating hot aisles for removal from the data center (see Figure 21.2). This data center organization provides greater efficiency in thermal management by allowing supply ducts to serve all cold aisles and exhaust ducts to collect and draw away heated air.

Overcooling causes condensation on equipment, and too-dry environments lead to excessive static. In addition to monitoring temperature, organizations should monitor humidity. Humidity is a measure of moisture content in the air. A high level of humidity can cause components to rust and degrade electrical resistance or thermal conductivity. A low level of humidity can subject components to electrostatic discharge (ESD), causing damage; at extremely low levels, components might be affected by the air itself. The American Society of Heating, Refrigerating and Air-Conditioning Engineers (ASHRAE) recommends optimal humidity levels in the range of 40 to 55 percent.

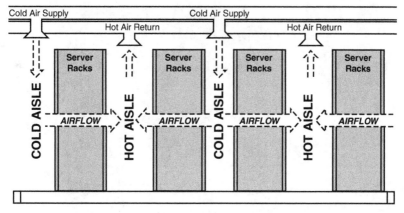

FIGURE 21.2 **A simplified hot aisle/cold aisle data center layout with overhead HVAC supply and exhaust ducts**

Environmental monitoring solutions can raise alerts or trigger automated responses as needed. Alerting systems must be capable of sustaining operations during the event, so a water-sensing monitor should be able to function and raise an alert even when the environment is filled with water.

Monitoring systems must also be able to communicate in the event of service disruption so that alerts can be passed to responders even if the email server cluster has shut down from thermal overload conditions. If the monitoring solution relies on networking for sensor measurement or raising alerts, environmental issues that degrade or prevent network communications might go unnoticed or alerts might not reach responders in a timely manner.

What Next?

If you want more practice on this chapter's exam objectives before you move on, remember that you can access all the Cram Quiz questions on the Pearson Test Prep software. You can also create a custom exam by objective. Note any objective you struggle with and go to that objective material in this chapter.

Cram Quiz

These review questions cover material related to Chapters 13–21, which cover objectives falling under Domain 3, "Architecture and Design," of the Security+ exam.

1. Using a combination of firewalls, intrusion detection systems, content filters, encryption, and auditing procedures in the organization for protection against intrusions is an example of which of the following?

    - ○ **A.** Defense in depth
    - ○ **B.** Infrastructure as a Service
    - ○ **C.** Community cloud
    - ○ **D.** Layered security

2. Which of the following types of control is a surveillance system?

    - ○ **A.** Logical control
    - ○ **B.** Technical control
    - ○ **C.** Physical control
    - ○ **D.** Management control

3. Which of the following are the most compelling reasons that secure configuration baselines have been established? (Select all correct answers.)

    - ○ **A.** Industry standards
    - ○ **B.** Organizational requests
    - ○ **C.** Governmental mandates
    - ○ **D.** Regulatory bodies

4. Which of the following devices is used to accept encrypted connections from users and then send the connection to the server unencrypted?

    - ○ **A.** VPN
    - ○ **B.** DMZ
    - ○ **C.** DDoS mitigation appliance
    - ○ **D.** SSL accelerator

5. You are setting up a switched network and want to group users by department. Which technology should you implement?

    - ○ **A.** DMZ
    - ○ **B.** VPN

○ C. VLAN

○ D. NAT

6. You are setting up a web server that both the internal employees and external customers need to access. What type of architecture should you implement?

○ A. VLAN

○ B. DMZ

○ C. NAT

○ D. VPN

7. An organization has a sensitive network that needs to have physically isolated machines. Which of the following practices would be used to meet this requirement?

○ A. Air gap

○ B. VLAN

○ C. RAS

○ D. Honeynet

8. An organization is experiencing a large amount of electromagnetic interference (EMI). Which of the following is the best method to provide continuous operations?

○ A. extra shielding

○ B. A generator

○ C. A redundant electric connection

○ D. A RAID configuration

9. Which of the following best describes the result of adding an email address to the blocked list?

○ A. It is considered part of the whitelist.

○ B. It is considered part of the blacklist.

○ C. It is considered part of the graylist.

○ D. It is considered part of the brownlist.

10. Which of the following can result in the exploitation of a BIOS vulnerability? (Select all correct answers.)

○ A. Hard drive failure occurs

○ B. System cannot boot

○ C. System locks up

○ D. Denial of service occurs

11. Which of the following uses a secure cryptoprocessor to authenticate hardware devices such as a PC or laptop?

   ○ **A.** Public key infrastructure

   ○ **B.** Full disk encryption

   ○ **C.** File-level encryption

   ○ **D.** Trusted platform module

12. Which of the following provides a sandboxed environment that can be used to investigate unsafe executables?

   ○ **A.** Virtualization

   ○ **B.** Network storage

   ○ **C.** Host software baselining

   ○ **D.** Application baselining

13. Which of the following is considered good practice for separation of development and test environments? (Select two correct answers.)

   ○ **A.** Different physical locations

   ○ **B.** Firewall

   ○ **C.** VPN

   ○ **D.** VLAN

14. In which of the following are attestation challenges from computed hashes of system or application information used to obtain confidence in the trustworthiness and identity of a platform or software?

   ○ **A.** Application baselines

   ○ **B.** Integrity measurement

   ○ **C.** Staging environments

   ○ **D.** Sandboxing

15. A vulnerability assessment has revealed that legacy internal heart monitors of a hospital's intensive care unit (ICU) are visibly exposed to the Internet. Which of the following should be implemented?

   ○ **A.** Network segmentation

   ○ **B.** Code wrappers

   ○ **C.** Control diversity

   ○ **D.** Manual updates

16. Which of the following operating systems is run in a SoC environment?

   ○ **A.** Windows Server 2016

   ○ **B.** RedHat Enterprise Linux (RHEL)

   ○ **C.** CAN bus

   ○ **D.** RTOS

17. Which of the following is most likely to use network segmentation as a security method?

   ○ **A.** SCADA systems

   ○ **B.** Mainframes

   ○ **C.** Android devices

   ○ **D.** Gaming consoles

18. In which of the following phases should code security first be implemented?

   ○ **A.** Testing

   ○ **B.** Review

   ○ **C.** Implementation

   ○ **D.** Design

19. Buffer overflows, format string vulnerabilities, and utilization of shell escape codes can be mitigated by using which of the following practices to test an application?

   ○ **A.** Fuzzing

   ○ **B.** Testing

   ○ **C.** Input validation

   ○ **D.** Browser-initiated token request

20. The organization is building a new application and is more interested in being able to use a rigorous methodical process to verify each phase along the way than it is in selecting a fast delivery method. Which of the following should the organization choose?

   ○ **A.** IaC

   ○ **B.** Agile

   ○ **C.** Waterfall

   ○ **D.** Continuous integration

21. An organization is interested in using a vendor SaaS application but is concerned about the lack of cloud security. What type of cloud architecture is the most appropriate?

   ○ **A.** Public
   ○ **B.** Private
   ○ **C.** Hybrid
   ○ **D.** Community

22. Which of the following methods of cloud computing allows the client to literally outsource everything that would normally be in a typical IT department?

   ○ **A.** SaaS
   ○ **B.** IaaS
   ○ **C.** PaaS
   ○ **D.** DaaS

23. An organization wants to use a service provider to implement processes for the organization such as identity and access management (IAM) and encryption. Which of the following should the organization choose?

   ○ **A.** IaaS
   ○ **B.** SecaaS
   ○ **C.** DRaaS
   ○ **D.** SaaS

24. An organization that operates a small web-based photo backup business is evaluating single points of failure. The organization has three servers, four switches, and 100 client systems. Which of the following is the most likely component(s) to be the single point of failure?

   ○ **A.** Servers
   ○ **B.** ISP connection
   ○ **C.** Client systems
   ○ **D.** Switches

25. An organization is implementing a data availability solution based on a striped disk array without redundancy. Which of the following best describes this implementation?

   ○ **A.** RAID 0
   ○ **B.** RAID 1
   ○ **C.** RAID 5
   ○ **D.** RAID 10

26. Because of seasonal business fluctuations, an organization uses cloud environments to purchase resources for a short period of time based on demand. Which of the following terms best describes this principle?

   - ○ **A.** Snapshots
   - ○ **B.** Elasticity
   - ○ **C.** Scalability
   - ○ **D.** Server redundancy

27. Which type of fire extinguisher is best for putting out burning wires?

   - ○ **A.** Water
   - ○ **B.** Carbon dioxide
   - ○ **C.** Sodium chloride
   - ○ **D.** Copper powder

28. What is the plenum?

   - ○ **A.** A mesh enclosure designed to block EMI
   - ○ **B.** A mechanism for controlling condensation
   - ○ **C.** A type of dry-pipe fire control system
   - ○ **D.** A mechanism for thermal management

29. The ASHRAE recommends humidity levels in which range?

   - ○ **A.** 25%–40%
   - ○ **B.** 40%–55%
   - ○ **C.** 55%–70%
   - ○ **D.** 70%–85%

30. An organization that has several small branches in North Dakota, Minnesota, and Ontario, Canada, is planning for a fire-suppression system installation. Which of the following best fits the needs of the organization?

   - ○ **A.** Dry pipe
   - ○ **B.** Wet pipe
   - ○ **C.** Deluge
   - ○ **D.** Preaction

Cram Quiz Answers

1. **D.** Layered security is based on the premise that, by implementing security at different levels or layers to form a complete security strategy, better protection is provided than by implementing an individual security defense. Answer A is

incorrect. Defense in depth is rooted in military strategy and requires a balanced emphasis on people, technology, and operations to maintain information assurance (IA). Answer B is incorrect because Infrastructure as a Service (IaaS) is the delivery of computer infrastructure in a hosted service model over the Internet. Answer C is incorrect because a community cloud provides collaborative business processes in a cloud environment.

2. **C.** Physical controls form the outer line of defense against direct access to data, such as protection of backup media; secure output and mobile file storage devices; and facility design details such as layout, doors, guards, locks, and surveillance systems. Answer A is incorrect because logical controls are the same as technical controls. Answer B is incorrect because technical controls include logical access control systems, security systems, encryption, and data classification solutions. Answer D is incorrect because management and administrative controls include business and organizational processes and procedures, such as security policies and procedures, personnel background checks, security awareness training, and formal change management procedures.

3. **A, C, and D.** Security baselines are often established by governmental mandate, regulatory bodies, or industry representatives—for example, think of the PCI requirements established by the credit card industry for businesses that collect and transact using credit information. Answer B is incorrect because organizational requests are merely requests, and security baselines are often established to comply with some type of regulation or standard.

4. **D.** SSL accelerators are devices that accept SSL connections from users and then send the connection to the server unencrypted. They are typically positioned in-line between the users and a server. Answer A is incorrect because a VPN is a network connection that allows you access via a secure tunnel created through an Internet connection. Answer B is incorrect because a DMZ is a small network between the internal network and the Internet that provides a layer of security and privacy. Answer C is incorrect because DDoS mitigation appliances are used to mitigate DDoS attacks and can be implemented through external ISP- based solutions, on- premises solutions, or third-party based solutions.

5. **C.** The purpose of a VLAN is to unite network nodes logically into the same broadcast domain, regardless of their physical attachment to the network. Answer A is incorrect because a DMZ is a small network between the internal network and the Internet that provides a layer of security and privacy. Answer B is incorrect because a VPN is a network connection that allows you access via a secure tunnel created through an Internet connection. Answer D is incorrect because NAT acts as a liaison between an internal network and the Internet.

6. **B.** A DMZ is a small network between the internal network and the Internet that provides a layer of security and privacy. For example, web servers are often placed in a DMZ. Answer A is incorrect because the purpose of a VLAN is to unite network nodes logically into the same broadcast domain, regardless of their physical attachment to the network. Answer C is incorrect because NAT acts as a liaison between an internal network and the Internet. Answer D is incorrect because a VPN is a network connection that allows access via a secure tunnel created through an Internet.

7. **A.** Air gaps are physically isolated machines or networks. They should not have any connection to the Internet or any machine that connects to the Internet. Answer B is incorrect because a virtual local-area network (VLAN) unites network nodes logically into the same broadcast domain, regardless of their physical attachment to the network. Answer C is incorrect because Remote Access Services (RAS) lets you connect your computer from a remote location, such as your home or any on-the-road location, to a corporate network. Answer D is incorrect because honeynets are used to distract attackers from valid network content, to study the attacker's methods, and to provide early warning of attack attempts.

8. **A.** Shielding is used to reduce EMI output. Extra shielding contains a metallic sheath that surrounds surrounding connection wires for mouse devices, keyboards, and video monitor connectors. Answer B is incorrect because a generator is used for rolling blackouts, emergency blackouts, or electrical problems. Answer C is incorrect because most electric companies service only one area. If it is possible to contract with another service provider, the cost will most likely be prohibitive. Answer D is incorrect because RAID does not protect against electrical failures.

9. **B.** In general, an email address added to the approved list is never considered spam. This is also known as a whitelist. Using whitelists allows more flexibility in the type of email you receive. Putting the addresses of your relatives or friends in your whitelist allows you to receive any type of content from them. An email address added to the blocked list is always considered spam. This is also known as a blacklist. Answer A is incorrect because whitelisting is allowing an email address. Answer C is incorrect because graylisting is related to whitelisting and blacklisting. Each time a given mailbox receives an email from an unknown contact (IP), that mail is rejected with a "try again later." Answer D is incorrect because brownlisting is a concept based on a CBL type system driven by tokens from blocked sites.

10. **B and D.** A vulnerability in the BIOS can allow local users to cause a denial of service and result in the system not booting. Answer A is incorrect because a hard drive failure has to do with the hard disk itself and nothing to do with the BIOS. Answer C is incorrect because system lockup implies that the machine was already booted; this is associated more with attacks that happen after the machine is up and running.

11. **D.** TPM refers to a secure cryptoprocessor used to authenticate hardware devices such as a PC or laptop. The idea behind TPM is to allow any encryption-enabled application to take advantage of the chip. Answer A is incorrect because the public key infrastructure (PKI) is a set of hardware, software, policies, and procedures needed to create, manage, distribute, use, store, and revoke digital certificates. Answer B is incorrect because full disk encryption involves encrypting the operating system partition on a computer and then booting and running with the system drive encrypted at all times. Answer C is incorrect because, in file- or folder-level encryption, individual files or folders are encrypted by the file system itself.

12. **A.** A virtualized sandboxed environment can help in computer security research, which studies the effects of unsafe executables without the possibility of compromising the host system. Answer B is incorrect because network storage has nothing to do with desktop management. Answer C is incorrect because host software baselining can be done for a variety of reasons, including monitoring malware and

creating system images. Answer D is incorrect because application baselining is used to monitor changes in application behavior.

13. **B and D.** In a physical isolation environment, a firewall normally separates the environments from each other and the outside world. In VLAN segmentation, VLANs are often mapped into security zones. Traffic between zones must pass through a firewall, which enforces the segmentation rules between the environments. Answer A is incorrect because physical separation, unless air gapped, does not guarantee that the two environments cannot access each other. Answer C is incorrect because a VPN is used for remote access.

14. **B.** Integrity measurement is a method that uses attestation challenges from computed hashes of system or application information to obtain confidence in the trustworthiness and identity of a platform or software. Answer A is incorrect because application baselining is similar to operating system baselining: It provides a reference point for normal and abnormal activity. Answer C is incorrect because a staging environment is primarily used to unit test the actual deployment of code. Answer D is incorrect because the basic idea of sandboxing is to provide a safe execution environment for untrusted programs.

15. **A.** Network segmentation is one of the most effective controls an organization can implement to mitigate the effect of a network intrusion. In sensitive systems such as SCADA networks, applying segmentation in layers, from the data link layer through the application layer, can go a long way in protecting vital infrastructure services. Answer B is incorrect because wrappers are used in several types of implementations, such as smart grids and integration of legacy systems. They reduce the risk of web-based attacks. Answer C is incorrect because control diversity refers to having multiple versions of software packages in which redundant software versions differ. Answer D is incorrect because although manual updates are inconvenient, they might also be necessary when the system contains sensitive data and is segmented.

16. **D.** A real-time operating system (RTOS) is a small operating system used in embedded systems and IoT applications that is typically run in a SoC environment. Answer A is incorrect because Windows 2016 is a server operating system. Answer B is incorrect because Red Hat Enterprise Linux (RHEL) is a server operating system. Answer C is incorrect because a CAN bus is associated with internal vehicle communications.

17. **A.** SCADA systems would most likely use network segmentation. Answer B is incorrect because mainframes would most likely use security layers. Answer C is incorrect because Android would most likely use security layers. Answer D is incorrect because most gaming consoles only run signed code, encrypt memory, and use firmware updates to patch vulnerabilities.

18. **D.** It is important to implement security from the very beginning. In the early design phase, potential threats to the application must be identified and addressed. Ways to reduce the associated risks must also be taken into consideration. Therefore, answers A, B, and C are incorrect.

19. **C.** Input validation tests whether an application properly handles input from a source outside the application destined for internal processing. Answer A is incorrect because fuzzing allows the injection of random-looking data into a program to see if it can cause the program to crash. Answer B is incorrect because testing is a generic term that encompasses more than what the question is asking.

Answer D is incorrect because it is a method used to mitigate cross-site request forgery (XSRF) attacks.

20. **C.** The Waterfall SDLC model is traditional, starting with a defined set of requirements and a well-developed plan with adjustments confined to the current development stage. Answer A is incorrect because Infrastructure as Code (IaC) is also known as programmable infrastructure, meaning that infrastructure configuration can be incorporated into application code. Answer B is incorrect because the Agile SDLC model starts with less rigorous guidelines and allows for adjustments during the entire process. Answer D is incorrect because continuous integration (CI) is a process in which the source code updates from all developers working on the same project are continually monitored and merged from a central repository when a new commit is detected.

21. **C.** A hybrid cloud environment is the best choice when an organization offers services that need to be configured for diverse vertical markets or wants to use a SaaS application but is concerned about security. Answer A is incorrect because using a public cloud increases concern about security. Answer B is incorrect because a private cloud does not allow the public vendor SaaS implementation. Answer D is incorrect because a community cloud provides collaborative business processes in a cloud environment.

22. **B.** Infrastructure as a Service (IaaS) is the delivery of computer infrastructure in a hosted service model over the Internet. This method of cloud computing allows the client to literally outsource everything that would normally be in a typical IT department. Answer A is incorrect because Software as a Service (SaaS) is the delivery of a licensed application to customers over the Internet for use as a service on demand. Answer C is incorrect. Platform as a Service (PaaS) is the delivery of a computing platform, often an operating system with associated services, that is delivered over the Internet without downloads or installation. Answer D is incorrect because Desktop as a Service (DaaS), also called virtual desktop or hosted desktop services, is the outsourcing of a virtual desktop infrastructure (VDI) to a third-party service provider.

23. **B.** In SecaaS, a security service provider uses a subscription-based model to implement security for the organization. SecaaS providers offer a wide variety of security services, including but not limited to identity and access management (IAM), email security, and encryption. Answer A is incorrect because IaaS is a cloud computing model in which hardware, storage, and networking components are virtualized and provided by an outsourced service provider. Answer C is incorrect because DRaaS is the replication and hosting of physical or virtual servers by a third party to provide failover in case of a man-made or natural catastrophe. Answer D is incorrect because SaaS is a cloud computing model in which software applications are virtualized and provided by an outsourced service provider.

24. **B.** Neglecting single points of failure can prove disastrous. A single point of failure is any piece of equipment that can bring your operation down if it stops working. Based on this, the Internet connection would be the single point of failure. Answers A, C, and D are incorrect; the system has more than one of each of these pieces of equipment, so they are not single points of failure.

25. A. RAID Level 0 is a striped disk array without fault tolerance. Answer B is incorrect because RAID Level 1 is mirroring and duplexing. This solution requires a minimum of two disks and offers 100 percent redundancy because all data is written to both disks. Answer C is incorrect because RAID Level 5 consists of independent data disks with distributed parity blocks. In RAID 5, each entire block of the data and the parity is striped. Answer D is incorrect because RAID Level 10 is high reliability combined with high performance. This solution is a striped array that has RAID 1 arrays.

26. B. Elasticity is most often found in cloud environments where resources can be purchased for a short period of time, based on demand, and then deleted when they are no longer needed. Answer A is incorrect because a snapshot preserves the entire state and data of the virtual machine at the time it is taken. Answer C is incorrect because scalability is the capacity to expand the amount of production from the current infrastructure without negatively impacting performance. Answer D is incorrect because server redundancy is implemented to ensure high availability and reliability.

27. B. The carbon dioxide extinguisher replaces the halon extinguisher for putting out electrical (Class C) fires. Answer A is incorrect because water is used for Class A fires (trash, wood, and paper). Answers C and D are incorrect because both sodium chloride and copper-based dry powder extinguishers are used for Class D (combustible materials) fires.

28. D. A plenum is the space below a raised floor or above a drop ceiling that can be used in hot aisle/cold aisle server rooms to efficiently manage thermal dissipation. Answer A is incorrect because a grounded mesh enclosure for EMI shielding is called a Faraday cage. Answer B is incorrect because management of condensation is handled as part of the HVAC function as air is cooled. Answer C is incorrect because a dry-pipe system is a fire-extinguishing system that uses pressurized air as a triggering mechanism for water.

29. B. The Air-Conditioning Engineers (ASHRAE) recommendation for optimal humidity levels is between 40 percent and 55 percent to minimize electrostatic discharge and condensation. Answer A is incorrect because it specifies a low range that would be dangerous for static discharge. Answers C and D are incorrect because they represent too high of a humidity level that could result in the buildup of condensation on cool components and boards.

30. A. One reason for using a dry-pipe system is that, when the outside temperature drops below freezing, any water in the pipes will freeze, causing them to burst. Therefore, answer B is incorrect. Answer C is incorrect because deluge systems are used in places that are considered high hazard areas, such as power plants, aircraft hangars, and chemical storage or processing facilities. Deluge systems are needed where high-velocity suppression is necessary to prevent fire spread. Answer D is incorrect because conventional preaction systems are relatively complex and expensive. That tends to preclude the benefits of their use in low-cost, water-sensitive applications such as small areas and residential applications where the need to avoid inadvertent water damage is as important as providing protection against fire damage.

Identity and Access Management

For more information on the official CompTIA Security+ SY0-501 exam topics, see the "About the CompTIA Security+ SY0-501 Exam" section in the Introduction.

Part III, "Architecture and Design," covered secure architecture and design. It outlined how various components fit into a secure design and addressed the connection between the components of that design. This part focuses on the four main principles of identity and access management. It covers the fundamental identity and access management concepts, selecting the appropriate identity and access service solution, implementing identity and access management controls, and following account management best practices.

Identity and access management (IAM) is the security principle that defines the proper authentication, authorization, and access to resources for users. This security principle is a vital part of the overall management of the enterprise. IAM addresses the essential need to provide the appropriate level of access to resources across diverse technological environments while meeting organizational and regulatory compliance requirements. IAM encompasses creating unique identities for individuals and systems, and then associating system and application-level accounts with these identities. It requires the alignment of people, processes, technology, and business goals. The advantage of using IAM systems is that they reduce organizational identity management costs and allow the organization to be more flexible when new business initiatives arise.

CHAPTER 22

Identity and Access Management Concepts

This chapter covers the following official Security+ exam objective:

4.1 Compare and contrast identity and access management concepts.

- ▶ Identification, authentication, authorization and accounting (AAA)
- ▶ Multifactor authentication
  - ▪ Something you are
  - ▪ Something you have

- ▪ Something you know
- ▪ Somewhere you are
- ▪ Something you do
- ▶ Federation
- ▶ Single sign-on
- ▶ Transitive trust

Essential Terms and Components

- ▶ accounting
- ▶ authentication
- ▶ authorization
- ▶ federation

- ▶ identification
- ▶ multifactor authentication
- ▶ transitive trust

CramSaver

If you can correctly answer these questions before going through this section, save time by skimming the Exam Alerts in this chapter and then completing the Cram Quiz at the end of Part 4.

1. What distinguishes single-factor from multifactor authentication?

   _____

2. What is the primary advantage of using federated identity systems for authentication?

   _____

3. How does a transitive trust relationship work?

   _____

Answers

1. Multifactor identification involves two or more different types of authentication (something you have versus something you know, for example). Two or more of the same type of authentication remains a single-factor solution (as in the case of username and password, which are both something you know).

2. In a federated identity system, the user never supplies credentials directly to any application or service except the originating identity provider. The user's credentials are always stored with the originating organization or identify provider.

3. When a trust is configured so that any domain trusting Domain A will then trust all other domains that Domain A trusts, this connection is called a transitive trust.

Identification, Authentication, Authorization, and Accounting (AAA)

It is necessary to discern the differences in the actions of identification, authentication, authorization, and accounting because you will be tested on all these concepts. *Identification* occurs when a user or device presents information such as a username, a process ID, a smart card, or another unique identifier and claims an identity. *Authentication* is the process of validating an identity. This occurs when the user provides appropriate credentials, such as the correct password with a username.

When identification through the presentation and acceptance of credentials is accomplished, the credentials must be measured against a listing of all known credentials by the authentication service to determine *authorization* of the request before access rights during the session can be established. Authorization is based on security policy.

Accounting keeps track of the resources a user accesses by keeping a record of events of authentication and authorization actions. Accounting functions log session statistics and usage information, which then can be used for management tasks such as access control and resource utilization. Additional capabilities include billing, trend analysis, and capacity planning. Implementing the accounting component of AAA requires special server considerations.

These are the core components of AAA:

▶ The device that wants to access the network is known as the client.

▶ The Policy Enforcement Point (PEP) is the authenticator. The PEP enforces the conditions of the client's access.

▶ The Policy Information Point (PIP) holds data relevant to the decision on whether to grant access to the client.

▶ The Policy Decision Point (PDP) is the crux of the AAA decision. The PDP is responsible for making the final decision of whether to grant access to the client.

▶ The Accounting and Reporting System tracks the client network usage and reports the "who, what, where, when, and why."

Core AAA components are logical functions that can be combined and are not necessarily physical devices.

Multifactor Authentication

A method for authenticating users must be designed and implemented properly for the organization to achieve established business goals and security control objectives. Several common factors are used for authentication: something you know, something you have, something you are, something you do, and somewhere you are. Authentication factors provide a means of implementing multifactor authentication. *Multifactor authentication* provides additional security because account access is no longer possible with only a password.

ExamAlert

Forms of authentication credentials can be generally broken into five basic categories, depending on what is required to identify the access requester:

▶ Something you *know* (passwords, account logon identifiers)

▶ Something you *have* (smart cards, synchronized shifting keys)

▶ Something you *are* (fingerprints, retinal patterns, hand geometry)

▶ Something you *do* (gait and handwriting kinematics)

▶ Some*where* you *are* (you are in a trusted or less trusted location)

Location-specific logons from a particular GPS zone, time-of-day restrictions, and restricted console terminal requirements can also be factors when limiting access to requests.

The most common form of authentication combines two "something you know" forms of authentication: a username and a password or passphrase. This form is easily implemented across many types of interfaces, including standard keyboards and assistive technology interfaces. If both values match the credentials associated within the authorization system's database, the credentials can be authenticated and authorized for a connection.

An organization's authentication needs are relative to the value assigned to a particular resource's security. Additional authentication layers required for access increase both the administrative overhead necessary for management and the difficulty users have trying to reach needed resources. Consider, for example, the differences in authentication requirements for access to a high-security solution such as the Department of Energy's power grid control network and those needed to access an unprivileged local account at a public kiosk.

In the first scenario, to establish authentication for rightful access, the use of a combination of multiple biometric, token-based, and password form authentication credentials might be mandatory. You can also use these access methods with more complex forms of authentication, such as dedicated lines of communication, time-of-day restrictions, synchronized shifting-key hardware encryption devices, and redundant-path comparison. You use these to ensure that each account attempting to make an access request is properly identified. In the second scenario, authentication might be as simple as an automatic anonymous guest logon that all visitors share.

Each mechanism for authentication provides different levels of identification, security over data during the authentication exchange, and suitability to different authentication methods such as wireless or dial-up network access requests.

Multiple authentication factors can be combined to improve the overall strength of the access control mechanism.

Automated teller machines (ATMs) use a common example of a multifactor authentication system, requiring both a "something you have" physical key (your ATM card) and a "something you know" personal identification number (PIN). Similar issues with payment card systems have arisen following public attacks on vendors such as Target, resulting in an expanded effort to enable two-factor authentication using electronic chips in the cards (something you have) and a PIN (something you know). By combining two or more types of authentication, you improve access security above a single-factor authentication such as your "something you have" car key, which can be used alone without any additional credentials beyond simply possessing the physical key or its duplicate.

The difficulty involved in gaining unauthorized access increases as more types of authentication are used, although the difficulty also increases for users who want to authenticate themselves. Administrative overhead and cost of support also increase with the complexity of the authentication scheme, so a solution should be reasonable based on the sensitivity of data being secured.

> **ExamAlert**
>
> The exam might ask you to distinguish between single-factor and multifactor authentication solutions. A multifactor authentication scenario involves two or more *types* of authentication (something you know, have, are, or do or somewhere you are), not simply multiple credentials or keys of the same type. The common logon/password combination is single-factor ("something you know") authentication using two separate keys of the same authentication type.

Federation, Single Sign-On, and Transitive Trust

The proper identification of a person, device, or group is important to protect and maintain the confidentiality, integrity, and availability of the organization's assets and infrastructure. Based on business policies, identification and access controls can be created to authenticate users and devices. Various methodologies are used to validate identification and grant resource access. Federation, single sign-on, and transitive trust are the three most popular methods of object identification and access validation.

Single Sign-On

Distributed enterprise networks often include many different resources, each of which might require a different mechanism or protocol for authentication and access control. To reduce user support and authentication complexity, a single sign-on (SSO) capable of granting access across multiple services might be desirable. SSO solutions can use a central metadirectory service or can sequester services behind a series of proxy applications, as with the service-oriented architecture (SOA) approach. In the SOA network environment, the client-facing proxy application provides a standard mechanism for interacting with each service (called a *wrapper*), handling specialized logon, authentication, and access control functions behind the scenes and out of sight of the consuming user or service.

> **ExamAlert**
>
> With SSO, a user can log in to multiple applications during a session while authenticating only once.

All applications still require a password for login, but the software stores the password. When an application requires a login, the software automatically retrieves the password and provides it to the application on the user's behalf, resulting in an automatic login. The user still has a password for each system that must be changed based on organizational policy.

Federation

Federation is a way to connect identity management systems by allowing identities to cross multiple jurisdictions. A political federation involves myriad equal participants, collaborating through agreements and agreed-upon rules or mediators who can represent their own political agenda. In the United Nations, for example, each governmental body assigns its own ambassador to speak for the country's interests. A federated identity management solution transfers this idea into technology by assigning an administrative account capable of enumerating local security principals and resources. The federation system is accessible from each domain. Thus, accounts in one area can be granted access rights to any other resource, whether local or remote within the communicating domains. This enables enterprises to exchange identity information securely across Internet domains and can integrate access to applications across distinct business units within a single organization.

ExamAlert

In a federated identity system, the user never supplies credentials directly to any application or service except the originating identity provider. The user's credentials are always stored with the originating organization or identity provider.

When the user logs into a service, the service provider trusts the identity provider to validate the credentials instead of providing credentials to the service provider. This type of enterprise solution provides flexibility for organizations when acquisitions happen or when individual business units maintain independent authentication mechanisms across applications.

Federation and *SSO* are often used together but are two distinct and different concepts. Many federated identity management solutions provide some form of SSO, and many SSO systems are implemented using federated identity management. The two don't have to be intertwined; they can be used entirely separate from each other. The main difference is that federation eliminates the requirement to use a password. The federation server stores the username in each application and presents that application with a token that is then used for authentication.

Transitive Trust

In addition to the aforementioned mechanisms for provisioning identification and access control, transitive trust relationships can be configured to allow users to traverse domains. This provides access across an enterprise or multiple enterprises, connecting resources with users across multiple resource pools. Two domains can be configured to share a trust by configuring the administrative connection between two resource pools.

ExamAlert

A one-way trust (Domain A trusts Domain B) allows resources in Domain A to be accessed by security principals (users, services, and so on) in Domain B. A two-way trust allows each domain to trust members of either domain. (Domain A and Domain B resources can be accessed by authorized requests from user accounts in either Domain A or Domain B.)

Within compatible domains, a limited form of interoperation can be assigned directly between two resource pools though administrative actions within each, to specifically designate the other as a trusted resource pool and allow enumeration of accounts and available resources. Access control over any resource can then be granted or denied to any account in either domain. This connection is termed a *trust*, which is like a direct agreement between allied countries. If the trust is configured so that any domain trusting Domain A will then trust all other domains that Domain A trusts, this connection is called a *transitive trust*. This is like having your siblings trust a friend of your father, and the arrangement turns transitive if you and your siblings agree to trust everyone your father trusts.

What Next?

If you want more practice on this chapter's exam objectives before you move on, remember that you can access all the Cram Quiz questions on the Pearson Test Prep software. You can also create a custom exam by objective. Note any objective you struggle with and go to that objective material in this chapter.

CHAPTER 23

Identity and Access Services

Essential Terms and Components

- ▶ LDAP
- ▶ Kerberos
- ▶ TACACS+
- ▶ CHAP
- ▶ PAP
- ▶ MSCHAP
- ▶ RADIUS
- ▶ SAML
- ▶ OpenID Connect
- ▶ OAuth
- ▶ Shibboleth

CramSaver

If you can correctly answer these questions before going through this section, save time by skimming the Exam Alerts in this chapter and then completing the Cram Quiz at the end of Part 4.

1. Which directory services protocol would be implemented to protect against man-in-the-middle data interception attacks?

   _____

2. Which AAA protocol would be used if reliability and flexibility were implementation requirements?

   _____

3. What is the main difference between the functions of OAuth and the functions of OpenID or SAML?

   _____

Answers

1. The Kerberos protocol supports mutual authentication between two systems, protecting against man-in-the-middle forms of data interception or manipulation by ensuring that both network endpoints are authenticated to one another.

2. The TACACS+ protocol is an open standard that uses TCP as a transport method and communicates on port 49. TACACS+ tends to be more reliable because it uses TCP instead of UDP. TACACS+ uses the AAA architecture to perform authorization and accounting with separate authentication methods. RADIUS combines the authentication and authorization features of AAA, making it difficult to use the functions separately.

3. OAuth does not provide authentication services. It is used exclusively for authorization services, making it different than OpenID and SAML.

The following section discusses the various identity and access services and explores how they are used. This includes services that use tickets, such as Kerberos; services that use challenge mechanisms, such as Challenge Handshake Authentication Protocol (CHAP); remote access services, such as RADIUS; and federated services, such as OAuth.

Authentication Protocols

Password Authentication Protocol (PAP) is a simple authentication protocol in which the username and password are sent to the remote access server in plain-text form. PAP offers no protection from playback or trial-and-error attacks. The remote server is in control of the frequency and timing of the login attempts. Using PAP is strongly discouraged because user passwords are easily readable from the PPP packets exchanged during the authentication process. The default status of any PPP link is not to require authentication of the remote host. PAP is typically used only when connecting to older UNIX-based remote access servers that do not support more secure authentication protocols.

Challenge Handshake Authentication Protocol (CHAP) can be used to provide on-demand authentication within an ongoing data transmission. CHAP uses a one-way hashing function that first involves a service requesting a CHAP response from the client. The client creates a hashed value that is derived using the Message Digest (MD5) hashing algorithm and sends this value to the service, which also calculates the expected value itself. The server, referred to as the *authenticator*, compares these two values. If they match, the transmission continues. This process is repeated at random intervals during a session of data transaction to help eliminate the possibility of a replay attack. The process of authenticating is called a *three-way process*. Actually, four steps are involved because the first step is establishing the connection, but the authentication process itself is a three-way process.

CHAP is an improvement over PAP because it hashes the password but still sends the username in clear text. CHAP functions over Point-to-Point Protocol (PPP) connections. PPP is a protocol for communicating between two points using a serial interface, providing service at the second layer of the OSI model, the data link layer.

Microsoft CHAP (MSCHAP) is an encrypted authentication mechanism that is similar to CHAP. It comes in two versions, MSCHAPv1 and MSCHAPv2. MSCHAPv1 is a one-way authentication method in which the server requires authentication from the client. This version should not be used. MSCHAPv2 provides stronger security because it uses a new string each time the authentication is challenged. In MSCHAPv2, the client and server mutually authenticate and use two encryption keys, one for sending data and one for receiving data.

PAP, CHAP, and MSCHAP are authentication protocols intended for use primarily by hosts and routers that connect to a PPP or PPPoE network server via switched circuits or dial-up lines. These are all older, less secure protocols. In August 2012, Microsoft advised against using MSCHAPv2 and recommended using either MS-CHAP with Protected Extensible Authentication Protocol (PEAP) or more secure alternatives, such as L2TP/IPsec.

When implementing security for a legacy protocol such as MSCHAPv2, Extensible Authentication Protocol (EAP) can be used. EAP is a password-based authentication framework. In this implementation, the client doesn't need to have a certificate, but the authentication server has one. Passwords from the clients are sent using hashes to the authentication server.

If the environment allows for a stronger authentication method, PEAP can be used. PEAP acts as a TLS/SSL tunnel and protects the authentication traffic. PEAP uses a certificate on the authentication server and optionally a certificate on the client.

Directory Services Protocols

NTLM (NT LAN Manager) is an older Microsoft authentication protocol that requires Active Directory and relies on Microsoft Windows user credentials in the authentication process. NTLM was replaced with Kerberos starting with Windows 2000. NTLM authentication is similar to CHAP and MSCHAP, in that authentication is validated by means of a random challenge generated by the server. NTLM also differs from CHAP and MSCHAP because it is specific to a Microsoft network environment, as opposed to data link layer connections. Consider the NTLM authentication steps:

1. The client sends the username to the server.

2. A server-generated challenge is returned to the client.

3. Using the user's password, the client encrypts the challenge and sends a response to the server.

4. For local accounts, the server validates the user's response based on information in the Security Account Manager (SAM).

5. For domain user accounts, the server forwards the response to a domain controller for validation of the user account based on group policy. Then the server creates an access token and establishes a session.

NTLM is easily exploitable and puts organizations at risk for a breach. All NTLM versions use a relatively weak cryptographic scheme. Because a user must respond to a challenge from the target to authenticate to a machine, the password is exposed to offline cracking. Because NTLM is password-based, it lacks effective support for multifactor authentication solutions and is subject to replay and man-in-the-middle attacks.

Microsoft's guide to restricting NTLM recommends first auditing all NTLM traffic and then conducting an analysis of servers and users that are using NTLM. NTLM authentication could potentially be eliminated using options that aren't necessarily organization-driven. For example, the organization might be required to conform to current regulations such as Sarbanes-Oxley that require the use of a stronger authentication mechanism than NTLM.

To avoid sending the open plain-text logon information across an unsecured network, one solution is the symmetric key authentication protocol known as *Kerberos* (created by the Athena project at MIT and named for the three-headed dog Cerberus that guarded Hades). Kerberos is an authentication protocol that has been around for decades and is an open standard. *Symmetric key* means that both the client and the server must agree to use a single key in the encryption and decryption processes.

> **ExamAlert**
>
> Kerberos is primarily a UDP protocol, although it falls back to TCP for large Kerberos tickets. Kerberos clients send UDP and TCP packets on port 88 and receive replies from the Kerberos servers. Port 88 is the standard port for Kerberos V5 for the KDC, and port 749 is used for the administrative server.

In Kerberos authentication, a client sends its authentication details not to the target server, but to a key distribution center (KDC), as follows:

1. The client first contacts a certification authority (CA).

2. The CA creates a time-stamped session key with a limited duration (by default, 8 hours) using the client's key and a randomly generated key that includes the identification of the target service.

3. This information is sent back to the client in the form of a ticket-granting ticket (TGT).

4. The client submits the TGT to a ticket-granting server (TGS).

5. This server generates a time-stamped key encrypted with the service's key and returns both to the client.

6. The client uses its key to decrypt its ticket, contacts the server, and offers the encrypted ticket to the service.

7. The service uses its key to decrypt the ticket and verify that the time stamps match and the ticket remains valid.

8. The service contacts the KDC and receives a time-stamped, session-keyed ticket that it returns to the client.

9. The client decrypts the keyed ticket using its key. When both agree that the other is the proper account and that the keys are within their valid lifetime, communication is initiated.

ExamAlert

The short lifespan of a ticket ensures that if someone attempts to intercept the encrypted data to try to break its keys, the key will have changed before the attacker can reasonably succeed in breaking the key using cryptographic algorithms. The handshaking between the client and the KDC and between the service and the KDC verifies that the current session is valid, without requiring the transmission of logons or passwords directly between client and service.

Kerberos V5 includes support for a process known as mutual authentication, in which both client and server verify that the computer with which they are communicating is the proper system. This process helps prevent man-in-the-middle attacks, in which an unauthorized party intercepts communications between two systems and masquerades as the other system. The unauthorized part might pass some data intact, modify other data, or insert entirely new sets of values to accomplish desired tasks.

In mutual authentication, one system creates a challenge code based on a random number and then sends this code to the other system. The receiving system generates a response code using the original challenge code and creates a challenge code of its own; it sends both back to the originating system. The originating system verifies the response code as a value and returns its own response code to the second system, generated from the challenge code returned with the first response code. After the second system has verified its returned response code, it notifies the originating system. Both systems then consider themselves mutually authenticated.

The strength of Kerberos authentication comes from its time-synchronized connections and the use of registered client and service keys within the KDC. These also create some drawbacks, such as the need to use a standard synchronized time base for all systems involved. Difficulties arise if the KDC is unavailable or the cached client and service credentials were accessed directly from the granting servers. An important advantage of time-stamped credentials is that they help prevent spoofing and replay attacks.

ExamAlert

Not all authentication services provide the same functions, so aligning the proper service with the right environment requires knowledge of the basics of each service. Remember that Microsoft Active Directory networks rely on Kerberos for credentials exchange, so all systems must share a common time service to maintain synchronization.

Kerberos is more secure than NTLM because it uses stronger encryption. Its implementation consumes less bandwidth and Kerberos tickets support identity delegation.

Lightweight Directory Access Protocol (LDAP) provides access to directory services, including those used by the Microsoft Active Directory. LDAP was created as a "lightweight" alternative to earlier implementations of the X.500 Directory Access Protocol and communicates on port 389. The main purpose of LDAP is to query user directories. Its widespread use influences many other directory systems, including the Directory Service Markup Language (DSML), Service Location Protocol (SLP), and Microsoft Active Directory and Secure LDAP variations.

LDAP is used for queries, so the LDAP process is simple. The client sends an authentication request to the LDAP server. The server queries the database to determine whether the client can authenticate. After authenticating, the client requests access to resources. The server again queries a database to determine whether the client has permissions to access the requested resources. In Microsoft environments, LDAP is used to read from and write to Active Directory.

By default, LDAP traffic is transmitted unsecured and is subject to the following vulnerabilities:

▶ Buffer overflow vulnerabilities can be used to enact arbitrary commands on the LDAP server.

▶ Format string vulnerabilities might result in unauthorized access to enact commands on the LDAP server or impair its normal operation.

▶ Improperly formatted requests can be used to create an effective denial-of-service (DoS) attack against the LDAP server, preventing it from responding to normal requests.

LDAP traffic can be made confidential and secure by using Secure Sockets Layer (SSL)/Transport Layer Security (TLS) technology. You can enable LDAP over SSL (LDAPS) by installing a properly formatted certificate from either a Microsoft certification authority (CA) or a non-Microsoft CA. The following are reasons for enabling Lightweight Directory Access Protocol (LDAP) over SSL/TLS (also known as LDAPS):

▶ Protection of the authentication session when an application authenticates with Active Directory Domain Services (AD DS) through simple BIND

▶ The use of proxy binding or password change over LDAP, which requires LDAPS

▶ The use of encrypted communications, which are required by applications that integrate with LDAP servers (such as Active Directory or Active Directory domain controllers)

AAA Protocols and Services

Two prominent security protocols used to control access in networks are TACACS+ and RADIUS. The *Remote Authentication Dial-In User Service (RADIUS)* remote access control system provides authentication and access control within an enterprise network, using UDP transport to a central network access server. In turn, this provides credentials for client access to resources within the extended enterprise. RADIUS was originally developed for use in dial-up connectivity over telephony, and you might still find RADIUS servers in larger enterprises where logons must span resources located in multiple logon realms.

A protected network segment might implement a virtual private network (VPN) or remote access server (RAS) gateway connection to allow an authenticated external service request to reach a protected server by communicating with a RADIUS server. The requesting account must provide its credentials to the RADIUS server, which then authorizes the access request. A RADIUS server supports a variety of authentication methods including PPP, PAP, CHAP, and UNIX login authentication mechanisms.

> **ExamAlert**
>
> The RADIUS service provides authentication and authorization functions as well as network access accounting functions. However, it does not provide further access control.

The RADIUS service can forward authentication and authorization requests between authentication domains (called *realms*) and thus can facilitate cross-enterprise authentication, often as part of a single sign-on (SSO) solution.

Terminal Access Controller Access Control System Plus (TACACS+) is a protocol that was developed by Cisco and released as an open standard beginning in 1993. Although it derives from TACACS, TACACS+ is a separate protocol that handles authentication, authorization, and accounting (AAA) services. TACACS+ is similar to RADIUS but uses TCP as a transport method; it uses port 49 as the default port. TACACS+ takes a client/server model approach. The client first queries the server. The client is typically a router or a firewall used to determine whether the user has proper authorization to access the network. The server sends back a reply stating whether the user passed authentication.

Both TACACS+ and RADIUS contain an accounting function, so if a device were intentionally compromised, an audit trail would show the originating IP address and the user account logged into the device. TACACS+ offers several advantages over RADIUS:

- ▶ TACACS+ tends to be more reliable because it uses TCP instead of UDP.

- ▶ TACACS+ encrypts the entire body of the packet in the original access request packet. RADIUS encrypts only the password, leaving information such as the username subject to the compromise.

- ▶ TACACS+ uses the AAA architecture. This allows the use of TACACS+ for authorization and accounting with separate authentication methods. RADIUS combines the authentication and authorization features of AAA, making it difficult to use the functions separately.

- ▶ TACACS+ provides methods to control the authorization of router commands. RADIUS is not as useful for router management or as flexible for terminal services because it does not allow users to control the commands that can be executed.

Consider an example of when TACACS+ should be used instead of RADIUS: An organization requires the use of Kerberos authentication but also needs authorization and accounting functions. In this instance, the network access server (NAS) informs the TACACS+ server that it has successfully authenticated on a Kerberos server. The server then provides authorization information without having to reauthenticate.

TACACS+ servers should not be running other applications, to minimize the chance of compromising the entire user/password database. Proper access control lists should be implemented and additional security steps (such as using TCP wrappers) should be taken, to prevent the ability to connect to the TACACS+ server in case an internal device is compromised.

Federated Services

Technologies used for federated identity include Security Assertion Markup Language (SAML), OAuth, OpenID, Simple Web Tokens, and JSON Web Tokens. These technologies use secure tokens. Token authentication is a better approach to authentication because it is stateless. Instead of authenticating with the username and password for each resource, the user authenticates once with the username and password and then receives a secure token. The token is then used for further authentication and expires after a set amount of time. This method prevents storage of user information on the server or in a session. Using tokens provides restrictive permissions to third-party applications such as Twitter and Facebook.

Security Assertion Markup Language (SAML) is an Extensible Markup Language (XML) framework for creating and exchanging security information between online partners. It is a product of the OASIS Security Services Technical Committee. Most cloud and Software as a Service (SaaS) Service Providers favor SAML because it provides authentication assertion, attribute assertion, and authorization assertion. Authentication assertion validates the user's identity. Attribute assertion contains information about the user, and authorization assertion identifies what the user is authorized to do.

The main purpose of SAML is single sign-on for enterprise users. The SAML framework defines three main functions:

▶ The user seeking to verify its identity is the principal.

▶ The entity that can verify the identity of the end user is the Identity Provider.

▶ The entity that uses the Identity Provider to verify the identity of the end user is the Service Provider.

These functions happen with single sign-on:

1. The user accesses a resource.

2. The Service Provider issues an authentication request.

3. The Identity Provider authenticates the user.

4. The Identity Provider issues an authentication response.

5. The Service Provider checks the authentication response.

6. When validation is complete, the resource returns the content.

The main difference between SAML and other identity mechanisms is that SAML relies on assertions about identities. The weakness in the SAML identity chain is the integrity of users. SAML uses SAM, XML, HTTP, and SOAP protocols. To mitigate risk, SAML systems need to use timed sessions, HTTPS, and SSL/TLS.

Open Authorization (OAuth) is a framework used for Internet token-based authorization. The main purpose of OAuth is API authorization between applications. Two versions are used; the most current is version 2.0.

The OAuth framework consists of the following:

1. The resource owner

2. The OAuth provider, which is the hosting resource server

3. The OAuth consumer, which is the resource consumer

OAuth 2.0 defines four roles: resource owner, authorization server, resource server, and client. It creates separate roles for the resource server and authorization server. OAuth 2.0 obtains authorization by the user via an access token and then uses that token to make user requests. Flows are ways to get an access token. The flows in OAuth 2.0 are called grant types:

▶ The *authorization code* grant type is used for server-side applications. The user is prompted to authorize the application, the Identity Provider supplies an authorization code, and the application server exchanges the authorization code for an access token.

▶ The *implicit* grant type is used for client-side web applications. This grant type doesn't have a server-side component. It skips the authorization code generation step. Immediately after the user authorizes the application, an access token is returned.

▶ The *password credentials* grant type is used for first-class web applications or mobile applications. This grant type is to be used only for native web or mobile applications because it allows applications to collect the user's username and password and exchange them for an access token.

▶ The *client credentials* grant type is used for application code to allow an application to access its own resources. The application makes a request using its own credentials to receive an access token.

OAuth2.0 uses the JSON and HTTP protocols. Because it only provides authorization services, it does not support secure methods such as client verification, encryption, or channel binding. OAuth 2.0 relies on underlying technologies, implementers, and other protocols to protect the exchange of data. TLS/SSL is recommended to prevent any eavesdropping during the data exchange. If a user was not logged into the server before the OAuth initiation request, resource providers should automatically log the user out after handling the third-party OAuth authorization flow, to prevent session management exploits.

> **ExamAlert**
>
> OAuth does not provide authentication services. It is used exclusively for authorization services, making it different than OpenID and SAML.

OpenID Connect is an identity layer based on OAuth 2.0 specifications that is used for consumer single sign-on. OpenID Connect is similar to the open standard OpenID, sponsored by Facebook, Microsoft, Google, PayPal, Ping Identity, Symantec, and Yahoo!. In 2015, Google recommended switching from OpenID to OpenID Connect. OpenID Connect implements authentication as an extension to the OAuth 2.0 authorization process and provides additional mechanisms for signing, encryption of identity data, and session management.

The OpenID Connect protocol specifications guide states this process for validation:

▶ The client sends a request to the OpenID provider (OP).

▶ The OP authenticates the end user and obtains authorization.

▶ The OP responds with an ID token and an access token.

▶ The client sends a request with the access token to the UserInfo endpoint.

▶ The UserInfo endpoint returns claims about the end user.

OpenID Connect uses an ID token structure that contains an authorization server's claims about the authentication of an end user via a JSON web token (JWT). A JWT is used to prove that the sent data was created by an authentic source. The flows determine how the ID token and access token are returned to the client. Authentication takes place through one of three flows:

▶ The authorization code flow returns an authorization code to the client, which then exchanges it for an ID token and an access token.

▶ The implicit flow eliminates the token endpoint. All tokens are returned from the authorization endpoint.

▶ The hybrid flow can have some tokens returned from the authorization endpoint and some returned from the token endpoint.

The OpenID Connect specification takes attacks into consideration and resolves many of the security issues with OAuth 2.0. However, if guidelines are not followed to implement it securely, broken end user authentication can result.

Shibboleth is a SAML-based, open source federated identity solution that provides single sign-on (SSO) capabilities and federated services popular in research and educational institutions. Ongoing development, support, and maintenance are performed by the Shibboleth Consortium. Shibboleth works similarly to other SSO systems, allowing access across or within organizational boundaries. Shibboleth uses the following three elements:

▶ The Identity Provider (IdP), located in the home organization, authenticates the user.

▶ The Service Provider (SP), located at the resource organization, performs the resource SSO process.

▶ The Discovery Service (DS) is useful for finding the user's IdP. It can be located anywhere on the web and is not a required component.

The functions that happen with Shibboleth SSO are the same as described for SAML. Shibboleth is a flexible solution because it is based on standards. Some federated systems are designed to work only when the Identity Provider and the Service Provider are in the same organization, but Shibboleth works across organizations. This flexibility enlarges the attack surface. The Shibboleth Consortium maintains a current list of security advisories issued from incorrect configurations by Service or Identity Providers.

What Next?

If you want more practice on this chapter's exam objectives before you move on, remember that you can access all the Cram Quiz questions on the Pearson Test Prep software. You can also create a custom exam by objective. Note any objective you struggle with and go to that objective material in this chapter.

CHAPTER 24

Identity and Access Controls

This chapter covers the following official Security+ exam objective:

4.3 Given a scenario, implement identity and access management controls.

- ▶ Access control models
  - ■ MAC
  - ■ DAC
  - ■ ABAC
  - ■ Role-based access control
  - ■ Rule-based access control
- ▶ Physical access control
  - ■ Proximity cards
  - ■ Smart cards
- ▶ Biometric factors
  - ■ Fingerprint scanner
  - ■ Retinal scanner
  - ■ Iris scanner
  - ■ Voice recognition

- ■ Facial recognition
- ■ False acceptance rate
- ■ False rejection rate
- ■ Crossover error rate
- ▶ Tokens
  - ■ Hardware
  - ■ Software
  - ■ HOTP/TOTP
- ▶ Certificate-based authentication
  - ■ PIV/CAC/smart card
  - ■ IEEE 802.1X
- ▶ File system security
- ▶ Database security

Essential Terms and Components

- ▶ ABAC
- ▶ CAC
- ▶ DAC
- ▶ HOTP

- ▶ MAC
- ▶ RBAC
- ▶ smart card
- ▶ TOTP

CramSaver

If you can correctly answer these questions before going through this section, save time by skimming the Exam Alerts in this chapter and then completing the Cram Quiz at the end of Part 4.

1. Would a high-security biometric sensor measuring palm geometry, fingerprints, blood vessel patterns, and blood oxygenation be a multifactored authentication solution?

   _____

2. What are the two meanings of RBAC controls?

   _____

3. What are three file system protections that an organization can implement to protect the environment?

   _____

Answers

1. No, all the measures are of a biological nature and thus represent a complex but single-factor, biometric (something you are) authentication mechanism. If a personal identification number (PIN) or smart card (something you have) type of validator was also required, the solution would be considered multifactor.

2. RBAC refers to rule-based access control or role-based access control. The exam will expect you to use role-based access control anytime RBAC is paired with discretionary access control (DAC) and mandatory access control (MAC) measures.

3. File system protections include encryption, RAID, and access controls.

Access Control Models

Access control generally refers to the process of making resources available to accounts that should have access, while limiting that access to only what is required. You need to know these forms of access control:

▶ Mandatory access control (MAC)

▶ Discretionary access control (DAC)

▶ Attribute-based access control (ABAC)

▶ Rule-based access control (RBAC)

▶ Role-based access control (RBAC)

The most basic form of access control involves assigning labels to resources and accounts (examples include SENSITIVE, SECRET, and PUBLIC). If the labels on the account and resource do not match, the resource remains unavailable in a nondiscretionary manner. This type of access control, called *mandatory access control* (MAC, also referred to as *multilevel access control*), is often used within governmental systems, where resources and access are granted based on categorical assignments as classified, secret, or top secret. Mandatory access control applies to all resources within the network and does not allow users to extend access rights by proxy.

A slightly more complex system of access control involves restricting access for each resource in a discretionary manner. *Discretionary access control (DAC)* scenarios allow individual resources to be individually made available or secured from access. Access rights are configured at the discretion of the accounts that have the authority over each resource, including the capability to extend administrative rights through the same mechanism. In DAC, a security principal (account) has complete control over the objects that it creates or otherwise owns, unless this is restricted through group or role membership. The owner assigns security levels based on objects and subjects and can make his or her own data available to others as desired. A common scenario for DAC is online social network users choosing who can access their data.

The Trusted Computer System Evaluation Criteria (TCSEC) specification that many government networks use explicitly specifies only the MAC and DAC forms of access control. The TCSEC is sometimes referred to as the Orange Book because of the original color of its printed manual's cover (DoD 5200.28-STD).

The designation RBAC is sometimes used to refer to *rule-based access control* in addition to *role-based access control*. Rule-based access control dynamically assigns roles to users based on criteria that the data custodian or system administrator defines. Rule-based access control includes controls such as the time of day, the day of the week, specific terminal access, and GPS coordinates of the requester, along with other factors that might overlay a legitimate account's access request. Implementation of rule-based access control might require that rules be programmed using code instead of allowing traditional access control by checking a box.

In a role-based access control (RBAC) scenario, access rights are first assigned to roles. Then accounts are associated with these roles, without the direct assignment of resource access rights. This solution provides the greatest level of scalability within large enterprise scenarios, where explicitly granting rights to each individual account could rapidly overwhelm administrative staff and increase the potential for accidentally granting unauthorized permissions.

RBAC combines some direct access aspects of mandatory access control and varying discretionary access rights based on role membership. Delegated administration over rights granted through RBAC is itself managed by specialized administration roles instead of through ownership or direct control over the individual resources, as in strictly DAC solutions.

> **ExamAlert**
>
> Remember that the exam might include alternative uses for the RBAC acronym, referring to rule-based access controls. In a rule-based access control solution, access rights can vary by account, time of day, the trusted OS, or other forms of conditional testing. Exam items that deal with conditional testing for access (for example, time-of-day controls) are examining rule-based access control. Items that involve assigning rights to groups for inheritance by group member accounts are focusing on role-based access control.

As the RBAC specification became popular and allowed the central management of enterprise access control, the need for access control lists (ACLs) was reduced. RBAC does not easily support multifactor decisions and lacks the capability to associate roles with access control requirements. This makes long-term maintenance difficult.

Attribute Based Access Control (ABAC) is a logical access control model that the Federal Identity, Credential, and Access Management (FICAM) Roadmap recommends as the preferred access control model for information sharing among diverse organizations. ABAC is based on the Extensible Access Control Markup Language (XACML). The reference architecture is similar to the core components of AAA. The ABAC authorization process is determined by evaluating rules and policies against attributes associated with an entity, such as the subject, object, operation, or environment condition. Attributes are characteristics that define specific aspects of the entity. When an access request is made, the access decision is based on the evaluation of attributes and access control rules by the attribute-based access control mechanism.

ABAC is a more dynamic access control method. When attribute values change, the access is changed based on the attribute changes. ABAC systems are capable of enforcing both DAC and MAC models. ABAC is well suited for large and federated enterprises, making it more complicated and costly to implement and maintain than simple access control models.

Physical Access Controls

The relative strength of an authentication system involves making it difficult to falsify or circumvent its process. Anonymous or open access represents the weakest possible form of authentication, whereas the requirement for both a logon identifier and a password might be considered the simplest form of actual account verification. The highest levels of authentication might involve not only account logon, but also criteria measuring whether the logon is occurring from specific network addresses, or perhaps whether some type of additional physical security measure is present.

Proximity and smart cards are the most basic form of physical access controls. Proximity cards have an embedded microchip and hold very little information. The main purpose of the card is to determine access by matching the card identification number to information in a database. If the number is in the database, access is granted. The most common use of a proximity card is for door access. Proximity cards are also used for applications that require quick processing, such as toll booths and parking garages.

Smart cards are a form of "something you have" authentication that uses a standard wallet card with an embedded chip that can automatically provide an authenticating cryptographic key to its reader. Smart cards might also contain useful data for other forms of authentication, such as biometric measures, that is too large for high-volume remote authentication solutions. A smart card typically displays a picture of the cardholder and has a programmable chip that provides identification and authentication. Communication between the card and reader occurs either through direct physical contact or with a remote contactless electromagnetic field. The upcoming section "Certificate-based Authentication" discusses contactless smart cards. Implementing smart cards into physical security improves overall security by allowing additional identification methods such as biometrics to be used for authentication.

In theory, the strongest security is offered by combining biometric (body-measuring) keys that are unique to a particular user's physical characteristics (such as fingerprints and retinal or iris patterns) with other authentication methods that involve either access passwords or token-based security requiring the possession of a physical smart card key.

The most unique qualities of an individual can be obtained by measuring and identifying the person's unique physical characteristics in "something you are" forms of bio measurement (biometric) authentication, such as fingerprints, retinal patterns, iris patterns, blood vessel patterns, bone structure, and other forms of physiological qualities unique to each person. Other "something you do" values can be measured, such as voice pattern recognition, movement kinematics, or high-resolution cardiac patterns. However, because these can change based on illness, injury, or exertion, they suffer high rates of false rejection (valid attempts at authentication that are returned as failures).

Many systems are available to authenticate users by their body measurements (biometrics). Those measures are compared to values stored within an authorization system's database, to provide authentication only if the biometric values match those previously measured. Another alternative is to store biometric data on smart card tokens, which the localized authentication service can pair with the requisite physical measurement without requiring a centralized database for comparison. Under this scenario, users must be authenticated within a widely distributed scheme when transactions against a central server storing large and complex biometric values might be difficult.

Table 24.1 describes some of the most common biometric methods.

TABLE 24.1 **A Comparison of Common Biometric Measures**

Method	Process	Issues
Fingerprint	Scans and identifies the swirls and loops of a fingerprint	Injury, scars, or loss of a finger might create false rejection results. Unless paired with other measures, the pattern alone can be easily counterfeited.
Hand/ palm geometry	Measures the length and width of a hand's profile, including hand and bone measures	Loss of fingers or significant injury might create false rejection results.
Voiceprint	Measures the tonal and pacing patterns of a spoken phrase or passage	Allergies, illnesses, and exhaustion can distort vocal patterns and create false rejection results.
Facial recognition	Identifies and measures facial characteristics, including eye spacing, bone patterns, chin shape, and forehead size and shape	This method is subject to false rejection results if the scanner is not aligned precisely with the scanned face.
Iris	Scans and identifies the unique patterns in the colored part of the eye that surrounds the pupil	Lighting conditions, alcohol, and medications can affect the pupil's dilation and present false rejections.

Method	Process	Issues
Retina	Scans and identifies the unique blood vessel and tissue patterns at the back of the eye	Illness or inaccurate placement of the eye against the scanner's cuff can result in false rejection results.
Blood vessels	Identifies and measures unique patterns of blood vessels in the hand or face	Environmental conditions, clothing, and some illnesses can render false rejection results due to measurement inaccuracies.
Signature	Records and measures the speed, shape, and kinematics of a signature provided to an electronic pad	Attitude, environment, injury, and use of alcohol or medication can create variations in personal signature and might render false rejection results.
Gait	Records and measures the unique patterns of weight shift and leg kinematics while walking	Variations in gait due to attitude, environment, injury, and alcohol or medication use might render false rejection results.

ExamAlert

The exam might include questions about the various biometric methods, so be sure you are familiar with the categories in Table 24.1 and their limitations. Remember that combinations of biometric solutions, such as readers for both hand geometry and blood vessel patterns, remain a single-factor "something you are" authentication solution unless they are also paired with something else, such as a "something you have" key card.

Biometric devices are susceptible to false acceptance and false rejection rates. The *false acceptance rate (FAR)* measures the likelihood that the access system will wrongly accept an access attempt (in other words, allow access to an unauthorized user). The *false rejection rate (FRR)* is the percentage of identification instances in which false rejection occurs. In false rejection, the system fails to recognize an authorized person and rejects that person as unauthorized. The *crossover error rate (CER)* is the percentage at which the FAR and FRR are equal. CER will increase if routine maintenance procedures on biometric devices are not performed. Generally, the lower the CER, the higher the accuracy of the biometric system. The lower the FAR and FRR, the better the system.

Biometric data is basically information stored in a database that is used for comparison functions, to protect the database against compromise. Forgery of biometric mechanisms can be an issue, especially where fingerprint technology is concerned.

Tokens

One of the best methods of "something you have" authentication involves using a token, which can be either a physical device or a one-time password issued to the user seeking access. In the case of credit cards, this is an embedded chip in the card itself that must be paired with a "something you know" PIN code to avoid the $18.5 million exploit Target suffered in 2013. Tokens include solutions such as a chip-integrated smart card or a digital token (such as RSA Security's SecurID token) that provides a numeric key that changes every few minutes and is synchronized with the authentication server. Without the proper key or physical token, access is denied. Because the token is unique and granted only to the user, pretending to be the properly authorized user (that is, spoofing) is more difficult. Digital tokens are typically used only one time or are valid for a very short period of time to prevent capture and later reuse. Most token-based access control systems pair the token with a PIN or other form of authentication, to protect against unauthorized access using a lost or stolen token.

Telecommuters might also use an electronic device known as a key fob that provides one part of a three-way match to log on over an unsecure network connection to a secure network. This kind of key fob might have a keypad on which the user must enter a PIN to retrieve an access code, or it could be a display-only device such as a VPN token that algorithmically generates security codes as part of a challenge/response authentication system.

One-time passwords (OTPs) are passwords that can be used only one time. An OTP is considered safer than a regular password because the password keeps changing, providing protection against replay attacks. The two main standards for generating OTPs are TOTP and HOTP. Both standards are governed by the Initiative for Open Authentication (OATH). The time-based one-time password (TOTP) algorithm relies on a shared secret and a moving factor or counter, which is the current time. The moving factor constantly changes based on the time that has passed since an epoch.

The HMAC-based one-time password (HOTP) algorithm relies on a shared secret and a moving factor or counter. When a new OTP is generated, the moving factor is incremented, generating a different password each time.

The main difference between HOTP and TOTP is that HOTP passwords can be valid for an unknown amount of time. In contrast, TOTP passwords keep changing and are valid for only a short period of time. Because of this difference, TOTP is considered more secure.

Certificate-based Authentication

Certificate-based authentication uses a digital certificate to identify a user or device before granting access to a resource. Certificate-based authentication is based on "something you have," which is the user's private key, and "something you know," which is the password that protects the private key.

IEEE 802.1X authentication allows only authorized devices to connect to the network. The most secure form of IEEE 802.1X authentication is certificate-based authentication. When this authentication model is used, all clients must have a certificate to validate their identity. When implementing 802.1X with wired networks, using a public key infrastructure (PKI) to deploy certificates is recommended. PKI infrastructure is covered in depth in Chapter 37, "Public Key Infrastructure."

A personal identity verification (PIV) card is a contactless smart card used to identify federal employees and contractors. NIST developed the standard Personal Identity Verification (PIV) of Federal Employees and Contractors, published as *Federal Information Processing Standards (FIPS) Publication 201*. A PIV card contains the necessary data for the cardholder to be granted access to federal facilities and information systems, including separation of roles and strong biometric binding. A smart card becomes a common access card (CAC) if it is used by the U.S. Department of Defense; a CAC is for DoD users. Civilian users who work for the federal government use PIV cards.

The common access card (CAC) is a credit card–sized "smart" card. This is the standard identification for active duty uniformed service personnel, selected reserve personnel, DoD civilian employees, and eligible contractor personnel. It is also the principal card used to enable physical access to buildings and controlled spaces, and it provides access to DoD computer networks and systems. Homeland Security Presidential Directive 12 (HSPD 12) established the policies for a common identification standard for federal employees and contractors. DoD Instruction (DoDI) 1000.13 states that the common access card (CAC) shall serve as the federal personal identity verification (PIV) card for DoD implementation of HSPD 12. HSPD 12 requires PIV cards to have secure components, including PKI digital certificates and biometrics. When a CAC is inserted into a smart card reader and the associated PIN is entered, the information on the card's chip is compared with data on a government server. Access then is either granted or denied.

ExamAlert

The exam might include questions about two new forms of smart card required for U.S. federal service identity verification under the Homeland Security Presidential Directive 12 (HSPD 12):

▶ **Common access card (CAC):** A smart card used in military, reserve officer, and military contractor identity authentication systems

▶ **Personal identity verification (PIV) card**: A smart card used for federal employees and contractors

---

Using public key cryptography merely verifies that a private key corresponds to the public key in a certificate. Certificate-based authentication is digital and does not address physical access to devices or passwords. Ensuring the physical security of a device and keeping the password for the private key secure are just as important.

File System Security

Operating system security includes planning against both accidental and directed attacks, such as using fault-tolerant hardware and software solutions. In addition, choosing the proper file system is important so that you implement an effective method for file-level security. This includes encrypted file support and a secured file system that allows the proper level of access control. For example, the Microsoft New Technology File System (NTFS) allows file-level access control, whereas most File Allocation Table (FAT)–based file systems allow only share-level access control.

Also be sure to include regular update reviews for all deployed file and operating systems, to address newly identified exploits and apply security patches, hotfixes, and service packs. Many automated attacks make use of common vulnerabilities, often ones for which patches and hotfixes are already available but not yet applied. Failure to update applications on a regular basis or to update auditing can result in an unsecure solution that gives an attacker access to additional resources throughout an organization's network.

IP Security (IPsec) and public key infrastructure (PKI) implementations must also be properly configured and updated to maintain key and ticket stores. Some systems can be hardened to include specific levels of access, thus gaining the C2 security rating that many government deployment scenarios require.

The Trusted Computer System Evaluation Criteria (TCSEC) rating of C2 indicates a discretionary access control environment with additional requirements, such as individual logon accounts and access logging. You can find an explanation of the TCSEC rating system here, in a NIST document: http://csrc.nist.gov/publications/history/dod85.pdf.

Operating system protections includes configuring log files and auditing, changing default administrator account names and default passwords, and instituting account lockout and password policies to guarantee strong passwords that can resist brute-force attacks. File-level security and access control mechanisms isolate access attempts within the operating system environment. Make sure you understand the principle of least privilege, which states that every user or service of a system should operate with the minimal set of privileges required to fulfill their job duty or function.

File system protections include encryption, RAID, and access controls. Distributed file system and encrypted file system solutions might require bandwidth planning and proper user authentication to allow even basic access. Security planning for these solutions might also include placing users who access authenticating servers close to the file servers, to decrease delays created by authentication traffic.

Database Security

Databases are the largest repository of sensitive information in many organizations. Organizational databases contain data ranging from personally identifiable customer information to intellectual property. Lost or stolen customer data can ultimately result in such severe, permanent damage that the organization goes out of business.

> **ExamAlert**
>
> Although database security is a top priority for organizations, traditional database security methods such as firewalls are no longer sufficient to protect organizational data, especially against insider threat. Database encryption can mitigate security breach risk and comply with regulations.

For example, in the financial sector, organizations must comply with the Payment Card Industry Data Security Standard (PCI DSS). PCI DSS creates policies that define what data needs to be encrypted, tell how it is to be encrypted, and define requirements for key management. One of the biggest challenges associated with database encryption is key management.

This is especially true for organizations that have to meet policies requiring Federal Information Processing Standard (FIPS) validated key storage. Database encryption is most often accompanied by a centralized method of defining key policy and enforcing key management, creating a center of trust. If this trust is breached, the ramifications can be far-reaching, as recently seen with the RSA breach and subsequent Lockheed Martin attack.

With the use of cloud computing environments, rapidly expanding organizations such as financial services, healthcare, utilities, and telecommunications companies are moving toward managing big data with NoSQL database technologies. NoSQL encompasses a wide variety of database technologies. When compared to relational databases, NoSQL systems are more scalable and provide superior performance. Protecting NoSQL data from both internal and external breaches is a concern because the NoSQL design does not see security as a high priority; NoSQL also lacks confidentiality and integrity. This means that the application accessing the data must be relied upon to provide confidentiality and integrity. Relational database security, on the other hand, includes features that protect confidentiality, integrity, and availability. These features include role-based security, encryption, and access control through user-level permissions on stored procedures. Best practices for protecting NoSQL databases include changing the default ports, binding the interface to only one IP, and encrypting data in the application before writing it to the database. Databases such as MongoDB have added support for Kerberos authentication, more granular access controls, and SSL encryption. If the organization selects a NoSQL database technology that is lacking security, it is recommended that organizations implement their own authorization, authentication, and auditing methodologies.

Although a defense-in-depth strategy can help, encryption of data should occur both at rest and in transit. For example, application-level encryption can be used to encrypt information before it is stored in the database. This can prevent sensitive database information from being disclosed by either unauthorized access or theft. Database-level encryption by means of encrypting the entire contents written to the database can have unintended consequences, such as limiting access control and auditing capabilities, so it is important to evaluate any solution before implementation.

ExamAlert

Database encryption must also be accompanied by key management to provide a high level of security. Other solutions to protect encrypted databases include permission restrictions on database and root administrators, as well as restrictions on encryption key administration.

Hardware security modules (HSMs), which were discussed in Chapter 15, "Secure Systems Design," can enforce the separation of duties for key management by separating database and security administration.

What Next?

If you want more practice on this chapter's exam objectives before you move on, remember that you can access all the Cram Quiz questions on the Pearson Test Prep software. You can also create a custom exam by objective. Note any objective you struggle with and go to that objective material in this chapter.

CHAPTER 25

Account Management Practices

CramSaver

If you can correctly answer these questions before going through this section, save time by skimming the Exam Alerts in this chapter and then completing the Cram Quiz at the end of the section.

1. What is the best model for access rights assignment in a large, distributed enterprise?

   _____

2. What policy prevents accidental access or denial rights from continuing after role reassignment?

   _____

3. What is the best practice for handling the user account of a user who has been terminated?

   _____

Answers

1. The *role/group-based* model is best for large, complex enterprises because each group can have associated access rights that are inherited by individuals and other groups assigned to that group.

2. User access reviews allow the identification of misapplied changes or other access control adjustments through direct assignment or inherited nesting of role access rights. Regular reviews can identify and rectify accidents or malicious attempts to gain unauthorized access rights.

3. Disable user accounts as soon as a user leaves the company. The advantage of disabling user accounts is that all settings, files, and folders remain intact, and you can access information tied to the user account anytime by reenabling the account.

Account Types

The access level users are given directly affects the level of network protection you have. You might find it strange to think that you need to protect the network from its own users. However, internal users have the greatest access to data and, therefore, the greatest opportunity to either deliberately sabotage it or accidentally delete it. Upon logon, organizations should show a logon banner statement that network access is granted under certain conditions and that activities might be monitored. This helps the organization be sure that legal ramifications are covered and that users can be expected to follow security policy protocols.

IT organizations often use shared accounts for privileged users, administrators, or applications. This practice presents security and compliance risks. One of the first steps in providing a secure account access environment is to eliminate the use of shared accounts. With these accounts, use cannot be attributed to a particular user's credentials, so determination of specific access rights and audit of access use is impossible. Providing each set of access credentials to a single principal, either a user or a machine service, enables you to measure every use of data access, to determine a baseline of expected and acceptable use. You then can monitor these baselines for variations that indicate potential misuse of enterprise resources or data access.

Users with administrative functions should not rely on their with-privileges accounts for everyday use (email and so on) because an unexpected piece of malware encountered through normal business functions runs under the access control restrictions of the accessing account. Issuing these users both a common account for normal access and a separate administrative credential set to use when needed limits the span of control for their operational account. Linux users have been doing this for some time, using **sudo** (superuser do) to perform administrative functions from their session account.

Certain groups and accounts are installed by default. As an administrator, you should know what these are. Service accounts often are installed as well, for interaction with the operating system. Local service accounts typically interact with the Windows OS and tend to have default passwords.

In dealing with individual accounts, the administrative account should be used only in administering the server. Granting users this type of access is a disaster waiting to happen. An individual using the administrative account can put a company's entire business in jeopardy if he or she accesses a malware-infected website or reads the wrong email. In addition, generic accounts used by multiple users must be prohibited.

By knowing which accounts are installed by default, you can determine which are really needed and which can be disabled to make the system more secure. You should also know which accounts, if any, are installed with blank or well-established passwords. Common machine accounts used in web-based access systems are common targets for unauthorized access attempts, particularly when left in default or well-known configuration states (as with the Oracle database Scott/Tiger access credential combination).

The security settings in many of the newer operating systems do not allow blank passwords. However, accounts in older operating systems might still have a blank password or a well-known default, as with the admin/admin logon in older routers. User rights are applied to security groups to determine what members of that group can do within the scope of a domain or forest. User rights are assigned through security options that apply to user accounts.

> **ExamAlert**
>
> The User Account Control (UAC) technology that the Windows operating system uses ensures that software applications cannot perform privileged access without additional authorization from the user. Within the Microsoft environment, lesser accounts may perform privileged processes using the **run as** option to specify the explicit use of a privileged account from within the unprivileged account logon. This is similar to the sudo shell operation under UNIX operating systems.

Default credentials and unmonitored accounts such as the guest or admin account commonly established in older equipment and software soften security because they provide one component of access credentials to potential attackers or their tools. Replacing a default administrative account named admin with one that uses a more generic or obscure name adds another obstacle. Attackers then must break both the account name and its associated authentication keys.

General Concepts

When an employee joins or leaves an organization, the process of onboarding/offboarding happens. *Onboarding* is the process of creating an identity profile and the necessary information required to describe that identity. Onboarding can also include registering the user's assets, such as a computer and mobile devices, and provisioning them so they can be used to access the corporate network. In BYOD cases, many organizations use a self-service method through a preconfigured profile to minimize IT intervention. As part of best-practice onboarding procedures, some solutions offer integration with Active Directory. This offers a simplified way to identify domain user groups that are permitted to onboard their devices. *Offboarding* is the opposite process. User identities that no longer require access to the environment are disabled or deactivated and then deleted from the environment, based on organizational policy. When an employee is terminated, retires, or quits, segregating and retrieving organizational data and applications can be difficult if the user's own devices were used. BYOD policies should address how data and corporate-owned applications will be retrieved during the offboarding process. In some instances, the organization might opt for a total device wipe.

Least privilege is an access control practice in which a logon is provided only the minimum access to the resources required to perform its tasks. Remember the phrase *less is more* when considering security principles: Grant no more access than is necessary to perform assigned tasks.

User access reviews allow you to identify misapplied changes or other access control adjustments through direct assignment or inherited nesting of role access rights. In these reviews, you can find and rectify accidents or malicious attempts to gain unauthorized access rights. Periodic access reviews for access management can help ensure that the necessary personnel have access to essential systems and unauthorized employees do not. A more formal form of user access review is called *access recertification*. Access recertification is typically the responsibility of the organization's Chief Information Security Officer (CISO) because it involves stating that current access adheres to the organization's internal policies and compliance regulations.

Best practices dictate that access to high-risk applications should be reviewed quarterly and that every application have a review conducted at least annually. A baseline must be established to account for normal line-of-business operations and be updated regularly to reflect changes in the organization's processes and software applications. Examples include identifying the business owners of every application and classifying the data within applications. This allows you to identify unusual activity and to regularly review all accounts (including "permanent" machine and service accounts) to disable and remove any unneeded credentials. Access reviews should also be conducted for group membership and role/group alignment for organization assignment. In this way, you can correct accidental access rights assignment through role and group membership. Users should also be notified of their access rights and the need to alert the IT staff if their access appears to be greater than allowed by their role.

Education and regular operational control reviews should be part of the organization's continuous improvement program, to ensure that users comply with security protections and understand the requirements demanded by both their acceptance and use of data access credentials. Understanding requirements is inherent in any attempt to control data access to conform to those requirements. Technical controls must be continuously monitored to protect against violation of policy through purposeful or accidental access. An important best practice is to make sure separation of duties among developers, data custodians, and IT administration is well defined and documented.

The purpose of continuous monitoring is to ensure that the processes for user account provisioning, life cycle management, and termination are followed and enforced. Continuous monitoring begins with knowing what user account activity should be present. Continuously monitoring user access enables you to detect unauthorized access from attackers using a system backdoor, averting a wide-scale incident. Industry regulations might require continuous monitoring. For example, PCI DSS compliance requires that an organization have well-defined processes in place to review and reassess security practices, even in highly dynamic business environments.

Monitoring practices should consist of a process to record and monitor significant changes to user accounts and groups, to ensure that access is not granted outside of a formal approval process. Activities that should be monitored and reviewed include the business need for each active account, reconciliation of existing active accounts with account access requests, and account and privilege updates. Close attention should paid to administrative privilege updates because these can signify compromised accounts.

By default, all domain users can log in at any time. Many times, restricting logon hours is necessary for maintenance purposes. For example, consider that the backup runs at 11:00 p.m. each night. In this case, you might want to be sure that everyone is off the system. In another example, if databases get reindexed on a nightly basis, you might have to confirm that no one is changing information or locking records during the reindexing process.

This is also a good way to be sure that a hacker is not logging in with stolen passwords during off-peak hours. You can restrict logon hours by days of the week, hours of the day, or both. You can also assign time-of-day restrictions to ensure that employees use computers only during specified hours. This setting proves useful for organizations when users require supervision, when security certification requires it, or when employees are mainly temporary or shift workers.

> ### ExamAlert
>
> Each OS is different, so the effect of the restrictions differs if the user is currently logged on when the restriction time begins. In a Microsoft environment, the Automatically Log Off Users setting determines whether users are forced to log off when their logon hours expire. In other environments, the user might be allowed to stay logged on, but once logged off, the user cannot log back on. The logon schedule is enforced by the Kerberos group policy setting Enforce User Logon Restrictions, which is enabled by default in Windows Active Directory environments.

Because employees have become more mobile, organizations now often implement BYOD policies. *Location-based policies* allow organizations to set policies that permit users to access resources in both organizational and personal location settings. Location-based policies are policies based on where a device is located. One example is a web filtering policy that prevents inappropriate surfing in the workplace but allows employees to have unrestricted access to web content when they are outside the corporate environment.

When dealing with user access, a fine line often exists between sufficient access to get the job done and too much access. In this section, you examine how to manage user access by using groups and group policies. Keep the "least privilege" best practice in mind when comparing access control options.

A user account holds information about the specific user. It can contain basic information such as name, password, and level of permission the user has in the associated access control lists (ACLs). User accounts should follow standard naming conventions and can also contain more specific information, such as the department the user works in, a home phone number, and the days and hours the user is allowed to log on to specific workstations. Groups are created to make the sharing of resources more manageable. A group contains users who share a common need for access to a particular resource; it can be nested in other groups, in turn, to better aggregate access permissions for multiple roles. Even though the connotations might differ within each operating system, all of these terms still refer to the access that a user or group account is specifically granted or denied.

When working with logical controls, two models exist for assigning permissions and rights: the user-based model and the role- or group-based model. Within a user-based model, permissions are uniquely assigned to each user account. One example of this is a peer-to-peer network, or a workgroup in which access is granted based on individual needs. This access type is also found in government and military situations and in private companies where patented processes and trademark products require protection. User-based privilege management is usually used for specific parts of the network or specific resources. This type of policy is time-consuming and difficult for administrators to handle, and it does not work well in large environments. You will find that creating groups and assigning users to these groups makes the administration process much easier.

ExamAlert

In Windows environments, Active Directory Domain Services provides flexibility by allowing two types of groups: security groups and distribution groups:

▶ Security groups are used when assigning rights and permissions to groups for resource access.

▶ Distribution groups are assigned to a user list for applications or non-security-related functions, such as an email distribution list that functions as a LISTSERV in the UNIX environment.

When working with groups, remember a few key items: No matter what OS you are working with, if you are giving a user full access in one group and deny access in another group, the result is deny access. However, group permissions are cumulative. Therefore, if a user belongs to two groups and one has more liberal access, the user will have the most liberal access, except where the deny access permission is involved. If a user has difficulty accessing information after he or she has been added to a new group, the first item to check for is conflicting permissions.

> **ExamAlert**
>
> When assigning user permissions, remember that if the groups to which the user is assigned have liberal access and another group has no access, the result is no access.

Access control over large numbers of user accounts can be more easily accomplished by managing the access permissions on each group, which are then inherited by the group's members. In this type of access, permissions are assigned to groups, and user accounts become members of the groups based on their organizational roles. Each user account has access based on the combined permissions inherited from its various group memberships. These groups often reflect divisions or departments of the company, such as human resources, sales, development, and management. In enterprise networks, groups can also be nested. Group nesting can simplify permission assignment if you know how to use hierarchical nesting. On the other hand, group nesting can complicate troubleshooting if you do not know what was set up for each level or why, and thus do not know where a deny or allow permission is assigned.

Account Policy Enforcement

As the number of systems and users grows in an organization, account policy enforcement becomes critical. Therefore, you should set account policies that define strong security for your systems. Account policies are a subset of the policies configurable in group policy.

Credentials must also be assigned for a given time period, with an automatic failover to access denial if they are not renewed, to ensure that provisioned accounts are used and then cease to operate. This is often necessary in workforces of short-term or temporary workers, whose accounts could otherwise be left intact and unmonitored after the workers rotate to new positions. Such an account presents a target for brute force types of attacks on logon passwords, which can then be spread over a long period of time to avoid detection intrusion prevention measures.

ExamAlert

The account expires attribute specifies when an account expires. You can use this setting under the same conditions as mentioned previously for the time-of-day restrictions. Temporary or contract workers should have user accounts that are valid for only a certain amount of time. This way, when the account expires, it can no longer be used to log on to any service. Statistics show that many temporary accounts are never disabled. Limiting the time an account is active for such employees should be part of the policies and procedures. In addition, user accounts should be audited on a regular basis for deprovisioning or reprovisioning based on role change.

All credentials, whether simple logon passwords or complex encryption keys, should carry a built-in lifetime that ensures their termination even if they are lost or forgotten. Auditing procedures need to reveal long-term inactive accounts and machine accounts that should be routinely expired and reestablished to protect against long-term attacks and limit exploitation if they are compromised during the normal period of use.

Active Directory domains use group policy objects (GPOs) to store a wide variety of configuration information, including password policy settings. Domains have their own password policy in addition to the local password policy. Domain password policies can control password settings. The Account Policies settings in Group Policy are applied at the domain level. The domain Account Policies settings become the default local Account Policies settings of any Windows-based computer that is a member of the domain. The only exception to this rule occurs when another Account Policies setting is defined for an organizational unit (OU). The Account Policies settings for the OU affect the local policy on any computers that the OU contains.

ExamAlert

In organizations that use Windows or a similar directory service architecture for enterprise management, group policy assignment of access controls can mandate that security configuration technical controls be applied based on organizational unit or domain membership, to handle all accounts within an organization or to establish default configuration settings.

Password policy settings for the domain are defined in the root container for the domain. The default domain policy is linked to the root container. It contains a few critical domain-wide settings, including the default password policy settings.

Of course, passwords are one of the best methods of gaining successful access to services and resources, so password length, duration, history, and complexity requirements are all important to the security of the network. When setting up user accounts, take into account proper planning and policies. Passwords are one of the first pieces of information a user enters. Passwords that contain only alphanumeric characters are easy to compromise by using publicly available tools. To prevent this, passwords should contain additional characters and meet complexity requirements.

Passwords must meet the complexity requirements policy setting in Windows operating systems to determine whether passwords meet certain criteria for a strong password. Enabling this policy setting requires passwords to meet the following requirements:

▶ The password may not contain the user's account or full name value.

▶ The password must contain three of the following: uppercase letters, lowercase letters, numbers, nonalphanumeric characters (special characters), and any Unicode character that is categorized as an alphabetic character but is not uppercase or lowercase.

Complexity requirements are enforced when passwords are changed or created. This policy setting, combined with a minimum password length of 8, ensures that there are at least 218,340,105,584,896 different possibilities for a single password. This makes a brute force attack difficult but still not impossible.

In the normal course of business, you might sometimes create domain user accounts for a short duration. This type of account is useful for contractors or temporary employees, for example. With this kind of user, accounts should automatically expire after a specified date. When an account expires, the user then is no longer allowed to log on to the domain, and the operating system displays an error message informing the user that the account has expired.

Account provisioning policies for the creation, update, and removal of accounts must be integrated into an organization's HR process and regularly audited to ensure continued compliance. Legacy access groups should be similarly expired when they are no longer appropriate to the organization's operational structure. This helps eliminate potential avenues of unauthorized access through normal line-of-business operations. During separation procedures, passwords and other security credentials should be automatically expired to prevent unauthorized access after they are no longer appropriate. During termination proceedings, this is typically coordinated between managers and the IT department, to protect against a terminated employee carrying out retributive or exploitive actions on organizational resources.

When a user forgets a password, two options exist: password recovery or a password reset. Password resets are also performed when a new account is created, to set an initial password. Password recovery and resets can take place in several ways, ranging from an in-person visit with an IT staff member to a fully automated self-service utility. If the identity of the user requesting a password recovery or reset is not properly verified, an attacker could easily pose as a user and gain access to that user's password. All recovery and reset mechanisms should first verify the user's identity using methods. Common methods include using predetermined challenge response questions set during account creation, emailing recovery information, or texting a code to the user's cellphone.

Never store passwords or access credentials in an unsecure location or use a reversible form of encryption. Sometimes a company wants a list of machine accounts or fundamental server recovery administrative passwords. However, this list might end up in the wrong hands if it is not properly secured along with the disaster recovery documentation. If a user forgets a password, administrators should not be able to recover the old password. Instead, they should issue new credentials after verifying the proper identity.

Rename or disable the administrator account and guest account in each domain to prevent attacks on your domains. Disable user accounts as soon as a user leaves the company. The advantage of disabling user accounts is that all the settings, files, and folders of that account remain intact; you can then access information tied to the user account anytime by reenabling the account. It is good policy to not reuse or rename the account of a terminated user. When a user leaves the organization, the account can simply be disabled and moved, if necessary. Depending on company policy, the user account might need to be kept for a certain period of time. For example, some organizations keep disabled accounts for 90 days and then delete them.

The account lockout policy settings help prevent attackers from guessing users' passwords and decrease the likelihood of successful attacks on your network. An account lockout policy disables a user account when an incorrect password is entered a specified number of times over a certain time period. Account lockout policy settings control the threshold for this response and the actions to be taken when the threshold is reached.

The Account lockout duration policy setting determines the number of minutes that a locked-out account remains locked out before it is automatically unlocked. The available range is from 1 through 99,999 minutes. A lockout duration value of 0 specifies that the account will be locked out until an administrator explicitly unlocks it. The lockout threshold can be set to any value from 0 to 999. If the lockout threshold is set to 0, accounts will not be locked out due to invalid logon attempts. The Reset Account Lockout Counter After policy setting determines the number of minutes that must elapse from the time a user fails to log on before the failed logon attempt counter is reset to 0. If the account lockout threshold is set to a number greater than 0, this reset time must be less than or equal to the value of account lockout duration. A disadvantage of configuring these settings too restrictively is that users might have to make excessive help desk calls. General best practices dictate that you should lock user accounts out after three to five failed logon attempts. This policy stops programs from deciphering the passwords on locked accounts by repeated brute force attempts.

The Maximum password age policy setting determines the number of days that a password can be used before the system requires the user to change it. You can set passwords to expire after any number of days between 1 and 999, or you can specify that passwords never expire by setting the number of days to 0. Microsoft operating systems use both a maximum password age and a minimum password age. If the maximum password age is set, the minimum password age must be less than the maximum password age. When the maximum password age is set to 0, the minimum password age can be any value between 0 and 998 days. Good policy is to set the maximum password age to a value between 30 and 90 days, depending on your environment. Try to expire the passwords between major business cycles, to prevent work loss. Configure minimum password age so that you do not allow passwords to be changed immediately. This way, an attacker has a limited amount of time in which to compromise a user's password and gain access to your network resources.

Password reuse is an important concern in any organization. When allowed, users tend to reuse the same password over a long period of time. The longer the same password is used for a particular account, the greater the chance that an attacker will be able to determine the password through brute force attacks. Allowing users to reuse an old password greatly reduces the effectiveness of a good password policy.

Most operating systems have settings that do not allow users to reuse a password for a certain length of time or a certain number of password changes. The enforce password history policy setting in Windows operating systems determines the number of unique new passwords that must be associated with a user account before an old password can be reused. Specifying a low number for this setting allows users to continually use the same small number of passwords repeatedly. Configure the server to not allow users to use the same password this way. Setting the enforce password history setting to 24 helps mitigate vulnerabilities caused by password reuse.

Making the password length at least eight characters and requiring combinations of uppercase and lowercase letters, numbers, and special characters is good practice. In Windows operating systems, the Minimum Password Length policy setting determines the least number of characters that can make up a password for a user account. You can set a value of between 1 and 14 characters, or you can establish that no password is required by setting the number of characters to 0.

In most environments, an eight-character password is recommended because it is long enough to provide adequate security but still short enough for users to easily remember it. Adding complexity requirements helps reduce the possibility of a dictionary attack. Although longer passwords are more effective against attacks, requiring long passwords can cause account lockouts from mistyping and can actually decrease the security of an organization because users might be more likely to write down their passwords. User education on the proper way to make long passwords that they can easily remember is the best solution.

ExamAlert

The key aspects of password controls include required complexity, password length, and account lockout/expiration terms.

ExamAlert

Password policies help secure the network and define the responsibilities of users who have been given access to company resources. You should have all users read and sign security policies as part of their employment process. Domain password policies affect all users in the domain. The effectiveness of these policies depends on how and where they are applied. The three areas that can be configured are password, account lockout, and Kerberos policies.

You can use the account lockout policy to secure the system against attacks by disabling the account after a certain number of attempts for a certain period of time. Use the Kerberos policy settings for authentication services. In most environments, the default settings should suffice. If you do need to change them, remember that they are applied at the domain level and are more finely controlled by access denial for the particular group policy applied for specific groups.

Require users to change passwords every 90 to 180 days, depending on how secure the environment needs to be. Remember that the more often users are required to change passwords, the greater the chance that they will write them down, potentially exposing them to unauthorized use.

What Next?

If you want more practice on this chapter's exam objectives before you move on, remember that you can access all the Cram Quiz questions on the Pearson Test Prep software. You can also create a custom exam by objective. Note any objective you struggle with and go to that objective material in this chapter.

Cram Quiz

These review questions cover material related to Chapters 22–25, which cover objects falling under Domain 4, "Identity and Access Management," of the Security+ exam.

1. If you have a smart card that contains details of your iris coloring and retinal patterns, which two types of authentication would be involved in a successful access request?

   ○ **A.** Something you have and something you do

   ○ **B.** Something you do and something you are

   ○ **C.** Something you are and something you know

   ○ **D.** Something you have and something you are

2. Which of the following best describes the Policy Enforcement Point (PEP) component of AAA functions?

   ○ **A.** Data holder

   ○ **B.** Final decision maker

   ○ **C.** Authenticator

   ○ **D.** Auditor

3. If an organization wants to implement an enterprise access solution that does not require a user to remember passwords across multiple distinct business units, which of the following is the best choice?

   ○ **A.** Federation

   ○ **B.** Single sign-on

   ○ **C.** Transitive trusts

   ○ **D.** Retinal scanning

4. Which of the following processes occurs when the user provides appropriate credentials such as the correct password and a username?

   ○ **A.** Identification

   ○ **B.** Authentication

   ○ **C.** Authorization

   ○ **D.** Accounting

5. Which of the following best describes the Policy Decision Point (PDP) component of AAA functions?

   ○ **A.** Data holder

   ○ **B.** Final decision maker

   ○ **C.** Authenticator

   ○ **D.** Auditor

6. Which of the following processes occurs first when a user or device presents information such as a username, a process ID, a smart card, or another unique identifier?

   ○ **A.** Identification

   ○ **B.** Authentication

   ○ **C.** Authorization

   ○ **D.** Accounting

7. An organization that relies heavily on cloud and SaaS service providers, such as Salesforce.com, WebEx, or Google, would have security concerns about which of the following?

   ○ **A.** TACACS+

   ○ **B.** SAML

   ○ **C.** LDAP

   ○ **D.** OpenID Connect

8. An educational institution requires a secure solution that is capable of interfacing with state systems and other state-run universities. Which of the following is the best solution?

   ○ **A.** OAuth

   ○ **B.** SAML

   ○ **C.** Shibboleth

   ○ **D.** OpenID Connect

9. An organization is implementing a server-side application using OAuth 2.0. Which of the following grant types should be used?

   ○ **A.** Authorization code

   ○ **B.** Implicit

   ○ **C.** Password credentials

   ○ **D.** Client credentials

10. Which of the following is used with OAuth 2.0 as an extension to the authorization process?

   ○ **A.** Shibboleth

   ○ **B.** NTLM

   ○ **C.** LDAP

   ○ **D.** OpenID Connect

11. An organization is implementing an application that needs service access to its own resources using OA 2.0. Which of the following grant types should be used?

   ○ **A.** Authorization code

   ○ **B.** Implicit

   ○ **C.** Password credentials

   ○ **D.** Client credentials

12. Which of the following is a nonproprietary protocol that provides authentication and authorization in addition to accounting of access requests against a centralized service for the authorization of access requests?

   ○ **A.** TACACS+

   ○ **B.** SAML

   ○ **C.** LDAP

   ○ **D.** OAuth

13. Which type of "something you have" factor do U.S. federal governmental employees and contractors use under HSPD 12?

   ○ **A.** Smart card

   ○ **B.** CAC

   ○ **C.** PIV

   ○ **D.** SecurID

14. Which of the following token-based solutions is considered the most secure?

   ○ **A.** OTP

   ○ **B.** TOTP

   ○ **C.** HOTP

   ○ **D.** OATH

15. Which of the following is the best way to secure NoSQL databases such as MongoDB?

    ○ **A.** Implement separate authentication methods

    ○ **B.** Use the default port

    ○ **C.** Bind the interface to multiple IPs

    ○ **D.** Encrypt the data after it is written to the database

16. Which of the following best describes a biometric false acceptance rate (FAR)?

    ○ **A.** The point at which acceptances and rejections are equal

    ○ **B.** Rejection of an authorized user

    ○ **C.** Access allowed to an unauthorized user

    ○ **D.** Failure to identify a biometric image

17. Which of the following best describes a biometric false rejection rate (FRR)?

    ○ **A.** The point at which acceptances and rejections are equal

    ○ **B.** Rejection of an authorized user

    ○ **C.** Access allowed to an unauthorized user

    ○ **D.** Failure to identify a biometric image

18. Which directory services protocol should be implemented to protect against man-in-the-middle data interception attacks?

    ○ **A.** Kerberos

    ○ **B.** NTLM

    ○ **C.** LDAP

    ○ **D.** Shibboleth

19. Which of the following is a type of "something you have" that uses a time-shifting key token?

    ○ **A.** Smart card

    ○ **B.** CAC

    ○ **C.** PIV

    ○ **D.** SecurID

20. Which type of password policy protects against reuse of the same password?

    ○ **A.** Account lockout

    ○ **B.** Password complexity

    ○ **C.** Expiration

    ○ **D.** Password history

21. A user calls the help desk saying that she changed her password yesterday. She did not get any email on her mobile phone last night and she cannot log on this morning. Which password policy is most likely at fault for her difficulties?

    ○ **A.** Account lockout

    ○ **B.** Password complexity

    ○ **C.** Expiration

    ○ **D.** Password history

22. Which of the following reduces the effectiveness of a good password policy?

    ○ **A.** Account lockout

    ○ **B.** Password recovery

    ○ **C.** Account disablement

    ○ **D.** Password reuse

23. Which of the following is considered best practice when formulating minimum standards for developing password policies?

    ○ **A.** Password length set to six characters

    ○ **B.** Required password change at 90 days

    ○ **C.** Maximum password age set to 0

    ○ **D.** Account lockout threshold set to 0

24. Which of the following is one of the first steps that must be taken to provide a secure account access environment?

    ○ **A.** Set user-assigned privileges

    ○ **B.** Implement user access reviews

    ○ **C.** Eliminate the use of shared accounts

    ○ **D.** Initiate continuous account monitoring

25. Which of the following is used to create a user identity profile and get the necessary information required to describe the identity?

    ○ **A.** Least privilege

    ○ **B.** Offboarding

    ○ **C.** Onboarding

    ○ **D.** Recertification

Cram Quiz Answers

1. **D.** The smart card is an example of "something you have," and the biometric measures are an example of "something you are." Answer A is incorrect because there are no biometrics relating to "something you do"—only simple measurements of bodily configuration. Answer B is incorrect for the same reason; no "something you do" metric is present. Answer C is incorrect because no PIN or password is employed as a "something you know" factor.

2. **C.** The Policy Enforcement Point (PEP) is the authenticator. The PEP enforces the conditions of the client's access. Answer A is incorrect because the Policy Information Point (PIP) holds data relevant to the decision of whether to grant access to the client. Answer B is incorrect because the Policy Decision Point (PDP) is responsible for making the final decision on whether to grant access to the client. Answer D is incorrect because the accounting and reporting system tracks the client network usage and reports the "who, what, where, when, and why."

3. **A.** Federation eliminates the requirement to use a password. The federation server stores the username in each application and presents that application with a token that is then used for authentication. Answer B is incorrect because SSO still requires the user to remember passwords. Answer C is incorrect because transitive trusts work only across trusted domains. Answer D is incorrect because retinal biometric identification involves the scanning and identification of blood vessels and tissues in the back of the eye, requiring specialized equipment.

4. **B.** Authentication is the process of validating an identity. This occurs when the user provides appropriate credentials such as the correct password and a username. Answer A is incorrect because identification occurs when a user or device presents information such as a username, a process ID, a smart card, or another unique identifier, claiming an identity. Answer C is incorrect because after identification and authentication, authorization of the request is determined before access rights during the session can be established. Authorization is based on security policy. Answer D is incorrect because accounting keeps track of the resources a user accesses by keeping a record of events of authentication and authorization actions.

5. **B.** The Policy Decision Point (PDP) is responsible for making the final decision on whether to grant access to the client. The PEP enforces the conditions of the client's access. Answer A is incorrect because the Policy Information Point (PIP) holds data relevant to the decision of whether to grant access to the client. Answer C is incorrect because the Policy Enforcement Point (PEP) is the authenticator. Answer D is incorrect because the accounting and reporting system tracks the client network usage and reports the "who, what, where, when, and why."

6. **A.** Identification occurs when a user or device presents information such as a username, a process ID, a smart card, or another unique identifier, claiming an identity. Answer B is incorrect because authentication is the process of validating an identity. This occurs when the user provides appropriate credentials such as the correct password and a username. Answer C is incorrect because after identification and authentication, authorization of the request is determined before access rights during the session can be established. Authorization is based on security policy. Answer D is incorrect because accounting keeps track of the

resources a user accesses by keeping a record of events of authentication and authorization actions.

7. **B.** SAML (Security Assertion Markup Language) is an Extensible Markup Language (XML) framework for creating and exchanging security information between online partners. The weakness in the SAML identity chain is the integrity of users. To mitigate risk, SAML systems need to use timed sessions, HTTPS, and SSL/TLS. Answer A is incorrect because the TACACS+ protocol provides authentication and authorization in addition to accounting of access requests against a centralized service for authorization of access requests. Answer C is incorrect because LDAP is used for directory services. Answer D is incorrect because OpenID Connect uses a JSON Web Token (JWT) for authentication.

8. **C.** Shibboleth is a flexible solution because it is based on standards. Some federated systems are designed to work only when the identity provider and the service provider are in the same organization. Shibboleth, however, works across organizations. Answer A is incorrect because OAuth provides only authorization services; it does not support secure methods such as client verification, encryption, or channel binding. Answer B is incorrect because the main purpose of SAML is single sign-on for enterprise users; it has a weakness in handling the integrity of users. Answer D is incorrect because OpenID Connect is an identity layer based on OAuth 2.0 specifications used for consumer single sign-on.

9. **A.** The authorization code grant type is used for server-side applications. Answer B is incorrect because the implicit grant type is used for client-side web applications. This grant type does not have a server-side component. Answer C is incorrect because the password credentials grant type is used for first-class web applications or mobile applications. Answer D is incorrect because the client credentials grant type is used for application code to allow an application to access its own resources.

10. **D.** OpenID Connect takes attacks into consideration and resolves many of the security issues with OAuth 2.0. Answer A is incorrect because Shibboleth is a SAML-based, open-source federated identity solution that provides single sign-on capabilities and federated services popular in research and educational institutions. Answer B is incorrect because NTLM is an older Microsoft authentication protocol that requires Active Directory and relies on Microsoft Windows user credentials in the authentication process. Answer C is incorrect because LDAP is used for directory services.

11. **D.** The client credentials grant type is used for application code to allow an application to access its own resources. Answer A is incorrect because the authorization code grant type is used for server-side applications. Answer B is incorrect because the implicit grant type is used for client-side web applications. This grant type does not have a server-side component. Answer C is incorrect because the password credentials grant type is used for first-class web applications or mobile applications.

12. **A.** TACACS+, released as an open standard, is a protocol that provides authentication and authorization, as well as accounting of access requests against a centralized service for authorization of access requests. TACACS+ is similar to RADIUS but uses TCP instead of UDP transport. Answer B is incorrect because SAML (Security Assertion Markup Language) is an Extensible Markup Language

(XML) framework for creating and exchanging security information between online partners. Answer C is incorrect because LDAP is a directory services protocol. Answer D is incorrect because OAuth is an authorization framework.

13. **C.** The personal identity verification (PIV) card is used by U.S. federal employees and contractors under HSPD 12. Answer A is incorrect because A, B, and C are all smart card variations, but only C is specifically used for federal employees and contractors under HSPD 12. Answer B is incorrect because the common access card (CAC) is used by U.S. military, military reserve, and military contractors. Answer D is incorrect because the RSA SecurID is an example of a time-shifting key token.

14. **B.** TOTP passwords keep changing and are valid for only a short period of time. Because of this difference, TOTP is considered to be more secure. Answer A is incorrect because one-time passwords (OTPs) are passwords that can be only used one time. The term is too generic because the two main standards for generating OTPs are TOTP and HOTP. Answer C is incorrect because HOTP passwords can be valid for an unknown amount of time, making it less secure than TOTP. Answer D is incorrect because OAUTH is the Initiative for Open Authentication that governs TOTP and HOTP.

15. **A.** The best way to secure NoSQL databases such as MongoDB is to implement separate authentication methods. Best practices for protecting NoSQL databases include changing the default ports, binding the interface to only one IP, and encrypting data in the application before writing it to the database. Databases such as MongoDB have added support for Kerberos authentication, more granular access controls, and SSL encryption, which allows for the implementation of separate authentication methods. Based on the explanation for answer A, answers B, C, and D are incorrect.

16. **C.** The false acceptance rate (FAR) is a measure of the likelihood that the access system will wrongly accept an access attempt. Answer A is incorrect because the crossover error rate (CER) is the percentage at which the FAR and FRR are equal. Answer B is incorrect because the false rejection rate (FRR) is the percentage of identification instances in which false rejection occurs. Answer D is incorrect because the failure to acquire rate (FTA) is the rate of recognition attempts in which a biometric system fails to identify a biometric image.

17. **B.** The false rejection rate (FRR) is the percentage of identification instances in which false rejection occurs. Answer A is incorrect because the crossover error rate (CER) is the percentage at which the FAR and FRR are equal. Answer C is incorrect because the false acceptance rate (FAR) is a measure of the likelihood that the access system will wrongly accept an access attempt. Answer D is incorrect because the failure to acquire rate (FTA) is the rate of recognition attempts in which a biometric system fails to identify a biometric image.

18. **A.** The Kerberos protocol supports mutual authentication between two systems, protecting against man-in-the-middle forms of data interception or manipulation by ensuring that both network endpoints are authenticated to one another. Answer B is incorrect because NTLM is an older Microsoft authentication protocol that requires Active Directory and relies on Microsoft Windows user credentials in the authentication process. Answer C is incorrect because LDAP is used for directory services and is not secure. Answer D is incorrect because Shibboleth is an

open source federated identity solution that provides single sign-on (SSO) capabilities and federated services popular in research and educational institutions.

19. D. The RSA SecurID is an example of a time-shifting key token. Answer A is incorrect because it is a generic term and many smart card variations exist. Answer B is incorrect because the common access card (CAC) is used by the U.S. military, the military reserve, and military contractors. Answer C is incorrect because the personal identity verification (PIV) card is used by U.S. federal employees and contractors under HSPD 12.

20. D. The password history policy prevents reuse of the same passwords. Account lockout deactivates an account after a certain number of failed access attempts, making answer A incorrect. Answer B is incorrect because password complexity is a policy that determines how many types of characters must be used to create a strong password (lower- and uppercase letters, numbers, and symbols are the four general types of characters possible on a standard keyboard). Account expiration policies ensure that unused or no-longer-used accounts are properly disabled, making answer C incorrect.

21. A. If the user failed to also change her password on her phone, its repeated attempts to access email during the night would have triggered the account lockout protections and temporarily disabled her account. Password complexity and history would not lock out her account after successfully changing it, making answers B and D incorrect. Answer C is incorrect because, although account expiration is possible, it is unlikely that this happened unless it was near the end of her employment.

22. D. The longer the same password is used for a particular account, the greater the chance that an attacker will be able to determine the password through brute force attacks. Allowing users to reuse an old password greatly reduces the effectiveness of a good password policy. Answer A is incorrect because making the password length at least eight characters and requiring the use of the account lockout policy settings helps you prevent attackers from guessing users' passwords. This decreases the likelihood of successful attacks on your network. Answer B is incorrect because it is used when a user forgets a password. Generally, two options exist for this: password recovery or a password reset. Answer C is incorrect because disabling user accounts is used when there might be a need to keep the settings, files, and folders intact so that the company can later access information tied to the user account by reenabling the account.

23. B. Require users to change passwords every 90 to 180 days, depending on how secure the environment needs to be. Remember that the more often users are required to change passwords, the greater the chance that they will write them down, potentially exposing them to unauthorized use. Answer A is incorrect because making the password length at least eight characters and requiring the use of combinations of uppercase and lowercase letters, numbers, and special characters is good practice. Answer C is incorrect because good policy is to set the maximum password age to a value between 30 and 90 days. Answer D is incorrect because if the lockout threshold is set to zero, accounts will not be locked out due to invalid logon attempts.

24. **C.** One of the first steps that must be taken to provide a secure account access environment is to eliminate the use of shared accounts. Their use cannot be attributed to a particular user's credentials, which precludes the determination of specific access rights and audit of access use. Answers A, B, and D are incorrect because they should be considered after original configuration and after the shared accounts have been eliminated. Answer A is incorrect because, in a user-based model, permissions are uniquely assigned to each user account; this happens after any shared accounts are eliminated. This access type is also found in government and military situations, as well as in private companies where patented processes and trademark products require protection. Answer B is incorrect because user access reviews allow the identification of misapplied changes or other access control adjustments through direct assignment or inherited nesting of role access rights. This is done after accounts are created. Answer D is incorrect because the purpose of continuous monitoring is to ensure that the processes for user account provisioning, life cycle management, and termination are followed and enforced. This process happens after the accounts have been secured.

25. **C.** Onboarding is the process for creating an identity profile and the necessary information required to describe the identity. Answer A is incorrect because least privilege is an access control practice in which a logon is provided only the bare minimum access to resources required to perform its tasks. Answer B is incorrect because offboarding is the process used when user identities that no longer require access to the environment are disabled or deactivated. Answer D is incorrect because access recertification is a more formal form of user access review.

PART V

Risk Management

For more information on the official CompTIA Security+, SY0-501 exam topics, see the "About the CompTIA Security+, SY0-501 Exam" section in the Introduction.

Risk is often difficult, if not impossible, to completely avoid. Thus, effective risk management strategies must be applied to mitigate (reduce) the likelihood and impact of "bad risks" or to enhance (improve) the likelihood and results of "good risks." A "good risk" might be the chance of a windfall profit or other beneficial outcome. Most risks that the exam addresses, however, are of the "bad risk" type. In these cases, an attacker seeks unauthorized access to data or services. This part covers important concepts related to risk management.

Managing risk requires strong governance with an understanding of the goals of the organization, an understanding of the critical functions performed within the organization, and a comprehensive assessment of the risk the organization faces. From this understanding, organizations can develop appropriate policies, plans, and procedures related to organizational security that are commensurate with the overall goals and acceptable risk tolerance and threshold of the organization.

CHAPTER 26

CHAPTER 26

Policies, Plans, and Procedures Related to Organizational Security

This chapter covers the following official Security+ exam objective:

5.1 Explain the importance of policies, plans and procedures related to organizational security.

- ▶ Standard operating procedure
- ▶ Agreement types
  - BPA
  - SLA
  - ISA
  - MOU/MOA
- ▶ Personnel management
  - Mandatory vacations
  - Job rotation
  - Separation of duties
  - Clean desk
  - Background checks
  - Exit interviews
  - Role-based awareness training

- ▶ Data owner
- ▶ System administrator
- ▶ System owner
- ▶ User
- ▶ Privileged user
- ▶ Executive user
  - NDA
  - Onboarding
  - Continuing education
  - Acceptable use policy/ rules of behavior
  - Adverse actions
- ▶ General security policies
  - Social media networks/ applications
  - Personal email

Essential Terms and Components

- standard operating procedure (SOP)
- business partner agreement (BPA)
- service level agreement (SLA)
- interconnection security agreement (ISA)
- nondisclosure agreement (NDA)
- memorandum of understanding (MOU)
- memorandum of agreement (MOA)
- acceptable use policy (AUP)

CramSaver

If you can correctly answer these questions before going through this chapter, save time by skimming the Exam Alerts in this chapter and then completing the Cram Quiz at the end of this part of the book.

1. Name and describe examples of interoperability agreements.

   _____

2. Why is it important to understand the different user types interacting across systems before developing and delivering training?

   _____

3. Name a reason why conducting exit interviews is important.

   _____

Answers

1. Four examples of interoperability agreements are SLAs, BPAs, MOUs/MOAs, and ISAs. These are all contracts or agreements that involve third parties. The agreements serve as tools for organizations to manage risk, particularly as related to dealings with third parties.

2. Understanding the different user types makes the training more effective. Specific training can be tailored to the specific roles and responsibilities, based on user type.

3. Exit interviews are important because they help identify reasons employees leave, provide potential competitive intelligence, and they help ensure that employees continue to be positive ambassadors for the organization.

To ensure that proper risk management is coordinated, updated, communicated, and maintained, it is important to establish clear and detailed security policies that are ratified by an organization's management and brought to the attention of its users through regular security-awareness training. Policies that the users do not know about are rarely effective, and those that lack management support can be unenforceable. Several policies can support risk management within the organization, as described in the following sections.

To protect information and the organization, the risk management framework includes various components:

▶ **Policy:** Provides the foundation upon which everything else is built. Policies are general management statements.

▶ **Standard:** Describe specific mandatory controls, based on a given policy.

▶ **Guideline:** Provides recommendation or good practices.

▶ **Procedure:** Provides instructions and greater specifics, detailing how a policy, standard, and guideline will be implemented.

A procedure also is known as a *standard operating procedure* (SOP). Sometimes the two are the same, but SOPs tend to have a further level of specificity in providing step-by-step instructions to ensure a standardized and repeatable method for performing a task. Policies tend to be higher-level and more descriptive, whereas procedures—and, more specifically, SOPs—are prescriptive.

Human Resource Management Policies

Human resources (HR) policies and practices should reduce the risk of theft, fraud, or misuse of information facilities by employees, contractors, and third-party users. The primary legal and HR representatives should review all policies, especially privacy issues, legal issues, and HR enforcement language. Many, if not most, organizations require legal and HR review of policies.

Background Checks

Organizational policies often drive the need to hire trustworthy, competent employees. As a result, an organization might require background checks before offering employment. Background checks can be quite simple, requiring only reference checks, or can involve more stringent checks, such as verifying educational credentials, checking for criminal records, verifying employment history, and conducting drug testing.

Onboarding

The hiring process should also include provisions for making new employees aware of acceptable use, data handling, and disposal policies, as well as sanctions that could be enacted if violations occur. An organization should also institute a formal code of ethics to which all employees must subscribe, particularly privileged users and those with broad administrative rights.

Mandatory Vacations

Users should be required to take vacations and rotate positions or functional duties as part of the organization's security policy. These policies outline the way a user is associated with necessary information and system resources and the way access is rotated between individuals. Employees must be able to do each other's jobs, to avoid corruption, validate cross-checks, and minimize the effect of personnel loss. All employees must be adequately cross-trained and should have only the minimal level of access necessary to perform their normal duties (least privilege). Another benefit of mandatory vacations is that they help identify gaps in employee capabilities.

Separation of Duties

Too much power can lead to corruption, whether in politics or network administration. Most governments and other organizations implement some type of balance of power through separation of duties. It is important to include a separation of duties when planning for security policy compliance. Without this separation, all areas of control and compliance could end up in the hands of a single individual. The idea of separation of duties hinges on the concept that a scenario in which multiple people conspire to corrupt a system is less likely than a scenario in which a single person seeks to corrupt it. This is often the case in financial institutions: To violate the security controls, all the participants in the process have to agree to compromise the system.

> **ExamAlert**
>
> For physical or operational security questions, avoid giving one individual complete control of a transaction or process from beginning to end. Also implement policies such as job rotation, mandatory vacations, and cross-training. These practices also protect against the loss of a critical skill set due to injury, death, or another form of personnel separation.

Job Rotation

As an extension of the separation of duties best practice, rotating administrative users between roles both improves awareness of the mandates of each role and also ensures that fraudulent activity cannot be sustained. This is also the reason users with administrative access might be required to take mandatory vacations, allowing other administrators to review standard operating practices and protocols in place. You can easily remember this with the Latin phrase *Quis custodiet ipsos custodies?*, which translates to "Who will guard the guardians themselves?"

Clean Desk Policies

A clean desk policy is one of the top strategies to reduce the risk of security breaches in the workplace. Training should include details of the organization's clean desk policy, encouraging users to avoid jotting down hard-to-recall passphrases or details from electronic systems that might contain PII. A clean desk policy can also increase employee awareness about protecting sensitive information. Users should understand why taping a list of their logons and passwords under their keyboards is a bad idea.

> **ExamAlert**
>
> A clean desk policy can be a vital tool in protecting sensitive and confidential materials in the hands of end users. A clean desk policy requires that users remove sensitive and confidential materials from workspaces when they leave and lock away items they are not using.

Role-Based Awareness and Training

For organizations to protect the integrity, confidentiality, and availability of information in today's highly diverse network environments, each person involved needs to understand his or her roles and responsibilities. NIST Special Publication 800-16 outlines the advantages of role- and performance-based security training and presents models for the two training models. All employees need fundamental training in IT security concepts and procedures. Training can then be broken into three levels: beginning, intermediate, and advanced. Each level is linked to roles and responsibilities, based on the skills and abilities required to perform the required responsibilities. Of course, individuals might perform more than one role within the organization, so they might need intermediate or advanced IT security training in their primary job role but require only beginning training in their secondary role.

Understand that awareness is different from training. The primary difference is that training is more active. Awareness deals with recognition, specifically helping employees recognize IT security concerns. A common example of security awareness might be distributing pens and posters with security slogans or exhortations. Training relates more specifically to the specific competencies required of the individual. Effective training requires an understanding of user types who interact across information systems. From there, specific training can be tailored to the specific role and responsibilities.

Users can be the following types:

▶ **General user:** These users typically make up most of the user population. They have general nonprivileged access to use and transact across information systems.

▶ **Privileged user:** These users have access to otherwise restricted data and system functions.

▶ **System administrator:** This user is the custodian of the data and has responsibility for technical control over the systems that contain and process data.

▶ **Executive user:** These users are more likely to have privileged access to sensitive data but also nonprivileged access to systems. These users have overall accountability for the security efforts of the organization.

▶ **Data owner:** This user often is responsible for a specific information asset and many times is a senior person within a department or division. For example, the Vice President of Human Resources might be the data owner for all employee data.

▶ **System owner:** This user is responsible for the systems that contain and process data. Typically, the system owner oversees the employees who are responsible for the technical control and operations of such systems. The system owner also works closely with the data owner to ensure that data is secure across its lifecycle.

Executive users, data owners, and system owners all have positions that require them to be responsible for drafting and promulgating security policies, standards, and procedures related to the information systems.

ExamAlert

You must understand the differences among the different user types. Specifically, be sure you understand that each role requires different training. Executive users, data owners, and system owners, in particular, are responsible for drafting and promulgating security policies.

Continuing Education

User education and training is required to ensure that users are made aware of expectations, options, and requirements related to secure access within an organization's network. These programs should continue beyond the onboarding process and be a part of regular cadence. Education can include many different forms of communication, including the following:

▶ New employees and contract agents should be educated in security requirements as a part of the hiring process.

▶ Reminders and security-awareness newsletters, emails, and flyers should be provided to raise general security awareness.

▶ General security policies should be defined, documented, and distributed to employees.

▶ Regular focus group sessions and on-the-job training should be provided for users regarding changes to the user interface, application suites, and general policies.

▶ General online security-related resources should be made available to users through a simple, concise, and easily navigable interface.

ExamAlert

Combining security training during employee orientation with ongoing training is ideal to ensure that employees recognize and retain information, along with gaining necessary skills and understanding.

User training should ensure that operational guidelines, restrictions on data sharing, disaster recovery strategies, and operational mandates are clearly conveyed to users and refreshed regularly. Policies might also require refresher training during transfers between organizational components or between roles/job duties under the rotation policy. Details such as information classification (high, medium, low, confidential, private, public), sensitivity of data and handling guidelines, legal mandates related to data forms such as personally identifiable information (PII) in financial or healthcare settings, best practices, and consumption standards can vary widely among organizational units. The proper protocols for access, storage, and disposal should vary accordingly. In response to the continued expansion of electronic technology provided by users in bring your own device (BYOD) settings, security awareness training is key to managing user habits and expectations developed as a result of the prevalence of computing equipment at home and mobile devices.

Acceptable Use Policy/Rules of Behavior

An organization's *acceptable use policy* (AUP) must provide details that specify what users may do with their network access. Such rules help protect the organization's data and guard against legal liability. This includes email and instant messaging usage for personal purposes, limitations on access times, and the storage space available to each user. Such policies generally also include rules of behavior or a code of conduct to ensure that users behave in a manner that is legal, ethical, and within the cultural expectations of the organization.

An acceptable use policy should contain these main components:

▶ Clear, specific language

▶ Detailed standards of behavior

▶ Detailed enforcement guidelines and standards

▶ Acceptable and unacceptable uses

▶ Consent forms

▶ Privacy statement

▶ Disclaimer of liability

Organizations should be sure that the acceptable use policy complies with current state and federal legislation and does not create unnecessary business risk to the company from employee misuse of resources. Upon logon, users should see a statement that network access is granted under certain conditions and that all activities could be monitored. This way, you can be sure to cover any legal ramifications. Such policies commonly also address use of the Internet, covered next.

Internet Usage

Organizations set expectations on appropriate use of the Internet through an acceptable use policy or, explicitly, an Internet use policy. In addition to protecting the organization's data, such policies help ensure employee productivity and discourage disruptive and illegal activities. Obvious examples include guidelines that prohibit accessing or transmitting threatening or illegal material. In the past, organizations commonly prohibited the use of personal email and disallowed other nonbusiness use of corporate systems and Internet access. Many policy statements today do provide for personal use but limit such usage, especially when personal use is excessive. Internet usage policies also often govern the appropriate use of email and social media.

Email and social media provide open platforms that enable seamless data sharing, allowing organizations and partners to interface and extend network services and applications. Organizations use email for communication inside and outside the organization. Social media is often used beyond the organization to communicate externally and garner opinions about products and services. Such technologies improve collaboration and communication within and across partners and also raise the level of productivity and interaction between workers. Although such tools allow instant collaboration and increase productivity, they pose serious privacy concerns. Organizations must be cautious because of potential negative impacts such as damage to brand recognition and liability for online defamation and libel claims.

> ### ExamAlert
>
> Organizations must carefully consider risks versus benefits when deciding on a social media strategy. Risks must be evaluated for using social media as a business tool to communicate with affiliates, granting employee access to social media sites while on the corporate network, and allowing employee use of social media tools from corporate-issued mobile devices.

Strategies to address the risks of email and social media usage should focus on user behavior by developing policies and supporting user training and awareness programs. Technical controls can assist in policy enforcement and in blocking, preventing, or identifying potential incidents. Examples of technical controls include mobile device management (MDM) and mobile application management (MAM). These are enterprise solutions that you can use in social media application security, protection, and asset management.

Controls should be monitored to ensure that they are effective. In addition, the organization can engage a brand protection firm that scans the Internet and looks for misuse of the organization's brand. This approach maintains awareness of potential fraud and establishes clear guidelines about what information should be posted as part of a social media presence.

Nondisclosure Agreements

A *nondisclosure agreement* (NDA) is a legally binding document that organizations might require of both their own employees and anyone else who comes into contact with confidential information. This can include vendors, consultants, and contractors. The purpose of an NDA is to protect an organization's intellectual property and trade secrets. As a legally binding document, it protects the information from being improperly disclosed, even after the relationship is terminated. This applies, for example, to employees who move to a competing organization or partners who work across competing organizations.

Disciplinary and Adverse Actions

Policies are the first step in enforcement and should specify consequences for violations. Policies often can be enforced through technical controls, such as content and web filters. The most common and simple example of a policy is a statement such as, "An employee found to be in violation of this policy may be subject to disciplinary action, including termination of employment." Again, policy awareness and training are required here. In most cases, disciplinary actions depend on the nature of the violation and the status of the individual involved. Most violations are handled within management, the information technology team, and the human resources department. However, civil and criminal violations need to be governed outside the organization. As a result, policy statements should also include the jurisdiction responsible for interpreting applicable laws.

Exit Interviews

Exit interviews are a vital tool to help an organization identify workplace factors that cause employees to leave. These interviews provide a feedback loop to allow human resources personnel to improve the current situation, as well as adapt programs to ensure that the company can continue to recruit and hire the best talent. Other benefits include potentially learning more about competing organizations (for example, are others paying more?) and ensuring that the employee has a positive exit experience. A member of the human resources department typically conducts an exit interview in a one-on-one setting with the exiting employee. Exit interviews are typically voluntary and confidential, to help ensure candid responses from the employee.

Interoperability Agreements

Integrating systems and data with third parties or partners can combine complexity and inefficiency, leading to increased risk for the organization. Risks in partnerships are usually analyzed only during the onboarding process; after the relationship is established, organizations often forget about associated risks. Security policies and procedures need to be followed, however, to identify risks and security controls that will be implemented to protect the confidentiality, integrity, and availability of any connected systems and the data that will pass between them or be accessed. Controls should be appropriate for the environment and should contain a centralized platform to monitor the range of assessments, tasks, and responsibilities of all parties. Policies should define ownership and accountability. Both organizations must maintain clear lines of regular communication. Regular risk assessments and audits should occur, and a record of compliance should be established so that documentation pertains to the due diligence performed. In addition, changes in the legal and regulatory environment should be monitored for changes that impact the partnership or third-party agreement.

Third-party risk can vary greatly, depending on each individual third-party arrangement. Sometimes the risks are clear-cut. Other times, the risks seem unclear. To establish responsibilities in collaboration or the delivery of services, interoperability agreements are used. Agreements can be tailored to the circumstances and requirements of the participating parties, the various collaborative arrangements agreed upon, or the complexity of the service relationship. These agreements help create a common understanding about the agreement and each party's responsibilities. The following list describes several agreements commonly used in business:

▶ **Service level agreement (SLA):** A *service level agreement* is a contract between a service provider and a customer that specifies the nature of the service to be provided and the level of service that the provider will offer to the customer. An SLA often contains technical and performance parameters, such as response time and uptime, but it generally does not include security measures.

▶ **Business partner agreement (BPA):** A *business partner agreement* is a contract that establishes partner profit percentages, partner responsibilities, and exit strategies for partners. This is strictly a business arrangement that specifies partner financial and fiduciary responsibilities. It does not cover security measures.

▶ **Memorandum of understanding (MOU):** A *memorandum of understanding* (sometimes called MOA or memorandum of agreement) is a document that outlines the terms and details of an agreement between parties, including each party's requirements and responsibilities. An MOU that expresses mutual accord on an issue between two or more organizations does not need to contain legally enforceable promises; it can be legally enforceable based on the intent of the parties.

▶ **Interconnection security agreement (ISA):** An *interconnection security agreement* is an agreement between organizations that have connected or shared IT systems. The purpose of the ISA is to document the technical requirements of the interconnection, such as identifying the basic components of an interconnection, methods and levels of interconnectivity, and potential security risks associated with an interconnection. The ISA also supports an MOU between the organizations.

Another agreement commonly encountered is a Health Insurance Portability and Accountability Act (HIPAA) business associate agreement (BAA). This contract is signed between a HIPAA-covered entity and a HIPAA business associate (BA), to protect personal health information (PHI) in accordance with HIPAA guidelines.

Organizations can take additional steps to ensure that they are meeting compliance and performance standards:

▶ Annually approve and review third-party arrangements and performance

▶ Maintain an updated list of all third-party relationships and periodically review the list

▶ Take appropriate action with any relationship that presents elevated risk

▶ Review all contracts for compliance with expectations and obligations

The organization might also consider requiring an annual attestation by the partner or third party, stating adherence to the contract and its established controls, policies, and procedures.

> **ExamAlert**
>
> Third-party risk includes determining expectations, which can then be spelled out in SLAs, BPAs, MOUs, and ISAs. Depending on the situation, an SLA, MOU, and ISA might all be necessary. An ISA is the only document that specifically outlines any technical solution and addresses security requirements.

What Next?

If you want more practice on this chapter's exam objectives before you move on, remember that you can access all the Cram Quiz questions on the Pearson Test Prep software. You can also create a custom exam by objective. Note any objective you struggle with and go to that objective material in this chapter.

CHAPTER 27

Business Impact Analysis

Essential Terms and Components

- ▶ business impact analysis (BIA)
- ▶ business continuity plan (BCP)
- ▶ continuity of operations plan (COOP)
- ▶ mission-essential functions
- ▶ recovery point objective (RPO)

- ▶ recovery time objective (RTO)
- ▶ mean time to recovery (MTTR)
- ▶ mean time to failure (MTTF)
- ▶ mean time between failures (MTBF)
- ▶ privacy impact assessment (PIA)
- ▶ privacy threshold assessment

CramSaver

If you can correctly answer these questions before going through this chapter, save time by skimming the Exam Alerts in this chapter and then completing the Cram Quiz at the end of this part of the book.

1. A business impact analysis is a critical component of what type of plan that ensures uninterrupted operations for an organization after a disaster?

   _____

2. What are MTBF and MTTF? Describe a key difference between the two.

   _____

3. Under what conditions should an organization conduct a privacy impact analysis?

   _____

Answers

1. A business continuity plan (BCP) or continuity of operations plan (COOP) helps ensure uninterrupted operations for organizations and relies upon the business impact analysis.

2. MTBF is mean time between failures. MTTF is mean time to failure. MTBF relates to a component that can be repaired. MTTF relates to a component that cannot be repaired.

3. If an organization collects, uses, stores, or processes personal information, the organization should conduct a privacy impact analysis.

Business impact analysis (BIA) is the process of determining the potential impacts resulting from the interruption of time-sensitive or critical business processes. IT contingency planning for both disaster recovery and operational continuity relies on conducting a BIA as part of the overall plan to ensure continued operations and the capability to recover from disaster. Unlike a risk assessment, the BIA focuses less on the relative likelihood of potential threats to an organization. Instead, it focuses on the relative impact on critical business functions from the loss of operational capability. Conducting a business impact analysis involves identifying critical business functions and the services and technologies required for each, along with determining the cost associated with the loss of each and the maximum acceptable outage period.

For hardware-related outages, the assessment should also include the current age of existing solutions, along with standards for the expected average time between failures, based on vendor data or accepted industry standards.

Planning strategies are intended to minimize this cost by arranging recovery actions to restore critical functions in the most effective manner based on cost, legal or statutory mandates, and calculations of the mean time to restore.

Critical Functions

A business impact analysis is a key component in ensuring continued operations. For that reason, it is a major part of a business continuity plan (BCP) or continuity of operations plan (COOP). The focus is ensuring the continued operation of key mission and business processes. U.S. government organizations commonly use the term *mission-essential functions* to refer to functions that need to be immediately functional at an alternate site until normal operations can be restored. Essential functions for any organization require resiliency. Organizations also must identify the dependent systems for both the functions and the process that are critical to the mission or business.

Identification of Critical Systems

A BCP must identify critical systems and components. If a disaster is widespread or targets an Internet service provider (ISP) or key routing hardware point, an organization's continuity plan should detail options for alternate network access. This should include dedicated administrative connections that might be required for recovery. Continuity planning should include considerations for recovery, in case existing hardware and facilities are rendered inaccessible or unrecoverable. Also consider the hardware configuration details, network requirements, and utilities agreements for alternate sites.

Single Points of Failure

A single point of failure is a potential risk posed by a flaw in business continuity planning that allows one fault or malfunction to take down an entire system or enterprise. Single points of failure are avoided with redundancy and various fault-tolerant protocols. For example, single points of failure can be removed by using server clustering technology, redundant switches, and redundant network connections.

Naturally, systems that support critical missions or business processes should not be subject to a single point of failure. High availability (HA) describes the process for ensuring system redundancy and proper failover. Maintaining such systems requires more resources and is more expensive. As a result, HA is ideal for mission-critical systems that cannot be unavailable.

> **ExamAlert**
>
> Ensuring the continued operation of critical functions, or mission-essential functions, is a major component of the risk management process. This task starts with identifying and understanding systems that are directly relevant to the mission or goals of the organization. Such systems should be designed for high availability and should not be subject to a single point of failure.

Recovery Objectives

Recovery point objective (RPO) and recovery time objective (RTO) are crucial in risk mitigation planning. RPO specifically refers to data backup capabilities. RPO is the amount of time that can elapse during a disruption before the quantity of data lost during that period exceeds business continuity planning's maximum allowable threshold. Simply put, RPO specifies the allowable data loss. It determines up to what point in time data recovery can happen before business is disrupted. For example, if an organization does a backup at 10:00 p.m. every day and an incident happens at 7:00 p.m. the following day, everything that changed since the last backup would be lost. The RPO in this context is the backup from the previous day. If the organization set the threshold at 24 hours, the RPO would be within the threshold because it is less than 24 hours.

The RTO is the amount of time within which a process must be restored after a disaster to meet business continuity requirements. The RTO is how long the organization can go without a specific application; it defines how much time is needed to recover after a notification of process disruption.

> **ExamAlert**
>
> Be certain that you understand the distinction between RPO and RTO. RPO designates the amount of data that will be lost or will have to be re-entered because of network downtime. RTO designates the amount of actual time that can pass before the disruption begins to seriously impede normal business operations.

MTTR

When systems fail, one of the first questions asked is, how long will it take to get things back up? It is better to know the answer to such a question *before* disaster strikes. Fortunately, established mechanisms can help you determine this answer and others. Understanding these components is a big part of the overall analysis of business impact.

The mean time to recovery, or mean time to repair (MTTR), is the average time required to fix a failed component or device and return it to production status. MTTR is corrective maintenance. The calculation includes preparation time, active maintenance time, and delay time. Because of the uncertainty of these factors, MTTR is often difficult to calculate. It is usually part of a maintenance contract, with the user paying more for a system MTTR. Some systems have redundancy built in so that when one subsystem fails, another takes its place and keeps the whole system running, to reduce the MTTR.

Other risk calculations involve determining the lifespan and failure rates of components. These calculations help an organization measure the reliability of a product.

MTTF and MTBF

Mean time to failure (MTTF) is the length of time a device or product is expected to last in operation. It represents how long a product can reasonably be expected to perform, based on specific testing. MTTF metrics supplied by vendors about their products or components might not have been collected by running one unit continuously until failure. Instead, MTTF data is often collected by running many units for a specific number of hours and then is calculated as an average based on when the components fail.

MTTF is one of many ways to evaluate the reliability of hardware or other technology and is extremely important when evaluating mission-critical systems hardware. Knowing the general reliability of hardware is vital, especially when it is part of a larger system. MTTF is used for nonrepairable products. When MTTF is used as a measure, repair is not an option.

Mean time between failures (MTBF) is the average amount of time that passes between hardware component failures, excluding time spent repairing components or waiting for repairs. MTBF is intended to measure only the time a component is available and operating. MTBF is similar to MTTF, yet it is important to understand the difference. MTBF is used for products that can be repaired and returned to use. MTTF is used for nonrepairable products. MTBF is calculated as a ratio of the cumulative operating time to the number of failures for that item.

MTBF ratings can be predicted based on product experience or data supplied by the manufacturer. MTBF ratings are measured in hours and are often used to determine the durability of hard drives and printers. For example, typical hard drives for personal computers have MTBF ratings of about 500,000 hours.

> **ExamAlert**
>
> Mean time between failures (MTBF) is the average time before a product requires repair. On the other hand, mean time to failure (MTTF) is the average time before a product fails and cannot be repaired. MTBF considers a component that can be repaired, whereas MTTF considers a component that cannot be repaired.

Impact

As the name suggests, a businesses impact analysis requires careful examination of the potential business impact. The loss of a business process or function will likely result in some sort of impact, which is measured as part of a BIA to understand the severity. This can simply include an impact rating of low, medium, or high. A more complex analysis considers the different types of impacts that result from the loss of a functional business process. Consider, for example, the importance of availability to an e-commerce site. Most obvious is the loss of sales and income if web servers are not available. You likely can imagine other potential consequences.

When measuring impact, an organization should consider potential consequences across a broad set of categories, including these:

▶ Life and safety

▶ Facilities and physical property

▶ Intellectual property

▶ Finance

▶ Reputation

The preceding example of the loss of web servers for an e-commerce site clearly shows a potentially severe impact on finance. Additionally, the company's reputation would be impacted. The loss of web servers might not impact personal life and safety, but the loss of emergency management systems might. Subsequently, the loss of fire suppression systems could certainly have a significant impact on facilities and physical property. Taken as a whole, that could further impact an organization financially.

Further assessing impact requires drilling down into the specifics and other calculations. How long can the web servers be down? How much money will be lost per hour? How long can the business remain viable as a result? If an entire facility is destroyed, do alternate sites exist from which to do business?

> **ExamAlert**
>
> Understanding the impact of an adverse event is a key component of risk manage-
> ment. Impact should consider life, property, safety, finance, and reputation.

Privacy

In today's world, information systems are a part of almost everything an organization does. The loss of such systems and information through the examples
shown (and many more) can have a real impact on various organizational
processes and functions. A further subset that requires careful consideration is
analysis of privacy.

A *privacy impact assessment (PIA)* is needed for any organization that collects,
uses, stores, or processes personal information. This includes, for example, the
data of employees, partners, and customers. Specific types of sensitive data
include Personally Identifiable Information (PII) and Personal Health Information (PHI). Chapter 33, "Data Security and Privacy Practices," discusses both
types further. The PIA is an important first step to help identify such information assets. A *privacy threshold assessm*ent can determine whether a system contains such information. This assessment is required before analyzing impact and
determining how to best protect the information. A privacy threshold assessment can be as simple as distributing a questionnaire to system and application
owners. The assessment might consist of an assortment of specific data fields
for the owner to select. Examples could include name, social security number,
gender, citizenship, place of birth, address, phone number, credit card number,
driver's license number, race, income, banking information, and so on.

As demonstrated, an analysis of the impact of loss or disclosure is needed. A
common consequence might include regulatory fines. Consider, though, that
other consequences might be worse. For example, imagine the consequences of
the unauthorized disclosure of personnel information for operatives working
undercover for a federal agency.

What Next?

If you want more practice on this chapter's exam objectives before you move
on, remember that you can access all the Cram Quiz questions on the Pearson
Test Prep software. You can also create a custom exam by objective. Note any
objective you struggle with and go to that objective material in this chapter.

CHAPTER 28

Risk Management Processes and Concepts

This chapter covers the following official Security+ exam objective:

5.3 Explain risk management processes and concepts.

- ▶ Threat assessment
  - Environmental
  - Manmade
  - Internal vs. external
- ▶ Risk assessment
  - SLE
  - ALE
  - ARO
  - Asset value
  - Risk register
  - Likelihood of occurrence
  - Supply chain assessment
  - Impact
  - Quantitative
  - Qualitative
  - Testing
    - Penetration testing authorization
    - Vulnerability testing authorization
  - Risk response techniques
    - Accept
    - Transfer
    - Avoid
    - Mitigate
- ▶ Change management

Essential Terms and Components

- ▶ single loss expectancy (SLE)
- ▶ annual rate of occurrence (ARO)
- ▶ annual loss expectancy (ALE)
- ▶ risk register
- ▶ risk avoidance
- ▶ risk transference
- ▶ risk acceptance
- ▶ risk mitigation

CramSaver

If you can correctly answer these questions before going through this chapter, save time by skimming the Exam Alerts in this chapter and then completing the Cram Quiz at the end of this part of the book.

1. Purchasing an insurance plan to cover the costs of a stolen computer is an example of which risk management strategy?

   _____

2. If an event occurs about once every 4 years and has an asset value of $100,000, assuming that the asset would have to be fully replaced after the event, explain how to calculate the ARO, SLE, and ALE.

   _____

3. When a dollar value is assigned during the risk analysis process, what type of analysis has been done?

   _____

Answers

1. This is an example of transference. The cost of the risk is actualized and transferred to the insurance company. However, the risk is not reduced; its cost effect merely has been transferred. Other issues, such as client loss of trust, might produce second-order effects.

2. ARO identifies how often in a single year the attack will occur. With an ARO of 25 percent, this risk is expected to occur once every 4 years, on average. The SLE is $100,000 per event because the asset would require full replacement. SLE is the amount of loss expected for any single successful threat attack on any given asset. With an ARO of 25 percent, the ALE is equal to the SLE ($100,000) times the ARO (.25), or $25,000.

3. Quantitative analysis assigns a dollar value during the risk analysis process; qualitative analysis does not.

Risk is the possibility of or exposure to loss or danger. Risk management is the process of identifying and reducing risk to a level that is acceptable and then implementing controls to maintain that level.

Risk analysis helps align security objectives with business objectives. This involves dealing with how to calculate risk and return on investment. Risk comes in a variety of forms. Risk analysis identifies risks, estimates the effect of potential threats, and identifies ways to reduce the risk without the cost of the prevention outweighing the risk. Risk is a function of threats, vulnerabilities, and potential impact. Assessing the level of risk is often portrayed through the following simple equation:

$$\text{Risk} = \text{Threat} \times \text{Vulnerability} \times \text{Impact}$$

To determine the relative danger of an individual threat, or to measure the relative value across multiple threats to better allocate resources designated for risk mitigation, it is necessary to map the resources, identify threats to each, and establish a metric for comparison. The previous chapter reviewed the first step: the business impact analysis (BIA). The BIA is not only a technical matter of identifying services and technology assets; it is also a business process by which the relative value of each identified asset can be determined if it fails one or more of the CIA requirements (confidentiality, integrity, and availability). The failure to meet one or more of the CIA requirements is often a sliding scale, with increased severity as time passes. Keep in mind that recovery point objectives (RPOs) and recovery time objectives (RTOs) in incident handling, business continuity, and disaster recovery must be considered when calculating risk.

Threat Assessment

Before discussing the risk assessment, you must consider the threat assessment. Part I, "Threats, Attacks, and Vulnerabilities," discussed and compared the different types of threats and vulnerabilities.

When assessing threats, consider a threat as the potential that a vulnerability will be identified and exploited. A threat vector is the method a threat uses to get to the target. Threat vectors include those from Part I: viruses, botnets, drive-by downloads, malware, phishing attacks, and keyloggers. Analyzing threats can help the organization develop security policies and prioritize securing resources. Threat assessments are performed to determine the best approaches to securing the environment against a threat or class of threat. Threats might exist, but if an environment has no vulnerabilities, it faces little or no risk. Likewise, little or no risk affects environments that have vulnerability without threat. Consider the simple analogy of a hurricane. Few would argue that a hurricane represents a threat. However, now consider a home on the coast in Florida, versus a home inland in the Midwest. The former is certainly vulnerable to a hurricane, whereas the latter is not.

Probability is the likelihood that an event will occur. In assessing risk, it is important to estimate the probability or likelihood that a threat will occur. Assessing the likelihood of occurrence of some types of threats is easier than assessing other types. For example, you can use the frequency data to estimate the probability of natural disasters. You might also be able to use MTTF and MTBF to estimate the probability of component problems. Determining the probability of attacks by human threat sources is difficult. Threat source likelihood is assessed using skill level, motive, opportunity, and size. Vulnerability likelihood is assessed using ease of discovery, ease of exploit, awareness, and intrusion detection.

Chapter 3, "Threat Actor Types and Attributes," covered the adversarial and accidental threat actors. However, threat source types can be classified into a total of four areas:

▶ **Adversarial:** Individuals, groups, organizations, and nation states

▶ **Accidental:** Actions by regular and privileged users that are not of malicious intent but that occur inadvertently

▶ **Structural:** Equipment and software failure

▶ **Environmental:** Natural and manmade disasters, such as fire, flood, hurricanes, infrastructure failures, and other unusual events

Particularly with the last category, understanding the difference and overlap between natural and manmade disasters is important. Typically, a natural disaster such as a tornado is beyond an organization's control. A fire, on the other hand, can be caused by either a lightning storm or arson.

Furthermore, consider the internal versus external component of the threat source. In fact, across all four preceding categories, the threat source can be either internal or external. The adversary might be an insider or outsider looking to cause harm. Even accidental threats, which is mostly associated as being internal, can be caused externally (by a customer, for example). Structural threats are commonly internal, yet in today's interconnected world, organizations depend on the systems of many partners and third parties that are external to the organization. Finally, even environmental threats such as a fire or flood can be caused by an insider or an outsider.

ExamAlert

Threat assessments must consider internal and external categorizations of threats. Either of these can apply to environmental and manmade threats.

Risk Assessment

Recall that assessing risk is largely a function of threat, vulnerability, and impact. However, an important factor must be considered between the threat and the vulnerability: the likelihood that a threat will occur to exploit a vulnerability. As a result, the overall risk assessment consists of the following five steps:

1. Identify threats.

2. Identify vulnerabilities.

3. Determine the likelihood of occurrence.

4. Determine the magnitude of the impact.

5. Determine the risk.

Having already performed a threat assessment and vulnerability assessment, you must consider the likelihood that the threats identified might actually occur. To most accurately gauge the probability of an event occurring, use a combination of estimation and historical data. Most risk analyses use a fiscal year to set a time limit of probability and confine proposed expenditures, budget, and depreciation.

A common categorization resulting from likelihood assessment might be based on a qualitative probability of high, medium, or low. Be sure to consider the motivation and capability of the threat source, the nature of the vulnerability, and the existence and effectiveness of current controls to mitigate the threat. Often the three values are translated into numeric equivalents for use in quantitative analytical processes: high (1.0), medium (0.5), low (0.1). The next section further compares qualitative and quantitative measures.

Responses must be coupled with the likelihood determined in the risk analysis. For example, the risk analysis might have advocated putting corrective measures in place as soon as possible for all high-level threats. Medium-level threats might require an action plan for implementation as soon as is reasonable, and low-level threats might be dealt with as possible or simply accepted.

By nature, risk always has the potential for negative impact. Given a particular likelihood of occurrence, organizations must next determine the magnitude of the impact. A simple measure of impact can range from very low to very high, or from negligible impact to catastrophic impact. The size of the impact varies in terms of cost and impact on critical factors. Considering both the impact assessment and the risk assessment together best helps you assess the probabilities and consequences of risk events if they are realized. Examine Table 28.1 to understand the level of risk as either low, medium, or high for both likelihood and impact. You can then prioritize risks based on the assessment to establish an importance ranking of most critical to least critical. Ranking risks in terms of their criticality or importance is an important business function because it provides insight into where resources might be needed to mitigate the realization of high-probability risk events.

TABLE 28.1   **Level of Risk Based on Likelihood and Impact**

Likelihood	Level of Impact				
	Very Low (1)	**Low (2)**	**Moderate (3)**	**High (4)**	**Very High (5)**
Very High (5)	5 (Medium)	10 (High)	15 (High)	20 (High)	25 (High)
High (4)	4 (Low)	8 (Medium)	12 (High)	16 (High)	20 (High)
Moderate (3)	3 (Low)	6 (Medium)	9 (Medium)	12 (High)	15 (High)
Low (2)	2 (Low)	4 (Low)	6 (Medium)	8 (Medium)	10 (High)
Very Low (1)	1 (Low)	2 (Low)	3 (Low)	4 (Low)	5 (Medium)

Qualitative Versus Quantitative Measures

The preceding discussions are largely qualitative because they do not attempt to assign dollar values to the risk analysis process. Quantitative measures give the clearest measure of relative risk and expected return on investment, or risk reduction on investment. Not all risk can be measured quantitatively, though, so qualitative risk assessment strategies are needed. The culture of an organization greatly affects whether its risk assessments can be performed via quantitative (numeric) or qualitative (subjective/relative) measures.

Qualitative risk assessment can involve brainstorming, focus groups, surveys, and other similar processes to determine asset worth and valuation to the organization. Uncertainty is also estimated, allowing for a relative projection of qualitative risk for each threat, based on its position in a risk matrix that plots the probability (very low to very high) and impact (very low to very high). Numeric values can be assigned to each state (very low = 1, low = 2, moderate = 3, and so on) to perform a quasi-quantitative analysis, but because the categories are subjectively assigned, the result remains qualitative.

Quantitative results are generally easier for senior management to understand, but they require intensive labor to gather all related measurements and are more time-consuming to determine. Qualitative measures tend to be less precise, more subjective, and more difficult in assigning direct costs for measuring ROI/RROI (return on investment/rate of return on investment).

Because a quantitative assessment is less subjective, the process requires assigning a value to all the various components. To perform a quantitative risk assessment, an estimation of potential losses is calculated. Next, the likelihood of some unwanted event is quantified, based on the threat analysis. Finally, depending on the potential loss and likelihood, the quantitative process arrives at the degree of risk. Each step relies on the concepts of single loss expectancy (SLE), annual rate of occurrence (ARO), and annual loss expectancy (ALE).

> **ExamAlert**
>
> Remember the difference between quantitative (numeric) and qualitative (subjective/relative) measures. Quantitative (think quantity) is expressed numerically, whereas qualitative (think quality) is expressed as "good" or "bad."

Single Loss Expectancy

Single loss expectancy (SLE) is the expected monetary loss every time a risk occurs. The SLE, asset value, and exposure factor here. SLE equals asset value multiplied by the threat exposure factor. The exposure factor is the percent of the asset lost from a successful attack. The formula looks like this:

$$\text{Asset value} \times \text{Exposure factor} = \text{SLE}$$

Consider an example of SLE using denial-of-service (DoS) attacks. Firewall logs indicate that the organization was hit hard one time per month by a DoS attack in each of the past 6 months. You can use this historical data to estimate that you likely will be hit 12 times per year. This information helps you calculate the SLE and the ALE. The ALE is explained in greater detail shortly.

An asset is any resource that has value and must be protected. Determining an asset's value can most simply mean determining the cost to replace the asset if it is lost. Simple property examples fit well here, but figuring asset value is not always so straightforward. Other considerations could be necessary, including the value of the asset to adversaries, the value of the asset to the organization's mission, and the liability issues if compromised.

The exposure factor is the percentage of loss that a realized threat could have on a certain asset. In the DoS example, imagine that 25 percent of business would be lost if a DoS attack succeeded. The daily sales from the website are $100,000, so the SLE would be $25,000 (SLE = $100,000 × .25). The possibility of certain threats is greater than that of others. Historical data presents the best method of estimating these possibilities.

Annual Rate of Occurrence

The annual rate of occurrence (ARO) is the estimated possibility of a specific threat taking place in a one-year time frame. The possible range of frequency values is from 0.0 (the threat is not expected to occur) to some number whose magnitude depends on the type and population of threat sources. When the probability that a DoS attack will occur is 50 percent, the ARO is 0.5. After you calculate the SLE, you can calculate the ALE. This gives you the probability of an event happening over a single year.

Annual Loss Expectancy

The annual loss expectancy (ALE) is the expected monetary loss that can be expected for an asset from risk over a one-year period. ALE equals the SLE times the ARO:

$$SLE \times ARO = ALE$$

ALE can be used directly in a cost-benefit analysis. Going back to the example, if the SLE is estimated at $25,000 and the ARO is .5, the ALE is $12,500. ($25,000 × .5 = $12,500). Spending more than $12,500 might not be prudent because the cost would outweigh the risk.

> **ExamAlert**
>
> Calculating risk includes the following formulas:
>
> Risk = Threat × Vulnerability × Impact
>
> SLE = Asset value × Exposure factor
>
> ALE = SLE × ARO

Supply Chain Assessment

In today's business environment, finding organizations that need to consider just their own security and risk management process is difficult. Our global economy, combined with the importance of the Internet, requires organizations to consider all the third parties with whom they share data, networks, and processes.

Part of the risk assessment process needs to include an organization's supply chain, which includes various processes related to the business that also touch those outside the organization. For example, hiring a cleaning service for your home requires that you reconsider your risk as a homeowner. Consider the following common examples. How many different third-party organizations provide such services? What due diligence has been performed? In each example, risk also needs to be assessed because any of these can have an impact upon an organization.

- ▶ Software

- ▶ Hardware

- ▶ Integration services

- ▶ Telecommunications and data services

- ▶ Hosted computing and cloud application services

In today's connected world, consider the rapid adoption of cloud applications for email and file sharing (for example, those provided by Microsoft and Google), or think about how compute infrastructure is managed completely within the cloud through Amazon Web Services or Microsoft Azure. The idea of a shared responsibility model is more relevant than ever. It's critical that organizations consider the risks and understand the shared responsibilities through proper assessment and processes.

Change Management

As mentioned earlier, change is inevitable. Organizations grow and seek new opportunities. As a result, the risk assessment process needs to adapt and keep up. To embrace change is also to embrace risk. Risk is inevitable—the proper management of risk is important. Information technology also is dynamic and constantly changing, even in lieu of strategic shifts. As a result, the risk assessment process is critical to change management.

Within information technology, change can impact the systems and services provided. Change includes anything added, modified, or removed. The goal of a good change management process is to allow for change without disruption, or with only minimal disruption, to these systems and services. Three change types are generally accepted within information technology:

- ▶ **Normal:** Changes that must go through the change approval process. After approval, they go from design through operation. Replacing an HR system from one vendor with another vendor's system is an example.

- ▶ **Standard:** Preapproved changes with known low risks that follow the same process each time. Resetting a user password is an example.

- ▶ **Emergency:** Urgent changes that need to be implemented as soon as possible.

Many changes are proactive. Again, organizations grow and evolve, and they might continually be seeking to improve or stake out new opportunities. Change is required to achieve such goals. On the other hand, change can be reactive. Consider the requirement to patch operating systems to shore up recently identified vulnerabilities. For many organizations, this process is part of normal change management procedures. In some instances, such as zero day or high-risk vulnerabilities, patches require an emergency change. This highlights one of the most important aspects of change management related to the risk assessment: Any change to a process or system potentially incurs additional risks. This is why, for example, patching systems is first tested in a lab before production deployment. Have you ever patched your own personal system or even installed new software that subsequently created problems? Now consider an emergency change. Why might it make sense to implement a patch in production before testing? Proper assessment might show that the risk of not doing anything now outweighs any operational risk incurred as a result of an immediate patch.

Testing Authorization

By now, you should clearly see that vulnerability and penetration testing play an integral role in the risk assessment process. Part I touched on the dangers incurred throughout the testing process. For most organizations, however, the tradeoffs favor testing, or at least vulnerability testing. In any case, the risk assessment process must consider the potential impacts and should require authorization prior to conducting such tests. This authorization should clearly provide an overview and purpose, specifically highlighting the need for such tests to ensure the security of information assets and also reiterating the possibility that these scans could cause system disruption. In addition, the authorization should provide enough details about the testing. Common details included in such signed authorizations could be the following:

▶ Goals

▶ Type of assessment

▶ Tools to be used

▶ Authorized systems for testing

▶ Individuals authorized to perform the work

▶ Effective dates of the testing

▶ Agreed-upon declarations or prerequisites

▶ Appropriate signatures of management staff with authorization

ExamAlert

Before executing vulnerability tests or penetration tests, always get written authorization, particularly because these tests can have a negative impact on information systems.

Risk Register

Risk assessment should not be a one-time event. As an organization evolves, change is inevitable. Risk management needs to be part of a continual framework from which risk can easily be communicated and then can be continually adapted.

A risk register, usually implemented as a specialized software program, cloud service, or master document, gives organizations a way to record information about the identified risks. Risk registers often include enterprise- and IT-related risks. With threats and vulnerabilities identified, the organizations can then implement controls to manage the risk appropriately. The next section discusses these techniques. The risk register should contain the specific details about the risks, especially any residual risks the organization faces as a result of controls or mitigation techniques employed. Common contents of a risk register include the following:

- ▶ Risk categorization groupings
- ▶ Name and description of the risk
- ▶ The measure of the risk through a risk score
- ▶ The impact to the organization if the risk is realized
- ▶ The likelihood of the risk being realized
- ▶ Mitigating controls
- ▶ Residual risk
- ▶ Contingency plans that cover what happens if the risk is realized

The risk register is a strategic component for organizations. The register also helps ensure that an organization's risk tolerance and appetite is correctly aligned with the goals of the business. As a result, reporting from a risk register should be clear and understandable. The outputs should be available and visible across the business, including to management and senior executives responsible for strategy, budget, and operations.

> **ExamAlert**
>
> A risk register provides a single point of entry to record information about identified risks to the organization. Organizations might have one risk register for information systems and another risk register for enterprise risks, but the two are increasingly being combined.

Risk Response Techniques

Risk management involves creating a risk register document that details all known risks and their related mitigation strategies. Creating the risk register involves mapping the enterprise's expected services and data sets, as well as identifying vulnerabilities in both implementation and procedures for each. Risk cannot be eliminated outright in many cases, but mitigation strategies can be integrated with policies for user awareness training ahead of an incident. Formal risk management deals with the alignment of four potential responses to each identified risk:

- ▶ **Avoidance:** This response seeks to eliminate the vulnerability that gives rise to a particular risk. This is the most effective solution, but it often is not possible because of organizational requirements. For example, eliminating email to avoid the risk of email-borne viruses is an effective solution but is not likely a realistic approach.

- ▶ **Transference:** A risk or the effect of its exposure can be transferred by moving to hosted providers who assume the responsibility for recovery and restoration. Alternatively, organizations can acquire insurance to cover the costs of equipment theft or data exposure.

- ▶ **Acceptance:** An organization recognizes a risk, identifies it, and then accepts that it is sufficiently unlikely or of such limited impact that corrective controls are not warranted. Risk acceptance must be a conscious choice that is documented, approved by senior administration, and regularly reviewed.

- ▶ **Mitigation/deterrence:** Risk mitigation involves reducing the likelihood or impact of a risk's exposure. Risk deterrence involves putting into place systems and policies to mitigate a risk by protecting against the exploitation of vulnerabilities that cannot be eliminated. Most risk management decisions focus on mitigation and deterrence, balancing costs and resources against the level of risk and mitigation that will result.

Bruce Schneier, a well-known cryptographer and security expert, was asked after the tragic events of 9/11 if it was possible to prevent the events from happening again. "Sure," he replied. "Simply ground all the aircraft." Schneier gave an example of risk avoidance, albeit one he acknowledged as impractical in today's society. Consider the simple example of an automobile and its associated risks. If you drive a car, you have likely considered those risks. The option to not drive deprives you of the many benefits the car provides that are strategic to your individual goals in life. As a result, you have come to appreciate mitigating controls such as seat belts and other safety features. You accept the residual risks and might even transfer some of the risk through a life insurance policy. Certainly, when it comes to the risks of the vehicle itself, insurance plays a vital role. Not carrying insurance even carries risk itself because insurance is often required by law. Examples abound of people who have even accepted that risk, making a conscious choice to drive without insurance.

Finally, the choices you make related to risk often result in residual risk. Living in a high-crime neighborhood might spur someone to put bars on the home windows. That's one problem seemingly mitigated. Yet in case of a fire, common egress points in the home are no longer accessible.

ExamAlert

Remember that risk can be avoided, transferred, accepted or mitigated. Be sure you understand the different examples of when each would apply.

What Next?

If you want more practice on this chapter's exam objectives before you move on, remember that you can access all the Cram Quiz questions on the Pearson Test Prep software. You can also create a custom exam by objective. Note any objective you struggle with and go to that objective material in this chapter.

CHAPTER 29

Incident Response Procedures

This chapter covers the following official Security+ exam objective:

5.4 Given a scenario, follow incident response procedures.

- ▶ Incident response plan
  - Documented incident types/category definitions
  - Roles and responsibilities
  - Reporting requirements/ escalation
  - Cyber-incident response teams
  - Exercise

- ▶ Incident response process
  - Preparation
  - Identification
  - Containment
  - Eradication
  - Recovery
  - Lessons learned

Essential Terms and Components

- ▶ computer/cyber incident response team (CIRT)

CramSaver

If you can correctly answer these questions before going through this chapter, save time by skimming the Exam Alerts in this chapter and then completing the Cram Quiz at the end of this part of the book.

1. Instead of planning for every possibility regarding an incident, how should an organization manage its response strategies?

   _____

2. How will individuals understand what to do during a suspected or known incident?

   _____

3. What four phases are part of the overall incident response process, and what are the loops between the phases?

   _____

Answers

1. Planning for every possibility is impractical. Response strategies should be considered based on broader categories of attack vectors.

2. Broadly, the incident response plan should provide guidance and direction on what to do. Specifically defined roles and responsibilities provide further clarity. Furthermore, previously provided training and education will provide the knowledge—and even practice—on what to do.

3. The incident response process consists of four primary phases: 1) preparation; 2) identification and analysis; 3) containment, eradication, and recovery; and 4) post-incident events. The third step can lead to further work within the second step, and the final step feeds back into the first.

Incidents do happen from time to time in most organizations, no matter how strict their security policies and procedures are. Planning for such events is vital to ensure effective incident handling and response when the time comes. Proper planning makes the difference in being able to recover quickly instead of ruining the business.

Incident response guidelines, change management procedures, security procedures, and many other security-related factors require extensive planning and documentation. Incident response documentation should include identifying both the required forensic and data-gathering procedures and the proper reporting and recovery procedures for each type of security-related incident.

The components of an incident response plan should include preparation, roles, rules, and procedures. Incident response procedures should define how to maintain business continuity while defending against further attacks. Some organizations have a specific team of technical and security investigators that respond to and investigate security incidents, but many do not. If an organization has no such explicitly defined team, first responders need to handle the scene and the response. Systems should be secured to prevent as many incidents as possible and should be monitored to detect security breaches as they occur.

ExamAlert

The National Institute of Standards and Technology (NIST) has issued a report on incident response guidelines that can help an organization spell out its own internal procedures. These guidelines serve as best practices and can be found at http://nvlpubs.nist.gov/nistpubs/SpecialPublications/NIST.SP.800-61r2.pdf.

Incident Response Plan

Organizational policies and practices provide the structural guidance to ensure quality and efficiency in the workplace. To properly preserve evidence, organizations must put together an incident response team that knows how to handle incidents. Incident response plans help this team intelligently react to an intrusion. If a plan is not in place and duties are not clearly assigned, the organization could end up in a state of panic. The plan provides a formal approach for how the organization will respond to incidents. Incident response methodologies typically emphasize preparation so that the organization is ready to not only respond to incidents, but also prevent them by ensuring that systems, networks, and applications are sufficiently secure. The components of an incident response plan should include preparation, roles, rules, and procedures. More specifically, the *NIST Computer Security Incident Handling Guide* (SP 800-61) provides guidance on exact elements to include:

▶ Mission, strategies, and goals of incident response

▶ Senior management approval

▶ Approach to incident response

▶ Response team communications

▶ Metrics for measuring response capabilities and effectiveness

▶ Roadmap for maturing response capability

▶ How the incident response program fits into the organization

The plan starts with the mission, strategies, and goals of incident response because this lays the groundwork for the required capabilities. The plan then can be immediately implemented. Of course, the plan also should continually evolve to make sure it meets the defined mission, strategies, and goals. Occasionally revisiting the plan helps ensure that the program continues to mature based on the defined roadmap. Keep in mind, however, that an organization's mission and strategies can change. For this reason, companies should revisit the program at least annually, to assess such changes and adjust accordingly.

Documented Incident Type/Category Definitions

Planning for every conceivable type of incident is impractical. Still, incidents vary, which requires different types of response strategies. This is not unlike common incidents that take place in the real world. For example, terrorism might be further classified by attack vector, but focusing and planning incident response to every potential tactic is not feasible. Even at the airport, for example, security might face the threat of liquids one day, shoes the next, and so on. The following are common attack vectors, each potentially meriting its own incident response procedures:

▶ **Web and cloud:** Attacks perpetrated through websites and cloud-based applications and infrastructure

▶ **Email:** Attacks through email, such as with phishing and dangerous attachments

▶ **Improper usage:** Incidents that violate acceptable use policies, Internet policies, and other organizational policies (see Chapter 26, "Policies, Plans, and Procedures Related to Organizational Security")

▶ **Equipment damage, loss, or theft:** Incidents that involve computing equipment, including laptops and mobile devices, as well as other information systems

Roles and Responsibilities

An incident response program must define roles and responsibilities. Even with proper communication and notification following an incident, plans will be less effective if any confusion surrounds what role people are supposed to play and what they must do. Formal definition also grants clear authority for actions to be taken during an incident. Consider who can perform the following actions:

- ▶ Confiscate computers and other information systems

- ▶ Disconnect data networks and other information systems

- ▶ Monitor systems for further analysis and activity

- ▶ Communicate with the press

Reporting Requirements and Escalation

The plan should be clear about how an incident or potential incident should be reported and escalated. Incident identification involves gathering events from various sources (such as log files, intrusion detection systems, and firewalls) to procure evidence on whether an event is an incident. When an incident is analyzed and prioritized, the incident response team needs to notify the appropriate individuals so that all people who need to be involved can play their roles.

The exact reporting requirements vary among organizations, but parties that are typically notified include the Chief Information Officer (CIO), Chief Information Security Officer (CISO), other internal incident response team members, system owners, human resources officials, public affairs officers, legal department personnel, federal agencies, and law enforcement personnel, when necessary.

In 2013, a data breach incident at Target put some 110 million people at risk of credit fraud and identity theft. Companies such as Neiman Marcus, eBay, Home Depot, and Sony have recently made headlines due to large-scale data breaches. One of the most important points about a data breach is that mitigation of further data loss is necessary. Organizations need to conduct a thorough investigation of the suspected or confirmed loss or theft of account information within 24 hours of the compromise. Incident notification is often a legal requirement in responding to a data breach. Data breach notification laws provide direction on steps to take following a data breach and might define both responsibilities and liabilities involved in a breach. A key challenge in responding to a data breach is determining whether and when notification is an appropriate response; the legal team often makes this determination. Data breach notification laws are continually changing, and businesses should consider the statutes of all states in which they do business or where residents have personal information.

Cyber-incident Response Teams

The cyber-incident response team (CIRT) has a key role defined as part of an incident response plan. The team should consist of technical and security investigators who respond to and look into security incidents. When a suspected or confirmed incident occurs, the CIRT should be notified to handle the situation and execute the incident response process.

> **Note**
>
> A CIRT is also referred to as a computer incident response team, a computer security incident response team (CSIRT), a cyber-security incident response team, or simply an incident response team (IRT).

Most large organizations have response teams that are made up of full-time employees. However, many of these same organizations also partially outsource some of the responsibilities, particularly for more serious incidents. Other organizations choose to outsource the entire team and process. Varying structures are used, depending on the team's makeup. Most structures fall within one of the three models provided by NIST:

- ▶ **Central:** A single team is responsible for incidents. This model is common to smaller organizations, particularly companies that aren't geographically dispersed.

- ▶ **Distributed:** Multiple teams are involved. Each team might be assigned specific areas, based on different components of the organization or physical geography.

- ▶ **Coordinating:** As in the central model, a single team is established. However, this team only provides guidance for other teams. In this way, a coordinating model takes on attributes of the distributed model.

Regardless of the model, the CIRT needs to collaborate with others during an incident. Management, information security, physical security, support, legal, human resources, public affairs, privacy, and potentially other personnel are critical to the CIRT's success. These groups have specific expertise and responsibilities that can assist each other throughout the response process.

Training, Tests, and Exercises

An incident response plan should include requirements for training, tests, and simulated exercises. Mature incident response programs also likely have dedicated plans that focus on these activities. Executing these activities has two primary purposes: to ensure effectiveness during an incident and to identify any deficiencies that should be addressed or mitigated.

Proper training is critical to the success of any formal program. Specific to incident response, training starts with clear communication of the roles and responsibilities discussed earlier. Within each role, the specific set of skills needed to perform the corresponding responsibilities should be considered. Each role must get adequate training.

Tests, unlike exercises (discussed next), apply specifically to systems that are usually operational. For example, this might include the capability to recover a system from a backup. Where possible, tests should include the actual systems in operation. For example, if failover is to be tested, the system should be cut to determine whether it actually cuts over to the next system as expected.

Exercises tend to be used simulations—that is, they don't affect operational systems. Exercises are scenario-based. For example, an exercise might involve an attacker exfiltrating a database of customer data. The two primary types of exercises include tabletop and functional exercises. As the name implies, in tabletop exercises, the appropriate individuals and teams are brought together (for instance, around the tabletop) for a discussion. In an exercise on a customer data breach, for example, the group would discuss their individual roles and how they would coordinate. Contrast this with functional exercises. In this type of exercise, participants go through the motions of their response as they would during an actual emergency. Again, however, the response is simulated, so it does not affect systems in operation.

ExamAlert

Incident response exercises are either discussion-oriented (as with tabletop exercises) or more focused on simulated response (as with functional exercises).

Consider the simple analogy of a fire alarm response. Children and staff members in school are trained on what to do when they hear the fire alarm. Tests are conducted to ensure that the fire alarms function. Exercises are performed to ensure that the staff and students can execute what they have been trained for, by actually exiting the building and congregating at a specified location.

Incident Response Process

Processes generally consist of a series of steps or phases. The incident response process is a lifecycle of four primary phases:

▶ Preparation

▶ Identification and analysis

▶ Containment, eradication, and recovery

▶ Post-incident events

Figure 29.1 illustrates the flow and loops of this process. As mentioned earlier, the key components of an incident response plan should include preparation, roles, rules, and procedures that are critical to the incident response process and life cycle.

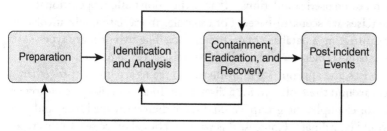

FIGURE 29.1　**Incident Response Process**

Preparation

Organizational policies and practices offer structural guidance designed to ensure quality and efficiency in the workplace. To properly preserve evidence, an organization should have an incident response team that knows how to handle incidents. Incident response methodologies typically emphasize preparation so that the organization is ready to not only respond to incidents, but also prevent incidents by ensuring that systems, networks, and applications are sufficiently secure.

Various tools and resources are needed to handle an incident. Proper preparation starts with ensuring that these resources are defined and available. The *NIST Computer Security Incident Handling Guide* (SP 800-61) provides a wealth of information to use as a baseline, highlighting specific tools and resources.

The following list covers the broad categories of resources incident handlers need, along with some examples:

▶ **Communications and facilities:** Contact information, encrypted communications, secure storage facility, phones

▶ **Hardware and software for analysis and mitigation:** Forensics workstations, protocol analyzers, portable printer, cameras, blank media

▶ **Ancillary analysis resources:** Port lists, documentation, network diagrams, existing system baselines

A jump kit is common among incident response teams. Similar to a first-aid kit, a jump kit is pre-prepared and available for immediate use in case of an incident. The jump kit should contain tools and resources from the categories just listed.

Incident Identification and Analysis

Many risks to enterprise networks relate both to vulnerabilities present in system and service configurations and to network and user logon weaknesses. Signs of an incident are either precursors or indicators. A precursor is a sign that an incident might occur in the future. An indicator is a sign that an incident might have occurred or might be occurring now. Not every precursor or indicator is guaranteed to be accurate. For example, intrusion detection systems can produce false positives. Thousands or millions of indicators can be generated daily, and each indicator must be evaluated to determine its legitimacy. An accurate indicator does not necessarily mean that an incident has occurred, so determining whether an event is truly an incident is a matter of judgment.

The first step is to analyze and validate the incident or incidents. When the response team has determined that an incident has occurred, the next step involves taking a comprehensive look at the incident activity to determine its scope. Documentation is important to eliminate errors and ensure an efficient process. A proper determination of the scope of the incident helps prioritize potential needs for deeper analysis, as well as the next step in the process for containment. To help with prioritization efforts, the response team should consider and categorize the impact and recoverability effort. This includes the following:

▶ **Functional impact of the incident:** A categorization that uses varying degrees of impact severity, from none (no effect) to high (unable to provide critical services).

▶ **Information impact of the incident:** The type of impact on information. For example, if personally identifiable information of individuals was accessed, this might be categorized as a privacy breach.

▶ **Recoverability from the incident:** The extent of the recoverability efforts. This can include a defined category, from simplest, in which recovery is well understood and does not require additional resources, to severe, in which recovery is not possible.

Finally, the incident response team should notify the proper individuals and teams, according to procedures defined in the incident response program.

Containment, Eradication, and Recovery

The process by which evidence is handled at the scene is often much more important than the laboratory analysis work done later. First responders are the first ones to arrive at the incident scene. The success of data recovery and potential prosecution depends on the actions of the individual who initially discovers the computer incident. How the evidence scene is handled can severely affect the organization's capability to successfully prosecute the perpetrator. Police officers are trained to have a good understanding of the limits of applicable laws, but many system administrators and network security personnel are not. The entire work area is a potential crime scene, not just the computer itself. Evidence might include removable media, voicemail messages, and handwritten notes. The work area should be secured and protected to maintain its integrity. Under no circumstances should anyone be allowed to remove items from the scene without proper authorization.

Isolating systems or devices involved in an incident gives a forensics team time to develop a tailored remediation strategy. The infected systems need to be isolated and quarantined. Quarantining involves finding each infected machine and disconnecting, removing, or blocking it from the network so that it cannot infect other unpatched machines on the network.

For example, when a malware-infected machine that regularly reports back to a designated host fails to report as expected, the malware might overwrite or encrypt all the data on the host's hard drive. Incident response personnel should not assume that they have prevented further damage to the host simply because they have disconnected a host from the network. In cases such as this, the organization can redirect the attacker to a sandbox, where the team can monitor the attacker's activity to gather additional evidence and more clearly understand the attack. This approach comes with additional risks, of course, including possible legal ramifications.

> **ExamAlert**
>
> Although removing the device from the network is generally advisable, this process can cause additional damage when sophisticated malware is involved.

Incident response functions can take many forms, depending on the severity of the incident and the organizational policy. The response team might send out recommendations for mitigation, recovery, containment, and prevention to systems and network administrators, who then complete the response steps. Alternatively, team members might perform the mitigation actions themselves.

In keeping with the severity of the incident, the organization can mitigate the impact of the incident by containing it and eventually restoring operations to normal. Mitigation is important before an incident damages resources. Because of the quick need to act, mitigation is often based on judgment and fast decision making. Decisions are easier to make if strategies and procedures for incident mitigation are already in place. Organizations should define acceptable risks in dealing with incidents and develop strategies accordingly. The incident type determines the mitigation type. Organizations should create separate mitigation strategies for each major incident type, with criteria clearly documented.

> **ExamAlert**
>
> *Mitigation* refers to the action of minimizing the impact of an incident. Accurately determining the cause of each incident is important so that the team can fully contain the attack and any exploited vulnerabilities, to prevent similar incidents from occurring in the future.

Depending on the nature of the incident, the organization might opt for destruction of physical property. In these cases, rebuilding or reconstituting the organization could be necessary. Reconstitution options include continuing to operate from the current alternate site, beginning an orderly phased return to the original site, and beginning to establish a reconstituted organization at another location. In recovery, administrators restore systems to normal operation and confirm that the systems are functioning normally.

Higher levels of system logging or network monitoring are often part of the recovery process. After a resource is successfully attacked, it is often attacked again, or other resources within the organization are attacked in a similar manner. Eradication and recovery should be done in a phased approach that prioritizes remediation steps. Eradication means removing elements of the incident, such as malware. Recovery is about restoring systems to normal, which often includes restoring from backups or rebuilding systems. For large-scale incidents, recovery can take months.

> **ExamAlert**
>
> Not all incidents require eradication. Sometimes systems only need to be recovered. On the other hand, sometimes eradication goes hand-in-hand with recovery. For example, whereas eradication might include disabling breached user accounts, recovery would include changing passwords.

Post-Incident Activities

After mitigating the incident, the organization issues a report containing details about the incident, such as the cause, the cost, and recommendations for preventing future incidents. Incident reporting allows the organization to review and adjust its processes, to help reduce additional incidents and losses. Organizations might be subject to industry requirements for reporting certain types of incidents. In this case, requirements and guidelines cover external communications and information sharing (what can be shared with whom, when, and over what channels), and they identify the handoff and escalation points in the incident management process. In addition, forensic analysis of information might require further reporting to law enforcement or clients, depending on the findings and evidentiary data.

The follow-up response can involve sharing information and lessons learned with other response teams and appropriate organizations and sites. One of the most important parts of incident response is lessons learned. A lesson-learned meeting should be conducted within a few days of a major incident; alternatively, a lesson learned report can be filed. A lesson-learned meeting or report provides incident closure by reviewing what occurred, describing the action taken to mitigate and contain the incident, and summarizing how well the mitigation worked. Lessons-learned reports provide valuable information for updating incident response policies and procedures. Post-mortem analysis of incident handling often reveals a missing step or procedure.

Following a data breach, a company typically incurs costs for notifying customers and for processing claims for damages. The following expenses can be incurred when a data breach results in the loss or theft of third-party information:

- ▶ A forensic examination to determine the severity and scope of the breach
- ▶ Notification of third parties
- ▶ Call center hotline support

▶ Credit or identity monitoring

▶ Public relations, for damage control

▶ Legal defense

▶ Regulatory proceedings, fines, and penalties

In addition, regulatory settlements might require the breached organization to produce or implement a comprehensive written information security program that is subject to periodic audits.

What Next?

If you want more practice on this chapter's exam objectives before you move on, remember that you can access all the Cram Quiz questions on the Pearson Test Prep software. You can also create a custom exam by objective. Note any objective you struggle with and go to that objective material in this chapter.

CHAPTER 30

Forensics

This chapter covers the following official Security+ exam objective:

5.5 Summarize basic concepts of forensics.

- ▶ Order of volatility
- ▶ Chain of custody
- ▶ Legal hold
- ▶ Data acquisition
  - ▪ Capture system image
  - ▪ Network traffic and logs
  - ▪ Capture video
  - ▪ Record time offset
  - ▪ Take hashes
- ▪ Screenshots
- ▪ Witness interviews
- ▶ Preservation
- ▶ Recovery
- ▶ Strategic intelligence/ counterintelligence gathering
  - ▪ Active logging
- ▶ Track man-hours

Essential Terms and Components

- ▶ e-discovery
- ▶ order of volatility
- ▶ chain of custody
- ▶ active logging

CramSaver

If you can correctly answer these questions before going through this chapter, save time by skimming the Exam Alerts in this chapter and then completing the Cram Quiz at the end of this part of the book.

1. What is the order of volatility?

   _____

2. What provides a clear record of the path evidence takes from acquisition to disposal?

   _____

3. What are several things that should be gathered during data forensics acquisition?

   _____

Answers

1. Order of volatility is the evidence collection process that requires collection from the most volatile component to the least volatile component.

2. The chain of custody provides a clear record of the path evidence takes from acquisition to disposal.

3. Data acquisition involves gathering forensics evidence, including system images, network logs, traffic logs, video, time offset, hashes, screenshots, and documented witness interviews.

The forensics process of preserving evidence and collecting data involves several important components. During the process, the following actions should be performed:

▶ Document an investigation from initial notification through conclusion.

▶ Locate data and any devices of potential evidentiary value.

▶ Identify data of interest.

▶ Establish an order of volatility to identify the first level of data capture desired.

▶ Eliminate external mechanisms of modification.

▶ Collect all data of potential evidentiary value.

▶ Create forensic duplicates of data for review.

▶ Store original data and devices in a manner that preserves integrity.

▶ Perform forensic evaluation and document findings (or lack thereof).

▶ Report findings as appropriate.

Forensics of information systems relates to both e-discovery and data recovery. E-discovery concerns the discovery of electronically stored information. Data recovery involves retrieving lost or corrupted data from media when it is otherwise inaccessible by typical means. During the forensics process, many requirements and methods are similar, particularly because incidents can be a part of legal matters. Data recovery is commonly associated with common failures (such as hard drive crashes), but the forensics process also involves data recovery when data might have been deleted or encrypted.

> **ExamAlert**
>
> From a forensics standpoint, preservation is a common theme, especially as it relates to evidence and legal proceedings.

Strategic Intelligence/ Counterintelligence Gathering

The forensics process places heavy emphasis on proper preservation and collection. Incidents such as a breach might require further intelligence gathering and counterintelligence considerations. Considering the complexity of computer systems, it is necessary after a breach occurs to make sure that attackers do not still have footprints within the organization. For example, attackers could remain active within the environment or might have placed persistent threats for subsequent access. Active logging is a common intelligence gathering tool used during the forensics process. Active logging cannot tell you what happened in the past, however—it can only examine what has happened since it was put into operation.

Many organizations might have these capabilities in place already. Forensically, this can be compared to a DVR system or video recording: Investigators can easily replay what happened across the computer networks. Considering counterintelligence is also important when using such tools. The forensics process might seek to keep adversaries from knowing they are being monitored.

Track Man-hours

The cost of a forensics investigation can run into thousands of dollars. As soon as the work proposal or court order is executed, man-hour tracking and administrative work begins. Costs are an important part of project planning. Calculating the number of man-hours and other related expenses provides a way to estimate the investigation costs with the budgeted amount. The costs include the acquisition, investigation, and reporting of time and expenses. An organization assesses the costs of the investigation against the potential benefits to determine whether it is cost-effective and technically feasible.

Order of Volatility

When a potential security breach must be reviewed, the digital forensics process comes into play. Data of potential evidentiary value can be stored in many different forms within a subject system. Some of these storage locations preserve the data even when a system is powered off, whereas others hold data for only a brief interval before it is lost or overwritten. Even the process of evaluation can modify or overwrite these volatile storage areas. Shutting off a running system might completely wipe all data stored in active memory. In some cases, evidence that is relevant to a case might exist only temporarily.

Evidence collection should follow the order of volatility. Specifically, during the collection process, the forensics team should proceed from the most volatile evidence to the least volatile pieces. Evidence can be lost when a computer is powered down. If you can capture the volatile data before you unplug the computer, you get a snapshot of the system at the time you arrived on the scene. You should collect the following information:

▶ System date and time

▶ Current network connections

▶ Current open ports and applications listening on those ports

▶ Applications currently running

Data capture is highly dependent upon this order of volatility, in which the capture and examination of more durable storage can eliminate data of potential evidentiary value at more volatile levels. Consider the order of volatility for a typical system:

1. **Registers and caches:** Data stored within the CPU's registers and cache levels. It might remain for only nanoseconds before it is overwritten by normal system operations.

2. **Routing and process tables:** Data stored within networking and other active devices. Ongoing operations can modify this data externally.

3. **Kernel statistics:** Data regarding current kernel operations. This data can be in constant transit between cache and main memory.

4. **Main memory:** Data stored within the system's RAM storage.

5. **Temporary file systems:** Data stored within elements of system memory allocated as temporary file storage, such as a RAM disk, or within virtual system drives.

6. **Secondary memory:** Data stored in nonvolatile storage such as a hard drive or other form of media that retains data values after a system shutdown.

7. **Removable media:** Nonvolatile removable media such as backup tape storage media.

8. **Write-once storage:** Nonvolatile media that is not subject to later overwrite or modification, such as CD-Rs, DVD-Rs, and printouts.

ExamAlert

Order of volatility demands that evidence be collected first from the most volatile systems (such as registers and caches) and later from the least volatile systems (such as archival media).

Chain of Custody

The chain of custody provides a clear record of the path evidence takes from acquisition to disposal. Key to any form of forensic investigation is adherence to standards for the identification, collection, storage, and review of evidence. Chief among these involves creating a log of all actions taken, including any inferences and causative details used to identify data of potential evidentiary value. This log should support the chain of custody for any evidentiary data, as well as track man-hours, expense, details of identification, and contact data for any witnesses and statements provided during an investigation. For evidence to be useful, it must have five properties:

▶ **Admissible:** Evidence must be usable in court or within an organization's practices. It must follow all appropriate legal requirements and guidelines for identification, acquisition, examination, and storage.

▶ **Authentic:** Evidence must be proven to relate to the incident, with any changes accounted for in evidence review logs.

▶ **Complete:** In addition to data of evidentiary value, evidentiary gathering must include both directly related data and indirectly related data. An example might include a listing of all accounts logged into a server when an attack occurred, not just the logging details of the suspect's login.

▶ **Reliable:** Evidentiary identification, acquisition, review, and storage practices must ensure that the data remains authentic and unmodified to the best extent possible, based on the data's order of volatility.

▶ **Believable:** Evidence must be clear and easy to understand, but it also must be related to the original binary or encrypted data through a process that is equally clear, documented, and free of manipulation during transition. Raw hexadecimal data is difficult for juries to review, but a chart illustrating the same information must represent the evidentiary data in a manner that another forensic analyst can replicate with the same end result.

As with other forms of forensics, this process requires a vast knowledge of computer hardware, software, and media to protect the chain of custody over the evidence, avoid accidental invalidation or destruction of evidence, and preserve the evidence for future analysis. Computer forensics review involves applying investigative and analytical techniques to acquire and protect potential legal evidence. Therefore, a professional within this field needs a detailed understanding of the local, regional, national, and even international laws affecting the process of evidence collection and retention, especially in cases involving attacks waged from widely distributed systems located in separate regions.

The practice of forensics analysis is a detailed and exacting one. The information in this section enables an entering professional to recognize that precise actions must be taken during an investigation. These tasks must not be attempted without training in the hardware, software, network, and legal issues involved in forensics analysis. Consider the major concepts behind computer forensics:

▶ Identify the evidence.

▶ Determine how to preserve the evidence.

▶ Extract, process, and interpret the evidence.

▶ Ensure that the evidence is acceptable in a court of law.

Each state has its own laws that govern how cases can be prosecuted. For cases to be prosecuted, evidence must be properly collected, processed, and preserved. The corporate world focuses more on prevention and detection, whereas law enforcement focuses on investigation and prosecution.

Forensics analysis involves establishing a clear chain of custody over the evidence. This relates to the documentation of all transfers of evidence from one person to another, including the date, time, and reason for the transfer and the signatures of both parties involved in the transfer. In other words, it tells how the evidence made it from the crime scene to the courtroom, including documentation on how the evidence was collected, preserved, and analyzed. Every time data of possible evidentiary value is moved, accessed, manipulated, or reviewed, the chain of custody must be maintained and actions must be logged. Forensic analysis of information might require further actions with law enforcement, depending on findings and evidentiary data of interest.

> **Note**
>
> As organizations place more data on infrastructures that the organization does not own, security and forensic processes and tools require revaluation to properly protect data and gather forensic evidence.

If you are asked to testify about data that has been recovered or preserved, it is critical that you, the investigating security administrator, be able to prove that no other individuals or agents could have tampered with or modified the evidence. This requires careful collection and preservation of all evidence, including the detailed logging of investigative access and the scope of the investigation. Defining the scope is crucial to ensure that accidental privacy violations and unrelated exposure do not contaminate the evidence trail. After data is collected, you must secure it in such a manner that you, the investigating official, can state with certainty that the evidence could not have been accessed or modified during your custodial term.

> ### ExamAlert
>
> Proper chain of custody helps ensure that evidence is handled correctly and strictly secured. For evidence to be useful, it must be admissible, authentic, complete, reliable, and believable.

Legal Hold

A legal hold is a request to not destroy what might be relevant to a legal matter. Organizations should have a legal hold process to perform an e-discovery to preserve and gather such information. As stated in the previous discussion of chain of custody, a legal hold is closely related to the forensics process during an information breach.

Data Acquisition

Data acquisition is an important concept that relates to the forensics process. Data acquisition involves gathering data or copying data to an image or other media. Special forensics systems can more easily assist with the process and ensure that the original source media is not modified in any way. The data acquisition process includes gathering and capturing the following:

▶ System images

▶ Network traffic and logs

▶ Video

▶ Time offset

▶ Hashes

▶ Screenshots

▶ Witnesses

The following sections look at these in more detail.

Capture System Images

Drive imaging can be performed in several ways—from the disk to the disk image, from the disk to an image file, and from an image file to a disk.

Regardless of whether a direct device-to-device copy of the media or forensic evidence copies are created for examination, the process should be forensically sound. Examination of the media should be conducted in a forensically sound environment—that is, an environment over which the examiner has complete control. You can use a full system image to further examine data in an operational state, although you must put protections in place to prevent external communication through wired and wireless connectivity; you want to guard against external manipulation or the risk that a suspect will be alerted. When available, use a write-blocking device to access the suspect media to capture a system image. You can use software or hardware write blockers. Software write blockers stop any operating system write operations from modifying the media. Hardware write blockers are physical devices that sit between the drive itself and the controller card.

Data storage should be duplicated using verified forensic utilities. Then only the duplicate should reviewed in subsequent investigations, to protect the original from modification or corruption. Virtual machine (VM) images are acquired either by using tools specifically designed to capture a VM environment or by using vendor built-in tools. System images can usually be easily validated from a forensics standpoint. Other environments are more challenging, as in big data environments that contain unstructured data spread across diverse environments.

Capture Network Traffic and Logs

Analysts can use data from network traffic to reconstruct and analyze network-based attacks. When deciding what evidence to capture, first identify potential sources where the breach might have occurred within the networking environment. These resources typically include network traffic and files. After identifying the resources, gather the log files that capture network traffic flows, management devices, servers, workstations, and wireless and mobile devices. Network traffic data is usually recorded to a log or stored in a packet capture file; the examiner can collect the logs along with the packet capture. Remote access logging occurs on the remote access server or the application server, but in some cases, the client also logs information related to the connection. Each system has its own method for tracking and logging access, so capturing all related log files is important. Keep in mind that collecting network traffic can pose legal issues, especially if you must capture information that involves privacy or security implications. If logs will be needed as court evidence, organizations might want to collect copies of the original log files, the centralized log files, and interpreted log data, in case questions arise about the accuracy of the copying and interpretation processes.

Capture Video

If at all possible, videotape the entry of all persons into the affected area. Recording the actual entrance of a forensics team into the area helps you refute claims that evidence was planted at the scene. You might also want to take photographs of the actual evidence and make notes at the scene. For example, in the case of an intrusion, you might want to take a photograph of the monitor. If the computer will be dissembled onsite for imaging, pictures of the computer should be taken from all angles to document the system hardware components and how they are connected. Carefully photograph the inside of the machine and note the serial number, internal drives, and peripheral components. Label the evidence and then photograph the evidence again after you attach the labels. It might be a good idea to use a 35mm camera for your photographs. Digital images are easy to manipulate, and film negatives can validate the pictures if questions arise over whether the images were altered. Ideally, one person documents while another person handles the evidence. You want to be able to prove that you did not alter any of the evidence.

You can find valuable evidence about physical access through the recordings of closed-circuit television (CCTV) systems. However, some organizations must deploy adequate signage to state whether camera systems are monitored or merely present for the later prosecution of wrongdoing. Otherwise, individuals who signal to the cameras for assistance during an emergency can later sue the organization because they expected live monitoring of security cameras. Some CCTV systems might employ non-visible-spectrum cameras, such as thermal imaging systems that can spot heat blooms and body heat sources even when those sources are otherwise concealed. CCTV systems should be configured to observe access paths and location areas without displaying data, password entry, and similar details.

Record Time Offset

Records should be kept of all data and devices collected, including details such as system time offset from a verified time standard, nonstandard hardware or equipment configurations, and codecs available for video manipulation and running services (if the system is in operation). Recording the time offset is critical to an accurate examination when dates and times are at issue, and this should be done at the beginning of any examination. Just because a computer was seized in a particular time zone does not mean that it is configured for that time zone. Computers can be moved from one zone to another, can be incorrectly configured, and can be deliberately altered, so the time and time zone offset might not be accurate. When computers are examined, their date and time settings should be recorded and compared with the current time, to calculate the difference between the two. This difference is then used as an offset and applied to all the time evidence on the computer. For example, when a computer that is imaged in Mountain Standard Time is analyzed with a tool that is in Eastern Standard Time, the time zone is adjusted to accurately reflect the time of the imaged drive. To resolve these issues, you need to know the machine's BIOS time and the time zone offset for which it is configured so that you can apply the correct time zone offset to your case. The time zone offset in Windows operating systems is stored in the Registry.

ExamAlert

Time offset adjustments cannot reveal anything about the accuracy of the events on the computer. The time offset adjustment establishes only the accuracy of the date and time record of the device when it was acquired.

Take Hashes

You should generate hashes of all data and applications before and after any in-depth analysis is performed, to validate that the forensic analysis itself has not produced unexpected modifications of evidentiary data. When the image of the drive is complete, a hash value of the image is taken and then compared against the hash of the original drive. If they are the same, this proves that you did not change anything.

The most common method of taking a hash of a drive is to calculate a hash of the entire drive. Most forensic tool sets include a utility to calculate either a cyclic redundancy check (CRC) or a Message Digest 5 (MD5) hash value. Other valid methods are available to generate a single value for a file or collection of files, but the CRC and MD5 hash values are the most common. Both algorithms examine the input and generate a single value. Any changes to the input result in a different value.

After you have ensured the physical integrity of the media, you can mount the media and access it in read-only mode. It is important that you explicitly separate the suspect media from other media during any access to the data. The only safe way to ensure that nothing changes the data on the drive is to use trusted tools to access the media only once. The only reason to directly access suspect media is to copy it for analysis.

Capture Screenshots

You should capture screenshots during the investigation and include them in forensic documentation for later reporting or testimony of the process and resulting findings. These should supplement photographs of the scene prior to evidentiary gathering and video of the collection and analysis process itself. Whenever possible, you should capture and preserve network traffic and logs to aid in the identification of related processes, remote virtual storage systems, and distributed computing functions that might relate to the investigation.

Collect Witness Interviews

Witnesses are an important part of any crime scene. If you interviewed anyone, you should create a list of whom you interviewed, including their names, email addresses, and what they saw (when, where, and how). The interviewer should minimize physical distractions such as noise or the presence of other persons. Witnesses should be encouraged to volunteer information without prompting. In cases such as the release of malware, denial-of-service (DoS) attacks, or theft of information, you can sometimes obtain more information than you expect just by asking. You might even end up with a confession if the threat came from an insider.

> **ExamAlert**
>
> Be certain you are comfortable with the items to be acquired during the forensics process: system images, network traffic and logs, videos, time offset, hashes, screenshots, and witness interviews.

What Next?

If you want more practice on this chapter's exam objectives before you move on, remember that you can access all the Cram Quiz questions on the Pearson Test Prep software. You can also create a custom exam by objective. Note any objective you struggle with and go to that objective material in this chapter.

CHAPTER 31

Disaster Recovery and Continuity of Operations

This chapter covers the following official Security+ exam objective:

5.6 Explain disaster recovery and continuity of operation concepts.

► Recovery sites
- Hot site
- Warm site
- Cold site

► Order of restoration

► Backup concepts
- Differential
- Incremental
- Snapshots
- Full

► Geographic considerations
- Off-site backups

- Distance
- Location selection
- Legal implications
- Data sovereignty

► Continuity of operation planning
- Exercises/tabletop
- After-action reports
- Failover
- Alternate processing sites
- Alternate business practices

Essential Terms and Components

► recovery site
► hot site
► cold site
► warm site
► order of restoration
► differential backup

► incremental backup
► full backup
► snapshot
► disaster recovery plan (DRP)

CramSaver

If you can correctly answer these questions before going through this chapter, save time by skimming the Exam Alerts in this chapter and then completing the Cram Quiz at the end of this part of the book.

1. Name the three types of recovery sites. Which one is usually the most expensive, at least initially?

   _____

2. With a differential backup, what other type of backup or backups are required to fully restore a system?

   _____

3. If a full backup of a server must be taken, how far away should the backup be stored?

   _____

Answers

1. Recovery sites include hot, warm, and cold. Hot sites are the most expensive, at least initially, because they are fully operational and ready to go.

2. Restoring from a differential backup tape also requires a full backup tape. The differential backup provides only the data that has changed since the last full backup; it is incomplete without the full backup.

3. The recommended distance from the storage location of a tape backup to the server from which it was taken depends on various risk factors and goals. Distance and geography should be given proper consideration. Storage in the same location is fine if it mitigates the risk of the hard disk crashing. The threat of an earthquake, however, might require a much greater distance.

In Chapter 27, "Business Impact Analysis," you learned about the importance of contingency planning for disaster recovery and operational continuity. Put simply, organizations need to be prepared for disasters so that they can continue operating and recover from the disaster. IT contingency planning is designed to sustain and recover critical IT services following an emergency. IT contingency planning is a broad plan that includes organizational and business process continuity and recovery planning. Organizations integrate a sequence of plans covering response, recovery, and continuity activities to prepare for disruptions to business processes, loss of IT systems, and damage to the facility. An IT contingency plan requires a long-term planning strategy and program management plan, especially when national security matters or military branches are involved. The planning process outlines how the organization will designate resources, define short- and long-term goals and objectives, forecast budgetary requirements, anticipate and address issues and potential obstacles, discuss essential functions, and establish planning milestones.

Business continuity plans (BCP) and continuity of operations plans (COOP) ensure the restoration of organizational functions in the shortest possible time, even if services resume at a reduced level of effectiveness or availability. Disaster recovery plans (DRPs) extend this process to ensure a full recovery of operational capacity following a disaster (natural or Manmade). Instructions and details for recovery should occur before an incident. Plans not only should be determined, but they also should be regularly updated and tested to ensure that communication plans can be implemented and that responders can properly execute response and recovery plans. These plans should address different scenarios for incident handling responses and notification procedures following identification, short-term recovery of key service and operational data access functions as part of continuity of operation preparedness, and long-term sustained recovery to full operational status in disaster recovery planning. A business recovery plan, business resumption plan, and contingency plan are also considered part of business continuity planning. If an incident occurs, an organization might also need to restore equipment (in addition to data) or personnel lost or rendered unavailable by the nature or scale of the disaster.

Disaster Recovery

Too many organizations realize the criticality of disaster recovery planning only after a catastrophic event (such as a hurricane, flood, or terrorist attack). However, disaster recovery is an important part of overall organization security planning for every organization. Natural disasters and terrorist activity can bypass even the most rigorous physical security measures. Common hardware failures and even accidental deletions might require some form of recovery capability. Failure to recover from a disaster could destroy an organization. Disaster recovery involves many aspects, including the following:

- ▶ **Disaster recovery plan:** A DRP is a written document that defines how the organization will recover from a disaster and how to restore business with minimal delay. The document also explains how to evaluate risks; how data backup and restoration procedures work; and the training required for managers, administrators, and users. A detailed disaster recovery plan should address various processes, including backup, data security, and recovery.

▶ **Disaster recovery policies:** These policies detail responsibilities and procedures to follow during disaster recovery events, including how to contact key employees, vendors, customers, and the press. They should also include instructions for situations in which bypassing the normal chain of command might be necessary, to minimize damage or the effects of a disaster.

▶ **Service level agreements:** SLAs are contracts with ISPs, utilities, facilities managers, and other types of suppliers that detail the minimum levels of support that must be provided (including during failure or disaster).

Fundamental to any disaster recovery plan is the need to provide for regular backups of key information, including user file and email storage; database stores; event logs; and security principal details such as user logons, passwords, and group membership assignments. Without a regular backup process, loss of data through accidents or directed attack could severely impair business processes.

Disaster recovery planning should include detailed system restoration procedures, particularly in complex clustered and virtualized environments. This planning should explain any general or specific configuration details that might be required to restore access and network function.

A restoration plan also should include contingency planning to recover systems and data in case of administration personnel loss or lack of availability. This plan should include procedures on what to do if a disgruntled employee changes an administrative password before leaving. Statistics show that more damage to a network comes from inside than outside. Therefore, any key root-level account passwords and critical procedures should be properly documented so that another equally trained individual can manage the restoration process. This documentation must also include back-out strategies to implement if the most recent backup proves unrecoverable or if alternative capacity and type of equipment is all that remains available.

As part of redundancy and recovery planning, an organization can contract annually with a company that offers redundancy services (for a monthly service charge or one that is otherwise negotiated). When contracting services from a provider, be sure to carefully read the contract. Daily fees and other incidental fees might apply. In addition, in a large-scale incident, the facility could well become overextended.

In the beginning stages of the organizational security plan, the organization must decide how it will operate and how it will recover from any unfortunate incidents that affect its capability to conduct business. Redundancy planning encompasses the effects of both natural and Manmade catastrophes. Often these catastrophes result from unforeseen circumstances. Site planning for recovery is key.

Recovery Sites

The type of recovery site an organization chooses depends on the criticality of recovery and budget allocations. Three types of recovery sites exist:

▶ Hot site

▶ Warm site

▶ Cold site

Hot, warm, and cold sites can provide a means for recovery in case an event renders the original building unusable. The following sections discuss these individually.

Hot Site

A hot site is a location that is already running and available 7 days a week, 24 hours a day. These sites allow the company to continue normal business operations, usually within a minimal period after the loss of a facility. This type of site functions like the original site and is equipped with all necessary hardware, software, network, and Internet connectivity fully installed, configured, and operational. Data is regularly backed up or replicated to the hot site so that it can be made fully operational in a minimal amount of time in case a disaster occurs at the original site. The business can resume without significant delay. In case of a catastrophe, people simply need to drive to the site, log on, and begin working.

Hot sites are the most expensive to operate and are mostly found in businesses that operate in real time and for which any downtime might mean financial ruin.

Warm Site

A warm site is a scaled-down version of a hot site. The site is generally configured with power, phone, and network jacks. The site might have computers and other resources, but they are not configured and ready to go. In a warm site, the data is replicated elsewhere for easy retrieval. However, you still must do something to be able to access the data. This "something" might include setting up systems so that you can access the data or taking special equipment to the warm site for data retrieval. It is assumed that the organization itself will configure the devices, install applications, and activate resources, or that it will contract with a third party for these services. Because the warm site is generally office space or warehouse space, the site can serve multiple clients simultaneously. The time and cost for getting a warm site operational is somewhere between the time and cost needed for a hot site versus a cold site.

Cold Site

A cold site is the weakest of the recovery plan options but also the cheapest. It is less costly in the short term, but remember that equipment purchased for a cold site after a disaster might be more expensive or difficult to obtain. These sites are merely a prearranged request to use facilities if needed. Electricity, bathrooms, and space are about the only facilities a cold site contract provides. Therefore, the organization is responsible for providing and installing all the necessary equipment. If the organization chooses this type of facility, it will require additional time to secure equipment, install operating systems and applications, and contract services such as Internet connectivity.

ExamAlert

Be familiar with various types of site descriptions. Understand different scenarios that require you to choose a hot, warm or cold site solution. Remember that a hot backup site is a full duplicate of the source data center and has the fastest recovery time and highest cost. On the other hand, a cold backup site is the opposite: It has a longer recovery window with a lower cost.

Backups

The backup procedures in use can also affect what is recovered following a disaster. Disaster recovery plans should identify the type and regularity of the backup process. The following sections cover the types of backups you can use and different backup schemes.

The following types of backups are used:

- ▶ Full
- ▶ Differential

▶ Incremental

▶ Copies and snapshots

When choosing a backup strategy, a company should consider the following factors:

▶ How often will data need to be restored? As a matter of convenience, if files are restored regularly, a full backup might be chosen because it can be done with one tape.

▶ How fast does the data need to be restored? If large amounts of data are backed up, the incremental backup method might work best.

▶ How long does the data need to be kept before it is overwritten? In a development arena where data is constantly changing, a differential backup method might be the best choice.

> **Note**
>
> Snapshots and copies are appropriate for certain use cases but should not be considered formal backup options, especially for transactional systems.

When the backups are complete, they must be clearly marked or labeled so that they can be properly safeguarded. In addition to these backup strategies, organizations employ tape rotation and retention policies. The various methods of tape rotation include the following:

▶ **Grandfather-father-son backup:** This is the most common rotation scheme for rotating backup media. The basic method is to define three sets of backups. The first set, the son, represents daily backups. A second set, the father, is used to perform full backups. The final set of three tapes, the grandfather, is used to perform full backups on the last day of each month.

▶ **Tower of Hanoi:** Based on the mathematics of the Tower of Hanoi puzzle, this is a recursive method in which every tape is associated with a disk in the puzzle. The disk movement to a different peg corresponds with a backup to a tape.

▶ **Ten-tape rotation:** This simpler and more cost-effective method for small businesses provides a data history of up to 2 weeks. Friday backups are full backups. Monday through Thursday backups are incremental.

All tape-rotation schemes can protect your data, but each one has different cost considerations. The Tower of Hanoi is more difficult to implement and manage but costs less than the grandfather-father-son method. In some instances, it might be more beneficial to copy or image a hard drive for backup purposes. For example, in a development office, where large amounts of data change constantly, spending money on a complex backup system to back up all the developers' data might not be the best plan. The company might find it less expensive and more efficient to buy another hard drive for each developer and have the developers back up data that way. If the drive is imaged, then a machine that suffers a hard drive failure can be swiftly returned to good running order.

Recovery planning documentation and backup media contain many details that an attacker can exploit when seeking access to an organization's network or data. Therefore, planning documentation, backup scheduling, and backup media must include protections against unauthorized access or potential damage. The data should be protected by at least a password, and preferably encryption. When the backups are complete, they must be clearly labeled so that they can be properly safeguarded. Imagine having to perform a restore for an organization that stores its backup tapes unlabeled in a plastic bin in the server room. The rotation is supposed to be on a 2-week basis. When you go to get the needed tape, you discover that the tapes are not marked, nor are they in any particular order. How much time will you spend just trying to find the proper tape? Also, is it a good practice to keep backup tapes in the same room with the servers? What happens if a fire occurs?

Considering how backup media is handled is just as important as determining how it should be marked. You certainly don't want to store optical media in a place where it can easily be scratched or store tapes in a high-temperature area. Make sure that you also have offsite copies of your backups stored where they are protected from unauthorized access, as well as fire, flood, and other environmental hazards that might affect the main facility. Normal backups should include all data that cannot be easily reproduced. Secure recovery services are another method of offsite storage and security for organizations to consider. In military environments, a common practice is to have removable storage media locked in a proper safe or container at the end of the day.

Full Backups

A full backup is a complete backup of all data. This is the most time- and resource-intensive form of backup, requiring the largest amount of data storage. In the event of a total loss of data, restoration from a complete backup is faster than other methods. A full backup copies all selected files and resets the archive bit, a file attribute used to track incremental changes to files for the purpose of the backup. The operating system sets the archive bit any time changes occur, such as when a file is created, moved, or renamed. This method enables you to restore using just one tape. Therefore, order of restoration doesn't matter: It is just a single restore. Theft poses the most risk because all data resides on one tape; only encryption can protect the data at that point.

Differential Backups

A differential backup is incomplete for full recovery without a valid full backup. For example, if the server dies on Thursday, two tapes are needed: the full backup from Friday and the differential from Wednesday. Differential backups require a variable amount of storage, depending on the regularity of normal backups and the number of changes that occur during the period between full backups. Theft of a differential tape is riskier than with an incremental tape because larger chunks of sequential data can be stored on the tape the further away it is from the last full backup.

> **ExamAlert**
>
> A differential backup includes all data that has changed since the last full backup, regardless of whether or when the last differential backup was made, because this backup does not reset the archive bit.

Incremental Backups

An incremental backup is incomplete for full recovery without a valid full backup and all incremental backups since the last full backup. For example, if the server dies on Thursday, four tapes are needed: the full backup from Friday and the incremental tapes from Monday, Tuesday, and Wednesday. Incremental backups require the smallest amount of data storage and require the least amount of backup time, but they can take the most time during restoration. If an incremental tape is stolen, it might not be valuable to the offender, but it still represents risk to the company.

> **ExamAlert**
>
> An incremental backup includes all the data that has changed since the last incremental backup. This type of backup resets the archive bit.

Copies and Snapshots

A copy or snapshot is like a full backup, in that it copies all selected files. However, it doesn't reset the archive bit. From a security perspective, losing a tape with a copy backup is the same as losing a tape with a full backup. Some important considerations separate these types of backups from the others. First, a copy or snapshot often resides on the same system from which it was taken. Certainly, this can be useful. For example, a snapshot was taken from a virtual machine image, you now need to revert to that image. Or consider a simpler example of a copy of a document being stored on the same computer in case the original gets corrupted. Neither of these situations helps if disaster strikes the entire primary hard drive of the system, though.

Next, traditional backup solutions are integrated within the operating system. This is important to be able to interact with other transactional applications, such as databases, where data might be processing and residing only in memory. Therefore, a copy is only a very specific point in time capture at the storage level and thus might not be enough to perform a restoration.

> **Note**
>
> Many organizations choose to back up data to a cloud environment using one of the many services available. Cloud services offer continuous backup options so that you can easily recover your files without losing data associated with normal backup procedures and without having offsite storage not immediately available. Enterprise solutions have options for protecting physical and virtual environments that include software, appliance, and offsite replication.

Geographic Considerations

Consideration of geography is critical for disaster recovery and continued operations. Think about alternate site planning, for example. The site should be located far enough from the original facility to avoid disaster striking both facilities. A good example of this concerns an earthquake or a flood. The range of a flood depends on its category and other factors, such as wind and the amount of rain that follows. A torrential flood can sink and wash away buildings and damage various other property, such as electrical facilities. If the hot site is within this range, the hot site will be affected, too.

The same applies to backups. Think about your own personal home computer. Assuming you have made backups, where is that backup? Sure, a copy that exists on the same computer might protect you if the original is deleted. But what if the hard drive crashes? Perhaps you considered this and moved the backup to a remote disk that resides in another room. If your house is consumed by fire, though, both will be lost. This is why many organizations must consider off-site backups. This option involves offsite tape storage through trusted third parties. Vendors offer a wide range of offsite tape-vaulting services, highly secure facilities that can include secure transportation services, chain of custody control for tapes in transit, and environmentally controlled storage vaults.

Finally, legal implications such as data sovereignty laws might dictate the extent to which geographies are considered. Data sovereignty applies to data that is subject to the laws of the geography (most often a specific country) where the data resides. For example, if an organization is legally bound to specific data within its country's borders, the idea of off-shore processing or backups is not feasible.

ExamAlert

Geography must be considered when planning for disaster recovery as it pertains to backups and alternate processing sites. In addition to ensuring separate geographic locations, organizations must factor in adequate distances and locations, as well as any legal implications.

Continuity of Operation Planning

Business continuity is mostly synonymous with continuity of operations planning (COOP). Specifically, COOP is an initiative that U.S. President George W. Bush issued in 2007 to ensure that government departments and agencies can continue operation of their essential functions under circumstances involving natural, Manmade, and technological threats and national security emergencies. Continuity of operations is generally viewed as the same as business continuity, but it primarily focuses on government and public sectors. Policies and procedures are designed to ensure that an organization can recover from a potentially destructive incident and resume operations as quickly as possible following that event.

The main goal of preventing and effectively dealing with any type of disruption is to ensure availability. This primarily includes making sure of the following:

▶ Failover is available for required system redundancy. This can be automatic or manual.

▶ Alternate processing sites are available that are geographically different from the primary facilities.

▶ Alternate business practices are available, in case systems or logistics prevent normal operating practices.

Organizations should also include contingencies for personnel replacement in the event of loss (death, injury, retirement, termination, and so on) or lack of availability. Succession planning is a process in which an organization ensures that it recruits and develops employees to fill each key role within the organization. Clear lines of succession and cross-training in critical functions are key. Organizations also need communications plans for alternative mechanisms of contact, to alert individuals of the need for succession. Such considerations are imperative for meeting recovery time objectives (RTOs) and recovery point objectives (RPOs).

Proper continuity of operations planning should allow for training and tabletop exercises, similar to the tabletop exercise discussed in Chapter 29, "Incident Response Procedures," for incident response. Tabletop exercises involve key personnel participating in an informal, simulated scenario setting. The exercises are conducted to evaluate an organization's capability to execute one or more portions of a business continuity or disaster recovery plan. Tabletop exercises should be conducted on a regular basis to accomplish the following:

▶ Test and evaluate business continuity or disaster recovery policies, as well as procedures to identify plan weaknesses and resource gaps.

▶ Train personnel and clearly define roles and responsibilities to improve performance, communication, and coordination.

▶ Meet regulatory requirements.

A progressive exercise program is made up of gradually more complex exercises, with each one building on the previous one until the exercises are as close to reality as possible. When escalated to a full-scale exercise, this should involve a wide range of organizations, including fire, law enforcement, and emergency management personnel, as well as, when necessary, other entities such as local public health and public safety agencies.

ExamAlert

Any disaster recovery or business continuity plan that involves contingencies, backup and recovery, or succession must include regular testing of restoration and recovery processes. The organization must ensure that personnel can transition and that backup media and procedures can adequately restore lost functionality.

Finally, recall from Chapter 29 that lessons learned plays a key role after incident response. The same applies with continuity of operations. After training exercises and actual events, it is important to debrief and identify what went well and where improvement is needed. Some organizations, particularly government agencies, refer to these as after-action reports. In addition to identifying strengths and weaknesses, these reports should maintain a clear outline of what occurred.

What Next?

If you want more practice on this chapter's exam objectives before you move on, remember that you can access all the Cram Quiz questions on the Pearson Test Prep software. You can also create a custom exam by objective. Note any objective you struggle with and go to that objective material in this chapter.

CHAPTER 32

Controls

This chapter covers the following official Security+ exam objective:

5.7 Compare and contrast various types of controls.

- ▶ Deterrent
- ▶ Preventive
- ▶ Detective
- ▶ Corrective
- ▶ Compensating
- ▶ Technical
- ▶ Administrative
- ▶ Physical

Essential Terms and Components

- ▶ deterrent control
- ▶ preventive control
- ▶ detective control
- ▶ corrective control
- ▶ compensating control
- ▶ administrative control
- ▶ physical control

CramSaver

If you can correctly answer these questions before going through this chapter, save time by skimming the Exam Alerts in this chapter and then completing the Cram Quiz at the end of this part of the book.

1. Name three control types based on their function.

2. What is the difference between a technical preventive control and a management preventive control?

3. What type of control can be used when required controls cannot be put in place?

Answers

1. Functional control types include deterrent, preventive, detective, and corrective.

2. The technical preventive control is a technical system that precludes an attack by inhibiting the use of technical resources. For example, operating system access control could technically limit someone from deleting files. A management preventive control is also preventive, but it is not technical. Instead, it is administrative in nature and relies on processes and procedures. Proper training on the use of operating systems is an example.

3. Mitigating controls can be used when required controls cannot be put in place or when an alternate control is needed.

To compare controls, understanding the general taxonomy of controls is helpful. First, a control is simply a defense or countermeasure put in place to manage risk. Chapter 28, "Risk Management Processes and Concepts," highlighted several strategies for dealing with risk. If a risk cannot be completely avoided or transferred, but the organization is not willing to completely accept the risk, the most appropriate action is to mitigate the risk. Controls can be classified in several ways. Furthermore, some controls can apply across various types. At a high level, controls are classified as technical, management, or operational. Controls can be further classified by their functional use, or according to the time they are acted upon. For example, functionally, they can be classified as deterrent, preventive, detective, or corrective controls.

Nature of Controls

You can apply three general classifications of controls to mitigate risks, typically by layering defensive controls to protect data with multiple control types, when possible. This technique is called a layered defensive strategy, or *defense in depth*. The three types of controls are technical, management, and operational:

▶ **Technical/logical:** Technical controls are security controls put in place that are executed by technical systems. Technical controls include logical access control systems, security systems, encryption, and data classification solutions.

▶ **Management/administrative:** Management or administrative controls include business and organizational processes and procedures, such as security policies and procedures, personnel background checks, security awareness training, and formal change-management procedures. They are usually controlled by and promulgated with people.

▶ **Operational/physical:** Operational controls include organizational culture and physical controls that form the outer line of defense against direct access to data, such as protecting backup media; securing output and mobile file storage devices; and paying attention to facility design details, including layout, doors, guards, locks, and surveillance systems.

Functional Use of Controls

The preceding categories of controls can be further classified by their functional use, or within a phased approached based on the time they are in use. The following section outlines these controls and provides examples of each type of control.

▶ Deterrent

▶ Preventive

▶ Detective

▶ Corrective

Consider the importance of having both detection controls and prevention controls. In a perfect world, we would need only prevention controls. Unfortunately, not all malicious activity can be prevented. As a result, it is important to make detection controls part of a layered security approach. For example, the best protected banks use both detective and preventive controls. In addition to the locks, bars, and security signs, the bank probably has various detection controls, such as motion detectors and cash register audits.

> **ExamAlert**
>
> Controls work together as a security system and provide layered defense mechanisms, for defense in depth.

Deterrent

Deterrent controls are intended to discourage individuals from intentionally violating information security policies or procedures. Deterrents do not necessarily have to be designed to stop unauthorized access. As the name implies, they need to help deter the access. These usually take the form of some type of punishment or consequence that makes performing unauthorized activities undesirable. Deterrence involves detecting violations that are attached to some form of punishment that the intruder fears. Examples of deterrent controls are warnings indicating that systems are being monitored. Perhaps you have seen or know someone who has a "Beware of Dog" sign but doesn't actually have a dog.

Preventive

Preventive controls attempt to avoid unwanted events by inhibiting the free use of computing resources. Preventive controls are often hard for users to accept because they restrict free use of resources. Examples of preventive administrative controls include security awareness, separation of duties, access control, security policies and procedures, intrusion prevention systems, firewalls, and antimalware.

Detective

Physical detective controls warn that physical security measures are being violated. Detective controls attempt to identify unwanted events after they have occurred. Common technical detective controls include audit trails, intrusion detection systems, system monitoring, checksums, and antimalware. Common physical detective controls include motion detectors, CCTV monitors, and alarms. Administrative detective controls are used to determine compliance with security policies and procedures. They can include security reviews and audits, mandatory vacations, and rotation of duties.

Corrective

Corrective controls are reactive and provide measures to lessen harmful effects or restore the system being impacted. Examples of corrective controls include operating system upgrades, data backup restores, vulnerability mitigation, and antimalware.

Did you notice that antimalware is listed among all three types of controls? It is preventive because it can block certain potentially dangerous file types from being downloaded. It is detective because it can identify and alert administrators when a file is infected with malware. Finally, it is corrective because it can quarantine or fix the infected file.

ExamAlert

Some controls can be multiple types. A visible camera, for example, serves as a detection control (if actively monitored) and also a deterrent to a would-be attacker, which makes it preventive as well. Without active monitoring by a security guard, however, cameras are likely useful only for later analysis to identify the actor and means following an incident. Security guards, on the other hand, easily serve as both a preventive and a detective control. In addition, a security guard can be a corrective control, initiating an immediate response to an incident and potentially alerting others about the identified threat.

Compensating Controls

Compensating controls are alternate controls that are intended to reduce the risk of an existing or potential control weakness. Compensating controls are not a shortcut to compliance or security. They come into play when a business or technological constraint exists and an effective alternate control is used in the current security threat landscape. For example, if separation of duties is required but duties cannot be separated because of company size, compensating controls should be in place. These can include audit trails and transaction logs that someone in a higher position reviews.

We need look no further than our daily lives to find examples and analogies of the various types of controls and compensating controls we encounter every day. In your digital life, you might have met someone who doesn't want to incur the cost (monetary and perceived technical) of running antimalware software. That person might compensate, for example, by being extra careful and navigating to only well-known, trusted websites. Or consider parents traveling with a baby but without the normal control of a crib's high rails. Perhaps you can already see the compensating control of the child sleeping in between the parents in bed or among pillows on the floor.

In another practical example, consider that most organizations have well-defined standards for controls that are commensurate with the risk. One such standard might require third-party web-based applications to enforce at least 12-character alphanumeric passwords. If the vendor does not support this, of course, an organization can try to demand it, but until it is a real possibility, the organization can decide not to use that vendor or perhaps consider a temporary exception. This could include, for example, detailed logging and monitoring of session events or frequent password changes.

What Next?

If you want more practice on this chapter's exam objectives before you move on, remember that you can access all the Cram Quiz questions on the Pearson Test Prep software. You can also create a custom exam by objective. Note any objective you struggle with and go to that objective material in this chapter.

CHAPTER 33

Data Security and Privacy Practices

This chapter covers the following official Security+ exam objective:

5.8 Given a scenario, carry out data security and privacy practices.

- ▶ Data destruction and media sanitization
  - ■ Burning
  - ■ Shredding
  - ■ Pulping
  - ■ Pulverizing
  - ■ Degaussing
  - ■ Purging
  - ■ Wiping
- ▶ Data sensitivity labeling and handling
  - ■ Confidential
  - ■ Private

- ■ Public
- ■ Proprietary
- ■ PII
- ■ PHI
- ▶ Data roles
  - ■ Owner
  - ■ Steward/custodian
  - ■ Privacy officer
- ▶ Data retention
- ▶ Legal and compliance

Essential Terms and Components:

- ▶ personally identifiable information (PII)
- ▶ personal health information (PHI)
- ▶ Health Insurance Portability and Accountability Act (HIPAA)
- ▶ General Data Protection Regulation (GDPR)
- ▶ Personal Information Protection and Electronics Document Act (PIPEDA)
- ▶ Payment Card Industry Data Security Standard (PCI DSS)
- ▶ data disposal
- ▶ data sensitivity

CramSaver

If you can correctly answer these questions before going through this chapter, save time by skimming the Exam Alerts in this chapter and then completing the Cram Quiz at the end of this part of the book.

1. How would you dispose of sensitive paper documents at the highest classification? The unauthorized disclosure of this data would cause grave harm to the business.

   _____

2. You have been assigned as the privacy officer for a small insurance company. What type of data should you be concerned with, considering privacy laws within the United States?

   _____

3. Why might you choose to keep or delete personal information being stored but not used?

   _____

Answers

1. Shredding, pulping, pulverizing, and burning are common methods of data destruction. If you chose shredding, you should ensure that the shredder is not so coarse that the documents can be potentially put back together.

2. Regulatory requirements as promulgated by HIPAA protect personal health information (PHI). As the privacy officer, you need to ensure that you are in compliance with all applicable laws and regulations regarding such protected data, including personally identifiable information (PII).

3. Although varying circumstances apply, legal and compliance requirements might dictate a specific duration for retention. On the other hand, pending no requirements, the data needs to be secured. You can reduce your risk and burden by getting rid of the data. You should also consider the risk to the business as it relates to potential opportunities to add value to the business through leveraging the data.

Ensuring the confidentiality, integrity, and availability of data is at the fundamental core of an information security risk management program. Organizations are tasked with many data security and privacy practices that need to be carried out as defined within data handling and data management policies. These data policies are based on organizational requirements and regulatory compliance. Data policies are also used to govern overall IT administrative tasks.

Policies for data protection should include how to classify, handle, store, and destroy data. The important point to remember here is to document your security objectives. Then you can change and adjust that policy when and as needed. You might have a reason to make new classifications as business goals change—just make sure that gets into your documentation. This is an ongoing, ever-changing process.

Data protection scenarios begin with proper classification of the data, based upon the impact of its loss or unauthorized access. Organizational data assets might also fall under legal discovery mandates, so a careful accounting is vital to ensure that data can be located if requested and that it is protected against destruction or recycling. Proper data handling also ensures that data storage media can be properly processed for reuse or disposal when appropriate. Special requirements for sensitive data might require the outright destruction of the storage device and logging of its destruction in the inventory catalog.

Data Sensitivity Labeling and Handling

Information must be classified according to its value and level of sensitivity so that the appropriate level of security can be used and access to data can be controlled. A system of classification should be effective and easy to administer and should be uniformly applied throughout the organization. A common data classification scheme among organizations includes the following classifications:

- ▶ **Public:** Nonsensitive data that has the least, if any, negative impact on the organization. Press releases and marketing material are two common examples.

- ▶ **Proprietary:** Data disclosed outside the organization on a limited basis. Proprietary data often includes information that is exchanged with prospective customers and business partners, for example. Such data is usually protected by a signed nondisclosure agreement (NDA).

- ▶ **Private:** Compartmental data used within a specific division, such as human resources. Typically, private data does not cause the company much damage if it is disclosed, but it should be protected for confidentiality reasons. An example of this type of data is the year-end bonus payout for each employee.

- ▶ **Confidential:** Data that might cause damage to the organization if it were exposed. Confidential data might be widely distributed within an organization, but is typically reserved for employees only and should not be shared outside. Examples might include competitive battle cards and employee training presentations.

▶ **Sensitive:** Data that would have a severe impact to an organization. Sensitive data typically should not be broadly shared internally or externally. Access to sensitive data should be limited and tightly controlled.

The United States government uses a similar classification system, with Top Secret and Secret among the most sensitive classifications. The information in these categories could have grave or severe consequences for national security if it fell into the wrong hands. Keep in mind that data does not necessarily always stay within one classification. Information about a project under consideration might be considered sensitive until the project plans are finalized. At that point, it might require a lesser classification. As another example, consider a publicly traded company's financial reports. Eventually, the company will publicly release its quarterly financial statements. However, while the reports are being gathered and prepared, such data is considered sensitive.

> **ExamAlert**
>
> An NDA should be in place to protect proprietary data that an organization still needs to share with an outside entity.

The preceding discussion focused mainly on the confidentiality of data. However, data classification should also consider the impact upon integrity and availability. For example, data classified as public will likely have no confidentiality implications. However, this does not remove such data from the considerations of integrity and availability. Public financial reports available to the public could certainly have a significant impact on an organization if the integrity of that data is compromised. Furthermore, if the information is not properly made available, this also could have consequences. Similarly, private data needs to be protected for integrity, availability, and confidentiality as well.

> **ExamAlert**
>
> Be sure to consider confidentiality, integrity, and availability in any scenario that involves data classification. Although public data does not require confidentiality, it still might necessitate concern for its integrity and availability.

Understanding and documenting how classifications correlate to security objectives is important. When classifications are established, they should be adhered to and closely monitored, and employees should be trained so that they understand the information classifications. Data classifications can also help when submitting discoverable information that is subject to the Federal Rules of Civil Procedure, if the organization will be involved in a lawsuit.

Privacy Laws and Regulatory Compliance

Particularly in light of various privacy laws regarding sensitive data about individuals, organizations have implemented processes to identify and label data that is potentially subject to such laws and regulations. Two of the most common examples include personally identifiable information (PII) and personal health information (PHI). PII is, broadly, any data that can be used to identify an individual. More specifically, the United States Office of Management and Budget defines PII as "information which can be used to distinguish or trace an individual's identity, such as their name, social security number, biometric records, etc. alone, or when combined with other personal or identifying information which is linked or linkable to a specific individual, such as date and place of birth, mother's maiden name, etc."

To be considered PII, information must be specifically associated with an individual person. Gender and state of residence, for example, don't identify an individual by themselves. Information that is either provided anonymously or not associated with its owner before collection is not considered PII. Unique information, such as a personal profile, a unique identifier, biometric information, and an IP address that is associated with PII, can also be considered PII. The definition of PII is not anchored to any single category of information or technology. An organization must train employees to recognize that non-PII data can become PII data whenever additional information is made publicly available (in any medium and from any source) that, when combined with other available information, could be used to identify an individual. Organizations should require all employees and contractors to complete privacy training annually within a set number of days after the start of employment.

ExamAlert

PII is information about a person that contains some unique identifier from which the identity of the person can be determined. Examples of PII include name, address, phone number, fax number, email address, financial profile, social security number, and credit card information. PII is not limited to these examples and includes any other personal information that is linked or linkable to an individual.

PHI applies to specific organizations that create and collect health information, as covered under the Privacy Rule of the Health Insurance Portability and Accountability Act (HIPAA). HIPAA's Privacy Rule regulates the use and disclosure of PHI for organizations. Organizations must understand their responsibilities regarding such data and also know the practices they must abide by. For example, PHI must be protected for 50 years after the individual's death. In other examples, the Privacy Rule specifically requires that the covered entities abide by the following regarding PHI:

▶ Organizations must disclose PHI to individuals within 30 days, upon request.

▶ Individuals must be notified of uses regarding their PHI.

▶ A patient's written authorization is required before PHI is disclosed for treatment or payment.

▶ Must take reasonable steps to ensure the confidentiality of communications with individuals.

▶ Reasonable efforts must be made to disclose minimal information to achieve its purpose.

▶ Disclosures of PHI must be tracked, and privacy and policy procedures must be documented.

> **Note**
>
> Many other privacy and regulatory requirements affect the safeguarding and handling of personal information. In the United States, examples include the Gramm-Leach-Bliley Act, the Fair Credit Reporting Act, and the Children's Online Privacy Protection Act. Related examples include the General Data Protection Regulation (GDPR) and the Personal Information Protection and Electronic Documents Act (PIPEDA). As of May 2018, GDPR strengthens and unifies data protection for individuals within the European Union. PIPEDA is a Canadian law that governs the collection and use of personal information.

For many organizations, privacy policies are mandatory, have detailed requirements, and carry significant legal penalties for noncompliance. As a result, organizational privacy policies will play a big role in helping to drive compliance. The privacy policy itself must contain the following features:

▶ A list of the categories of PII the operator collects

▶ A list of the categories of third parties with whom the operator might share such PII

▶ A description of the process by which consumers can review and request changes to their PII collected by the operator

▶ A description of the process by which the operator notifies consumers of material changes to the operator's privacy policy

By limiting the collection of personal information to the least amount necessary to conduct business, an organization limits potential negative consequences in case of a data breach involving PII. Organizations should consider the types, categories, and total amount of PII used, collected, and maintained. When PII is no longer relevant or necessary, it should be properly destroyed in accordance with any litigation holds and the Federal Records Act. Organizations should also ensure that retired hardware has been properly sanitized before disposal.

Data Roles

All data in your organization should have assigned data roles. This starts with data ownership. The owner is responsible for determining how much risk to accept. On the surface, data ownership might seem to be a simple matter. However, one look at a transaction that involves third parties proves otherwise. When an employee purchases an airline ticket for business travel, processing intermediaries such as payment systems, ticket processors, and online booking tools assert a right to capture and distribute travel data. These intermediaries might also make data available to third-party aggregators. The question of rightful ownership remains murky. Depending on whom you ask, the data being collected could belong to the organization, the booking agency, or the airline.

The organization must decide who will be permitted to access data and how they will use it. To protect organizational data, when the organization enters any third-party agreement, the topic of data ownership and data aggregation must be addressed.

Some cloud services offer data ownership agreements that specifically identify the data owner and outline ownership of relevant data. When assessing data ownership, especially when the organization is using a cloud provider, consider the following points:

▶ A determination of what is relevant data

▶ Provisions for exercising rights of ownership over the data

▶ Access to the organization's environments

▶ Costs associated with exercising rights of ownership over the data

▶ Contract term and termination conditions

▶ Liability of the cloud provider

Data classification and appropriate data ownership are key elements in an organization's security policy. These concepts must be extended to third-party entities to properly protect data that belongs to the organization. A key component of any security program includes clearly defined roles and responsibilities. Pertaining specifically to the data, you should be familiar with three primary roles:

▶ **Data owner:** This user often is responsible for a specific information asset. This is often a senior person within a department or division. For example, the vice president of Human Resources could be the data owner for all employee data. The data owner is responsible for determining the classification level of the data.

▶ **Data custodian:** The data custodian is responsible for implementing the data classification and security controls, given the classification determined by the data owner. The data custodian is also known as the data steward.

▶ **Privacy officer:** The privacy officer is responsible for legal compliance with data privacy regulations and manages data protection risk that relates to ensuring the proper management of personal and protected information. For example, in addition to the requirements mentioned in the previous section, HIPAA also requires covered entities to designate a privacy officer.

ExamAlert

Data owners determine the level of classification for their data, and the data custodians implement the classification and security controls for the data.

Data Retention and Disposal

Sensitive and privacy-related data (including log files, physical records, security evaluations, and other operational documentation) should be managed within an organization's retention and disposal policies. These should include specifications for access authorization, term of retention, and requirements for disposal. Depending on the relative level of data sensitivity, retention and disposal requirements can become extensive and detailed.

Retention

Industry best practices and laws can also affect the retention and storage of data, log files, and audit logs. For example, in the United States, the Federal Rules of Civil Procedure (FRCP) have implications for data retention policies. They govern the conduct and procedure of all civil actions in federal district courts. Organizations can face issues related to the discovery, preservation, and production of digitally stored information. For example, if an organization is sued by a former employee for wrongful termination, the department might be compelled during the discovery phase of the suit to produce all documents that relate to that individual's work performance. This used to mean personnel records and copies of any written correspondence (such as memos and letters) concerning the performance of that employee. Previously, debate sometimes arose over what a document was, given that most records now reside in electronic format. The FRCP changes establish that electronic data is clearly subject to discovery. It goes further to say that all data is subject to discovery regardless of storage format or location: email, instant messaging, mobile devices, voice mail, and so on all fall under this.

Consideration must be given regarding the burden placed on organizations when they are required to produce data, as well as the economics and advantage of data retained. Consider the Payment Card Industry Data Security Standard (PCI DSS) requirements governing the use and storage of credit card data. An organization that processes and stores credit card data is likely to be subject to these regulations. However, choosing to forego the burden by outsourcing credit card processing and not storing the data could impact personalized business and other value-add services that the company could offer its clients.

Data retention policies should consider the requirements surrounding retention of data. In lieu of any requirements, the policies need to balance the needs for proper safeguarding and potential legal burdens against the value of retaining the data. At a minimum, these policies should clearly describe which data is retained and for how long.

Disposal

Clear policies and procedures should be put into place for properly disposing of data and associated hardware. Such practices should dictate that equipment the organization uses should be disposed of only in accordance with approved procedures, including independent verification that the relevant security risks have been mitigated. Procedures should be in place when disposing of old computer hardware, whether for recycle, disposal, donation, or resale.

The most prominent example of a security risk is a hard drive inside a computer that has not been completely or properly wiped. Some concerns about data erasure sufficiency in new solid-state drives (SSDs) might require organizations to destroy drives instead of simply erasing them for normal disposal channels.

With the secure disposal of equipment, a wide range of scenarios needs to be considered:

▶ Breaches of health and safety requirements

▶ Inadequate disposal planning that results in severe business loss

▶ Remnants of legacy data from old systems that might still be accessible

▶ Disposal of old equipment that is necessary to read archived data

▶ Theft of equipment in use during cleanup of unwanted equipment

Proper disposal of removable media is just as important. Organizations must properly handle removable media when the data should be overwritten or is no longer useful or pertinent to the organization. Generally, all electronic storage media should be sanitized or purged when it is no longer necessary for business use, as well as before its sale, donation, or transfer of ownership. Sanitization and purging is the process of removing the contents from the media as fully as possible, making it extremely difficult (or close to impossible) to restore. The following methods are acceptable for some forms of media sanitation:

▶ **Declassification:** This is a formal process of assessing the risk involved in discarding information.

▶ **Degaussing:** This method uses a tool to reduce or remove the magnetic field of the storage media.

▶ **Wiping:** This method applies to magnetic storage devices. It writes over all data on the media (often multiple times) and destroys what was originally recorded.

▶ **Encryption:** This method requires a strong key, effectively making the data unrecoverable without the key. This process can be combined with crypto shredding by purposely purging the key used to encrypt the data.

▶ **Destruction:** This process physically destroys both the media and the information stored on it. For USB flash drives and other solid-state non-ferric removable storage, this might be the only solution acceptable for certain controls and legal mandates. For paper records, destruction is the only viable option.

> **ExamAlert**
>
> An organization's information sensitivity policy defines the requirements for the classification and security of data and hardware resources, based on their relative level of sensitivity. Some resources, such as hard drives, might require extensive preparations before they can be discarded.

Paper records that contain sensitive information need to be destroyed. In addition to organizational requirements, regulations often have specific rules and recommendations. For example, in addition to electronic PHI, HIPAA requires PHI in paper records to be properly disposed. Methods of media and paper destruction include the following:

▶ **Burning:** Government organizations commonly use this method. Sensitive data is temporarily contained within burn bags and then incinerated.

▶ **Shredding:** This common method involves destruction using blades, with varying degrees of effectiveness. Simple, low-cost solutions present problems because shredded documents sometimes can be reassembled.

▶ **Pulping:** This process dissolves paper, reducing it to its cellulose fibers. Organizations that provide shredding services often later pulp the shredded material to then recycle it.

▶ **Pulverizing:** Special systems that contain rotating hammers crush materials at high speed before passing them through a sizing screen to turn them into tiny particles, even dust.

What Next?

If you want more practice on this chapter's exam objectives before you move on, remember that you can access all the Cram Quiz questions on the Pearson Test Prep software. You can also create a custom exam by objective. Note any objective you struggle with and go to that objective material in this chapter.

PART V
Cram Quiz

These review questions cover material related to Chapters 26–33, which cover objectives falling under Domain 5, "Risk Management," of the Security+ exam.

1. Which of the following policies addresses the need for other employees who can do the job of each employee so that corruption does not occur, and also helps minimize the impact when personnel leave their jobs?

   ○ **A.** Acceptable use

   ○ **B.** Least privilege

   ○ **C.** Mandatory vacations

   ○ **D.** Privacy policy

2. An organization is partnering with another organization that requires shared systems. Which of the following documents outlines how the shared systems will interface?

   ○ **A.** SLA

   ○ **B.** BPA

   ○ **C.** MOU

   ○ **D.** ISA

3. Which of the following are steps an organization can take to be sure compliance and performance standards are met in third-party or partner agreements? (Select two correct answers.)

   ○ **A.** Implement an acceptable use policy

   ○ **B.** Take appropriate action if the relationship presents elevated risk

   ○ **C.** Review third-party arrangements and performance annually

   ○ **D.** Sign a data ownership agreement

4. Which of the following requires users to remove sensitive and confidential materials from workspaces and lock items that are not in use when they leave their workstations?

   ○ **A.** Data handling policy

   ○ **B.** Clean desk policy

○ **C.** Tailgating training

○ **D.** Phishing attack training

5. Which of the following designates the amount of data loss that is sustainable and up to what point in time data recovery could happen before business is disrupted?

○ **A.** RTO

○ **B.** MTBF

○ **C.** RPO

○ **D.** MTTF

6. Eliminating email to avoid the risk of email-borne viruses is an effective solution but is not likely to be a realistic approach for which of the following?

○ **A.** Risk avoidance

○ **B.** Risk transference

○ **C.** Risk acceptance

○ **D.** Risk mitigation

7. Which of the following parties typically are notified first when a confirmed incident has occurred? (Select two correct answers.)

○ **A.** Press

○ **B.** CISO

○ **C.** End users

○ **D.** Legal

8. In which of the following types of analysis might an examiner have difficulty proving that the evidence is original?

○ **A.** Disk-to-image file

○ **B.** Disk-to-disk image

○ **C.** Big data

○ **D.** Log files

9. Which of the following information should be collected when collecting volatile data? (Select all correct answers.)

○ **A.** System date and time

○ **B.** Current network connections

○ **C.** Current open ports and applications listening on those ports

○ **D.** Full disk image

10. Which of the following provides a clear record of the path evidence takes from acquisition to disposal?

   ○ **A.** Video capture

   ○ **B.** Chain of custody

   ○ **C.** Hashes

   ○ **D.** Witness statements

11. Which recovery site has only power, telecommunications, and networking active all the time?

   ○ **A.** Hot site

   ○ **B.** Cold site

   ○ **C.** Warm site

   ○ **D.** Shielded site

12. If an organization takes a full backup every Sunday morning and a daily differential backup each morning, what is the fewest number of backups that must be restored following a disaster on Friday?

   ○ **A.** 1

   ○ **B.** 2

   ○ **C.** 5

   ○ **D.** 6

13. Which one of the following best provides an example of detective controls versus prevention controls?

   ○ **A.** IDS/camera versus IPS/guard

   ○ **B.** IDS/IPS versus camera/guard

   ○ **C.** IPS/camera versus IDS/guard

   ○ **D.** IPS versus guard

14. Which one of the following federal laws addresses privacy, data protection, and breach notification?

   ○ **A.** HIPAA

   ○ **B.** Gramm-Leach-Bliley Act

   ○ **C.** Children's Online Privacy Protection Act

   ○ **D.** All of the above

15. Which of the following individual items are examples of PII? (Choose all correct answers.)

   ○ **A.** Social security number

   ○ **B.** Home address

   ○ **C.** Gender

   ○ **D.** State of residence

16. Which of the following is information that is unlikely to result in a high-level financial loss or serious damage to the organization but whose confidentiality should
still be protected?

   ○ **A.** Public data

   ○ **B.** Confidential data

   ○ **C.** Sensitive data

   ○ **D.** Private data

Cram Quiz Answers

1. **C.** Mandatory vacations addresses the need for other employees who can do the
job of each employee. This helps mitigate corruption and minimizes the impact
when personnel resign from their positions. Answer A is incorrect because an
organization's acceptable use policy provides details specifying what users may
do with their network access. Answer B is incorrect. Least privilege addresses
access rights for user accounts, mandating that only the minimum permissions
necessary to perform work should be assigned to a user. Answer D is incorrect
because privacy policy describes federal and state legislation requiring owners of
commercial websites or online services to post how they collect and protect
personal data.

2. **D.** An interconnection security agreement (ISA) is an agreement between organizations that have connected IT systems. Answer A is incorrect because a service
level agreement (SLA) is a contract between a service provider and a customer
that specifies the nature of the service to be provided and the level of service that
the provider will offer to the customer. Answer B is incorrect because a business
partner agreement (BPA) is a contract that establishes partner profit percentages,
partner responsibilities, and exit strategies for partners. Answer C is incorrect
because a memorandum of understanding (MOU) is a document that outlines the
terms and details of an agreement between parties, including each party's requirements and responsibilities.

3. **B and C.** Some additional steps an organization can take to ensure that compliance and performance standards are met include approving and reviewing third-
party arrangements and performance annually, maintaining an updated list of
all third-party relationships and reviewing the list periodically, taking appropriate
action with any relationship that presents elevated risk, and reviewing all contracts
for compliance with expectations and obligations. Answer A is incorrect because
an acceptable use policy is geared toward terms a user must agree to follow to
be provided with access service. Answer D is incorrect because a data ownership
agreement is an agreement that some cloud service providers offer that specifically identifies the data owner and outlines ownership of relevant data.

4. **B.** A clean desk policy requires users to remove sensitive and confidential materials from workspaces and to also lock items that are not in use when they leave their workstations. Answer A is incorrect because a data handling policy should address legal or regulatory requirements for accessing, transporting, storing, or disposing of data and data storage devices. Answer C is incorrect because tailgating involves following an authorized individual to avoid having to provide personal authorization credentials. Answer D is incorrect because phishing attacks training teaches users to avoid the natural response of opening every email that seems to be coming from family members, a boss, or coworkers.

5. **C.** The recovery point objective (RPO) is the amount of time that can elapse during a disruption before the quantity of data lost during that period exceeds business continuity planning's maximum allowable threshold. Simply put, RPO specifies the allowable data loss. It determines up to what point in time data recovery can happen before business is disrupted. Answer A is incorrect because the recovery time objective (RTO) is the amount of time within which a process must be restored after a disaster to meet business continuity. It defines how much time it takes to recover after notification of process disruption. Answer B is incorrect because mean time between failures (MTBF) is the average amount of time that passes between hardware component failures, excluding time spent waiting for or undergoing repairs. Answer D is incorrect because mean time to failure (MTTF) is the length of time a device or product is expected to last in operation.

6. **A.** Risk avoidance involves eliminating the vulnerability that gives rise to a particular risk so that it is avoided altogether. This is the most effective solution, but is often not possible due to organizational requirements. Answer B is incorrect because risk transference involves either moving the risk to hosted providers who assume the responsibility for recovery and restoration or acquiring insurance to cover the costs from a risk. Answer C is incorrect because risk acceptance involves recognizing a risk, identifying it, and then accepting that it is sufficiently unlikely or of such limited impact that corrective controls are not warranted. Answer D is incorrect because risk mitigation involves reducing the likelihood or impact of a risk's exposure by putting systems and policies into place to mitigate a risk and guard against the exploitation of vulnerabilities.

7. **B and D.** The exact reporting requirements vary among organizations, but parties that are typically notified include the Chief Information Officer (CIO), Chief Information Security Officer (CISO), other internal incident response team members, human resources officers, public affairs personnel, the legal department, and law enforcement officers, when necessary. Answer A is incorrect because the press is not normally notified when an incident occurs. Answer C is incorrect because the users are not normally notified initially when an incident occurs.

8. **C.** Because big data is unstructured and located in diverse environments, the examiner might have difficulty proving that the evidence is original: The data has neither a validating hash nor a forensic image of the device. Answer A is incorrect because disk-to-image files are hashed to prove originality. Answer B is incorrect because disk-to-disk images are hashed to prove originality. Answer D is incorrect because when logs are needed as court evidence, organizations can collect copies of the original log files, the centralized log files, and interpreted log data.

9. **A, B, and C.** The following volatile information should be collected: system date and time, current network connections, current open ports and applications listening on those ports, and applications currently running. Answer D is incorrect because a full disk image is not volatile data.

10. **B.** The chain of custody provides a clear record of the path evidence takes from acquisition to disposal. Answer A is incorrect because videotaping the actual entrance of a forensics team into the area helps refute claims that evidence was planted at the scene. Answer C is incorrect because hashes allow validation that the forensic analysis itself has not produced unexpected modifications of evidentiary data. Answer D is incorrect because witnesses provide statements about what they saw, including when, where, and how.

11. **C.** The warm site has basics such as power, networking, and telecommunications active all the time. Although alternate computers might be present, they are not loaded and operational as in a hot site, making answer A incorrect. Answer B is incorrect because a cold site generally includes only power and physical space when not in use. Answer D is incorrect because any of the recovery site types might or might not be shielded against electromagnetic interference.

12. **B.** With a differential backup scheme, only the last full and last differential backups need to be restored. Therefore, daily full backups would require only the last full backup, making Answer A incorrect in this configuration. Answer C is incorrect because only the last full and last differential backups need to be restored. Answer D is incorrect because six is correct for an incremental backup instead of a differential backup, where the last full backup and all intervening incremental backups must be restored for recovery.

13. **A.** Both IDS and a camera are examples of detective controls. IPS and a guard are examples of prevention controls. Answers B, C, and D are incorrect because they do not properly align the detective control against the prevention control.

14. **D.** Federal laws addressing privacy, data protection, and breach notification include HIPAA and HITECH, the Gramm-Leach-Bliley Act, the Fair Credit Reporting Act, and the Children's Online Privacy Protection Act.

15. **A and B.** Examples of personally identifiable information (PII) are name, address, phone number, fax number, email address, financial profiles, social security number, and credit card information. PII is not limited to these examples: It includes any other personal information that is linked or linkable to an individual. Answers C and D are incorrect because, individually, they are not considered to be PII; only when combined with other information could they become PII.

16. **D.** Private data is information that is unlikely to result in a high-level financial loss or serious damage to the organization but that still should be protected. Answer A is incorrect because the unauthorized disclosure, alteration, or destruction of public data would result in little or no risk to the organization. Answer B is incorrect because confidential information is internal information that defines the way in which the organization operates. Security should be high. Answer C is incorrect because sensitive data is considered confidential data.

PART VI

Cryptography and PKI

> **This part covers the following official CompTIA Security+ SY0-501 exam objectives for Domain 6, "Cryptography and PKI":**
>
> ▶ 6.1 Compare and contrast basic concepts of cryptography.
>
> ▶ 6.2 Explain cryptography algorithms and their basic characteristics.
>
> ▶ 6.3 Given a scenario, install and configure wireless security settings.
>
> ▶ 6.4 Given a scenario, implement public key infrastructure.

For more information on the official CompTIA Security+, SY0-501 exam topics, see the "About the CompTIA Security+, SY0-501 Exam" section in the Introduction.

Cryptography dates to the ancient Assyrians and Egyptians. In the beginning, the systems of cryptography were manually performed. During the twentieth century, machines and mechanical cryptography were born. Both this part and the exam focus on modern cryptography, which began with the advent of the computer.

Today we rely upon modern cryptography in various facets of our lives. Increasing concern involves the security of data, which continues to rapidly grow across information systems and traverses and resides in many different locations. This, combined with more sophisticated attacks and a growing economy around computer-related fraud and data theft, makes the need to protect the data itself even more important than in the past.

One practical way to secure this data is to use cryptography in the form of encryption algorithms applied to data that is passed around networks and to data at rest.

The chapters in this part discuss the concepts of cryptography and look at many popular encryption methods and their applications. In addition to being able to explain these fundamental cryptography concepts, you will begin to understand how cryptography works as a tool to protect and authenticate all types of information, including how this protection applies to systems with no prior contact residing in separate geographical locations.

CHAPTER 34

Cryptography

This chapter covers the following official Security+ exam objective:

6.1 Compare and contrast basic concepts of cryptography.

- ▶ Symmetric algorithms
- ▶ Modes of operation
- ▶ Asymmetric algorithms
- ▶ Hashing
- ▶ Salt, IV, nonce
- ▶ Elliptic curve
- ▶ Weak/deprecated algorithms
- ▶ Key exchange
- ▶ Digital signatures
- ▶ Diffusion
- ▶ Confusion
- ▶ Collision
- ▶ Steganography
- ▶ Obfuscation
- ▶ Stream vs. block
- ▶ Key strength
- ▶ Session keys
- ▶ Ephemeral key
- ▶ Secret algorithm
- ▶ Data-in-transit
- ▶ Data-at-rest

- ▶ Data-in-use
- ▶ Random/pseudo-random number generation
- ▶ Key stretching
- ▶ Implementation vs. algorithm selection
  - ▪ Crypto service provider
  - ▪ Crypto modules
- ▶ Perfect forward secrecy
- ▶ Security through obscurity
- ▶ Common use cases
  - ▪ Low power devices
  - ▪ Low latency
  - ▪ High resiliency
  - ▪ Supporting confidentiality
  - ▪ Supporting integrity
  - ▪ Supporting obfuscation
  - ▪ Supporting authentication
  - ▪ Supporting non-repudiation
  - ▪ Resource vs. security constraints

Essential Terms and Components

▶ symmetric key
▶ asymmetric key
▶ encryption algorithm
▶ cipher
▶ cryptographic module
▶ cryptography
▶ hash value
▶ hashing
▶ key exchange
▶ key management
▶ message digest
▶ private key
▶ public key
▶ steganography
▶ digital certificate
▶ salt
▶ initialization vector (IV)

▶ diffusion
▶ confusion
▶ obfuscation
▶ stream cipher
▶ block cipher
▶ session keys
▶ key stretching
▶ cryptographic module
▶ perfect forward secrecy
▶ key derivation function
▶ security through obscurity
▶ encryption
▶ decryption
▶ ephemeral key
▶ stream cipher
▶ block cipher

CramSaver

If you can correctly answer these questions before going through this chapter, save time by skimming the Exam Alerts in this chapter and then completing the Cram Quiz at the end of this part of the book.

1. What are the differences between symmetric and asymmetric cryptography?

   _____

2. What is the fundamental difference between a block cipher and a stream cipher?

   _____

Answers

1. Symmetric cryptography uses a shared key; asymmetric cryptography uses different, mathematically related keys. Symmetric key cryptography is more efficient, yet asymmetric cryptography helps overcome the challenges associated with key management and key distribution.

2. Block ciphers operate on a fixed-length group of bits, which are called blocks. The resulting cipher text corresponds to the input length. Stream ciphers are more efficient and plain-text bits are encrypted one at a time.

A cryptosystem or cipher system provides a method for protecting information by disguising it in a format that only authorized systems or individuals can read. The use and creation of such systems is called cryptography. Cryptography involves turning plain text into cipher text (encryption), and then cipher text into plain text (decryption). More specifically, encryption protects confidentiality and safeguards data integrity.

Related to cryptography, an *algorithm* is the mathematical procedure or sequence of steps taken to perform the encryption and decryption. Practically speaking, you can think of an algorithm as a cooking recipe, with the ingredients needed and step-by-step instructions. These algorithms are used in conjunction with a key to encrypt and decrypt. Combined, the process of encryption is based upon the following two important principles:

▶ **Confusion:** The plain-text input should be significantly changed in the resulting cipher text. More technically, each bit of the resulting cipher text should depend on numerous parts of the key. This hides any connection between the two, making it difficult to reverse from cipher text to plain text without the key.

▶ **Diffusion:** If the plain text is changed, no matter how minor, then at least half of the cipher text should also change, and vice versa. As in confusion, diffusion makes things more difficult for an attacker. Specifically, diffusion mitigates the capability to identify patterns that might help break the cipher.

Keys

Cryptographic algorithms and keys work together. These keys determine the output of a cryptographic algorithm and consist of a random string of bits. Keys used in cryptography provide for secrecy. In fact, a principle known as Kerckhoff's principle (from the nineteenth century) states that "only secrecy of the key provides security." This is particularly important in relation to the associated algorithms. The algorithm itself does not need to be (and should not be) kept secret. Depending on the type of algorithm used, either the same key is used for both encryption and decryption, or else different yet mathematically related keys are used.

Keys also need to be of an appropriate *key strength* or length to prevent against a brute force attack. Key size is expressed by the number of bits in the key used by the algorithm. The longer the key, the more difficult it is to crack the key. When keys are generated, they need to be done so in a way that contains enough entropy or randomness. Modern cryptography relies upon random numbers. *Pseudo-random numbers* however, are commonly used. This process appears to be random, at least statistically, but is not truly so. An *initialization vector* (IV) is a fixed-size input of a random or pseudo-random value. Within cryptography, an IV, for example, helps ensure that each message encrypts differently. You would not want the same message, encrypted with the same key, to have the same resulting cipher text. A *nonce* can also be used as an IV. A nonce is a random or pseudo-random number that used only once and associated with a time stamp. A nonce is more common with authentication protocols to ensure that older authentication messages cannot be reused.

Passwords are often thought of as keys because they act as such. For example, a password might be needed before encrypting a document. At least in reliable cryptographic systems, the password is used as an input to a key derivation function (KDF), which is used to derive the actual key based on the password as just the origin point. Additional random data can be applied or a *key stretching* technique can be used. An eight-character password contains only 64 bits. Key stretching runs the password through an algorithm to produce an enhanced key, usually at least 128 bits long.

In most instances, keys are static and used repeatedly up to a year or even longer. In other cases, keys are used only for a single session. This type of key is known as an ephemeral key. Ephemeral keys are common to ephemeral key agreement protocols, which the next chapter covers.

Key Exchange

An important concept in any discussion of encryption is understanding the importance of key exchange. Historically, the challenge is that, to get a secret, you must share a secret. Consider a simple analogy of a password as the key. Imagine that you are friends with a kid who requires the secret password to gain secret access. Perhaps that password is "open sesame." The problem is, at some point, that secret password has to be shared with you. This process is likely not going to be secure and will be subject to eavesdropping. It could even be whispered to you, but that is still subject to eavesdropping. Even in this scenario, the challenge is that you have to meet face to face. Regardless, you will likely receive the key "out of band," not when you are waiting at the door to gain entry.

Modern cryptography solves this age-old challenge of key exchange. Exchanging keys in many applications happens securely "in band" when you need to establish a secure session. Any type of out-of-band key exchange relies on having shared in advance—that is, the key is delivered outside the network or process from which it will actually be used.

Symmetric Algorithms

Symmetric key cryptography is a system that uses a common shared key between the sender and receiver. The primary advantages of such a system are that it is easier to implement than an asymmetric system and also typically is faster. However, the two parties must first somehow exchange the key securely. Assume, for example, that you have a friend located thousands of miles away from you. To exchange secure messages, you send messages back and forth in a secure lockbox; you both have a copy of the key to the lockbox. This works, but how do you securely deliver the key to your friend? Somehow the key must have been communicated or delivered to your friend, which introduces additional challenges of logistics and ways to ensure that the key is not compromised in the process. Asymmetric cryptography helps overcome these challenges.

Now imagine a system in which more than two parties are involved. In this scenario, every party participating in communications must have the exact same key to compare the information. If the key is compromised at any point, guaranteeing a secure connection is impossible.

> **Note**
>
> Symmetric key algorithms are often referred to as secret key algorithms, private key algorithms, and shared secret algorithms.

Even given the possible risks involved with symmetric key encryption, the method is used often today mainly because of its simplicity and easy deployment. In addition, this is generally considered a strong encryption method if the source and destination that house the key information are kept secure.

> **ExamAlert**
>
> A symmetric key is a single cryptographic key used with a secret key (symmetric) algorithm. The symmetric key algorithm uses the same private key for both operations of encryption and decryption.

Symmetric encryption uses two primary types of methods for encrypting plain-text data:

- ▶ **Stream cipher:** The plain-text bits are encrypted a single bit at a time. These bits are also combined with a stream of pseudo-random characters. Stream ciphers are known for their speed and simplicity.

- ▶ **Block cipher:** Plain text is encrypted in blocks, which is a fixed-length group of bits. The block of plain text is encrypted into a corresponding block of cipher text. For example, a 64-bit block of plain text would output as a 64-bit block of cipher text. Because most plain text does not fit within the precise block size, leftover text is padded to complete the block.

Block ciphers can be further described by their *mode of operation*. Because block ciphers encrypt based on the specified block size, the mode of operation defines how the cipher is continually applied to encrypt data larger than the specific block size.

Most block cipher modes require an initialization vector (IV), a fixed-size input of a random or pseudo-random value. Within cryptography, an IV helps ensure that each message encrypts differently. You do not want the same message, encrypted with the same key, to have the same resulting cipher text.

Table 34.1 outlines the differences between block ciphers and stream ciphers.

TABLE 34.1 A Comparison of Block Ciphers and Stream Ciphers

Block Cipher	Stream Cipher
Encryption performed on a fixed-length block of plain text (for example, 128 bits)	Encryption performed bit by bit
More complex and not as fast	High performance, requiring fewer resources
Requires padding to complete a block	Does not require padding because each bit is processed and is the smallest unit
High diffusion	Low diffusion
Less susceptible to malicious insertions	Susceptible to malicious insertions
Most symmetric algorithms are block ciphers	Block ciphers can operate in modes, essentially making them stream ciphers
A single error can corrupt an entire block	A single error in a bit not likely to affect subsequent bits

Asymmetric Algorithms

An asymmetric encryption algorithm has two keys: a public key and a private key. The public key is made available to whomever will encrypt the data sent to the holder of the private key. The private key is maintained on the host system or application. Often the public encryption key is made available in a number of ways, such as email or centralized servers that host a pseudo-address book of published public encryption keys. One challenge, however, is ensuring the authenticity of the public key. To address this, a public key infrastructure (PKI) is often used. A PKI uses trusted third parties that certify or provide proof of key ownership (see Chapter 37, "Public Key Infrastructure"). Figure 34.1 illustrates the asymmetric encryption process.

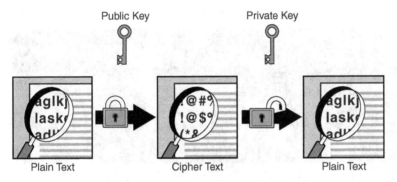

FIGURE 34.1   **An Example of Asymmetric Encryption**

Asymmetric algorithms are often referred to as public key algorithms because they use the public key as the focal point for the algorithm.

As an example of asymmetric encryption, think about the secure exchange of an email. When someone wants to send a secure email to someone else, he or she obtains the target user's public encryption key and encrypts the message using this key. Because the message can be unencrypted only with the private key, only the target user can read the information held within. Ideally, for this system to work well, everyone should have access to everyone else's public keys. Refer again to Figure 34.1. Note that the public key and the private key shown both belong to the recipient. The key difference is that anyone can use the public key to encrypt; only that person with the private key (that is, the recipient) can decrypt.

Imagine a postal mailbox that enables the letter carrier to insert your mail via an open slot, but only you have the key to get the mail out. This is analogous to an asymmetric system. The open slot is the public key. If you are concerned about the security of your mail, this is much easier than ensuring that every letter carrier has a copy of your mailbox key. The letter carrier is also thankful he or she is not required to carry hundreds of different keys to complete mail delivery.

Keep the following points in mind regarding keys in asymmetric encryption:

▶ **Public keys encrypt and private keys decrypt:** For example, Alice can encrypt a message with Bob's public key. Bob decrypts the message with his private key, which only he has.

▶ **Private keys sign and public keys verify signatures:** For example, Alice signs the message with her private key. Bob verifies the message's signature with Alice's public key.

ExamAlert

Some general rules for asymmetric algorithms include the following:

▶ The public key can never decrypt a message that it was used to encrypt with.

▶ With proper design, public keys should never be able to determine private keys.

▶ Each key should be capable of decrypting a message made with the other. For instance, if a message is encrypted with the private key, the public key should be able to decrypt it.

Public key encryption has proven useful on networks such as the Internet. This is primarily because the public key is all that needs to be distributed. Because nothing harmful can be done with the public key, it is useful over unsecured networks where data can pass through many hands and is vulnerable to interception and abuse. Symmetric encryption works fine over the Internet, too, but the limitations on providing the key securely to everyone who requires it can be difficult. In addition, asymmetric key systems can verify digital signatures, which provide assurance that communications have not been altered and that the communication arrived from an authorized source.

ExamAlert

In an asymmetric key system, each user has a pair of keys: a private key and a public key. Sending an encrypted message requires you to encrypt the message with the recipient's public key. The recipient then decrypts the message with his or her private key.

Elliptic Curve and Quantum Cryptography

Two other cryptosystems are *elliptic curve* cryptography (ECC) and still-emerging quantum cryptography. ECC is a public-key cryptosystem based on complex mathematical structures. ECC uses smaller key sizes than traditional public-key cryptosystems. As a result, it is faster and consumes fewer resources, making it more ideal for mobile and wireless devices.

Unlike elliptic curves and other cryptosystems, quantum cryptography does not rely on mathematics. Instead, it relies on physics. Although this cryptosystem is slower, its primary advantage is increased security. Quantum mechanics protects against data disturbance because no one can measure the quantum state of the photons. The mere observation of a quantum system changes the system.

> **ExamAlert**
>
> Elliptic curve cryptography is an example of an asymmetric public-key cryptosystem. It is often used for mobile and wireless devices.

Session Keys

Session keys, sometimes called *symmetric keys*, are a randomly generated keys to perform both encryption and decryption during the communication of a session between two parties. They are described as being symmetric because the key is used for both encryption and decryption. When a session key is generated, the key is valid only during that one communication session. As a result, you can think of a session key as being temporary, for one-time use.

Session keys are deleted after the communication ends, but the key exchange mechanism used to establish these keys (most notably, RSA) often relies on a private key. This can be the web server's private key, which is used to establish a secure session with the client. Although this is efficient, the challenge is that gaining access to the server's private key allows an adversary to decrypt the communications. The benefit, however, is that organizations can use this private key so that security systems (for example, IDS and web application firewalls) have visibility into the traffic.

This method of obtaining a symmetric key for a session completely depends on the secrecy of the private key. Because of this, *perfect forward secrecy* (PFS), or just forward secrecy, provides a mechanism to prevent the compromise of a private key used to create new session keys from past session keys that were compromised. As a result, PFS eliminates the vulnerability where a compromised private key can be used to go back and decrypt all previous key exchange conversations. This is important because with a decrypted key exchange, previously used encryption keys could then be retrieved to reveal entire transactions or messages.

This method gained popularity in 2013, as revelations about government monitoring became public. It made mainstream news when Twitter announced that it would adopt forward secrecy to protect recorded traffic from potentially being decrypted later.

Nonrepudiation and Digital Signatures

Nonrepudiation is intended to provide, through encryption, a method of accountability that makes it impossible to refute the origin of data. It guarantees that the sender cannot later deny being the sender and that the recipient cannot deny receiving the data. This definition, however, does not factor into the possible compromise of the workstation or system used to create the private key and the encrypted digital signature. The following list outlines four key elements that nonrepudiation services provide on a typical client/server connection:

▶ **Proof of origin:** The host gets proof that the client is the originator of particular data or an authentication request from a particular time and location.

▶ **Proof of submission:** The client gets proof that the data (or authentication, in this case) has been sent.

▶ **Proof of delivery:** The client gets proof that the data (or authentication, in this case) has been received.

▶ **Proof of receipt:** The client gets proof that the data (or authentication, in this case) has been received correctly.

Digital signatures provide integrity and authentication. In addition, digital signatures provide nonrepudiation with proof of origin. Although authentication and nonrepudiation might appear to be similar, the difference is that, with non-repudiation, proof can be demonstrated to a third party.

A sender of a message signs a message using his or her private key. This provides unforgeable proof that the sender did indeed generate the message. Nonrepudiation is unique to asymmetric systems because the private (secret) key is not shared. Remember that, in a symmetric system, both parties involved share the secret key; therefore, any party can deny sending a message by claiming that the other party originated the message.

Digital signatures attempt to guarantee the identity of the person sending the data from one point to another. The digital signature acts as an electronic signature used to authenticate the identity of the sender and to ensure the integrity of the original content (to ensure that it has not been changed).

> **Note**
>
> Do not confuse a digital signature with a digital certificate (Chapter 37 has further details). In addition, do not confuse digital signatures with encryption. Digital signatures and encryption use related concepts, but their intentions and operations differ significantly. Finally, do not confuse a digital signature with the block of identification information that is often appended to an email, such as the sender's name and telephone number or digitally created image.

Digital signatures can easily be transported and are designed so that no one else can copy them. This ensures that something signed cannot be repudiated.

A digital signature does not have to accompany an encrypted message. It can simply be used to assure the receiver of the sender's identity and confirm that the message's integrity was maintained. The digital signature contains the digital signature of the certificate authority (CA) that issued the certificate for verification.

The point of this verification is to prevent or alert the recipient to any data tampering. Ideally, if a packet of data is digitally signed, it can bear only the original mark of the sender. If this mark differs, the receiver knows that the packet differs from what it is supposed to be, and either the packet is not unencrypted or it is dropped altogether. This works based on the encryption algorithm principles discussed previously. If you cannot determine what the original data was in the encrypted data (in this case, the signature), faking the data and convincing the receiver that it is legitimate data is much harder.

Suppose, for example, that you need to digitally sign a document sent to your stockbroker. You need to ensure the integrity of the message and assure the stockbroker that the message is really from you. The exchange looks like this:

1. You type the email.

2. Using software built in to your email client, you obtain a hash (which you can think of as digital fingerprint) of the message.

3. You use your private key to encrypt the hash. This encrypted hash is your digital signature for the message.

4. You send the message to your stockbroker.

5. Your stockbroker receives the message. Using software, he makes a hash of the received message.

6. The stockbroker uses your public key to decrypt the message hash.

7. A match of the hashes proves that the message is valid.

Hashing

A *hash* is a generated summary from a mathematical rule or algorithm, commonly used as a "digital fingerprint" to verify the integrity of files and messages. Hashing ensures message integrity and provides authentication verification. In other words, hashing algorithms are not encryption methods, but they offer additional system security via a "signature" for data to confirm the original content.

Hash functions work by taking a string (for example, a password or email) of any length and producing a fixed-length string for output. Keep in mind that hashing works one-way. Although you can create a hash from a document, you cannot re-create the document from the hash. If this all sounds confusing, the following example should help clear things up. Suppose that you want to send an email to a friend, and you also want to ensure that, during transit, it cannot be read or altered. You use software that generates a hash value of the message to accompany the email and then encrypts both the hash and the message. After receiving the email, the recipient's software decrypts the message and the hash, and then produces another hash from the received email. The two hashes are compared, and a match indicates that the message was not tampered with. (Any change in the original message produces a change in the hash.)

Password hashes can use a *salt*, an additional input of random data to a function that hashes a password. This salting, as it is known, helps defend against specific attacks in which hashed values are precomputed. Some of the attacks mentioned here work because users who have the same password would also have the same resulting hash. This problem can be overcome by making the hashes more random. Salting uses a prefix consisting of a random string of characters to passwords before they are hashed. Such a countermeasure makes it more difficult or impractical to attack passwords unless the attacker knows the value of the salt that needs to be removed.

Cryptographic hashes are susceptible to collisions and, thus, *collision* attacks. Recall the example in Chapter 1, "Indicators of Compromise and Malware Types," about the birthday attack used to find collisions within hash functions. Such an attack tries to find two input strings of a hash function that have the same output. Although collisions are not likely, they can occur because hash functions produce a predefined output length, despite taking in an infinite input length.

Use of Proven Technologies and Implementation

Because of the sensitive nature of cryptography, using well-known, proven technologies is crucial. Backdoors and flaws, for example, can undermine any encryption algorithm. Vendors might have their own encryption solutions, and most of these depend on well-known, time-tested algorithms; you should be skeptical of any vendor using a proprietary unproven algorithm.

Recall from earlier that Kerckhoff's principle states that a cryptosystem should be secure even if everything about the system is known except for the key. Proven technologies are well-designed cryptosystems. Systems that require keeping the algorithms secret not only introduce additional measures related to what needs to be protected, but often are referred to as *security through obscurity*.

In addition to avoiding *secret algorithms*, or "snake oil" cryptography, be sure to steer clear of *weak or deprecated algorithms*. Even once-proven technologies can weaken over time. Only algorithms that are public and have been thoroughly reviewed and approved should be used. The National Institute of Standards and Technology (NIST) maintains publications and guidance for the use of approved cryptographic and hashing algorithms. The following is a summary of this and other good practices:

▶ Use well-known and approved cryptographic algorithms.

▶ Adhere to required minimum key guidance for the chosen algorithm.

▶ Use approved cryptographic modes.

▶ Use strong random number generators.

NIST's Federal Information Publication Standard 140-2 (FIPS 140-2) covers the secure design and implementation of cryptographic modules, and NIST provides a program to validate such modules to this standard. Cryptographic modules, or cryptographic service providers (CSPs), are the hardware, software, or firmware that implements cryptographic functions such as encryption, decryption, digital signature, random number generation, authentication, and key management.

Applications and systems can interface with these secure cryptographic modules, helping to ensure a sound implementation based on vetted and sound cryptographic modules. Many modules, however, provide varying security levels and options, particularly because different algorithms can be encapsulated within the module. Thus, consideration must be given to algorithm selection and the application, to ensure an appropriate level of security. For example, a cryptography algorithm based on factoring and prime numbers uses more bits for keys than cryptography based on the algebraic structure of elliptic curves. As a result, the former requires compute resources, which makes the latter more ideal for mobile devices.

Obfuscation

Obfuscation is the act of making something difficult to understand. Obfuscation relies upon mechanisms that are not known or widely discovered. Obfuscation is likened to the phrase "security through obscurity." The words *obfuscation* and *obscurity* share Latin origins and tend to carry a negative connotation. However, particularly in software engineering and when layered with other controls, security through obscurity can provide value, depending upon the situation. Still, it's generally accepted that organizations should not rely solely on obfuscation or obscurity. As you see in the next chapter, obfuscation techniques do play an important role in accepted cryptographic algorithms. Again, however, they play a *part* and should not be relied upon by themselves.

As with encryption, obfuscation can use an algorithm. The key difference here is the key. Encoding data, for example, is the process of transforming data from one form into another form using a known algorithm so that it can be reversed easily—no key is required. Obfuscation techniques are generally similar. They use an algorithm without a key, but the obscurity depends on the algorithm being not known or available to others. Did you ever speak in pig Latin or another made-up language as a youth (or perhaps as an adult with young children)? The success of your ability to communicate secretly depended on only you and your partner knowing the algorithm, and hopefully no one else.

A common used method of obfuscating data, particularly within media types such as audio and image files, and other documents, is *steganography*.

Steganography is a word of Greek origin that means "hidden writing." It involves hiding messages so that unintended recipients are not even aware of any message. Compare this to cryptography, which does not seek to hide the fact a message exists—cryptography just makes the message unreadable by anyone other than the intended recipients. Writing a letter using plain text but in invisible ink is an example of steganography. The content is not scrambled in any way; it is just hidden. Another interesting example, albeit a bit cumbersome, is the historical use of writing a secret message on the scalp of one's bald head, allowing the hair to grow back, and then ultimately having it shaved again upon arrival at the intended recipient.

> **ExamAlert**
>
> Steganography and other obfuscation techniques are not cryptography. For example, steganography hides the presence of a message, whereas the purpose of cryptography is to transform a message from its readable plain text into an unreadable form known as cipher text.

Of course, steganography is useless if someone other than the intended recipient knows where to look. Therefore, steganography is best used when combined with encryption. If attackers do not even know the message exists in the first place, they cannot attempt to crack it. As a result, steganography is not just the stuff of child's play or far-fetched spy movies.

Steganography actually entered mainstream media after the terrorist attacks of 9/11. Various reports indicated that the terrorists were (and others still are) using this practice to secretly hide messages. Modern uses include hiding messages in digital media and using digital watermarking. In addition, printers have used steganography, using tiny dots that reveal serial numbers and time stamps.

Use Cases

Cryptography has many potential use cases. The following are common examples:

- ▶ **Confidentiality:** Ensures the privacy of data. This is the most common use case, or at least the one that many tend to think of during discussions on cryptography.

- ▶ **Integrity:** Ensures the accuracy of the data. Hashing, discussed earlier, is a common mechanism to ensure integrity. Assurance of message integrity, for example, might apply regardless of whether a message was encrypted.

▶ **Nonrepudiation:** Ensures accountability so that the origin of the data cannot be refuted. Nonrepudiation is needed to affirm the authenticity of a digital signature and verify that a message was indeed sent by the originator.

▶ **Authentication:** Ensures the secure transfer of authentication data between two entities or systems. Cryptographic authentication protocols are required here. Additionally, encryption and authentication work together. Both have their own responsibilities when it comes to securing communications and data.

Protecting data through encryption and yet maintaining the capability for decryption can be broadly categorized into three high-level areas, based on the state of the data:

▶ **Data at rest:** Represents data in its stored or resting state, which is typically on some type of persistent storage such as a hard drive or tape.

▶ **Data in transit:** Represents data moving across a network or from one system to another. Data in transit is also commonly known as data in motion.

▶ **Data in use:** Represents data being processed in memory or cache. It includes the presentation of data, such as that on a monitor.

ExamAlert

Cryptography supports the confidentiality and integrity of data across several states, such as at rest, in transit, and in use.

The distinctions can be blurred, particularly when talking about data at rest and data in use. This has led some to refer to data in use as being "active data," and further defining data at rest as being in one of potentially two substates. Data at rest is static, in that it is inactive and does not change, such as in archives. Data at rest is constant or inactive yet does occasionally change. Consider a simple example for the three states. This chapter is an unstructured document on my laptop. When I turn off my laptop, the document is encrypted because I have full-disk encryption that protects the entire contents of my hard drive. This is data-at-rest encryption. When I arrive at the coffee shop to continue completing this chapter, the document is decrypted and is now considered data in use. After I have completed the chapter, I will send the document via upload to a file repository or through email. The transport mechanism I use, such as HTTPS or FTPS, provides transport layer encryption. This is data-in-transit encryption.

You may have noticed that the document was not encrypted while in use. Encryption of data in use is difficult to achieve, and this is typically reserved for specific situations to meet certain requirements. For example, data-in-use encryption is better suited to structured data, such as fields within a database. Certainly, maintaining the referential integrity a database requires is not trivial, but there are methods (often involving other security or usability tradeoffs) to encrypt data or protect data through a means other than encryption, such as through tokenization (assigning a random surrogate value with no mathematical relationship).

Other specific use cases, or certainly needs, continue to exist. Although it is considered not secure on its own, obfuscation is commonly used with encryption. This includes, for example, first encrypting the obfuscated data. A primary use case for obfuscation without encryption involves trying to protect source code from reverse engineering. Further research in combining obfuscation and encryption to protect source code continues.

Strong cryptographic implementations demonstrate resiliency to leakage and subsequent attacks, but research and development into highly resilient cryptography or leakage-resilient cryptography is continuing. For example, the physical implementation of cryptographic algorithms could leak information (for example, electromagnetic and power consumption), which can be leveraged to break the system.

Resource Constraints

Security systems are often about managing and making appropriate tradeoffs. Cryptography, for example, consumes additional resources in a system and carries a cost. Modern computer systems and algorithms work well together. Furthermore, cryptographic implementations have made management easier. In fact, several sources have recently reported that more than half of the web is now encrypted using HTTPS. When it comes to modern cryptography, performance and security have always been two important factors. Simply put, how is it possible to increase the security robustness of an algorithm or system without sacrificing speed and introducing more latency? More recently, especially with smaller and lower-power devices, the tradeoffs and resource constraints are continually being considered in the search for lighter-weight cryptography. A few factors need to be considered:

▶ Security

▶ Performance

▶ Power

Particularly with the advent of the Internet of Things (IoT), an increasing number of smart objects now require low power, including ones using radio frequency tags. These devices require the same security demands, but are at odds with strong cryptography usually requiring significant amounts of resources. Or consider embedded cryptography, such as chips with integrated circuits on smart cards and credit cards. Essentially, these are tiny computers with a limited area, capable of performing limited cryptographic functions. Research in these areas and the evolution of secure ciphers will continue to seek to sustain high levels of security while minimizing latency and meeting power and surface area requirements.

What Next?

If you want more practice on this chapter's exam objectives before you move on, remember that you can access all the Cram Quiz questions on the Pearson Test Prep software. You can also create a custom exam by objective. Note any objective you struggle with and go to that objective material in this chapter.

CHAPTER 35

Cryptography Algorithms

This chapter covers the following official Security+ exam objective:

6.2 Explain cryptography algorithms and their basic characteristics.

- ▶ Symmetric algorithms
  - AES
  - DES
  - 3DES
  - RC4
  - Blowfish/Twofish
- ▶ Cipher modes
  - CBC
  - GCM
  - ECB
  - CTM
  - Stream vs. block
- ▶ Asymmetric algorithms
  - RSA
  - DSA
  - Diffie-Hellman
- ▶ Groups

- ▶ DHE
- ▶ ECDHE
  - Elliptic curve
  - PGP/GPG
- ▶ Hashing algorithms
  - MD5
  - SHA
  - HMAC
  - RIPEMD
- ▶ Key stretching algorithms
  - BCRYPT
  - PBKDF2
- ▶ Obfuscation
  - XOR
  - ROT13
  - Substitution ciphers

Essential Terms and Components

- Advanced Encryption Standard (AES)
- Data Encryption Standard (DES)
- Rivest Cipher (RC)
- Blowfish
- Twofish
- counter mode
- cipher block chaining (CBC)
- Galois/Counter Mode (GCM)
- Electronic Codebook (ECB)
- elliptic curve cryptography (ECC)
- RSA algorithm
- Diffie-Hellman key exchange (D-H)
- Diffie-Hellman Ephemeral (DHE)
- Elliptic Curve Diffie-Hellman Ephemeral (ECDHE)
- El Gamal

- Digital Signature Algorithm (DSA)
- Pretty Good Privacy (PGP)
- GNU Privacy Guard (GPG)
- Secure Hash Algorithm (SHA)
- Message Digest Algorithm
- RACE Integrity Primitives Evaluation Message Digest (RIPEMD)
- message authentication code (MAC)
- hash-based message authentication code (HMAC)
- Password-Based Key Derivation Function 2 (PBKDF2)
- Bcrypt
- XOR
- ROT13

CramSaver

If you can correctly answer these questions before going through this chapter, save time by skimming the Exam Alerts in this chapter and then completing the Cram Quiz at the end of this part of the book.

1. What technique encodes ABCDEFGHIJKLM as NOPQRSTUVWXYZ, and vice versa?

   _____

2. Name at least three symmetric algorithms and three asymmetric algorithms.

   _____

3. PBKDF2 and Bcrypt are examples of what?

   _____

Answers

1. ROT13 rotates each letter by 13 places. The shift of half the 26 letters in the alphabet makes ROT13 simple to encode and decode.

2. The most common symmetric algorithms include DES, 3DES, AES, Blowfish, Twofish, and RC4. Common asymmetric algorithms include RSA, D-H, DHE, ECDHE, El Gamal, and DSA.

3. PBKDF2 and Bcrypt are key derivation functions that are known for their capability to perform key stretching.

Cryptographic algorithms can broadly be divided into the following three groups: symmetric, asymmetric, and hash functions. Cryptosystems are made up of a combination of these algorithms, providing capabilities to ensure confidentiality and integrity. Be sure that you understand the differences in the various algorithms and their operations so that you select strong and appropriate cryptosystems.

Obfuscation Techniques

Before diving into the details of cryptographic algorithms, it's worth exploring means of obfuscation. Recall from the last chapter that obfuscation by itself usually doesn't provide strong security. However, obfuscation techniques play a role in many of the algorithms used.

The first cryptographic cipher learned is often some type of *substitution cipher*. Chapter 2, "Attack Types," gave an example in which the letter *a* was substituted for the letter *b*, and *b* for *c*, and so on. ROT13 (rotate by 13 places) is an example of such a cipher. Keep in mind that although ROT13 has found its way into even modern applications, it does not provide any cryptographic security. With the shift of 13, each letter is encoded 13 places. For example, the letter *A* then becomes the letter *N*. A unique aspect of ROT13 is that the number 13 is half the number of letters in the alphabet. This inverse nature makes it simple to encode and decode (see Figure 35.1).

FIGURE 35.1 **ROT13 Substitution Cipher**

Another simple cipher with valuable application to modern cryptography is *XOR* (exclusive or). In this next example, *ABCD* is converted to its ASCII binary equivalent, and XOR is applied using all 1s.

01000001 01000010 01000011 01000100

11111111 11111111 11111111 11111111

101111110 101111101 101111100 101111011

The result (in bold) demonstrates that a "true" value (the number 1) is derived only when the two comparisons are mutually *exclusive*. They are exclusive *or* they are not—in which case, the output is false (the number 0). Despite the lack of confusion and diffusion, this type of streaming operation is commonly used with advanced cryptographic algorithms, where pseudo-random numbers are used in place of the string of ones in the preceding example. The XOR operation usually comes before or follows another encryption operation. Because XOR works bit by bit in a stream, it lends itself well to working with different cryptographic modes of operations, to turn block ciphers into stream ciphers.

Symmetric Algorithms

The last chapter introduced you to the concept of symmetric key encryption, in which the sender and receiver use a common shared key or identical key. Symmetric algorithms can be classified as either block ciphers or stream ciphers. As the name implies, a stream cipher encrypts the message bit by bit, one at a time. A block cipher encrypts the message in chunks.

Several symmetric key algorithms are in use today. The more commonly used algorithms include the following:

▶ **Data Encryption Standard (DES):** *DES* was adopted for use by the National Institute of Standards and Technology (NIST) in 1977. DES is a block cipher that uses a 56-bit key and 8 bits of parity on each 64-bit chunk of data. Although it is considered a strong algorithm, it is limited in use because of its relatively short key length limit.

▶ **Triple Data Encryption Standard (3DES):** *3DES*, also known as Triple DES, dramatically improves on DES by using the DES algorithm three times with three distinct keys. This provides a total bit strength of 168 bits. 3DES superseded DES in the late 1990s.

▶ **Advanced Encryption Standard (AES):** *AES* is also known as Rijndael, which is the name originally given to the cipher upon which AES is based. NIST chose this block cipher as the successor to DES. AES is similar to DES because it can create keys from 128 bits to 256 bits in length and can perform the encryption and decryption of up to 128-bit chunks of data (in comparison to the 64-bit chunks of the original DES). As in 3DES, the data passes through three layers, each with a specific task, such as generating random keys based on the data and the bit strength being used. The data is then encrypted with the keys through multiple encryption rounds, as in DES, and then the final key is applied to the data.

▶ **Blowfish Encryption Algorithm:** *Blowfish* is a block cipher that can encrypt using any size chunk of data. Blowfish also can perform encryption with any length of encryption key (up to 448 bits), making it a flexible and secure symmetric encryption algorithm. Succeeding Blowfish is *Twofish*, which was a finalist successor to DES.

▶ **Rivest Cipher (RC2, RC4, RC5, RC6):** The Rivest Cipher (RC) encryption algorithms are some of the most commonly implemented commercial ciphers for encryption security. RC2, RC5, and RC6 are block ciphers, whereas RC4 is a stream cipher. *RC4* was widely used around the world, but it has been discovered to have several vulnerabilities.

Table 35.1 compares different algorithms, their cipher types, and their supported key lengths.

TABLE 35.1 **A Comparison of Symmetric Key Algorithms**

Algorithm	Cipher Type	Key Length
DES	Block	56 bits
Triple-DES (3DES)	Block	168 bits
AES (Rijndael)	Block	128, 192, or 256 bits
Blowfish	Block	32–448 bits
Twofish	Block	128, 192, or 256 bits
RC4	Stream	40–2048 bits

ExamAlert

Be sure that you understand the differences in various symmetric key algorithms. Note that these are symmetric, not asymmetric. RC4 is the only stream cipher of those mentioned.

Cipher Modes

Block ciphers have many different modes of operation. The following list gives some of the more common modes, especially the ones you should be familiar with.

- ▶ **Counter (CTR) Mode:** This mode essentially turns a block cipher into a stream cipher. Each block combines a nonce or IV with a sequentially assigned number to produce a unique counter block that is then encrypted. That result is then obfuscated with the plain text to produce cipher text. Note that the cipher is used to generate a keystream. It never encrypts the plain text directly, but encrypts only the numbered counter.

- ▶ **Cipher Block Chaining (CBC):** This commonly used mode provides for confidentiality only, not integrity. CBC uses an IV with the first block. Thereafter, each block of plain text is obfuscated with the cipher text from the previous block before it is encrypted.

- ▶ **Galois/Counter Mode (GCM):** This efficient mode offers both integrity and confidentiality and works in 128-bit blocks. GCM uses CTR. With this mode, each 128-bit block is given a number, and that number is encrypted. That result is then obfuscated with the plain text, producing the cipher text. For each encrypted stream, an IV is required.

- ▶ **Electronic Codebook (ECB):** This simple deterministic mode divides the message into blocks and then encrypts each block on its own. ECB is not recommended for use because the same plain-text block is encrypted into the same cipher-text block each time.

Asymmetric Algorithms

Various asymmetric algorithms have been designed, but few have gained the widespread acceptance of symmetric algorithms. As you read this section, keep in mind that some asymmetric algorithms have unique features, including built-in digital signatures. In addition, because of the extra overhead generated by using two keys for encryption and decryption, asymmetric algorithms require more resources than symmetric algorithms. As a result, these algorithms are primarily used for digital signatures and for the secure exchange of a shared key that symmetric algorithms subsequently use.

Elliptic curve cryptography (ECC) describes a technique in which elliptic curves are used to calculate simple but difficult-to-break encryption keys for use in general-purpose encryption. A key benefit of ECC encryption algorithms is that they have a compact design because of the advanced mathematics involved. For instance, an ECC encryption key of 160-bit strength is actually equal in strength to a 1024-bit RSA encryption key.

Popular asymmetric cryptographic algorithms include the following:

▶ **Rivest, Shamir, and Adleman (RSA):** *RSA*, named after the three men who developed it, is a well-known cryptography system used for encryption and digital signatures. Because of performance constraints, RSA is not often used to encrypt data. Instead, it is primarily used to share a secret key. From there, a symmetric algorithm is used to encrypt communications. The RSA key can be of any length, and the algorithm works by multiplying two large prime numbers. In addition, through other operations in the algorithm, RSA derives a set of numbers: one for the public key and the other for the private key. Although RSA can be used for digital signatures, it is slower when compared to other algorithms.

▶ **Diffie-Hellman key exchange (D-H):** The *Diffie-Hellman* key exchange (also called *exponential key agreement*) is an early key exchange design in which two parties, without prior arrangement, can agree on a secret key that is known only to them. The keys are passed in such a way that they are not compromised, using encryption algorithms to verify that the data is arriving at its intended recipient. Note that this algorithm does not handle encryption or signing; it is used simply to generate a shared key.

▶ **Diffie-Hellman Ephemeral (DHE):** DHE is an ephemeral version of the D-H key exchange. DHE uses a different key for every conversation and supports perfect forward secrecy.

▶ **Elliptic Curve Diffie-Hellman Ephemeral (ECDHE):** ECDHE is a variant of the Diffie-Hellman key agreement protocol for ECC that uses an ephemeral mode of operation and supports perfect forward secrecy.

▶ **El Gamal:** El Gamal works as an extension to the Diffie-Hellman design. In 1985, Dr. El Gamal began investigating the design requirements of using encryption to develop digital signatures. Instead of focusing on just the key design, El Gamal designed a complete public key encryption algorithm using some of the key exchange elements from Diffie-Hellman and incorporating encryption on those keys. The resultant encrypted keys reinforced the security and authenticity of public key encryption design and later led to advances in asymmetric encryption technology.

▶ **Digital Signature Algorithm (DSA):** *DSA* is a U.S. standard for the generation and verification of digital signatures to ensure authenticity. DSA does not encrypt, except when implemented with products such as RSA or El Gamal. DSA's strength lies in its performance in digital signing. However, it is slower at verifying signatures. When verification performance is required, RSA might be preferred.

▶ **Pretty Good Privacy (PGP) and GNU Privacy Guard (GPG):** *PGP* derives from the Pretty Good Privacy application developed by Phillip R. Zimmerman in 1991 and is an alternative to S/MIME. Basically, it encrypts and decrypts email messages using asymmetric encryptions schemes such as RSA. Another useful feature of the PGP program is that it can include a digital signature that validates that the email has not been tampered with (thus assuring the recipient of the email's integrity).

ExamAlert

DHE and ECDHE are ephemeral key agreement protocols that, although computationally slower, provide perfect forward secrecy.

Some systems incorporate a mixed approach, using both asymmetric and symmetric encryption to take advantage of the benefits that each provides. For example, asymmetric algorithms might be used at the beginning of a process to securely distribute symmetric keys. From that point, after the private keys have been securely exchanged, they can be used for encryption and decryption (thus solving the issue of key distribution). PGP is an example of such a system. PGP was originally designed to handle the encryption and decryption of email and to digitally sign emails. PGP and other similar hybrid encryption systems, such as the GNU Privacy Guard (GnuPG or GPG) program, follow the OpenPGP format and use a combination of public key and private key encryption. *GPG* provides an alternative to PGP under a free software license.

Note

In 2000, the RSA algorithm was released into the public domain. This release permitted developers to create products by incorporating their own implementation of the algorithm, without being subject to license and patent enforcement.

Throughout this section on encryption algorithms, you have learned how each type of symmetric and asymmetric algorithm performs. You have not yet seen how their bit strengths compare to each other. The following list reveals why symmetric algorithms are favored for most applications and why asymmetric algorithms are widely considered very secure but often too complex and resource intensive for every environment. The following examples compare a symmetric key and an RSA or Diffie-Hellman asymmetric key:

▶ 64-bit symmetric key strength = 512-bit asymmetric key strength

▶ 112-bit symmetric key strength = 1792-bit asymmetric key strength

▶ 128-bit symmetric key strength = 2304-bit asymmetric key strength

▶ 256-bit symmetric key strength = 15360-bit asymmetric key strength

You can see a dramatic difference in the strength and, consequently, the overall size of asymmetric encryption keys. For many environments today, 128-bit strength is considered adequate; therefore, symmetric encryption often suffices. If you want to simplify how you distribute keys, however, asymmetric encryption might be the better choice.

> **Note**
>
> In the early 1990s, the U.S. government tried to suppress the use of PGP, which was gaining popularity and exposure in the media. The government tried to force the software to be taken down and made unavailable to public consumption. (PGP is the email program that uses encryption and is available to anyone who wants to download it within North America.)
>
> Part of the government's argument against PGP was that it could not control the information people were sending. For example, criminals could use encryption and seemingly be able to hide their online activities and data from the prying eyes of the government. Eventually, the public's right to use encryption (and PGP, in particular) won out.

Hashing Algorithms

Numerous hash functions exist, and many published algorithms are known to be unsecure. However, you should be familiar with the following three hash algorithms:

▶ **Secure Hash Algorithm (SHA, SHA-1, SHA-2, SHA-3):** These hash algorithms were pioneered by the National Security Agency and are widely used in the U.S. government. SHA-1 can generate a 160-bit hash from any variable-length string of data, making it very secure but also resource-intensive. Subsequently, four additional hash functions were introduced. These were named after their digest lengths: SHA-224, SHA-256, SHA-384, and SHA-512. Together, these four hash functions are known as *SHA-2*. In 2007, a contest was announced to design a hash function (SHA-3) to replace the aging SHA-1 and SHA-2 hash functions. Cryptographers from Belgium and Italy created an algorithm known as Keccak that went on to become known as SHA-3.

▶ **Message Digest Algorithm (MD2, MD4, MD5):** This series of encryption algorithms created by Ronald Rivest (founder of RSA Data Security, Inc.) was designed to be fast, simple, and secure. The MD series generates a hash of up to 128-bit strength out of any length of data.

▶ **RACE Integrity Primitives Evaluation Message Digest (RIPEMD):** RIPEMD was developed within academia and is based on the design of MD4. The more commonly used 160-bit version of the algorithm, RIPEMD-160, performs comparably to SHA-1, although it is less used.

Both SHA and the MD series are similar in design; however, keep in mind that the higher bit strength of the SHA algorithm means that it processes 20 to 30 percent more slowly than the MD family of algorithms.

A message authentication code (MAC) provides for authentication of a message and works like a hash used to detect tampering. The MAC is a small piece of data known as an *authentication tag* that is derived by combining a message or file with a secret key. A MAC is generated and verified using the same secret key. A MAC based on a cryptographic hash function is known as a *hash-based message authentication code* (HMAC). The sender of a message uses an HMAC function to produce the MAC. Essentially, HMAC uses a hash function such as MD5 with the secret key.

Although MACs and HMACs are similar, HMAC increases security by using an additional integrity check on the data being transmitted. SHA-3 can be used to calculate an HMAC, which results in what is called *HMAC-SHA3*. (If MD5 is used, it is called *HMAC-MD5*.) The fact MD5 is vulnerable to collision attacks should not impede its use with HMAC. Unlike MD5 alone, HMACs are not as affected by collisions.

ExamAlert

A hash-based MAC is a bit of a misnomer. Remember that, in addition to providing authentication services, HMAC (and MAC) also provides for data integrity.

ExamAlert

Hashing within security systems ensures the integrity of transmitted messages (that is, to be certain they have not been altered) and password verification. Be able to identify both the SHA and MD series as hashing algorithms.

The Message Digest Algorithm has been refined over the years (hence the version numbers). The most commonly used version is MD5, which is faster than the others. Both MD4 and MD5 produce a 128-bit hash; however, the hash in MD4 has been successfully broken. This security breach spurred the development of MD5, which features a redeveloped cipher that makes it stronger than the MD4 algorithm while still featuring a 128-bit hash. Since the mid-2000s, several advances on breaking MD5 have occurred. Although MD5 is still commonly used, U.S. government agencies have stated that MD5 should be considered compromised. Meanwhile, the recommendation is to use the SHA-2 family of hash functions, at least until its successor is formally announced.

Key Derivation Function

In the last chapter, you learned that something known, such as a password, is ideally used only as an input to obtain a strong key. Key derivation functions (KDFs) work like this. They also provide other capabilities:

▶ Key separation to generate multiple keys from a single key

▶ Key expansion to create a longer key

▶ Key whitening to generate a key of a fixed size

▶ Key stretching to derive a key from a password

As with the other algorithms previously discussed, KDFs have their strengths and weaknesses. The last capability in the previous list is the ideal domain of the following algorithms, which are the most widely used *key stretching algorithms*:

▶ **PBKDF2 (Password-Based Key Derivation Function 2):** This algorithm applies a pseudo-random function to the password, combined with a salt of at least 64 bits, and then repeats the process at least 1,000 times.

▶ **Bcrypt:** Based on the Blowfish cipher, Bcrypt provides an adaptive hash function. This function, based on what Bcrypt calls a key factor, compensates for increasing compute power used for brute force attacks. The process used doesn't necessarily make Bcrypt useful for other KDF functions, however.

What Next?

If you want more practice on this chapter's exam objectives before you move on, remember that you can access all the Cram Quiz questions on the Pearson Test Prep software. You can also create a custom exam by objective. Note any objective you struggle with and go to that objective material in this chapter.

CHAPTER 36

Wireless Security Settings

This chapter covers the following official Security+ exam objective:

6.3 Given a scenario, install and configure wireless security settings.

- ▶ Cryptographic protocols
  - WPA
  - WPA2
  - CCMP
  - TKIP
- ▶ Authentication protocols
  - EAP
  - PEAP
  - EAP-FAST

- EAP-TLS
- EAP-TTLS
- IEEE 802.1X
- RADIUS Federation
- ▶ Methods
  - PSK vs. Enterprise vs. Open
  - WPS
  - Captive portals

Essential Terms and Components

- ▶ Wi-Fi Protected Access (WPA)
- ▶ Wi-Fi Protected Access Version 2 (WPA2)
- ▶ Wi-Fi Alliance
- ▶ Wired Equivalent Privacy (WEP)
- ▶ IEEE 802.1X
- ▶ WPA-Personal
- ▶ WPA-Enterprise
- ▶ Temporal Key Integrity Protocol (TKIP)
- ▶ Counter Mode with Cipher Block Chaining Message Authentication Code Protocol (CCMP)

- ▶ EAP-Transport Layer Security (EAP-TLS)
- ▶ Protected EAP (PEAP)
- ▶ EAP Tunneled Transport Layer Security (EAP-TTLS)
- ▶ EAP Flexible Authentication via Secure Tunneling (EAP-FAST)
- ▶ Remote Authentication Dial-in User Service (RADIUS)
- ▶ captive portal

CramSaver

If you can correctly answer these questions before going through this chapter, save time by skimming the Exam Alerts in this chapter and then completing the Cram Quiz at the end of this part of the book.

1. What are three types of methods for accessing wireless networks, and in what environment are you likely to find each?

   _____

2. What wireless protocol uses a shared key used by all devices on the wireless network and requires a password consisting of 8 to 63 characters?

   _____

3. Which EAP protocol, when compared to others, is difficult to deploy and requires both the client and server to have a certificate?

   _____

Answers

1. Authenticating to wireless networks is accomplished typically via one of the following three access methods: open authentication, shared authentication, or EAP authentication. Typical environments include public hotspots such as coffee shops, homes and small businesses, and large organizations.

2. WPA-PSK, or WPA-Personal, requires a password consisting of 8 to 63 characters. All devices on the wireless network must use this same password.

3. EAP-TLS uses mutual certificate-based authentication between client and server. Compared with PEAP, EAP-TTLS, and EAP-FAST, it is more difficult to deploy.

Cryptography plays a vital role in wireless networks, so wireless security is more important than ever. Because these types of networks are so ubiquitous, users expect to be able to connect with minimal friction and, of course, steer clear of evolving threats. Wireless security fundamentally needs to enable a seamless experience for "disconnected" devices while also preventing unauthorized access.

The need for wireless security extends even beyond the wireless network. Most networks are a combination of both wired and wireless technologies. As a result, misconfigured or poor security practices and methods for wireless networks can grant adversaries unauthorized access.

Access Methods

Authentication to wireless networks is typically accomplished through one of the following three methods:

▶ Open authentication

▶ Shared authentication

▶ Extensible Authentication Protocol (EAP) authentication

Although it is not as common as it once was, the simplest option for many wireless networks is to forge authentication and use an "open" network. Open networks do not provide encryption; they do not even require a password to connect. In fact, open networks do not attempt to provide any security at all. Users simply select the network name or the Service Set Identifier (SSID) for the network. This configuration is not recommended.

Some open networks first require the user to connect through a *captive portal*. A captive portal is a web page that is launched first when connecting through a network. It usually requires some type of interaction before being allowed access to other networking or Internet sites. Open networks might use captive portals for advertising or to provide terms of use for the connecting user. Such portals are common in public places such as airports and coffee shops. The user simply clicks Accept, views an advertisement, provides an email address, or performs some other required action. The network then grants access to the user and no longer holds the user captive to that portal.

Shared authentication uses a *pre-shared key (PSK)*. Essentially, the key on the wireless access device is the same key that each user will use to connect to the network.

Extensible Authentication Protocol (EAP) is more typical within larger organizations. The authentication process is a bit more involved because an authentication server is required. EAP is an extension of Point-to-Point Protocol (PPP) and allows for flexibility in authentication; this includes authentication methods beyond just a username and a password. Instead of using PPP, however, the IEEE 802.1X standard defines using EAP over both wired Ethernet and wireless networks.

EAP is a challenge response protocol that can be run over secured transport mechanisms. It is a flexible authentication technology and can be used with smart cards, one-time passwords, and public key encryption. EAP also provides support for public certificates that are deployed using auto-enrollment or smart cards. These security improvements enable access control to Ethernet networks in public places such as malls and airports.

Wireless Cryptographic Protocols

To properly manage the risk of wireless networks and prevent unauthorized access, you must understand the wireless cryptographic protocols available. Organizations of all sizes—even home users—need to be aware of the available technologies. This industry has done a lot to help make technology simple and easy to use. However, this same industry has introduced vulnerable technologies to make the setup and configuration of wireless clients mindlessly simple.

Consider, for example, *Wi-Fi Protected Setup (WPS)*, originally known as Wi-Fi Simple Config. WPS is an extension of the wireless standards whose purpose was to simplify for end users the process of establishing secure wireless home networks. As Wi-Fi devices entered the mainstream, setup previously was complex. Consequently, users often ran with default configurations, leaving the wireless networks wide open and easy to exploit.

WPS provides two certified modes of operation. The first requires the user to enter a PIN code when connecting devices. The second method requires the user to simply push a button on the AP and the connecting wireless device. In 2011, however, a major security vulnerability was exposed—in fact, the vulnerability was so severe that the solution was to turn off WPS capabilities altogether. In this vulnerability, the user's PIN could be recovered through brute-force attack in as few as 11,000 guesses or within several hours. In some cases, disabling WPS might not be enough to prevent such attacks. A firmware upgrade then is required to completely disable the feature.

> **ExamAlert**
>
> Wi-Fi Protected Setup should not be used to prevent attacks. Instead, it should be disabled, at a minimum.

WPS aside, several protocols have been developed to protect wireless networks. The primary goals of these cryptographic protocols are to protect the authentication and connection process and to also ensure the confidentiality of data sent through the air. Three common protocols have worked to achieve these goals:

▶ **Wired Equivalent Privacy (WEP):** This original wireless encryption standard should not be used today, but it still occasionally is. Its goal was to provide security on par with wired networks, but WEP has many known security issues. It was superseded in 2003 by WPA.

▶ **Wi-Fi Protected Access (WPA):** WPA was developed in response to security concerns over WEP. WPA is implemented using a couple different options for encryption.

▶ **Wi-Fi Protected Access Version 2 (WPA2):** WPA2 further improved upon WPA. Since 2006, it has been required for Wi-Fi certified devices. WPA2 introduced the use of the Advanced Encryption Standard (AES) for encryption.

> **Note**
>
> The Wi-Fi Alliance is a consortium of companies that has a major impact on wireless technologies. It contributes to the standards process and is responsible for certifying wireless devices. The alliance coined the term *Wi-Fi* and still claims it as a registered trademark.

Wireless Equivalent Privacy

WEP is the most basic form of encryption that can be used on IEEE 802.11–based wireless networks to ensure that data sent between a wireless client and its access point remains private. Originally, wireless networks generally were based on the IEEE 802.11 standard, which had serious data transmission security shortcomings. When this standard was put into place, the 802.11 committee adopted the WEP cryptographic protocol.

To understand WEP's shortcomings, you need to know how it operates. WEP uses a stream cipher for encryption called RC4. RC4 uses a shared secret key to generate a long sequence of bytes from a generator. This stream is then used to produce the encrypted ciphertext. Early 802.11b networks used 40-bit encryption because of government restrictions. However, hackers can crack a 40-bit key in a few hours. Breaking RC4 encryption is much easier if an attacker can isolate a second instance of encryption with a single key. In other words, the weakness is that the same keys are used repeatedly.

> **Note**
>
> IEEE 802.11 is the family of standards for wireless networks maintained by the Institute of Electrical and Electronics Engineers (IEEE).

Wi-Fi Protected Access

Similar to WEP, *Wi-Fi Protected Access (WPA)* includes a method to encrypt wireless traffic between wireless clients and wireless access points. WPA has been included in 802.11-based products since WEP was deprecated in 2004.

WPA includes a strategy for restricting network access and encrypting network traffic based on a shared key. The Wi-Fi Alliance developed WPA to replace the WEP protocol after security flaws were found in WEP. WPA protects networks by incorporating a set of enhanced security features. WPA-protected networks require users to enter a passkey to access the wireless network. WPA has two different modes:

▶ **WPA-Personal:** Known also as *WPA-PSK* (pre-shared key), WPA-Personal requires a password consisting of 8 to 63 characters. All devices on the wireless network must use this same password.

▶ **WPA-Enterprise:** Known also as *WPA-802.1X mode*, WPA-Enterprise requires security certificates and uses an authentication server from which the keys can be distributed.

WPA-Personal and WPA-Enterprise target different users and are applicable to both WPA and WPA2. WPA-Personal is designed for home and small office use; it uses a pre-shared key and does not require a separate authentication server. WPA-Enterprise, in contrast, is better suited for larger organizations because it provides increased security. This comes with a tradeoff, of course. WPA-Enterprise requires a Remote Authentication Dial-In User Service (RADIUS) authentication server, which demands additional effort for setup and maintenance.

ExamAlert

Remember that WPA2 provides a greater level of protection over WPA and WEP. Furthermore, WEP has been deprecated and is no longer considered secure.

Note

In October 2017 details of a severe replay attack were published. This vulnerability affects WPA2 and all variants of WPA. WPA2 users should apply available software and firmware updates.

Temporal Key Integrity Protocol

WPA adopted the *Temporal Key Integrity Protocol (TKIP)*. Based on RC4, TKIP was designed to overcome many limitations of WEP and delivered huge improvements in message integrity and confidentiality. TKIP uses a unique key with each packet, unlike WEP, which used the same key. In addition, TKIP provides a more robust method of doing integrity checks to prevent man-in-the-middle attacks. WPA with TKIP is a huge improvement over WEP, but TKIP has been deprecated since 2012 and is no longer considered secure.

Counter Mode with Cipher Block Chaining Message Authentication Code Protocol

With the introduction of WPA2, TKIP was essentially replaced with *Counter Mode Cipher Block Chaining Message Authentication Code Protocol (CCMP)*, based on the Advanced Encryption Standard (AES) encryption cipher. While CCMP is more resource-intensive, it supported much longer keys and more advanced security for data confidentiality, user authentication, and user access control. CCMP is based on the AES encryption algorithm and provides significant security improvements over TKIP. WPA is usually associated with TKIP, and WPA2 is typically linked to AES, but this pairing isn't necessary.

Wi-Fi Protected Access Version 2

WPA2, based on the IEEE 802.11i standard, provides government-grade security by implementing the AES block cipher encryption algorithm and 802.11-based authentication. WPA2 incorporates stricter security standards and is configurable in either the PSK or enterprise mode. As with WPA, two versions of WPA2 exist: WPA2-Personal and WPA2-Enterprise. WPA2-Personal protects unauthorized network access via a password. WPA2-Enterprise verifies network users through a server. WPA2 is backward-compatible with WPA and supports strong encryption and authentication for both infrastructure and ad-hoc networks. Additionally, as in WPA, WPA2 supports CCMP based on both AES and TKIP.

Authentication Protocols

Four protocols are used with EAP and provide authentication for wireless networks. Table 36.1 provides a summary comparison

- ▶ EAP-Transport Layer Security (EAP-TLS)

- ▶ Protected EAP (PEAP)

- ▶ EAP Tunneled Transport Layer Security (EAP-TTLS)

- ▶ EAP Flexible Authentication via Secure Tunneling (EAP-FAST)

EAP-Transport Layer Security (EAP-TLS) uses certificate-based mutual authentication, negotiation of the encryption method, and encrypted key determination between the client and the authenticating server.

EAP messages are encapsulated into 802.1X packets and are marked as EAP over LAN (EAPOL). After the client sends a connection request to a wireless access point, the authenticator marks all initial communication with the client as unauthorized. Only EAPOL messages are accepted while in this mode. All other types of communication are blocked until credentials are verified with an authentication server. Upon receiving an EAPOL request from the client, the wireless access point requests logon credentials and passes them to an authentication server. RADIUS is usually employed for authentication purposes; however, 802.1X does not make it mandatory. RADIUS federation allows a user's valid authentication to be shared across trusted entities. This trust must be established beforehand, and the RADIUS server makes assertions about the user identity and other attributes. This enables users to seamlessly roam across different wireless networks without having to reauthenticate with unique credentials of another entity.

Protected EAP (PEAP) provides several additional benefits within TLS, including an encrypted authentication channel, dynamic keying material from TLS, a fast reconnect capability using cached session keys, and server authentication that guards against unauthorized access points. PEAP offers a means of protecting another EAP method within a Transport Layer Security (TLS) tunnel. PEAP is thus basically a secure wrapper around EAP and is essential in preventing attacks on password-based EAP methods. As part of PEAP negotiation, the client establishes a TLS session with a RADIUS server. Using a TLS session as part of PEAP serves several purposes:

▶ The client can authenticate the RADIUS server—that is, the client establishes the session only with a server that holds a certificate trusted by the client.

▶ It protects the authentication protocol from packet snooping.

▶ Negotiation of the TLS session generates a key that the client and RADIUS server can use to establish common master keys. These keys then derive the keys used to encrypt the WLAN traffic.

Secured within the PEAP channel, the client authenticates itself to the RADIUS server using the EAP protocol. During this exchange, the traffic within the TLS tunnel is visible only to the client and the RADIUS server; it is never exposed to the wireless AP.

EAP Tunneled Transport Layer Security (EAP-TTLS) is similar to PEAP but further builds upon TLS. With an established secure tunnel, the server authenticates the client using authentication attributes within the TLS wrapper.

EAP Flexible Authentication via Secure Tunneling (EAP-FAST) is a proposed replacement to the Lightweight Extensible Authentication Protocol (LEAP), which for years has been known to contain vulnerabilities. The goal of EAP-FAST is to provide a replacement that is also lightweight but secure. EAP-FAST also works like PEAP but does not require client or server certificates. Instead, it uses a Protected Access Credential (PAC), which is essentially a shared secret between the client and the authentication server to establish a tunnel where authentication is then performed. For many organizations that don't want to manage certificates, EAP-FAST might be an ideal alternative to LEAP.

Table 36.1 compares the various flavors of EAP authentication protocols.

TABLE 36.1 **Comparing EAP Authentication Protocols**

	EAP-TLS	PEAP	EAP-TTLS	EAP-FAST
Client certificate required	Yes	No	No	No
Server certificate required	Yes	Yes	Yes	No
Ease of deployment	Difficult	Moderate	Moderate	Easy
Security	High	Medium	Medium	Medium

Each protocol is developed and backed by specific vendors. An organization's choice of vendors might dictate the choice of solution. Organizations do not have to manage a certificate infrastructure or deploy certificates, which greatly reduces the burden for many.

> **ExamAlert**
>
> EAP-TLS requires client and server certificates for mutual authentication. Both PEAP and EAP-TTLS eliminate the requirement to deploy client certificates. EAP-FAST does not require any certificates.

What Next?

If you want more practice on this chapter's exam objectives before you move on, remember that you can access all the Cram Quiz questions on the Pearson Test Prep software. You can also create a custom exam by objective. Note any objective you struggle with and go to that objective material in this chapter.

CHAPTER 37

Public Key Infrastructure

This chapter covers the following official Security+ exam objective:

6.4 Given a scenario, implement public key infrastructure.

► Components
- CA
- Intermediate CA
- CRL
- OCSP
- CSR
- Certificate
- Public key
- Private key
- Object identifiers (OID)
- Concepts
- Online vs. offline CA
- Stapling
- Pinning
- Trust model
- Key escrow
- Certificate chaining

► Types of certificates
- Wildcard
- SAN
- Code signing
- Self-signed
- Machine/computer
- Email
- User
- Root
- Domain validation
- Extended validation

► Certificate formats
- DER
- PEM
- PFX
- CER
- P12
- P7B

Essential Terms and Components:

▶ Certificate Authority (CA)

▶ certificate revocation list (CRL)

▶ registration authority (RA)

▶ certification practice statement (CPS)

▶ key escrow

▶ X.509

▶ object identifier (OID)

▶ certificate signing request (CSR)

▶ certificate policy

▶ DV certificate

▶ OV certificate

▶ EV certificate

▶ PEM

▶ DER

▶ PFX

▶ CER

▶ P12

▶ P7B

▶ Online Certificate Status Protocol (OCSP)

▶ OCSP stapling

▶ pinning

CramSaver

If you can correctly answer these questions before going through this chapter, save time by skimming the Exam Alerts in this chapter and then completing the Cram Quiz at the end of this part of the book.

1. What components are required to implement a PKI?

   _____

2. What is the purpose of a Certificate Authority?

   _____

3. Why is it best to take a root Certificate Authority offline?

   _____

4. What are DV, OV, and EV certificates?

   _____

Answers

1. PKI consists of an infrastructure of hardware, software, policies, and processes. These components provide for the management and use of digital certificates. Core components include Certificate Authorities, certificate policies, digital certificates, and certification practice statements.

2. A Certificate Authority is a key component of a PKI. The primary purpose of a Certificate Authority is to verify the holder of a digital certificate, issue certificates, and ensure that the holder of a certificate is who they claim to be.

3. Certificate Authorities operate on a hierarchical trust model. If the root Certificate Authority is compromised, the entire architecture is compromised. If the root Certificate Authority is offline and a subordinate Certificate Authority is compromised, however, the root Certificate Authority can be used to revoke the subordinate.

4. DV, or domain validation, is the quickest and least expensive option because only ownership of a specific domain name is validated. OV, or organizational validation, certificates provide stronger assurance over just domain verification because the organization and not just the domain is verified. Finally, EV, or extended validation, certification provides the highest level of trust and security features.

To begin to understand the applications and deployment of a public key infrastructure (PKI), you should understand the various pieces that make up a PKI. A PKI is a vast collection of varying technologies and policies for the creation and use of digital certificates. A PKI encompasses Certificate Authorities, digital certificates, and the tools, systems, and processes to bring it all together. As previous chapters showed, digital certificates are a critical component to provide secure systems. For example, in the previous chapter, you learned that many implementations of EAP in wireless networks require digital certificates to verify the identity of the client or server. Digital signatures are digitally signed data blocks, which provide several potential functions but most notably are used for identification and authentication purposes. The requirement for certificates adds complexity. This chapter introduces the many concepts of how these certificates are generated and managed.

The basic concepts of the public and private keys you learned about earlier in this part play an important role in PKI. This infrastructure makes use of both types of keys and lays the foundation for binding keys to an identity via a Certificate Authority (CA). This gives the system a way to securely exchange data over a network using an asymmetric key system. For the most part, this system consists of digital certificates and the CAs that issue the certificates. These certificates identify individuals, systems, and organizations that have been verified as authentic and trustworthy.

Recall that symmetric key cryptography requires a key to be shared. For example, suppose the password to get into the clubhouse is "open sesame." At some point in time, this key or password needs to be communicated to other participating parties before it can be implemented. PKI provides confidentiality, integrity, and authentication by overcoming this challenge. With PKI, it is not necessary to exchange the password, key, or secret information in advance. This is useful when involved parties have no prior contact or when exchanging a secure key is neither feasible nor secure.

PKI is widely used to provide the secure infrastructure for applications and networks, including access control, resources from web browsers, secure email, and much more. PKI protects information by providing the following:

▶ Identity authentication

▶ Integrity verification

▶ Privacy assurance

▶ Access authorization

▶ Transaction authorization

▶ Nonrepudiation support

> **ExamAlert**
>
> A public key infrastructure is a vast collection of varying technologies and policies for the creation and use of digital certificates. PKI encompasses certificate authorities; digital certificates; and the tools, systems, and processes to bring it all together.

Certificate Authority (CA)

Certificate Authorities are trusted entities and an important concept within PKI. Aside from the third-party CAs (such as those provided by Symantec, for example), an organization can establish its own CA, typically for use only within the organization. The CA's job is to issue certificates, verify the holder of a digital certificate, and ensure that holders of certificates are who they claim to be. A common analogy is to compare a CA to a passport-issuing authority. To obtain a passport, you need the assistance of another (for example, a customs office) to verify your identity. Passports are trusted because the issuing authority is trusted.

Registration authorities (RA) provide authentication to the CA on the validity of a client's certificate request; in addition, the RA serves as an aggregator of information. For example, a user contacts an RA, which then verifies the user's identity before issuing the request of the CA to go ahead and issue a digital certificate.

ExamAlert

A CA is responsible for issuing certificates. Remember that an RA initially verifies a user's identity and then passes along to the CA the request to issue a certificate to the user.

CAs follow a chained hierarchy, or certificate chain, when verifying digital certificates, to form what's known as a chain of trust. Starting with a trust anchor, known as the root CA, certificates are trusted transitively through one or many certificates within the chain. This trust is transitive across the chain. For example:

▶ The root certificate verifies certificate A.

▶ Certificate A verifies certificate B.

▶ Certificate B verifies certificate C.

This also works in reverse:

▶ Certificate C references certificate B.

▶ Certificate B references certificate A.

▶ Certificate A references the root certificate.

Certification Practice Statement

A *certification practice statement* (CPS) is a legal document that a CA creates and publishes for the purpose of conveying information to those who depend on the CA's issued certificates. The information within a CPS provides for the general practices the CA follows in issuing certificates and customer-related information about certificates, responsibilities, and problem management. It is important to understand that these statements are described in the context of operating procedures and system architecture. Certificate policies, on the other hand, indicate the rules that apply to an issued certificate. A CPS includes the following items:

▶ Identification of the CA

▶ Types of certificates issued and applicable certificate policies

▶ Operating procedures for issuing, renewing, and revoking certificates

▶ Technical and physical security controls that the CA uses

Trust Models

Certificate authorities within a PKI follow several models or architectures. The simplest model is the single-CA architecture, in which only one CA exists to issue and maintain certificates. This model might benefit smaller organizations because of its administrative simplicity, but it can present many problems. For example, if the CA fails, no other CA can quickly take its place. Another problem can arise if the private key of the CA becomes compromised; in this scenario, all the issued certificates from that CA would then be invalid. A new CA would have to be created, which, in turn, would need to reissue all the certificates.

A more common model, and one that reduces the risks inherent with a single CA, is the hierarchical CA model. In this model, an initial root CA exists at the top of the hierarchy and subordinate CAs, or *intermediate CAs,* reside beneath the root. The subordinate CAs provide redundancy and load balancing in case any of the other CAs fail or need to be taken offline. Because of this model, you might hear PKI referred to as a trust hierarchy.

A root CA differs from subordinate CAs because the root CA is usually offline. Remember, if the root CA is compromised, the entire architecture is compromised. If a subordinate CA is compromised, however, the root CA can revoke the subordinate CA.

An alternative to this hierarchical model is the cross-certification model, often referred to as a *web of trust.* In this model, CAs are considered peers to each other. Such a configuration, for example, might exist at a small company that started with a single CA. As the company grew, it continued to implement other single-CA models and then decided that each division of the company needed to communicate with the others. To achieve secure exchange of information across the company, each CA established a peer-to-peer trust relationship with the others. As you might imagine, such a configuration could become difficult to manage over time.

> **ExamAlert**
>
> The root CA should be taken offline to reduce the risk of key compromise. It should be made available only to create and revoke certificates for subordinate CAs. A compromised root CA compromises the entire system.

A solution to the complexity of a large cross-certification model is to implement a *bridge CA model.* Remember that, in the cross-certification model, each CA must trust the others. By implementing bridging, however, you can have a single CA, known as the *bridge CA,* serve as the central point of trust.

> **ExamAlert**
>
> Certificates rely on a hierarchical chain of trust. If the CA's root key is compromised, any keys issued by that CA are compromised as well.

Key Escrow

Key escrow occurs when a CA or other entity maintains a copy of the private key associated with the public key signed by the CA. This scenario allows the CA or escrow agent to have access to all information encrypted using the public key from a user's certificate and to create digital signatures on behalf of the user. Therefore, key escrow is a sensitive topic within the PKI community. Harmful results might occur if the private key is misused. Because of this issue, key escrow is not a favored PKI solution.

Despite public concerns about escrow for private use, key escrow is often considered a good idea in corporate PKI environments. In most cases, an employee of an organization is bound by the information security policies of that organization (which usually mandate that the organization has a right to access all intellectual property generated by a user and to any data that an employee generates). In addition, key escrow enables an organization to overcome the large problem of forgotten passwords. Instead of revoking and reissuing new keys, an organization can generate a new certificate using the private key stored in escrow.

Digital Certificate

A digital certificate is a digitally signed block of data that allows public key cryptography to be used for identification purposes. The most common type of certificate is the SSL or TLS certificates used on the web. Essentially, these certificates ensure secure communications. This occurs when a website uses https:// instead of just http:// in the browser address bar, accompanied by a closed padlock.

CAs issue these certificates, which are signed using the CA's private key. Most certificates are based on the X.509 standard. Although most certificates follow the X.509 Version 3 hierarchical PKI standard, the PGP key system uses its own certificate format. X.509 certificates to be signed contain the following information:

- ▶ **Version number:** This identifies the version of the X.509 standard that the certificate complies with.

- ▶ **Serial number:** The CA that creates the certificate is responsible for assigning a unique serial number.

▶ **Signature algorithm identifier:** This identifies the cryptographic algorithm used by the CA to sign the certificate. An *object identifier* (OID) is used. OIDs are hierarchical globally unique identifiers for an object.

▶ **Issuer name:** This identifies the directory name of the entity signing the certificate, which is typically a CA.

▶ **Period of validity:** This identifies the time frame for which the private key is valid, if the private key has not been compromised. This period is indicated with both a start and an end time; it can be of any duration, but it is often set to 1 year.

▶ **Subject or owner name:** This is the name of the entity that is identified in the public key associated with the certificate. This name uses the X.500 standard for globally unique naming and is often called the distinguished name (DN) (for example, CN=Sri Puthucode, OU=Sales, O=CompTIA, C=US).

▶ **Subject or owner's public key:** This includes the public key of the entity named in the certificate, in addition to a cryptographic algorithm identifier and optional key parameters associated with the key.

▶ **Extensions:** The extensions field optionally provides methods in X.509 v3 certificates to associate additional attributes. This field must not be present in previous versions. Common extensions include specific key usage requirements, such as allowing the public key of the certificate to be used only for certificate signing.

▶ **Signature value:** This value provides the computed digital signature from the signed certificate's body, used as an input. The signature ensures the validity of the certificate.

You likely have used the most common application of digital certificates: Websites that ask for personal information, especially credit card information, use digital certificates. (Not necessarily all do, but they should.) The traffic from your computer to the website is secured using a protocol called Secure Sockets Layer (SSL), and the web server uses a digital certificate for the secure exchange of information. This is easily identified by a small padlock located in the bottom status bar of most browsers. By clicking this icon, you can view the digital certificate and its details.

> **ExamAlert**
>
> Remember the components of an X.509 certificate. You might be required to recognize the contents of a certificate.

Refer to Figure 37.1 for an example of a digital certificate as viewed through a web browser by clicking on the lock icon in the browser address bar. Specifically, note that the certificate applies to comptia.org, including any subdomains, and note that this certificate is chained to an intermediary CA's certificate (RapidSSL), which is chained to the root CA's certificate (GeoTrust Global CA). Next, note the different fields, many of which the text just covered.

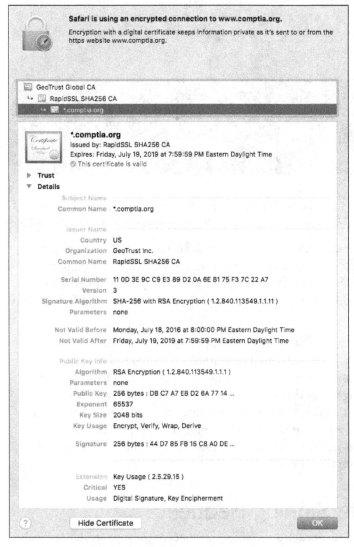

FIGURE 37.1   **Details of a Digital Certificate**

Public and Private Key Usage

Digital certificates and key pairs can be used for various purposes, including privacy and authentication. The security policy of the organization that is using the key or the CA defines the purposes and capabilities for the certificates issued.

To achieve privacy, users require the public key of the individual or entity they want to communicate with securely. This public key is used to encrypt the data that is transmitted, and the corresponding private key is used on the other end to decrypt the message.

> **ExamAlert**
>
> You obtain another's public key (freely available to anyone), which you use to encrypt a message to that person. As a result, that person can use his or her private key, which no one else has. This private key decrypts the message. The public and private keys are mathematically related.

Authentication is achieved by digitally signing the message being transmitted. To digitally sign a message, the signing entity requires access to the private key.

In short, the key usage extension of the certificate specifies how the private key can be used—either to enable the exchange of sensitive information or to create digital signatures. In addition, the key usage extension can specify that an entity can use the key both for the exchange of sensitive information and for signature purposes.

In some circumstances, dual or multiple key pairs might be used to support distinct and separate services. For example, an individual in a corporate environment might require one key pair just for signing and another just for encrypting messages. Another example is a reorder associate who has one key pair to use for signing and sending encrypted messages, and another one restricted to ordering equipment worth no more than a specific dollar amount. Multiple key pairs require multiple certificates because the X.509 certificate format does not support multiple keys.

Certificate Signing Request

To install a digital certificate, a specific request needs to be generated and submitted to the CA. This request to apply for a digital certificate is known as a *certificate signing request* (CSR); it is requested from the applicant to the CA.

Included within the request is the applicant's public key, along with information about the applicant. Typical information includes the following:

- ▶ Fully qualified domain name
- ▶ Legally incorporated name of the company
- ▶ Department name
- ▶ City, state, and country
- ▶ Email address

Before submitting a CSR, the applicant generates a key pair consisting of a public and private key. The public key is provided with the request, and the applicant signs the request with the private key. If all is successful, the CA returns a digital certificate that is signed with the CA's private key.

Certificate Policy

A *certificate policy* indicates specific uses applied to a digital certificate and other technical details. Not all certificates are created equal. Digital certificates are issued that often follow different practices and procedures and are issued for different purposes. Therefore, the certificate policy provides the rules that indicate the purpose and use of an assigned digital certificate. For example, one certificate might have a policy indicating its use for electronic data interchange to conduct e-commerce, whereas another certificate might be issued to only digitally sign documents.

Remember that a certificate policy identifies the purpose for which the certificate can be used. You should also be able to identify the other types of information that can be included within a certificate policy:

- ▶ Legal issues often used to protect the CA
- ▶ Mechanisms for how the CA will authenticate users
- ▶ Key management requirements
- ▶ Instructions for what to do if the private key is compromised
- ▶ Lifetime of the certificate
- ▶ Certificate enrollment and renewal
- ▶ Rules regarding exporting the private key
- ▶ Private and public key minimum lengths

ExamAlert

The applicant's public key is submitted along with the CSR.

Certificate Types

For TLS certificates, three types of validated certificates exist, each with their own level of trust:

▶ **Domain validation (DV):** This type of certificate includes only the domain name. DVs can easily be issued, just as a domain name lookup can easily be performed against WHOIS, a database of registered domains. DV certificates are inexpensive and quick to acquire, so if trust is important or a public-facing website is desired, organizations should consider another type of validated certificate.

▶ **Organizational validation (OV):** This certificate type provides stronger assurance. Organizations are vetted against official government sources, and this is a common certificate type for many organizational public-facing websites. Unlike a DV certificate, verification requires a more manual review and verification process; this can take days to process.

▶ **Extended validation (EV):** This certificate type provides a high level of trust and security features. EV certificates are easily identified: The business name in the address bar is green. EVs are designed to provide assurance against phishing attacks. As the name implies, this certificate requires a comprehensive validation of the business; this can take up to a couple weeks to acquire.

ExamAlert

DV certificates are the quickest and least expensive. EV certificates can take a couple weeks and are the most expensive, but they also provide the highest level of trust.

Special certificates you should be familiar with include the following:

▶ **Wildcard:** This certificate provides any number of subdomains for a single registered domain. The name for the certificate thus might look like *.example.com, which would be valid for www.example.com, sub.example.com, and so on. Refer to Figure 37.1, which uses a wildcard certificate example.

▶ **SAN:** This type of certificate takes advantage of the subject alternate name (SAN) extension. It provides for the use of multiple domain names or even IP addresses within a single certificate. This certificate is also known as a unified communications (UC) certificate.

▶ **Code signing:** This type of certificate is required to digitally sign software packages. It provides assurance that the software is authentic and has not been tampered with.

▶ **Self-signed:** Self-signed certificates are often used for testing purposes or when trust is not a concern. Certificates are typically signed by another entity or CA. Self-signed certificates are recognized by web browsers, which provide an alert to the user that the connection is not trusted.

▶ **Email:** This type of certificate is also known as an S/MIME (Secure/Multipurpose Internet Mail Extensions) certificate. An email certificate is required to digitally sign or encrypt email messages.

▶ **Root signing:** A root signing certificate is usually provided by a recognized CA. Organizations with a root signing certificate thus can sign for themselves any number of certificates. These certificates, in turn, will be trusted by those outside the organization, because web browsers include, by default, many trusted certificates for recognized CAs. For example, an organization that wants to run its own CA in-house, particularly when trust needs to be extended outside the organization, should purchase a root signing certificate.

▶ **User:** Known also as client certificates, a user certificate identifies an individual. Just as a website's TLS certificate authenticates the website to the user, a user certificate can authenticate the user to the remote server. This works much like a password does.

▶ **Machine/computer:** Similar to the user certificate, a machine/computer certificate authenticates a client system. This is primarily used with machine-to-machine communications.

Certificate Formats

Certificates can have various file extension types. Some extension types are interchangeable, but not all are. Be sure to determine whether the certificate is binary or Base64 ASCII encoded. Table 37.1 provides a brief comparison of common certificate formats.

The most common format and extension for certificates is PEM, which is mostly associated with Apache web servers. The PEM format is a Base64 ASCII-encoded text file, which make copying the contents from one document to another simple. A PEM file might contain several certificates and private keys within a single file, although having each component (that is, each certificate and key) as its own file is common. A single certificate includes a header of BEGIN CERTIFICATE, preceded and followed by five dashes; and a footer of END CERTIFICATE, preceded and followed by five dashes. A single private key includes a header of BEGIN ENCRYPTED PRIVATE KEY, preceded and followed by five dashes; and a footer of END ENCRYPTED PRIVATE KEY, preceded and followed by five dashes. In addition to using the PEM file extension, .crt, .cer, and .key extensions can be used. However, the latter is typically used when the file contains only the private key.

Another Base64-encoded certificate format is P7B, also known as PKCS#7. This format uses the .p7b or .p7c file extension, which is commonly supported on the Windows operating system and Java Tomcat. This format includes a header of BEGIN PKCS7 and a footer of END PKCS7; each is preceded and followed by five dashes.

The binary form of a PEM certificate is DER. In addition to the .der extension, .cer and .crt extensions can be used for DER-encoded certificates. DER-encoded certificates are common on Java platforms.

Another binary certificate format is PFX, also known as PKCS#12. Extensions for PFX-encoded certificates include .pfx or .p12. This type of certificate is common to the Windows operation system for importing and exporting certificates and private keys. PFX supports a private key and can store one or more certificates within a single binary file.

Table 37.1 provides an overview of the certificate formats.

TABLE 37.1 **Summary of Certificate Formats**

Certificate Format	Encoding	Systems	Extensions
DER	Binary	Java	.der .cer .crt
PEM	Base64 ASCII	Apache HTTP	.pem .cer .crt
PFX (PKCS#12)	Binary	Windows	.pfx .p12
P7B (PKCS#7)	Base64 ASCII	Windows and Java Tomcat	.p7b .p7c

ExamAlert

DER and PFX certificates are binary-encoded and cannot be edited with a plain-text editor, such as the Base64 ASCII–encoded PEM and P7B certificates.

Certificate Revocation

Digital certificates also can be revoked. Revoking a certificate invalidates a certificate before its expiration date. Digital certificates contain a field indicating the date to which the certificate is valid. This date is mandatory, and the validity period can vary from a short period of time up to several years. Revocation occurs for several reasons. For example, a private key might become compromised, the private key might be lost, or the identifying credentials might no longer be valid. Other reasons for revocation include fraudulently obtained certificates or a change in the holder's status, which could indicate less trustworthiness. Revoking a certificate is just not enough, however. The community that trusts these certificates must be notified that the certificates are no longer valid. This is accomplished via a *certificate revocation list (CRL)* or the *Online Certificate Status Protocol (OCSP)*, as follows:

- ▶ **CRL:** A mechanism for distributing certificate revocation information. A CRL is used when verification of the digital certificate takes place to ensure the validity of a digital certificate. A limitation of CRLs is that they must be constantly updated at least every two weeks; otherwise, certificates might be accepted despite having been recently revoked.

- ▶ **OCSP:** A newer mechanism for identifying revoked certificates. OCSP checks certificate status in real time instead of relying on the end user to have a current copy of the CRL.

Both OCSP and CRLs are used to verify the status of a certificate. Three basic status levels exist in most PKI solutions: valid, suspended, and revoked. You can check the status of a certificate by going to the CA that issued the certificate or to an agreed-upon directory server that maintains a database indicating the status level for the set of certificates. In most cases, however, the application (such as a web browser) has a function available that initiates a check for certificates.

OCSP Stapling

Although OCSP provides for real-time status checking, it requires the CA to respond to every client request to validate a site's certificate. High-traffic websites burden the CA with these requests because they need to respond potentially to an overwhelming number of certificate validity requests. A mechanism known as OCSP *stapling* helps reduce this load by allowing the web server to instead "staple" a time-stamped OCSP response as part of the TLS handshake with the client. The web server is now responsible for handling OCSP requests instead of the CA. The OCSP stapling process involves the following steps:

1. A TLS-encrypted web server presents its certificate to the CA to check the validity.

2. The CA responds with the certificate status that includes a digitally signed time stamp.

3. The web server "staples" the CA's signed time stamp to the certificate when a client web browser connects.

4. The client web browser verifies the signed time stamp.

OCSP stapling provides several benefits. First, it improves performance of the secure connection. Next, privacy concerns are reduced because the end user's browser does not need to potentially contact a third-party CA to verify the certificates and reveal the browsing history. Finally, reliability is improved. If the client were unable to connect to an overburdened CA, for example, the client would otherwise accept a potentially invalid certificate—or simply end the connection.

> **ExamAlert**
>
> A certificate revocation list (CRL) is not as efficient as OCSP. The lists need to be frequently updated and are not reliable if they are outdated.

Before it is revoked, a certificate might be suspended. Certificate suspension occurs when a certificate is under investigation to determine whether it should be revoked. This mechanism allows a certificate to stay in place, but it is not valid for any type of use. Users and systems are notified of suspended certificates. New credentials do not need to be retrieved, however; it is only necessary to be notified that current credentials have had a change in status and are temporarily not valid for use.

Pinning

Certificate *pinning* provides a method that extends beyond certificate validation (already discussed) to thwart man-in-the-middle attacks. Hashes of public keys for popular web servers are built in to applications such as web browsers. A similar variation, known as HTTP Public Key Pinning (HPKP), uses public key pins, which are essentially hashed values of the public key communicated to the browser client from the server in the HTTP header. After obtaining the server certificate, the client verifies the public key against the hash of the public key.

What Next?

If you want more practice on this chapter's exam objectives before you move on, remember that you can access all the Cram Quiz questions on the Pearson Test Prep software. You can also create a custom exam by objective. Note any objective you struggle with and go to that objective material in this chapter.

Cram Quiz

This Cram Quiz covers material related to Chapters 34–37, which cover objectives falling under Domain 6, "Cryptography and PKI," of the Security+ exam.

1. Which one of the following best describes diffusion?

   ○ **A.** A principle that the plain-text input should be significantly changed in the resulting cipher text

   ○ **B.** A principle that if the plain text is changed, no matter how minor, then at least half of the cipher text should change

   ○ **C.** A principle that states only secrecy of the key provides security

   ○ **D.** A key stretching technique in which a password is used as part of a KDF

2. Which of the following are elements provided by nonrepudiation? (Choose three correct answers.)

   ○ **A.** Proof of origin

   ○ **B.** Proof of submission

   ○ **C.** Proof of delivery

   ○ **D.** Proof of concept

3. Which of the following algorithms are examples of a symmetric encryption algorithm? (Choose three correct answers.)

   ○ **A.** Rijndael

   ○ **B.** Diffie-Hellman

   ○ **C.** RC6

   ○ **D.** AES

4. Which of the following algorithms are examples of an asymmetric encryption algorithm? (Choose two correct answers.)

   ○ **A.** Elliptic curve

   ○ **B.** 3DES

   ○ **C.** AES

   ○ **D.** RSA

5. You are tasked with configuring your web server with strong cipher suites. Which of the following should you choose as part of your cipher suite? (Choose three correct answers.)

   ○ **A.** RSA

   ○ **B.** RC4

○ **C.** AES

○ **D.** SHA

6. Which one of the following EAP authentication protocols should you deploy to avoid having to deploy client or server certificates?

○ **A.** EAP-TLS

○ **B.** PEAP

○ **C.** EAP-TTLS

○ **D.** EAP-FAST

7. Which of the following statements is true when comparing CCMP and TKIP?

○ **A.** TKIP is more resource-intensive than CCMP, but it supports longer keys.

○ **B.** CCMP is more resource-intensive than TKIP, but it supports longer keys.

○ **C.** CCMP is less resource-intensive than TKIP, and it supports longer keys.

○ **D.** TKIP is less resource-intensive than CCMP, and it supports longer keys.

8. To check the validity of a digital certificate, which one of the following is used?

○ **A.** Corporate security policy

○ **B.** Certificate policy

○ **C.** Certificate revocation list

○ **D.** Expired domain names

9. Which of the following is not a certificate trust model for arranging Certificate Authorities?

○ **A.** Bridge CA architecture

○ **B.** Sub-CA architecture

○ **C.** Single-CA architecture

○ **D.** Hierarchical CA architecture

10. Which of the following are included within a digital certificate? (Choose all the correct answers.)

○ **A.** User's public key

○ **B.** User's private key

○ **C.** Information about the user

○ **D.** Digital signature of the issuing CA

11. Which of the following is not true about the expiration dates of certificates?

○ **A.** Certificates may be issued for a week.

○ **B.** Certificates are issued only at 1-year intervals.

○ **C.** Certificates may be issued for 20 years.

○ **D.** Certificates must always have an expiration date.

12. What type of certificate supplies mechanisms to help prevent phishing attacks and provides the highest level of trust?

   ○ **A.** DV

   ○ **B.** OV

   ○ **C.** EV

   ○ **D.** SAN

13. Which one of the following is not true regarding DER-encoded certificates?

   ○ **A.** They are binary-encoded.

   ○ **B.** They include the BEGIN CERTIFICATE header.

   ○ **C.** The .cer and .crt extensions can be used instead of .der.

   ○ **D.** They are common to Java platforms.

14. Which one of the following mechanisms places the responsibility for handling certificate status requests on the web server instead of the CA?

   ○ **A.** OCSP pinning

   ○ **B.** OCSP stapling

   ○ **C.** CRL pinning

   ○ **D.** CRL stapling

Cram Quiz Answers

1. **B.** Diffusion is the principle that, if plain text is changed, even if just a little, then at least half the cipher text should also change. Answer A is incorrect because this describes the principle of confusion. Answer C is incorrect because this describes Kerckhoff's principle. Answer D is incorrect as well: A KDF is a function that provides the capability to perform key stretching.

2. **A, B, and C.** Proof of origin, proof of submission, proof of delivery, and proof of receipt are the key elements nonrepudiation services provide. Answer D is incorrect because proof of concept is not a valid choice.

3. **A, C, and D.** Because Rijndael and AES are now the same, they both can be called symmetric encryption algorithms. RC6 is symmetric, too. Answer B is incorrect because Diffie-Hellman uses public and private keys, so it is considered an asymmetric encryption algorithm.

4. **A and D.** In this case, both elliptic curve and RSA are types of asymmetric encryption algorithms. Although the elliptic curve algorithm is typically a type of algorithm that is incorporated into other algorithms, it falls into the asymmetric family of algorithms because of its use of public and private keys, just like the RSA algorithm. Answers B and C are incorrect because 3DES and AES are symmetric encryption algorithms.

5. **A, C, and D.** RSA, AES, and SHA comprise a suite for strong key exchange, authentication, bulk cipher, and message authentication. Answer B is incorrect because RC4 is considered a weak bulk cipher.

6. **D.** EAP-FAST does not require either client or server certificates; instead, it uses a Protected Access Credential (PAC). Answer A is incorrect because EAP-TLS requires both client and server certificates. Answer B is incorrect because PEAP requires a server certificate. Answer C is incorrect because EAP-TTLS requires a server certificate.

7. **B.** CCMP replaced TKIP with the introduction of WPA2, providing for much longer keys and more advanced security. Although CCMP is more resource intensive, modern systems can handle the additional resources required. Answer A is entirely incorrect. Answer C is incorrect because although CCMP does support longer keys, it is not less resource-intensive than TKIP. Answer D is also incorrect because TKIP does not support longer keys, although it is less resource-intensive.

8. **C.** A CRL provides a detailed list of certificates that are no longer valid. A corporate security policy does not provide current information on the validity of issued certificates; therefore, answer A is incorrect. A certificate policy does not provide information on the validity of issued certificates, either; therefore, answer B is incorrect. Finally, an expired domain name has no bearing on the validity of a digital certificate; therefore, answer D is incorrect.

9. **B.** Sub-CA architecture does not represent a valid trust model. Answers A, C, and D all represent legitimate trust models. Another common model is cross-certification; however, implementing a bridge architecture usually makes more sense than using this type of model.

10. **A, C, and D.** Information about the user, the user's public key, and the digital signature of the issuing CA are all included within a digital certificate. A user's private key should never be contained within the digital certificate and should remain under tight control; therefore, answer B is incorrect.

11. **B.** Digital certificates contain a field indicating the date until which the certificate is valid. This date is mandatory, and the validity period can vary from a short period of time up to a number of years; therefore, answers A, C, and D are true statements.

12. **C.** EV, or extended validation, provides the highest level of trust and security features. Included are also mechanisms to prevent phishing attacks. DV certificates validate only the domain. OV certificates provider stronger validation over DV certificates, but the validation is not as comprehensive as for EV certificates. Thus, answers A and B are incorrect. Answer D is incorrect because a SAN certificate provides for multiple domain names or IP addresses with a single certificate, and is not considered a validated certificate type.

13. **B.** Because they are binary encoded and not Base64 ASCII, DER certificates cannot be edited with a text editor and do not contain such text, as PEM certificates do, for example. Answers A, C, and D are incorrect because these are all true of DER-encoded certificates.

14. **B.** OCSP stapling allows the web server to instead "staple" a time-stamped OCSP response as part of the TLS handshake with the client. The web server is now responsible for handling OCSP requests instead of the CA. Answers A, C, and D are incorrect. A CRL provides a mechanism for distributing certificate revocation information, and certificate pinning helps mitigate man-in-the-middle attacks.

Index

Numbers

A

D

T

REGISTER YOUR PRODUCT at PearsonITcertification.com/register
Access Additional Benefits and SAVE 35% on Your Next Purchase

- Download available product updates.

- Access bonus material when applicable.

- Receive exclusive offers on new editions and related products.
  (Just check the box to hear from us when setting up your account.)

- Get a coupon for 35% for your next purchase, valid for 30 days. Your code will
  be available in your PITC cart. (You will also find it in the Manage Codes
  section of your account page.)

Registration benefits vary by product. Benefits will be listed on your account page
under Registered Products.

PearsonITcertification.com–Learning Solutions for Self-Paced Study, Enterprise, and the Classroom
Pearson is the official publisher of Cisco Press, IBM Press, VMware Press, Microsoft Press,
and is a Platinum CompTIA Publishing Partner–CompTIA's highest partnership accreditation.
At **PearsonITcertification.com** you can

- Shop our books, eBooks, software, and video training.
- Take advantage of our special offers and promotions (pearsonitcertifcation.com/promotions).
- Sign up for special offers and content newsletters (pearsonitcertifcation.com/newsletters).
- Read free articles, exam profiles, and blogs by information technology experts.
- Access thousands of free chapters and video lessons.

Connect with PITC – Visit PearsonITcertifcation.com/community
Learn about PITC community events and programs.

PEARSON IT CERTIFICATION

Addison-Wesley • Cisco Press • IBM Press • Microsoft Press • Pearson IT Certification • Prentice Hall • Que • Sams • VMware Press

ALWAYS LEARNING   **PEARSON**

To receive your 10% off
Exam Voucher, register
your product at:

www.pearsonitcertification.com/register

and follow the instructions.